U0496559

雅思阅读

全薇机经

刘薇 编著

IELTS
阅读备考
专项突破

Vicky

资深教师 精心力作

55篇 题型专项练习 + **5套** 完整试题，刷题必备

源于真题，再现真题

文章、题目均源自官方题库，雅思考试真题答案精准再现

石油工业出版社

图书在版编目（CIP）数据

雅思阅读全薇机经 / 刘薇编著. —北京：石油工业出版社, 2018.12
　ISBN 978-7-5183-1614-4

Ⅰ.①雅… Ⅱ.①刘… Ⅲ.①IELTS—阅读教学—自学参考资料 Ⅳ.①H319.37

中国版本图书馆CIP数据核字（2018）第265282号

雅思阅读全薇机经
刘　薇　编著

出版发行：石油工业出版社
　　　　　（北京安定门外安华里2区1号　100011）
网　　址：www.petropub.com
编　辑　部：(010) 64253667　图书营销中心：(010) 64523633
经　　销：全国新华书店
印　　刷：北京中石油彩色印刷有限责任公司

2018年12月第1版　2023年10月第8次印刷
787×1092毫米　开本：16　印张：33
字数：1000千字

定价：78.00元
（如发现印装质量问题，我社图书营销中心负责调换）
版权所有，翻印必究

推荐序

移动互联网是由每一位有志青年做起来的，它的发展是面向未来的。虽然我不是互联网专家，但是我懂年轻人、懂创业者，也懂得如果几个人有一个梦想，并且坚持不懈，就能够做出了不起的事业。同时，我们也愿意和优秀创业者一起去寻找未来。而刘薇正是我们想要与之合作的优秀创业者的典范。

她的教学生涯贯穿了中国雅思发展从无到有，从低潮到辉煌，从线下到线上，又从线上到线下的全过程。她先是在被称为"胡雅思"的胡敏老师身边工作，后来加盟北京雅思学校，又在"环球雅思"把控整个集团教学质量走向，再后来掌管"小站雅思"，而现在她率领精英团队创建了"土豆教育"。

土豆教育虽成立不到半年时间，却在这个行业引发了不小的震荡，其中，刘薇身上那股坚定、果敢、严谨、不断求新的劲儿是主要原因。从创立开始，她带领平均行业从业经验十年的团队，低调投入到产品研发中，不断打磨，升级迭代，待到站在公众面前的时候，已是成熟的姿态，走在主流培训机构的前面。在这个精英教育时代，需要像刘薇及其团队所具备的这种低头勤恳做事、抬头改变未来的精气神儿。

继《雅思口语全薇机经（PLUS 版）》《雅思写作全薇机经》之后，《雅思阅读全薇机经》如期和大家见面，我依旧推荐这本满是诚意和体现刘薇精气神儿的作品。这本以及后续马上和大家见面的《雅思听力全薇机经》，如果不是积累了足够的教学经验、不是深谙雅思出题考官出题思路、不是拥有足够的对教研的热爱和足够沉稳的教研的心态，是无法写出这样的作品的。所以，每位考生，这本备考书，需要研习！

相信，在刘薇的带领下，刘薇的团队和她的书会引领这个行业的发展，会帮助更多学子走出国门看世界！

徐小平

真格基金创始人

前 言

雅思机经是参加雅思考试的考生对考试内容的回忆。机经，在雅思领域的重要性不亚于真题，这是因为：

一、机经弥补了"剑桥真题"系列题量的不足。 不同于国内考试，学生可以很容易买到近5年或近10年的真题来备考，雅思考试真题素材偏少。雅思出题方剑桥大学考试委员会在2015年之前每两年才会出一本真题册，虽然从2016年"加速"到每年出一本，但是到目前为止，更新到"剑桥雅思"系列17，去除前三本历史久远且题型老套、没有太大参考意义的真题册，仅有14本书56套题可供考生参考。而这56套题，再去除考前的集中模拟测试，可供技巧提升练习训练的题目并不充足。所以机经的存在，弥补了这一点，丰富了考生的备考题库。

二、机经弥补了"剑桥真题"系列不会再考的"缺憾"。 雅思每场考试的题目来自一个庞大的题库，即真题库，计算机从真题库中随机抽取而组成一套真题。"剑桥真题"系列的题目即是选自于这个真题大题库。然而，一旦入选剑桥雅思系列丛书，就不会再被放回题库中，即再也不会被抽中重考。而机经则不同，有机会被再考到，所以对于考生来说有更大的参考意义，也就是说考生有可能会在未来的考试中遇到这些题目。

编写《雅思阅读全薇机经》的初衷及过程：

雅思共分为听说读写四科。四科的机经中，阅读和听力的机经，尤其是还原机经更为难得，为什么呢？写作和口语，题目短小，且答案含有主观性，只要回顾问题就好，这对考生来说不难。而后续的考生只需找到相应的高分写作范文、高分口语答案学习和借鉴就可以了（这也是我们出版《雅思口语全薇机经PLUS版》《雅思写作全薇机经》的原因）。

但阅读和听力则不同。以阅读为例，因为考生参加考试专注于做题，并且拥有"天才枪手"记忆力的考生毕竟稀有，所以大部分的考试回顾仅限于每篇文章考了什么、有几个题型、答案是什么，而且这个答案很可能不正确（毕竟是全凭回忆）。没有原文、没有完整的题目，只有片面的信息，没有办法达到有效借鉴和学习备考的目的。所以，能够精准还原所有正确答案且还原所有题目甚至原文的机经就更加弥足珍贵。

而开心的是，这件事情，我们做到了。

首先，我和我的团队收集了近10年、近500场考试、近1,500篇文章的近10个回忆版本，集中对比、筛选，还原完整的答案，并从中首先筛选出我们认为最有可能在近一两年内出现以及对大家而言最有学习和参考意义的 70 篇阅读文章。

接下来，我们再根据考生对文章内容、主题的回忆到国外网站及国外原版杂志"海选"原文，确定原文，并进行删减、修改、加工，使之从长难度、段落分布、信息量无限趋近于真题。

然后，我们将题目按照真题的出题模式"修复"完整，从题型、题目的长度、考点方向极致还原，使之"真题化"。

最后，初稿出来后，我邀请我的考官朋友们从头到尾审核内容，从文章到题目再到答案，直至他们都认为没有问题才最终定稿，所以就有了这本竭尽所能还原答案、还原题目、还原阅读完整文章的《雅思阅读全薇机经》。

具体而言，《雅思阅读全薇机经》：

选材——雅思考试中近两年考过的阅读题目重考的概率较小，所以在选材上，我们注意到了这点，选择了很多两年之前考过的文章。对于这些阅读文章，考生务必加以重视，因为它们在未来重考的可能性更高。

数量——我们还原了70篇文章，是目前雅思图书市场上阅读还原题目非常多的一本书，足够大家充分练习、备考。

布局——基于阅读机经的内容，我们将本书分成了题型专项练习和套题两大部分。题型专项练习部分是特殊设计，因为雅思阅读题型多样，不限于我们国内学生所熟悉的选择题，其中小标题、配对题等题型难度比较大，所以设置这一部分给大家题型突破之用；套题部分不言而喻，是帮助大家在开始备考和冲刺阶段自测、模拟之用。

内容——全书共分为三部分：第一部分，对雅思阅读时间、评分标准、题型等的介绍；第二部分，八大题型的专项练习；第三部分，五套完整机经试题。

其中，专项练习是依据八大种题型的分类为考生提供还原度极高的练习题，这些题型分别是判断题、小标题、配对题、选择题、摘要填空题、完成句子题、图表题和简答题。根据近年来各题型在实际考试中出现的频率，我们针对不同题型配以不同的文章和练习数量，如判断题包含10篇，小标题包含10篇，配对题11篇，选择题8篇，摘要填空题6篇，完成句子题2篇，简答题4篇，图表题4篇。

每篇真题除了完整的文章和专项题目之外，还有【核心词】【高频同义替换】【题目解析】和【参考答案】四个板块。

☑【核心词】从文章中提取的关键词汇，通常也是雅思阅读考试中同类话题文章中的代表和经典词汇。此外，核心词中还有一部分拓展词汇，这些拓展词汇是以核心词为基础，拓展出其对应的不同词性词汇、反义词或短语等，帮助考生尽可能多地熟悉单词与词群之间的连接，更加便于记忆。

☑【高频同义替换】是本书独特的一个版块，这部分选取真题文章中的单词或短语,提供数个对应的同义替换，并且不仅仅拘泥于与已有单词同词性之间的替换，而是包含了与已有单词之间不同词性、短语，甚至是从句形式的替换，帮助考生丰富自己的词汇储备，对于不同单词、词性和词形之间的切换更加自如。

☑【题目解析】针对所有题目进行抽丝剥茧式的分析，首先从题目中提炼定位词，再根据定位词寻找文中对应点，呈现答案全部出现的过程，最后锁定答案。本书的解析言简意赅，语言风格深入浅出，确保不同分数段的雅思考生均能准确理解。

☑ **【参考答案】**将答案清晰罗列，一目了然。

各位考生在进行专项练习时，可以首先针对自己的弱势题型进行强化训练，可选择每天完成2篇机经阅读，将核心词和高频同义替换部分的内容牢记于心，随后结合自己的实际情况，按需调节每天的练习量。考生在学习较难的题型，如小标题和配对题时，一定要将书中的题目反复训练，把阅读机经的练习价值最大化。

本书第三部分涵盖5套完整套题和答案，每套题与雅思阅读考试的形式、版式、难度完全一致。各位考生可以在进行专项练习之前，先完成两套试题，以系统、全面地对自己的雅思阅读水平进行自测。随后再针对自己的薄弱环节进行集中练习，以达到事半功倍的效果。建议考生在做机经套题时严格按照考试时间。

做完题目后，考生可以对照后面的参考答案进行核对；对于做错的题目，可以参考本书给出的答案对应句及翻译，纠正错题。

另外，需要特殊说明的是，如果有需要按照文章话题进行学习的考生或者老师，可以参考前言后面的《雅思阅读全薇机经》文章、话题对照表，找到相应的位置进行研习。

最后想要告诉各位考生的是，阅读是很多雅思考生非常恐惧的一项，因为相对于国内考试，文章长（三篇文章2,000多词）、题型多（8大题型）、题目难（题目对原文进行了转换）、要求词汇量大（8,000词左右）。但是，只要坚定信念，充分练习，相信一定会在成绩单上看到经历汗水之后足以让你微笑的成绩！

(Vicky)

《雅思阅读全薇机经》文章、话题对照表

话题分类	文章名称	题型	页码
人类行为研究类	The Sense for Flavour	判断题	45
	The Impact of Environment on Children		70
	Food for Thought	小标题	107
	Intelligence and Giftedness	配对题	167
	Decision Making and Happiness		186
	Optimism and Health		172
	Implication of False Belief Experiments		179
	The Adolescents		198
	Activities for Children	选择题	204
	Smell and Memory		217
	Compliance or Noncompliance for Children		229
	London Swaying Footbridge	摘要填空题	269
	What Are You Laughing At?		281
	The Effect of Living in a Noisy World	简答题	305
	What Does the Consumer Think?	小标题 / 配对题 / 摘要填空题	367
	Finding Our Way	配对题 / 选择题 / 判断题	374
	Communicating Conflict!	小标题 / 判断题 / 选择题	383
	Can Scientists Tell Us: What Happiness Is?	配对题 / 摘要填空题 / 选择题	402
教育类	Mental Gymnastics	判断题	57
	New Ways of Teaching History	小标题	119
	Education Philosophy		131
	Children's Acquiring the Principles of Mathematics and Science	选择题	235
人物传记类	Andrea Palladio — Italian Architect	判断题	14
	Paul Nash	选择题	240
	Thomas Young: The Last True Know-It-All	简答题	317
商业类	Economic Evolution	判断题	20
	Design the Mat and Foot Health		51
	Carlill VS Carbolic Smoke Ball Company		64
	Fossil Files 'The Paleobiology Database'	小标题	83
	Corporate Social Responsibility		95
	Text the Television		125
	Grey Workers	选择题	210
	Aqua Product: New Zealand's Algae Biodiesel	配对题	142
	Plain English Campaign	摘要填空题	263
	The Success of Cellulose	配对题 / 判断题 / 摘要填空题	378
	Paper or Computer?	小标题 / 摘要填空题 / 选择题	371
科技类	Asian Space Satellite Technology	小标题	77

续表

科技类	Inspired by Mimicking Mother Nature	判断题	26
	Man or Machine	配对题	161
	Flight from Reality	摘要填空题	257
	Spider Silk	图表题	323
	Water Filter		329
	Radio Automation—Forerunner of the Integrated Circuit		335
	Detection of a Meteorite Lake	判断题	358
		图表题	
		摘要填空题	
	Life Code: Unlocked	小标题	391
		判断题	
		摘要填空题	
	Sunny Days for Silicon	配对题	394
		判断题	
		摘要填空题	
动植物类	Koalas	判断类	33
	Otter	配对题	148
	Extinct: the Giant Deer		192
	The Culture of Chimpanzee	简答题	311
	The Dugong: Sea Cow	摘要填空题	354
		判断题	
		简答题	
	Finches on Islands	图表题	362
		摘要填空题	
		判读题	
	Hunting Perfume in Madagascar!	配对题	386
		判断题	
		图表题	
	Coral Reefs	配对题	398
		判断题	
		选择题	
文化艺术类	Tattoo in Tikopia	判断题	39
	Save Endangered Language	小标题	113
	Ancient Chinese Chariots	完成句子题	287
	Is Graffiti Art or Crime?		293
发展史类	Exploring British Village	小标题	89
	Ancient Storytelling	配对题	136
	The Origin of Ancient Writing	选择题	223
	Making Copier	摘要填空题	275
	The Concept of Childhood in the Western Countries	简答题	299
	Travel Accounts	图表题	342
医学类	Magnetic Therapy	小标题	101
	Knowledge in Medicine	配对题	155
环境资源类	Coastal Archaeology of Britain	选择题	245
	Global Warming: Prevent Poles from Melting	摘要填空题	251
	Crisis! Fresh Water	判断题	350
		配对题	
		摘要填空题	
	Changes in Air	配对题	406
		判断题	
		摘要填空题	

Contents / 目录

Part 1
雅思阅读简介

1. 考试类型 / **2**
2. 作答方式 / **3**
3. 考试时间 / **3**
4. 评分标准 / **3**
5. 题目类型 / **4**

Part 2
雅思阅读专项练习

第一章　判断题

READING PASSAGE 1　Andrea Palladio — Italian Architect / **14**
READING PASSAGE 2　Economic Evolution / **20**
READING PASSAGE 3　Inspired by Mimicking Mother Nature / **26**
READING PASSAGE 4　Koalas / **33**
READING PASSAGE 5　Tattoo in Tikopia / **39**
READING PASSAGE 6　The Sense for Flavour / **45**
READING PASSAGE 7　Design the Mat and Foot Health / **51**

READING PASSAGE 8　　Mental Gymnastics / **57**
READING PASSAGE 9　　Carlill VS Carbolic Smoke Ball Company / **64**
READING PASSAGE 10　　The Impact of Environment on Children / **70**

第二章　　小标题

READING PASSAGE 1　　Asian Space Satellite Technology / **77**
READING PASSAGE 2　　Fossil Files 'The Paleobiology Database' / **83**
READING PASSAGE 3　　Exploring British Village / **89**
READING PASSAGE 4　　Corporate Social Responsibility / **95**
READING PASSAGE 5　　Magnetic Therapy / **101**
READING PASSAGE 6　　Food for Thought / **107**
READING PASSAGE 7　　Save Endangered Language / **113**
READING PASSAGE 8　　New Ways of Teaching History / **119**
READING PASSAGE 9　　Text the Television / **125**
READING PASSAGE 10　　Education Philosophy / **131**

第三章　　配对题

READING PASSAGE 1　　Ancient Storytelling / **136**
READING PASSAGE 2　　Aqua Product: New Zealand's Algae Biodiesel / **142**
READING PASSAGE 3　　Otter / **148**
READING PASSAGE 4　　Knowledge in Medicine / **155**
READING PASSAGE 5　　Man or Machine / **161**
READING PASSAGE 6　　Intelligence and Giftedness / **167**

Contents / 目录

READING PASSAGE 7   Optimism and Health / *172*
READING PASSAGE 8   Implication of False Belief Experiments / *179*
READING PASSAGE 9   Decision Making and Happiness / *186*
READING PASSAGE 10   Extinct: the Giant Deer / *192*
READING PASSAGE 11   The Adolescents / *198*

第四章　选择题

READING PASSAGE 1   Activities for Children / *204*
READING PASSAGE 2   Grey Workers / *210*
READING PASSAGE 3   Smell and Memory / *217*
READING PASSAGE 4   The Origin of Ancient Writing / *223*
READING PASSAGE 5   Compliance or Noncompliance for Children / *229*
READING PASSAGE 6   Children's Acquiring the Principles of Mathematics and Science / *235*
READING PASSAGE 7   Paul Nash / *240*
READING PASSAGE 8   Coastal Archaeology of Britain / *245*

第五章　摘要填空题

READING PASSAGE 1   Global Warming: Prevent Poles from Melting / *251*
READING PASSAGE 2   Flight from Reality / *257*
READING PASSAGE 3   Plain English Campaign / *263*
READING PASSAGE 4   London Swaying Footbridge / *269*
READING PASSAGE 5   Making Copier / *275*
READING PASSAGE 6   What Are You Laughing At? / *281*

第六章　完成句子题

READING PASSAGE 1   Ancient Chinese Chariots / *287*
READING PASSAGE 2   Is Graffiti Art or Crime? / *293*

第七章 简答题

READING PASSAGE 1 The Concept of Childhood in the Western Countries / **299**
READING PASSAGE 2 The Effect of Living in a Noisy World / **305**
READING PASSAGE 3 The Culture of Chimpanzee / **311**
READING PASSAGE 4 Thomas Young: The Last True Know-It-All / **317**

第八章 图表题

READING PASSAGE 1 Spider Silk / **323**
READING PASSAGE 2 Water Filter / **329**
READING PASSAGE 3 Radio Automation—Forerunner of the Integrated Circuit / **335**
READING PASSAGE 4 Travel Accounts / **342**

Part 3
雅思阅读机经套题及解析

第一章 机经套题

TEST 1

READING PASSAGE 1 Crisis! Fresh Water / **350**

Contents / 目录

READING PASSAGE 2	The Dugong: Sea Cow / **354**
READING PASSAGE 3	Detection of a Meteorite Lake / **358**

TEST 2

READING PASSAGE 1	Finches on Islands / **362**
READING PASSAGE 2	What Does the Consumer Think? / **367**
READING PASSAGE 3	Paper or Computer? / **371**

TEST 3

READING PASSAGE 1	Finding Our Way / **374**
READING PASSAGE 2	The Success of Cellulose / **378**
READING PASSAGE 3	Communicating Conflict! / **383**

TEST 4

READING PASSAGE 1	Hunting Perfume in Madagascar! / **386**
READING PASSAGE 2	Life Code: Unlocked / **391**
READING PASSAGE 3	Sunny Days for Silicon / **394**

TEST 5

READING PASSAGE 1	Coral Reefs / **398**
READING PASSAGE 2	Can Scientists Tell Us: What Happiness Is? / **402**
READING PASSAGE 3	Changes in Air / **406**

第二章　机经套题解析

TEST 1

READING PASSAGE 1 / **410**

READING PASSAGE 2 / **417**

READING PASSAGE 3 / **424**

TEST 2

READING PASSAGE 1 / *431*
READING PASSAGE 2 / *438*
READING PASSAGE 3 / *444*

TEST 3

READING PASSAGE 1 / *450*
READING PASSAGE 2 / *457*
READING PASSAGE 3 / *463*

TEST 4

READING PASSAGE 1 / *469*
READING PASSAGE 2 / *476*
READING PASSAGE 3 / *482*

TEST 5

READING PASSAGE 1 / *488*
READING PASSAGE 2 / *494*
READING PASSAGE 3 / *501*

Vicky IELTS Practices

Part 1

雅思阅读简介

雅思考试（IELTS），全称为国际英语测试系统（International English Language Testing System），是著名的国际性英语标准化水平测试之一，包含四门学科，即听力（Listening）、阅读（Reading）、写作（Writing）和口语（Speaking）。

对于大多数考生来说阅读是雅思考试中较难的单项，因为考生在一个小时内不仅要阅读三篇平均篇幅 800 词左右的文章，还要做出 40 道题型多样的题目。俗话说"想要攻城，先破其门"，下面就一起了解一下雅思阅读的基本信息吧！

1. 考试类型

类型	文章数量	文章背景	题目数量
Academic	Reading Passage 1	学术背景	13~14
	Reading Passage 2	学术背景	13~14
	Reading Passage 3	学术背景	13~14
General Training	Section 1	日常事务（两篇或三篇）	14
	Section 2	培训内容（两篇）	13
	Section 3	说明文（一篇）	13

雅思阅读考试根据出国的目的分为两类。凡是计划出国留学，攻读学士、硕士或博士学位的考生应参加 Academic 类（简称 A 类）的考试。申请移民或参加短期交流式培训的考生要参加 General Training 类（简称 G 类）的考试。

A 类的阅读考试有三篇文章，文章的内容包含即将学习本科、研究生课程或进行职业注册的考生所感兴趣的、与其认知程度相符的常见话题。其中，至少有一篇文章为文科题材（与社会、经济等文科专业有关），另外两篇涉及理、工、农、医，一般与科技相关。每篇文章有 13~14 道题，三篇文章共 40 道题，总长度约在 2,000 到 2,750 字之间。所有的文章均出自英美刊物或书籍。

G 类的阅读考试由三部分组成。第一部分通常包含 2 到 3 篇短文或者若干段文字（如广告），内容选自通知、广告、时间表、宣传品、以及其他类似的内容，共计 14 道题；第二部分通常有 2 篇文章，内容选自大学招生简章、课程介绍、图书馆指引、规定、以及其他类似的内容，共计 13 道题；第三部分则为一段较长的文章，内容选自报纸、杂志、期刊、小说或非虚构的书籍以及其他类似的内容，共计 13 道题。文章总长度约在 2,400 字左右。

本书收集的文章，题材主要是针对 A 类的考试，但是 G 类试题中第三部分的长篇文章的长度、题型均与 A 类试题非常接近。因此，本书中的许多文章也适用于准备参加 G 类考试的考生。

2. 作答方式

答案写在答题卡上，写在试卷上不计入成绩。雅思的评分标准是按照做对题目的个数计分，错题不会扣分，所以答题卡上千万不要留空。

3. 考试时间

60 分钟，包含了把答案写在答题卡上的时间。对于多数考生来说，要以同样的细致程度完成三篇文章的阅读是有困难的，最好的安排是花 45 分钟左右将其中的两篇做得较细，使答题的正确率高一些，将剩余的时间（10 分钟）用在另一篇文章中。

4. 评分标准

题目数（A类）	分数（A类）	题目数（G类）	分数（G类）
39-40	9.0	40	9.0
37-38	8.5	39	8.5
35-36	8.0	38	8.0
33-34	7.5	36-37	7.5
30-32	7.0	34-35	7.0
27-29	6.5	32-33	6.5
23-26	6.0	30-31	6.0
20-22	5.5	26-29	5.5
16-19	5.0	23-25	5.0
13-15	4.5	19-22	4.5
10-12	4.0	15-18	4.0
6-9	3.5	12-14	3.5
4-5	3.0	8-11	3.0

5. 题目类型

雅思阅读的题型共分八大类：判断题、小标题、配对题、选择题、摘要填空题、完成句子题、简答题、图表题。

题型一：判断题

判断题是雅思阅读考试中的经典题型，也是每一次雅思阅读考试中都会出现的高频题型。判断题考查考生的原文定位能力和逻辑分析能力，很多考生分不清楚 FALSE/NO 与 NOT GIVEN。题目要求考生对原文给出的信息或作者的观点进行判断。此题的答题要求有两种 TRUE/FALSE/NOT GIVEN 和 YES/NO/NOT GIVEN，切记不要写混！

样例：

Do the following statements agree with the information given in Reading Passage 1?

In boxes 1–4 on your answer sheet, write

TRUE　　　　　if the statement agrees with the information
FALSE　　　　if the statement contradicts the information
NOT GIVEN　if there is no information on this

或者

Do the following statements agree with the views of the writer in Reading Passage 1?

In boxes 1–4 on your answer sheet, write

YES　　　　　if the statement agrees with the claims of the writer
NO　　　　　if the statement contradicts the claims of the writer
NOT GIVEN　if it is impossible to say what the writer thinks about this

判断题有以下特点：

（1）出题顺序：一般情况下会遵循顺序性原则，即题目的根据在原文中按顺序出现，但偶尔也会有乱序的情况出现。

（2）在三种选项中，NOT GIVEN 所占的比例一般最小，题目中的关键词在原文中没有出现或者只是部分出现。

（3）判断题属于细节题，大多数题目不需要考生对上下文进行理解，只阅读定位到的相关句子进行判断即可。

题型二：小标题

小标题也是一种高频题型，平均每两次考试中就会出现一次，有时甚至连续出现。但是这种题型很容易出现一种情况就是连带错误，导致错误率急速上升。

样例：

Reading Passage 2 has eight paragraphs, **A–H**.

*Choose the correct heading for paragraphs **A** and **C–H** from the list of headings below.*

*Write the correct number, **i–xi**, in boxes 14–20 on your answer sheet.*

List of Headings

i	Scientists' call for a revision of policy
ii	An explanation for reduced water use
iii	How a global challenge was met
iv	Irrigation systems fall into disuse
v	Environmental effects
vi	The financial cost of recent technological improvements
vii	The relevance to health
viii	Addressing the concern over increasing populations
ix	A surprising downward trend in demand for water
x	The need to raise standards
xi	A description of ancient water supplies

Example	Answer
Paragraph B	iii

14 Paragraph **A**

15 Paragraph **C**

16 Paragraph **D**

17 Paragraph **E**

18 Paragraph **F**

19 Paragraph **G**

20 Paragraph **H**

小标题有以下特点：

（1）小标题的题目出现在文章的前面。

（2）要求给每个段落或部分找一个小标题，有时候一个部分包含多个段落。

（3）罗马数字选项个数一般多于题目个数。

（4）因为题目正确答案具有唯一性，所以例子中出现的罗马数字选项，将不会再被其他题目选择。

题型三：配对题

配对题包含：段落配信息题、属性配对题、句尾配对题。段落配信息题是指题干给出原文的若干条细节信息，要求考生找出文中分别有这些信息的段落。属性配对题一般考查的是某专家的言论或观点、某组织与其对应的功能、某事件对应的年代等。句尾配对题这种题型，题干为不完整句子，需要从选项中找出剩余信息补全句子。配对题相比于其他题型较难，对考生的定位能力要求较高。

样例：

Questions 37–40

Look at the following statements (Questions 37–40) and the list of scientists below.

Match each statement with the correct scientist, **A–D**.

Write the correct letter, **A–D**, in boxes 37–40 on your answer sheet.

37 The effects of geo-engineering may not be long-lasting.

38 Geo-engineering is a topic worth exploring.

39 It may be necessary to limit the effectiveness of geo-engineering projects.

40 Research into non-fossil-based fuels cannot be replaced by geo-engineering.

List of Scientists
A Roger Angel
B Phil Rasch
C Dan Lunt
D Martin Sommerkorn

配对题有以下特点：

（1）出题顺序：

i. 段落配信息题为乱序题型，定位难度较大。题目表达：Which paragraph contains

the following information?

ii. 属性配对题包括专家与观点、组织与功能、时代与事件等，这类配对题比较容易定位。需要注意的是属性配对题有时乱序，有时顺序。题目表达：Match.../Classify...

iii. 句尾配对题大多数为顺序，偶尔有乱序情况。题目表达：Complete each sentence with the correct ending, **A–I**, below.

（2）题目要求中 **NB** You may use any letter more than once. 表明一般情况下有两道题目答案相同。

题型四：选择题

雅思考试中的选择题可以说是考生最熟悉的一种题型。选择题分为单选题和多选题两种形式。单选题一般要求考生四个选项中选择一个正确的选项，但剑桥雅思真题中也出现过特殊的情况，比如剑 4 TEST 1 Reading Passage 1 Question14 中要求考生从五个选项中选择一个正确选项。多选题在剑桥真题中就是多选多，常出现的情况有：五个选项中选择两个正确选项，七个选项中选择三个正确选项和十个或十一个选项中选择五个正确选项。

样例：

Choose **THREE** letters, **A–G**.

Which **THREE** topics does Sandra agree to include in the proposal?

    A   climate change

    B   field trip activities

    C   geographical features

    D   impact of tourism

    E   myths and legends

    F   plant and animal life

    G   social history

选择题有以下特点：

（1）出题顺序：一般情况下会遵循顺序性原则，但偶尔也会有乱序的情况出现。

（2）因为每道题目都有干扰项，一般干扰项具有以下几个特征：

i. 选项内容和原文表述一样，但答非所问

ii. 选项内容和原文意思相近，但个别词有问题

（3）一般正确答案为原文信息的同义改写

注意：因为选择题耗时比较长，所以在没有时间的情况下，猜答案时可以选择：

i. 带有否定词的选项

ii. TWINS 原则（两个相反选项，选其中一个作为答案）

题型五：摘要填空题

这种题型是一小段文字，是原文全文或原文中的几个段落主要内容的缩写或改写，我们称之为摘要。摘要中有几个空白部分要求考生填空。

样例：

Complete the summary below.

Choose **NO MORE THAN TWO WORDS** from the passage for each answer.

Write your answers in boxes 8–13 on your answer sheet.

Additional Evidence for Theory of Kite-lifting

The Egyptians had **8** .... which could lift large pieces of **9** ...., and they knew how to use the energy of the wind from their skill as **10** .... The discovery on one pyramid of an object which resembled a **11** .... suggests they may have experimented with **12** .... In addition, over two thousand **years ago** kites were used in China as weapons, as well as for sending **13** ....

摘要填空题有以下特点：

（1）题目字数要求有限制（这点在其他填空题型中也需注意）

答案书写要求	举例说明
Write **ONE WORD ONLY**	答案是一个单词，举例：eighteen
Write **NO MORE THAN TWO WORDS OR A NUMBER** for each answer	答案是两个单词；或者答案是一个数字 e.g. twelve trees（对）；12 trees（错）
Write **NO MORE THAN TWO WORDS AND/OR A NUMBER** for each answer	答案是两个单词；或者答案是一个数字；或者答案是两个单词+一个数字的组合e.g. twelve trees或12 trees

（2）题目中出现字数限制时（e.g. NO MORE THAN XXX WORDS），需注意以下三点：

i. 满足字数要求

ii. 空内答案为原文原词

iii. 题目之间符合顺序原则

（3）题目中出现选项信息时（e.g. Complete the summary using the list of words, **A–E**, below.），需注意以下两点：

　　i. 选项中答案信息与原文对应，一般为同义替换

　　ii. 个别题目之间为乱序，建议同时检查两道题目

题型六：完成句子题

　　完成句子题型是先给出句子的一部分，未给出部分需要在文章中寻找。这种题型较难，要花一点时间仔细查看文章中的相关部分。

样例：

Complete the sentences below.

*Choose **NO MORE THAN TWO WORDS** from the passage for each answer.*

Write your answers in boxes 10–13 on your answer sheet.

10 Long before the invention of radar, ……………… had resulted in a sophisticated radar-like system in bats.

11 Radar is an inaccurate term when referring to bats, because ……………… are not in their navigation system.

12 Radar and sonar are based on similar ……………… .

13 The word 'echolocation' was first used by someone working as a ……………… .

完成句子题的特点：

（1）出题顺序：一般情况下会遵循顺序性原则，但偶尔也会有乱序的情况出现。

（2）每个题目都是一个陈述句，但留有一个或两个空格，要求根据原文填空。目前考试中，绝大部分是一个空格。

（3）大部分的题目要求中有字数限制，一般不会超过四个字。

（4）该题型的解题难度在于题目中的关键词和原文中的相应词对应不明显。

题型七：简答题

　　简答题属于填空类题型，该题型难度偏低，要求考生根据文章内容回答由特殊疑问词引导的疑问句，主要考查考生的英语基本能力（包括单词量和对基础语法的掌握程度）和对雅思阅读解题基本方法的掌握情况。因此，考生要突破该题型相对较容易。

样例：

Questions 12 and 13

Answer the questions below.

Choose **NO MORE THAN THREE WORDS AND/OR A NUMBER** from the passage for each answer.

Write your answers in boxes 12 and 13 on your answer sheet.

12 What is produced to help an athlete plan their performance in an event?
13 By how much did some cyclists' performance improve at the 1996 Olympic Games?

简答题一般具有以下三个特点：

（1）提问词为特殊疑问词，包括 what，when，where，who，which，why 和 how 等。考生要明确每道题询问的疑问词是什么，然后有针对性地答题，不能答非所问。

（2）题目遵循顺序一致原则。也就是说，题目顺序与题目答案在原文中出现的顺序一致。

（3）答案多为名词性原词重现。简答题的题目答案绝大多数都是名词性质的词（包括名词、动名词等），而且答案都是来自于原文中的原词，考生作答时一般无需作任何改动。

题型八：图表题

图表题是雅思考试的特色题型之一，相对于雅思阅读的其他题型而言，图表题的难度不高，出题的频率较低。其出题总的形式是：根据阅读文章所给出的信息，填补图表内所缺失的内容。考查的是考生快速寻读找位，并理解细节信息的阅读能力。它又分成三种类型，即统计表 (Table)、原理图 (Diagram) 和流程图 (Flow Chart)。前几年的阅读考试图表题以 Table 居多，而近一两年 Diagram 和 Flow Chart 出现次数较多。

样例：

Questions 4–8

Complete the flow-chart below.

Choose **ONE WORD ONLY** from the passage for each answer.

Write your answers in boxes 4–8 on your answer sheet.

The Production of Bakelite

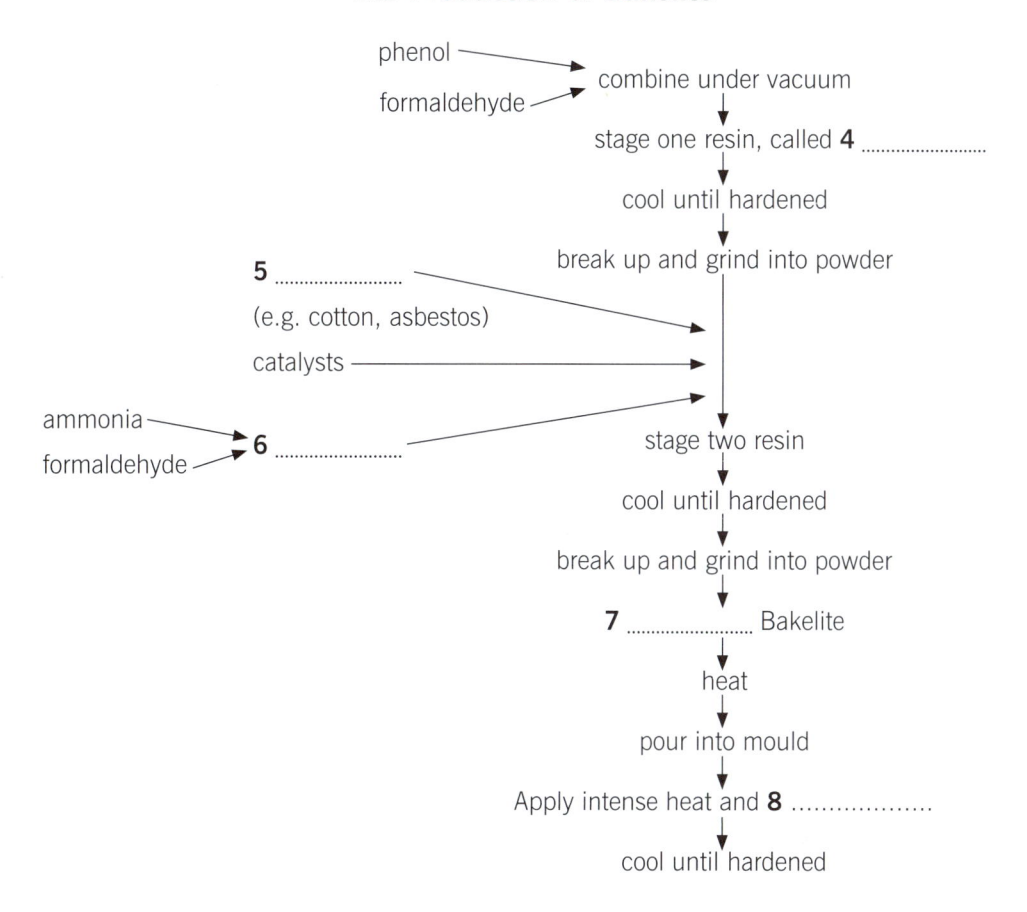

```
phenol ─────────────┐
                    ▼
formaldehyde ──► combine under vacuum
                    │
                    ▼
            stage one resin, called 4 ..................
                    │
                    ▼
             cool until hardened
                    │
                    ▼
         break up and grind into powder

5 ..................
(e.g. cotton, asbestos)
catalysts

ammonia ─────┐
             ▼
formaldehyde ► 6 ..................
                    │
                    ▼
              stage two resin
                    │
                    ▼
             cool until hardened
                    │
                    ▼
         break up and grind into powder
                    │
                    ▼
          7 .................. Bakelite
                    │
                    ▼
                   heat
                    │
                    ▼
              pour into mould
                    │
                    ▼
      Apply intense heat and 8 ..................
                    │
                    ▼
             cool until hardened
```

图表题所填内容一般有以下特点：

（1）图表中所需要填充的词可能会涉及时间、事件及人物。有时也可能只考其中的一项或两项，但是时间往往只涉及年代，不会涉及具体的日期。

（2）文章的某一段提到了一个物体，讲述了它的构造和各部分的功能。题目是该物体的简图，给出一些部件的名称及功能，要求填其余部件的名称及功能。所填信息常常集中于原文中的一个段落。

（3）文章的某一段提到了做一件事情的过程，题目以流程图的形式描述这个过程，要求填其中几个环节的内容。

以上这八大题型是雅思阅读的核心题型，本书第二部分是针对这些题型的专项练习，大家可以集中练习、攻克。

Vicky

IELTS R

Practices

Part 2

雅思阅读专项练习

第一章 判断题

READING PASSAGE 1

Andrea Palladio – Italian Architect

A new exhibition celebrates Palladio's architecture 500 years on

A Vicenza is a pleasant, prosperous city in the Veneto, 60km west of Venice. Its grand families settled and farmed the area from the 16th century. But its principal claim to fame is Andrea Palladio, who is such an influential architect that a neoclassical style is known as Palladian. The city is a permanent exhibition of some of his finest buildings, and as he was born — in Padua, to be precise — 500 years ago, the International Centre for the Study of Palladio's Architecture has an excellent excuse for mounting la grande mostra, the big show.

B The exhibition has the special advantage of being held in one of Palladio's buildings, Palazzo Barbaran da Porto. Its bold facade is a mixture of rustication and decoration set between two rows of elegant columns. On the second floor the pediments are alternately curved or pointed, a Palladian trademark. The harmonious proportions of the atrium at the entrance lead through to a dramatic interior of fine fireplaces and painted ceilings. Palladio's design is simple, clear and not over-crowded. The show has been organised on the same principles, according to Howard Bums, the architectural historian who co-curated it.

C Palladio's father was a miller who settled in Vicenza, where the young Andrea was apprenticed to a skilled stonemason. How did a humble miller's son become a world-renowned architect? The answer in the exhibition is that, as a young man, Palladio excelled at carving decorative stonework on columns, doorways and fireplaces. He was plainly intelligent, and lucky enough to come across a rich patron, Gian Giorgio Trissino, a landowner and scholar, who organised his education, taking him to Rome in the 1540s, where he studied the masterpieces of classical Roman and Greek architecture and the work of other influential architects of the time, such as Donato Bramante and Raphael.

D Burns argues that social mobility was also important. Entrepreneurs, prosperous from agriculture in the Veneto, commissioned the promising local architect to design their country villas and their urban mansions. In Venice, the aristocracy were anxious to co-opt talented artists, and Palladio was given the chance to design the buildings that have made him famous — the churches of San Giorgio Maggiore and the Redentore, both easy to admire because they can be seen from the city's historical centre across a stretch of water.

E He tried his hand at bridges — his unbuilt version of the Rialto Bridge was decorated with the large pediment and columns of a temple — and, after a fire at the Ducal Palace, he offered an alternative design which bears an uncanny resemblance to the Banqueting House in Whitehall in London. Since it was designed by Inigo Jones, Palladio's first foreign disciple, this is not as surprising as it sounds.

F Jones, who visited Italy in 1614, bought a trunk full of the master's architectural drawings; they passed through the hands of the Dukes of Burlington and Devonshire before settling at the Royal Institute of British Architects in 1894. Many are now on display at Palazzo Barbaran. What they show is how Palladio drew on the buildings of ancient Rome as models. The major theme of both his rural and urban building was temple architecture, with a strong pointed pediment supported by columns and approached by wide steps.

G Palladio's work for rich landowners alienates unreconstructed critics on the Italian left, but among the papers in the show are designs for cheap housing in Venice. In the wider world, Palladio's reputation has been nurtured by a text he wrote and illustrated, 'Quattro Libri dell Architettura'. His influence spread to St Petersburg and to Charlottesville in Virginia, where Thomas Jefferson commissioned a Palladian villa he called Monticello.

H Vicenza's show contains detailed models of the major buildings and is leavened by portraits of Palladio's teachers and clients by Titian, Veronese and Tintoretto; the paintings of his Venetian buildings are all by Canaletto, no less. This is an uncompromising exhibition; many of the drawings are small and faint, and there are no sideshows for children, but the impact of harmonious lines and satisfying proportions is to impart in a viewer a feeling of benevolent calm. Palladio is history's most therapeutic architect.

'Palladio, 500 Anni: La Grande Mostra' is at Palazzo Barbaran da Porto, Vicenza, until January 6th 2009. The exhibition continues at the Royal Academy of Arts, London, from January 31st to April 13th, and travels afterwards to Barcelona and Madrid.

Questions 1–7

Do the following statements agree with the information given in the passage?

In boxes 1–7 on your answer sheet, write

> **TRUE**   *if the statement agrees with the information*
> **FALSE**   *if the statement contradicts the information*
> **NOT GIVEN**   *if there is no information on this*

1   The building where the exhibition is staged has been newly renovated.

2   Palazzo Barbaran da Porto typically represents the Palladio's design.

3   Palladio's father worked as an architect.

4   Palladio's family refused to pay for his architectural studies.

5   Palladio's alternative design for the Ducal Palace in Venice was based on an English building.

6   Palladio designed for both wealthy and poor people.

7   The exhibition includes paintings of people by famous artists.

核心词汇

A 段

prosperous [ˈprɒspərəs] *adj.* 富裕的；繁荣的
fame [feɪm] *n.* 名声，名望
influential [ˌɪnfluˈenʃl] *adj.* 有影响力的；有权势的
permanent [ˈpɜːmənənt] *adj.* 永久性的，永恒的
mount [maʊnt] *vt.* 准备；安排；组织 *vi.* 渐渐增加，逐渐增长 *vi. & vt.* 骑上，跨上

B 段

pediment [ˈpedɪmənt] *n.* 三角顶饰
alternately [ɔːlˈtɜːnətli] *adv.* 交互，轮流地

C 段

apprentice [əˈprentɪs] *n.* 学徒，徒弟
renowned [rɪˈnaʊnd] *adj.* 有名的；享有声誉的
plainly [ˈpleɪnli] *adv.* 明显地，清楚地；坦白地
come across 偶遇，偶然发现
patron [ˈpeɪtrən] *n.* 赞助者，资助人
masterpiece [ˈmɑːstəpiːs] *n.* 杰作，名作

D 段

mobility [məʊˈbɪləti] *n.* 移动性，流动性
commission [kəˈmɪʃn] *vt.* 委任，授予 *n.* 委员会；佣金

E 段

uncanny [ʌnˈkæni] *adj.* 离奇的，不可思议的
resemblance [rɪˈzembləns] *n.* 相似，类似

H 段

leaven [ˈlevn] *vt.* 使生动
faint [feɪnt] *adj.* 模糊的；虚弱的
benevolent [bəˈnevələnt] *adj.* 乐善好施的；仁爱的
therapeutic [ˌθerəˈpjuːtɪk] *adj.* 使人放松的；治疗的

高频同义替换

principal ▸ primary, chief, major

precise ▸ accurate, exact, pinpoint, meticulous

interior ▸ inside, inner, inherent, intrinsic

contain ▸ involve, include, comprise, consist of

题目解析

1 定位词：building where the exhibition is staged

文中对应点：B 段第一句

题目解析：题干说，举行展览的建筑物被重新装修了。通过定位词 building where exhibition is staged 定位到 B 段第一句 "The exhibition has the special advantage of being held in one of Palladio's buildings, Palazzo Barbaran da Porto."。其中，exhibition…being held in one of Palladio's buildings 与 building where the exhibition is staged 为同义替换。句意为，这次展览有一个特别的优势，那就是在帕拉第奥的一座建筑物里举办。在随后的句子中详细地描述了建筑物的特点，并未提及建筑物是否于最近翻修（newly renovated），因此答案为 NOT GIVEN。

2 定位词：Palazzo Barbaran da Porto, represent, Palladio's design

文中对应点：B 段第三句

题目解析：题干说，芭芭拉波尔图宫是帕拉第奥设计的典型代表。通过定位词 Palazzo Barbaran da Porto, represent, Palladio's design 定位到 B 段第三句 "On the second floor the pediments are alternately curved or pointed, a Palladian trademark."。这句是对芭芭拉波尔图宫的进一步补充说明。其中，Palladian 对应 Palladio's design，trademark 对应 represent。句意为，二层的三角顶饰是用曲线或点状交替装饰的，这是帕拉第奥式建筑的标志。因此答案为 TRUE。

3 定位词：Palladio's father, architect

文中对应点：C 段第一句

题目解析：题干说，帕拉第奥的父亲是一位建筑师。通过定位词 Palladio's father 定位到 C 段第一句 "Palladio's father was a miller who settled in Vicenza, where the young Andrea was apprenticed to a skilled stonemason."。其中，miller 与题干中的 architect 矛盾。句意为，帕拉第奥的父亲是定居在维琴察的一位磨坊主，在这里，年轻的安德里亚给一位技术熟练的石匠当学徒。因此答案为 FALSE。

4 定位词：pay, architectural studies

文中对应点：C 段最后一句

题目解析：题干说，帕拉第奥的家人拒绝支付帕拉第奥学习建筑的费用。通过定位词 pay, architectural studies 定位到 C 段最后一句 "He was plainly intelligent, and lucky enough to come across a rich patron, …where he studied the masterpieces of classical Roman and Greek architecture and the work of other influential architects of the time, such as Donato Bramante and Raphael."。其中，patron 对应 pay，studied the masterpieces of… 与 architectural studies 为同义替换，

但文中并未提及帕拉第奥的家人是否拒绝支付帕拉第奥学习费用的相关信息。句意为，帕拉第奥相当聪明，也足够幸运遇到了一位赞助人，……在罗马他研究了古典罗马和希腊建筑的杰作，以及当时其他有影响力的建筑师的作品，比如多纳托·布拉曼特和拉斐尔。因此答案为 NOT GIVEN。

5. 定位词：alternative design, Ducal Palace, an English building
   文中对应点：E 段第一句
   题目解析：题干说，帕拉第奥在威尼斯的公爵宫殿的替代设计是以一座英国建筑为基础的。通过定位词 alternative design, Ducal Palace, an English building 定位到 E 段第一句 "…after a fire at the Ducal Palace, he offered an alternative design which bears an uncanny resemblance to the Banqueting House in Whitehall in London."。其中，the Banqueting House in Whitehall in London 对应 an English building。句意为，公爵宫殿发生火灾后，帕拉第奥提出了一种替代方案，与伦敦白厅的宴会厅有着惊人的相似性。因此答案为 TRUE。

6. 定位词：wealthy and poor people
   文中对应点：G 段第一句
   题目解析：题干说，帕拉第奥既为富人做设计也为穷人做设计。通过关键词 wealthy and poor people 定位到 G 段第一句 "Palladio's work for rich landowners alienates unreconstructed critics on the Italian left, but among the papers in the show are designs for cheap housing in Venice."。其中，rich landowners 和 cheap housing 对应 wealthy and poor people。句意为，尽管帕拉第奥为富有地主们创作的作品受到意大利左翼保守评价家们的抵制，但在本次展出的这些图纸中，有很多却是为威尼斯的廉价住房而设计的。因此答案为 TRUE。

7. 定位词：exhibition, paintings of people
   文中对应点：H 段第一句
   题目解析：题干说，此次展览包括著名艺术家的人物绘画作品。由题干中的定位词 exhibition, paintings of people 定位到 H 段第一句 "Vicenza's show contains detailed models of the major buildings and is leavened by portraits of Palladio's teachers and clients by Titian, Veronese and Tintoretto; the paintings of his Venetian buildings are all by Canaletto, no less."。其中，Vicenza's show 对应 exhibition，portraits of Palladio's teachers and clients 对应 paintings of people，portraits 与 paintings 为同义替换。另外，原文中的 Titian, Veronese and Tintoretto 是一些著名艺术家的名字，对应题目中的 famous artists。句意为，维琴察的展览包括帕拉第奥设计的主要建筑的详细模型，还有一些由提香、维罗纳和丁托列托所绘的帕拉第奥的老师和客人们的肖像。题干的表述符合原文意思，因此答案为 TRUE。

参考答案

1 NOT GIVEN　2 TRUE　3 FALSE　4 NOT GIVEN　5 TRUE　6 TRUE　7 TRUE

READING PASSAGE 2

Economic Evolution

A Living along the Orinoco River that borders Brazil and Venezuela are the Yanomam people, hunter-gatherers whose average annual income has been estimated at the equivalent of $90 per person per year. Living along the Hudson River that borders New York State and New Jersey are the Manhattan people, consumer-traders whose average annual income has been estimated at $536,000 per person per year. That dramatic difference of 400 times, however, pales in comparison to the differences in Stock Keeping Units (SKUs, a measure of the number of types of retail products available), which has been estimated at $300 for the Yanomam and $10 billion for the Manhattans, a difference of 33 million times.

B How did this happen? According to economist Eric D. Beinhocker, who published these calculations in his revelatory work *The Origin of Wealth* (Harvard Business School Press, 2006), the explanation is to be found in complexity theory. Evolution and economics are not just analogous to each other, but they are actually two forms of a larger phenomenon called complex adaptive systems, in which individual elements, parts or agents interact, then process information and adapt their behaviour to changing conditions. Immune systems, ecosystems, language, the law and the Internet are all examples of complex adaptive systems.

C In biological evolution, nature selects from the variation produced by random genetic mutations and the mixing of parental genes. Out of that process of cumulative selection emerges complexity and diversity. In economic evolution, our material economy proceeds through the production and selection of numerous permutations of countless products. Those 10 billion products in the Manhattan village represent only those variations that made it to market, after which there is a cumulative selection by consumers in the marketplace for those deemed most useful: VHS over Betamax, DVDs over VHS, CDs over vinyl records, flip phones over brick phones, computers over typewriters, Google over Altavista, SUVs over station wagons, paper books over e-books (still), and Internet news over network news (soon). Those that are purchased 'survive' and 'reproduce' into the future through repetitive use and remanufacturing.

D As with living organisms and ecosystems, the economy looks designed — so just as humans naturally deduce the existence of a top-down intelligent designer, humans also (understandably) infer that a top-down government designer is needed in nearly every aspect of the economy. But just as living organisms are shaped from the bottom up by natural selection, the economy is molded from the bottom up by the invisible hand. The correspondence between evolution and economics is not perfect, because some top-down institutional rules and laws are needed to provide a structure within which free and fair trade can occur. But too much top-down interference into the marketplace makes trade neither free nor fair. When such attempts have been made in the past, they have failed — because markets are far too complex, interactive and autocatalytic to be designed from the top down. In his 1922 book, *Socialism*, Ludwig Von Mises spelled out the reasons why, most notably the problem of 'economic calculation' in a planned socialist economy. In capitalism, prices are in constant and rapid flux and are determined from below by individuals freely exchanging in the marketplace. Money is a means of exchange, and prices are the information people use to guide their choices. Von Mises demonstrated that socialist economies depend on capitalist economics to determine what prices should be assigned to goods and services. And they do so cumbersomely and inefficiently. Relatively free markets are, ultimately, the only way to find out what buyers are willing to pay and what sellers are willing to accept.

E Economics helps to explain how Yanomam-like hunter-gatherers evolved into Manhattan-like consumer-traders. In the nineteenth century French economist Frederic Bastiat well captured the principle: 'Where goods do not cross frontiers, armies will.' In addition to being fierce warriors, the Yanomam are also sophisticated traders, and the more they trade the less they fight. The reason is that trade is a powerful social adhesive that creates political alliances. One village cannot go to another village and announce that they are worried about being conquered by a third, more powerful village — that would reveal weakness. Instead they mask the real motives for alliance through trade and reciprocal feasting. And, as a result not only gain military protection but also initiate a system of trade that — in the long run — leads to an increase in both wealth and SKUs.

F Free and fair trade occurs in societies where most individuals interact in ways that provide mutual benefit. The necessary rules weren't generated by wise men in a sacred temple, or lawmakers in congress, but rather evolved over generations and were widely accepted and practiced before the law was ever written. Laws that fail this test are ignored. If enforcement becomes too onerous, there is rebellion. Yet the concept that human interaction must, and can be controlled by a higher force is universal. Interestingly, there is no widespread agreement on who the 'higher force' is. Religious people ascribe good behaviour to god's law. They cannot conceive of an orderly society of atheists. Secular people credit the government. They consider anarchy to be synonymous with barbarity. Everyone seems to agree on the concept that orderly society requires an omnipotent force. Yet, everywhere there is evidence that this is not so. An important distinction between spontaneous social order and social anarchy is that the former is developed by work and investment, under the rule of law and with a set of evolved morals while the latter is chaos. The classical liberal tradition of Von Mises and Hayek never makes the claim that the complete absence of top-down rules leads to the optimal social order. It simply says we should be sceptical about our ability to manage them in the name of social justice, equality, or progress.

Questions 1–5

Do the following statements agree with the information given in the passage?

In boxes 1–5 on your answer sheet, write

    TRUE   if the statement agrees with the information
    FALSE   if the statement contradicts the information
    NOT GIVEN if there is no information on this

1   SKUs is a more precise measurement to demonstrate the economic level of a community.

2   No concrete examples are presented when the author makes the statement concerning economic evolution.

3   Evolution and economics show a defective homolog.

4   Martial actions might be taken to cross the borders if trades do not work.

5   Profit is the invisible hand to guide the market.

核心词汇

A 段

equivalent [ɪˈkwɪvələnt] *adj.* 等价的；相等的 *n.* 等价物；相等物

B 段

evolution [ˌiːvəˈluːʃn] *n.* 进化，演变

phenomenon [fəˈnɒmɪnən] *n.* 现象；奇迹

C 段

genetic [dʒəˈnetɪk] *adj.* 基因的，遗传的

cumulative [ˈkjuːmjələtɪv] *adj.* 积累的；渐增的

diversity [daɪˈvɜːsəti] *n.* 多样化，多元化

D 段

deduce [dɪˈdjuːs] *vt.* 推论，推断；演绎

intelligent [ɪnˈtelɪdʒənt] *adj.* 聪明的，机智的；理解力强的

invisible [ɪnˈvɪzəbl] *adj.* 无形的；看不见的

correspondence [ˌkɒrəˈspɒndəns] *n.* 通信；信件；联系；关系

interference [ˌɪntəˈfɪərəns] *n.* 干预，干涉；介入

capitalism [ˈkæpɪtəlɪzəm] *n.* 资本主义

cumbersomely [ˈkʌmbəsəmli] *adv.* 笨重地；累赘地；冗长地

E 段

principle [ˈprɪnsəpl] *n.* 原理；原则；行为准则

sophisticated [səˈfɪstɪkeɪtɪd] *adj.* 复杂的；富有经验的；精通的

adhesive [ədˈhiːsɪv] *n.* 黏合剂 *adj.* 带黏性的

F 段

enforcement [ɪnˈfɔːsmənt] *n.* 执行；强制

rebellion [rɪˈbeljən] *n.* 造反，叛乱

conceive [kənˈsiːv] *vi.* & *vt.* 想象，设想；怀孕 *vt.* 构思

omnipotent [ɒmˈnɪpətənt] *adj.* 无所不能的，全能的

spontaneous [spɒnˈteɪniəs] *adj.* 自发的；率性的

sceptical [ˈskeptɪkl] *adj.* 不相信的，怀疑的

题目

defective [dɪˈfektɪv] *adj.* 有缺陷的

homolog [ˈhɒməˌlɒg] *n.* 相当或相同的事物

高频同义替换

diversity ▸ difference, multiplicity, variety

intelligent ▸ wise, bright, clever, smart

cumbersomely ▸ clumsily

interference ▸ conflict, disturbance, obstacle, collision

rebellion ▸ revolution, insurrection, revolt, muting, uprising

题目解析

1 定位词：SKUs, measurement
文中对应点：A 段最后一句
题目解析：题干说，SKUs 是一种更精确的测量，以展示一个社区的经济水平。根据定位词 SKUs, measurement 定位到 A 段最后一句 "…(SKUs, a measure of the number of types of retail products available), which has been estimated at \$300 for the Yanomam and \$10 billion for the Manhattans, a difference of 33 million times."。其中，a measure 对应 measurement，但并未说明 SKUs 是否是一种更为精准的测量方式。句意为，……（库存单位是可售零售商品类型数量的一种指标），据估算，雅诺马马人的年收入为 300 美元，曼哈顿岛人的年收入为 100 亿美元，相差 3,300 万倍。因此答案为 NOT GIVEN。

2 定位词：no concrete examples, economic evolution
文中对应点：B 段最后两句
题目解析：题干说，作者发表关于经济发展的声明时，没有给出具体的例子。根据定位词 no concrete examples, economic evolution 定位到 B 段最后两句 "Evolution and economics are not just analogous to each other, but they are actually two forms of a larger phenomenon called complex adaptive systems… Immune systems, ecosystems, language, the law and the Internet are all examples of complex adaptive systems."。其中，Evolution and economics 对应 economic evolution，Immune systems, ecosystems, language, the law and the Internet are all examples 与题干中的 no concrete examples（没有具体例子）矛盾。句意为，进化和经济不仅仅是相互类似，它们其实是一个被称作复杂适应系统的更大的现象的两种形式……免疫系统、生态系统、语言、法律和互联网均是复杂适应系统的例子。因此答案为 FALSE。

3 定位词：evolution and economics, defective homolog
文中对应点：D 段第三句
题目解析：题干说，进化和经济学显示出一种有缺陷的同系物。根据定位词 evolution and economics, defective homolog 定位到 D 段第三句 "The correspondence between evolution and economics is not perfect, because some top-down institutional rules and laws are needed to provide a structure within which free and fair trade can occur."。其中，not perfect 与 defective 为同义替换，correspondence 对应 homolog。句意为，进化和经济学之间的关系并不完善，因为需

要一些自上而下的规章制度和法律提供一个能进行公平自由贸易的结构。原文与题干意义一致，因此答案为 TRUE。

4 定位词：martial actions, cross the borders, trades
文中对应点：E 段第二句
题目解析：题干说，如果交易不成，可能会采取军事行动跨越边境。根据定位词 martial actions, cross the borders, trades 定位到 E 段第二句 "In the nineteenth century French economist Frederic Bastiat well captured the principle: 'Where goods do not cross frontiers, armies will.'"。其中，cross frontiers 与 cross the borders 为同义替换，goods 对应 trades，armies 对应 martial actions。句意为，十九世纪法国经济学家弗雷德里克·巴师夏很好地抓住了其中的原理："商品穿越不了的国界，军队可以。"原文与题干意义一致，因此答案为 TRUE。

5 定位词：profit, invisible hand
文中对应点：D 段第二句
题目解析：题干说，利润是引导市场的无形之手。根据定位词 invisible hand 定位到 D 段第二句 "But just as living organisms are shaped from the bottom up by natural selection, the economy is molded from the bottom up by the invisible hand."。文中仅提到经济（economy）是由无形的手塑造的，并未提及利润（profit）是无形的手。句意为，但正如生物体是根据自然选择自上而下形成的，经济也是由无形的手自上而下塑造的。因此答案为 NOT GIVEN。

参考答案

1 NOT GIVEN **2** FALSE **3** TRUE **4** TRUE **5** NOT GIVEN

READING PASSAGE 3

Inspired by Mimicking Mother Nature

Using the environment not as an exploitable resource, but as a source of inspiration

A   Researchers and designers around the globe endeavour to create new technologies that, by honouring the tenets of life, are both highly efficient and often environmentally friendly. And while biomimicry is not a new concept (Leonardo da Vinci looked to nature to design his flying machines, for example, and pharmaceutical companies have long been miming plant organisms in synthetic drugs), there is a greater need for products and manufacturing processes that use a minimum of energy, materials, and toxins. What's more, due to technological advancements and a newfound spirit of innovation among designers, there are now myriad ways to mimic Mother Nature's best assets.

B   'We have a perfect storm happening right now,' says Jay Harman, an inventor and CEO of PMX Scientific, which designs fans, mixers, and pumps to achieve maximum efficiency by imitating the natural flow of fluids. 'Shapes in nature are extremely simple once you understand them, but to understand what geometries are at play, and to adapt them, is a very complex process. We only just recently have had the computer power and manufacturing capability to produce these types of shapes.' 'If we could capture nature's efficiencies across the board, we could decrease dependency on fuel by at least 50 percent,' says Harman. 'What we're finding already with the tools and methodology we have right now is that we can reduce energy consumption by between 30 and 40 percent.'

C   It's only recently that mainstream companies have begun to equate biomimicry with the bottom line. Daimler Chrysler, for example, introduced a prototype car modeled on a coral reef fish. Despite its boxy, cube-shaped body, which defies a long-held aerodynamic standard in automotive design (the raindrop shape), the streamlined boxfish proved to be aerodynamically ideal and the unique construction of its skin — numerous hexagonal, bony plates — a perfect recipe for designing a car of maximum strength with minimal weight.

D   Companies and communities are flocking to Janine Benyus, author of the landmark book *Biomimicry: Innovation Inspired by Nature* (Perennial, 2002) and cofounder of the Biomimicry Guild, which seats biologists at the table with researchers and designers at companies such as Nike, Interface Carpets, Novell, and Procter & Gamble. Their objective is to marry industrial problems with natural solutions.

E   Benyus, who hopes companies will ultimately transcend mere product design to embrace nature on a more holistic level, breaks biomimicry into three tiers. On a basic (albeit complicated) level, industry will mimic nature's precise and efficient shapes, 30 structures, and geometries. The microstructure of the lotus leaf, for example, causes raindrops to bead and run off immediately, while self-cleaning and drying its surface — a discovery that the British paint company Sto has exploited in a line of building paints. The layered structure of a butterfly wing or a peacock plume, which creates iridescent colour by refracting light, is being mimicked by cosmetics giant L'Oreal in a soon-to-be-released line of eye shadow, lipstick, and nail varnish.

F The next level of biomimicry involves imitating natural processes and biochemical 'recipes': engineers and scientists are now looking at the nasal glands of seabirds to solve the problem of desalination; the abalone's ability to self-assemble its incredibly durable shell in water, using local ingredients, has inspired an alternative to the conventional, and often toxic, 'heat, beat, and treat' manufacturing method. How other organisms deal with harmful bacteria can also be instructive: researchers for the Australian company Biosigmal, for instance, observed a seaweed that lives in an environment teeming with microbes to figure out how it kept free of the same sorts of bacterial colonies, called biofilms, that cause plaque on your teeth and clog up your bathroom drain. They determined that the seaweed uses natural chemicals, called furanones, that jam the cell-to-cell signaling systems that allow bacteria to communicate and gather.

G Ultimately, the most sophisticated application of biomimicry, according to Benyus, is when a company starts seeing itself as an organism in an economic ecosystem that must make thrifty use of limited resources and creates symbiotic relationships with other like organisms. A boardroom approach at this level begins with imagining any given company, or collection of industries, as a forest, prairie, or coral reef, with its own 'food web' (manufacturing inputs and outputs) and asking whether waste products from one manufacturing process can be used, or perhaps sold, as an ingredient for another industrial activity. For instance, Geoffrey Coates, a chemist at Cornell, has developed a biodegradable plastic synthesised from carbon dioxide and limonene (a major component in the oil extracted from citrus rind) and is working with a cement factory to trap their waste CO_2 and use it as an ingredient.

H Zero Emissions Research and Initiatives (ZERI), a global network of scientists, entrepreneurs, and educators, has initiated eco-industrial projects that attempt to find ways to reuse all wastes as raw materials for other processes. Storm Brewing in Newfoundland, Canada — in one of a growing number of projects around the world applying ZERI principles — is using spent grains, a by-product of the beer-making process, to make bread and grow mushrooms.

I As industries continue to adopt nature's models, entire manufacturing processes could operate locally, with local ingredients — like the factories that use liquefied beach sand to make windshields. As more scientists and engineers begin to embrace biomimicry, natural organisms will come to be regarded as mentors, their processes deemed masterful.

Questions 1–8

Do the following statements agree with the information given in the passage?

In boxes 1–8 on your answer sheet, write

> **TRUE** if the statement agrees with the information
> **FALSE** if the statement contradicts the information
> **NOT GIVEN** if there is no information on this

1. Biomimicry is a totally new concept which has been unveiled recently.
2. Leonardo da Vinci has been the first designer to mimic nature.
3. Scientists believe that it involves more than mimicking the shape to capture the design in nature.
4. We can save the utilisation of energy by up to 40% if we take advantage of the current findings.
5. Daimler Chrysler's prototype car modeled on a coral reef fish is a best-seller.
6. Some great companies and communities themselves are seeking solutions beyond their own industrial scope.
7. The British paint company Sto did not make the microstructure of the lotus leaf applicable.
8. A Canadian beer company increased the production by applying ZERI principles.

核心词汇

A 段

endeavour [ɪnˈdevə(r)] *vi.* 努力；尽力 *n.* 努力；尝试
tenet [ˈtenɪt] *n.* 原理；原则；信条；宗旨
biomimicry [ˌbaɪɒmɪˈmɪkri] *n.* 仿生学
synthetic [sɪnˈθetɪk] *adj.* 合成的；人造的
process [ˈprəʊses] *n.* 过程；进程；变化过程 *vt.* 处理；加工
innovation [ˌɪnəˈveɪʃn] *n.* 创新，革新；新发明

B 段

imitate [ˈɪmɪteɪt] *vt.* 模仿，仿效
dependency [dɪˈpendənsi] *n.* 依赖，依靠；从属（国）
consumption [kənˈsʌmpʃn] *n.* 消费；消耗；消耗量

C 段

mainstream [ˈmeɪnstriːm] *adj.* 主流的；主要的 *n.* 主流
prototype [ˈprəʊtətaɪp] *n.* 原型；标准，模范
aerodynamic [ˌeərəʊdaɪˈnæmɪk] *adj.* 空气动力学的
standard [ˈstændəd] *n.* 标准；水准 *adj.* 标准的；正常的；符合规格的

E 段

ultimately [ˈʌltɪmətli] *adv.* 最后，最终

F 段

durable [ˈdjʊərəbl] *adj.* 耐用的；持久的
ingredient [ɪnˈɡriːdiənt] *n.* 成分；原料；要素；组成部分
instructive [ɪnˈstrʌktɪv] *adj.* 有益的；有教育性的；有启发性的
determine [dɪˈtɜːmɪn] *vt.* 决定，断定；查明

G 段

sophisticated [səˈfɪstɪkeɪtɪd] *adj.* 复杂的；精密的；久经世故的；富有经验的

H 段

initiate [ɪˈnɪʃieɪt] *vt.* 开始实施；发起，开创

I 段

entire [ɪnˈtaɪə(r)] *adj.* 全部的，全体的
embrace [ɪmˈbreɪs] *vt.* 拥抱；信奉；包含 *vi.* 拥抱 *n.* 拥抱

高频同义替换

mimic ▸ imitate, copy, simulate

involve ▸ include, embrace, contain

capture ▸ snatch, captivate, catch

seek ▸ find, search, explore

题目解析

1 定位词：biomimicry, new concept
   文中对应点：A 段第二句
   题目解析：题干说，仿生学是一个最近才被揭晓的全新概念。由题干中的定位词 biomimicry, new concept 定位到 A 段第二句 "And while biomimicry is not a new concept…, there is a greater need for products and manufacturing processes that use a minimum of energy, materials, and toxins." 其中，biomimicry，new concept 为原文重现。句意为，虽然仿生学并不是一个新概念，但对使用最少的能量、材料和毒性物质的产品和制造过程的需求更大。明确说明仿生学不是一个新概念（a new concept），题干中的 "a totally new concept" 与此意义矛盾，因此答案为 FALSE。

2 定位词：Leonardo da Vinci, designer
   文中对应点：A 段第二句
   题目解析：题干说，Leonardo da Vinci 是第一个模仿自然的设计师。由题干中的定位词 Leonardo da Vinci 定位到 A 段第二句括号里的内容 "…Leonardo da Vinci looked to nature to design his flying machines, for example, and pharmaceutical companies have long been miming plant organisms in synthetic drugs…"。其中，design 与 designer 为同根词。虽然原文提到了达·芬奇发明了他的飞行器，但并没有指出是不是第一个，因此答案为 NOT GIVEN。

3 定位词：more than mimicking the shape
   文中对应点：A 段倒数第一句
   题目解析：题干说，科学家认为这不仅仅是模仿形状来捕捉自然界的设计。由题干中的定位词 more than mimicking the shape 定位到 A 段倒数第一句 "What's more, due to technological advancements and a newfound spirit of innovation among designers, there are now myriad ways to mimic Mother Nature's best assets."。其中，myriad ways to mimic Mother Nature's best assets 与 more than mimicking the shape 为同义替换。句意为，更重要的是，由于技术的进步和在设计师身上新发现的创新精神，现在有无数种方法来效仿大自然的财富。题干中的不仅仅是模仿形状（more than mimicking the shape）与原文意思相符，因此答案为 TRUE。

4 定位词：utilisation of energy, up to 40%
   文中对应点：B 段倒数第二句
   题目解析：题干说，如果我们利用目前的发现，可以节省高达 40% 的能源利用。由题干中的定位词 utilisation of energy, up to 40% 定位到 B 段倒数第二句 "If we could capture nature's efficiencies across the board, we could decrease dependency on fuel by at least 50 percent,' says Harman."。其中，dependency on fuel 对应 utilisation of energy，at least 50% 与 up to 40% 矛盾。句意为，如果我们能够抓住自然之效，就能将对化石燃料的依赖至少减少了 50%。因此答案为 FALSE。

5 定位词：Daimler Chrysler, coral reef fish
   文中对应点：C 段第二句
   题目解析：题干说，Daimler Chrysler 以珊瑚礁鱼为蓝本的原型车是最畅销的车型。由题干中的定位词 Daimler Chrysler, coral reef fish 定位到 C 段第二句 "Daimler Chrysler, for example, introduced a prototype car modeled on a coral reef fish."。其中，Daimler Chrysler, coral reef fish 为原文重现。句意为，克莱斯勒公司引进了一种模仿珊瑚鱼的原型车。但是原文没有提及这种汽车的销售情况，因此答案为 NOT GIVEN。

6 定位词：companies and communities, seeking solutions
   文中对应点：D 段第一句
   题目解析：题干说，一些伟大的公司和社团正在自己工业范围外寻求解决方案。由题干中的定位词 companies and communities 定位到 D 段第一句 "Companies and communities are flocking to Janine Benyus, author of the landmark book *Biomimicry: Innovation Inspired by Nature* (Perennial, 2002) and cofounder of the Biomimicry Guild, which seats biologists at the table with researchers and designers at companies such as Nike, Interface Carpets, Novell, and Procter & Gamble."其中，companies and communities 为原文重现，seeking solutions 与 seats biologists at the table 对应。句意为，许多公司和社团追随珍妮·班纳斯，使得生物学家和来例如 Nike, Interface carpets, Novell 和 Procter & Gamble 公司的研究人员和设计师共聚一堂。与题干中的 "在自己工业范围外寻求解决方案" 与原文相符，因此答案为 TRUE。

7 定位词：Sto, microstructure of the lotus leaf
   文中对应点：E 段第三句
   题目解析：题干说，英国油漆公司 Sto 没有使荷叶的微观结构实用化。由题干中的定位词 Sto, microstructure of the lotus leaf 定位到 E 段第三句 "The microstructure of the lotus leaf, for example, causes raindrops to bead and run off immediately, while self-cleaning and drying its surface — a discovery that the British paint company Sto has exploited in a line of building paints."。其中, has exploited in a line of building paints 与题干中的 did not make...applicable 矛盾。句意为，荷叶的微观结构使得它可以将雨点变成水珠，并立即滑落，从而自我清洁并使得叶片表面干燥。而这项发现已经被英国油漆公司 Sto 开发应用在一系列的建筑油漆上。因此答案为 FALSE。

8 定位词：Canadian beer company, ZERI principles
   文中对应点：H 段第二句
   题目解析：题干说，一家加拿大啤酒公司通过应用 ZERI 原理增加了产量。由题干中的定位词 Canadian beer company, ZERI principles 定位到 H 段第二句 "Storm Brewing in Newfoundland, Canada — in one of a growing number of projects around the world applying ZERI principles — is

using spent grains, a byproduct of the beer-making process, to make bread and grow mushrooms."。其中，Canadian beer company 与 Storm Brewing in Newfoundland, Canada 对应，to make bread and grow mushrooms 与 increased the production 相矛盾。句意为，加拿大纽芬兰的风暴酿酒厂是全球越来越多应用 ZERI 原则的项目中的一个。他们利用啤酒制造过程中的副产品——酒糟，来生产面包和种植蘑菇。因此答案为 FALSE。

参考答案

1 FALSE　**2** NOT GIVEN　**3** TRUE　**4** FALSE　**5** NOT GIVEN　**6** TRUE　**7** FALSE　**8** FALSE

READING PASSAGE 4

Koalas

A Koalas are just too nice for their own good. And except for the occasional baby taken by birds of prey, koalas have no natural enemies. In an ideal world, the life of an arboreal couch potato would be perfectly safe and acceptable.

B Just two hundred years ago, koalas flourished across Australia. Now they seem to be in decline, but exact numbers are not available as the species would not seem to be 'under threat'. Their problem, however, has been men, more specifically, the white man. Koalas and aborigine had co-existed peacefully for centuries.

C Today koalas are found only in scattered pockets of southeast Australia where they seem to be at the risk on several fronts. The koala's only food source, the eucalyptus tree, has declined. In the past 200 years, a third of Australia's eucalyptus forests have disappeared. Koalas have been killed by parasites, chlamydia epidemics and a tumour-causing retrovirus. And every year 11,000 are killed by cars, ironically most of them in wildlife sanctuaries, and thousands are killed by poachers. Some are also taken illegally as pets. The animals usually soon die, but they are easily replaced.

D Bush fires pose another threat. The horrific ones that raged in New South Wales recently killed between 100 and 1,000 koalas. Many that were taken into sanctuaries and shelters were found to have burnt their paws on the glowing embers. But zoologists say that the species should recover. The koalas will be aided by the eucalyptus, which grows quickly and is already burgeoning forth after the fires. So the main problem to their survival is their slow reproductive rate — they produce only one baby a year over a reproductive lifespan of about nine years.

E The latest problem for the species is perhaps more insidious. With plush, grey fur dark amber eyes and button nose, koalas are cuddliness incarnate Australian zoos and wildlife parks have taken advantage of their uncomplaining attitudes, and charge visitors to be photographed hugging the furry bundles. But people may not realise how cruel this is, but because of the koala's delicate disposition, constant handling can push an already precariously balanced physiology over the edge.

F Koalas only eat the foliage of certain species of eucalyptus trees, between 600 and 1,250 grams a day. The tough leaves are packed with cellulose, tannins, aromatic oils and precursors of toxic cyanides. To handle this cocktail, koalas have a specialised digestive system. Cellulose-digesting bacteria in the caecum break down fibre, while a specially adapted gut and liver process the toxins. To digest their food properly, koalas must sit still for 21 hours every day.

G Koalas are the epitome of innocence and inoffensiveness. Although they are capable of ripping open a man's arm with their needle-sharp claws, or giving a nasty nip, they simply wouldn't. If you upset a koala, it may blink or swallow, or hiccup. But attack? No way! Koalas are just not aggressive. They use their claws to grip the hard smooth bark of eucalyptus trees.

H   They are also very sensitive, and the slightest upset can prevent them from breeding, cause them to go off their food, and succumb to gut infections. Koalas are stoic creatures and put on a brave face until they are at death's door. One day they may appear healthy, the next they could be dead. Captive koalas have to be weighed daily to check that they are feeding properly. A sudden loss of weight is usually the only warning keepers have that their charge is ill. Only two keepers plus a vet were allowed to handle London Zoo's koalas, as these creatures are only comfortable with people they know. A request for the koala to be taken to meet the Queen was refused because of the distress this would have caused the marsupial. Sadly, London's Zoo no longer has a koala. Two years ago the female koala died of a cancer caused by a retrovirus. When they come into heat, female koalas become more active, and start losing weight, but after about sixteen days, heat ends and the weight piles back on. London's koala did not. Surgery revealed hundreds of pea-sized tumours.

I   Almost every zoo in Australia has koalas — the marsupial has become the Animal Ambassador of the nation, but nowhere outside Australia would handling by the public be allowed. Koala cuddling screams in the face of every rule of good care. First, some zoos allow koalas to be passed from stranger to stranger, many children who love to squeeze. Second, most people have no idea of how to handle the animals: they like to cling on to their handler, all in their own good time and use his or her arm as a tree. For such reasons, the Association of Fauna and Marine parks, an Australian conservation society is campaigning to ban koala cuddling. Policy on koala handling is determined by state government authorities, and the largest of the numbers in the Australian Nature Conservation Agency, with the aim of instituting national guidelines. Following a wave of publicity, some zoos and wildlife parks have stopped turning their koalas into photo.

Questions 1–7

Do the following statements agree with the views of the writer in the passage?

In boxes 1–7 on your answer sheet, write

> **YES** if the statement agrees with the views of the writer
> **NO** if the statement contradicts the views of the writer
> **NOT GIVEN** if it is impossible to say what the writer thinks about this

1 New coming human settlers caused danger to koalas.

2 Koalas can still be seen in most of the places in Australia.

3 It takes decades for the eucalyptus trees to recover after the fire.

4 Koalas will fight each other when food becomes scarce.

5 It is not easy to notice that koalas are ill.

6 Koalas are easily infected with human contagious disease via cuddling.

7 Koalas like to hold a person's arm when they are embraced.

核心词汇

A 段

prey [preɪ] *n.* 猎物 [拓] be/fall prey to sb./sth. 受某人／某事所伤害（影响）
arboreal [ɑːˈbɔːriəl] *adj.* 树木的
couch potato 成天躺着或坐在沙发上看电视的人

B 段

flourish [ˈflʌrɪʃ] *vi.* 繁荣，兴旺；茁壮成长 *vt.* 挥动 *n.* 兴旺 [拓] in all flourish 在全盛时
aborigine [ˌæbəˈrɪdʒəni] *n.* 土著居民

D 段

ember [ˈembə(r)] *n.* 余烬

E 段

insidious [ɪnˈsɪdiəs] *adj.* 暗中为害的；阴险的 [拓] insidiously *adv.* 潜伏地；阴险地
disposition [ˌdɪspəˈzɪʃn] *n.* 性情，性格；意向
precariously [prɪˈkeəriəsli] *adv.* 不安全地 [拓] precarious *adj.* 不稳定的
physiology [ˌfɪziˈɒlədʒi] *n.* 生理学 [拓] physiological *adj.* 生理学的；生理的

F 段

foliage [ˈfəʊliɪdʒ] *n.* 叶子
pack with 满含……；挤满……

G 段

epitome [ɪˈpɪtəmi] *n.* 典型；概括；缩影 [拓] epitomise *vt.* 摘要，概括
innocence [ˈɪnəsns] *n.* 天真；清白，无罪 [拓] innocent *adj.* 无辜的；无知的
inoffensiveness [ˌɪnəˈfensɪvnəs] *n.* 无效，不起作用
hiccup [ˈhɪkʌp] *vi.* 打嗝；暂时中断 *n.* 打嗝；短暂耽搁
aggressive [əˈgresɪv] *adj.* 有进取心的，有冲劲的；好斗的

H 段

surgery [ˈsɜːdʒəri] *n.* 外科手术 [拓] surgeon *n.* 外科医生
reveal [rɪˈviːl] *vt.* 显示；揭示，揭露；展现

I 段

squeeze [skwiːz] *vt.* 捏；挤压；榨出 *n.* 拥挤；塞满

高频同义替换

flourish	▸	thrive, prosper, boom, flower
epitome	▸	image, abstract, symbol, summary
aggressive	▸	invasive, enterprising, forceful, determined
reveal	▸	conceal, uncover, display, show

题目解析

1 定位词：new coming human settlers, danger
文中对应点：B 段第二、三句
题目解析：题干说，新来的定居者给考拉带来了危险。由题干中的定位词 new coming human settlers, danger 定位到 B 段第二、三句 "Now they seem to be in decline, but exact numbers are not available as the species would not seem to be 'under threat'. Their problem, however, has been men, more specifically, the white man."。其中，danger 对应 in decline，相对土著居民，new coming human settlers 则是指文中的 the white man。句意为，现在它们的数量似乎在减少，虽然数量是不确切的，因为这个物种似乎不会受到"威胁"。然而，它们的问题是人类，更确切地说，是白人。所以答案为 YES。

2 定位词：seen, most of the places
文中对应点：C 段第一句
题目解析：题干说，考拉仍然可以在澳大利亚大部分地方看到。由题干中的定位词 seen, most of the places 定位到 C 段第一句 "Today koalas are found only in scattered pockets of southeast Australia where they seem to be at the risk on several fronts."。其中，are found 与 seen 为同义替换，原文中 only 与 most of the places 意思相反。句意为，现在考拉只在澳大利亚东南部零散的区域里被发现，它们似乎在多个方面都处于危险之中。原文提及考拉现只是在澳洲的东南部分散存在着，与题干所说的能在澳洲大部分地方看到不符。所以答案为 NO。

3 定位词：eucalyptus, after the fire
文中对应点：D 段倒数第二句
题目解析：题干说，桉树在火灾后恢复需要几十年的时间。由题干中的定位词 eucalyptus, after the fire 定位到 D 段倒数第二句 "The koalas will be aided by the eucalyptus, which grows quickly and is already burgeoning forth after the fires."。其中，eucalyptus, after the fire 为原文重现。句意为，桉树能够帮助考拉，因为桉树生长速度快，能在火灾后迅速萌发新芽。这与题目表达的桉树在火灾后需要数十年才能恢复不符，所以答案为 NO。

4 定位词：fight each other, food, scarce
文中对应点：无
题目解析：题目说当食物紧缺时，考拉会相互打斗。文中并未提及此类信息，所以答案为 NOT GIVEN。

5　定位词：not easy to notice, ill
　　文中对应点：H 段第三句
　　题目解析：题干说，很难通过观察来辨别考拉是否生病。由题干中的定位词 not easy to notice, ill 定位到 H 段第三句 "One day they may appear healthy, the next they could be dead."。其中，dead 对应 ill。句意为，它们可能某天看起来很健康，但是第二天可能就死了。说明很难通过观察来辨别考拉是否生病，所以答案为 YES。

6　定位词：human contagious disease, cuddling
　　文中对应点：无
　　题目解析：题目说考拉容易通过拥抱感染到人类的传染性疾病。文中并未提及此类信息，所以答案为 NOT GIVEN。

7　定位词：a person's arm, embraced
　　文中对应点：I 段第四句
　　题目解析：题干说，考拉被抱着的时候喜欢抓住人的手臂。由题干中的定位词 a person's arm, embraced 定位到 I 段第四句 "Second, most people have no idea of how to handle the animals: they like to cling on to their handler, all in their own good time and use his or her arm as a tree." 其中，his or her arm 与 a person's arm 相对应，use his or her arm as a tree 与 embraced 相对应。句意为，其次，大多数人对于如何抱动物没有任何概念：考拉喜欢紧贴着它们的饲养者，舒服的时候会把他／她的手臂当作树。与题目中的被抱着的时候抓住人的手臂意思一致，所以答案为 YES。

参考答案

1 YES　2 NO　3 NO　4 NOT GIVEN　5 YES　6 NOT GIVEN　7 YES

Tattoo in Tikopia

A There are still debates about the origins of Polynesian culture but one thing we can ensure is that Polynesia is not a single tribe but a complex one. Polynesians, which include Marquesans, Samoans, Niueans, Tongans, Cook Islanders, Hawaiians, Tahitians, and Miori, are genetically linked to indigenous peoples of parts of Southeast Asia. It's a sub-region of Oceania, comprising of a large grouping of over 1,000 islands scattered over the central and southern Pacific Ocean, within a triangle that has New Zealand, Hawaii and Easter Island as its corners.

B Polynesian history has fascinated the Western world since Pacific cultures were first contacted by European explorers in the late 18th century. The small island of Tikopia, for many people — even for many Solomon Islanders — is so far away that it seems like a mythical land, a place like Narnia, that magical land in C. S. Lewis' classic, *The Chronicles of Narnia*. Maybe because of it — Tikopia, its people, and their cultures have long fascinated scholars, travellers, and casual observers. Like the pioneers Peter Dillion, Dumont D'Urville and John Colleridge Patterson who visited and wrote about the island in the 1800s, Raymond Firth is one of those people captured by the alluring attraction of Tikopia. As a result, he had made a number of trips to the island since 1920s and recorded his experiences, observations and reflections on Tikopia, its people, cultures and the changes that have occurred.

C While engaged in study of the kinship and religious life of the people of Tikopia, Firth made a few observations on their tattooing. Brief though these notes are they may be worth putting on record as an indication of the sociological setting of the practice in this primitive Polynesian community. The origin of the English word 'tattoo' actually comes from the Tikopia word 'tatau'. The word for tattoo marks in general is *tau*, and the operation of tattooing is known as *ta tau*, *ta* being the generic term for the act of striking.

D The technique of tattooing was similar throughout Polynesia. Traditional tattoo artists create their indelible tattoos using pigment made from the candlenut or kukui nut. First, they burn the nut inside a bowl made of half a coconut shell. They then scrape out the soot and use a pestle to mix it with liquid. Bluing is sometimes added to counteract the reddish hue of the carbon-based pigment. It also makes the outline of the inscribed designs bolder on the dark skin of tattooing subjects.

E For the instruments used when tattooing, specialists used a range of chisels made from albatross wing bone which were hafted onto a handle which was made from the heart wood of the bush and struck with a mallet. The tattooer began by sketching with charcoal a design on the supine subject, whose skin at that location was stretched taut by one or more apprentices. The tattooer then dipped the appropriate points either a single one or a whole comb into the ink (usually contained in a coconut-shell cup) and tapped it into the subject's skin, holding the blade handle in one hand and tapping it with the other. The blood that usually trickled from the punctures was wiped away either by the tattooer or his apprentice, the latter having also served by restraining a pain-wracked subject from moving, for the operation was inevitably painful — a test of fortitude that tattooers sought to shorten by working as fast as possible. In fact, tattoos nearly always festered and often led to sickness and in some cases death.

F In ancient Polynesian society, nearly everyone was tattooed. It was an integral part of ancient culture and was much more than a body ornament. Tattooing indicated one's genealogy and/or rank in society. It was a sign of wealth, of strength and of the ability to endure pain. Those who wait without them were seen as persons of lower social status. As such, chiefs and warriors generally had the most elaborate tattoos. Tattooing was generally begun at adolescence, and would often not be completed for a number of years. Receiving tattoo constituted an important milestone between childhood and adulthood, and was accompanied by many rites and rituals. Apart from signaling status and rank, another reason for the practice in traditional times was to make a person more attractive to the opposite sex.

G The male facial tattoo is generally divided into eight sections of the face. The centre of the forehead designated a person's general rank. The area around the brows designated his position. The area around the eyes and the nose designated his *hapu*, or sub-tribe rank. The area around the temples served to detail his marital status, like the number of marriages. The area under the nose displayed his signature. This signature was once memorised by tribal chiefs who used it when buying property, signing deeds, and officiating orders. The cheek area designated the nature of the person's work. The chin area showed the person's mana. Lastly, the jaw area designated a person's birth status.

H A person's ancestry is indicated on each side of the face. The left side is generally the father's side, and the right side was the mother's. The manutahi design is worked on the men's back. It consists of two vertical lines drawn down the spine, with short vertical lines between them. When a man had the manutahi on his back, he took pride in himself. At gatherings of the people he could stand forth in their midst and display his tattoo designs with songs. And rows of triangles design on the men's chest indicate his bravery.

I Tattoo was a way delivering information of its owner. It's also a traditional method to fetch spiritual power, protection and strength. The Polynesians use this as a sign of character, position and levels in a hierarchy. Polynesian peoples believe that a person's mana, their spiritual power or life force, is displayed through their tattoo.

Questions 1–4

Do the following statements agree with the views of the writer in the passage?

In boxes 1–4 on your answer sheet, write

> **YES** if the statement agrees with the views of the writer
> **NO** if the statement contradicts the views of the writer
> **NOT GIVEN** if it is impossible to say what the writer thinks about this

1. Scientists like to do research in Tikopia because this tiny place is of great remoteness.

2. Firth was the first scholar to study on Tikopia.

3. Firth studied the cultural differences on Tikopia as well as on some other islands of the Pacific.

4. The English word 'tattoo' is evolved from the local language of the island.

核心词汇

A 段

origin [ˈɒrɪdʒɪn] *n.* 起源；来源；血统

indigenous [ɪnˈdɪdʒɪnəs] *adj.* 本土的；生来的，固有的

B 段

fascinate [ˈfæsɪneɪt] *vt.* 使着迷；入迷

capture [ˈkæptʃə(r)] *vt.* 俘虏；捕获；逮捕；捕捉；拍摄 *n.* 捕获；占领；抢占

alluring [əˈlʊrɪŋ] *adj.* 迷人的；吸引人的

reflection [rɪˈflekʃn] *n.* 想法，见解；映像；（光或热等的）反射

C 段

kinship [ˈkɪnʃɪp] *n.* 亲属关系，家属关系

primitive [ˈprɪmətɪv] *adj.* 原始的；未开化的；古老的

D 段

technique [tekˈniːk] *n.* 工艺；方法；技巧

pigment [ˈpɪɡmənt] *n.* 颜料；色素

counteract [ˌkaʊntərˈækt] *vt.* 中和；抵消；对抗

E 段

instrument [ˈɪnstrəmənt] *n.* 器具，器械；仪器；乐器；方法，手段

charcoal [ˈtʃɑːkəʊl] *n.* 炭笔；木炭

apprentice [əˈprentɪs] *n.* 学徒；徒弟

restrain [rɪˈstreɪn] *vt.* 阻止；抑制；控制

inevitably [ɪnˈevɪtəbli] *adv.* 不可避免地

fortitude [ˈfɔːtɪtjuːd] *n.* 坚韧；刚毅

F 段

integral [ˈɪntɪɡrəl] *adj.* 必不可少的；完整的

ornament [ˈɔːnəm(ə)nt] *n.* 装饰；装饰物

indicate [ˈɪndɪkeɪt] *vt.* 暗示；表明；指出

constitute [ˈkɒnstɪtjuːt] *vt.* 构成，组成；设立

milestone [ˈmaɪlstəʊn] *n.* 重大事件；里程碑

ritual [ˈrɪtʃəl] *n.* 仪式；典礼；惯例 *adj.* 仪式的；礼节性的

G 段

designate [ˈdezɪɡneɪt] *vt.* 表示；任命；指派

H 段

ancestry [ˈænsestri] *n.* 祖先；血统

I 段

hierarchy [ˈhaɪərɑːki] *n.* 等级制度；统治集团

高频同义替换

tiny	▶	small, minute, few, little, micro
remoteness	▶	distant, lonely, aloof, far away
study	▶	investigate, survey, examine, scrutiny
evolve	▶	develop, grow, advance
local	▶	native, regional

题目解析

1 定位词：scientists, tiny place, remoteness
文中对应点：B 段第二、三句
题目解析：题干说，科学家们喜欢在 Tikopia 作研究，因为这个小地方非常偏远。由题干中的定位词 scientists, tiny place, remoteness 定位到 B 段第二、三句 "The small island of Tikopia, for many people — even for many Solomon Islanders — is so far away that it seems like a mythical land, a place like Narnia, that magical land in C. S. Lewis' classic, *The Chronicles of Narnia*. Maybe because of it — Tikopia, its people, and their cultures have long fascinated scholars, travellers, and casual observers."。其中，small island 对应 tiny place，so far away 对应 remoteness，scholars, travellers, and casual observers 与 scientists 相对应。句意为，Tikopia 岛非常远，即使对许多所罗门群岛的岛民来说也像是神话中的岛屿，因此一直以来 Tikopia 以及当地的人和文化都深深地吸引着学者、旅行者和非正式的观察家。所以答案为 YES。

2 定位词：Firth, the first scholar, study
文中对应点：B 段倒数第一、二句
题目解析：题干说，Firth 是第一个研究 Tikopia 的学者。由题干中的定位词 Firth, first scholar, study 定位到 B 段倒数第一、二句 "Like the pioneers Peter Dillion, Dumont D'Urville and John Colleridge Patterson who visited and wrote about the island in the 1800s, Raymond Firth is one of those people captured by the alluring attraction of Tikopia. As a result, he had made a number of trips to the island since 1920s and recorded his experiences, observations and reflections on

Tikopia, its people, cultures and the changes that have occurred."。其中，最早来到 Tikopia 的学者包括 Peter Dillion 和 Dumont D'Urville 以及 John Colleridge Patterson 等人，时间为 19 世纪，而 Raymond Firth 是从 20 世纪 20 年代才开始观察、研究。题干与原文意义不一致，所以答案为 NO。

3　定位词：Firth, cultural differences, other islands of the Pacific
　　文中对应点：原文未提及
　　题目解析：题干说，Firth 研究了 Tikopia 以及太平洋上其他岛屿的文化差异。Firth 不但研究了 Tikopia 岛上的文化差异，还研究了太平洋上其他岛屿的文化差异，这一点在原文中未找到对应信息，所以答案为 NOT GIVEN。

4　定位词：English word 'tattoo', evolved from, local language of the island
　　文中对应点：C 段倒数第二句
　　题目解析：题干说，英语单词 'tattoo' 是从岛上的当地语言演变而来的。由题干中的定位词 English word, tattoo, local language 定位到 C 段倒数第二句 "The origin of the English word 'tattoo' actually comes from the Tikopia word 'tatau'."。其中，English word 'tattoo' 为原文重现，comes from 与 evolved from 为同义替换，Tikopia word 'tatau' 对应 local language of the island。句意为，英文单词 tattoo 一词实际来源于 Tikopia 语言中的 tatau 一词。题干与原文意义一致。所以答案为 YES。

参考答案

1 YES　　**2** NO　　**3** NOT GIVEN　　**4** YES

READING PASSAGE 6

The Sense for Flavour

A   Scientists now believe that human beings acquired the sense of taste as a way to avoid being poisoned. Edible plants generally taste sweet; deadly ones, bitter. Taste is supposed to help us differentiate food that's good for us from food that's not. The taste buds on our tongues can detect the presence of half a dozen or so basic tastes, including: sweet, sour, bitter, salty, and umami (a taste discovered by Japanese researchers, a rich and full sense of deliciousness triggered by amino acids in foods such as shellfish, mushrooms, potatoes and seaweed). Taste buds offer a limited means of detection, however, compared with the human olfactory system, which can perceive thousands of different chemical aromas. Indeed, flavour, is primarily the smell of gases being released by the chemicals you've just put in your mouth. The aroma of food can be responsible for as much as 90% of its flavour.

B   The act of drinking, sucking or chewing a substance releases its volatile gases. They flow out of the mouth and up the nostrils, or up the passageway at the back of the mouth, to a thin layer of nerve cells called the olfactory epithelium, located at the base of the nose, right between the eyes. The brain combines the complex smell signals from the epithelium with the simple taste signals from the tongue, assigns a flavour to what's in your mouth, and decides if it's something you want to eat.

C   Babies like sweet tastes and reject bitter ones; we know this because scientists have rubbed various flavours inside the mouths of infants and then recorded their facial reactions. A person's food preferences, like his or her personality, are formed during the first few years of life, through a process of socialisation. Toddlers can learn to enjoy hot and spicy food, bland health food, or fast food, depending upon what the people around them eat. The human sense of smell is still not fully understood. It is greatly affected by psychological factors and expectations. The mind filters out the overwhelming majority of chemical aromas that surround us, focusing intently on some, ignoring others. People can grow accustomed to bad smells or good smells; they stop noticing what once seemed overpowering.

D   Aroma and memory are somehow inextricably linked. A smell can suddenly evoke a long-forgotten moment. The flavours of childhood foods seem to leave an indelible mark, and adults often return to them, without always knowing why. These 'comfort foods' become a source of pleasure and reassurance of a fact that fast-food chains work hard to promote childhood memories of Happy Meals can translate into frequent adult visits to McDonalds', like those of the chain's 'heavy users', the customers who eat there four or five times a week.

E   The human craving for flavour has been a large unacknowledged and unexamined force in history. Royal empires have been built, unexplored lands have been traversed, great religions and philosophies have been forever changed by the spice trade. In 1492, Christopher Columbus set sail in order to try to find new seasonings and thus to make his fortune with this most desired commodity of that time. Today, the influence of flavour in the world marketplace is no less decisive. The rise and fall of corporate empires, soft-drink companies, snack-food companies and fast-food chains is frequently determined by how their products taste.

F   The flavour industry emerged in the mid-1800s, as processed foods began to be manufactured on a large scale. Recognising the need for flavour additives, the early food processors turned to perfume companies that had years of experience working with essential oils and volatile aromas. The great perfume houses of England, France and the Netherlands produced many of the first flavour compounds. In the early part of the 20th century, Germany's powerful chemical industry assumed the lead in flavour production. Legend has it that a German scientist discovered methyl anthranilate, one of the first artificial flavours, by accident while mixing chemicals in his laboratory. Suddenly, the lab was filled with the sweet smell of grapes. Methyl anthranilate later became the chief flavouring compound of manufactured grape juice.

G   The quality that people seek most of all in a food — its flavour, is usually present in a quantity too infinitesimal to be measured by any traditional culinary terms such as ounces or teaspoons. Today's sophisticated spectrometres, gas chromatographs and headspace vapour analysers provide a detailed map of a food's flavour components, detecting chemical aromas in amounts as low as one part per billion. The human nose, however, is still more sensitive than any machine yet invented. A nose can detect aromas present in quantities of a few parts per trillion. Complex aromas, such as those of coffee or roasted meat, may be composed of gases from nearly a thousand different chemicals. The chemical that provides the dominant flavour of bell pepper can be tasted in amounts as low as 0.02 parts per billion; one drop is sufficient to add flavour to the amount of water needed to fill five average-size swimming pools.

Questions 1–5

Do the following statements agree with the information given in the passage?

In boxes 1–5 on your answer sheet, write

> **TRUE** if the statement agrees with the information
> **FALSE** if the statement contradicts the information
> **NOT GIVEN** if there is no information on this

1 The brain determines which aromas we are aware of.

2 The sense of taste is as efficient as the sense of smell.

3 Personal tastes in food are developed in infancy.

4 Christopher Columbus found many different spices on his travels.

5 In the mid-1880s, man-made flavours were originally invented on purpose.

核心词汇

A 段

acquire [əˈkwaɪə(r)] vt. 获得，取得；学到

poison [ˈpɔɪzn] vt. 毒害，毒杀 n. 毒药

differentiate [ˌdɪfəˈrenʃieɪt] vi. & vt. 区分，区别 vi. 区别对待 vt. 使……不同

trigger [ˈtrɪɡər] vt. 引发；激发；触发 n. 扳机

olfactory [ɒˈfæktəri] adj. 嗅觉的；味道的 n. 嗅觉器官

perceive [pəˈsiːv] vt. 察觉；理解 vi. 感知；认识到 [拓] perception n. 知觉

aroma [əˈrəʊmə] n. 芳香，香味

release [rɪˈliːs] vt. 释放；发射；公开发表 n. 释放；发布

B 段

volatile [ˈvɒlətaɪl] adj. 易变的；易挥发的

C 段

reject [rɪˈdʒekt] vt. 排斥；拒绝；抵制；丢弃 n. 被弃之物或人；次品

overwhelming [ˌəʊvəˈwelmɪŋ] adj. 压倒性的；势不可挡的

intently [ɪnˈtentli] adv. 专心地，一心一意地

D 段

indelible [ɪnˈdeləbl] adj. 难忘的；擦不掉的

E 段

unacknowledged [ˌʌnəkˈnɒlɪdʒd] adj. 未公开承认的，不被承认的；未答复的 [拓] acknowledge vt. 承认；答谢

traverse [ˈtrævəs] n. 穿过；横贯 vt. 穿过，跨过，横穿

decisive [dɪˈsaɪsɪv] adj. 决定性的；果断的

F 段

additive [ˈædətɪv] n. 添加剂；添加物

compound [ˈkɒmpaʊnd] n. 化合物；混合物 vt. 恶化，加剧 adj. 复合的；混合的

artificial [ˌɑːtɪˈfɪʃl] adj. 人造的；仿造的；虚伪的；武断的

G 段

culinary [ˈkʌlɪnəri] adj. 烹调用的；厨房的

vapour [ˈveɪpə(r)] n. 蒸气；水蒸气

compose [kəmˈpəʊz] vi. & vt. 构成；作曲 [拓] composition n. 作文；作曲；合成物

dominant [ˈdɒmɪnənt] adj. 占优势的；显性的；支配的；统治的 [拓] dominance n. 优势；统治；支配

高频同义替换

determine ▸ ensure, confirm, decide, make sure, ascertain

develop ▸ cultivate, form, foster, grow

man-made ▸ artificial, factitious, unnatural

originally ▸ first, initially, at the beginning

题目解析

1 定位词：brain, aromas, aware of
文中对应点：B 段最后一句
题目解析：题干说，大脑决定了我们所感知的气味。利用由题干中的定位词 brain, aromas, aware of 定位至 B 段最后一句 "The brain combines the complex smell...if it's something you want to eat." 其中，smell 对应 aromas，want to 对应 aware of。句意为，大脑将来自上皮的复杂气味信号和来自舌头的简单味觉信号结合起来，给你嘴里的东西分配一种味道，并决定它是否是你想吃的东西。文章并没有提到大脑是否可以决定我们意识感知到的味道。因此答案为 NOT GIVEN。

2 定位词：sense of taste, efficient, sense of smell
文中对应点：无
题目解析：题干说，味觉和嗅觉有一样的效果。文中多次提到 smell 及 taste，但并没有一处将两者进行对比。找不到题干对应点。因此答案为 NOT GIVEN。

3 定位词：personal tastes, developed, in infancy
文中对应点：C 段第二句
题目解析：题干说，对于食物的个人口味是在婴儿时期发展起来的。由题干中的定位词 personal tastes, in infancy 定位至 C 段第二句 "A person's food preferences, like his or her personality, are formed during the first few years of life, through a process of socialisation."。其中，person's food preferences 与 personal tastes 对应，formed 对应 developed，during the first few years of life 与 in infancy 为同义替换。句意为，一个人的食物偏好就像他或她的性格一样，是在人生最初几年的社会化过程中形成的。题干的整体意义与原文相符。因此答案为 TRUE。

4 定位词：Christopher Columbus, spices, on his travels
文中对应点：E 段第三句
题目解析：题干说，Christopher Columbus 在旅行中发现了许多不同的香料。由题干中的定位词 Christopher Columbus, spices, on his travels 定位至 E 段第三句 "In 1492, Christopher Columbus set sail in order to try to find new seasonings and thus to make his fortune with this most desired commodity of that time."。其中，spices 与 seasonings 为同义替换，set sail 与 on his travels 对应。句意为，1492 年，克里斯托弗·哥伦布起航试图寻找新的调味料，以利用这一当时最抢手的商品为自己带来财富。原文并没有提到旅途中是否发现了很多不同的调味料。因此答案为 NOT GIVEN。

5 定位词：man-made flavours, on purpose

文中对应点：F 段倒数第三句

题目解析：题干说，在 19 世纪 80 年代中期，人造香料最初是人们刻意发明的。由题干中的定位词 man-made flavours, on purpose 定位至 F 段倒数第三句 "Legend has it that a German scientist discovered methyl anthranilate, one of the first artificial flavours, by accident while mixing chemicals in his laboratory." 。其中，artificial flavours 与 man-made flavours 为同义替换，by accident 与 on purpose 意思相反。句意为，传说一位德国科学家在实验室混合化学试剂时，偶然发现了首批人造香味剂之一的邻氨基苯甲酸甲酯。原文中说是偶然发现，而题干却说是刻意发明的。由此可知，题干与原文意义不符。因此答案为 FALSE。

参考答案

1 NOT GIVEN　**2** NOT GIVEN　**3** TRUE　**4** NOT GIVEN　**5** FALSE

READING PASSAGE 7

Design the Mat and Foot Health

A You've scoured the innovations website and gadget shops, trawled a dozen more sites offering 'alternative' gifts, spent hours on eBay, and still you haven't found that perfect something. When just about everyone you know has just about everything, coming up with a present that is both novel and useful gets harder every year. But fear not. There is something worth having that most of us lack — something that could improve the quality of our lives immeasurably. If you really care, give the gift of a wobbly walk.

B Seriously, the feet of a typical urbanite rarely encounter terrain any more undulating than a crack in the pavement. While that may not seem like a problem, it turns out that this flatearth business is not doing us any good. By ironing all the bumps out of our urban environment we have put ourselves at risk of a surprising number of chronic illnesses and disabilities. Fortunately, the free market has come to the rescue. You can now buy the solution — in fact, there is even a choice of products. Indoor types will appreciate the cobblestone walkway, a knobbly textured plastic mat that they can wobble along in the comfort of their own homes. And for the more adventurous, there are shoes designed to throw you off balance.

C The technology may be cutting edge, but its origins are deep and exotic. Research into the idea that flat floors could be detrimental to our health was pioneered back in the late 1960s. While others in Long Beach, California, contemplated peace and love, podiatrist Charles Brantingham and physiologist Bruce Beekman were concerned with more pedestrian matters. They reckoned that the growing epidemic of high blood pressure, varicose veins and deep-vein thromboses might be linked to the uniformity of the surfaces that we tend to stand and walk on.

D The trouble, as they saw it, was that walking continuously on flat floors, sidewalks and streets concentrates forces on just a few areas of the foot. As a result, these surfaces are likely to be far more conducive to chronic stress syndromes than natural ones, where the foot meets the ground in a wide variety of orientations. The anatomy of the foot parallels that of the human hand — each having 26 bones, 33 joints and more than 100 muscles, tendons and ligaments. Modern lifestyles waste all this flexibility in your socks. Brantingham and Beekman became convinced that damage was being done simply by people standing on even surfaces and that this could be rectified by introducing a wobble.

E 'In Beijing and Shanghai city dwellers take daily walks on cobbled paths to improve their health.' To test their ideas, they got 65 clerks and factory workers to try standing on a variable terrain floor — spongy mats with different amounts of give across the surface. This modest irregularity allowed the soles of the volunteers' feet to deviate slightly from the horizontal each time they shifted position. As the researchers hoped, this simple intervention turned out to make a huge difference over just a few weeks. Just a slight wobble from the floor activated a host of muscles in people's legs, which in turn helped to pump blood back to their hearts. The muscle action prevented the pooling of blood in their feet and legs, reducing the stress on the entire cardiovascular system.

And two-thirds of the volunteers reported feeling much less tired. Yet decades later, the flooring of the world's workplaces remains relentlessly smooth.

F Earlier this year, however, the idea was given a new lease of life when researchers in Oregon announced findings from a similar experiment with people over 60. John Fisher and colleagues at the Oregon Research Institute in Eugene designed a mat intended to replicate the effect of walking on cobblestones. In tests funded by the National Institute of Aging, they got some 50 adults to walk on the mats in their stockinged feet for less than an hour three times a week. After 16 weeks, these people showed marked improvements in balance and mobility, and even a significant reduction in blood pressure. People in a control group who walked on ordinary floors also improved but not as dramatically.

G The mats are now on sale at $35. 'Our first 1,000 cobblestone mats sold in three weeks,' Fisher says, 'Production is now being scaled up.' Even so, demand could exceed supply if this foot-stimulating activity really is a 'useful non-pharmacological approach for preventing or controlling hypertension of older adults', as the researchers believe. They are not alone in extolling the revitalising powers of cobblestones. Reflexologists have long advocated walking on textured surfaces to stimulate so-called 'acupoints' on the soles of the feet. Practitioners of this unorthodox therapy believe that pressure applied to particular spots on the foot connects directly to corresponding organs and somehow enhances their function. In China, spas, hotels, apartment blocks and even factories promote their cobblestone paths as healthful amenities. Fisher admits he got the idea from regular visits to the country. In Beijing and Shanghai, city dwellers take daily walks along cobbled paths to improve their health. 'In the big cities, people take off their shoes and walk on these paths for 5 or 10 minutes, perhaps several times a day,' Fisher says.

H The idea is now taking off in Europe too. People in Germany, Austria and Switzerland can visit 'barefoot parks' and walk along 'paths of the senses' with mud, logs, stone and moss underfoot to receive what's known there as reflexion-massage. And it is not difficult to construct your own 'health pathway'. American reflexologists Barbara and Kevin Kunz, based in Albuquerque, New Mexico, advise that you cobble together a walkway using broom handles, bamboo poles, hosepipes, gravel, pebbles, dried peas, driftwood, fallen logs, sand, door mats and strios of turf.

I If your enthusiasm for DIY doesn't stretch to this, and Fisher's cobblestone mats are all sold out, there is another option. A new shoe on the market claims to transform flat, hard, artificial surfaces into something like natural uneven ground. 'These shoes have an unbelievable effect,' says Benno Nigg, an exercise scientist at the human performance laboratory of Calgary University in Canada, which has done contract research for the shoe's manufacturers. 'They are one of the best things to have happened to humankind for years.' Known as Masai Barefoot Technology, or MBTs, the shoes have rounded soles that cause you to rock slightly when you stand still, exercising the small muscles around the ankle that are responsible for fore-aft stability. Forces in the joint are reduced, putting less strain on the system, Nigg claims.

J Perhaps this all sounds a bit high-tech. If so, hang consumerism and go for the radical solution: search out a patch of Mother Earth that has yet to be concreted over and walk around on it for a few hours. You can even take your shoes off first, at no extra charge. But hurry: this offer is available for a limited period only.

Questions 1–5

Do the following statements agree with the information given in the passage?

In boxes 1–5 on your answer sheet, write

> **TRUE**   if the statement agrees with the information
> **FALSE**   if the statement contradicts the information
> **NOT GIVEN** if there is no information on this

1. Charles Brantingham and Bruce Beekman are the first researchers on the connection between damage to health and conditions of floor.

2. John Fisher and his colleagues found that those who walked on cobblestones suffered a worsening physical condition.

3. Manufacture of Fisher's cobblestone mats booms with high demand of this product.

4. The research works such as customised pathway from Barbara and Kevin Kunz were inspired from an oversea trip.

5. Benno Nigg suggests that shoes of Masai Barefoot Technology have specific age limitation.

核心词汇

A 段

scour [ˈskaʊə(r)] *vt.* 四处搜索；冲刷；洗涤
gadget [ˈgædʒɪt] *n.* 小配件；装置
trawl [trɔːl] *vi. & vt.* 搜寻 *n.* 查阅；施网
immeasurably [ɪˈmeʒərəbli] *adv.* 不可测量地；无法估量地
wobble [ˈwɒbl] *vi. & vt.* （使）摇晃，（使）摇摆

C 段

cutting edge 尖端，最前沿
contemplate [ˈkɒntəmpleɪt] *vi. & vt.* 深思，细想 *vt.* 考虑；打算
podiatrist [pəˈdaɪətrɪst] *n.* 足部医生
be concerned with 干预；关心
reckon [ˈrekən] *vt.* 估计；料想
epidemic [ˌepɪˈdemɪk] *n.* 流行病 *adj.* 流行性的，极为盛行的
uniformity [ˌjuːnɪˈfɔːməti] *n.* 单调；无变化

D 段

be conducive to 有利于，有助于
anatomy [əˈnætəmi] *n.* 解剖；分解

E 段

dweller [ˈdwelə(r)] *n.* 居民，居住者
deviate [ˈdiːvieɪt] *vi.* 脱离；违背；误入歧途 [拓] deviate from 偏离……
intervention [ˌɪntəˈvenʃn] *n.* 介入，干涉

G 段

scale up 按……的比例增加
exceed [ɪkˈsiːd] *vt.* 超出，超过；超越

I 段

stand still 停滞不前；站着不动

高频同义替换

encounter	▷	face, confront, be confronted with, be faced with
detrimental	▷	adverse, disadvantageous, unfavourable
tend to	▷	be prone to, be liable to, intend to

ordinary	➡	plain, general, average, normal
dramatic	➡	sharp, drastic, significant, serious

题目解析

1. 定位词：Charles Brantingham, Bruce Beekman, first researchers, damage to health
   文中对应点：C 段第二、三句
   题目解析：题干说，Charles Brantingham 和 Bruce Beekman 是第一个关于健康损害和地板状况之间关系的研究人员。由题干定位词 Charles Brantingham, Bruce Beekman 定位到 C 段第二、三句 "Research into the idea that flat floors...podiatrist Charles Brantingham and physiologist Bruce Beekman were concerned with more pedestrian matters."。其中，first researchers 与原文中的 pioneered 对应，damage to health 与 detrimental to our health 对应。句意为，平地可能对我们的健康有害这一想法最早是于 20 世纪 60 年代提出的，而足部医生 Charles Brantingham 和生理学家 Bruce Beekman 更多考虑的是与行人有关的问题。因此答案为 TRUE。

2. 定位词：John Fisher and his colleagues, cobblestones
   文中对应点：F 段第二、四句
   题目解析：题干说，John Fisher 和他的同事们发现那些在鹅卵石路上行走的人的身体状况正在恶化。由题干定位词 John Fisher 定位到 F 段第二句 "John Fisher and colleagues at the Oregon Research Institute in Eugene designed a mat intended to replicate the effect of walking on cobblestones."。其中，John Fisher and his colleagues, cobblestone 均为原文重现。句意为，John Fisher 和他的同事们设计了一种垫子，试图复制走在鹅卵石上的效果；接着第四句 "After 16 weeks, these people showed marked improvements in balance and mobility, and even a significant reduction in blood pressure."。句意为，16 周后，这些人在平衡性和灵活性方面均有显著提高，血压也有明显下降。题干中的 worsening physical condition 与原文意思矛盾，因此答案为 FALSE。

3. 定位词：Fisher's cobblestone mats, high demand
   文中对应点：G 段第二、三句
   题目解析：题干说，Fisher 的鹅卵石垫子的生产在这款产品需求旺盛的情况下显得非常繁荣。由题干定位词可以定位到 G 段第二、三句 "'Our first 1,000 cobblestone mats sold in three weeks,' Fisher says, 'Production is now being scaled up.' Even so, demand could exceed supply if this foot-stimulating activity really is a 'useful non-pharmacological approach for preventing or controlling hypertension of older adults', as the researchers believe."。其中，demand could exceed supply 对应 high demand。句意为，首批的 1,000 块鹅卵石垫子在 3 周内售罄，现在生产也在扩大规模。研究者相信即使如此，仍可能出现供不应求的情况。因此答案为 TRUE。

4. 定位词：Barbara and Kevin Kunz
   文中对应点：H 段最后一句
   题目解析：题干说，Barbara 和 Kevin Kunz 定制课程的研究灵感来自一次海外之旅。由题干定位词 Barbara and Kevin Kunz 定位到 H 段倒数第一句 "American reflexologists Barbara and Kevin Kunz,

based in Albuquerque, New Mexico, advise that you cobble together a walkway using broom handles, bamboo poles, hosepipes, gravel, pebbles, dried peas, driftwood, fallen logs, sand, door mats and strios of turf."。文中并没有提及他们的灵感是否来自一次海外旅行，而且在文中也没有其他与之对应的句子，因此答案为 NOT GIVEN。

5   定位词：Benno Nigg
    文中对应点：I 段第三句
    题目解析：题干说，Benno Nigg 认为 Masai 赤脚技术的鞋子有特定的年龄限制。由题干定位词 Benno Nigg 定位到 I 段第三句 "These shoes have an unbelievable effect,' says Benno Nigg, an exercise scientist at the human performance laboratory of Calgary University in Canada, which has done contract research for the shoe's manufacturers." 句意为，加拿大卡尔加里大学人类行为实验室的运动科学家 Benno Nigg 说："这些鞋子有令人难以置信的效果。"他曾为鞋厂的制造商做过合同研究。I 段第三句到 I 段最后一句是 Benno Nigg 关于鞋子的观点，但是并没有提及鞋子是否应该有明确的年龄限制，因此答案为 NOT GIVEN。

参考答案

1 TRUE   2 FALSE   3 TRUE   4 NOT GIVEN   5 NOT GIVEN

READING PASSAGE 8

Mental Gymnastics

A The working day has just started at the head office of Barclays Bank in London. Seventeen staff are helping themselves to a buffet breakfast as young psychologist Sebastian Bailey enters the room to begin the morning's training session. But this is no ordinary training session. He's not here to sharpen their finance or management skills. He's here to exercise their brains.

B Today's workout, organised by a company called the Mind Gym in London, is entitled 'having presence'. What follows is an intense 90-minute session in which this rather abstract concept is gradually broken down into a concrete set of feelings, mental tricks and behaviours. At one point the bankers are instructed to shut their eyes and visualise themselves filling the room and then the building. They finish up by walking around the room acting out various levels of presence, from low-key to over the top.

C It's easy to poke fun. Yet similar mental workouts are happening in corporate seminar rooms around the globe. The Mind Gym alone offers some 70 different sessions, including ones on mental stamina, creativity for logical thinkers and 'zoom learning'. Other outfits draw more directly on the exercise analogy, offering 'neurobics' courses with names like 'brain sets' and 'cerebral fitness'. Then there are books with titles like *Pumping*, full of brainteasers that claim to 'flex your mind', and software packages offering memory and spatial-awareness games.

D But whatever the style, the companies' sales pitch is invariably the same — follow our routines to shape and sculpt your brain or mind, just as you might tone and train your body. And, of course, they nearly all claim that their mental workouts draw on serious scientific research and thinking into how the brain works.

E One outfit, Brainergy of Cambridge, Massachusetts (motto: 'Because your grey matter matters') puts it like this: 'Studies have shown that mental exercise can cause changes in brain anatomy and brain chemistry which promote increased mental efficiency and clarity. The neuroscience is cutting-edge.' And on its website, Mind Gym trades on a quote from Susan Greenfield, one of Britain's best known neuroscientists: 'It's a bit like going to the gym, if you exercise your brain it will grow.'

F Indeed, the Mind Gym originally planned to hold its sessions in a local health club, until its founders realised where the real money was to be made. Modern companies need flexible, bright thinkers and will seize on anything that claims to create them, especially if it looks like a quick fix backed by science. But are neuronic workouts really backed by science? And do we need them?

G Nor is there anything remotely high-tech about what Lawrence Katz, co-author of *Keep Your Brain Alive*, recommends. Katz, a neurobiologist at Duke University Medical School in North Carolina, argues that just as many of us fail to get enough physical exercise, so we also lack sufficient mental stimulation to keep our brain in trim. Sure we are busy with jobs, family and housework. But most of this activity is repetitive routine. And any leisure time is spent slumped in front of the TV.

H So, read a book upside down. Write or brush your teeth with your wrong hand. Feel your way around the room with your eyes shut. Sniff vanilla essence while listening intently to orchestral music. Anything, says Katz, to break your normal mental routine. It will help invigorate your brain, encouraging its cells to make new connections and pump out neurotrophins, substances that feed and sustain brain circuits.

I Well, up to a point it will. 'What I'm really talking about is brain maintenance rather than bulking up your IQ.' Katz adds. Neurobics, in other words, is about letting your brain fulfill its potential. It cannot create super-brains. Can it achieve even that much, though? Certainly the brain is an organ that can adapt to the demands placed on it. Tests on animal brain tissue, for example, have repeatedly shown that electrically stimulating the synapses that connect nerve cells thought to be crucial to learning and reasoning, makes them stronger and more responsive. Brain scans suggest we use a lot more of our grey matter when carrying out new or strange tasks than when we're doing well-rehearsed ones. Rats raised in bright cages with toys sprout more neural connections than rats raised in bare cages — suggesting perhaps that novelty and variety could be crucial to a developing brain. Katz, and neurologists have proved time and again that people who lose brain cells suddenly during a stroke often sprout new connections to compensate for the loss especially if they undergo extensive therapy to overcome any paralysis.

J Guy Claxton, an educational psychologist at the University of Bristol, dismisses most of the neurological approaches as 'neuro-babble'. 'Nevertheless there are specific mental skills we can learn,' he contends. 'Desirable attributes such as creativity, mental flexibility, and even motivation, are not the fixed faculties that most of us think.' They are thought habits that can be learned. The problem, says Claxton, is that most of us never get proper training in these skills. We develop our own private set of mental strategies for tackling tasks and never learn anything explicitly. Worse still, because any learned skill — even driving a car or brushing our teeth — quickly sinks out of consciousness, we can no longer see the very thought habits we're relying upon. Our mental tools become invisible to us.

K Claxton is the academic adviser to the Mind Gym. So not surprisingly, the company espouses his solution — that we must return our thought patterns to a conscious level, becoming aware of the details of how we usually think. Only then can we start to practise better thought patterns, until eventually these become our new habits. Switching metaphors, picture not gym classes, but tennis or football coaching.

L In practice, the training can seem quite mundane. For example, in one of the eight different creativity workouts offered by the Mind Gym — entitled 'creativity for logical thinkers', one of the mental strategies taught is to make a sensible suggestion, then immediately pose its opposite. So, asked to spend five minutes inventing a new pizza, a group soon comes up with no topping, sweet topping, cold topping, price based on time of day, flat-rate prices and so on.

M Bailey agrees that the trick is simple. But it is surprising how few such tricks people have to call upon when they are suddenly asked to be creative: 'They tend to just label themselves as uncreative, not realising that there are techniques that every creative person employs.' Bailey says the aim is to introduce people to half a dozen or so such strategies in a session so that what at first seems like dauntingly abstract mental task becomes a set of concrete, learnable behaviours. He admits this is not a short cut to genius. Neurologically, some people do start with quicker circuits or greater handling capacity. However, with the right kind of training he thinks we can dramatically increase how efficiently we use it.

N It is hard to prove that the training itself is effective. How do you measure a change in an employee's creativity levels, or memory skills? But staff certainly report feeling that such classes have opened their eyes. So, neurological boosting or psychological training? At the moment you can pay your money and take your choice. Claxton for one believes there is no reason why schools and universities shouldn't spend more time teaching basic thinking skills, rather than trying to stuff heads with facts and hoping that effective thought habits are somehow absorbed by osmosis.

Questions 1–5

Do the following statements agree with the views of the writer in the passage?

In boxes 1–5 on your answer sheet, write

> **YES** if the statement agrees with the views of the writer
> **NO** if the statement contradicts the views of the writer
> **NOT GIVEN** if it is impossible to say what the writer thinks about this

1. Mind Gym coach instructed employees to imagine that they are the building.

2. Mind Gym uses the similar marketing theory that is used all round.

3. Susan Greenfield is the founder of Mind Gym.

4. All business and industries are using Mind Gym's session globally.

5. According to Mind Gym, extensive scientific background supports their mental training sessions.

核心词汇

A 段

buffet [ˈbʊfeɪ] *n.* 自助餐；小卖部
psychologist [saɪˈkɒlədʒɪst] *n.* 心理学家
session [ˈseʃn] *n.* 会议；开庭

B 段

entitle [ɪnˈtaɪtl] *v.* 使有权利；使有资格
concrete [ˈkɒnkriːt] *adj.* 具体的；混凝土的
trick [trɪk] *n.* 诡计；恶作剧

C 段

seminar [ˈsemɪnɑː(r)] *n.* 讨论会，研讨班
outfit [ˈaʊtfɪt] *n.* 全套服装；全套设备
analogy [əˈnælədʒi] *n.* 类比；类推
cerebral [ˈserəbrəl] *adj.* 脑的，大脑的

D 段

invariably [ɪnˈveəriəbli] *adv.* 始终不变地；总是
sculpt [skʌlpt] *v.* 雕刻，雕塑

E 段

anatomy [əˈnætəmi] *n.* 解剖学；剖析
promote [prəˈməʊt] *v.* 促进；提升
clarity [ˈklærəti] *n.* 清楚；清晰
neuroscientist [ˈnjʊərəʊsaɪəntɪst] *n.* 神经系统学家

F 段

flexible [ˈfleksəbl] *adj.* 灵活的；易弯曲的
neuronic [njʊəˈrɒnɪk] *adj.* 神经生物学的
workout [ˈwɜːkaʊt] *n.* 锻炼；练习；试验

G 段

remotely [rɪˈməʊtli] *adv.* 稍微，略微；偏远地
stimulation [ˌstɪmjuˈleɪʃn] *n.* 刺激；激励
trim [trɪm] *v.* 修剪；削减

repetitive [rɪˈpetətɪv] *adj.* 重复的

slump [slʌmp] *v.* 倒下；跌倒

H 段

shut [ʃʌt] *v.* 关闭；停业；幽禁

orchestral [ɔːˈkestrəl] *adj.* 管弦乐的；管弦乐队的

I 段

synapse [ˈsaɪnæps] *n.* 突触

nerve [nɜːv] *n.* 神经；勇气

sprout [spraʊt] *v.* 发芽；长芽

therapy [ˈθerəpi] *n.* 治疗，疗法

J 段

dismiss [dɪsˈmɪs] *v.* 解散；解雇；开除；让……离开

attribute [əˈtrɪbjuːt] *v.* 认为……属于；把……归咎于

consciousness [ˈkɒnʃəsnəs] *n.* 意识；知觉

K 段

academic [ˌækəˈdemɪk] *adj.* 学术的

espouse [ɪˈspaʊz] *v.* 支持；赞成；信奉

conscious [ˈkɒnʃəs] *adj.* 意识到的；神志清醒的

metaphor [ˈmetəfə(r)] *n.* 暗喻，隐喻

L 段

creativity [ˌkriːeɪˈtɪvəti] *n.* 创造力；创造性

sensible [ˈsensəbl] *adj.* 明智的；通情达理的

pose [pəʊz] *v.* 造成；形成

M 段

dauntingly [ˈdɔːntɪŋli] *adv.* 令人生畏地；吓人地

N 段

neurological [ˌnjʊərəˈlɒdʒɪkl] *adj.* 神经病学的；神经学上的

osmosis [ɒzˈməʊsɪs] *n.* 渗透；渗透作用

高频同义替换

staff ▸ employee, clerk, personnel

ordinary ▸ common, usual, general

cause ▸ lead to, result in, bring about

sufficient ▸ enough, plenty, adequate, ample

intently ▸ devotedly, attentively

achieve ▸ accomplish, carry out, perform, complete, fulfil

immediately ▸ at once, straight away, right away, in a moment

admit ▸ acknowledge, recognise, grant, concede

dramatically ▸ remarkably, markedly, significantly

prove ▸ demonstrate, certify, testify

题目解析

1 定位词：instructed, employees, imagine, the building

文中对应点：B 段第三句

题目解析：题干说，心灵健身房教练引导员工把自己想象成大楼。通过定位词 Mind Gym, employees, imagine, the building 定位到 B 段第三句 "At one point the bankers are instructed to shut their eyes and visualise themselves filling the room and then the building." 其中，bankers 对应 employees，visualise 与 imagine 为同义替换。句意为，银行工作人员被要求闭上眼睛，想象他们填满了房间，然后填满了大楼。题干中的"引导工作人员把自己想象成大楼"与原文表述不一致，所以答案为 NO。

2 定位词：similar, marketing theory

文中对应点：D 段第一句

题目解析：题干说，心灵健身房使用了类似的被广泛使用的营销理论。通过定位词 similar, marketing theory 定位到 D 段第一句 "But whatever the style, the companies' sales pitch is invariably the same…" 其中，the same 与 similar 为同义替换，sales pitch 对应 marketing theory。句意为，在出售产品时，不管什么类型的公司，所有的销售说辞都是一致的。题干"心灵健身房使用了类似的被广泛使用的营销理论"，与原文信息表述一致，因此答案为 YES。

3 定位词：Susan Greenfield

文中对应点：E 段倒数第一句

题目解析：题干说，Susan Greenfield 是心灵健身房的创始人。通过定位词 Susan Greenfield 定位到 E 段倒数第一句 "Mind Gym trades on a quote from Susan Greenfield, one of Britain's best known neuroscientists…" 其中，Susan Greenfield 为英国最著名的神经科学家之一，但是，题干中说她是心灵健身房公司的创始人，是无法从原文得出的。句意为，心灵健身房在其网站上引用了英国最著名的神经科学家之一 Susan Greenfield 的一句话……因此答案为 NOT GIVEN。

4 定位词：business and industries

文中对应点：无

题目解析：题干说，所有的企业和行业都在全球范围内使用心灵健身房的课程。题干定位词在原文中没有出现，所以答案为 NOT GIVEN。

5 定位词：extensive scientific background

文中对应点：F 段第二句到第四句

题目解析：题干说，根据心灵健身房，广泛的科学背景支持他们的心理训练课程。通过定位词 extensive scientific background 定位到 F 段第二句到第四句 "Modern companies need flexible, bright thinkers and will seize on anything that claims to create them, especially if it looks like a quick fix backed by science. But are neuronic workouts really backed by science? And do we need them?" 其中，really backed by science 与 extensive scientific background 对应。句意为，现代企业需要灵活的、聪明的思想者，他们会抓住任何声称可以帮助他们的东西，特别是它如果看起来是有科学依据的速成法。但是神经运动真的有科学依据吗？我们需要它们吗？综上，题干中说关于大脑锻炼课程有大量的科学依据，原文中并没有明确说明有没有相关科学依据，所以答案为 NOT GIVEN。

参考答案

1 NO **2** YES **3** NOT GIVEN **4** NOT GIVEN **5** NOT GIVEN

READING PASSAGE 9

Carlill VS Carbolic Smoke Ball Company

A The Carbolic Smoke Ball Company made a product called the 'smoke ball'. It claimed to be a cure for influenza and a number of other diseases, in the context of the 1889–1890 flu pandemic (estimated to have killed 1 million people). The bottle was a patented design and the nozzle part was mental one with the gauze inside which filter the air flux. The smoke ball was a rubber ball with a tube attached. It was filled with carbolic acid (or phenol). The tube would be inserted into a user's nose and squeezed at the bottom to release medicine powder (the vapours) hold inside the rubber ball bottle. The nose would run, ostensibly flushing out viral infections.

B The Company published advertisements in the *Pall Mall Gazette* and other newspapers on November 13, 1891, claiming that it would pay £100 to anyone who got sick with influenza after using its product according to the instructions set out in the advertisement.

> '£100 reward will be paid by the Carbolic Smoke Ball Company to any person who contracts the increasing epidemic influenza colds, or any disease caused by taking cold, after having used the ball three times daily for two weeks, according to the printed directions supplied with each ball.
>
> £1,000 is deposited with the Alliance Bank, Regent Street, showing our sincerity in the matter.
>
> During the last epidemic of influenza many thousand carbolic smoke balls were sold as preventives against this disease, and in no ascertained case was the disease contracted by those using the carbolic smoke ball.
>
> One carbolic smoke ball will last a family several months, making it the cheapest remedy in the world at the price. 10s, post free. The ball can be refilled at a cost of 5s. Address: "Carbolic Smoke Ball Company", 27, Princes Street. Hanover Square. London.'

C Mrs Louisa Elizabeth Carlill saw the advertisement, bought one of the balls and used it three times daily for nearly two months until she contracted the flu on 17 January 1892. She claimed £100 from the Carbolic Smoke Ball Company. They ignored two letters from her husband, a solicitor. On a third request for her reward, they replied with an anonymous letter that if it is used properly the company had complete confidence in the smoke ball's efficacy, but 'to protect themselves against all fraudulent claims' they would need her to come to their office to use the ball each day and be checked by the secretary. Mrs Carlill brought a claim to court. The barristers representing her argued that the advertisement and her reliance on it was a contract between her and the company, and so they ought to pay. The company argued it was not a serious contract.

D The Carbolic Smoke Ball Company, despite being represented by HH Asquith, lost its argument at the Queen's Bench. It appealed straight away. The Court of Appeal unanimously rejected the company's arguments and held that there was a fully binding contract for £100 with Mrs Carlill. Among the reasons given by the three judges were (1) that the advert was a unilateral offer to all the world (2) that satisfying conditions for using the smoke ball constituted acceptance of the offer (3) that purchasing or merely using the smoke ball constituted good consideration, because it was a distinct detriment incurred at the behest of the company and, furthermore, more people buying smoke balls by relying on the advert was a clear benefit to Carbolic (4) that the company's claim that £1,000 was deposited at the Alliance Bank showed the serious intention to be legally bound.

E   Lord Justice Lindley gave the first judgment, after running through the facts again. He makes short shrift of the insurance and wagering contract arguments that were dealt with in the Queen's Bench. He believed that the advert was intended to be issued to the public and to be read by the public. How would an ordinary person reading this document construe it? It was intended unquestionably to have some effect. He followed on with essentially five points. First, the advert was not 'mere puff' as had been alleged by the company, because the deposit of £1,000 in the bank evidenced seriousness. Second, the advertisement was an offer to the world. Third, communication of acceptance is not necessary for a contract when people's conduct manifests an intention to contract. Fourth, that the vagueness of the advert's terms was no insurmountable obstacle. And fifth, the nature of Mrs Carlill's consideration (what she gave in return for the offer) was good, because there is both an advantage in additional sales in reaction to the advertisement and a 'distinct inconvenience' that people go to use a smoke ball.

F   Lord Justice Bowen LJ's opinion was more tightly structured in style and is frequently cited. Five main steps in his reasoning can be identified. First, he says that the contract was not too vague to be enforced, because it could be interpreted according to what ordinary people would understand by it. He differed slightly to Lindley LJ on what time period one could contract flu and still have a claim (Lindley LJ said a 'reasonable time' after use, while Bowen LJ said 'while the smoke ball is used') but this was not a crucial point, because the fact was that Mrs Carlill got flu while using the smoke ball. Second, like Lindley LJ, Bowen LJ says that the advert was not mere puff because £1,000 was deposited in the bank to pay rewards. Third, he said that although there was an offer to the whole world, there was not a contract with the whole world. Therefore, it was not an absurd basis for a contract, because only the people that used it would bind the company. Fourth, he says that communication is not necessary to accept the terms of an offer; conduct is and should be sufficient. Fifth, there was clearly good consideration given by Mrs Carlill because she went to the 'inconvenience' of using it, and the company got the benefit of extra sales.

G   Carlill is frequently cited as a leading case in the common law of contract, particularly where unilateral contracts are concerned. This is perhaps due to the ingenuity of Counsel for the Defendant in running just about every available defense, requiring the court to deal with these points in turn in the judgment. It provides an excellent study of the basic principles of contract and how they relate to everyday life till modern world. The case remains good law. It still binds the lower courts of England and Wales and is cited by judges with approval. However, in addition to the contractual remedy afforded to users, the same facts would give rise to a number of additional statutory remedies and punishments were an individual to place an advert in the same terms today.

Questions 1–4

Do the following statements agree with the information given in the passage?

In boxes 1–4 on your answer sheet, write

> **TRUE**　　　if the statement agrees with the information
> **FALSE**　　if the statement contradicts the information
> **NOT GIVEN**　if there is no information on this

1　Influenza epidemic was more rampant in London City than in rural areas.

2　A letter has replied to Mrs. Carlill bearing no signed name to claim the company's innocence.

3　The Carbolic Smoke Ball Company lost its lawsuit then the company accepted the sentence straight away.

4　The new patented carbolic acid product can be poisonous and viral infectious.

核心词汇

A 段

carbolic [kɑːˈbɒlɪk] *adj.* 碳的；石炭酸的
influenza [ˌɪnfluˈenzə] *n.* 流行性感冒（简写 flu）
pandemic [pænˈdemɪk] *adj.* 全国流行的；普遍的
nozzle [ˈnɒzl] *n.* 喷嘴；管口
gauze [gɔːz] *n.* 纱布；薄纱
flush [flʌʃ] *v.* 使发红；用水冲洗

B 段

contract [ˈkɒntrækt] *v.* 感染；收缩；订约

C 段

efficacy [ˈefɪkəsi] *n.* 功效，效力
fraudulent [ˈfrɔːdjələnt] *adj.* 欺骗性的；不正的
reliance [rɪˈlaɪəns] *n.* 信赖；信心

D 段

distinct [dɪˈstɪŋkt] *adj.* 明显的；独特的；有区别的
detriment [ˈdetrɪmənt] *n.* 损害；伤害；损害物
incur [ɪnˈkɜː(r)] *v.* 招致，引发；蒙受

E 段

unquestionably [ʌnˈkwestʃənəbli] *adv.* 无可非议地；确凿地
puff [pʌf] *v.* 膨胀；张开；鼓吹；夸张
manifest [ˈmænɪfest] *v.* 显示，出现
vagueness [ˈveɪgnəs] *n.* 模糊；含糊；茫然
insurmountable [ˌɪnsəˈmaʊntəbl] *adj.* 不能克服的；不能超越的；难以对付的

F 段

absurd [əbˈsɜːd] *adj.* 荒谬的；可笑的

G 段

unilateral [ˌjuːnɪˈlætrəl] *adj.* 单边的；单系的
ingenuity [ˌɪndʒəˈnjuːəti] *n.* 心灵手巧；独创性
contractual [kənˈtræktʃuəl] *adj.* 契约的；合同的
remedy [ˈremədi] *n.* 补救；治疗；赔偿
statutory [ˈstætʃətri] *adj.* 法定的；法令的

题目

rampant [ˈræmpənt] *adj.* 蔓延的；猖獗的
innosence [ˈɪnəsns] *n.* 清白，无罪
poisonous [ˈpɔɪzənəs] *adj.* 有毒的

高频同义替换

cure	▸	remedy, therapy, medical treatment, treat
supply	▸	provide, offer, furnish with, afford
reliance	▸	dependence, trust, have confidence in, rely on
distinct	▸	obvious, evident, visible, apparent
furthermore	▸	moreover, besides, additionally, in addition
manifest	▸	indicate, prove, demonstrate, reveal
crucial	▸	key, important, considerable, critical
frequently	▸	often, continually, regularly, constantly

题目解析

1 定位词：influenza epidemic
  文中对应点：A 段第二句
  题目解析：题干说，相比农村地区，伦敦市区的流感更为肆虐。由定位词 influenza epidemic 定位到 A 段第二句 "It claimed to be a cure for influenza and a number of other diseases, in the context of the 1889—1890 flu pandemic (estimated to have killed 1 million people)." 其中，flu pandemic 与 influenza epidemic 为同义替换。但是 A 段第二句并未用数据强调其造成的严重后果，而且通篇并没有一处对比说明伦敦市区和农村地区各自的灾情状况。句意为，在 1889—1890 年流感肆虐的情况下（据估已造成一百万人死亡），据称，它是能够治愈流感及其他很多疾病的一种疗法。题干的表述在原文中并没有相关的对应信息，因此答案为 NOT GIVEN。

2 定位词：letter, replied, innocent
  文中对应点：C 段第四句
  题目解析：题干说，该公司匿名给卡里尔女士回了一封信，以此声明公司是没有过错的。由定位词 letter, replied, claim 定位到 C 段第四句 "On a third request for her reward, they replied with an anonymous letter that if it is used properly the company had complete confidence in the smoke ball's efficacy, but 'to protect themselves against all fraudulent claims' they would need her to come to their office to use the ball each day and be checked by the secretary." 其中，they replied with an anonymous letter 与 a letter has replied to Ms. Carlill bearing no signed name 为同义替换，innocent 对应 to protect themselves against all fraudulent claims，本句后半部分提及的公司行为也正是其想证明自己并无过错的一种表现。句意为，当卡里尔第三次写信要求赔偿时，她收到了公司

的一份匿名信，信中提到如果使用合理，他们对产品的药效是很有信心的；但为了避免欺骗性索赔，他们需要卡里尔每天到办公室使用该产品并接受秘书的检查。题干的表述符合原文意思，因此答案为 TRUE。

3 定位词：lost its lawsuit, accepted the sentence straight away
文中对应点：D 段第一、二句
题目解析：题干说，碳烟球公司败诉后当即就接受了判决。由定位词 lost, straight away 定位到 D 段第一、二句 "The Carbolic Smoke Ball Company, despite being represented by HH Asquith, lost its argument at the Queen's Bench. It appealed straight away." 其中，lost its argument 与 lost its lawsuit 为同义替换，appealed（上诉）straight away 对应 accepted the sentence（接受判决）straight away，但意思完全相反。句意为，尽管是由 HH Asquith 代表碳烟球公司在英国高等法院进行辩论，官司还是没能打赢，它立即上诉。题干后半部分的表述与原文意思相反，因此答案为 FALSE。

4 定位词：patented, carbolic acid
文中对应点：A 段第三句和第五句
题目解析：题干说，新专利碳酸产品可能有毒，而且具有病毒感染性。由定位词 patented 定位到 A 段第三句 "The bottle was a patented design..." 瓶子是专利设计……由定位词 carbolic acid 定位到 A 段第五句 "It was filled with carbolic acid (or phenol)." 烟球中充满了石碳酸。所以，文中提到了该产品的具体构造，并没有相关信息证明药物本身具有毒性或会引起病毒性感染，且之后的案例纠纷中也没有提及药物本身存在的问题。因此，答案为 NOT GIVEN。

参考答案

1 NOT GIVEN　**2** TRUE　**3** FALSE　**4** NOT GIVEN

READING PASSAGE 10

The Impact of Environment on Children

A What determines how a child develops? In reality, it would be impossible to account for each and every influence that ultimately determines who a child becomes. What we can look at are some of the most apparent influences such as genetics, parenting, experiences, friends, family relationships and school to help us understand the influences that help contribute to a child's growth.

B Think of these influences as building blocks. While roost people tend to have the same basic building blocks, these components can be put together in an infinite number of ways. Consider your own overall personality. How much of who you are today was shaped by your genetic inheritance, and how much is a result of your lifetime of experiences? This question has puzzled philosophers, psychologists and educators for hundreds of years and is frequently referred to as the nature versus nurture debate. Generally, the given rate of influence to children is 40 % to 50%. It may refer to all of siblings of a family. Are we the result of nature (our genetic background) or nurture (our environment)? Today, most researchers agree that child development involves a complex interaction of both nature and nurture, while some aspects of development may be strongly influenced by biology, environmental influences may also play a role. For example, the timing of when the onset of puberty occurs is largely the results of heredity, but environmental factors such as nutrition can also have an effect.

C From the earliest moments of life, the interaction of heredity and the environment works to shape who children are and who they will become. While the genetic instructions a child inherits from his parents may set out a road map for development, the environment can impact how these directions are expressed, shaped or event silenced. The complex interaction of nature and nurture does not just occur at certain moments or at certain periods of time; it is persistent and lifelong.

D The shared environment (also called common environment) refers to environmental influences that have the effect of making siblings more similar to one another. Shared environmental influences can include shared family experiences, shared peer groups, and sharing the same school and community. In general, there has not been strong evidence for shared environmental effects on many behaviours, particularly those measured in adults. Possible reasons for this are discussed. Shared environmental effects are evident in children and adolescents, but these effects generally decrease across the life span. New developments in behaviour genetic methods have made it possible to specify shared environments of importance and to tease apart familial and nonfamilial sources of shared environmental influence. It may also refer to all of siblings of a family, but the rate of influence is less than 10 per cent.

E The importance of non-shared environment lay hidden within quantitative genetic studies since they began nearly a century ago. Quantitative genetic methods, such as twin and adoption methods, were designed to tease apart nature and nurture in order to explain family resemblance. For nearly all complex phenotypes, it has emerged that the answer to the question of the origins of family resemblance is nature — things run in families primarily for genetic reasons. However, the best available evidence for the importance of environmental influence comes from this same quantitative genetic research because genetic influence never explains all of the variance for complex phenotypes, and the remaining variance must be ascribed to environmental influences. Non-shared environment, it may refer to part of siblings of a family, the rate of influence to children is 40 % to 50%.

F Yet it took many decades for the full meaning of these findings to emerge. If genetics explains why siblings growing up in the same family are similar, but the environment is important, then it must be the case that the salient environmental effects do not make siblings similar. That is, they are not shared by children growing up in the same family — they must be 'non-shared'. This implication about non-shared environmental import lay fallow in the field of quantitative genetics because the field's attention was then firmly on the nature-nurture debate. 'Nurture' in the nature-nurture debate was implicitly taken to mean shared environment because from Freud onwards, theories of socialisation had assumed that children's environments are doled out on a family-by-family basis. In contrast, the point of non-shared environment is that environments are doled out on a child-by-child basis. Note that the phrase 'non-shared environment' is shorthand for a component of phenotypic variance — it refers to 'effects' rather than 'events', as discussed later. Research in recent years suggested that the impact from parents will be easy to be interrupted by the influence from the children of the same age. That also showed that variations of knowledge that children get from other culture is increasing. A number of interests between, whatever, fathers and mothers or parents and their children are conflicting.

G Because siblings living in the same home share some but not all of the potential genetic and environmental factors that influence their behaviours, teasing apart the potential influences of genetic and non-genetic factors that differentiate siblings is very difficult. Turkheimer and Waldron (2000) have noted that non-shared environmental influences — which include all of the random measurement error — may not be systematic, but instead may operate idiosyncratically and in ways that cannot be ascertained. Thus, the question is whether or not quasi-experimental behavioural genetic designs can be used to actually identify systematic non-shared environmental mechanisms cross sectionally and longitudinally. This is the impetus for the current study.

Questions 1–4

Do the following statements agree with the views of the writer in the passage?

In boxes 1–4 on your answer sheet, write

> **YES** if the statement agrees with the views of the writer
> **NO** if the statement contradicts the views of the writer
> **NOT GIVEN** if it is impossible to say what the writer thinks about this

1 The more children there are in a family, the more impacts of environment it is.

2 Methods based on twin studies still meet unexpected differences that cannot be ascribed purely to genetic explanation.

3 Children prefer to speak the language from the children of the same age to the language spoken by their parents.

4 The study of non-shared environmental influences can be a generally agreed idea among researchers in the field.

核心词汇

A 段

apparent [əˈpærənt] *adj.* 显然的；表面上的

genetics [dʒəˈnetɪks] *n.* 遗传学

B 段

inheritance [ɪnˈherɪtəns] *n.* 继承；遗传；遗产

philosopher [fəˈlɒsəfə(r)] *n.* 哲学家

nurture [ˈnɜːtʃə(r)] *v. & n.* 养育；鼓励；培植

sibling [ˈsɪblɪŋ] *n.* 兄弟姐妹

interaction [ˌɪntərˈækʃn] *n.* 相互作用；交互作用

puberty [ˈpjuːbəti] *n.* 青春期；开花期

heredity [həˈredəti] *n.* 遗传，遗传性

C 段

persistent [pəˈsɪstənt] *adj.* 固执的；坚持的

D 段

adolescent [ˌædəˈlesnt] *n.* 青少年

tease apart 梳理

E 段

quantitative [ˈkwɒntɪtətɪv] *adj.* 定量的；数量的

resemblance [rɪˈzembləns] *n.* 相似；相似之处

phenotype [ˈfiːnətaɪp] *n.* 表型；显型

variance [ˈveəriəns] *n.* 差异；不一致；变化幅度

F 段

salient [ˈseɪliənt] *adj.* 显著的；突出的；跳跃的

fallow [ˈfæləʊ] *adj.* 休耕的；不活跃的

implicitly [ɪmˈplɪsɪtli] *adv.* 含蓄地；暗中地

shorthand [ˈʃɔːthænd] *n.* 速记；速记法

G 段

idiosyncratically [ˌɪdɪəsɪŋˈkrætɪkəlɪ] *adv.* 独特地

ascertain [ˌæsəˈteɪn] *v.* 确定；查明

quasi-experimental [ˌkweɪzaɪˌɪkˌsperɪˈment(ə)l] *adj.* 准实验的

mechanism [ˈmekənɪzəm] *n.* 机制；机构

longitudinally [ˌlɒŋgɪˈtjuːdɪnəli] *adv.* 长度上；经度上

impetus [ˈɪmpɪtəs] *n.* 动力；促进；冲力

题目

ascribe [əˈskraɪb] *vt.* 归因于；归咎于 [拓] ascribe A to B 将 A 的原因归结于 B

高频同义替换

in reality	▸	in fact, actually, as it is, virtually, practically
account for	▸	interpret, explain, give reasons for
ultimately	▸	finally, eventually, lastly, in the end
complex	▸	complicated, sophisticated, intricate
impact	▸	affect, influence, work on, have an effect on
nearly	▸	almost, virtually, practically
primarily	▸	basically, mainly, mostly, largely
note	▸	notice, pay attention to, observe
suggest	▸	show, indicate, manifest, demonstrate

题目解析

1. 定位词：the more children, impacts of environment
   文中对应点：D 段、E 段
   题目解析：题干说，一个家庭里的孩子越多，环境的影响就越大。由定位词 the more children, impacts of environment 定位到 D 段、E 段，D 段、E 段分别介绍了共同环境和非共同环境的影响，没有提到兄弟姐妹越多，孩子受到环境的影响越大，题干信息无法从原文得出，所以答案为 NOT GIVEN。

2. 定位词：cannot be ascribed to purely, genetic, explanation
   文中对应点：E 段第四句
   题目解析：题干说，基于双胞胎研究的方法仍然会遇到意想不到的差异，而这些差异不能被归结为纯粹的基因解释。由定位词 cannot be ascribed to purely, genetic, explanation 定位到 E 段第四句 "However, the best available evidence for the importance of environmental influence comes from this same quantitative genetic research because genetic influence never explains all of the variance for complex phenotypes, and the remaining variance must be ascribed to environmental influences."。其中，never explains all of the variance for 与 can not be ascribed to purely 对应，explains 为 explanation 的动词形式。句意为，但是最好的对后天环境影响的重要性的解释恰恰也来自同样的定量基因研究，因为单纯基因的影响不能解释复杂多变型行为的所有差异，还有一部分归因于后天环境。题干的表述与原文一致，所以答案为 YES。

3 定位词：children of the same age, parents

   文中对应点：F 段倒数第三句

   题目解析：题干说，孩子们更喜欢同龄孩子的语言，而不是父母们所说的语言。通过定位词 children of the same age, parents 定位到 F 段倒数第三句 "Research in recent years suggested that the impact from parents will be easy to be interrupted by the influence from the children of the same age."。其中，children of the same age, parents 皆为原文重现。句意为，近些年来的研究表明父母对孩子的影响很容易被同龄人对孩子的影响所扰乱。题干的表达与原文对应信息既不一致也不矛盾，所以答案是 NOT GIVEN。

4 定位词：non-shared environmental influences, agreed idea

   文中对应点：G 段第二句

   题目解析：题干说，对非共享环境影响的研究可以成为该领域研究人员普遍认同的观点。通过定位词 non-shared environment influence 定位到 G 段第二句 "Turkheimer and Waldron (2000) have noted that non-shared environmental influences — which include all of the random measurement error — may not be systematic, but instead may operate idiosyncratically and in ways that cannot be ascertained."。其中，cannot be ascertain 与 agreed idea 意思相反。句意为，Turkheimer 和 Waldron（2000）提出，包括全部随机测量错误的非共同环境影响，可能不是呈系统性的，而是呈现特殊性而且是不确定的。题干"非共享环境影响的研究已经达成共识"与原文对应信息矛盾，所以答案为 NO。

参考答案

1 NOT GIVEN   **2** YES   **3** NOT GIVEN   **4** NO

第二章　小标题

READING PASSAGE 1

Questions 1–6

The passage has six paragraphs, **A–F**.

Choose the correct heading for each paragraph from the list of headings below.

Write the correct number, *i–x*, in boxes 1–6 on your answer sheet.

List of Headings

i	Western countries provide essential assistance
ii	Unbalanced development for an essential space technology
iii	Innovative application compelled by competition
iv	An ancient invention which is related to the future
v	Military purpose of satellite
vi	Rocket application in ancient China
vii	Space development in Asia in the past
viii	Non-technology factors count
ix	Competitive edge gained by more economically feasible satellite
x	Current space technology development in Asia

1　Paragraph **A**

2　Paragraph **B**

3　Paragraph **C**

4　Paragraph **D**

5　Paragraph **E**

6　Paragraph **F**

Asian Space Satellite Technology

A. Rocket technology has progressed considerably since the days of 'fire arrows' (bamboo poles filled with gunpowder) first used in China around 500 BC, and, during the Sung Dynasty, to repel Mongol invaders at the battle of Kaifeng (Kai-fung fu) in AD 1232. These ancient rockets stand in stark contrast to the present-day Chinese rocket launch vehicles, called the 'Long March', intended to place a Chinese astronaut in space by 2005 and, perhaps, to achieve a Chinese moon landing by the end of the decade.

B. In the last decade there has been a dramatic growth in space activities in Asia both in the utilisation of space-based services and the production of satellites and launchers. This rapid expansion has led many commentators and analysts to predict that Asia will become a world space power. The space age has had dramatic effects worldwide with direct developments in space technology influencing telecommunications, meteorological forecasting, earth resource, and environmental monitoring, and disaster mitigation (flood, forest fires, and oil spills). Asian nations have been particularly eager to embrace these developments.

C. New and innovative uses for satellites are constantly being explored with potential revolutionary effects, such as in the field of health and telemedicine, distance education, crime prevention (piracy on the high seas), food and agricultural planning and production (rice crop monitoring). Space in Asia is very much influenced by the competitive commercial space sector, the emergence of low-cost mini-satellites, and the globalisation of industrial and financial markets. It is not evident how Asian space will develop in the coming decades in the face of these trends. It is, however, important to understand and assess the factors and forces that shape Asian space activities and development in determining its possible consequences for the region.

D. At present, three Asian nations, Japan, China, and India, have comprehensive end-to-end space capabilities and possess a complete space infrastructure: space technology, satellite manufacturing, rockets, and spaceports. Already self-sufficient in terms of satellite design and manufacturing, South Korea is currently attempting to join their ranks with its plans to develop a launch site and spaceport. Additionally, nations in Southeast Asia as well as those bordering the Indian subcontinent (Nepal, Pakistan, and Bangladesh) have, or are starting to develop indigenous space programmes. The Association of Southeast Asian Nations (ASEAN) has, in varying degrees, embraced space applications using foreign technology and over the past five years or so its space activities have been expanding. Southeast Asia is predicted to become the largest and fastest growing market for commercial space products and applications, driven by telecommunications (mobile and fixed services), the Internet, and remote sensing applications. In the development of this technology, many non-technical factors, such as economics, politics, culture and history, interact and play important roles, which in turn affect Asian technology.

E. Asia, and Southeast Asia in particular, suffers from a long list of recurrent large-scale environmental problems including storms and flooding, forest fires and deforestation, and crop failures. Thus the space application that has attracted the most attention in this region is remote sensing. Remote sensing satellites equipped with instruments to take photographs of the ground at different wavelengths provide essential information for natural resource accounting, environmental management, disaster prevention and monitoring, land-use mapping, and sustainable development planning. Progress in these applications has been rapid and impressive. ASEAN members, unlike Japan, China, and India, do not have their own remote sensing satellites, however, most of its member nations have facilities to receive, process, and interpret such data from American and European satellites. In particular, Thailand, Malaysia, and Singapore have world-class remote sensing processing facilities and research programmes. ASEAN has plans to develop (and launch) its own satellites and in particular remote sensing satellites.

Japan is regarded as the dominant space power in Asia and its record of successes and quality of technologies are equal to those of the West. In view of the technological challenges and high risks involved in space activities, a very long, and expensive, learning curve has been followed to obtain those successes achieved. Japan's satellite manufacturing was based on the old and traditional defence and military procurement methodologies as practiced in the US and Europe.

F In recent years there have been fundamental changes in the way satellites are designed and built to drastically reduce costs. The emergence of 'small satellites' and their quick adoption by Asian countries as a way to develop low-cost satellite technology and rapidly establish a space capability has given these countries the possibility to shorten their learning curve by a decade or more. The global increase of technology transfer mechanisms and use of readily available commercial technology to replace costly space and military standard components may very well result in a highly competitive Asian satellite manufacturing industry.

核心词汇

A 段

astronaut [ˈæstrənɔːt] *n.* 宇航员，航天员

B 段

utilisation [ˌjuːtəlaɪˈzeɪʃn] *n.* 利用，使用 [拓] utilise *vt.* 利用，使用
satellite [ˈsætəlaɪt] *n.* 卫星，人造卫星
meteorological [ˌmiːtɪərəˈlɒdʒɪkəl] *adj.* 气象学的，气象的
mitigation [mɪtɪˈgeɪʃ(ə)n] *n.* 减轻，缓和 [拓] mitigate *vt.* 减轻，缓和
embrace [ɪmˈbreɪs] *vi. & vt.* 拥抱 *vt.* 欣然接受；包括，涉及

C 段

telemedicine [ˈtelɪˌmedɪsɪn] *n.* 远程医疗
consequence [ˈkɒnsɪkwəns] *n.* 后果，结果

D 段

comprehensive [ˌkɒmprɪˈhensɪv] *adj.* 综合的，全面的；彻底的
indigenous [ɪnˈdɪdʒənəs] *adj.* 本地的，土生土长的 [拓] indigenous population 土著

E 段

deforestation [ˌdiːˌfɒrɪˈsteɪʃn] *n.* 砍伐森林
remote sensing 遥感
sustainable [səˈsteɪnəbl] *adj.* 可持续的，不破坏环境的 [拓] sustainable growth 可持续增长
interpret [ɪnˈtɜːprɪt] *vi. & vt.* 口译 *vt.* 解释，阐释
procurement [prəˈkjʊəmənt] *n.* 采购；购买

F 段

mechanism [ˈmekənɪzəm] *n.* 机械装置；构造；机制
component [kəmˈpəʊnənt] *n.* 零件；成分

高频同义替换

progress	▸	advancement, improvement, growth, development
dramatic	▸	attractive, exciting, impressive, striking, spectacular
evident	▸	apparent, plain, observable, visible, obvious
essential	▸	fundamental, necessary, basic, crucial
component	▸	module, element, constituent

题目解析

1 关键词：ancient rockets, present-day Chinese rocket launch vehicles
文中对应点：A 段第二句
题目解析：A 段先介绍古代"火箭"的用途，进而将它与现代火箭进行比较。由 A 段的关键词 ancient rockets 可找到两个选项 iv 和 vi，iv 和 vi 中的 ancient 为原词重现，vi 中的 China 也为原词重现。但是 A 段第二句""These ancient rockets stand in stark contrast to the present-day Chinese rocket launch vehicles..."中的 ancient rockets 和 present-day Chinese rocket launch vehicles 表明本段的重点在于古代"火箭"与现代火箭的比较。iv 中的 ancient invention 和 future 分别与 ancient rockets 和 present-day Chinese rocket launch vehicles 对应。句意为，这些古老的火箭与当今中国的火箭发射车形成了鲜明的对比……因此本题答案为 iv。

2 关键词：in the last decade, a dramatic growth in space activities, Asia
文中对应点：B 段第一句
题目解析：B 段主要内容为亚洲的太空活动的急剧发展。由 B 段的关键词 in the last decade 和 a dramatic growth in space activities 可找到选项 vii。vii 中的 in the past 与原文中的 in the last decade 为同义替换，space development 与原文中的 a dramatic growth in space activities 对应，Asia 为原词重现。B 段第一句 "In the last decade there has been a dramatic growth in space activities in Asia both in the utilisation of space-based services and the production of satellites and launchers." 句意为，在过去的十年中，亚洲的空间活动在利用天基服务和生产卫星和发射装置方面急剧发展。因此答案为 vii。

3 关键词：innovative uses for satellites, competitive
文中对应点：C 段第一句
题目解析：C 段主要讲述的是卫星用途在各个领域的探索与创新。由 C 段的关键词可找到选项 iii 和 ix。iii 中的 competition 为 competitive 的名词形式，ix 中的 competitive 为原词复现。但是 C 段第一句提到 "New and innovative uses for satellites are constantly being explored with potential revolutionary effects..." 卫星在许多领域正在被不断探索创新性的用途。原文中的 innovative uses for satellites 与选项 iii 中的 innovative application 为同义替换，且 iii 项"竞争迫使的创新应用"更能概括 C 段的表述，因此答案为 iii。

4 关键词：Asian nations, space capabilities, South Korea
文中对应点：D 段第一至三句
题目解析：D 段主要说明亚洲各个国家在太空能力方面的发展情况。由 D 段的关键词 Asian nations, space capabilities, South Korea 可找到选项 x，x 中的 space technology development 对应 space capabilities，并且 D 段提及的国家均在亚洲。D 段第一至三句 "...three Asian nations, Japan, China, and India, have comprehensive end-to-end space capabilities and possess a complete space infrastructure...South Korea is currently attempting to join their ranks with its plans to develop a launch site and spaceport...nations in Southeast Asia...have, or are starting to develop indigenous space programmes" 句意为，当前有三个亚洲国家，即日本、中国和印度，具备综合太空能力和一套完整的太空设施。……韩国和东南亚的部分国家能够设计和制造卫星，或已有或开始发展太空项目。因此答案为 x。

5. **关键词**：attracted the most attention
   文中对应点：E 段第二句和第五句
   题目解析：E 段主要说明亚洲与美国、欧洲在太空遥感技术方面的发展差异。由 E 段的关键词 attracted the most attention 可找到选项 ii，attracted the most attention 与 ii 中的 essential space technology 对应，而且亚洲、美国和欧洲在这项技术的发展方面是不平衡的，对应 unbalanced development。E 段第二句 "Thus the space application that has attracted the most attention in this region is remote sensing." 句意为，亚洲，尤其是东南亚，长期遭受诸如洪灾、森林火灾等环境问题，所以十分关注太空技术应用中的遥感技术；而第五句 "In particular, Thailand, Malaysia, and Singapore have world-class remote sensing processing facilities and research programmes." 句意为，许多东盟国家没有自己的遥感卫星，但是可以接收、处理和解读来自美国和欧洲卫星探测的信息。因此答案为 ii。

6. **关键词**：low-cost，given these countries the possibility
   文中对应点：F 段第二句
   题目解析：F 段主要介绍 "小型卫星" 为亚洲国家发展低成本卫星技术带来契机。由 F 段的关键词 low-cost, given these countries the possibility 可找到选项 ix。F 段第二句 "The emergence of 'small satellites' and their quick adoption by Asian countries as a way to develop low-cost satellite technology and rapidly establish a space capability has given these countries the possibility to shorten their learning curve by a decade or more." 中的 low-cost 对应 ix 中的 economically，given these countries the possibility 对应 feasible。句意为，小型卫星的出现以及它们迅速被亚洲国家采用，作为开发低成本卫星技术和迅速建立空间能力的一种方式，使这些国家有可能缩短其 10 年或更长时间的学习曲线。选项 ix 意为 "更为经济合算的卫星给亚洲国家带来的优势"，因此答案为 ix。

参考答案

1 iv **2** vii **3** iii **4** x **5** ii **6** ix

READING PASSAGE 2

Questions 1–6

The passage has eight paragraphs, **A–H**.

*Choose the correct heading for paragraphs **A–F** from the list of headings below.*

*Write the correct number, **i–vii**, in boxes 1–6 on your answer sheet.*

List of Headings

i	Potential error exists in the database
ii	Supporter of database recleared its value
iii	The purpose of this paleobiology database
iv	Reason why some certain species were not included in it
v	Duplication of breed but with different names
vi	Achievement of Paleobiology Database
vii	Criticism on the project which is a waste of fund

1. Paragraph **A**
2. Paragraph **B**
3. Paragraph **C**
4. Paragraph **D**
5. Paragraph **E**
6. Paragraph **F**

Fossil Files 'The Paleobiology Database'

A Are we now living through the sixth extinction as our own activities destroy ecosystems and wipe out diversity? That's the doomsday scenario painted by many ecologists, and they may well be right. The trouble is we don't know for sure because we don't have a clear picture of how life changes between extinction events or what has happened in previous episodes. We don't even know how many species are alive today, let alone the rate at which they are becoming extinct. A new project aims to fill some of the gaps. The Paleobiology Database aspires to be an online repository of information about every fossil ever dug up. It is a huge undertaking that has been described as biodiversity's equivalent of the Human Genome Project. Its organisers hope that by recording the history of biodiversity they will gain an insight into how environmental changes have shaped life on Earth in the past and how they might do so in the future. The database may even indicate whether life can rebound no matter what we throw at it, or whether a human induced extinction could be without parallel, changing the rules that have applied throughout the rest of the planet's history.

B But already the project is attracting harsh criticism. Some experts believe it to be seriously flawed. They point out that a database is only as good as the data fed into it, and that even if all the current fossil finds were catalogued, they would provide an incomplete inventory of life because we are far from discovering every fossilised species. They say that researchers should get up from their computers and get back into the dirt to dig up new fossils. Others are more sceptical still, arguing that we can never get the full picture because the fossil record is riddled with holes and biases.

C Fans of the Paleobiology Database acknowledge that the fossil record will always be incomplete. But they see value in looking for global patterns that show relative changes in biodiversity. 'The fossil record is the best tool we have for understanding how diversity and extinction work in normal times,' says John Alroy from the National Centre for Ecological Analysis and Synthesis in Santa Barbara. 'Having a background extinction estimate gives us a benchmark for understanding the mass extinction that's currently under way. It allows us to say just how bad it is in relative terms.'

D To this end, the Paleobiology Database aims to be the most thorough attempt yet to come up with good global diversity curves. Every day between 10 and 15 scientists around the world add information about fossil finds to the database. Since it got up and running in 1998, scientists have entered almost 340,000 specimens, ranging from plants to whales to insects to dinosaurs to sea urchins. Overall totals are updated hourly at *www.paleodb.org*. Anyone can download data from the public part of the site and play with the numbers to their heart's content. Already, the database has thrown up some surprising results. Looking at the big picture, Alroy and his colleagues believe they have found evidence that biodiversity reached a plateau long ago, contrary to the received wisdom that species numbers have increased continuously between extinction events. 'The traditional view is that diversity has gone up and up and up,' he says. 'Our research is showing that diversity limits were approached many tens of millions of years before the dinosaurs evolved, much less suffered extinction.' This suggests that only a certain number of species can live on Earth at a time, filling a prescribed number of niches like spaces in a multi-storey car park. Once it's full, no more new species can squeeze in until extinctions free up new spaces or something rare and catastrophic adds a new floor to the car park.

E   Alroy has also used the database to reassess the accuracy of species names. His findings suggest that irregularities in classification inflate the overall number of species in the fossil record by between 32 and 44 per cent. Single species often end up with several names, he says, due to misidentification or poor communication between taxonomists in different countries. Repetition like this can distort diversity curves. 'If you have really bad taxonomy in one short interval, it will look like a diversity spike — a big diversification followed by a big extinction — when all that has happened is a change in the quality of names.' says Alroy. For example, his statistical analysis indicates that of the 4,861 North American fossil mammal species catalogued in the database, between 24 and 31 per cent will eventually prove to be duplicates.

F   Of course, the fossil record is undeniably patchy. Some places and times have left behind more fossil-filled rocks than others. Some have been sampled more thoroughly. And certain kinds of creatures — those with hard parts that lived in oceans, for example, are more likely to leave a record behind, while others, like jellyfish, will always remain a mystery. Alroy has also tried to account for this. He estimates, for example, that only 41 per cent of North American mammals that have ever lived are known from fossils, and he suspects that a similar proportion of fossils are missing from other groups, such as fungi and insects.

G   Not everyone is impressed with such mathematical wizardry. Jonathan Adrain from the University of Iowa in Iowa City points out that statistical wrangling has been known to create mass extinctions where none occurred. It is easy to misinterpret data. For example, changes in sea level or inconsistent sampling methods can mimic major changes in biodiversity. Indeed, a recent and thorough examination of the literature on marine bivalve fossils has convinced David Jablonsky from the University of Chicago and his colleagues that their diversity has increased steadily over the past 5 million years.

H   With an inventory of all living species, ecologists could start to put the current biodiversity crisis in historical perspective. Although creating such a list would be a task to rival even the Paleobiology Database, it is exactly what the San Francisco-based ALL Species Foundation hopes to achieve in the next 25 years. The effort is essential, says Harvard biologist Edward O. Wilson, who is alarmed by current rates of extinction. 'There is a crisis. We've begun to measure it, and it's very high,' Wilson says. 'We need this kind of information in much more detail to protect all of biodiversity, not just the ones we know well.' Let the counting continue.

核心词汇

A 段

doomsday [ˈduːmzdeɪ] *n.* 世界末日；最后的审判日
paleobiology [ˌpælɪəubaɪˈɔlədʒi] *n.* 古生物学
biodiversity [ˌbaɪəudaɪˈvɜːsəti] *n.* 生物多样性
rebound [rɪˈbaʊnd] *v.* 回升；弹回
induce [ɪnˈdjuːs] *v.* 引诱；说服

B 段

flawed [flɔːd] *adj.* 有缺陷的；有瑕疵的
sceptical [ˈskeptɪkl] *adj.* 怀疑的；怀疑论的；习惯怀疑的
riddled [ˈrɪdld] *adj.* 充满的

C 段

benchmark [ˈbentʃmɑːk] *n.* 基准

D 段

specimen [ˈspesɪmən] *n.* 样品，样本；标本
sea urchin 海胆

E 段

misidentification [ˈmisaɪˌdentifiˈkeiʃən] *n.* 错误识别
taxonomist [tækˈsɒnəmɪst] *n.* 分类学者
duplicate [ˈdjuːplɪkeɪt] *n.* 副本；复制品

F 段

patchy [ˈpætʃi] *adj.* 不完整的；零散的
fungus [ˈfʌŋɡəs] *n.* 真菌；菌类（复数形式为 fungi）

G 段

wizardry [ˈwɪzədri] *n.* 杰出成就，非凡才能
wrangle [ˈræŋɡl] *v.* 争吵
bivalve [ˈbaɪvælv] *n.* 双壳类动物

H 段

rival [ˈraɪvl] *v.* 与……相匹敌；比得上

高频同义替换

purpose ▸ aim, objective, intention, goal

reason ▸ cause, excuse, ground, explanation

previous ▸ preceding, former, prior

aspire ▸ desire, long for, feel like

indicate ▸ show, suggest, demonstrate, imply, reveal

sceptical ▸ suspicious, incredulous

allow ▸ permit, enable

perspective ▸ viewpoint, standpoint, view, opinion

题目解析

1. 关键词：Paleobiology Database, aspires to be, its organisers hope
   文中对应点：A 段第五至九句
   题目解析：A 段主要讲述的是生态学家关于物种灭绝的预测，然后通过对该预测的质疑提到了"古生物学数据库"项目及其研发目标。由 A 段的关键词 Paleobiology Database, aspires to be, its organisers hope 可找到选项 iii 和 vi，vi 中的 achievement 意为"成就"，文中只是在表达该数据库想要取得的成就，并不是已经取得的成就，所以可排除 vi。iii 中的 purpose 对应 aspires to be, its organisers hope 用以说明建立该数据库的目的所在，因此答案为 iii。

2. 关键词：criticism, seriously flawed
   文中对应点：B 段第一、二句
   题目解析：B 段主要讲述的是数据库项目因存在严重错误而招致相关人士的严厉批评，并具体说明了导致这种错误的原因。由 B 段的关键词 criticism, seriously flawed 可找到选项 i 和 vii，i 中的 error 对应 seriously flawed，vii 中的 criticism 为原词复现。B 段第一句提到 "But already the project is attracting harsh criticism." 但该项目已经招致严厉的批评，之后所提及的具体批评中并没有涉及浪费钱（a waste of fund）的问题，所以排除 vii。B 段第二句提到 "Some experts believe it to be seriously flawed." 一些专家认为数据库存在严重错误，i 项"数据库中有潜在错误"是对该句的同义替换，且精准概括了 B 段的表述，因此答案为 i。

3. 关键词：fans, acknowledge, see value in
   文中对应点：C 段第二句
   题目解析：C 段主要讲述的是数据库的粉丝们承认化石记录不完整，但他们仍然能看到数据库在证实生物多样性变化方面的价值。由 C 段的关键词 fans, acknowledge, see value in 可找到选项 ii，ii 中的 supporter 对应 fans，recleared its value 与 see value in 为同义替换，且 ii 项"数据库的支持者再次承认了它的价值"与 C 段的观点完全一致。因此答案为 ii。

4 关键词：Our research is showing that..., This suggests that...
   文中对应点：D 段第一句
   题目解析：D 段内容紧接上一段，主要继续说明为实现数据库价值所做的努力和取得的成果。D 段第一句提到"To this end, the Paleobiology Database aims to be the most thorough attempt yet to come up with good global diversity curves."为了这个目的，古生物学数据库计划了最全面的尝试，以生成权威的全球物种多样性变化曲线，之后又提到了一些具体数据以及得出的重要结论（Our research is showing that.../ This suggests that...），这些都是数据库所取得的成就。vi 项"古生物学数据库的成就"能概括 D 段的表述，因此答案为 vi。

5 关键词：species, names
   文中对应点：E 段第三句
   题目解析：E 段主要讲述的是数据库中所列物种名字的准确性。由关键词 species，names 可找到选项 iv 和 v。iv 中的 species 和 v 中的 names 均为原词复现。但 E 段第三句提到"Single species often end up with several names, he says, due to misidentification or poor communication between taxonomists in different countries."。其中，single species often end up with several names 与选项 v 中的 duplication of breed but with different names 为同义替换。句意为，由于鉴定错误或者分类学者之间的沟通不畅，单一物种经常会有多个名字。v 项"同一种物种但命名不同"更能概括 E 段的表述，因此答案为 v。

6 关键词：patchy, certain kinds of creatures
   文中对应点：F 段第一句、第五句
   题目解析：F 段主要解释了为什么说化石记录是不完整的。由 F 段的关键词 patchy，certain kinds of creatures 可找到选项 iv。iv 中的 certain 为原词复现，species 与 kinds of creatures 为同义替换。F 段第一句提到"Of course, the fossil record is undeniably patchy."当然化石记录肯定是不完整的。原文中的 patchy 与选项 iv 中的 were not included in it 为同义替换，且 F 段第五句提到"Alroy has also tried to account for this."Alroy 也在尝试对此作出解释，这与 iv 中的 reason why 也是同义替换，因此答案为 iv。

参考答案

1 iii　2 i　3 ii　4 vi　5 v　6 iv

READING PASSAGE 3

Questions 1–7

The passage has eight paragraphs, **A–H**.

*Choose the correct heading for paragraphs **A–G** from the list of headings below.*

*Write the correct number, **i–x**, in boxes 1–7 on your answer sheet.*

List of Headings

i	Questions arise to be answered
ii	Contrast data between present and past
iii	Initial response of association on village
iv	Origin of a certain ancient building
v	Inner structure of the building
vi	Layout of village to persist in micro-environment
vii	Term of village explained
viii	Definition of village type
ix	Difference between village and town
x	Elements need to be considered in terms of village

1. Paragraph **A**
2. Paragraph **B**
3. Paragraph **C**
4. Paragraph **D**
5. Paragraph **E**
6. Paragraph **F**
7. Paragraph **G**

Exploring British Village

A The Neolithic long house was a long, narrow timber dwelling built by the first farmers in Europe beginning at least as early as the period 5000 to 6000 BC. The origin of the name blackhouse is of some debate. It could be less than 150 years old and may have been synonymous with inferior. On Lewis, in particular, it seems to have been used to distinguish the older blackhouses from some of the newer white-houses (Scottish Gaelic: taigh-geal, Irish: ti geal, ti ban), with their mortared stone walls. There may also be some confusion arising from the phonetic similarity between the 'dubh', which means black and tughadh, which means thatch. The houses in Scotland were built high rather than wide; however, some were built small and wide.

B The buildings were generally built with double walls, dry-stone walls packed with earth and wooden rafters covered with a thatch of turf with cereal straw or reed. The floor was generally flagstones or packed earth and there was a central hearth for the fire. There was no chimney for the smoke to escape though. Instead the smoke made its way through the roof. The blackhouse was used to accommodate livestock as well as people. People lived at one end and the animals lived at the other with a partition between them.

C It is estimated that there are over ten thousand villages in Britain, yet defining the term 'village' isn't as simple as it may at first sound. When does a hamlet become a village? And when does a village become a town?

D Strictly speaking, the term 'village' comes from the Latin 'villaticus', which roughly translates as 'a group of houses outside a villa farmstead'. Today a village is understood as a collection of buildings (usually at least 20) that is larger than a hamlet, yet smaller than a town, and which contains at least one communal or public building. This is most commonly the parish church, though it can be a chapel, school, public house, shop, post office, smithy or mill. Villagers will share communal resources such as access roads, a water supply, and usually a place of worship.

E A hamlet is a smaller grouping of buildings that doesn't necessarily have any public or service buildings to support it. A significant difference is that it won't have a parish church like a village does, and most hamlets contain only between three and twenty buildings.

F The point at which a village becomes a town is difficult to determine, and is probably best defined by those who live there. However, since the Middle Ages the term 'town' has been a legal term that refers to the fact that the community has a borough charter. The situation is confused by the fact that there are many town-like suburban communities calling themselves villages (for example, Oxton Village in Birkenhead), as well as designed suburban 'villages' such as those built under the Garden Village Movement.

G The 2001 census shows us that approx 80% of people in England live in an urban environment, with under 7% living in rural villages (the remainder live in rural towns or outside concentrated settlements). This is the exact opposite of the situation two centuries ago, when under 20% of the population lived in the town, and the majority lived in rural villages. As late as 1851 agriculture remained the largest single source of employment in Britain, yet today under 3% of us work on the land.

H It is essential to remember that villages were created and have evolved because of particular combinations of geographical, commercial, economic and social factors. They expand, decline, move and fluctuate with the times. This article introduces some of the common forms of village to be found in Britain.

核心词汇

A 段

dwelling [ˈdwelɪŋ] *n.* 住宅；寓所
distinguish [dɪˈstɪŋgwɪʃ] *vt.* 区分；辨别；使杰出，使表现突出 *vi.* 区别，区分；辨别

B 段

chimney [ˈtʃɪmni] *n.* 烟囱
livestock [ˈlaɪvstɒk] *n.* 牲畜；家畜
partition [pɑːˈtɪʃn] *n.* 隔墙，隔离物；分裂 *vt.* 分割；分隔；区分

C 段

estimate [ˈestɪmeɪt] *v.* 估计，估算
hamlet [ˈhæmlət] *n.* 小村庄

D 段

communal [kəˈmjuːnl] *adj.* 共有的，公共的；群体的，团体的
parish church 教区教堂
worship [ˈwɜːʃɪp] *n.* 敬神活动 *vt.* 景仰，崇拜

F 段

borough [ˈbʌrə] *n.* 自治市（镇）
suburban [səˈbɜːbən] *adj.* 郊区的，城郊的；乏味的；古板的

G 段

census [ˈsensəs] *n.* 人口普查，统计，调查

高频同义替换

arise	▶	occur, come out, appear
initial	▶	premier, original
definition	▶	concept
consider	▶	expect, feel, view

题目解析

1 关键词：Neolithic long house, 5000 to 6000 BC, blackhouses, white-houses

文中对应点：A 段第一、二句

题目解析：A 段主要内容为古建筑的起源和时代发展。由 A 段的关键词 5000 to 6000 BC 可找到选项 iv，iv 中的 origin 对应原文中的 5000 to 6000 BC，less than 150 years old 这些时间关键词，ancient building 对应原文中的 Neolithic long house，blackhouses, white-houses 这些古老的建筑。A 段第一到三句 "The Neolithic long house was a long, narrow timber dwelling built by the first farmers in Europe beginning at least as early as the period 5000 to 6000 BC. The origin of the name blackhouse is of some debate. It could be less than 150 years old and may have been synonymous with inferior." 句意为，至少早在公元前 5000 年到 6000 年之间，新石器时代的长屋是欧洲第一批农民就建造了的狭长的木材住宅。"黑房子"这个名字的起源是有争议的。它可能不到 150 年，可能是劣等的同义词。只有选项 iv 能够概括本段内容，因此答案为 iv。

2 关键词：double walls, floor, fire, chimney

文中对应点：B 段第二、三句

题目解析：B 段主要是对房子的结构进行描述，重点提到了房子的内部结构。由 B 段的关键词 double walls, floor, fire, chimney 可找到选项 v，v 中的 inner structure 与原文中对房子的内部结构（地板、壁炉、房顶和排烟形式等）描述对应。B 段第二、三句 "The floor was generally flagstones or packed earth and there was a central hearth for the fire. There was no chimney for the smoke to escape though." 句意为，地板通常是石板或坚实的泥土，并且有一个壁炉的中央灶台。不过，没有烟囱可以让烟雾逃脱。因此答案为 v。

3 关键词：When, And when

文中对应点：C 段第一句

题目解析：C 段主要提出如何定义"村庄"这一概念。由 C 段的关键词 When, And when 可找到选项 i，i 中的 questions 对应原文的两个疑问句。C 段第一句 "It is estimated that there are over ten thousand villages in Britain, yet defining the term 'village' isn't as simple as it may at first sound." 句意为，估算出了英国村庄的数量，但很难定义"村庄"这一概念；最后直接抛出了两个疑问句。因此答案为 i。

4 关键词：term 'village'

文中对应点：D 段第一、二句

题目解析：D 段主要内容为对 'village' 一词的理解。D 段内容紧接着上一段提出的疑问，因此逻辑上也应该是解答上面的疑问。由本段的关键词 term 'village' 可找到选项 vii，对应 vii 中的 term of village。D 段第一句 "Strictly speaking, the term 'village' comes from the Latin 'villaticus', which roughly translates as 'a group of houses outside a villa farmstead'." 句意为，"village" 这个单词来自于拉丁文，并说明现在对它的理解。因此答案为 vii。

5 关键词：hamlet, a significant difference

文中对应点：E 段第一、二句

题目解析：E 段主要是讲一种村庄的形式"hamlet"。由 E 段的关键词 hamlet 和 a significant difference

可找到选项 viii，原文具体讲述 hamlet 的含义以及与 "village" 的区别。E 段第一至二句 "A hamlet is a smaller grouping of buildings that doesn't necessarily have any public or service buildings to support it. A significant difference is that it won't have a parish church like a village does, and most hamlets contain only between three and twenty buildings." 句意为，一个 hamlet 是一个较小的建筑群，它不一定有任何公共或服务建筑来支持它。一个重要的区别是，它不会像一个村庄那样有一个教区教堂，而且大多数 hamlet 只容纳三到二十栋建筑。选项 viii 符合这个描述，因此答案为 viii。

6 关键词：village, town
文中对应点：F 段第二、三句
题目解析：F 段主要讲的是 "town" 的界定，并通过对比与 "village" 的差异来具体说明。由 F 段的关键词 village 和 town 可找到选项 ix，ix 中的 village，town 为原词重现。F 段第二、三句 "...since the Middle Ages the term 'town' has been a legal term that refers to the fact that the community has a borough charter. The situation is confused by the fact that there are many town-like suburban communities calling themselves villages…, as well as designed suburban 'villages' such as those built under the Garden Village Movement." 句意为，自中世纪以来，'town' 这个词一直是一个法律术语，指的是有自治宪章的社区。这种情况让人感到困惑，因为有许多像城镇一样的郊区社区自称为 villages，以及设计郊区的 'villages'，比如在 "花园村运动" 下建造的村庄。因此答案为 ix。

7 关键词：exact opposite, two centuries ago
文中对应点：G 段第二句
题目解析：G 段主要描述两个世纪以前与现在的人口的同类数据比较情况。由 G 段的关键词 exact opposite 和 two centuries ago 可找到选项 ii，ii 中的 present and past 与 two centuries ago 对应，contrast 与 opposite 为同义替换。G 段第二句 "This is the exact opposite of the situation two centuries ago, when under 20% of the population lived in the town, and the majority lived in rural villages." 句意为，这与两个世纪前的情况正好相反，当时有 20% 的人口居住在城镇，而大多数人住在农村。因此答案为 ii。

参考答案

1 iv   2 v   3 i   4 vii   5 viii   6 ix   7 ii

READING PASSAGE 4

Questions 1–7

The passage has seven paragraphs, **A–G**.

Choose the correct heading for each paragraph from the list of headings below.

Write the correct number, *i–viii*, in boxes 1–7 on your answer sheet.

	List of Headings
i	An initiative of CSR even without financial rewards
ii	Tight combination of overall business strategy and CSR
iii	Business expansion benefited from CSR
iv	Lack of action by the state of social issues
v	Drives or pressures motivate companies to address CSR
vi	The past illustrates business are responsible for future outcomes
vii	Companies applying CSR should be selective
viii	Reasons that business and society benefit each other

1   Paragraph **A**

2   Paragraph **B**

3   Paragraph **C**

4   Paragraph **D**

5   Paragraph **E**

6   Paragraph **F**

7   Paragraph **G**

Corporate Social Responsibility

Broadly speaking, proponents of CSR have used four arguments to make their case: moral obligation, sustainability, license to operate, and reputation. The moral appeal — arguing that companies have a duty to be good citizens and to 'do the right thing' — is prominent in the goal of Business for Social Responsibility, the leading non-profit CSR business association in the United States. It asks that its members 'achieve commercial success in ways that honour ethical values and respect people, communities, and the natural environment'. Sustainability emphasises environmental and community stewardship.

A. An excellent definition was developed in the 1980s: Meeting the needs of the present without compromising the ability of future generations to meet their own needs. The notion of license to operate derives from the fact that every company needs tacit or explicit permission from governments, communities, and numerous other stakeholders to do business. Finally, reputation is used by many companies to justify CSR initiatives on the grounds that they will improve a company's image, strengthen its brand, enliven morale, and even raise the value of its stock.

B. To advance CSR, we must root it in a broad understanding of the interrelationship between a corporation and society. To say broadly that business and society need each other might seem like a cliché, but it is also the basic truth that will pull companies out of the muddle that their current corporate-responsibility thinking has created. Successful corporations need a healthy society. Education, health care, and equal opportunity are essential to a productive workforce. Safe products and working conditions not only attract customers but lower the internal costs of accidents. Efficient utilisation of land, water, energy, and other natural resources makes business more productive. Good government, the rule of law, and property rights are essential for efficiency and innovation. Any business that pursues its ends at the expense of the society in which it operates will find its success to be illusory and ultimately temporary. At the same time, a healthy society needs successful companies. No social programme can rival the business sector when it comes to creating the jobs, wealth, and innovation that improve standards of living and social conditions over time.

C. A company's impact on society also changes over time, as social standards evolve and science progresses. Asbestos, now understood as a serious health risk, was thought to be safe in the early 1900s, given the scientific knowledge then available. Evidence of its risks gradually mounted for more than 50 years before any company was held liable for the harms it can cause. Many firms that failed to anticipate the consequences of this evolving body of research have been bankrupt by the results. No longer can companies be content to monitor only the obvious social impacts of today. Without a careful process for identifying evolving social effects of tomorrow, firms may risk their very survival.

D. No business can solve all of society's problems or bear the cost of doing so. Instead, each company must select issues that intersect with its particular business. Corporations are not responsible for all the world's problems, nor do they have the resources to solve them all. Each company can identify the particular set of societal problems that it is best equipped to help resolve and from which it can gain the greatest competitive benefit. Addressing social issues by creating shared value will lead to self-sustaining solutions that do not depend on private or government subsidies. When a well-run business applies its vast resources, expertise, and management talent to problems that it understands and in which it has a stake, it can have a greater impact on social good than any other institution or philanthropic organisation.

E   The best corporate citizenship initiatives involve far more than writing a check: they specify clear, measurable goals and track results over time. A good example is GE's programme to adopt underperforming public high schools near several of its major U.S. facilities. The company contributes between $250,000 and $1 million over a five-year period to each school and makes in-kind donations as well. GE managers and employees take an active role by working with school administrators to assess needs and mentor or tutor students. The graduation rate of these schools almost doubled during this time period. Effective corporate citizenship initiatives such as this one create goodwill and improve relations with local governments and other important constituencies. What's more, GE's employees feel great pride in their participation. The effect is inherently limited, however. No matter how beneficial the programme is, it remains incidental to the company's business, and the direct effect on GE's recruiting and retention is modest.

F   Microsoft is a good example of a shared-value opportunity arising from investments in context. The shortage of information technology workers is a significant constraint on Microsoft's growth; currently, there are more than 450,000 unfilled IT positions in the United States alone. Community colleges, representing 45% of all U.S. undergraduates, could be a major solution. Microsoft recognises, however, that community colleges face special challenges: IT curricula are not standardised. Technology used in classrooms is often outdated, and there are no systematic professional development programmes to keep faculty up to date. In addition to contributing money and products, Microsoft sent employee volunteers to colleges to assess needs, contribute to curriculum development and create faculty development institutes. Note that in this case, volunteers and assigned staff were able to use their core professional skills to address a social need, a far cry from typical volunteer programmes. Microsoft has achieved results that have benefited many communities while having a direct — and potentially significant — impact on the company.

G   At the heart of any strategy is a unique value proposition: a set of needs a company can meet for its chosen customers that others cannot. The most strategic CSR occurs when a company adds a social dimension to its value proposition, making social impact integral to the overall strategy. Consider Whole Foods Market, whose value proposition is to sell organic, natural, and healthy food products to customers who are passionate about food and the environment. Whole Foods' commitment to natural and environmentally friendly operating practices extends well beyond sourcing. Stores are constructed using a minimum of virgin raw materials. Recently, the company purchased renewable wind energy credits equal to 100% of its electricity use in all of its stores and facilities, the only Fortune 500 Company to offset its electricity consumption entirely. Spoiled produce and biodegradable waste are trucked to regional centres for composting. Whole Foods' vehicles are being converted to run on biofuels. Even the cleaning products used in its stores are environmentally friendly. And through its philanthropy, the company has created the Animal Compassion Foundation to develop more natural and humane ways of raising farm animals. In short, nearly every aspect of the company's value chain reinforces the social dimensions of its value proposition, distinguishing Whole Foods from its competitors.

核心词汇

A 段

tacit ['tæsɪt] *adj.* 默示的，心照不宣的；无言的
explicit [ɪk'splɪsɪt] *adj.* 明确的，清楚的
permission [pə'mɪʃn] *n.* 允许，批准
initiative [ɪ'nɪʃətɪv] *n.* 主动性，主动精神
strengthen ['streŋθn] *vt.* 加强，巩固
enliven [ɪn'laɪvn] *vt.* 使有生气，使生动
morale [mə'rɑːl] *n.* 士气，精神面貌

B 段

interrelationship [ˌɪntərɪ'leɪʃnʃɪp] *n.* 相互关系，相互关联
muddle ['mʌdl] *n.* 糊涂；困惑；混乱
illusory [ɪ'luːsəri] *adj.* 貌似真实的，错觉的
temporary ['temprəri] *adj.* 临时的，暂时的

C 段

asbestos [æs'bestəs] *n.* 石棉
mount [maʊnt] *vt. & vi.* 登上，骑上 *vt.* 准备；安排；组织 *vi.* 渐渐增加，逐渐增长
be liable for 对……应负责任

D 段

expertise [ˌekspɜː'tiːz] *n.* 专门知识或技能
stake [steɪk] *n.* 股份，（在公司，计划等中的）重大利益 [拓] at stake 有风险
institution [ˌɪnstɪ'tjuːʃn] *n.* 机构；制度
philanthropic [ˌfɪlən'θrɒpɪk] *adj.* 博爱的，慈善的

E 段

specify ['spesɪfaɪ] *vt.* 指定；详述 *vi.* 明确提出，详细说明
assess [ə'ses] *vt.* 评定；估价
incidental [ˌɪnsɪ'dentl] *adj.* 附属的；易发生的
retention [rɪ'tenʃn] *n.* 保留；记忆力

F 段

shortage ['ʃɔːtɪdʒ] *n.* 不足，缺点

G 段

proposition [ˌprɒpəˈzɪʃn] *n.* 命题；建议；主张

reinforce [ˌriːɪnˈfɔːs] *vt.* 加固，强化；增援

题目

initiative [ɪˈnɪʃətɪv] *n.* 新方案；倡议

高频同义替换

notion	▶	conviction, belief, faith, view
obvious	▶	apparent, evident, distinct
constraint	▶	restriction, limitation, restraint

题目解析

1. 关键词：needs, tacit or explicit permission
   文中对应点：A 段第二句
   题目解析：A 段主要说明许可经营的缘由和取得方式。由 A 段的关键词 needs 可找到选项 v，v 中的 motivate 与 needs 对应。A 段第二句 "The notion of license to operate derives from the fact that every company needs tacit or explicit permission from governments, communities, and numerous other stakeholders to do business." 中的 governments, communities, and numerous other stakeholders 对应选项 v 中的 drives or pressures。句意为，公司要想取得营业执照，必须得到第三方的许可，因此公司必须践行 CSR 原则，以取得第三方的信任。因此答案为 v。

2. 关键词：interrelationship, corporation, society
   文中对应点：B 段第一句
   题目解析：B 段主要描述企业与社会之间的相互依存关系。由 B 段的关键词 interrelationship, corporation, society 可找到选项 viii，viii 中的 each other 对应原文中的 interrelationship，business 与 corporation 为同义替换，society 为原词重现。B 段第一句 "To advance CSR, we must root it in a broad understanding of the interrelationship between a corporation and society." 句意为，为了推进企业社会责任，我们必须深入了解企业与社会之间的相互关系。后面提及企业与社会的关系是互惠互利的。因此答案为 viii。

3. 关键词：without a careful process, social effects
   文中对应点：C 段倒数第一句
   题目解析：C 段用石棉的例子来说明公司的发展需要国家对于社会问题的治理和监管。由 C 段的关键词 without a careful process, social effects 可找到选项 iv。C 段倒数第一句 "Without a careful process for identifying evolving social effects of tomorrow, firms may risk their very survival." 中的 without a careful process 对应选项 iv 中的 lack of action，social effects 对应 social issues。句意为，如果没有一个仔细甄别的过程来确定未来的社会影响，公司可能会有生存危机。因此答案为 iv。

4 关键词：select
　　文中对应点：D 段第一、二句
　　题目解析：D 段主要阐述公司从最适合帮助解决的特定社会问题中可获得最大的竞争优势。由 D 段的关键词 select 可找到选项 vii，vii 中的 selective 为 select 的形容词形式。D 段第一、二句 "No business can solve all of society's problems or bear the cost of doing so. Instead, each company must select issues that intersect with its particular business." 中的 intersect with 与选项 vii 中的 applying 对应。句意为，没有一家公司能够解决所有的社会问题，每家公司必须挑选和其业务相关的问题来解决。因此答案为 vii。

5 关键词：goodwill and improve relations
　　文中对应点：E 段第六句
　　题目解析：E 段以通用电气的计划为例说明积极的公司行为可以产生良好的效果。由 E 段的关键词 goodwill and improve relations 可找到选项 iii。E 段第六句 "Effective corporate citizenship initiatives such as this one create goodwill and improve relations with local governments and other important constituencies." 中的 goodwill and improve relations 对应 iii 中的 benefited from。句意为，像这样积极的公司行为在当地产生了良好的效果，也提升了和其他部门的关系。这是在践行 CSR 之后给公司带来的好处，与 iii 的表述"得益于 CSR 的业务扩展"一致。因此答案为 iii。

6 关键词：contributing money and products, employee volunteers
　　文中对应点：F 段第六句
　　题目解析：F 段主要以微软公司为例讲述微软缺乏信息技术工人，大学生能解决这一问题，但是大学生所学的知识相对落后，因此微软除了捐钱、捐产品，还派公司志愿者去大学帮忙。由 F 段的关键词 contributing money and products 可找到选项 i。F 段第六句 "In addition to contributing money and products, Microsoft sent employee volunteers to colleges to assess needs, contribute to curriculum development and create faculty development institutes." 中的 contributing money and products，employee volunteers 对应 i 中的 without financial rewards。句意为，除了提供资金和产品外，微软还派员工到大学来评估需求，为课程开发作出贡献，并创建教师发展机构。另外，F 段整段都没有提到经济回报，这符合选项 i "没有经济回报的"这一说法，因此答案为 i。

7 关键词：strategy
　　文中对应点：G 段第一、二句
　　题目解析：G 段主要提出任何战略的核心都是一个独特的价值主张的观点。由 G 段的关键词 strategy 可找到选项 ii，ii 中的 strategy 为原词重现。G 段第一、二句 "At the heart of any strategy is a unique value proposition: a set of needs a company can meet for its chosen customers that others cannot. The most strategic CSR occurs when a company adds a social dimension to its value proposition, making social impact integral to the overall strategy." 句意为，公司将社会添加到其价值体系中使得社会影响和总体的战略成为一体时才会有最有战略性的公司企业道德。选项 ii "整体商业战略和企业社会责任的紧密结合"与原文表达意思相符，因此答案为 ii。

参考答案

1 v　2 viii　3 iv　4 vii　5 iii　6 i　7 ii

READING PASSAGE 5

Questions 1–7

The passage has eight paragraphs, **A–H**.

*Choose the correct heading for paragraphs **A–G** from the list of headings below.*

*Write the correct number, **i–x**, in boxes 1–7 on your answer sheet.*

List of Headings

i	Earth itself as the biggest magnet
ii	Products based on magnetic therapy
iii	Utilisation of the power from natural magnetic field
iv	Initial applications of magnet in history
v	Brief introduction of active principle of the magnetic therapy
vi	Pain-reduction of how the magnetic therapy works
vii	Dispute about the curative effect of magnetic therapy
viii	An experiment on patients with chronic disease
ix	Acceptability of magnetic therapy in different countries
x	The possible effects of magnetic therapy

1 Paragraph **A**

2 Paragraph **B**

3 Paragraph **C**

4 Paragraph **D**

5 Paragraph **E**

6 Paragraph **F**

7 Paragraph **G**

Magnetic Therapy

A Magnetic therapy, which is a $5-billion market worldwide, is a form of alternative medicine which claims that magnetic fields have healing powers. Magnetic devices that are claimed to be therapeutic include magnetic bracelets, insoles, wrist and knee bands, back and neck braces, and even pillows and mattresses although scientific evidence of their effect had not been gathered until recently.

B People wear magnets to treat painful conditions including general pain, pain after surgery, low back pain, foot pain, heel pain, chronic fatigue syndrome and nerve pain caused by diabetes and sports injuries. Magnets are also worn for treating water retention, wounds, trouble sleeping (insomnia), ringing in the ears (tinnitus), cancer, Parkinson's disease, and many other conditions. Their annual sales are estimated at $300 million in the United States and more than a billion dollars globally. They have been advertised to cure a vast array of ills, particularly pains.

C The therapy works on the principle of balancing electrical energy in the body by pulsating magnetic waves through different parts of the body. The electrical currents generated by magnets increase the blood flow and oxygen which helps to heal many of the ailments. The natural effects of the Earth's magnetic field are considered to play an essential role in the health of humans and animals. It is generally accepted that our body draws some benefits from the Earth's magnetic field. To restore the balance within our body allows us to function at our optimum level. For example, when the first astronauts returned to Earth sick, NASA concluded that their illness resulted from the lack of a planetary magnetic field in outer space. To resolve the problem, NASA placed magnets in the astronauts' space suits and space travel vehicles, and astronauts have returned to Earth healthy ever since.

D Historically it is reported that magnets have been around for an extremely long time. The therapeutic power of magnets was known to physicians in ancient Greece, Egypt and China over 4,000 years ago, who used naturally magnetic rock — lodestone — to treat a variety of physical and psychological ailments. Cleopatra, the beautiful Egyptian queen, was probably the first celebrity to use magnets. It is documented that in order to prevent from aging, she slept on a lodestone to keep her skin youthful. Ancient Romans also used magnet therapy to treat eye disease.

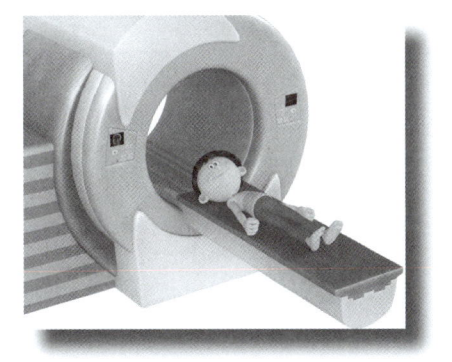

E The popularity of magnet therapy in the United States began to rise during the 1800s and soared in the post-Civil War era. Sears Roebuck advertised magnetic jewellery in its catalogue for the healing of virtually any ailment. An Austrian psychoanalyst by the name of Wilhelm Reich immigrated to the United States in 1939 and researched the effects of electromagnetism on humans. Today, Germany, Japan, Israel, Russia and at least 45 other countries consider magnetic therapy to be an official medical procedure for the treatment of numerous ailments, including various inflammatory and neurological problems.

F For those who practice magnetic therapy, they strongly believe that certain ailments can be treated if the patient is exposed to magnetic fields. While at the same time there is a strong resentment from the medical establishment and critics claim that most magnets don't have the strength to effect the various organs and tissues within the body, and it is a product of pseudoscience and is not based on proper research and analysis. However, there are few reported complications of magnetic therapy and the World Health Organisation says low level of magnetic energy is not harmful. Documented side effects are not life-threatening and include pain, nausea and dizziness that disappeared when the magnets were removed. If considering magnet therapy, as with any medical treatment, it is always advisable to consult one's regular physician first.

G Researchers at Baylor University Medical Centre recently conducted a double-blind study on the use of concentric-circle magnets to relieve chronic pain in 50 post-polio patients. A static magnetic device or a placebo device was applied to the patient's skin for 45 minutes. The patients were asked to rate how much pain they experienced when a 'trigger point was touched'. The researchers reported that the 29 patients exposed to the magnetic device achieved lower pain scores than did the 21 who were exposed to the placebo device. However, this study had significant flaws in their design. Although the groups were said to be selected randomly, the ratio of women to men in the experimental group was twice that of the control group; the age of the placebo group was four years higher than that of the control group; there was just one brief exposure and no systematic follow-up of patients.

H Magnet therapy is gaining popularity. However, the scientific evidence to support the success of this therapy is lacking. More scientifically sound studies are needed in order to fully understand the effects that magnets can have on the body and the possible benefits or dangers that could result from their use.

核心词汇

A 段

magnetic [mæg'netɪk] *adj.* 磁的；有磁性的；有吸引力的
healing ['hiːlɪŋ] *n.* 康复，痊愈；自然疗法
device [dɪ'vaɪs] *n.* 设备，装置

B 段

fatigue [fə'tiːg] *n.* 疲劳，疲乏
injury ['ɪndʒəri] *n.* 伤害，损害，受伤
array [ə'reɪ] *n.* 大批，大量；数组，排列 *vt.* 排列；部署；打扮 [拓] an array of 一批，大量

C 段

generate ['dʒenəreɪt] *v.* 产生，创造
ailment ['eɪlm(ə)nt] *n.* 小病，不适
restore [rɪ'stɔː(r)] *vt.* 恢复，修复
optimum ['ɒptɪməm] *adj.* 最适宜的，最优的

D 段

a variety of 种种，多种多样的

E 段

popularity [ˌpɒpju'lærəti] *n.* 普及，流行，受大众欢迎
procedure [prə'siːdʒə(r)] *n.* 程序，手续，步骤；手术

F 段

resentment [rɪ'zentmənt] *n.* 愤恨，不满，憎恶
consult [kə'zʌlt] *vt.* 查阅；商量；向……请教 *vi.* 请教；商议；当顾问

G 段

conduct [kə'dʌkt] *vt.* 实施，执行
relieve [rɪ'liːv] *vt.* 解除；减轻，缓解
static ['stætɪk] *adj.* 静止的，不变的 *n.* 静电
apply [ə'plaɪ] *vi.* 申请，（对）……适用 *vt.* 应用，运用，实施
flaw [flɔː] *n.* 缺陷，瑕疵；裂缝
randomly ['rændəmli] *adv.* 随便地，任意地，无目的地

高频同义替换

based on ▶ according to

dispute ▶ debate, argue, controversy, argument

effect ▶ influence, impact

题目解析

1 关键词：magnetic devices

文中对应点：A 段第二句

题目解析：A 段简单介绍磁疗的概念以及基本设备。由 A 段的关键词 magnetic devices 可找到选项 ii，ii 中的 products 与 magnetic devices 对应。A 段第二句 "Magnetic devices that are claimed to be therapeutic include magnetic bracelets, insoles, wrist and knee bands, back and neck braces, and even pillows and mattresses although scientific evidence of their effect had not been gathered until recently." 中的列举出了 magnetic bracelets, insoles, wrist and knee bands 等多种磁疗产品，与 ii "磁疗产品"表述一致，因此答案为 ii。

2 关键词：treat painful conditions

文中对应点：B 段第一、二句

题目解析：B 段主要介绍磁疗可能产生的治疗效果。由 B 段的关键词 treat painful conditions 可找到选项 x，x 中的 possible effects 与 treat painful conditions 对应。B 段第一、二句 "People wear magnets to treat painful conditions including general pain, pain after surgery, low back pain, foot pain, heel pain, chronic fatigue syndrome and nerve pain caused by diabetes and sports injuries. Magnets are also worn for treating water retention, wounds, trouble sleeping (insomnia), ringing in the ears (tinnitus), cancer, Parkinson's disease, and many other conditions." 中的列举出磁疗可以治疗的多种疼痛状况和其他健康问题，均是磁疗可能产生的治疗效果，因此答案为 x。

3 关键词：the therapy, principle

文中对应点：C 段第一句

题目解析：C 段解释了磁疗的工作原理。由 C 段的关键词 the therapy, principle 可找到选项 v，the therapy 对应 v 中的 the magnetic therapy，v 中的 principle 为原词重现。C 段第一句 "The therapy works on the principle of balancing electrical energy in the body by pulsating magnetic waves through different parts of the body." 句意为，这种疗法的原理是通过身体不同部位的脉动磁波来平衡身体的电能。v 项"磁疗的主动原理简介"可概述本段，因此答案为 v。

4 关键词：historically

文中对应点：D 段第二、三句

题目解析：D 段追溯了磁疗悠久的历史。由 D 段的关键词 historically 可找到选项 iv，iv 中的 in history 与 historically 对应。D 段第二、三句 "The therapeutic power of magnets was known to physicians in ancient Greece, Egypt and China over 4,000 years ago, who used naturally magnetic rock—lodestone—to treat a variety of physical and psychological ailments. Cleopatra, the beautiful Egyptian queen, was probably the first celebrity to use magnets." 句意为，四千多年前已经利用天然磁石治疗生理和心理疾病。并以埃及艳后 Cleopatra 和古罗马人为例，这与选项 iv 中的 initial application 对应，因此答案为 iv。

5. 关键词：countries
   文中对应点：E 段倒数第一句
   题目解析：E 段指出磁疗已在许多国家被视为正式的医疗程序。由 E 段的关键词 countries 可找到选项 ix，ix 中的 countries 为原词重现。E 段倒数第一句 "Today, Germany, Japan, Israel, Russia and at least 45 other countries consider magnetic therapy to be an official medical procedure for the treatment of numerous ailments, including various inflammatory and neurological problems." 句意为，直到今天，已有德、日、以、俄和其他至少 45 个国家将它视为正式的医疗程序。因此答案为 ix。

6. 关键词：resentment, critics, effect, pseudoscience
   文中对应点：F 段第一、二句
   题目解析：F 段主要介绍磁疗在治疗一些疾病方面存在争议。由 F 段的关键词 resentment, critics, effect, pseudoscience 可找到选项 vii，vii 中的 dispute 与 critics 为同义替换。F 段第一、二句 "For those who practice magnetic therapy, they strongly believe that certain ailments can be treated if the patient is exposed to magnetic fields. While at the same time there is a strong resentment from the medical establishment and critics claim that most magnets don't have the strength to effect the various organs and tissues within the body, and it is a product of pseudoscience and is not based on proper research and analysis." 指出磁疗的实施者坚信磁疗的作用，与此同时，也存在很多对于磁疗的质疑，认为它是 pseudoscience（伪科学）。这说明磁疗是有争议的，因此答案为 vii。

7. 关键词：a double-blind study, chronic pain
   文中对应点：G 段第一句
   题目解析：G 段阐述研究人员针对小儿麻痹症患者的磁疗实验。由 G 段的关键词 a double-blind study, chronic pain 可找到选项 viii，viii 中的 chronic disease 与 chronic pain 对应。G 段第一句 "Researchers at Baylor University Medical Centre recently conducted a double-blind study on the use of concentric-circle magnets to relieve chronic pain in 50 post-polio patients." 句意为，贝勒大学医学中心的研究人员最近对 50 名脊髓灰质炎后综合征患者的慢性疼痛进行了双盲研究。因此答案为 viii。

参考答案

1 ii   2 x   3 v   4 iv   5 ix   6 vii   7 viii

READING PASSAGE 6

Questions 1–7

The passage has seven paragraphs, **A–G**.

Choose the correct heading for each paragraph from the list of headings below.

Write the correct number, *i–xi*, in boxes 1–7 on your answer sheet.

List of Headings

i	Why better food helps students' learning
ii	A song for getting porridge
iii	Surprising use of school premises
iv	Global perspective
v	Brains can be starved
vi	Surprising academic outcome
vii	Girls are specially treated in the programme
viii	How food programme is operated
ix	How food programme affects school attendance
x	None of the usual reasons
xi	How to maintain academic standard

1   Paragraph **A**

2   Paragraph **B**

3   Paragraph **C**

4   Paragraph **D**

5   Paragraph **E**

6   Paragraph **F**

7   Paragraph **G**

Food for Thought

A   There are not enough classrooms at the Msekeni primary school, so half the lessons take place in the shade of yellow-blossomed acacia trees. Given this shortage, it might seem odd that one of the school's purpose-built classrooms has been emptied of pupils and turned into a storeroom for sacks of grain. But it makes sense. Food matters more than shelter.

B   Msekeni is in one of the poorer parts of Malawi, a landlocked southern African country of exceptional beauty and great poverty. No war lays waste Malawi, nor is the land unusually crowded or infertile, but Malawians still have trouble finding enough to eat. Half of the children under five are underfed to the point of stunting. Hunger blights most aspects of Malawian life, so the country is as good a place as any to investigate how nutrition affects development, and vice versa.

C   The headmaster at Msekeni, Bernard Kumanda, has strong views on the subject. He thinks food is a priceless teaching aid. Since 1999, his pupils have received free school lunches. Donors such as the World Food Programme (WFP) provide the food: those sacks of grain (mostly mixed maize and soybean flour, enriched with vitamin A) in that converted classroom. Local volunteers do the cooking — turning the dry ingredients into a bland but nutritious slop, and spooning it out on to plastic plates. The children line up in large crowds, cheerfully singing a song called 'We Are Getting Porridge'.

D   When the school's feeding programme was introduced, enrolment at Msekeni doubled. Some of the new pupils had switched from nearby schools that did not give out free porridge, but most were children whose families had previously kept them at home to work. These families were so poor that the long-term benefits of education seemed unattractive when set against the short-term gain of sending children out to gather firewood or help in the fields. One plate of porridge a day completely altered the calculation. A child fed at school will not howl so plaintively for food at home. Girls, who are more likely than boys to be kept out of school, are given extra snacks to take home.

E   When a school takes in a horde of extra students from the poorest homes, you would expect standards to drop. Anywhere in the world, poor kids tend to perform worse than their better-off classmates. When the influx of new pupils is not accompanied by any increase in the number of teachers, as was the case at Msekeni, you would expect standards to fall even further. But they have not. Pass rates at Msekeni improved dramatically, from 30% to 85%. Although this was an exceptional example, the nationwide results of school feeding programmes were still pretty good. On average, after a Malawian school started handing out free food, it attracted 38% more girls and 24% more boys. The pass rate for boys stayed about the same, while for girls it improved by 9.5%.

F   Better nutrition makes for brighter children. Most immediately, well-fed children find it easier to concentrate. It is hard to focus the mind on long division when your stomach is screaming for food. Mr. Kumanda says that it used to be easy to spot the kids who were really undernourished. 'They were the ones who stared into space and didn't respond when you asked them questions,' he says. More crucially, though, more and better food helps brains grow and develop. Like any other organ in the body, the brain needs nutrition and exercise. But if it is starved of the necessary calories, proteins and micronutrients, it is stunted, perhaps not as severely as a muscle would be, but stunted nonetheless. That is why feeding children at schools works so well. And the fact that the effect of feeding was more pronounced on girls than on boys gives a clue to who eats first in rural Malawian households. It isn't the girls.

G On a global scale, the good news is that people are eating better than ever before. Homo sapiens has grown 50% bigger since the industrial revolution. Three centuries ago, chronic malnutrition was more or less universal. Now, it is extremely rare in rich countries. In developing countries, where most people live, plates and rice bowls are also fuller than ever before. The proportion of children under five in the developing world who are malnourished to the point of stunting fell from 39% in 1990 to 30% in 2000, says the World Health Organisation (WHO). In other places, the battle against hunger is steadily being won. Better nutrition is making people cleverer and more energetic, which will help them grow more prosperous. And when they eventually join the ranks of the well off, they can start fretting about growing too fat.

核心词汇

A 段

shade [ʃeɪd] *n.* 树荫；阴影；细微的差别
make sense 有意义；有道理
shelter [ˈʃeltə(r)] *n.* 保护；住所；避难所

B 段

infertile [ɪnˈfɜːtaɪl] *adj.* 贫瘠的；不结果实的
stunting [ˈstʌntɪŋ] *n.* 发育不良，生长迟缓
blight [blaɪt] *vt.* 破坏；使……枯萎
vice versa 反之亦然；反过来也一样

C 段

priceless [ˈpraɪsləs] *adj.* 贵重的；无价的
bland [blænd] *adj.* （食物）清淡的；乏味的；没有生气的
porridge [ˈpɒrɪdʒ] *n.* 粥

D 段

switch [swɪtʃ] *v.* 转换；调换
plaintively [ˈpleɪntɪvli] *adv.* 悲痛地；伤心地

E 段

better-off *adj.* 较富裕的；经济状况良好的
influx [ˈɪnflʌks] *n.* 涌入；汇集

F 段

undernourished [ˌʌndəˈnʌrɪʃt] *adj.* 营养不良的
organ [ˈɔːɡən] *n.* 器官
stunt [stʌnt] *vt.* 阻碍……的正常发展
pronounced [prəˈnaʊnst] *adj.* 明显的；明确的；显眼的

G 段

Homo sapiens 人类
malnutrition [ˌmælnjuːˈtrɪʃn] *n.* 营养不良 [拓] malnourished *adj.* 营养不良的
fret [fret] *vt.&vi.* （使）烦恼；焦急

高频同义替换

odd ▸ unexpected, surprising

usual ▸ common, normal, regular

affect ▸ impact, change, alter, influence

help ▸ aid, assist, support, promote, improve

global ▸ worldwide, international, universal

题目解析

1. 关键词：classrooms, odd
   文中对应点：A 段第一、二句
   题目解析：A 段介绍 Meskeni 地区教室占用的问题。由 A 段的关键词 classrooms 可找到选项 iii，iii 中的 premises 指代原文中的 classrooms。A 段第一、二句 "There are not enough classrooms at the Msekeni primary school, so half the lessons take place in the shade of yellow-blossomed acacia trees. Given this shortage, it might seem odd that one of the school's purpose-built classrooms has been emptied of pupils and turned into a storeroom for sacks of grain." 句意为，学校没有足够的教室，因此一半的课程是在树下进行的。在这种教室紧缺的情况下，其中一间教室却变成了储存粮食的地方。这与选项 iii "学校房屋令人意外的用途" 对应，因此答案为 iii。

2. 关键词：no, nor
   文中对应点：B 段第一、二句
   题目解析：B 段列举了常见的导致饥荒的原因皆不是 Msekeni 饥荒的真正原因。由 B 段的关键词 no, nor 可找到选项 x，no 和 nor 对应选项 x 的 none。B 段第一、二句 "Msekeni is in one of the poorer parts of Malawi, a landlocked southern African country of exceptional beauty and great poverty. No war lays waste Malawi, nor is the land unusually crowded or infertile, but Malawians still have trouble finding enough to eat." 中列举了常见的导致饥荒的原因，如战争、疾患、人口拥挤等。但是，这些原因前都带有否定词 no 和 nor。因此，Msekeni 饥荒是一些非常见原因导致的。这对应选项 x "非常见的原因"。因此答案为 x。

3. 关键词：World Food Programme
   文中对应点：C 段第三句到段末
   题目解析：C 段以介绍 Msekeni 的校长为切入点，主要介绍 WFP 的项目以及项目是如何运作的。由关键词 World Food Programme 可找到选项 viii，viii 中的 food programme 与 World Food Programme 对应。C 段第三句 "Since 1999, his pupils have received free school lunches." 句意为，自 1999 年开始，学生就可以在学校获得免费午餐。第四句详细描述 WFP 等组织捐献食物，志愿者为孩子煮食物和孩子们领取食物。因此答案为 viii。

4 关键词：feeding programme, enrolment
   文中对应点：D 段第一句
   题目解析：D 段主要介绍食物援助项目的影响。由 D 段的关键词 enrolment 可找到选项 ix，ix 中的 school attendance 与 enrolment 为同义替换。D 段第一句 "When the school's feeding programme was introduced, enrolment at Msekeni doubled." 句意为，自从学校引入了食物项目后，Msekeni 的入学人数翻倍了。符合选项 ix "食物项目如何影响入学（人数）"，因此答案为 ix。

5 关键词：improved dramatically
   文中对应点：E 段第五句
   题目解析：E 段用大量的数据介绍学生成绩的提升，进一步阐述 food programme 对于 Msekeni 的积极影响。由 E 段的关键词 improved dramatically 可找到选项 vi，improved dramatically 与 vi 中的 surprising 对应。E 段第五句 "Pass rates at Msekeni improved dramatically, from 30% to 85%." 句意为，Msekeni 小学的通过率剧增，从原来的 30% 上升到现在的 85%。之后还提到全国范围内的结果都相当不错。联系定位句前的两句可知，这样的结果是出人意料的，因此答案为 vi。

6 关键词：better food, helps
   文中对应点：F 段第六句
   题目解析：F 段主要解释好的营养造就了好的孩子观点。由 F 段的关键词 better food, helps 可找到选项 i，i 中的 better food 和 helps 均为原词重现。F 段第六句 "More crucially, though, more and better food helps brains grow and develop." 句意为，更重要的是，更多、更好的食物有助于大脑的生长和发育。此句解释了"更好的食物有助于学习的原因"。因此答案为 i。

7 关键词：global scale
   文中对应点：G 段第一句
   题目解析：G 段主要利用数据解释全球范围内人们吃得都比以前更好。由 G 段的关键词 global scale 可找到选项 iv，iv 中的 global perspective 与 global scale 对应。G 段第一句 "On a global scale, the good news is that people are eating better than ever before." 句意为，在全球范围内，好消息是人们吃得都比以前更好。此后的内容都是相关的数据统计，因此答案为 iv。

参考答案

1 iii   2 x   3 viii   4 ix   5 vi   6 i   7 iv

READING PASSAGE 7

Questions 1–7

The passage has seven paragraphs, **A–G**.

Choose the correct heading for each paragraph from the list of headings below.

Write the correct number, *i–xi*, in boxes 1–7 on your answer sheet.

List of Headings

i	Data consistency needed for language
ii	Solution for dying out language
iii	Positive gains for protection
iv	Minimum requirement for saving a language
v	Potential threat to minority language
vi	Little progress in protection field
vii	Native language programme launched
viii	Subjective doubts as a negative factor
ix	Practice in several developing countries
x	Value of minority language to linguists
xi	Government participation in language field

1 Paragraph **A**

2 Paragraph **B**

3 Paragraph **C**

4 Paragraph **D**

5 Paragraph **E**

6 Paragraph **F**

7 Paragraph **G**

Save Endangered Language

A   Ten years ago Michael Krauss sent a shudder through the discipline of linguistics with his prediction that half the 6,000 or so languages spoken in the world would cease to be uttered within a century. Unless scientists and community leaders directed a worldwide effort to stabilise the decline of local languages, he warned, nine tenths of the linguistic diversity of humankind would probably be doomed to extinction. Krauss' prediction was little more than an educated guess, but other respected linguists had been clanging out similar alarms. Keneth L. Hale of the Massachusetts Institute of Technology noted in the same journal issue that eight languages on which he had done fieldwork had since passed into extinction. A 1990 survey in Australia found that 70 of the 90 surviving Aboriginal languages were no longer used regularly by all age groups. The same was true for all but 20 of the 175 Native American languages spoken or remembered in the U.S., Krauss told a congressional panel in 1992.

B   Many experts in the field mourn the loss of rare languages, for several reasons. To start, there is scientific self-interest: some of the most basic questions in linguistics have to do with the limits of human speech, which are far from fully explored. Many researchers would like to know which structural elements of grammar and vocabulary — if any — are truly universal and probably therefore hardwired into the human brain. Other scientists try to reconstruct ancient migration patterns by comparing borrowed words that appear in otherwise unrelated languages. In each of these cases, the wider the portfolio of languages you study, the more likely you are to get the right answers.

C   Despite the near constant buzz in linguistics about endangered languages over the past 10 years, the field has accomplished depressingly little. 'You would think that there would be some organised response to this dire situation — some attempt to determine which language can be saved and which should be documented before they disappear,' says Sarah G. Thomason, a linguist at the University of Michigan at Ann Arbor. 'But there isn't any such effort organised in the profession. It is only recently that it has become fashionable enough to work on endangered languages.' Six years ago, recalls Douglas H. Whalen of Yale University, 'When I asked linguists who were raising money to deal with these problems, I mostly got blank stares.' So Whalen and a few other linguists founded the Endangered Languages Fund. In the five years to 2001 they were able to collect only $80,000 for research grants. A similar foundation in England, directed by Nicholas Ostler, has raised just $8,000 since 1995.

D   But there are encouraging signs that the field has turned a corner. The Volkswagen Foundation, a German charity, just issued its second round of grants totaling more than $2 million. It has created a multimedia archive at the Max Planck Institute for Psycholinguistics in the Netherlands that can house recordings, grammars, dictionaries and other data on endangered languages. To fill the archive, the foundation has dispatched field linguists to document Aweti (100 or so speakers in Brazil), Ega (about 300 speakers in Ivory Coast), Waima'a (a few hundred speakers in East Timor), and a dozen or so other languages unlikely to survive the century. The Ford Foundation has also edged into the arena. Its contributions helped to reinvigorate a master-apprentice programme created in 1992 by Leanne Hinton of Berkeley and Native Americans who worried about the imminent demise of about 50 indigenous languages in California. Fluent speakers receive $3,000 to teach a younger relative (who is also paid) their native tongue through 360 hours of shared activities, spread over six months. 'So far about 5 teams have completed the programme,' Hinton says, 'transmitting at least some knowledge of 25 languages.' 'It's too early to call this language revitalisation,' Hinton admits. 'In California the death rate of elderly speakers will always be greater than the recruitment rate of young speakers. But at least we prolong the survival of the language.' That will give linguists more time to record these tongues before they vanish.

E Twenty years ago in New Zealand, Maori speakers set up 'language nests', in which preschoolers were immersed in the native language. Additional Maori-only classes were added as the children progressed through elementary and secondary school. A similar approach was tried in Hawaii, with some success — the number of native speakers has stabilised at 1,000 or so, reported by Joseph E. Grimes of SIL International, who is working on Oahu. Students can now get instruction in Hawaiian all the way through university.

F One factor that always seems to occur in the demise of a language is that the speakers begin to have collective doubts about the usefulness of language loyalty. Once they start regarding their own language as inferior to the majority language, people stop using it for all situations. Kids pick up on the attitude and prefer the dominant language. In many cases, people don't notice until they suddenly realise that their kids never speak the language, even at home.

G Linguists agree that ultimately, the answer to the problem of language extinction is multilingualism. Most Americans and Canadians, to the west of Quebec, have a gut reaction that anyone speaking another language in front of them is committing an immoral act. You get the same reaction in Australia and Russia. It is no coincidence that these are the areas where languages are disappearing the fastest. The first step in saving dying languages is to persuade the world's majorities to allow the minorities among them to speak with their own voices.

核心词汇

A 段

shudder [ˈʃʌdə(r)] *n.* 战栗，发抖，震颤 *vi.* 发抖，颤动，颤抖
discipline [ˈdɪsəplɪn] *n.* 学科；纪律；训练 *vt.* 处罚；训练；管教
linguistics [lɪŋˈgwɪstɪks] *n.* 语言学
utter [ˈʌtə(r)] *vt.* 发出，表达 *adj.* 完全的，十足的，彻底的
respected [rɪˈspektɪd] *adj.* 受尊敬的
alarm [əˈlɑːm] *n.* 警报；恐慌；闹钟 *vt.* 使不安，使恐慌
extinction [ɪkˈstɪŋkʃn] *n.* 灭绝，绝种，消亡
fieldwork [ˈfiːldwɜːk] *n.* 实地考察，野外考察

B 段

reconstruct [ˌriːkənˈstrʌkt] *vt.* 重建；重现
portfolio [pɔːtˈfəʊliəʊ] *n.* 公文包；文件夹；作品选集

C 段

buzz [bʌz] *vi.* 发出嗡嗡声 *n.* 嗡嗡声，喧闹
endangered [ɪnˈdeɪndʒəd] *adj.* 濒临灭绝的；有生命危险的
grant [ɡrɑːnt] *n.* 补助金，拨款，津贴 *vt.* 给予，授予；同意，承认

D 段

multimedia [ˌmʌltiˈmiːdiə] *adj.* 多媒体的 *n.* 多媒体
imminent [ˈɪmɪnənt] *adj.* 即将发生的，逼近的
demise [dɪˈmaɪz] *n.* 死亡；终止，结束
revitalisation [ˌriːˌvaɪtəlaɪˈzeɪʃn] *n.* 复兴，复苏；新生
vanish [ˈvænɪʃ] *vi.* 消失，突然不见

F 段

inferior to 不如，次于
dominant [ˈdɒmɪnənt] *adj.* 强大的，突出的；显性的

G 段

multilingualism [ˌmʌltɪˈlɪŋɡwəlɪzəm] *n.* 多语言，多语制度

高频同义替换

dominant	▸	ascendant, regnant, prevailing, predominant
utter	▸	release, project, let go, thorough, complete, absolute, total
reconstruct	▸	restore, rebuild, renovate, repair
reinvigorate	▸	revive, cheer, wake up, buck up, refresh, rekindle
be immersed in	▸	soak oneself in, immerse, be lost in, basking in
demise	▸	death, end, dying, termination, bequeath

题目解析

1. 关键词：decline, extinction
   文中对应点：A 段第二句
   题目解析：A 段主要讲几位语言学家发现了大量稀有语种逐渐灭绝的事实。由 A 段的关键词 decline, extinction 可找到选项 v，v 中的 threat 与 extinction 为同义替换。A 段第二句 "Unless scientists and community leaders directed a worldwide effort to stabilise the decline of local languages, he warned, nine tenths of the linguistic diversity of humankind would probably be doomed to extinction." 句意为，他曾警告，除非科学家和社区领导人为稳定当地语言种类的减少而作出全球性的努力，否则 90% 的人类语言多样性注定会灭绝。选项 v "稀有语种的潜在威胁"概括了原文，因此答案为 v。

2. 关键词：rare languages, linguistics
   文中对应点：B 段第一、二句
   题目解析：B 段着重讲述了研究语言学需要稀有语言的参与，稀有语言本身对科学研究具有重大意义。由 B 段的关键词 linguistics 可找到选项 x，x 中的 minority language 与 rare languages 对应，linguists 与 linguistics 为同根词。B 段第一、二句 "Many experts in the field mourn the loss of rare languages, for several reasons. To start, there is scientific self-interest: some of the most basic questions in linguistics have to do with the limits of human speech, which are far from fully explored." 句意为，有几个原因导致该领域的许多专家哀悼稀有语种的消失。首先，是科学自身的利益问题：语言学中一些最基本的问题必须涉及人类语言的极限，而这尚未被完全发掘。选项 x "稀有语言对语言学家的价值"概括了原文，因此答案为 x。

3. 关键词：the field, accomplished depressingly little
   文中对应点：C 段第一句
   题目解析：C 段举例说明了濒危语言的保护力度较弱。由 C 段的关键词 the field, accomplished 可找到选项 vi，vi 中的 protection field 与 the field 对应。C 段第一句 "Despite the near constant buzz in linguistics about endangered languages over the past 10 years, the field has accomplished depressingly little." 中的 accomplished depressingly little 与选项 vi 中的 Little progress 对应。句意为，尽管语言学系最近不断出现关于过去 10 年间濒危语言的流言，但该领域收获甚微。因此答案为 vi。

4 关键词：encouraging signs, turned a corner

文中对应点：D 段第一句

题目解析：D 段通过具体的例子说明人们正采取一系列措施来保护稀有语种，延缓其灭亡速度。由 D 段的关键词 encouraging signs 可找到选项 iii，iii 中的 positive 与 encouraging signs 对应。D 段第一句 "But there are encouraging signs that the field has turned a corner." 中的 turned a corner 与选项 iii 中的 gains 为同义替换。句意为，但是已经有一些振奋人心的迹象表明这个领域已出现转机。因此答案为 iii。

5 关键词：'language nests', native language

文中对应点：E 段第一句

题目解析：E 段以语言巢等为例表明使用稀有语种的人数已保持在稳定数量之内，一些语言项目已经发挥作用。由 E 段的关键词 'language nests', native language 可找到选项 vii，vii 中的 Native language programme 对应 'language nests'。E 段第一句 "Twenty years ago in New Zealand, Maori speakers set up 'language nests', in which preschoolers were immersed in the native language." 句意为，20 年前，在新西兰毛利语表达者建立了'语言巢'，学龄前儿童都会专注于他们的母语。选项 vii "母语项目启动"符合原文表述，因此答案为 vii。

6 关键词：one factor, doubts

文中对应点：F 段第一句

题目解析：F 段主要讲述人们对稀有语言价值的怀疑是导致其灭绝的一个重要因素。由 F 段的关键词 doubts 可找到选项 viii，viii 中的 doubts 为原词重现。F 段第一句 "One factor that always seems to occur in the demise of a language is that the speakers begin to have collective doubts about the usefulness of language loyalty." 句意为，语言灭亡的一个常见原因就是说话者开始集体质疑语言忠诚度的有效性。原文中的 one factor 与选项 viii 中的 a negative factor 对应，所以答案为 viii。

7 关键词：saving, dying language

文中对应点：G 段倒数第一句

题目解析：G 段说明了拯救濒危语言的第一步是转换人们的观念，为解决语言灭绝问题提供一种途径。由 G 段的关键词 dying language 可找到选项 ii，ii 中的 dying out language 与 dying language 对应。G 段倒数第一句 "The first step in saving dying languages is to persuade the world's majorities to allow the minorities among them to speak with their own voices." 句意为，拯救濒危语言的第一步就是劝导世界主流人群接受他们之中说不同语言的少数群体。原文中的 saving 与 solution 对应，因此答案为 ii。

参考答案

1 v   **2** x   **3** vi   **4** iii   **5** vii   **6** viii   **7** ii

READING PASSAGE 8

Questions 1–7

The passage has seven paragraphs, **A–G**.

Choose the correct heading for each paragraph from the list of headings below.

Write the correct number, *i–x*, in boxes 1–7 on your answer sheet.

	List of Headings
i	Unavoidable changing facts to be considered when picking up technology means
ii	A debatable place where the new technologies stand in for history teaching
iii	Hard to attract students in traditional ways of teaching history
iv	Display of the use of emerging multimedia as leaching tools
v	Both students and professionals as candidates did not produce decent results
vi	A good concrete example illustrated to show how multimedia animates the history class
vii	The comparisons of the new technologies applied in history class
viii	Enormous breakthroughs in new technologies
ix	Resistance of using new technologies from certain historian
x	Decisions needed on which technique to be used for history teaching instead of improvement in the textbooks

1   Paragraph **A**

2   Paragraph **B**

3   Paragraph **C**

4   Paragraph **D**

5   Paragraph **E**

6   Paragraph **F**

7   Paragraph **G**

New Ways of Teaching History

A In a technology and media-driven world, it's becoming increasingly difficult to get our students' attentions and keep them absorbed in classroom discussions. This generation, in particular, has brought a unique set of challenges to the educational table. Whereas youth are easily enraptured by high-definition television, computers, iPods, video games and cell phones, they are less than enthralled by what to them are obsolete textbooks and boring classroom lectures. The question of how to teach history in a digital age is often contentious. On the one side, the old guard thinks the professional standards history is in mortal danger from flash-in-the-pan challenges by the digital that are all show and no substance. On the other side, the self-styled 'disruptors' offer over-blown rhetoric about how digital technology has changed everything while the moribund profession obstructs all progress in the name of outdated ideals. At least, that's a parody (maybe not much of one) of how the debate proceeds. Both supporters and opponents of the digital share more disciplinary common ground than either admits.

B When provided with merely a textbook as a supplemental learning tool, test results have revealed that most students fail to pinpoint the significance of historical events and individuals. Fewer still are able to cite and substantiate primary historical sources. What does this say about the way our educators are presenting information? The quotation comes from a report of a 1917 test of 668 Texas students. Less than 10 percent of school-age children attended high school in 1917; today, enrolments are nearly universal. The whole world has turned on its head during the last century but one thing has stayed the same: Young people remain woefully ignorant about history reflected from their history tests. Guess what? Historians are ignorant too, especially when we equate historical knowledge with the 'Jeopardy' Daily Double. In a test, those specialising in American history did just fine. But those with specialties in medieval European and African history failed miserably when confronted by items about Fort Ticonderoga, the Olive Branch Petition, or the Quebec Act — all taken from a typical textbook. According to the testers, the results from the recent National Assessment in History, like scores from earlier tests, show that young people are 'abysmally ignorant' of their own history. Invoking the tragedy of last September, historian Diane Ravitch hitched her worries about our future to the idea that our nation's strength is endangered by youth who do poorly on such tests. But if she were correct, we could have gone down the tubes in 1917!

C There is a huge difference between saying 'Kids don't know the history we want them to know' and saying 'Kids don't know history at all'. Historical knowledge burrows itself into our cultural pores even if young people can't marshal it when faced by a multiple choice test. If we weren't such hypocrites (or maybe if we were better historians), we'd have to admit that today's students follow in our own footsteps. For too long we've fantasised that by rewriting textbooks we could change how history is learned. The problem, however, is not the content of textbooks but the very idea of them. No human mind could retain the information crammed into these books in 1917, and it can do no better now. If we have learned anything from history that can be applied to every time period, it is that the only constant is change. The teaching of history, or any subject for that matter, is no exception. The question is no longer whether to bring new technologies into everyday education;

now, the question is which technologies are most suitable for the range of topics covered in junior high and high school history classrooms. Fortunately, technology has provided us with opportunities to present our Civil War lesson plans or our American Revolution lesson plans in a variety of new ways.

D Teachers can easily target and engage the learners of this generation by effectively combining the study of history with innovative multimedia. PowerPoint and presentations in particular can expand the scope of traditional classroom discussion by helping teachers to explain abstract concepts while accommodating students' unique learning styles. PowerPoint study units that have been pre-made for history classrooms include all manner of photos, prints, maps, audio clips, video clips and primary sources which help to make learning interactive and stimulating. Presenting lessons in these enticing formats helps technology-driven students retain the historical information they'll need to know for standard exams.

E Whether you are covering Revolutionary War lesson plans or World War II lesson plans, PowerPoint study units are available in formats to suit the needs of your classroom. Multimedia teaching instruments like PowerPoint software are getting positive results the world over, framing conventional lectures with captivating written, auditory and visual content that helps students recall names, dates and causal relationships within a historical context.

F History continues to show us that new times bring new realities. Education is no exception to the rule. The question is not whether to bring technology into the educational environment. Rather, the question is which technologies are suitable for U.S. and world history subjects, from Civil War lesson plans to World War II lesson plans. Whether you're covering your American Revolution lesson plans or your Cold War lesson plans, PowerPoint presentations are available in pre-packaged formats to suit your classroom's needs.

G Meanwhile, some academic historians hold a different view on the use of technology in teaching history. One reason they hold is that not all facts can be recorded by film or videos and literature is relatively feasible in this case. Another challenge they have to be faced with is the painful process to learn new technology like the making of PowerPoint and the editing of audio and video clips which is also reasonable especially to some elderly historians.

核心词汇

A 段

enrapture [ɪnˈræptʃə(r)] *vt.* 使着迷，使陶醉
enthral [ɪnˈθrɔːl] *vt.* 迷住，着迷
obsolete [ˈɒbsəliːt] *adj.* 废弃的，淘汰的，过时的
contentious [kənˈtenʃəs] *adj.* 引起争论的，爱争论的
obstruct [əbˈstrʌkt] *vt.* 妨碍，阻塞
disciplinary [ˈdɪsəplɪnəri] *adj.* 有关纪律的，纪律性的

B 段

supplemental [ˌsʌplɪˈmentəl] *adj.* 补充的，追加的
substantiate [səbˈstænʃieɪt] *vt.* 证实，证明
ignorant [ˈɪgnərənt] *adj.* 无知的，愚昧的
endangered [ɪnˈdeɪndʒəd] *adj.* 濒临灭绝的；有生命危险的

C 段

retain [rɪˈteɪn] *vt.* 保持，保留，保存；记住
cram into 勉强塞入，填满
revolution [ˌrevəˈluːʃn] *n.* 革命，彻底变革；旋转

D 段

innovative [ˈɪnəveɪtɪv] *adj.* 革新的，创新的，新颖的
interactive [ˌɪntərˈæktɪv] *adj.* 交互式的；合作的
stimulating [ˈstɪmjuleɪtɪŋ] *adj.* 使人兴奋的；有刺激性的
entice [ɪnˈtaɪs] *vt.* 诱使；怂恿

E 段

conventional [kənˈvenʃənl] *adj.* 传统的，惯例的，守旧的
captivate [ˈkæptɪveɪt] *vt.* 迷住，迷惑，吸引

G 段

feasible [ˈfiːzəbl] *adj.* 可行的，可能的，行得通的

题目

animate [ˈænɪmeɪt] *vt.* 使有生气，使活泼

高频同义替换

supplemental ▸ supplementary, complementary, adscititious

tube ▸ underground, subway, metro

stimulate ▸ motivate, activate, needle

obstruct ▸ blockade, block, hinder, impede

innovative ▸ advanced, forward-looking, modern, groundbreaking

obsolete ▸ waste, dump, fall into disuse, outdated

entice ▸ lure, tempt, encourage

feasible ▸ viable, possible

题目解析

1 关键词：contentious
   文中对应点：A 段第四句
   题目解析：A 段主要阐述科技在历史教学中的使用引起争议。由 A 段的关键词 contentious 可找到选项 ii，contentious 与 debatable 为同义替换，并且 ii "A debatable place where the new technologies stand in for history teaching"（新技术支撑历史教学是一个值得商榷的问题）与 A 段第四句 "The question of how to teach history in a digital age is often contentious."（在数字时代如何教授历史的问题经常引起争议。）也是同义表达。接下来 On the one side,…On the other side,……主要论证前面提出的观点。只有选项 ii 准确概括该段的内容，因此答案为 ii。

2 关键词：test results
   文中对应点：B 段第一、五和六句
   题目解析：B 段主要是利用数据阐述年轻人以及历史学家对历史方面越来越无知。由 B 段关键词 test results 可找到选项 v，v 中的 results 为原词重现。B 段首先通过测试结果阐述学生在历史学习方面表现得不理想，接着指出本段的中心主题：年轻人以及历史学家对历史方面越来越无知，然后对测试的结果进行了详细的分析。只有选项 v 能够准确概括该段的内容，因此答案为 v。

3 关键词：not…but…, textbooks
   文中对应点：C 段第五、九句
   题目解析：C 段中首先提到我们幻想通过重写教科书来改变历史知识的学习，however 转折出段落的主旨，怎样的科技应该运用到历史课堂才是亟待解决的问题。由 C 段的关键词 textbooks 可找到选项 x，x 中的 instead of 与 not…but… 为同义替换。因此答案为 x。

4 关键词：innovative multimedia
   文中对应点：D 段第一句
   题目解析：D 段首句内容紧接着上一段提出的科技已经为我们提供以各种新的方式来介绍历史的机会，也就是将历史教学与多媒体技术相结合。由 D 段的关键词 innovative multimedia 可找到选项 iv，iv

项中的 emerging multimedia 与 innovative multimedia 为同义替换，因此答案为 iv。

5. 关键词：positive results
   文中对应点：E 段第二句
   题目解析：E 段主要是以 Revolutionary War lesson plans or World War II lesson plans 为例，说明 PowerPoint software 在历史课堂所能发挥的作用，对应了 vi 中的 concrete example。由 E 段中的关键词 positive results 也可找到选项 vi，vi 中的 animates the history class 与 positive results 对应。因此答案为 vi。

6. 关键词：new realities
   文中对应点：F 段第一、二、四句
   题目解析：F 段主要提到的是技术纳入教育的环境已是不争的事实。由 F 段的关键词 new realities 可找到选项 i，i 中的 changing facts 与 new realities 对应。接下来展开说明应该重视如何恰当地运用哪些技术于历史课堂，因此答案为 i。

7. 关键词：different view
   文中对应点：G 段第一句
   题目解析：G 段开始提到了一些历史学家对历史教学中使用的技术有不同的看法，之后给出相应的历史学家拒绝使用新科技的原因。由 G 段的关键词 different view 可找到选项 ix，ix 中的 Resistance of...from 与 different view 对应，并且选项 ix 的描述准确概括了 G 段的主旨。因此答案为 ix。

参考答案

1 ii 2 v 3 x 4 iv 5 vi 6 i 7 ix

READING PASSAGE 9

Questions 1–5

The passage has seven paragraphs, **A–G**.

Choose the correct heading for paragraphs **A–E** from the list of headings below.

Write the correct number, *i–ix*, in boxes 1–5 on your answer sheet.

List of Headings

i	An existed critical system into operating in a new way
ii	Overview of a fast growing business
iii	Profitable games gaining more concerns
iv	Netherlands taking the leading role
v	A new perspective towards sharing the business opportunities
vi	Opportunities for all round prevalent applications
vii	Revenue gains and bonus share
viii	The simpler technology prevails over complex ones
ix	Set-top box provider changed their mind

1. Paragraph **A**
2. Paragraph **B**
3. Paragraph **C**
4. Paragraph **D**
5. Paragraph **E**

Text the Television

A There was a time when any self-respecting television show, particularly one aimed at a young audience, had to have an e-mail address. But on Europe's TV screens, such addresses are increasingly being pushed aside in favour of telephone numbers to which viewers can send text messages from their mobile phones. And no wonder: according to research about to be published by Gartner, a consultancy, text messaging has recently overtaken Internet use in Europe. One of the fastest-growing uses of text messaging, moreover, is interacting with television. Gartner's figures show that 20% of teenagers in France, 11% in Britain and 9% in Germany have sent messages in response to TV shows.

B This has much to do with the boom in 'reality TV shows', such as '*Big Brother*', in which viewers' votes decide the outcome. Most reality shows now allow text-message voting, and in some cases, such as the most recent series of '*Big Brother*' in Norway, the majority of votes are cast in this way. But there is more to TV-texting than voting. News shows encourage viewers to send in comments; game shows allow viewers to compete; music shows take requests by text message; and broadcasters operate on-screen chatrooms. People tend to have their mobiles with them on the sofa, so 'it's a very natural form of interaction,' says Adam Daum of Gartner.

C It can also be very lucrative, since mobile operators charge premium rates for messages to particular numbers. The most recent British series of '*Big Brother*', for example, generated 5.4m text-message votes and £1.35m ($2.1m) in revenue. According to a report from Van Dusseldorp & Partners, a consultancy based in Amsterdam, the German edition of MTV's '*Videoclash*', which invites viewers to vote for one of two rival videos, generates up to 40,000 messages an hour, each costing euro 0.30 ($0.29). A text contest alongside the Belgian quiz show attracted 110,000 players in a month, each of whom paid euro 0.50 per question in an eight-round contest. In Spain, a clue is displayed before the evening news broadcast; viewers are invited to text in their answers at a cost of euro 1, for a chance to win a euro 300 prize. On a typical day, 6,000 people take part. TV-related text messaging now accounts for an appreciable share of mobile operators' data revenues. In July, a British operator, mm02, reported better-than-expected financial results, thanks to the flood of messages caused by '*Big Brother*'. Operators typically take 40–50% of the revenue from each message, with the rest divided between the broadcaster, the programme maker and the firm providing the message-processing system. Text-message revenues are already a vital element of the business model for many shows. Inevitably, there is grumbling that the operators take too much of the pie. Endemol, the Netherlands-based production company behind '*Big Brother*' and many other reality TV shows has started building its own database of mobile-phone users. The next step will be to establish direct billing relationships with them, and bypass the operator.

D Why has the union of television and text message suddenly proved so successful? One important factor is the availability of special four-, five- or six-digit numbers, called shortcodes. Each operator controls its own shortcodes, and only relatively recently have operators realised that it makes sense to co-operate and offer shortcodes that work across all networks. The availability of such common shortcodes was a breakthrough, says Lars Becker of Flytxt, a mobile-marketing firm, since shortcodes are far easier to remember when flashed up on the screen.

E The operators' decision to co-operate in order to expand the market is part of a broader trend, observes Katrina Bond of Analysis, a consultancy. Faced with a choice between protecting their margins and allowing a new medium to emerge, operators have always chosen the first WAP, a technology for reading cut-down web pages on mobile phones, failed because operators were reluctant to share revenue with content providers. Having learnt their lesson, operators are changing their tune. In France, one operator, Orange, has even gone so far as to publish a rate card for text-message revenue-sharing, a degree of transparency that would once have been unthinkable.

F At a recent conference organised by Van Dusseldorp & Partners, Han Weegink of CMG, a firm that provides text-message infrastructure, noted that all this is subtly changing the nature of television. Rather than presenting content to viewers, an increasing number of programmes involve content that reacts to the viewer's input. That was always the promise of interactive TV, of course. Interactive TV was supposed to revolve around fancy set-top boxes that plug directly into the television. But that approach has a number of drawbacks, says Mr.Daum. It is expensive to develop and test software for multiple and incompatible types of set-top box, and the market penetration, at 40% or less, is lower than that for mobile phones, which are now owned by around 85% of Europeans. Also, mobile-phone applications can be quickly developed and set up. 'You can get to market faster, and with fewer grasping intermediaries,' says Mr. Daum. Providers of set-top box technology are adding text-messaging capabilities to their products.

G The success of TV-related texting is a reminder of how easily an elaborate technology can be unexpectedly overtaken by a simpler, lower-tech approach. It does not mean that the traditional approach to interactive TV is doomed: indeed, it demonstrates that there is strong demand for interactive services. People, it seems, really do want to do more than just stare at the screen. If nothing else, couch potatoes like to exercise their thumbs.

核心词汇

A 段

overtake [ˌəʊvəˈteɪk] *v.* 赶上；超过

B 段

interaction [ˌɪntərˈækʃn] *n.* 互动；相互作用

C 段

lucrative [ˈluːkrətɪv] *adj.* 有利可图的，赚钱的；合算的
premium rate 高价
appreciable [əˈpriːʃəbl] *adj.* 相当可观的；可评估的
revenue [ˈrevənjuː] *n.* 收入；税收
inevitably [ɪnˈevɪtəbli] *adv.* 不可避免地；必然地

D 段

shortcode [ˈʃɔːtˌkəʊd] *n.* 简码

E 段

consultancy [kənˈsʌltənsi] *n.* 咨询公司
margin [ˈmɑːdʒɪn] *n.* 利润；边缘
transparency [trænsˈpærənsi] *n.* 透明，透明度

F 段

infrastructure [ˈɪnfrəstrʌktʃə(r)] *n.* 基础设施；公共建设
subtly [ˈsʌtli] *adv.* 精细地；巧妙地；敏锐地
plug [plʌg] *v.* 插入；塞住
incompatible [ˌɪnkəmˈpætəbl] *adj.* 不相容的；矛盾的
penetration [ˌpenəˈtreɪʃn] *n.* 渗透；穿透；进入；洞察力

G 段

reminder [rɪˈmaɪndə(r)] *n.* 暗示；起提醒作用的东西
doomed [duːmd] *adj.* 注定的

高频同义替换

favour ▸ acceptance, preference, good, mercy

decide ▸ resolve, determine

operate ▸ run, act, keep, produce

display ▸ exhibition, manifestation, reveal

co-operate ▸ team, collaborate

transparency ▸ clarity, lucency, clear

drawback ▸ defect, deficiency, disadvantage, vice, fault

demonstrate ▸ prove, give evidence of, certify

题目解析

1 关键词：fastest-growing uses
文中对应点：A 段第四句
题目解析：A 段首先介绍过去每个电视节目都有自己的邮箱，接着提出短信开始取代邮箱，在欧洲的电视节目中使用日益增加，其中一种就是和电视互动。由 A 段的关键词 fastest-growing uses 可找到选项 ii，选项 ii 中的 fast growing business 与原文中的 fastest-growing uses 为同义替换。A 段第四句 "One of the fastest-growing uses of text messaging, moreover, is interacting with television." 句意为，此外，短信增长速度最快的应用之一是与电视互动。因此答案为 ii。

2 关键词：boom
文中对应点：B 段第四句
题目解析：B 段首句交代电视短信盛行的原因：电视短信的广泛使用与电视真人秀的大量出现密切相关。由 B 段的关键词 boom 可找到选项 vi，boom 与 vi 中的 prevalent 为同义替换；B 段第四句 "News shows encourage viewers to send in comments; game shows allow viewers to compete; music shows take requests by text message; and broadcasters operate on-screen chatrooms." 列举了电视短信在其他各类节目中都成为节目与观众之间互动的主要形式，与 vi 中的 opportunities for all round 对应。因此答案为 vi。

3 关键词：lucrative
文中对应点：C 段第一、九句
题目解析：C 段首句提出本段主旨：短信为运营商带来巨大收益。由 C 段的关键词 lucrative（有利可图的）可找到选项 vii，lucrative 与选项 vii 中的 revenue gains 对应。C 段第一句 "It can also be very lucrative, since mobile operators charge premium rates for messages to particular numbers." 句意为，它也可以非常赚钱，因为移动运营商要收取高额费用。其后列举了不同节目中短信收益的例子。第九句 "Operators typically take 40–50% of the revenue from each message, with the rest divided between the broadcaster, the programme maker and the firm providing the message-processing system." 提到各方从短信收益中获取不同占比的利润，对应 vii 中的 bonus share。因此答案为 vii。

4　关键词：shortcodes

　　文中对应点：D 段第三句

　　题目解析：D 段主要阐述了为何电视和短信的联合突然取得成功的问题。由 D 段的关键词 shortcodes 可找到选项 i，选项 i 中的 critical system 与原文中的 shortcodes 为同义替换。D 段第三句 "Each operator controls its own shortcodes, and only relatively recently have operators realised that it makes sense to co-operate and offer shortcodes that work across all networks." 提出只是最近才有运营商意识到应该和别人合作，向网络提供简码，这与 i 选项中的 operating in a new way 信息相符。因此答案为 i。

5　关键词：revenue-sharing, unthinkable

　　文中对应点：E 段第四句

　　题目解析：E 段主要是阐述运营商的利益分配机制。由 E 段的关键词 revenue-sharing, unthinkable 可找到选项 v，选项 v 中的 A new perspective 对应原文中的 unthinkable，sharing the business opportunities 对应 revenue-sharing。E 段第四句 "In France, one operator, Orange, has even gone so far as to publish a rate card for text-message revenue-sharing, a degree of transparency that would once have been unthinkable." 句意为，在法国，一家名为 Orange 的运营商甚至已经发布了一份用于短信收入分享的费率卡，这在一定程度上是不可想象的。因此答案为 v。

参考答案

1 ii　2 vi　3 vii　4 i　5 v

READING PASSAGE 10

Questions 1–4

The passage has six paragraphs, **A–F**.

*Choose the correct heading for paragraphs **A** and **C–E** from the list of headings below.*

*Write the correct number, **i–vii**, in boxes 1–4 on your answer sheet.*

List of Headings

i	Reasons for unusual experiments implemented by several thinkers
ii	Children had to work to alleviate burden on family
iii	Why children are not highly valued
iv	Children died in hospital at their early age
v	Politics related philosophy appeared
vi	Creative learning method was applied on certain wild kid
vii	Emergence and spread of the so-called kindergarten

1   Paragraph **A**

Example	Answer
Paragraph **B**	ii

2   Paragraph **C**

3   Paragraph **D**

4   Paragraph **E**

Education Philosophy

A   In 1660s, while there are few accurate statistics for child mortality in the preindustrial world, there is evidence that as many as 30 percent of all children died before they were 14 days old. Few families survived intact. All parents expected to bury some of their children and they found it difficult to invest emotionally in such a tenuous existence as a newborn child. When the loss of a child was commonplace, parents protected themselves from the emotional consequences of the death by refusing to make an emotional commitment to the infant. How else can we explain mothers who call the infant 'it', or leave dying babies in gutters, or mention the death of a child in the same paragraph with a reference to pickles?

B   One of the most important social changes to take place in the Western world in the 18th century was the result of the movement from an agrarian economy to an industrial one. Increasingly, families left the farms and their small-town life and moved to cities where life was very different for them. Social supports that had previously existed in the smaller community disappeared, and problems of poverty, crime, sub-standard housing and disease increased. For the poorest children, childhood could be painfully short, as additional income was needed to help support the family and young children were forced into early employment. Children as young as 7 might be required to work full-time jobs, often under unpleasant and unhealthy circumstances, from factories to prostitution. Although such a role for children has disappeared in most economically strong nations, the practice of childhood employment has hardly disappeared entirely and remains in many undeveloped nations.

C   Over the course of the 1800s, the lives of children in the United States began to change drastically. Previously, children in both rural and urban families were expected to take part in the everyday labour of the home, as the bulk of manual work had to be completed there. However, establishing a background the technological advances of the mid-1800s, coupled with the creation of a middle class and the redefinition of roles of family members, meant that work and home became less synonymous over the course of time. People began to buy their children toys and books to read. As the country slowly became more dependent upon machines for work, both in rural and in urban areas, it became less necessary for children to work inside the home. This trend, which had been rising slowly over the course of the nineteenth century, took off exponentially after the Civil War, with the beginning of the Industrial Revolution. John Locke was one of the most influential writers of his period. His writings on the role of government are seen as foundational to many political movements and activities, including the American Revolution and the drafting of the *Declaration of Independence*. His ideas are equally foundational to several areas of psychology. As the father of 'British empiricism', Locke made the first clear and comprehensive statement of the 'environmental position' and, by so doing, became the father of modern learning theory. His teachings about childcare were highly regarded during the colonial period in America.

D   Jean Jacques Rousseau lived during an era of the American and French Revolution. His works condemn distinctions of wealth, property, and prestige. In the original state of nature, according to Rousseau, people were 'noble savages', innocent, free and uncorrupted. Rousseau conveyed his educational philosophy through his famous novel *Emile*, in 1762, which tells the story of a boy's education from infancy to adulthood. Rousseau observed children and adolescents extensively and spoke of children's individuality, but he based much of his developmental theory on observation in writing the book, and on the memories of his own childhood. Rousseau contrasts children to Developmental Psychology in Historical Perspective adults and describes age-specific characteristics. Johan Heinrich Pestalozzi lived during the early stages of Industrial Revolution, he sought to develop schools that would nurture children's development. He agreed with Rousseau that humans are naturally good but were spoiled by a corrupt society. Pestalozzi's approach to teaching can be divided into the general and special methods. The theory was designed to create an emotionally healthy homelike learning environment that had to be in place before more specific instruction occurred.

E   One of the best documented cases of all the so-called feral children concerned a young man who was captured in a small town in the south of France in 1800, and who was later named Victor. The young man had been seen in the area for months before his final capture — prepubescent, mute, and naked, perhaps 11 or 12 years old, foraging for food in the gardens of the locals and sometimes accepting their direct offers of food. Eventually he was brought to Paris, where it was hoped that he would be able to answer some of the profound questions about the nature of man, but that goal was quashed very early. Jean-Marc-Gaspard Itard, a young physician who had become interested in working with the deaf, was more optimistic about a future for Victor and embarked on a five-year plan of education to civilise him and teach him to speak. With a subsidy from the government, Itard spent an enormous amount of time and effort working with Victor. He was able to enlist the help of a local woman, Madame Guerin, to assist in his efforts and provide a semblance of a home for Victor. But, after five years and despite all of his efforts, Itard considered the experiment to be a failure. Although Victor had learned some elementary forms of communication, he never learned the basics of speech, which, for Itard, was the goal. Victor's lessons were discontinued, although he continued to live with Madame Guerin until his death, approximately at the age of 40.

F   Other educators were beginning to respond to the simple truth that was embedded in the philosophy of Rousseau. Identifying the stages of development of children was not enough. Education had to be geared to those stages. One of the early examples of this approach was the invention of the kindergarten ('the children's garden') — a word and a movement created by Friedrich Froebel in 1840, a German-born educator. Froebel placed particular emphasis on the importance of play in a child's learning. His invention, in different forms, would eventually find its way around the world. His ideas about education were initially developed through his association with Johann Heinrich Pestalozzi. Froebel spent five years teaching at one of Pestalozzi's model schools in Frankfurt, and later he studied with Pestalozzi himself. Eventually he was able to open his own schools to test his educational theories. One of his innovative ideas was his belief that women could serve as appropriate educators of young children — an unpopular view at the time. At the age of 58, after almost four decades as a teacher, Froebel introduced the notion of the kindergarten. It was to be a haven and a preparation for children who were about to enter the regimented educational system. A cornerstone of his kindergarten education was the use of guided or structured play. For Froebel, play was the most significant aspect of development at this time of life. Play served as the means for a child to grow emotionally and to achieve a sense of self-worth. The role of the teacher was to organise materials and a structured environment in which each child, as an individual, could achieve these goals. By the time of Froebel's death in 1852, dozens of kindergartens had been created in Germany. Their use increased in Europe and the movement eventually reached and flourished in the United States in the 20th century.

核心词汇

A 段

intact [ɪn'tækt] *adj.* 完整的；原封不动的；未受损伤的
tenuous ['tenjuəs] *adj.* 纤细的；薄的；缥缈的
commonplace ['kɒmənpleɪs] *n.* 司空见惯的事；老生常谈 *adj.* 常见的
gutter ['gʌtə(r)] *n.* 水沟，水槽

B 段

agrarian [ə'greəriən] *adj.* 土地的；耕地的；农业的

C 段

drastically ['dræstɪkli] *adv.* 彻底地；激烈地
manual ['mænjuəl] *adj.* 手工的；体力的
exponentially [ˌekspə'nenʃəli] *adv.* 以指数方式；呈指数地
empiricism [ɪm'pɪrɪsɪzəm] *n.* 经验主义；经验论

D 段

condemn [kən'dem] *v.* 谴责；定罪；声讨
adolescent [ˌædə'lesnt] *n.* 青少年

E 段

feral ['ferəl] *adj.* 野生的；凶猛的；阴郁的
prepubescent [priːpju'bes(ə)nt] *adj.* 青春期前的
quash [kwɒʃ] *v.* 撤销；制止
embark [ɪm'bɑːk] *v.* 从事，着手；上船或飞机

F 段

embed [ɪm'bed] *v.* 嵌入
regimented ['redʒɪmentɪd] *adj.* 受管制的

高频同义替换

accurate	▸	precise, mathematical, strict, rigid
intact	▸	whole, complete, integrated, full
existence	▸	presence, being, entity, life
disappear	▸	blank, vanish
unpleasant	▸	evil, rank, poisonous

circumstance	▶	context, situation, setting, event
establish	▶	build, found, constitute
regard	▶	view, honour
observation	▶	view, monitoring, watch
enormous	▶	huge, tremendous, massive
appropriate	▶	suitable, adequate
create	▶	produce, invent, generate

题目解析

1 关键词：difficult to invest, call the infant "it", reference to pickles
文中对应点：A 段倒数第一句
题目解析：A 段主要内容是父母并不是十分重视孩子的原因。由 A 段的关键词 difficult to invest，call the infant "it" 以及 reference to pickles（父母谈论孩子死亡经常是夹杂在谈论泡菜的内容里）可找到选项 iii，作者的主要情感走向是想说"孩子不受重视"，与 iii 中的 not highly valued 符合，同时 infants 也是主要谈论的内容。因此答案为 iii。

2 关键词：role of government, political movements and activities
文中对应点：C 段第八句
题目解析：C 段中主要阐述了中产阶级富足的生活促进了哲学相关的政治的出现。C 段第八句 "His writings on the role of government are seen as foundational to many political movements and activities, including the American Revolution and the drafting of the *Declaration of Independence*." 中的提到了 John Locke 关于 role of government 的文章以及 political movements and activities，与选项 v 中的 politics related philosophy appeared 相符合。因此答案为 v。

3 关键词：Jean Jacques Rousseau, Johan Heinrich Pestalozzi, Pestalozzi's approach
文中对应点：D 段最后两句
题目解析：文章中提到了两位思想家专门研究人类的青少年时期的个性发展，并且结合了自己成长的经历。由 D 段的人名关键词 Jean Jacques Rousseau 和 Johan Heinrich Pestalozzi 可找到选项 i，这两位与选项 i 中的 thinkers 对应，并且 Pestalozzi's approach 对应 i 中的 experiments。D 段后两句 "Pestalozzi's approach to teaching can be divided into the general and special methods. The theory was designed to create an emotionally healthy homelike learning environment that had to be in place before more specific instruction occurred." 句意为，佩斯塔洛齐的教学方法可以分为一般方法和特殊方法。这个理论的目的是在更具体的教学之前，创造一个情感健康的类似于家庭的学习环境。因此答案为 i。

4 关键词：Victor, five-year plan of education
文中对应点：E 段第四句
题目解析：E 段主要内容为有记录的一个案例中野人 Victor 被发现，后来一名医生制订了五年教育计划，对其进行教化，然而最后以失败告终。由 E 段的关键词 Victor 可找到选项 vi，Victor 与 vi 中的 certain wild kid 对应，同时 five-year plan of education（五年的教育计划）对应 vi 选项中的 method。E 段第四句 "Jean-Marc-Gaspard Itard, ..., was more optimistic about a future for Victor and embarked on a five-year plan of education to civilise him and teach him to speak." 句意为，Jean-Marc-Gaspard Itard 对 Victor 的未来更加乐观，他开始了一项为期五年的教育计划，教化他并教他说话。与选项 vi "创造性的学习方式被应用在了对野孩子的教育之中"的表述相符合。因此答案为 vi。

参考答案

1 iii **2** v **3** i **4** vi

第三章　配对题

READING PASSAGE 1

Ancient Storytelling

A   It was told, we suppose, to people crouched around a fire: a tale of adventure, most likely-relating some close encounter with death; a remarkable hunt, an escape from mortal danger; a vision, or something else out of the ordinary. Whatever its thread, the weaving of this story was done with a prime purpose. The listeners must be kept listening. They must not fall asleep. So, as the story went on, its audience should be sustained by one question above all. What happens next?

B   The first fireside stories in human history can never be known. They were kept in the heads of those who told them. This method of storage is not necessarily inefficient. From documented oral traditions in Australia, the Balkans and other parts of the world we know that specialised storytellers and poets can recite from memory literally thousands of lines, in verse or prose, verbatim — word for word. But while memory is rightly considered an art in itself, it is clear that a primary purpose of making symbols is to have a system of reminders or mnemonic cues — signs that assist us to recall certain information in the mind's eye.

C   In some Polynesian communities a notched memory stick may help to guide a storyteller through successive stages of recitation. But in other parts of the world, the activity of storytelling historically resulted in the development or even the invention of writing systems. One theory about the arrival of literacy in ancient Greece, for example, argues that the epic tales about the Trojan War and the wanderings of Odysseus — traditionally attributed to Homer — were just so enchanting to hear that they had to be preserved. So the Greeks, 750-700 BC, borrowed an alphabet from their neighbours in the eastern Mediterranean, the Phoenicians.

D   The custom of recording stories on parchment and other materials can be traced in many manifestations around the world, from the priestly papyrus archives of ancient Egypt to the birch-bark scrolls on which the North American Ojibway Indians set down their creation — myth. It is a well-tried and universal practice: so much so that to this day storytime is probably most often associated with words on paper. The formal practice of narrating a story aloud would seem — so we assume — to have given way to newspapers, novels and comic strips. This, however, is not the case. Statistically it is doubtful that the majority of humans currently rely upon the written word to get access to stories. So what is the alternative source?

E   Each year, over 7 billion people will go to watch the latest offering from Hollywood, Bollywood and beyond. The supreme storyteller of today is cinema. The movies, as distinct from still photography, seem to be an essentially modern phenomenon. This is an illusion, for there are, as we shall see, certain ways in which the medium of film is indebted to very old precedents of arranging 'sequences' of images. But any account of visual storytelling must begin with the recognition that all storytelling beats with a deeply atavistic pulse: that is, a 'good story' relies upon formal patterns of plot and characterisation that have been embedded in the practice of storytelling over many generations.

F   Thousands of scripts arrive every week at the offices of the major film studios. But aspiring screenwriters really need look no further for essential advice than die fourth-century BC Greek Philosopher Aristotle. He left some incomplete lecture notes on the art of telling stories in various literary and dramatic modes, a slim volume known as *The Poetics*. Though he can never have envisaged the popcorn-fuelled actuality of a multiplex cinema, Aristotle is almost prescient about the key elements required to get the crowds flocking to such a cultural hub. He analysed the process with cool rationalism. When a story enchants us, we lose the sense of where we are; we are drawn into the story so thoroughly that we forget it is a story being told. This is, in Aristotle's phrase, the suspension of disbelief.

G   We know the feeling. If ever we have stayed in our seats, stunned with grief, as the credits roll by, or for days after seeing that vivid evocation of horror have been nervous about taking a shower at home, then we have suspended disbelief. We have been caught, or captivated, in the storyteller's web. Did it all really happen? We really thought so for a while. Aristotle must have witnessed often enough this suspension of disbelief. He taught at Athens, the city where theatre developed as a primary form of civic ritual and recreation. Two theatrical types of storytelling, tragedy and comedy, caused Athenian audiences to lose themselves in sadness and laughter respectively. Tragedy, for Aristotle, was particularly potent in its capacity to enlist and then purge the emotions of those watching the story unfold on the stage, so he tried to identify those factors in the storyteller's art that brought about such engagement. He had, as an obvious sample for analysis, not only the fifth-century BC masterpieces of Classical Greek tragedy written by Aeschylus, Sophocles and Euripides. Beyond them stood Homer, whose stories even then had canonical status: *The Iliad* and *The Odyssey* were already considered literary landmarks — stories by which all other stories should be measured? So what was the secret of Homer's narrative art?

H   It was not hard to find. Homer created credible heroes. His heroes belonged to the past, they were mighty and magnificent, yet they were not, in the end, fantasy figures. He made his heroes sulk, bicker, cheat and cry. They were, in short, characters — protagonists of a story that an audience would care about, would want to follow, would want to know what happens next. As Aristotle saw, the hero who shows a human side — some flaw or weakness to which mortals are prone — is intrinsically dramatic by logging.

Questions 1–5

Reading Passage 1 has eight paragraphs, **A–H**.

Which paragraph contains the following information?

*Write the correct letter, **A–H**, in boxes 1–5 on your answer sheet.*

1   a misunderstanding of a modern way for telling stories

2   the typical forms mentioned for telling stories

3   the fundamental aim of storytelling

4   a description of reciting stories without any assistance

5   how to make story characters attractive

核心词汇

A 段

crouch [kraʊtʃ] *vi.* 蹲下；蹲伏；俯身接近
encounter [ɪnˈaʊtə(r)] *n.* 遭遇；经历；相遇，邂逅 *vt.* 遇到，遭遇；偶然碰到
mortal [ˈmɔːtl] *adj.* 致命的，终结的；终有一死的；极度的 *n.* 凡人
thread [θred] *n.* 贯穿的主线；思路，头绪；线 *vt.* 穿线于；装入
weave [wiːv] *vt.* 编造，编纂；组合 *vi. & vt.* 编，织 *n.* 织法；编织式样

B 段

specialised [ˈspeʃəlaɪzd] *adj.* 专门的；专用的
recite [rɪˈsaɪ] *vi. & vt.* 背诵；朗诵 *vt.* 列举；详述
literally [ˈlɪtərəli] *adv.* 按照原义，根据字面意思；的确，确实
mnemonic [nɪˈmɒnik] *adj.* 帮助记忆的 *n.* 帮助记忆的东西

C 段

successive [səkˈsesɪv] *adj.* 连续的，相继的
recitation [ˌresɪˈteɪʃn] *n.* 讲述；朗诵，背诵
literacy [ˈlɪtərəsi] *n.* 读写能力，识字
attribute to 认为……是……所做；把……归因于……
enchanting [ɪnˈtʃɑːtɪŋ] *adj.* 迷人的，令人陶醉的；令人愉悦的 [拓] enchant *vt.* 使陶醉，使入迷
alphabet [ˈalfəbet] *n.* 字母表

D 段

parchment [ˈpɑːtʃmənt] *n.* 羊皮纸；仿羊皮纸；（仿）羊皮纸文件
manifestation [ˌmænɪfeˈsteɪʃn] *n.* 明显迹象；表现；显示
comic strip 连环漫画，四格漫画

E 段

illusion [ɪˈluːʃn] *n.* 错误的观念；幻想；假象，错觉

F 段

multiplex [ˈmʌltɪpleks] *adj.* 复合的 [拓] multiplex cinema 多放映厅电影院，多屏幕电影院

G 段

narrative [ˈnærətɪv] *adj.* 叙事的 *n.* 叙述，记叙；叙事过程，叙事技巧

高频同义替换

remarkable ▶ outstanding, excellent, eminent, distinct

universal ▶ common, general, widespread

obvious ▶ apparent, distinct, clear, evident

flaw ▶ shortcoming, demerit, drawback, disadvantage

题目解析

1. 定位词：misunderstanding, modern way
   文中对应点：E 段第三、四句
   题目解析：题干说，对于讲故事的现代方式的误解。由 misunderstanding 和 modern way 定位到 E 段第三、四句 "The movies, as distinct from still photography, seem to be an essentially modern phenomenon. This is an illusion, for there are, as we shall see, certain ways in which the medium of film is indebted to very old precedents of arranging 'sequences' of images."。其中，modern phenomenon 与 modern way 为同义替换，illusion 对应 misunderstanding。句意为，与静止的摄影不同，电影似乎从根本上就是一种现代的现象。但这是一种错觉，因为正如我们看到的，从某些方面来看，电影媒介其实源于图像的顺序展示这一非常古老的方式。因此答案为 E。

2. 定位词：typical forms, telling stories
   文中对应点：G 段第八句
   题目解析：题干说，讲故事的典型形式。由 typical forms 和 telling stories 定位到 G 段第八句 "Two theatrical types of storytelling, tragedy and comedy, caused Athenian audiences to lose themselves in sadness and laughter respectively."。其中，theatrical types 对应题干中的 typical forms，storytelling 对应 telling stories。句意为，叙述故事的两种戏剧类型——悲剧和喜剧，使得雅典的观众们各自沉浸在悲伤和欢笑之中。因此答案为 G。

3. 定位词：fundamental aim
   文中对应点：A 段第二、三句
   题目解析：题干说，讲故事的根本目的。由 fundamental aim 定位到 A 段第二、三句 "Whatever its thread, the weaving of this story was done with a prime purpose. The listeners must be kept listening."。其中，prime purpose 对应 fundamental aim。句意为，无论故事的主线是什么，讲故事都只有一个主要目的——必须使聆听者保持聆听的状态。因此答案为 A。

4. 定位词：reciting stories without any assistance
   文中对应点：B 段第四句
   题目解析：题干说，在没有任何帮助的情况下对背诵故事的描述。由 reciting stories 和 without any assistance 定位到 B 段第四句 "From documented oral traditions in Australia, the Balkans and other parts of the world we know that specialised storytellers and poets can recite from memory literally thousands of lines, in verse or prose, verbatim-word for word."。其中，recite from memory

对应 reciting stories without any assistance。句意为，据澳大利亚、巴尔干半岛地区以及世界其他地区有关口述传统的文献记载，我们知道专业的故事讲述人和诗人可以凭借记忆正确地讲述成千上万行的故事。因此答案为 B。

5 定位词：characters, attractive
文中对应点：H 段第四、五句
题目解析：题干说，如何让故事的角色有吸引力。由 characters, attractive 定位到 H 段第四、五句 "He made his heroes sulk, bicker, cheat and cry. They were, in short, characters — protagonists of a story that an audience would care about, would want to follow, would want to know what happens next."。其中，sulk, bicker, cheat and cry 这些要素均是使得故事人物能够吸引人的（attractive）信息。句意为，他使他的主人公生气、争吵、欺骗和哭泣。简而言之，这样的主人公是观众会关心、愿意追随并且想要知道剧情发展的角色。因此答案为 H。

参考答案

1 E 2 G 3 A 4 B 5 H

READING PASSAGE 2

Aqua Product: New Zealand's Algae Biodiesel

A The world's first wild algae biodiesel, produced in New Zealand by Aquaflow Bionomic Corporation, was successfully test driven in Wellington by the Minister for Energy and Climate Change Issues, David Parker. In front of a crowd of invited guests, media and members of the public, the Minister filled up a diesel-powered Land Rover with Aquaflow B5 blend bio-diesel and then drove the car around the forecourt of Parliament Buildings in Central Wellington. Green Party co-leader, Jeanette Fitzsimons was also on board. Marlborough-based Aquaflow announced in May 2006 that it had produced the world's first bio-diesel derived from wild microalgae sourced from local sewage ponds.

B 'We believe we are the first company in the world to test drive a car powered by wild algae-based biodiesel. This will come as a surprise to some international bio-diesel industry people who believe that this breakthrough is still years away,' explains Aquaflow spokesperson Barrie Leay. 'A bunch of inventive Kiwis, and an Aussie, have developed this fuel in just over a year,' he comments. 'This is a huge opportunity for New Zealand and a great credit to the team of people who saw the potential in this technology from day one.'

C Bio-diesel based on algae could eventually become a sustainable, low cost, cleaner burning fuel alternative for New Zealand, powering family cars, trucks, buses and boats. It can also be used for other purposes such as heating or distributed electricity generation. There is now a global demand for billions of litres of biodiesel per year. Algae are also readily available and produced in huge volumes in nutrient rich waste streams such as at the settling ponds of Effluent Management Systems (EMS). It is a renewable indigenous resource ideally suited to the production of fuel and other useful by-products. The breakthrough comes after technology start-up, Aquaflow, agreed to undertake a pilot with Marlborough District Council late last year to extract algae from the settling ponds of its EMS based in Blenheim. By removing the main contaminant to use as a fuel feedstock, Aquaflow is also helping clean up the council's water discharge — a process known as bio-remediation. Dairy farmers, and many food processors too, can benefit in similar ways by applying the harvesting technology to their nutrient-rich waste streams.

D Blended with conventional mineral diesel, bio-diesel can run vehicles without the need for vehicle modifications. Fuel derived from algae can also help meet the Government B5 (5% blended) target, with the prospect of this increasing over time as bio-fuel production increases. 'Our next step is to increase capacity to produce one million litres of bio-diesel from the Marlborough sewerage ponds over the next year,' says Leay. Aquaflow will launch a prospectus pre-Christmas as the company has already attracted considerable interest from potential investors. The test drive bio-diesel was used successfully in a static engine test at Massey University's Wellington campus on Monday, December 11.

E   Today algae are used by humans in many ways; for example, as fertilisers, soil conditioners and livestock feed. Aquatic and microscopic species are cultured in clear tanks or ponds and are either harvested or used to treat effluents pumped through the ponds. Algaculture on a large scale is an important type of aquaculture in some places. Naturally growing seaweeds are an important source of food, especially in Asia. They provide many vitamins including: A, B, B2, B6, niacin and C, and are rich in iodine, potassium, iron, magnesium and calcium. In addition commercially cultivated microalgae, including both Algae and Cyan-bacteria, are marketed as nutritional supplements, such as Spirulina, Chlorella and the Vitamin-C supplements, Dunaliella, high in beta-carotene. Algae are national foods of many nations: China consumes more than 70 species, including fat choy, a cyano-bacterium considered a vegetable; Japan, over 20 species. The natural pigments produced by algae can be used as an alternative to chemical dyes and colouring agents.

F   Algae are the simplest organism that convert sunlight and carbon dioxide in the air around us into stored energy through the well understood process of photosynthesis. Algae are rich in lipids and other combustible elements and Aquaflow is developing technology that will allow these elements to be extracted in a cost effective way. The proposed process is the subject of a provisional patent. Although algae are good at taking most of the nutrients out of sewage, too much algae can taint the water and make it smell. So, councils have to find a way of cleaning up the excess algae in their sewerage outflows and then either dispose of it or find alternative uses for it. And that's where Aquaflow comes in.

G   Unlike some bio-fuels which require crops to be specially grown and thereby compete for land use with food production, and use other scarce resources of fuel, chemicals and fertiliser, the source for algae-based bio-diesel already exists extensively and the process produces a sustainable net energy gain by capturing free solar energy from the sun.

Questions 1–5

Reading Passage 2 has seven paragraphs, **A–G**.

Which paragraph contains the following information?

*Write the correct letter, **A–G**, in boxes 1–5 on your answer sheet.*

1. It is unnecessary to modify vehicles driven by bio-diesel.
2. Some algae are considered edible plants.
3. Algae could be part of a sustainable and recycled source.
4. Algae bio-diesel is superior to other bio-fuels in a lot of ways.
5. Overgrown algea can also be a potential threat to environment.

核心词汇

A 段

fill up 填补；装满；堵塞
derive from 来源于……
sewage ['suːɪdʒ] *n.* 污水；下水道；污物

B 段

potential [pəˈtenʃəl] *n.* 潜能；可能性；电势 *adj.* 潜在的；可能的；势的

C 段

indigenous [ɪnˈdɪdʒɪnəs] *adj.* 本土的，土著的
extract from 从……提取，从……取出

D 段

conventional [kəˈvenʃənl] *adj.* 传统的；常规的，守旧的

E 段

on a large scale 大规模地
scale [skeɪl] *n.* 规模，范围，程度 *vi.* 衡量；攀登 *vt.* 测量；攀登；缩放
aquaculture [ˈækwəkʌltʃə(r)] *n.* 水产养殖；水产业
alternative [ɔːlˈtɜːnətɪv] *n.* 二中择一；可供替代的选择 *adj.* 供选择的；选择性的，可替代的

F 段

convert into 使转变；把……转化成
combustible [kəmˈbʌstəbl] *adj.* 易燃的；可燃的
excess [ɪkˈses] *adj.* 额外的，过量的 *n.* 超额，过度，过量 [拓] **excessive** *adj.* 过多的，过度的

G 段

scarce [skeəs] *adj.* 缺乏的，不足的；稀有的 *adv.* 仅仅；几乎不；几乎没有 [拓] **scarcity** *n.* 不足，缺乏
extensively [ɪkˈstensɪvli] *adv.* 广阔地；广大地 [拓] **extensive** *adj.* 广泛的；大量的；广阔的

题目

superior [suːˈpɪəriə(r)] *adj.* 出众的，优秀的 [拓] **superior...to...** 优于，比……优越

高频同义替换

modify	▶	alter, improve
sustainable	▶	renewable, recycled
threat	▶	danger, intimidation

题目解析

1. 定位词：unnecessary to modify vehicles
   文中对应点：D 段第一句
   题目解析：题干说，不需要对生物柴油驱动的车辆进行改装。由 unnecessary to modify vehicles 定位到 D 段第一句 "Blended with conventional mineral diesel, bio-diesel can run vehicles without the need for vehicle modifications."。其中，without the need for vehicle modifications 与 unnecessary to modify vehicles 为同义替换。句意为，与传统的矿物柴油混合，汽车可以不进行改装就能使用生物柴油。因此答案为 D。

2. 定位词：edible plants
   文中对应点：E 段第四句
   题目解析：题干说，有些藻类被认为是可食用植物。由 edible plants 定位到 E 段第四句 "Naturally growing seaweeds are an important source of food, especially in Asia."。其中，source of food 对应 edible plants。句意为，自然生长的海藻为重要的食物来源，尤其是在亚洲。因此答案为 E。

3. 定位词：sustainable, recycled source
   文中对应点：C 段第一、五句
   题目解析：题干说，藻类可能是可持续再生资源的一部分。由定位词 sustainable 定位到 C 段第一句 "Bio-diesel based on algae could eventually become a sustainable, low cost, cleaner burning fuel alternative for New Zealand, powering family cars, trucks, buses and boats." 由定位词 recycled source 定位到 C 段第五句 "It is a renewable indigenous resource ideally suited to the production of fuel and other useful by-products."。其中，sustainable 在 C 段第一句原文再现，recycled source 与 C 段第五句中的 renewable resource 对应。C 段第一句意为，以藻类为基础的生物柴油最终可能成为新西兰可持续的、低成本的、更清洁的燃烧燃料替代品，为家庭轿车、卡车、公共汽车和船只提供动力。C 段第五句意为，它是一种可再生的本地资源，非常适合生产燃料和其他有用的副产品。因此答案为 C。

4. 定位词：superior to, other bio-fuels
   文中对应点：G 段
   题目解析：题干说，藻类生物柴油在很多方面都优于其他生物燃料。由定位词 superior to, other bio-fuels 定位到 G 段 "Unlike some bio-fuels which require crops to be specially grown and thereby compete for land use with food production, and use other scarce resources of fuel, chemicals and fertiliser, the source for algae-based bio-diesel already exists extensively and the process

produces a sustainable net energy gain by capturing free solar energy from the sun."。其中，unlike 对应 superior to, some bio-fuels 对应 other bio-fuels。句意为，有些生物柴油需要特殊种植的农作物，因此需要占用土地和使用其他稀缺资源，而基于藻类的生物柴油大量存在，只要利用太阳能就能产生可持续的能量。由此可见，它比其他生物柴油更有优势，因此答案为 G。

5 定位词：overgrown, threat to environment
文中对应点：F 段倒数第三句
题目解析：题干说，过度生长的海藻也可能对环境构成潜在的威胁。由定位词 overgrown, threat to environment 定位到 F 段倒数第三句"Although algae are good at taking most of the nutrients out of sewage, too much algae can taint the water and make it smell."。其中，overgrown 与 too much 对应，threat to environment 与 taint the water 对应。句意为，太多藻类会污染水源并使水产生臭味。这与题干"对环境造成潜在威胁"的意思一致，因此答案为 F。

参考答案

1 D 2 E 3 C 4 G 5 F

Otter

A Otters have long, thin bodies and short legs — ideal for pushing through dense undergrowth or hunting in tunnels. An adult male may be up to 4 feet long and 30lbs. Females are smaller typically. The Eurasian otter's nose is about the smallest among the otter species and has a characteristic shape described as a shallow 'W'. An otter's tail (or rudder, or stem) is stout at the base and tapers towards the tip where it flattens. This forms part of the propulsion unit when swimming fast under water. Otter fur consists of two types of hair: stout guard hairs which form a waterproof outer covering, and under-fur which is dense and fine, equivalent to an otter's thermal underwear. The fur must be kept in good condition by grooming. Sea water reduces the waterproofing and insulating qualities of otter fur when salt water in the fur. This is why freshwater pools are important to otters living on the coast. After swimming, they wash the salts off in the pools and then squirm on the ground to rub dry against vegetation.

B Scent is used for hunting on land, for communication and for detecting danger. Otterine sense of smell is likely to be similar in sensitivity to dogs. Otters have small eyes and are probably short-sighted on land. But they do have the ability to modify the shape of the lens in the eye to make it more spherical, and hence overcome the refraction of water. In clear water and good light otters can hunt fish by sight. The otter's eyes and nostrils are placed high on its head so that it can see and breathe even when the rest of the body is submerged. Underwater, the otter holds its legs against the body, except for steering, and the hind end of the body is flexed in a series of vertical undulations. River otters have webbing which extends for much of the length of each digit, though not to the very end. Giant otters and sea otters have even more prominent webs, while the Asian short-clawed otter has no webbing — they hunt for shrimps in ditches and paddy fields so they don't need the swimming speed. Otter ears are tiny for streamlining, but they still have very sensitive hearing and are protected by valves which close them against water pressure.

C A number of constraints and preferences limit suitable habitats for otters. Water is a must and the rivers must be large enough to support a healthy population of fish. Being such shy and wary creatures, they will prefer territories where man's activities do not impinge greatly. Of course, there must also be no other otter already in residence — this has only become significant again recently as populations start to recover. Coastal otters have a much more abundant food supply and ranges for males and females may be just a few kilometres of coastline. Because male ranges are usually larger a male otter may find his range overlaps with two or three females — not bad! Otters will eat anything that they can get hold of — there are records of sparrows and snakes and slugs being gobbled. Apart from fish the most common prey are crayfish, crabs and water birds. Small mammals are occasionally taken, most commonly rabbits but sometimes even moles.

D Eurasian otters will breed anytime there food is readily available. In places where condition is more severe, Sweden for example, where the lakes are frozen for much of winter, cubs are born in spring. This ensures that they are well grown before severe weather returns. In the Shetlands, cubs are born in summer when fish is more abundant. Though otters can breed every year, some do not. Again, this depends on food availability. Other factors such as food range and quality of the female may have an effect. Gestation for Eurasian otter is 63 days, with the exception of Lutra canadensis whose embryos may undergo delayed implantation. Otters normally give birth in more secure dens to avoid disturbances. Nests are lined with bedding to keep the cubs warm while mummy is away feeding.

E Litter size varies between 1 and 5. For some unknown reasons, coastal otters tend to produce smaller litters. At five weeks they open their eyes — a tiny cub of 700g. At seven weeks they're weaned onto solid food. At ten weeks they leave the nest, blinking into daylight for the first time. After three months they finally meet the water and learn to swim. After eight months they are hunting, though the mother still provides a lot of food herself. Finally, after nine months she can chase them all away with a clear conscience, and relax — until the next fella shows up.

F The plight of the British otter was recognised in the early 60s, but it wasn't until the late 70s that the chief cause was discovered. Pesticides, such as dieldrin and aldrin, were first used in 1955 in agriculture and other industries — these chemicals are very persistent and had already been recognised as the cause of huge declines in the population of peregrine falcons, sparrow hawks and other predators. The pesticides entered the river systems and the food chain — micro-organisms, fish and finally otters, with every step increasing the concentration of the chemicals. From 1962 the chemicals were phased out, but while some species recovered quickly, otter numbers did not — and continued to fall into the 80s. This was probably due mainly to habitat destruction and road deaths. Acting on populations fragmented by the sudden decimation in the 50s and 60s, the loss of just a handful of otters in one area can make an entire population unviable and spell the end.

G Otter numbers are recovering all around Britain — populations are growing again in the few areas where they had remained and have expanded from those areas into the rest of the country. This is almost entirely due to legislation, conservation efforts, slowing down and reversing the destruction of suitable otter habitat and reintroductions from captive breeding programmes. Releasing captive-bred otters is seen by many as a last resort. The argument runs that where there is no suitable habitat for them they will not survive after release and where there is suitable habitat, natural populations should be able to expand into the area. However, reintroducing animals into a fragmented and fragile population may add just enough impetus for it to stabilise and expand, rather than die out. This is what the Otter Trust accomplished in Norfolk, where the otter population may have been as low as twenty animals at the beginning of the 1980s. The Otter Trust has now finished its captive breeding programme entirely, great news because it means it is no longer needed.

Questions 1–8

The passage has seven paragraphs, **A–G**.

Which paragraph contains the following information?

*Write the correct letter, **A–G**, in boxes 1–8 on your answer sheet.*

NB   You may use any letter more than once.

1   social characteristic and restraint on the territory of otter

2   the fitness-purpose of otter's body

3   conservation and law that can really make a difference

4   the maturation stages of baby otters' development

5   the mention of a degenerated sense from underwater to on land

6   breeding habit chosen as strategy for combating cold

7   controversy arised to argument and example for a conservation resort

8   failure in recovering project due to agricultural practice around habitat

核心词汇

A 段

otter ['ɒtə(r)] *n.* 水獭

stout [staʊt] *n.* 结实的

thermal ['θɜːml] *adj.* 热量的

insulate ['ɪnsjuleɪt] *v.* 使绝缘，使隔热

squirm [skwɜːm] *v.* 蠕动

B 段

spherical ['sferɪkl] *adj.* 球形的

refraction [rɪ'frækʃn] *n.* 折射

nostril ['nɒstrəl] *n.* 鼻孔

submerged [səb'mɜːdʒd] *adj.* 水下的

steer [stɪə(r)] *v.* 掌舵

hind [haɪnd] *adj.* 后部的

prominent ['prɒmɪnənt] *adj.* 突出的，显著的

streamline ['striːmlaɪn] *v.* 使成流线型

valve [vælv] *n.* 瓣膜

C 段

impinge [ɪm'pɪndʒ] *v.* 侵犯

mole [məʊl] *n.* 鼹鼠

D 段

breed [briːd] *v.* 繁殖

cub [kʌb] *n.* 幼兽

embryo ['embriəʊ] *n.* 胚胎

implantation [ˌɪmplɑːn'teɪʃn] *n.* 移植

E 段

wean [wiːn] *v.* 使断奶

a clear conscience 问心无愧

F 段

phase out 逐步淘汰

G 段

fragmented ['frægməntɪd] *adj.* 碎片的；分裂的

legislation [ˌledʒɪsˈleɪʃn] *n.* 立法
conservation [ˌkɒnsəˈveɪʃən] *n.* 保护

题目

restrain [rɪˈstreɪn] *n.* 限制
territory [ˈterətri] *n.* 领地

高频同义替换

describe	▸	represent, trace, figure, depict
groom	▸	clean, train, dress up
detect	▸	explore, perceive, discover
prefer	▸	would rather, affect, fancy
abundant	▸	ample, plentiful, luxurious
availability	▸	validity, practicality, right
implantation	▸	transplantation, infusion
provide	▸	afford, furnish, supply, offer
recognise	▸	accept, identify, acknowledge
finish	▸	accomplish, achieve, complete

题目解析

1 定位词：restraint, territory
文中对应点：C 段第一句
题目解析：题干说，水獭领地的社会特征和约束。由定位词 restraint, territory 定位到 C 段第一句 "A number of constraints and preferences limit suitable habitats for otters."。其中，constraints 与 restraint 为同义替换；suitable habitats 与 territory 对应。句意为，许多约束和偏好限制了水獭的适宜居住地。因此答案为 C。

2 定位词：otter's body, fitness-purpose
文中对应点：A 段第一句
题目解析：题干说，水獭身体的健康目的。由定位词 otter's body 定位到 A 段第一句 "Otters have long, thin bodies and short legs — ideal for pushing through dense undergrowth or hunting in tunnels."。其中，otter's body 与 long, thin bodies and short legs 对应，ideal for 与 fitness-purpose 对应。句意为，水獭有细长的身体和短腿——这是一种理想的方式，可以穿过茂密的灌木丛或在隧道中狩猎。因此答案为 A。

3 定位词：conservation, law

文中对应点：G 段第二句

题目解析：题干说，保护和法律确实能带来改变。由 conservation, law 定位到 G 段第二句 "This is almost entirely due to legislation, conservation efforts, slowing down and reversing the destruction of suitable otter habitat and reintroductions from captive breeding programmes."。其中，legislation 与 law 对应，conservation 为原文重现。句意为，这几乎完全是由于立法、保护行动、减缓和逆转对水獭的适宜栖息地的破坏和圈养繁殖计划的重新引入。因此答案为 G。

4 定位词：maturation stages

文中对应点：E 段第三到末七句

题目解析：题干说，婴儿水獭发育的成熟阶段。由定位词 maturation stages 定位到 E 段第三到末句 "At five weeks they open their eyes — a tiny cub of 700g. At seven weeks they're weaned onto solid food. At ten weeks they leave the nest, blinking into daylight for the first time. After three months they finally meet the water and learn to swim. After eight months they are hunting, though the mother still provides a lot of food herself. Finally, after nine months she can chase them all away with a clear conscience, and relax — until the next fella shows up."。从 At five weeks... At seven weeks... At ten weeks... After three months... After eight months... Finally, after nine months... 的描述可以看出水獭发育的各阶段。因此答案为 E。

5 定位词：a degenerated sense

文中对应点：B 段第四句

题目解析：题干说，提及了一种从水下到陆地的退化的感观。由定位词 a degenerated sense 定位到 B 段第四句 "they do have the ability to modify the shape of the lens in the eye to make it more spherical, and hence overcome the refraction of water."。其中，the lens in the eye to make it more spherical 对应 a degenerated sense。句意为，他们确实有能力改变眼睛的晶状体形状使其更加球形，从而克服水的折射。因此答案为 B。

6 定位词：habit, cold

文中对应点：D 段第二句

题目解析：题干说，作为对抗寒冷的策略的选育习性。由定位词 habit, cold 定位到 D 段第二句 "In places where condition is more severe, Sweden for example, where the lakes are frozen for much of winter, cubs are born in spring."。其中，habit 与 cubs 对应，cold 与 frozen，winter 对应。句意为，在条件更糟糕的地方，情况更严重，比如瑞典，冬天大部分时间湖泊都被冻住，幼崽在春天出生。因此答案为 D。

7 定位词：argument, a conservation resort

文中对应点：G 段第四句

题目解析：题干说，出现在一个保护度假地的论证和例子中的争议。由定位词 argument, a conservation resort 定位到 G 段第四句 "The argument runs that where there is no suitable habitat for them they will not survive after release and where there is suitable habitat, natural populations should be able to expand into the area."。其中，a conservation resort 对应 suitable habitat，指

的是水獭的保护栖息地。句意为，他们的论点是如果没有合适的栖息地，他们将无法在出生后存活，在有合适栖息地的地方，自然种群应该能够扩展到该地区。因此答案为 G。

8 定位词：agricultural practice
文中对应点：F 段第二及最后两句
题目解析：题干说，由于栖息地周围的农业实践导致恢复项目的失败。由定位词 agricultural practice 定位到 F 段第二句 "Pesticides, such as dieldrin and aldrin, were first used in 1955 in agriculture and other industries — these chemicals are very persistent and had already been recognised as the cause of huge declines in the population of peregrine falcons, sparrow hawks and other predators."。其中，Pesticides...were first used 对应 agricultural practice。句意为，杀虫剂，如狄氏剂和艾氏剂，在 1955 年首次用于农业和其他行业——这些化学物质非常持久，已经被认为是游隼、麻雀鹰和其他食肉动物数量急剧下降的原因。接着后两句中的 did not—and continued to fall into the 80s，habitat destruction and road deaths，the loss 等描述表明 recovering project 的失败（failure）。因此答案为 F。

参考答案

1 C **2** A **3** G **4** E **5** B **6** D **7** G **8** F

Knowledge in Medicine

A What counts as knowledge? What do we mean when we say that we know something? What is the status of different kinds of knowledge? In order to explore these questions we are going to focus on one particular area of knowledge — medicine.

B How do you know when you are ill? This may seem to be an absurd question. You know you are ill because you feel ill; your body tells you that you are ill. You may know that you feel pain or discomfort but knowing you are ill is a bit more complex. At times, people experience the symptoms of illness, but in fact they are simply tired or over-worked or they may just have a hangover. At other times, people may be suffering from a disease and fail to be aware of the illness until it has reached a late stage in its development. So how do we know we are ill, and what counts as knowledge?

C Think about this example. You feel unwell. You have a bad cough and always seem to be tired. Perhaps it could be stress at work, or maybe you should give up smoking. You feel worse. You visit the doctor who listens to your chest and heart, takes your temperature and blood pressure, and then finally prescribes antibiotics for your cough.

D Things do not improve but you struggle on thinking you should pull yourself together, perhaps things will ease off at work soon. A return visit to your doctor shocks you. This time the doctor, drawing on years of training and experience, diagnoses pneumonia. This means that you will need bed rest and a considerable time off work. The scenario is transformed. Although you still have the same symptoms, you no longer think that these are caused by pressure at work. You now have proof that you are ill. This is the result of the combination of your own subjective experience and the diagnosis of someone who has the status of a medical expert. You have a medically authenticated diagnosis and it appears that you are seriously ill; you know you are ill and have evidence upon which to base this knowledge.

E This scenario shows many different sources of knowledge. For example, you decide to consult the doctor in the first place because you feel unwell — this is personal knowledge about your own body. However, the doctor's expert diagnosis is based on experience and training, with sources of knowledge as diverse as other experts, laboratory reports, medical textbooks and years of experience.

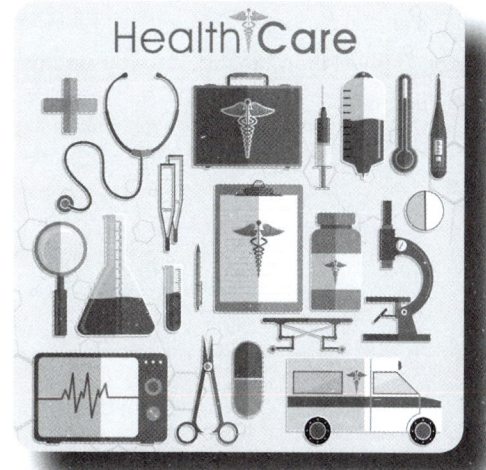

F One source of knowledge is the experience of our own bodies; the personal knowledge we have of changes that might be significant, as well as the subjective experience of pain and physical distress. These experiences are mediated by other forms of knowledge such as the words we have available to describe our experience and the common sense of our families and friends as well as that drawn from popular culture. Over the past decade, for example, Western culture has seen a significant emphasis on stress-related illness in the media. Reference to being 'stressed out' has become a common response in daily exchanges in the workplace and has become part of popular common-sense knowledge. It is thus not surprising that we might seek such an explanation of physical symptoms of discomfort.

G We might also rely on the observations of others who know us. Comments from friends and family such as 'you do look ill' or 'that's a bad cough' might be another source of knowledge. Complementary health practices, such as holistic medicine, produce their own sets of knowledge upon which we might also draw in deciding the nature and degree of our ill health and about possible treatments.

H Perhaps the most influential and authoritative source of knowledge is the medical knowledge provided by the general practitioner. We expect the doctor to have access to expert knowledge. This is socially sanctioned. It would not be acceptable to notify our employer that we simply felt too unwell to turn up for work or that our faith healer, astrologer, therapist or even our priest thought it was not a good idea. We need an expert medical diagnosis in order to obtain the necessary certificate if we need to be off work for more than the statutory self-certification period. The knowledge of the medical sciences is privileged in this respect in contemporary Western culture. Medical practitioners are also seen as having the required expert knowledge that permits them legally to prescribe drugs and treatment to which patients would not otherwise have access. However there is a range of different knowledge upon which we draw when making decisions about our own state of health.

I However, there is more than existing knowledge in this little story; new knowledge is constructed within it. Given the doctor's medical training and background, she may hypothesise 'Is this now pneumonia?' and then proceed to look for evidence about it. She will use observations and instruments to assess the evidence and — critically — interpret it in the light of her training and experience. This results in new knowledge and new experience both for you and for the doctor. This will then be added to the doctor's medical knowledge and may help in future diagnosis of pneumonia.

Questions 1–8

Reading Passage 4 has nine paragraphs, **A–I**.

Which paragraph contains the following information?

*Write the correct letter, **A–I**, in boxes 1–8 on your answer sheet.*

NB *You may use any letter more than once.*

1 The contrast between the nature of personal judgment and the nature of doctor

2 The reference of culture about pressure

3 Sick leave will not be permitted if employees are without the professional diagnosis

4 How doctors are regarded in the society

5 The symptom of the patients can be added as new information

6 What the situation will be if we come across knowledge from non-specialised outer sources

7 An example of collective judgment from personal experience and professional doctor

8 A reference about those people who do not realise their illness

核心词汇

A 段

count as 算作，看作
status ['steɪtəs] *n*. 重要性；社会地位，法律地位；身份，状况

B 段

absurd [əb'sɜːd] *adj*. 愚蠢的，荒谬的，荒唐的 [拓] absurdity *n*. 荒诞；悖理
symptom ['sɪmptəm] *n*. 症状；征兆

C 段

prescribe [prɪ'skraɪb] *vt*. 给……开处方；规定，指定 [拓] prescription *n*. 处方，药方；处方药；治疗方法
antibiotics [ˌæntibaɪ'ɒtɪks] *n*. 抗生素

D 段

pull oneself together 控制自己的情绪，让自己冷静
ease off 减轻；缓和
draw on 动用，利用
diagnose ['daɪəgnəʊz] *vt*. 诊断；判断 [拓] diagnosis *n*. 诊断
pneumonia [njuː'məʊniə] *n*. 肺炎
scenario [sə'nɑːriəʊ] *n*. 可能发生的事，可能出现的情况；剧情梗概
transform [træs'fɔːm] *vt*. 使变形；使改观；使转化
subjective [səb'dʒektɪv] *adj*. 主观的；主观想象的；主语的

H 段

statutory ['stætʃətri] *adj*. 依照法令的；法定的

I 段

hypothesise [haɪ'pɒθəsaɪz] *v*. 假定，假设

高频同义替换

personal ▸	subjective, individual, own
pressure ▸	stress, burden, tension
permit ▸	allow, approve, endorse
come across ▸	encounter, meet, see, discover
collective ▸	joint, combined, mutual, shared
realise ▸	be aware of, recognise, understand

题目解析

1 **定位词**：contrast, personal judgment, doctor

文中对应点：C 段第四句和最后一句

题目解析：题干说，个人判断和医生诊断的对比。由定位词 contrast, personal judgment, doctor 定位到 C 段第四句 "Perhaps it could be stress at work, or maybe you should give up smoking." 和 C 段最后一句 "You visit the doctor who listens to your chest and heart, takes your temperature and blood pressure, and then finally prescribes antibiotics for your cough."。其中，C 段第四句中的内容为个人判断，与题干中的 personal judgment 对应，doctor 在 C 段最后一句原文再现。C 段第四句意为，（咳嗽）可能是工作上有压力，也可能是你应该戒烟了。C 段最后一句意为，你去看医生，医生则会听听你的胸腔和心跳，给你测体温、量血压，最后给你开抗生素治疗咳嗽。由此可以看出对于咳嗽和疲惫，个人的判断和医生的判断是截然不同的，符合题干中的 contrast，因此答案为 C。

2 **定位词**：culture, pressure

文中对应点：F 段第三、四句

题目解析：题干说，关于压力的文化。由定位词 culture, pressure 定位到 F 段第三、四句 "Over the past decade, for example, Western culture has seen a significant emphasis on stress-related illness in the media. Reference to being 'stressed out' has become a common response in daily exchanges in the workplace and has become part of popular common-sense knowledge."。其中，stressed out 对应 pressure，Western culture 对应 culture。句意为，在过去的 10 年中，西方文化在媒体中非常强调与压力相关的疾病。"压力过大"已经成为工作场所日常交流的一个普遍反应，也已是大众常识的一部分。因此答案为 F。

3 **定位词**：sick leave, not be permitted, professional diagnosis

文中对应点：H 段第四、五句

题目解析：题干说，如果员工没有专业诊断是不允许请病假的。由 sick leave, not be permitted, professional diagnosis 定位到 H 段第四、五句 "It would not be acceptable to notify our employer that we simply felt too unwell to turn up for work or that our faith healer, astrologer, therapist or even our priest thought it was not a good idea. We need an expert medical diagnosis in order to obtain the necessary certificate if we need to be off work for more than the statutory self-certification period."。其中，not be acceptable 对应 not be permitted，expert medical diagnosis 对应 professional diagnosis，too unwell to turn up for work 对应 sick leave。句意为，告诉你的老板说你或你的信仰治疗师、占星家、理疗师甚至是牧师觉得你身体不好无法上班是不能被接受的。如果我们需要请假的时间超过了法定自行验证的时间，那就需要一份专业的医学诊断来获得必要的请假证明。因此答案为 H。

4 **定位词**：doctors, regarded, in the society

文中对应点：H 段第二、三句

题目解析：题干说，医生在社会上是如何被看待的。由 doctors 和 regarded 定位到 H 段第二、三句 "We expect the doctor to have access to expert knowledge. This is socially sanctioned."。其中，socially 对应 in the society，sanctioned 对应 regarded。句意为，我们期待医生拥有专业知识。

这是全社会都认可的。因此答案为 H。

5. 定位词：new information, be added
   文中对应点：I 段最后一句
   题目解析：题干说，病人的症状可以作为新信息被加入。由 new information, be added 定位到 I 段最后一句 "This will then be added to the doctor's medical knowledge and may help in future diagnosis of pneumonia."。其中，the doctor's medical knowledge 对应 new information。句意为，这会被加入到医生的医疗知识中，可能对于未来的肺炎诊断有所帮助。因此答案为 I。

6. 定位词：non-specialised outer sources
   文中对应点：G 段第一、二句
   题目解析：题干说，如果我们获取了非专业的外部来源的知识时会出现什么样的情形。由 non-specialised outer sources 定位到 G 段第一、二句 "We might also rely on the observations of others who know us. Comments from friends and family such as 'you do look ill' or 'that's a bad cough' might be another source of knowledge."。其中，comments from friends and family 对应 non-specialised outer sources。句意为，我们可能也会依靠那些了解我们的其他人的观察。朋友和家人的话可能也是另外的知识来源，比如 "你看起来像是生病了" 或 "咳嗽非常严重"。因此答案为 G。

7. 定位词：collective judgment, personal experience, professional doctor
   文中对应点：D 段倒数第二句
   题目解析：题干说，个人经验和专业医生共同判断的例子。由 collective judgment, personal experience, professional doctor 定位到 D 段倒数第二句 "This is the result of the combination of your own subjective experience and the diagnosis of someone who has the status of a medical expert."。其中，subjective experience 对应 personal experience，someone who has the status of a medical expert 对应 professional doctor，combination 对应 collective judgment。句意为，这是你的主观经验和医学专家诊断结合起来的结果。因此答案为 D。

8. 定位词：those people, do not realise their illness
   文中对应点：B 段倒数第二句
   题目解析：题干说，关于那些没有意识到自己生病的人。由 those people, do not realise their illness 定位到 B 段倒数第二句 "At other times, people may be suffering from a disease and fail to be aware of the illness until it has reached a late stage in its development."。其中，people 对应 those people，fail to be aware of the illness 对应 do not realise their illness 为同义替换。句意为，有时，人们可能已经生病，但没能意识到正在生病，直到发展到了晚期。因此答案为 B。

参考答案

1 C 2 F 3 H 4 I 5 I 6 G 7 D 8 B

Man or Machine

A   During July 2003, the Museum of Science in Cambridge, Massachusetts exhibited what Honda calls 'the world's most advanced humanoid robot', ASIMO (the Advanced Step in Innovative Mobility). Honda's brainchild is on tour in North America and delighting audiences wherever it goes. After 17 years in the making, ASIMO stands at four feet tall, weighs around 115 pounds and looks like a child in an astronaut's suit. Though it is difficult to see ASIMO's face at a distance, on closer inspection it has a smile and two large eyes that conceal cameras. The robot cannot work autonomously — its actions are 'remote controlled' by scientists through the computer in its backpack. Yet watching ASMIO perform at a show in Massachusetts it seemed uncannily human. The audience cheered as ASIMO walked forwards and backwards, side to side and up and downstairs. After the show, a number of people told me that they would like robots to play more of a role in daily life — one even said that the robot would be like 'another person'.

B   While the Japanese have made huge strides in solving some of the engineering problems of human kinetics and bipedal movements, for the past 10 years scientists at MIT's former Artificial Intelligence (AI) lab recently renamed the Computer Science and Artificial Intelligence Laboratory), CSAIL have been making robots that can behave like humans and interact with humans. One of MIT's robots, Kismet, is an anthropomorphic head and has two eyes (complete with eyelids), ears, a mouth, and eyebrows. It has several facial expressions, including happy, sad, frightened and disgusted. Human interlocutors are able to read some of the robot's facial expressions, and often change their behaviour towards the machine as a result — for example, playing with it when it appears 'sad'. Kismet is now in MIT's museum, but the ideas developed here continue to be explored in new robots.

C   Cog (short for Cognition) is another pioneering project from MIT's former AI lab. Cog has a head, eyes, two arms, hands and a torso — and its proportions were originally measured from the body of a researcher in the lab. The work on Cog has been used to test theories of embodiment and developmental robotics, particularly getting a robot to develop intelligence by responding to its environment via sensors, and to learn through these types of interactions.

D   MIT is getting furthest down the road to creating human-like and interactive robots. Some scientists argue that ASIMO is a great engineering feat but not an intelligent machine — because it is unable to interact autonomously with unpredicted abilities in its environment in meaningful ways, and learn from experience. Robots like Cog and Kismet and new robots at MIT's CSAIL and media lab, however, are beginning to do this.

E   These are exciting developments. Creating a machine that can walk, make gestures and learn from its environment is an amazing achievement. And watch this space: these achievements are likely rapidly to be improved upon. Humanoid robots could have a plethora of uses in society, helping to free people from everyday tasks. In Japan, for example, there is an aim to create robots that can do the tasks similar to an average human, and also act in more sophisticated situations as firefighters, astronauts or medical assistants to the elderly in the workplace and in homes — partly in order to counterbalance the effects of an ageing population.

F   Such robots say much about the way in which we view humanity, and they bring out the best and worst of us. On one hand, these developments express human creativity — our ability to invent, experiment, and to extend our control over the world. On the other hand, the aim to create a robot like a human being is spurred on by dehumanised ideas — by the sense that human companionship can be substituted by machines; that humans lose their humanity when they interact with technology; or that we are little more than surface and ritual behaviours, that can be simulated with metal and electrical circuits.

Questions 1–6

Reading Passage 5 has six paragraphs, **A–F**.

Which paragraph contains the following information?

Write the correct letter, **A–F**, in boxes 1–6 on your answer sheet.

NB You may use any letter more than once.

1 different ways of using robots

2 a robot whose body has the same proportion as that of an adult

3 the fact that human can be copied and replaced by robots

4 a comparison between ASIMO from Honda and other robots

5 the pros and cons of creating robots

6 a robot that has eyebrows

核心词汇

A 段

humanoid [ˈhjuːmənɔɪd] *n.* 人形机器人；类人动物
brainchild [ˈbreɪntʃaɪld] *n.* 思想结晶；创作成果
delight [dɪˈlaɪt] *v.* 使……感到高兴，使……感到愉快
backpack [ˈbækpæk] *n.* 背囊，背包
uncannily [ʌnˈkænɪli] *adj.* 奇怪地，离奇地；费解地

B 段

kinetics [kɪˈnetɪks] *n.* 动力学
bipedal [ˌbaɪˈpiːdl] *adj.* 双足行走的
anthropomorphic [ˌænθrəpəˈmɔːfɪk] *adj.* 人格化的，拟人的
interlocutor [ˌɪntəˈlɒkjətə(r)] *n.* 谈话者，参加对话者

C 段

pioneering [ˌpaɪəˈnɪərɪŋ] *adj.* 开创性的，先驱性的
torso [ˈtɔːsəʊ] *n.* （人体的）躯干
proportion [prəˈpɔːʃn] *adj.* 比例
embodiment [ɪmˈbɒdimənt] *n.* （品质，思想等的）典型，化身
sensor [ˈsensə(r)] *n.* （探测光、热等的）传感器，探测设备

E 段

a plethora of 大量；过剩
counterbalance [ˈkaʊntəˌbæl(ə)ns] *v.* 抗衡；抵消

F 段

spur [spɜː(r)] *v.* 促进，加速；推动
dehumanised [ˌdiːˈhjuːmənaɪzd] *adj.* 无人性的
substitute [ˈsʌbstɪtjuːt] *v.* 替代，替换

题目

pros and cons 正反面，赞成与反对

高频同义替换

suit	▸	clothes, coat; lawsuit
action	▸	movement, function, campaign

facial	▶	external, surface, superficial
particularly	▶	specifically, extra, especially
interaction	▶	reciprocity, mutual effect
improve	▶	further, gain, accelerate, promote
spur	▶	stimulate, encourage, motivate
simulate	▶	pattern, imitate, mimic

题目解析

1 定位词：different ways of using

文中对应点：E 段第四句

题目解析：题干说，使用机器人的不同方式。由 different ways of using 定位到 E 段第四句 "Humanoid robots could have a plethora of uses in society, helping to free people from everyday tasks."。其中，different ways of using 对应 a plethora of uses，using 与 uses 为同根词。句意为，类人机器人能在社会上具有广泛的用途：把人们从日常琐事中解放出来。因此答案为 E。

2 定位词：proportion, adult

文中对应点：C 段第二句

题目解析：题干说，一个身体与成人比例一样的机器人。由 proportion，adult 定位到 C 段第二句 "Cog has a head, eyes, two arms, hands and a torso — and its proportions were originally measured from the body of a researcher in the lab."。其中，proportions 为 proportion 的复数，the body of a researcher in the lab 对应 adult。句意为，Cog 有头、眼睛、两条胳膊、手臂和躯干，其比例最早是由实验室研究员的身体测量而来的。因此答案为 C。

3 定位词：be copied, replaced by

文中对应点：F 段最后一句

题目解析：题干说，人类可以被机器人复制和取代的事实。由 be copied, replaced by 定位到 F 段最后一句 "On the other hand, the aim to create a robot like a human being is spurred on by dehumanised ideas — by the sense that human companionship can be substituted by machines; that humans lose their humanity when they interact with technology; or that we are little more than surface and ritual behaviours, that can be simulated with metal and electrical circuits."。其中，be substituted by 与 replaced by 为同义替换，be simulated with 对应 be copied。句意为，另一方面，创造类人机器人的目标被去个性化的理念所刺激。人类友情将让路于机器。当人类与技术互动时，人类失去了人性。或者说，我们人类不过是具有能够被钢铁和电路所取代的外表和仪式行为而已。因此答案为 F。

4 定位词：comparison, ASIMO

文中对应点：D 段第二、三句

题目解析：题干说，本田的 ASIMO 和其他机器人的比较。由 ASIMO 定位到 D 段第二、三句 "Some scientists argue that ASIMO is a great engineering feat but not an intelligent machine — because it is unable to interact autonomously with unpredicted abilities in its environment in meaningful ways, and learn from experience. Robots like Cog and Kismet and new robots at MIT's CSAIL and media lab, however, are beginning to do this."。其中，Cog, Kismet, new robots at MIT's 与 other robots 对应，ASIMO 为原文重现。句意为，有些科学家争辩道：ASIMO 是一个伟大的工程，但并不算是智力机器——因为它不能自动以有意义的方式与未知情况互动，也不能从经验中学习。但 Cog 和 Kismet 以及在 MIT 的 CSAIL 媒体实验室的新机器人却是可以自发学习的。因此答案为 D。

5　定位词：pros and cons
　　文中对应点：F 段第一句
　　题目解析：题干说，创造机器人的优点和缺点。由 pros and cons 定位到 F 段第一句 "Such robots say much about the way in which we view humanity, and they bring out the best and worst of us."。其中，the best and worst 与 pros and cons 对应。句意为，这些机器人证明了我们看待人性的方式，它们也表现出了我们人类中最好的和最差的方面。因此答案为 F。

6　定位词：eyebrows
　　文中对应点：B 段第二句
　　题目解析：题干说，一个有眉毛的机器人。由 eyebrows 定位到 B 段第二句 "One of MIT's robots, Kismet, is an anthropomorphic head and has two eyes (complete with eyelids), ears, a mouth, and eyebrows."。其中，eyebrows 为原文重现。句意为，Kismet 是 MIT 的拟人机器人，有一个像人一样的头，有两只眼睛（也有眼睑）、耳朵、嘴巴、眉毛。因此答案为 B。

参考答案

1 E　2 C　3 F　4 D　5 F　6 B

READING PASSAGE 6

Intelligence and Giftedness

A   In 1904 the French minister of education, facing limited resources for schooling sought a way to separate the unable from the merely lazy. Alfred Binet got the job of devising selection principles and his brilliant solution put a stamp on the study of intelligence and was the forerunner of intelligence tests still used today. He developed a thirty-problem test in 1905, which tapped several abilities related to intellect, such as judgment and reasoning, the test determined a given child's mental age, the test previously established a norm for children of a given physical age. (For example, five-year-olds on average get ten items correct.) Therefore, a child with a mental age of five should score 10, which would mean that he or she was functioning pretty much as others of that age, the child's mental age was then compared to his physical age.

B   A large disparity in the wrong direction (e.g. a child of nine with a mental age of four) might suggest inability rather than laziness and mean he or she was earmarked for special schooling. Binet, however, denied that the test was measuring intelligence, its purpose was simply diagnostic, for selection only. This message was however lost, and caused many problems and misunderstanding later.

C   Although Binet's test was popular, it was a bit inconvenient to deal with a variety of physical and mental ages. So in 1912 Wilhelm Stern suggested simplifying this by reducing the two to a single number, he divided the mental age by the physical age, and multiplied the result by 100. An average child, irrespective of age, would score 100, a number much lower than 100 would suggest the need for help, and one much higher would suggest a child well ahead of his peer.

D   This measurement is what is now termed the IQ (for intelligence quotient) score and it has evolved to be used to show how a person, adult or child, performed in relation to others. (The term IQ was coined by Lewis M. Terman, professor of psychology and education of Stanford University, in 1916. He had constructed an enormously influential revision of Binet's test, called the Stanford-Bind test, versions of which are still given extensively.)

E   The field studying intelligence and developing tests eventually coalesced into a sub-field of psychology called psychometrics (psycho for 'mind' and metrics for 'measurements'). The practical side of psychometrics (the development and use of tests) became widespread quite early, by 1917, when Einstein published his grand theory of relativity, mass-scale testing was already in use. Germany's unrestricted submarine warfare (which led to the sinking of the *Lusitania* in 1915) provoked the United States to finally enter the First World War in the same year. The military had to build up an army very quickly; it had two million inductees to sort out. Who would become officers and who enlisted men? Psychometricians developed two intelligence tests that helped sort all these people out, at least to some extent, this was the first major use of testing to decide who lived and who died, as officers were a lot safer on the battlefield, the tests themselves were given under horrendously bad conditions, and the examiners seemed to lack common sense, a lot of recruits simply had no idea what to do and in several sessions most inductees scored zero! The examiners also came up with the quite astounding conclusion from the testing that the average American adult's intelligence was equal to that of a thirteen-year-old!

F   Intelligence testing enforced political and social prejudice, their results were used to argue that Jews ought to be kept out of the United States because they were so intelligently inferior that they would pollute the racial mix; and blacks ought not to be allowed to be breed at all. And so abuse and test bias controversies continued to plague psychometrics.

G   Measurement is fundamental to science and technology, science often advances in leaps and bounds when measurement devices improve. Psychometrics has long tried to develop ways to gauge psychological qualities such as intelligence and more specific abilities, anxiety, extroversion, emotional stability, compatibility with marriage partner, and so on. Their scores are often given enormous weight, a single IQ measurement can take on a life of its own if teachers and parents see it as definitive. It became a major issue in the 70s, when court cases were launched to stop anyone from making important decisions based on IQ test scores. The main criticism was and still is that current tests don't really measure intelligence, whether intelligence can be measured at all is still controversial, some say it cannot others say that IQ tests are psychology's greatest accomplishments.

Questions 1–4

Reading Passage 6 has seven paragraphs, **A–G**.

Which paragraph contains the following information?

*Write the correct letter, **A–G**, in boxes 1–4 on your answer sheet.*

1   IQ is just one single factor of human characteristics.

2   Discussion of methodology behind Professor Stern's test.

3   Inadequacy of IQ test from Binet.

4   The definition of IQ was created by a professor.

核心词汇

A 段

devise [dɪˈvaɪz] *v.* 设计

forerunner [ˈfɔːrʌnə(r)] *n.* 先驱

B 段

disparity [dɪˈspærəti] *n.* 不一致

earmark [ˈɪɑːmɑːk] *v.* 指定……的用途；预先安排

C 段

irrespective of 不考虑某事物

E 段

coalesce [ˌkəʊəˈles] *v.* 合并，联合

psychometrics [saɪkə(ʊ)ˈmetrɪks] *n.* 心理测验学

submarine [ˌsʌbməˈriːn] *adj.* 水下的

provoke [prəˈvəʊk] *v.* 激起；唤起

inductee [ˌɪndʌkˈtiː] *n.* 应召入伍的士兵

horrendously [həˈrendəsli] *adv.* 骇人听闻地，可怕地

astounding [əˈstaʊndɪŋ] *adj.* 令人震惊的

F 段

inferior [ɪnˈfɪəriə(r)] *adj.* 差劲的

plague [pleɪɡ] *v.* 折磨

G 段

in leaps and bounds 迅速地

gauge [ɡeɪdʒ] *v.* 测量

extroversion [ˌekstrəˈvɜːʃn] *n.* 外向性

高频同义替换

judgment ▸	estimate, assessment
pretty ▸	relatively, fairly, comparatively, reasonably, considerably
inability ▸	incapacity, incompetency, disability
physical ▸	personal, material, natural
construct ▸	institute, frame, structure

| extent | ▶ | boundary, region, territory |
| case | ▶ | situation, circumstance, instance |

题目解析

1 定位词：human characteristics

文中对应点：G 段第二句

题目解析：题干说，智商只是人类特征的一个单一因素。由 human characteristics 定位到 G 段第二句 "Psychometrics has long tried to develop ways to gauge psychological qualities such as intelligence and more specific abilities, anxiety, extroversion, emotional stability, compatibility with marriage partner, and so on."。其中，psychological qualities 对应 human characteristics。句意为，长期以来，心理测量学一直试图发展各种方法来衡量心理素质，比如智力和更具体的能力、焦虑、外向、情绪稳定性、与婚姻伴侣的相容性等。因此答案为 G。

2 定位词：Professor Stern

文中对应点：C 段第二句

题目解析：题干说，Stern 教授的测试背后的方法论讨论。由 Stern 定位到 C 段第二句 "So in 1912 Wilhelm Stern suggested simplifying this by reducing the two to a single number, he divided the mental age by the physical age, and multiplied the result by 100."。其中，Wilhelm Stern 与 Professor Stern 对应。句意为，所以在 1912 年，Wilhelm Stern 建议通过将两者减少到一个数字来简化这个问题，他将精神年龄除以生理年龄并将结果乘以 100。因此答案为 C。

3 定位词：inadequacy, Binet

文中对应点：B 段第一句

题目解析：题干说，来自 Binet 的智商测试的不足。由 inadequacy, Binet 定位到 B 段第一句 "A large disparity in the wrong direction (e.g. a child of nine with a mental age of four) might suggest inability rather than laziness and mean he or she was earmarked for special schooling."。其中，a large disparity 与 inadequacy 对应。句意为，在错误的方向上有很大的差异（例如，一个九岁的孩子，精神年龄却为四岁）可能暗含着无能而不是懒惰，这意味着他或她被指定去接受特殊教育。因此答案为 B。

4 定位词：definition of IQ

文中对应点：D 段第二句

题目解析：题干说，IQ 的定义是由一位教授创造的。由 definition of IQ 定位到 D 段第二句 "The term IQ was coined by Lewis M. Terman, professor of psychology and education of Stanford university, in 1916."。其中，the term IQ 与 definition of IQ 对应。句意为，"IQ" 这个词是由斯坦福大学心理学和教育学教授 Lewis M. Terman 在 1916 年创造的。因此答案为 D。

参考答案

1 G　2 C　3 B　4 D

Optimism and Health

Mindset is all. How you start the year will set the template for 2009, and two scientifically backed character traits hold the key: optimism and resilience (if the prospect leaves you feeling pessimistically spineless, the good news is that you can significantly boost both of these qualities).

A Faced with 12 months of plummeting economics and rising human distress, staunchly maintaining a rosy view might seem deucedly Pollyannaish. But here we encounter the optimism paradox. As Brice Pitt, an emeritus professor of the psychiatry of old age at Imperial College, London, told me: optimists are unrealistic. Depressive people see things as they really are, but that is a disadvantage from an evolutionary point of view. Optimism is a piece of evolutionary equipment that carried us through millennia of setbacks.

B It has been known that optimism has something to do with the long life, and optimists have plenty to be happy about. In other words, if you can convince yourself that things will get better, the odds of it happening will improve — because you keep on playing the game. In this light, optimism 'is a habitual way of explaining your setbacks to yourself', reports Martin Seligman, the psychology professor and author of *Learned Optimism*. The research shows that when times get tough, optimists do better than pessimists — they succeed better at work, respond better to stress, suffer fewer depressive episodes and achieve more personal goals.

C Studies also show that belief can help with the financial pinch. Chad Wallens, a social forecaster at the Henley Centre who surveyed middle-class Britons' beliefs about income, has found that 'the people who feel wealthiest, and those who feel poorest, actually have almost the same amount of money at their disposal. Their attitudes and behaviour patterns, however, are different from one another.'

D Optimists have something else to be cheerful about — in general, they are more robust. For example, a study of 660 volunteers by the Yale University psychologist Dr Becca Levy, found that thinking positively adds an average of 7 years to your life. Other American research claims to have identified a physical mechanism behind this. A Harvard Medical School study of 670 men found that the optimists have significantly better lung function. The lead author, Dr Rosalind Wright, believes that attitude somehow strengthens the immune system. 'Preliminary studies on heart patients suggest that, by changing a person's outlook, you can improve their mortality risk,' she says.

E Few studies have tried to ascertain the proportion of optimists in the world. But a 1995 nationwide survey conducted for the American magazine *Adweek* found that about half the population counted themselves as optimists, with women slightly more apt than men (53 per cent versus 48 per cent) to see the sunny side.

F   Although some optimists may be accurate in their positive beliefs about the future, others may be unrealistic — their optimism is misplaced, according to American Psychological Association. Research shows that some smokers exhibit unrealistic optimism by underestimating their relative chances of experiencing disease. An important question is whether such unrealistic optimism is associated with risk-related attitudes and behaviour. We addressed this question by investigating if one's perceived risk of developing lung cancer, over and above one's objective risk, predicted acceptance of myths and other beliefs about smoking. Hierarchical regressions showed that those individuals who were unrealistically optimistic were more likely to endorse beliefs that there is no risk of lung cancer if one only smokes for a few years and that getting lung cancer depends on one's genes.

G   Of course, there is no guarantee that optimism will insulate you from the crunch's worst effects, but the best strategy is still to keep smiling and thank your lucky stars. Because (as every good sports coach knows) adversity is character-forming — so long as you practise the skills of resilience. Research among tycoons and business leaders shows that the path to success is often littered with failure: a record of sackings, bankruptcies and blistering castigations. But instead of curling into a foetal ball beneath the coffee table, they resiliently pick themselves up, learn from their pratfalls and march boldly towards the next opportunity.

H   The American Psychological Association defines resilience as the ability to adapt in the face of adversity, trauma or tragedy. A resilient person may go through difficulty and uncertainty, but he or she will doggedly bounce back.

I   Optimism is one of the central traits required in building resilience, say Yale University investigators in the Annual Review of Clinical Psychology. They add that resilient people learn to hold on to their sense of humour and this can help them to keep a flexible attitude when big changes of plan are warranted. The ability to accept your lot with equanimity also plays an important role, the study adds.

J   One of the best ways to acquire resilience is through experiencing a difficult childhood, the sociologist Steven Stack reports in the *Journal of Social Psychology*. For example, short men are less likely to commit suicide than tall guys, he says, because shorties develop psychological defense skills to handle the bullies and mickey — taking that their lack of stature attracts. By contrast, those who enjoyed adversity-free youths can get derailed by setbacks later on because they've never been inoculated against agro.

K   Learning to overcome your fears. If you are handicapped by having had a happy childhood, then practising proactive optimism can help you to become more resilient. Studies of resilient people show that they take more risks; they court failure and learn not to fear it. And despite being thick-skinned, resilient types are also more open than average to other people. Bouncing through knock backs is all part of the process. It's about optimistic risk-taking — being confident that people will like you. Simply smiling and being warm to people can help. It's an altruistic path to self-interest — and if it achieves nothing else, it will reinforce an age-old adage: hard times can bring out the best in you.

Questions 1–5

Look at the following opinions or deeds (Questions **1–5**) and the list of people or organisations below.

Match each opinion or deed with the correct person or organisation, **A–G**.

Write the correct letter, **A–G**, in boxes 1–5 on your answer sheet.

1   Different optimism results found according to gender.

2   There is no necessary relationship between happiness and money.

3   Excessive optimism may be incorrect in everyday life.

4   Optimists are advantageous for human evolution.

5   Occurrence of emergency assists resilient people in a positive way.

List of People or Organisations	
A	Brice Pitt
B	American Psychological Association
C	Martin Seligman
D	Chad Wallens of Henley Centre
E	Annual Review of Clinical Psychology
F	Steven Stack
G	American magazine *Adweek*

核心词汇

A 段

plummeting [ˈplʌmɪtɪŋ] *adj.* 直线下降的
staunchly [ˈstɔːntʃli] *adv.* 坚定地；忠实地
deucedly [ˈdjuːsɪdli] *adv.* 非常；过度地
Pollyannaish [ˌpɒliˈænɪʃ] *adj.* 盲目乐观的
paradox [ˈpærədɒks] *n.* 悖论；自相矛盾的人或事
emeritus [iˈmerɪtəs] *adj.* 退休的；名誉退休的
psychiatry [saɪˈkaɪətri] *n.* 精神病学；精神病治疗法
millennia [mɪˈleniə] *n.* 千年期（millennium 的复数）；一千年
setback [ˈsetbæk] *n.* 挫折；周折

B 段

pessimist [ˈpesɪmɪst] *n.* 悲观主义者
episode [ˈepɪsəʊd] *n.* 插曲；一段情节

C 段

pinch [pɪntʃ] *n.* 匮乏；少量
disposal [dɪˈspəʊzl] *n.* 处理；支配；清理；安排

D 段

robust [rəʊˈbʌst] *adj.* 强健的；粗野的
preliminary [prɪˈlɪmɪnəri] *adj.* 初步的；开始的；预备的
outlook [ˈaʊtlʊk] *n.* 展望；观点；景色
mortality [mɔːˈtæləti] *n.* 死亡数，死亡率

E 段

ascertain [ˌæsəˈteɪn] *v.* 确定，查明

F 段

perceived [pəˈsiːvd] *adj.* 感知到的；感观的
hierarchical regression　层序式的回归分析
endorse [ɪnˈdɔːs] *v.* 认可；签署；赞同

G 段

insulate [ˈɪnsjuleɪt] *v.* 隔离，使孤立；使绝缘，使隔热
adversity [ədˈvɜːsəti] *n.* 逆境；不幸；灾难；灾祸

resilience [rɪˈzɪliəns] *n.* 恢复力；弹力；顺应力
tycoon [taɪˈkuːn] *n.* 企业界大亨，巨头
castigation [ˌkæstɪˈɡeɪʃn] *n.* 惩罚；苛评；修订
foetal [ˈfiːtl] *adj.* 胎儿的；似胎儿的
pratfall [ˈprætfɔːl] *n.* 丢脸（或可笑）的失误

H 段

trauma [ˈtrɔːmə] *n.* 创伤
doggedly [ˈdɒɡɪdli] *adv.* 顽强地；固执地

I 段

lot [lɒt] *n.* 命运
equanimity [ˌekwəˈnɪməti] *n.* 平静；镇定

J 段

stature [ˈstætʃə(r)] *n.* 身高；身材
derail [dɪˈreɪl] *v.* 使出轨，使脱轨
inoculate [ɪˈnɒkjuleɪt] *v.* 接种；嫁接；灌输

K 段

proactive [ˌprəʊˈæktɪv] *adj.* 有前瞻性的；积极主动的
altruistic [ˌæltruˈɪstɪk] *adj.* 利他的；无私心的
reinforce [ˌriːɪnˈfɔːs] *v.* 加强，加固；强化；补充
adage [ˈædɪdʒ] *n.* 格言，谚语；箴言

高频同义替换

rise	▸	raise, arise, tower
maintain	▸	claim, submit; sustain, keep
setback	▸	frustration, drawback, defeat
suffer	▸	endure, stand, experience
identify	▸	confirm, recognise, ascertain
outlook	▸	viewpoint, scenery, perspective
accurate	▸	precise, mathematical, strict
associate	▸	company, combine, mix
adversity	▸	disaster, tragedy, evil, grief
failure	▸	defeat, losing, fault, trouble

题目解析

1 定位词：optimism results, gender
文中对应点：E 段第二句
题目解析：题干说，不同的乐观结果是根据性别得出的。根据 optimism results, gender 定位到 E 段第二句 "But a 1995 nationwide survey conducted for the American magazine *Adweek* found that about half the population counted themselves as optimists, with women slightly more apt than men (53 per cent versus 48 per cent) to see the sunny side."。其中，*Adweek* found that... 对应 optimism results，women 和 men 对应 gender。此处出现大写 American magazine *Adweek*，对应选项 G。

2 定位词：happiness, money
文中对应点：C 段第二句
题目解析：题干说，幸福与金钱没有必然的关系。根据 happiness, money 定位到 C 段第二句 "Chad Wallens, a social forecaster at the Henley Centre who surveyed middle-class Britons' beliefs about income, has found that 'the people who feel wealthiest, and those who feel poorest, actually have almost the same amount of money at their disposal."。句意为，亨利中心的社会预测家查德·沃伦斯调查了英国中产阶级对收入的看法。他发现，那些感觉最富有的人，以及那些感觉最贫穷的人，实际上拥有的钱几乎和他们的可支配收入差不多。言外之意则是，幸福（happiness）与金钱（money）没有必然的关系。此处出现大写 Chad Wallens 和 Henley Centre，对应选项 D。

3 定位词：excessive optimism, incorrect
文中对应点：F 段第一句
题目解析：题干说，过度乐观可能在日常生活中是不正确的。根据 excessive optimism, incorrect 定位到 F 段第一句 "Although some optimists may be accurate in their positive beliefs about the future, others may be unrealistic — their optimism is misplaced, according to American Psychological Association."。其中，others may be unrealistic 对应 excessive optimism，misplaced 对应 incorrect。句意为，美国心理协会的研究显示，尽管一些乐观主义者对未来的积极信念可能是准确的，但其他人可能是不现实的——他们的乐观主义是错误的。此处出现大写 American Psychological Association，对应选项 B。

4 定位词：optimists, human evolution
文中对应点：A 段最后一句
题目解析：题干说，乐观主义者对人类的进化是有利的。根据 human evolution 定位到 A 段最后一句 "Optimism is a piece of evolutionary equipment that carried us through millennia of setbacks."。其中，optimism 对应 optimists，evolutionary equipment 对应 human evolution。句意为，乐观是一种进化的品质，它带着我们经历了几千年的挫折。这个观点在 A 段第三句由 Brice Pitt 提出，对应选项 A。

5 定位词：resilient, a positive way

文中对应点：I 段第一句

题目解析：根据 resilient, a positive way 定位到 I 段第一句 "Optimism is one of the central traits required in building resilience, say Yale University investigators in the Annual Review of Clinical Psychology."。其中，resilience 为 resilient 的名词形式，optimism 对应题干中的 a positive way。此处出现大写 Annual Review of Clinical Psychology，对应选项 E。

参考答案

1 G **2** D **3** B **4** A **5** E

Implication of False Belief Experiments

A A considerable amount of research since the mid-1980s has been concerned with what has been termed children's theory of mind. This involves children's ability to understand that people can have different beliefs and representations of the world — a capacity that is shown by four years of age. Furthermore, this ability appears to be absent in children with autism. The ability to work out what another person is thinking is clearly an important aspect of both cognitive and social development. Furthermore, one important explanation for autism is that children suffering from this condition do not have a theory of mind (TOM). Consequently, the development of children's TOM has attracted considerable attention.

B Wimmer and Pemer devised a 'false belief task' to address this question. They used some toys to act out the following story. Maxi left some chocolate in a blue cupboard before he went out. When he was away his mother moved the chocolate to a green cupboard. Children were asked to predict where Maxi will look for his chocolate when he returns. Most children under four years gave the incorrect answer, which Maxi will look in the green cupboard. Those over four years tended to give the correct answer, which Maxi will look in the blue cupboard. The incorrect answers indicated that the younger children did not understand that Maxi's beliefs and representations no longer matched the actual state of the world, and they failed to appreciate that Maxi will act on the basis of his beliefs rather than the way that the world is actually organised.

C A simpler version of the Maxi task was devised by Baron Cohen to take account of criticisms that younger children may have been affected by the complexity and too much information of the story in the task described above. For example, the child is shown two dolls, Sally and Anne, who have a basket and a box, respectively. Sally also has a marble, which she places in her basket, and then leaves to take a walk. While she is out of the room, Anne takes the marble from the basket, eventually putting it in the box. Sally returns, and the child is then asked where Sally will look for the marble. The child passes the task if she answers that Sally will look in the basket, where she put the marble; the child fails the task if she answers that Sally will look in the box, where the child knows the marble is hidden, even though Sally cannot know, since she did not see it hidden there. In order to pass the task, the child must be able to understand that another's mental representation of the situation is different from their own, and the child must be able to predict behaviour based on that understanding. The results of research using false-belief tasks have been fairly consistent: most normally-developing children are unable to pass the tasks until around age four.

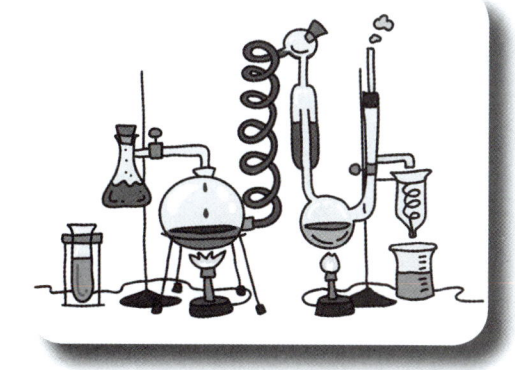

D Leslie argues that, before 18 months, children treat the world in a literal way and rarely demonstrate pretense. He also argues that it is necessary for the cognitive system to distinguish between what is pretend and what is real. If children were not able to do this, they would not be able to distinguish between imagination and reality. Leslie suggested that this pretend play becomes possible because of the presence of a decoupler that copies primary representations to secondary representations. For example, children, when pretending a banana is a telephone, would make a secondary representation of a banana. They would manipulate this representation and they would use their stored knowledge of 'telephone' to build on this pretense.

E There is also evidence that social processes play a part in the development of TOM. Meins and her colleagues have found that what they term mindmindedness in maternal speech to six-month-old infants is related to both security of attachment and TOM abilities. Mindmindedness involves speech that discusses infants' feelings and explains their behaviour in terms of mental states (e.g. you're feeling hungry).

F Lewis investigated older children living in extended families in Crete and Cyprus. They found that children who socially interact with more adults, who have more friends, and who have older siblings tend to pass TOM tasks at a slightly earlier age than other children. Furthermore, because young children are more likely to talk about their thoughts and feelings with peers than with their mothers, peer interaction may provide a special impetus to the development of a TOM. A similar point has been made by Dunn, who argues that peer interaction is more likely to contain pretend play and that it is likely to be more challenging because other children, unlike adults, do not make large adaptations to the communicative needs of other children.

G In addition, there has been concern that some aspects of the TOM approach underestimate children's understanding of other people. After all, infants will point to objects apparently in an effort to change a person's direction of gaze and interest; they can interact quite effectively with other people; they will express their ideas in opposition to the wishes of others; and they will show empathy for the feelings of others. All this suggests that they have some level of understanding that their own thoughts are different to those in another person's mind. Evidence to support this position comes from a variety of sources. When a card with a different picture on each side is shown to a child and an adult sitting opposite her, then three-year-olds understand that they see a different picture to that seen by the adult.

H Schatz studied the spontaneous speech of three-year-olds and found that these children used mental terms, and used them in circumstances where there was a contrast between, for example, not being sure where an object was located and finding it, or between pretending and reality. Thus the social abilities of children indicate that they are aware of the difference between mental states and external reality at ages younger than four.

I A different explanation has been put forward by Harris. He proposed that children use 'simulation'. This involves putting yourself in the other person's position, and then trying to predict what the other person would do. Thus success on false belief tasks can be explained by children trying to imagine what they would do if they were a character in the stories, rather than children being able to appreciate the beliefs of other people. Such thinking about situations that do not exist involves what is termed counterfactual reasoning.

Questions 1–7

Look at the following opinions or deeds (Questions **1–7**) and the list of people below.

Match each opinion or deed with the correct person, **A–G**.

Write the correct letter, **A–G**, in boxes 1–7 on your answer sheet.

List of People
A Baron Cohen
B Meins
C Wimmer and Perner
D Lewis
E Dunn
F Schatz
G Harris

1   gave an alternative explanation that children may not be understanding other's belief.

2   found that children under certain age can tell difference between reality and mentality.

3   designed an experiment and drew conclusion that young children under age of 4 were unable to comprehend the real state of the world.

4   found that children who get along with adults often comparatively got through test more easily.

5   revised an easier experiment ruling out the possibility that children might be influenced by sophisticated reasoning.

6   related social factor such as mother-child communication to capability act in TOM.

7   explained children are less likely to tell something interactive to their mothers than to their friends.

核心词汇

A 段
autism [ˈɔːtɪzəm] *n.* 孤独症；自我中心主义

B 段
devise [dɪˈvaɪz] *v.* 设计；想出；发明
appreciate [əˈpriːʃieɪt] *v.* 欣赏；感激

C 段
respectively [rɪˈspektɪvli] *adv.* 分别地；各自地，独自地

D 段
decoupler [diːˈkʌplə] *n.* 断开器，分离器
manipulate [məˈnɪpjuleɪt] *v.* 操纵；操作
pretense [prɪˈtens] *n.* 借口；虚假；炫耀

E 段
mindmindedness [ˌmaɪndˈmaɪndɪdnɪs] *n.* 将心比心
maternal [məˈtɜːnl] *adj.* 母亲的；母性的

F 段
sibling [ˈsɪblɪŋ] *n.* 兄弟姐妹
impetus [ˈɪmpɪtəs] *n.* 动力；促进；冲力

G 段
underestimate [ˌʌndərˈestɪmeɪt] *v.* 低估；看轻
empathy [ˈempəθi] *n.* 移情作用；执着

H 段
spontaneous [spɒnˈteɪniəs] *adj.* 自发的；自然的；无意识的
external [ɪkˈstɜːnl] *adj.* 外部的；表面的

I 段
simulation [ˌsɪmjuˈleɪʃn] *n.* 仿真；模拟；模仿
counterfactual [ˌkaʊntəˈfæktʃuəl] *adj.* 反事实的

题目
alternative [ɔːlˈtɜːnətɪv] *adj.* 供选择的，可替代的
sophisticated [səˈfɪstɪkeɪtɪd] *adj.* 复杂的；精致的

高频同义替换

suffer	●	stand, experience, tough, abide
considerable	●	crucial, important, material
predict	●	forecast, foretell, shadow
indicate	●	index, image, imply, figure
eventually	●	finally, ultimately, lastly
distinguish	●	differentiate, discriminate
primary	●	elementary, major, central, main
involve	●	contain, comprise, include
special	●	particular, extraordinary, technical
understand	●	absorb, seize, comprehend

题目解析

1 定位词：alternative explanation

文中对应点：I 段第一句

题目解析：题干说，给出孩子们可能不理解别人的信仰的另一种解释。由 alternative explanation 定位到 I 段第一句 "A different explanation has been put forward by Harris."。其中，alternative 与 different 对应，explanation 为原文重现。句意为，Harris 提出了一个不同的解释。由此可知提出该解释的人为 Harris，因此答案为 G。

2 定位词：tell difference between reality and mentality

文中对应点：H 段最后一句

题目解析：题干说，一定年龄以下的孩子可以区分现实和想法的发现。由 tell difference between reality and mentality 定位到 H 段最后一句 "Thus the social abilities of children indicate that they are aware of the difference between mental states and external reality at ages younger than four."。其中，are aware of difference between mental states and external reality 与 tell difference between reality and mentality 为同义替换。句意为，因此，儿童的社交能力表明他们在四岁以前是能意识到想法和现实的不同的。提出该观点的人为 Schatz，因此答案为 F。

3 定位词：young children, real state of the world

文中对应点：B 段最后一句

题目解析：题干说，设计了一个实验并得出结论：4 岁以下的幼儿无法理解世界的真实状态。由 young children, real state of the world 定位到 B 段最后一句 "The incorrect answers indicated that the younger children did not understand that Maxi's beliefs and representations no longer matched the actual state of the world, and they failed to appreciate that Maxi will act on the basis of his beliefs rather than the way that the world is actually organised."。其中，the younger children 与对应 young children，actual state of the world 与 real state of the world 为同义替换。

句意为，这些错误的答案表明年纪较小的孩子不能理解 Maxi 最初的想法和实际情况的不同，他们不能理解 Maxi 会以自己的想法来采取行动而不是依据实际情况。得出相关结论的人为 Wimmer and Perner，因此答案为 C。

4 定位词：get along with adults
文中对应点：F 段第二句
题目解析：题干说，与成年人相处的孩子往往更容易通过考试的研究发现。由 gets along with adults 定位到 F 段第二句 "They found that children who socially interact with more adults, who have more friends, and who have older siblings tend to pass TOM tasks at a slightly earlier age than other children."。其中，interact with more adults 对应 gets along with adults，tend to pass TOM tasks 与 got through test more easily 对应。句意为，他们发现平时和成人有比较多互动，有较多朋友以及其他年长的兄弟姐妹的儿童能够在较小的年纪通过 TOM 测试。由此可知进行该实验的人为 F 段第一句提及的 Lewis，因此答案为 D。

5 定位词：easier experiment
文中对应点：C 段第一句
题目解析：题干说，修正了一个更简单的实验：排除了孩子可能受到复杂推理的影响。由 easier experiment 定位到 C 段第一句 "A simpler version of the Maxi task was devised by Baron Cohen to take account of criticisms that younger children may have been affected by the complexity and too much information of the story in the task described above."。其中，a simpler version 与 easier experiment 对应，affected by 与 influenced by 对应，sophisticated reasoning 与 complexity 对应。句意为，Maxi 任务的一个更为简单的版本是由 Baron Cohen 设计的，考虑到了年幼的孩子可能会被原来实验的复杂性和其中过量的信息所影响的情况。由此可知此处提及的是 Baron Cohen 对前人的实验进行简化，因此答案为 A。

6 定位词：social factor, mother-child communication
文中对应点：E 段第一、二句
题目解析：题干说，相关的社会因素如母子交流能力在儿童心理理论中所起到的作用。由 social factor, mother-child communication 定位到 E 段第一、二句 "There is also evidence that social processes play a part in the development of TOM. Meins and her colleagues have found that what they term mindmindedness in maternal speech to six-month old infants is related to both security of attachment and TOM abilities."。其中，social factor 对应 social processes，maternal speech to six-month old infants 与 mother-child communication 对应。句意为，也有证据表明，社会过程在心理理论的发展中起着重要作用。Meins 和她的同事们发现，他们在对 6 个月大的婴儿的母亲讲话中所表达的思想意识，与依恋安全性和心理理论能力都有关。由此可知提出该观点的是 Meins，因此答案为 B。

7 定位词：tell something, mothers, friends
文中对应点：F 段倒数第一句
题目解析：题干说，与他们的母亲相比，孩子们愿意与他们的朋友互动。由 tell something, mother, friends 定位到 F 段倒数第一句 "Furthermore, because young children are more likely to talk about

their thoughts and feelings with peers than with their mothers, peer interaction may provide a special impetus to the development of a TOM."。其中，talk about their thoughts and feelings 对应 tell something，peers 与 friends 为同义替换。句意为，此外，由于年幼的孩子更有可能与同龄人谈论他们的想法和感受，而不是和他们的母亲交流，同伴的互动可能会为心智理论的发展提供特殊的推动力。仅接着后一句中提到 "A similar point has been made by Dunn..." 由此可知提出该理论的是 Dunn，因此答案为 E。

参考答案

1 G   2 F   3 C   4 D   5 A   6 B   7 E

Decision Making and Happiness

A Americans today choose among more options in more parts of life than has ever been possible before. To an extent, the opportunity to choose enhances our lives. It is only logical to think that if some choice is good, more is better; people who care about having infinite options will benefit from them, and those who do not can always just ignore the 273 versions of cereal they have never tried. Yet recent research strongly suggests that, psychologically, this assumption is wrong. Although some choice is undoubtedly better than none, more is not always better than less.

B Recent research offers insight into why many people end up unhappy rather than pleased when their options expand. We began by making a distinction between 'maximisers' (those who always aim to make 'the best possible choice') and 'satisficers' (those who aim for 'good enough', whether or not better selections might be out there).

C In particular, we composed a set of statements — the Maximisation Scale — to diagnose people's propensity to maximise. Then we had several thousand people rate themselves from 1 to 7 (from 'completely disagree' to 'completely agree') on such statements as 'I never settle for second best.' We also evaluated their sense, of satisfaction with their decisions. We did not define a sharp cutoff to separate maximisers from satisficers, but in general, we think of individuals whose average scores are higher than 4 (the scale's midpoint) as maximisers and those whose scores are lower than the midpoint as satisficers. People who score highest on the test — the greatest maximisers — engage in more product comparisons than the lowest scorers, both before and after they make purchasing decisions, and they take longer to decide what to buy. When satisficers find an item that meets their standards, they stop looking. But maximisers exert enormous effort reading labels, checking out consumer magazines and trying new products. They also spend more time comparing their purchasing decisions with those of others.

D We found that the greatest maximisers are the least happy with the fruits of their efforts. When they compare themselves with others, they get little pleasure from finding out that they did better and substantial dissatisfaction from finding out that they did worse. They are more prone to experiencing regret after a purchase, and if their acquisition disappoints them, their sense of well-being takes longer to recover. They also tend to brood or ruminate more than satisficers do.

E Does it follow that maximisers are less happy in general than satisficers? We tested this by having people fill out a variety of questionnaires known to be reliable indicators of well-being. As might be expected, individuals with high maximisation scores experienced less satisfaction with life and were less happy, less optimistic and more depressed than people with low maximisation scores. Indeed, those with extreme maximisation ratings had depression scores that placed them in the borderline clinical range.

F Several factors explain why more choice is not always better than less, especially for maximisers. High among these are 'opportunity costs'. The quality of any given option cannot be assessed in isolation from its alternatives. One of the 'costs' of making a selection is losing the opportunities that a different option would have afforded. Thus an opportunity cost of vacationing on the beach in Cape Cod might be missing the fabulous restaurants in the Napa Valley. 'EARLY DECISION-MAKING RESEARCH' by Daniel Kahneman and Amos Tversky showed that people respond much more strongly to losses than gains. If we assume that opportunity costs reduce the overall desirability of the most preferred choice, then the more alternatives there are, the deeper our sense of loss will be and the less satisfaction we will derive from our ultimate decision.

G The problem of opportunity costs will be worse for a maximiser than for a satisficer. The latter's 'good enough' philosophy can survive thoughts about opportunity costs. In addition, the 'good enough' standard leads to much less searching and inspection of alternatives than the maximiser's 'best' standard. With fewer choices under consideration, a person will have fewer opportunity costs to subtract.

H Just as people fed sorrow about the opportunities they have forgone, they may also suffer regret about the option they settle on. My colleagues and I devised a scale to measure proneness to feeling regret, and we found that people with high sensitivity to regret are less happy, less satisfied with life, less optimistic and more depressed than those with low sensitivity. Not surprisingly, we also found that people with high regret sensitivity tend to be maximisers. Indeed, we think that worry over future regret is a major reason that individuals become maximisers. The only way to be sure you will not regret a decision is by making the best possible one. Unfortunately, the more options you have and the more opportunity costs you incur, the more likely you are to experience regret.

I In a classic demonstration of the power of sunk costs, people were offered season subscriptions to a local theatre company. Some were offered the tickets at full price and others at a discount. Then the researchers simply kept track of how often the ticket purchasers actually attended the plays over the course of the season. Full-price payers were more likely to show up at performances than discount payers. The reason for this, the investigators argued, was that the full-price payers would experience more regret if they did not use the tickets because not using the more costly tickets would constitute a bigger loss. To increase sense of happiness, we can decide to restrict our options when the decision is not crucial. For example, make a rule to visit no more than two stores when shopping for clothing.

Questions 1–4

Classify the following as typical of

    A maximiser
    B satisficer
    C both
    D neither of them

*Write the correct letter, **A**, **B**, **C**, or **D**, in boxes 1–4 on your answer sheet.*

1   finish transaction when the items match their expectation

2   buy the most expensive things when shopping

3   consider repeatedly until they make final decision

4   participate in the questionnaire of the author

核心词汇

A 段

enhance [ɪn'hɑːns] *vt.* 提高，改进，增强

assumption [ə'sʌmpʃn] *n.* 假定，假设；承担，就任

B 段

distinction [dɪ'stɪŋkʃn] *n.* 区别，差别；优秀，卓越；独特

satisficer ['sætɪsfaɪsə] *n.* 满足者

C 段

sharp cutoff 锐减

consumer [kən'sjuːmə(r)] *n.* 消费者，用户

D 段

substantial [səb'stænʃl] *adj.* 大量的；实质的

acquisition [ˌækwɪ'zɪʃn] *n.* 获得物，获得

disappoint [ˌdɪsə'pɔɪnt] *vi. & vt.* （使）失望 [拓] disappointment *n.* 失望，沮丧

well-being *n.* 幸福；舒适；繁荣

E 段

questionnaire [ˌkwestʃə'neə(r)] *n.* 问卷，调查

depressed [dɪ'prest] *adj.* 沮丧的；萧条的 [拓] depress *vt.* 使沮丧；使萧条

borderline ['bɔːdəlaɪn] *adj.* 边界的，临界的 *n.* 边界线，边界；中间地带

F 段

isolation [ˌaɪsə'leɪʃn] *n.* 隔离；隔离状态

alternative [ɔːl'tɜːnətɪv] *n.* 替代选择；可供选择的事物 *adj.* 可替代的；另外的；二者择一的

fabulous ['fæbjələs] *adj.* 难以置信的；极好的，绝妙的

desirability [dɪˌzaɪərə'bɪləti] *n.* 愿望；有利条件

ultimate ['ʌltɪmət] *adj.* 最终的，终极的

G 段

inspection [ɪn'spekʃn] *n.* 视察，检查

H 段

devise [dɪ'vaɪz] *vt.* 设计，想出，计划

optimistic [ˌɒptɪ'mɪstɪk] *adj.* 乐观的，乐观主义的

I 段

demonstration [ˌdemənˈstreɪʃn] *n.* 示范，证明，演示；游行示威

restrict [rɪˈstrɪkt] *vt.* 限制，约束，控制

crucial [ˈkruːʃl] *adj.* 重要的，决定性的

高频同义替换

option	▶	choice, selection, election
infinite	▶	very great in amount or degree, unlimited, boundless, limitless
expand	▶	become larger, swell, dilate, inflate, puff up
propensity	▶	tendency, trend, habit, inclination
purchase	▶	buy, procurement

题目解析

1 定位词：finish, match their expectation

文中对应点：C 段倒数第三句

题目解析：题干说，当物品条件满足期望即完成交易。由 finish, match their expectation 定位到 C 段倒数第三句 "When satisficers find an item that meets their standards, they stop looking."。其中，meets their standards 与 match their expectation 为同义替换，stop 对应 finish。句意为，当满足者找到满足他们标准的物品时，他们就停止寻找。故答案为 B。

2 定位词：most expensive things, shopping

文中对应点：无

题目解析：题干说，购物时买最贵的东西。文中在讲 maximiser 和 satisficer 的特征时，并未提及购买最贵的东西的人群划分，所以不属于任何一类，故答案为 D。

3 定位词：repeatedly, final decision

文中对应点：C 段第五句和第七句

题目解析：题干说，反复考虑直到作出最终决定。由 repeatedly, final decision 定位到 C 段第五句 "People who score highest on the test — the greatest maximisers — engage in more product comparisons than the lowest scorers, both before and after they make purchasing decisions, and they take longer to decide what to buy." 和第七句 "But maximisers exert enormous effort reading labels, checking out consumer magazines and trying new products."。在讲 maximiser 的特征时，讲到在作出购买决定前后反复对比各种标签、消费者杂志和尝试新品，可看出与题目意义基本一致，所以对应 maximiser 的特征。C 段第五句意为，在测试中得分最高的人——最大的最大化者——比得分最低的人进行更多的产品比较，无论是在他们作出购买决定之前还是之后，他们都要花更长的时间

来决定买什么。C 段第七句意为，但是，最大化者在阅读标签、查看消费者杂志和尝试新产品上付出了巨大的努力。故答案为 A。

4 定位词：questionnaire
   文中对应点：E 段第二句
   题目解析：题干说，参与作者的调查问卷活动。由 questionnaire 定位到 E 段第二句 "We tested this by having people fill out a variety of questionnaires known to be reliable indicators of well-being."。其中，questionnaire 为原文再现，E 段其他部分也讲到利用调查问卷，根据得分来划分两类人，可看出是两类人群都有参加，然后综合对比。句意为，我们通过让人们填写各种被认为是幸福的可靠指标的问卷来测试这一点。故答案为 C。

参考答案

1 B 2 D 3 A 4 C

Extinct: the Giant Deer

Toothed cats, mastodons, giant sloths, woolly rhinos, and many other big, shaggy mammals are widely thought to have died out around the end of the last Ice Age, since 10,500 years ago.

A The Irish elk is also known as the giant deer (Megaloceros giganteus). Analysis of ancient bones and teeth by scientists based in Britain and Russia show the huge herbivore survived until about 5,000 B.C. — more than three millennia later than previously believed. The research team says this suggests additional factors, besides climate change, probably hastened the giant deer's eventual extinction. The factors could include hunting or habitat destruction by humans.

B The Irish elk, so-called because its well-preserved remains are often found in lake sediment under peat bogs in Ireland, first appeared about 400,000 years ago in Europe and central Asia. Through a combination of radiocarbon dating of skeletal remains and the mapping of locations where the remains were unearthed, the team shows the Irish elk was widespread across Europe before the last 'big freeze'. The deer's range later contracted to the Ural Mountains, in modern-day Russia, which separates Europe from Asia.

C The giant deer made its last stand in western Siberia, since 3,000 years after the ice sheets receded, said the study's co-author, Adrian Lister, professor of palaeobiology at University College London, England. 'The eastern foothills of the Urals became very densely forested about 8,000 years ago, which could have pushed them on to the plain,' he said. He added that pollen analysis indicates the region then became very dry in response to further climactic change, leading to the loss of important food plants. 'In combination with human pressures, this could have finally snuffed them out,' Lister said.

D Hunting by humans has often been put forward as a contributory cause of extinctions of the Pleistocene megafauna. The team, though, said their new date for the Irish elk's extinction hints at an additional human-made problem — habitat destruction. Lister said, 'We haven't got just hunting 7,000 years ago — this was also about the time the first Neolithic people settled in the region. They were farmers who would have cleared the land.' The presence of humans may help explain why the Irish elk was unable to tough out the latest of many climatic fluctuations — periods it had survived in the past.

E Meanwhile, Lister cast doubt on another possible explanation for the deer's demise — the male's huge antlers. Some scientists have suggested this exaggerated feature — the result of females preferring stags with the largest antlers, possibly because they advertised a male's fitness — contributed to the mammal's downfall. They say such antlers would have been a serious inconvenience in the dense forests that spread northward after the last Ice Age. But, Lister said, 'That's a hard argument to make, because the deer previously survived perfectly well through wooded interglacials (warmer periods between ice ages).' Some research has suggested that a lack of sufficient high-quality forage caused the extinction of the elk. High amounts of calcium and phosphate compounds are required to form antlers, and therefore large quantities of these minerals are required for the massive structures of the Irish elk. The males (and male deer in general) met this requirement partly from their bones, replenishing them from food plants after the antlers were grown or reclaiming the nutrients from discarded antlers (as has been observed in extant deer). Thus, in the antler growth phase, Giant Deer were suffering from a condition similar to osteoporosis. When the climate changed at the end of the last glacial period, the vegetation in the animal's habitat also changed towards species that presumably could not deliver sufficient amounts of the required minerals, at least in the western part of its range.

F   The extinction of megafauna around the world was almost completed by the end of the last Ice Age. It is believed that megafauna initially came into existence in response to glacial conditions and became extinct with the onset of warmer climates. Tropical and subtropical areas have experienced less radical climatic change. The most dramatic of these changes was the transformation of a vast area of North Africa into the world's largest desert. Significantly, Africa escaped major faunal extinction as tropical and subtropical Asia did. The human exodus from Africa and our entrance into the Americas and Australia were also accompanied by climate change. Australia's climate changed from cold-dry to warm-dry. As a result, surface water became scarce. Most inland lakes became completely dry or dry in the warmer seasons. Most large, predominantly browsing animals lost their habitat and retreated to a narrow band in eastern Australia, where there was permanent water and better vegetation. Some animals may have survived until about 7,000 years ago. If people have been in Australia for up to 60,000 years, then megafauna must have co-existed with humans for at least 30,000 years. Regularly hunted modern kangaroos survived not only 10,000 years of Aboriginal hunting, but also an onslaught of commercial shooters.

G   The group of scientists led by A. J. Stuart focused on northern Eurasia, which he was taking as Europe, plus Siberia, essentially, where they've got the best data that animals became extinct in Europe during the Late Pleistocene. Some cold-adapted animals, go through into the last part of the cold stage, and then become extinct up there. So you've actually got two phases of extinction. Now, neither of these coincide — these are Neanderthals here being replaced by modern humans. There's no obvious coincidence between the arrival of humans or climatic change alone and these extinctions. There's a climatic change here, so there's a double effect here. Again, as animals come through to the last part of the cold stage, here there's a fundamental change in the climate, reorganisation of vegetation, and the combination of the climatic change and the presence of humans — of advanced Paleolithic humans — causes this wave of extinction. There's a profound difference between the North American data and that of Europe, which summarise that the extinctions in northern Eurasia, in Europe, are moderate and staggered, and in North America severe and sudden. And these things relate to the differences in the timing of human arrival. The extinctions follow from human predation, but only at times of fundamental changes in the environment.

Questions 1–4

Look at the following statements (Questions 1–4) and the list of continents below.

Match each statement with the correct continent, **A–D**.

Write the correct letter, **A–D**, in boxes 1–4 on your answer sheet.

1   the continent where humans imposed little impact on large mammal's extinction

2   the continent where the climatic change was mild and fauna remains

3   the continent where both humans and climatic change are the causes

4   the continent where the climatic change alone caused a massive extinction

List of Continents
A   Eurasia
B   Australia
C   Asia
D   Africa

核心词汇

A 段

mammal ['mæml] *n.* 哺乳动物

herbivore ['hɜːbɪvɔː] *n.* 食草动物

hasten ['heɪsn] *vt.* 加速，加紧 *vi.* 抢着，急忙，赶快

extinction [ɪkˈstɪŋ(k)ʃn] *n.* 灭绝，绝种；消亡

B 段

remains [rɪˈmeɪnz] *n.* （复数）剩余部分；遗迹；遗体

unearth [ʌnˈɜːθ] *vt.* 发掘；揭露；发现

C 段

recede [rɪˈsiːd] *vi.* 逐渐消失；消退，退去

D 段

contributory [kəˈtrɪbjətəri] *adj.* 促进的，促成的，起作用的 [拓] contribute *vi. & vt.* 捐献，捐赠；投稿 *vi.* 促成，造成 [拓] contribution *n.* 贡献；捐款；稿件

fluctuation [ˌflʌktʃuˈeɪʃn] *n.* 起伏，波动 [拓] fluctuate *vi.* 起伏，波动

E 段

cast doubt on 引起对……的怀疑；对……产生怀疑

antler [ˈæntlə(r)] *n.* 鹿角

exaggerated [ɪɡˈzædʒəreɪtɪd] *adj.* 夸大的，言过其实的；引人注目的 [拓] exaggerate *vi. & vt.* 夸大，夸张，言过其实

replenish [rɪˈplenɪʃ] *vt.* 补充；重新装满

discard [dɪˈskɑːd] *vt.* 扔掉，弃置

osteoporosis [ˌɒstiəʊpəˈrəʊsɪs] *n.* 骨质疏松（症）

vegetation [ˌvedʒəˈteɪʃn] *n.* 植物，草木

presumably [prɪˈzjuːməbli] *adv.* 大概；据推测 [拓] presume *vt.* 料想，认为；推定 *vi.* 擅作主张

F 段

onset [ˈɒnset] *n.* 某事的开始（尤指不好的事情）

exodus [ˈeksədəs] *n.* 离开，涌离

predominantly [prɪˈdɒmɪnəntli] *adv.* 主要地；绝大多数 [拓] predominant *adj.* 占优势的，占主导地位的；最突出的

onslaught [ˈɒnslɔːt] *n.* 猛攻；猛烈抨击

G 段

coincide [ˌkəʊɪn'saɪd] *vi.* 一致，相符；同时发生；相交 [拓] **coincidence** *n.* 巧合；一致；同时发生 [拓] **coincident** *adj.* 同时发生的；巧合的

profound [prə'faʊnd] *adj.* 深厚的；知识渊博的；强烈的

moderate ['mɒdərət] *adj.* 温和的；适度的；有节制的 *vi. & vt.* （使）缓和；节制，克制

predation [prɪ'deɪʃn] *n.* 捕食；捕食行为 [拓] **prey** *n.* 猎物 [拓] **predator** *n.* 捕食者

高频同义替换

impact	▸	influence, effect, affect
mild	▸	soft, moderate, gentle, temperate, slight, light
remains	▸	relic, fragment, ruin
massive	▸	huge, enormous, colossal, immense, tremendous

题目解析

1 **定位词**：little impact, large mammal's extinction

文中对应点：F 段第二及倒数第二句

题目解析：题干说，人类对大型哺乳动物灭绝影响甚微的大陆。由 large mammal's extinction 定位至 F 段第二句 "It is believed that megafauna initially came into existence in response to glacial conditions and became extinct with the onset of warmer climates."。其中，large mammal 与 megafauna 对应，extinction 为 extinct 的名词形式。句意为，据说巨型动物最初是伴随着冰川气候情况出现的，又随着气候变暖而灭绝。由 little impact 定位到 F 段倒数第二句 "If people have been in Australia for up to 60,000 years, then megafauna must have co-existed with humans for at least 30,000 years."。其中，megafauna must have co-existed with humans 与 little impact 对应。句意为，如果人们已经在澳大利亚生活了 6 万年，那么巨型动物群肯定已经和人类共存了至少 3 万年。由此可知澳大利亚大陆并不是人类活动使得大型食草动物灭绝的大陆，对应题干中的"人类对大型哺乳动物的灭绝产生较小影响的大陆"，因此答案为 B。

2 **定位词**：fauna, remains

文中对应点：F 段第五句

题目解析：题干说，这个大陆的气候变化温和，动物群仍然存在。由 fauna, remains 定位到 F 段第五句 "Significantly, Africa escaped major faunal extinction as tropical and sub-tropical Asia did."。其中，escaped major faunal extinction 与 remains 对应。句意为，值得注意的是，非洲同亚洲热带和亚热带地区一样，躲过了主要动物物种大灭绝。可见非洲仍有动物群存在，因此答案为 D。

3 定位词：both, humans, climatic change, causes
   文中对应点：G 段第七句
   题目解析：题干说，人类和气候变化都是大陆发生改变的原因。由 humans，climatic change 和 causes 定位到 G 段第七句 "Again, as animals come through to the last part of the cold stage, here there's a fundamental change in the climate, reorganisation of vegetation, and the combination of the climatic change and the presence of humans — of advanced Paleolithic humans — causes this wave of extinction."。其中，humans 和 climatic change 为原文再现，可知是人类和气候变化的共同作用导致了大灭绝，而这一段主要讲的是亚欧大陆，句意为，因为动物安然来到了寒冷期的最后一个阶段，该阶段在气候上有一个根本性改变，植被重组，再结合气候变化和先进的旧石器时代人类的出现，共同导致了这一波灭绝。因此答案为 A。

4 定位词：climatic change alone, a massive extinction
   文中对应点：F 段第三到五句
   题目解析：题干说，仅是气候变化就造成了大规模物种灭绝的大陆。由 climatic change alone, a massive extinction 定位到 F 段第三到五句 "Tropical and subtropical areas have experienced less radical climatic change. The most dramatic of these changes was the transformation of a vast area of North Africa into the world's largest desert. Significantly, Africa escaped major faunal extinction as tropical and sub-tropical Asia did."。其中，a massive extinction 与 major faunal extinction 对应，climatic change alone 与 radical climatic change 对应。句意为，热带和亚热带地区的气候变化不那么剧烈。这些变化中最引人注目的是北非的大片地区变成了世界上最大的沙漠。值得注意的是，非洲逃过了主要动物群的灭绝，亚洲的热带和亚热带也逃过了。因此答案为 C。

参考答案

1 B   2 D   3 A   4 C

The Adolescents

A The American Academy of Pediatrics recognises three stages of adolescence. There are early, middle and late adolescence, and each has its own developmental tasks. Teenagers move through these tasks at their own speed depending on their physical development and hormone levels. Although these stages are common to all teenagers, each child will go through them in his or her own highly individual ways.

B During the early years young people make the first attempts to leave the dependent, secure role of a child and to establish themselves as unique individuals, independent of their parents. Early adolescence is marked by rapid physical growth and maturation. The focus of adolescents' self-concepts are thus often on their physical self and their evaluation of their physical acceptability. Early adolescence is also a period of intense conformity to peers. 'Getting along', not being different, and being accepted seem somehow pressing to the early adolescent. The worst possibility, from the view of the early adolescent, is to be seen by peers as 'different'.

C Middle adolescence is marked by the emergence of new thinking skills. The intellectual world of the young person is suddenly greatly expanded. Their concerns about peers are more directed toward their opposite sexed peers. It is also during this period that the move to establish psychological independence from one's parents accelerates. Delinquency behaviour may emerge since parental views are no longer seen as absolutely correct by adolescents. Despite some delinquent behaviour, middle adolescence is a period during which young people are oriented toward what is right and proper. They are developing a sense of behavioural maturity and learning to control their impulsiveness.

D Late adolescence is marked by the final preparations for adult roles. The developmental demands of late adolescence often extend into the period that we think of as young adulthood. Late adolescents attempt to crystallise their vocational goals and to establish sense of personal identity. Their needs for peer approval are diminished and they are largely psychologically independent from their parents. The shift to adulthood is nearly complete.

E Some years ago, Professor Robert Havighurst of the University of Chicago proposed that stages in human development can best be thought of in terms of the developmental tasks that are part of the normal. He identified eleven developmental tasks associated with the adolescent transition. One developmental task an adolescent needs to achieve is to adjust to a new physical sense of self. At no other time since birth does an individual undergo such rapid and profound physical changes as during early adolescence. Puberty is marked by sudden rapid growth in height and weight. Also, the young person experiences the emergence and accentuation of those physical traits that make him or her a boy or a girl. The effect of this rapid change is that the young adolescent often becomes focused on his or her body.

F   Before adolescence, children's thinking is dominated by a need to have a concrete example for any problem that they solve. Their thinking is constrained to what is real and physical. During adolescence, young people begin to recognise and understand abstractions. The adolescent must adjust to increased cognitive demands at school. Adults see high school in part as a place where adolescents prepare for adult roles and responsibilities and in part as preparatory for further education. School curricula are frequently dominated by inclusion of more abstract, demanding material, regardless of whether the adolescents have achieved formal thought. Since not all adolescents make the intellectual transition at the same rate, demands for abstract thinking prior to achievement of that ability may be frustrating.

G   During adolescence, as teens develop increasingly complex knowledge systems and a sense of self, they also adopt an integrated set of values and morals. During the early stages of moral development, parents provide their child with a structured set of rules of what is right and wrong, what is acceptable and unacceptable. Eventually the adolescent must assess the parents' values as they come into conflict with values expressed by peers and other segments of society. To reconcile differences, the adolescent restructures those beliefs into a personal ideology.

H   The adolescent must develop expanded verbal skills. As adolescents mature intellectually, as they face increased school demands, and as they prepare for adult roles, they must develop new verbal skills to accommodate more complex concepts and tasks. Their limited language of childhood is no longer adequate. Adolescents may appear less competent because of their inability to express themselves meaningfully.

I   The adolescent must establish emotional and psychological independence from his or her parents. Childhood is marked by strong dependence on one's parents. Adolescents may yearn to keep that safe, secure, supportive, dependent relationship. Yet, to be an adult implies a sense of independence, of autonomy, of being one's own person. Adolescents may vacillate between their desire for dependence and their need to be independent. In an attempt to assert their need for independence and individuality, adolescents may respond with what appears to be hostility and lack of cooperation.

J   Adolescents do not progress through these multiple developmental tasks separately. At any given time, adolescents may be dealing with several. Further, the centrality of specific developmental tasks varies with early, middle, and late periods of the transition.

Questions 1–4

Complete the sentences below.

Choose the correct letter, **A–F**.

Write the correct letter in boxes 1–4 on your answer sheet.

1   One of Havighurst's research

2   High school courses

3   Adolescence is a time when young people

4   The developmental speed of thinking patterns

A	form(s) personal identity with a set of morals and values.
B	develop(s) a table and productive peer relationship.
C	are designed to be more challenging than some can accept.
D	varies / vary from people to people.
E	focus(es) on creating self-image.
F	become(s) an extension of their parents.

核心词汇

A 段

pediatrics [ˌpiːdiˈætrɪks] *n.* 小儿科

adolescence [ˌædəˈlesns] *n.* 青春期

B 段

maturation [ˌmætʃuˈreɪʃn] *n.* 成熟

conformity [kənˈfɔːməti] *n.* 一致；符合；相似

C 段

accelerate [əkˈseləreɪt] *v.* 加速；促进；增加

delinquency [dɪˈlɪŋkwənsi] *n.* 不良行为；违法犯罪

impulsiveness [ɪmˈpʌlsɪvnəs] *n.* 冲动

D 段

crystallise [ˈkrɪstəlaɪz] *v.* 结晶，形成结晶；明确；具体化

diminish [dɪˈmɪnɪʃ] *v.* 减少；削弱

E 段

accentuation [əkˌsentʃuˈeɪʃn] *n.* 强调；增强；重读

F 段

cognitive [ˈkɒgnətɪv] *adj.* 认知的，认识的

transition [trænˈzɪʃn] *n.* 转变；过渡

G 段

integrated [ˈɪntɪgreɪtɪd] *adj.* 综合的；完整的；互相协调的

segment [ˈsegmənt] *n.* 片段；段数

reconcile [ˈrekənsaɪl] *v.* 使一致；使和解；使顺从

ideology [ˌaɪdiˈɒlədʒi] *n.* 意识形态；思想意识

H 段

competent [ˈkɒmpɪtənt] *adj.* 胜任的；有能力的；能干的；足够的

I 段

autonomy [ɔːˈtɒnəmi] *n.* 自治；自治权

vacillate [ˈvæsəleɪt] *v.* 犹豫；踌躇；摇摆

hostility [hɒˈstɪləti] *n.* 敌意；战争行动

高频同义替换

- **secure** ▸ certain, safe, reliable
- **unique** ▸ distinct, characteristic, particular
- **accept** ▸ undertake, adopt, recognise, shoulder
- **correct** ▸ rectify, admonish, adjust, amend
- **attempt** ▸ essay, attack, push, try
- **rapid** ▸ forward, ready, quick
- **cognitive** ▸ recognitive, epistemic, sanctified
- **conflict** ▸ interference, difference, battle, collision
- **adequate** ▸ suitable, competent, appropriate

题目解析

1 定位词：Havighurst
文中对应点：E 段第三句
题目解析：由题干中的定位词 Havighurst 定位到 E 段第三句"One developmental task an adolescent needs to achieve is to adjust to a new physical sense of self."。其中，achieve 与 E 项中的 focuses on 对应，adjust to 与 E 项中的 creating 对应，a new physical sense of self 与 E 项中的 self image 对应。句意为，青少年需要完成的一项发展任务是适应一种新的身体感觉。因此可知道 Havighurst 的研究重点在自我形象上。因此答案为 E。

2 定位词：courses
文中对应点：F 段第六句
题目解析：由题干中的定位词 courses 定位到 F 段第六句"School curricula are frequently dominated by inclusion of more abstract, demanding material, regardless of whether the adolescents have achieved formal thought."。其中，curricula 与题干中的 courses 同义替换，are...dominated by 与 C 项中的 are designed to 对应，more abstract...regardless of whether 与 C 项中的 more challenging than 对应。句意为，学校的课程经常以包含更抽象、更苛刻的材料为主导，不管这些青少年是否已经形成有条理的想法。因此答案为 C。

3 定位词：a time when
文中对应点：G 段第一句
题目解析：由题干中的定位词 a time when 定位到 G 段第一句"During adolescence, as teens develop increasingly complex knowledge systems and a sense of self, they also adopt an integrated set of values and morals."。其中，during adolescence 对应题干中的 a time when，adopt 与 A 项中的 form 对应，A 项中的 a set of 和 moral and values 为原文重现。句意为，在青少年时期，随着青少年复杂知识体系和自我意识逐步发展，他们也采用了一套完整的价值观和道德观。因此答案就是 A。

4 定位词：speed, thinking patterns

文中对应点：F 段倒数第一句

题目解析：由题干中的定位词 speed, thinking patterns 定位到 F 段倒数第一句 "Since not all adolescents make the intellectual transition at the same rate, demands for abstract thinking prior to achievement of that ability may be frustrating."。其中，rate 对应题干中的 speed，abstract thinking 对应题干中的 thinking patterns，原文中的 not all...at the same rate 对应 D 项中的 vary。句意为，因为并不是所有的青少年都以同样的速度进行智力方面的过渡，所以对于抽象思维的形成要先于这种能力的要求可能是令人沮丧的。因此答案为 D。

参考答案

1 E **2** C **3** A **4** D

第四章　选择题

READING PASSAGE 1

Activities for Children

A Twenty-five years ago, children in London walked to school and played in parks and playing fields after school and at the weekend. Today they are usually driven to school by parents anxious about safety and spend hours glued to television screens or computer games. Meanwhile, community playing fields are being sold off to property developers at an alarming rate. 'This change in lifestyle has, sadly, meant greater restrictions on children,' says Neil Armstrong, Professor of Health and Exercise Sciences at the University of Exeter. 'If children continue to be this inactive, they'll be storing up big problems for the future.'

B In 1985, Professor Armstrong headed a five-year research project into children's fitness. The results, published in 1990, were alarming. The survey, which monitored 700 11-16-year-olds, found that 48 per cent of girls and 41 per cent of boys already exceeded safe cholesterol levels set for children by the American Heart Foundation. Armstrong adds, 'Heart is a muscle and needs exercise, or it loses its strength.' It also found that 13 per cent of boys and 10 per cent of girls were overweight. More disturbingly, the survey found that over a four-day period, half the girls and one-third of the boys did less exercise than the equivalent of a brisk 10-minute walk. High levels of cholesterol, excess body fat and inactivity are believed to increase the risk of coronary heart disease.

C Physical education is under pressure in the UK — most schools devote little more than 100 minutes a week to it in curriculum time, which is less than many other European countries. Three European countries are giving children a head start in PE, France, Austria and Switzerland — offering at least two hours in primary and secondary schools. These findings, from the European Union of Physical Education Associations, prompted specialists in children's physiology to call on European governments to give youngsters a daily PE programme. The survey shows that the UK ranks 13th out of the 25 countries, with Ireland bottom, averaging under an hour a week for PE. From age 6 to 18, British children received, on average, 106 minutes of PE a week. Professor Armstrong, who presented the findings at the meeting, noted that since the introduction of the national curriculum there had been a marked fall in the time devoted to PE in UK schools, with only a minority of pupils getting two hours a week.

D As a former junior football international, Professor Armstrong is a passionate advocate for sport. Although the government has poured millions into beefing up sport in the community, there is less commitment to it as part of the crammed school curriculum. This means that many children never acquire the necessary skills to thrive in team games. If they are no good at them, they lose interest and establish an inactive pattern of behaviour. When this is coupled with a poor diet, it will lead inevitably to weight gain. Seventy per cent of British children give up all sports when they leave school, compared with only 20 per cent of French teenagers. Professor Armstrong believes that there is far too great an emphasis on team games at school. 'We need to look at the time devoted to PE and balance it between individual and pair activities, such as aerobics and badminton as well as team sports.' He added that children need to have the opportunity to take part in a wide variety of individual, partner and team sports.

E The good news, however, is that a few small companies and children's activity groups have reacted positively and creatively to the problem. During the wild and chaotic hopper race across the studio floor, commands like this are issued and responded to with untrammelled glee. The sight of 13 bouncing seven-year-olds who seem about to launch into orbit at every bounce brings tears to the eyes. Uncoordinated, loud, excited and emotional, children provide raw comedy.

F Any cardiovascular exercise is a good option, and it doesn't necessarily have to be high intensity. It can be anything that gets your heart rate up: such as walking the dog, swimming, running, skipping, hiking. 'Even walking through the grocery store can be exercise,' Samis Smith said. What they don't know is that they're at a Fit Kids class, and that the fun is a disguise for the serious exercise plan they're covertly being taken through. Fit Kids trains parents to run fitness classes for children. 'Ninety per cent of children don't like team sports,' says company director, Gillian Gale.

G A prevention survey found that children whose parents keep in shape are much more likely to have healthy body weights themselves. 'There's nothing worse than telling a child what he needs to do and not doing it yourself,' says Elizabeth Ward, R.D., a Boston nutritional consultant and author of *Healthy Foods, Healthy Kids*. 'Set a good example and get your nutritional house in order first.' In the 1930s and '40s, kids expended 800 calories a day just walking, carrying water, and doing other chores, notes Fima Lifshitz, M.D., a pediatric endocrinologist in Santa Barbara. 'Now, kids in obese families are expending only 200 calories a day in physical activity,' says Lifshitz, 'Incorporate more movement in your family's life — park farther away from the stores at the mall, take stairs instead of the elevator, and walk to nearby friends' houses instead of driving.'

Questions 1–5

Choose the correct letter, **A**, **B**, **C** or **D**.

Write the correct letter in boxes 1–5 on your answer sheet.

1   According to Paragraph A, what does Professor Armstrong concern about?

    A   Spending more time on TV affects academic level.
    B   Parents have less time to stay with their children.
    C   British children will face health problem in the future.
    D   The speed of property's development increases.

2   What does Armstrong indicate in Paragraph B?

    A   We need to take a 10-minute walk every day.
    B   We should do more activities to exercise our hearts.
    C   Girls' situation is better than that of boys'.
    D   Exercise can cure many diseases.

3   The aim of Fit kids' training is

    A   to make profit by running several sessions.
    B   to only concentrate on one activity for each child.
    C   to guide parents how to organise activities for children.
    D   to spread the idea that team sport is better.

4   What did Lifshitz suggest at the end of this passage?

    A   Create opportunities to exercise your body.
    B   Taking the elevator saves your time.
    C   Kids should spend more than 200 calories each day.
    D   We should never drive but walk.

5   What is the main idea of this passage?

    A   Health of the children who are overweight is at risk in the future.
    B   Children in the UK need proper exercises.
    C   Government takes the mistaken approach for children.
    D   Parents play the most important role in children's activities.

核心词汇

A 段

anxious [ˈæŋkʃəs] *adj.* 焦虑的，不安的，紧张的 [拓] be anxious about sth./for sb. 为某事或某人担心

glue [gluː] *vt.* 粘合，黏合 *n.* 胶水

alarming [əˈlɑːmɪŋ] *adj.* 令人担忧的，令人恐慌的 [拓] alarmingly *adv.* 惊人地；让人担忧地 [拓] alarm *n.* 闹钟 *vt.* 使不安，使惊恐

inactive [ɪnˈæktɪv] *adj.* 不活动的；不工作的 [拓] inactively *adv.* 不活动地；无用地

B 段

exceed [ɪkˈsiːd] *vt.* 超过，胜过 [拓] exceed in 在……方面超过

disturbingly [dɪˈstɜːbɪŋli] *adv.* 令人不安地；使人震惊地 [拓] disturb *vt.* 打扰；妨碍

equivalent [ɪˈkwɪvələnt] *n.* 等价物，等价物 *adj.* 等同的，相当的 [拓] equivalence *n.* 等值，相等

cholesterol [kəˈlestərɒl] *n.* 胆固醇

coronary [ˈkɒrənri] *adj.* 心脏的，冠状动脉的 *n.* 冠状动脉病

C 段

prompt [prɒmpt] *vt.* 促使，激励，激起 *adj.* 迅速的，立刻的；及时的 *adv.* 准时地 *n.* 提词；提示符

D 段

passionate [ˈpæʃənət] *adj.* 有激情的，酷爱的 [拓] passion *n.* 热情；激情

advocate [ˈædvəkeɪt] *n.* 倡导者，支持者 *vi. & vt.* 主张，拥护

inevitably [ɪnˈevɪtəbli] *adv.* 必然地；不可避免地 [拓] inevitable *adj.* 必然的；不可避免的

E 段

untrammelled [ʌnˈtræmld] *adj.* 不受限制的，不受妨碍的

uncoordinated [ˌʌnkəʊˈɔːdɪneɪtɪd] *adj.* 不协调的；笨拙的

F 段

disguise [dɪsˈɡaɪz] *n.* 伪装物，伪装 *vt.* 装扮；掩饰，掩盖

G 段

nutritional [njuˈtrɪʃənl] *adj.* 有营养的；滋养的

高频同义替换

| exceed | ▶ | transcend, go beyond, overcome |
| equivalent | ▶ | equal, same |

| inevitably | ▸ | necessarily, unavoidably, surely |
| prompt | ▸ | motivate, inspire, spur |

题目解析

1. **定位词**：Paragraph A, parents, future, property's development
   文中对应点：A 段倒数第一、二句
   题目解析：由题干中的定位词 Paragraph A 定位到 A 段。A 项说花更多的时间在电视上会影响学习水平，在文中并未提及，所以排除。由 B 项中的 parents 定位到 A 段第二句 "Today they are usually driven to school by parents anxious about safety and spend hours glued to television screens or computer games."。其中，parents 为原文重现，但并未提及父母陪伴孩子的时间多少问题，所以排除。由 C 项中的 future 定位到 A 段倒数第一、二句 "'This change in lifestyle has, sadly, meant greater restrictions on children,' says Neil Armstrong, Professor of Health and Exercise Sciences at the University of Exeter. 'If children continue to be this inactive, they'll be storing up big problems for the future.'"。句意为，阿姆斯特朗教授指出这种生活方式的改变将会使孩子们受到更多的限制。如果孩子们继续这么不活跃，将会对未来造成大麻烦。C 项"英国儿童未来会面临健康问题"意思与原文相符，所以保留。由 D 项中的 property's development 定位到 A 段第三句 "Meanwhile, community playing fields are being sold off to property developers at an alarming rate." 句意为，与此同时，社区的运动场正以惊人的速度被卖给房地产开发商。D 项的"房地产开发增速"不是阿姆斯特朗教授所关注的重点，因此答案为 C。

2. **定位词**：Paragraph B, 10-minute walk, exercise, hearts, diseases
   文中对应点：B 段第四句
   题目解析：由题干中的定位词 Paragraph B 定位到 B 段。由 A 项中的 10-minute walk 定位到 B 段第六句 "More disturbingly, the survey found that over a four-day period, half the girls and one-third of the boys did less exercise than the equivalent of a brisk 10-minute walk."。句意为，调查发现更令人不安的是在四天的时间里，一半的女孩和三分之一的男孩的运动量少于 10 分钟的快步行走的运动量。这是调查的直接结果不是 indicate 的意思，所以排除。由 B 项中的 exercise, hearts 定位到 B 段第四句 "Armstrong adds, 'Heart is a muscle and needs exercise, or it loses its strength.'"。其中，hearts 为 heart 的复数形式。句意为，阿姆斯特朗教授指出心脏是一种肌肉，它需要锻炼，不然就会失去力量。选项 B "我们应该做更多的活动去锻炼心脏"与原文意思一致，所以保留。C 项"女孩的情况比男孩好"在文中并未提及，所以排除。由 D 项中的 diseases 定位到 B 段倒数第一句 "High levels of cholesterol, excess body fat and inactivity are believed to increase the risk of coronary heart disease."。句意为，高胆固醇、过多的身体脂肪和不活动被认为会增加患冠心病的风险。D 项"运动可以治疗许多疾病"在文中并未提及，所以排除。因此答案为 B。

3. **定位词**：Fit Kids' training, activity for children, team sport
   文中对应点：F 段倒数第二句
   题目解析：由题干中的定位词 Fit Kids' training 定位到 F 段。A 项"通过开展几节课来获利"在文中并未提及，所以排除。B 项"只专注于每个孩子的一项活动"在文中也未提及，所以排除。由 C 项

中的 activity for children 定位到 F 段倒数第二句 "Fit Kids trains parents to run fitness classes for children."。其中，activity for children 对应 fitness classes for children。句意为，Fit Kids 培养家长为他们的孩子组织健身课程。C 项 "指导父母如何组织儿童活动" 与原文意思一致，所以保留。由 D 项中的 team sport 定位到 F 段倒数第一句 "Ninety per cent of children don't like team sports."。其中，team sport 为原文出现。句意为，90% 的孩子不喜欢团队运动。但原文没有提及 team sport 更好的观点，所以排除。因此答案为 C。

4　定位词：Lifshitz, at end of this passage
　文中对应点：G 段倒数第一句
　题目解析：由题干中的定位词 Lifshitz，at end of this passage 定位到 G 段倒数第一句 "'Now, kids in obese families are expending only 200 calories a day in physical activity,' says Lifshitz, 'Incorporate more movement in your family's life — park farther away from the stores at the mall, take stairs instead of the elevator, and walk to nearby friends' houses instead of driving.'"。句意为，利夫希茨指出，如今肥胖家庭的孩子每天在户外运动中仅仅消耗 200 卡路里的热量，在家庭生活中要多动动——购物时停车停得远一些，多走楼梯而不是乘电梯，走路去拜访朋友而不是开车。B 项 "乘电梯可以节省时间" 没有在文中出现，所以排除。C 项 "孩子们每天应该摄入超过 200 卡路里的热量" 和 D 项 "我们不应该开车，而是步行" 都只是片面的一个点，而 A 项 "创造机会去锻炼身体" 概括了原文的意思，因此答案为 A。

5　定位词：main idea, this passage
　文中对应点：全篇总结
　题目解析：整篇文章围绕英国学生缺乏运动这一话题。选项 A "肥胖儿童的健康将在未来面临危险" 是 Professor Armstrong 的观点。选项 C "政府对于儿童采用了错误的方式" 原文没有提及。选项 D "家长在儿童活动中扮演着最重要的角色"，原文没有提及。选项 B "英国儿童需要适当的锻炼"，最能体现整篇文章的含义，因此答案为 B。

参考答案

1 C　2 B　3 C　4 A　5 B

Grey Workers

A Given the speed at which their workers are growing greyer, employers know surprisingly little about how productive they are. The general assumption is that the old are paid more in spite of, rather than because of, their extra productivity. That might partly explain why, when employers are under pressure to cut costs, they persuade the 55-year-olds to take early retirement. Earlier this year, Sun Life of Canada, an insurance company, announced that it was offering redundancy to all its British employees aged 50 or over 'to bring in new blood'.

B In Japan, says Mariko Fujiwara, an industrial anthropologist who runs a think-tank for Hakuhodo, Japan's second-largest advertising agency, most companies are bringing down the retirement age from the traditional 57 to 50 or thereabouts — and in some cases, such as Nissan, to 45. More than perhaps anywhere else, pay in Japan is linked to seniority. Given that the percentage of workers who have spent more than 32 years with the same employer rose from 11% in 1980 to 42% by 1994, it is hardly surprising that seniority-based wage costs have become the most intractable item on corporate profit-and-loss accounts.

C In Germany, Patrick Pohl, spokesman for Hoechst, expresses a widely held view: 'The company is trying to lower the average age of the workforce. Perhaps the main reason for replacing older workers is that it makes it easier to "defrost" the corporate culture. Older workers are less willing to try a new way of thinking. Younger workers are cheaper and more flexible.' Some German firms are hampered from getting rid of older workers as quickly as they would like. At SGL Carbon, a graphite producer, the average age of workers has been going up not down. The reason, says the company's Ivo Lingnau, is not that SGL values older workers more. It is collective bargaining: the union agreement puts strict limits on the proportion of workers that may retire early.

D Clearly, when older people do heavy physical work, their age may affect their productivity. But other skills may increase with age, including many that are crucial for good management, such as an ability to handle people diplomatically, to run a meeting or to spot a problem before it blows up. Peter Hicks, who coordinates OECD work on the policy implications of ageing, says that plenty of research suggests older people are paid more because they are worth more.

E And the virtues of the young may be exaggerated. 'The few companies that have kept on older workers find they have good judgment and their productivity is good,' says Mr. Peterson. 'Besides, their education standards are much better than those of today's young high-school graduates.' Companies may say that older workers are not worth training, because they are reaching the end of their working lives: in fact, young people tend to switch jobs so frequently that they offer the worst returns on training. 'The median age for employer-driven training is the late 40s and early 50s,' says Mr. Hicks. 'It goes mainly to managers.'

F Take away those seniority-based pay scales, and older workers may become a much more attractive employment proposition. But most companies (and many workers) are uncomfortable with the idea of reducing someone's pay in later life — although workers on piece-rates often earn less over time. So retaining the services of older workers may mean employing them in new ways.

G One innovation, described in Mr. Walker's report on combating age barriers, was devised by IBM Belgium. Faced with the need to cut staff costs, and having decided to concentrate cuts on 55–60-year-olds, IBM set up a separate company called SkillTeam, which re-employed any of the early retired who wanted to go on working up to the age of 60. An employee who joined SkillTeam at the age of 55 on a five-year contract would work for 58% of his time, over the full period, for 88% of his last IBM salary. The company offered services to IBM, thus allowing it to retain access to some of the intellectual capital it would otherwise have lost.

H The best way to tempt the old to go on working may be to build on such 'bridge' jobs: part-time or temporary employment that creates a more gradual transition from full-time work to retirement. Mr. Quinn, who has studied the phenomenon, finds that, in the United States, nearly half of all men and women who had been in full-time jobs in middle age moved into such 'bridge' jobs at the end of their working lives. 'In general, it is the best-paid and worst-paid who carry on working: there are', he says, 'two very different types of bridge job-holders — those who continue working because they have to and those who continue working because they want to, even though they could afford to retire.'

I If the job market grows more flexible, the old may find more jobs that suit them. Often, they will be self-employed. Sometimes, they may start their own businesses: a study by David Storey of Warwick University found that, in Britain, 70% of businesses started by people over 55 survived, compared with an average of only 19%. To coax the old back into the job market, work will not only have to pay. It will need to be more fun than touring the country in an Airstream trailer, or seeing the grandchildren, or playing golf. Only then will there be many more Joe Clarks.

Questions 1–5

Choose the correct letter, **A**, **B**, **C** or **D**.

Write the correct letter in boxes 1–5 on your answer sheet.

1   According to Paragraph F, the firms and workers still hold the opinion that

    A   older workers are more likely to attract other staff.
    B   people are not happy if pay gets lower in retiring age.
    C   older people have more retaining motivation than young people.
    D   young people often earn less for their piece-rates salary.

2   Which of the following movements did SkillTeam that has been founded by IBM conduct?

    A   Ask all the old workers to continue their jobs on former working hours' basis.
    B   Carry on the action of cutting off the elder's proportion of employment.
    C   Ask employees to work more hours in order to get extra pay.
    D   Re-hire old employees and keep the salary a bit lower.

3   Which of the followings is correct according to the research of Mr. Quinn?

    A   About 50% of all employees in America switched into 'bridge' jobs.
    B   Only the worst-paid continue to work.
    C   More men than women fell into the category of 'bridge' work.
    D   Some old people keep working for their motive rather than economic incentive.

4   Which of the followings is correct according to David Storey?

    A   70% of businesses will be successful if hiring more older people.
    B   The rate of success of self-employed business is getting lower.
    C   Self-employed elder people are more likely to survive.
    D   Older people's working hours are more flexible.

5   What is the main purpose of the author in writing this passage?

    A   There must be a successful retiring programme for the old.
    B   Older people should be correctly valued in employment.
    C   Old people should offer more help for young employees' growth.
    D   There should be more companies in the world that only employ older people.

核心词汇

A 段

assumption [əˈsʌmpʃn] *n.* 假定，设想；担任

redundancy [rɪˈdʌndənsi] *n.* 冗余，多余；裁员

B 段

think-tank *n.* 智囊团

thereabouts [ˈðeərəbaʊts] *adv.* 在那附近；大约

seniority [siːnɪˈɒrɪti] *n.* 资历，年资

intractable [ɪnˈtræktəbl] *adj.* 棘手的，难解决的

C 段

defrost [ˌdiːˈfrɒst] *vi. & vt.* 除霜，解冻

hamper [ˈhæmpər] *vt.* 妨碍，束缚

get rid of 摆脱，除去

collective [kəˈlektɪv] *adj.* 集体的，共同的，共有的 *n.* 集团；集体企业

D 段

crucial [ˈkruːʃl] *adj.* 重要的，决定性的

diplomatically [ˌdɪpləˈmætɪkli] *adv.* 圆滑地；婉转地；在外交上 [拓] diplomat *n.* 外交官

spot [spɒt] *vt.* 发现，注意，认出 *n.* 地点；斑点

E 段

virtue [ˈvɜːtʃuː] *n.* 美德；优点

exaggerate [ɪɡˈzædʒəreɪt] *vi. & vt.* 夸张，夸大

median [ˈmiːdiən] *adj.* 中值的；中央的 *n.* 中值，中位数

F 段

proposition [ˌprɒpəˈzɪʃ(ə)n] *n.* 主张，观点；提议 [拓] propose *vt.* 建议，提议

G 段

innovation [ˌɪnəˈveɪʃ(ə)n] *n.* 创新，革新 [拓] innovate *vi. & vt.* 创新，革新；改革

combat [ˈkɒmbæt] *vt.* 与……战斗；反对 *n.* 战斗；争论

retain [rɪˈteɪn] *vt.* 保持，保留；记住

capital [ˈkæpɪtl] *n.* 资金，资本；首都；大写字母 *adj.* 首都的；资金的；大写的

H 段

tempt [tempt] *vt.* 诱惑；劝说，鼓动

temporary ['temprəri] *adj.* 暂时的，临时的；短期的

I 段

coax [kəuks] *vt.* 劝诱，诱导

高频同义替换

get lower	▶	reduce, decrease, lessen, cut down
re-hire	▶	re-employ
incentive	▶	motivation, stimulation
self-employ	▶	start one's own business

题目解析

1 定位词：Paragraph F, attract, not happy, piece-rates

文中对应点：F 段第二句

题目解析：由题干中的定位词 Paragraph F 定位到 F 段。由 A 项中的 attract 定位到 F 段第一句 "Take away those seniority-based pay scales, and older workers may become a much more attractive employment proposition."。其中，attractive 为 attract 的形容词形式。句意为老员工更受企业的青睐，而非选项中的 attract other staff（吸引其他员工），所以排除。由 B 项中的 not happy 定位到 F 段第二句 "But most companies (and many workers) are uncomfortable with the idea of reducing someone's pay in later life — although workers on piece-rates often earn less over time."。其中，not happy 与 uncomfortable 为同义替换。B 项中的 pay gets lower in retiring age 对应 reducing someone's pay in later life，意思与原文相符，所以保留。C 项说老人比年轻人更有动力，在文中并未提及，所以排除。根据 D 项中的 piece-rates 同样定位到 F 段第二句 "...although workers on piece-rates often earn less over time."。句意为，尽管按计件的工人的收入通常会随着时间的推移而减少。D 项 "年轻人计件工资通常较低" 与原文表述不一致，所以排除。因此答案为 B。

2 定位词：SkillTeam, IBM, old workers, re-hire

文中对应点：G 段第二、三句

题目解析：由题干中的定位词 SkillTeam 定位到 G 段。由 A 项中的 old workers 定位到 G 段第二句 "Faced with the need to cut staff costs, and having decided to concentrate cuts on 55–60-year-olds, IBM set up a separate company called SkillTeam..."。其中，old workers 与 55–60-year-olds 对应。句意为面对削减员工成本的需要，并决定将裁员集中在 55 岁至 60 岁的人群中后，IBM 成立了一家名为 "技能团队" 的独立公司……但并未提及 continue their jobs，所以排除。B 项说继续采取削减老年人就业比例的行动，在文中并未提及，所以排除。C 项说要求员工多工作几个小时，以

获得额外的报酬，在文中并未提及，所以排除。由 D 项中的 re-hire 定位到 G 段第二句 "...IBM set up a separate company called SkillTeam, which re-employed any of the early retired who wanted to go on working up to the age of 60."。其中，原文中的 re-employed 对应 D 项中的 re-hire。句意为……IBM 成立了一家名为"技能团队"的独立公司，该公司重新聘用了那些想要工作到 60 岁的早期退休人员。G 段第三句 "An employee who joined SkillTeam at the age of 55 on a five-year contract would work for 58% of his time, over the full period, for 88% of his last IBM salary." 句意为加入 SkillTeam 的工人，工作 58% 的时间可以拿到他在 IBM 最后薪水的 88%，对应 D 项中的 a bit lower，所以答案为 D。

3 **定位词**：Mr. Quinn, switched into, worst-paid, rather than economic incentive
  文中对应点：H 段第二、三句
  题目解析：由题干中的定位词 Mr. Quinn 定位到 H 段。由 A 项中的 switched into 定位到 H 段第二句 "Mr. Quinn, who has studied the phenomenon, finds that, in the United States, nearly half of all men and women who had been in full-time jobs in middle age moved into such 'bridge' jobs at the end of their working lives."。其中，moved into 对应 switched into，但 A 项扩大了论述对象的范围，who had been in full-time jobs in middle age 与选项 A 中的 about 50% of all employees in America 描述不一致，所以排除。由 B 项中的 worst-paid 定位到 H 段第三句 "'In general, it is the best-paid and worst-paid who carry on working...'"。其中 worst-paid 为原文重现。句意为，不仅仅是工资低的人会继续工作，工资高的人也可能继续工作。B 项中的 only the worst-paid 只是抓住了原文的部分信息，表达上过于绝对化，和原文不一致，所以排除。C 项说进入 "bridge" 就业中的男性数量多于女性，原文并未涉及，所以排除。由 D 项中的 rather than economic incentive 定位到 H 段第三句 "...those who continue working because they want to, even though they could afford to retire."。其中，could afford to retire 对应 rather than economic incentive。句意为，一部分人工作只是因为他们想工作，即使他们有足够的钱享受退休生活。选项意思和原文表述一致，所以答案为 D。

4 **定位词**：David Storey, 70% of businesses, the rate of success, survive
  文中对应点：I 段第三句
  题目解析：由题干中的定位词 David Storey 定位到 I 段。由 A 项中的 70% of businesses 定位到 I 段第三句 "...a study by David Storey of Warwick University found that, in Britain, 70% of businesses started by people over 55 survived...."。句意为，英国华威大学的大卫·斯托里的一项研究发现，在英国，由 55 岁以上的人创办的企业七成可以存活。选项 A 中的雇佣更多的老年员工就能成功，表述与原文不一致，所以排除。由 B 项中的 the rate of success 定位到 I 段第三句 "..., compared with an average of only 19%."。原文并没有说明总体的平均变化是减少还是增多，选项 B 中的 is getting lower 用的是现在进行时，表示正在逐渐变少，描述的是一个动态变化的状态，所以排除。由 C 项中的 survive 同样定位到 I 段第三句 "...a study by David Storey of Warwick University found that, in Britain, 70% of businesses started by people over 55 survived..."。其中，70% of businesses started by people over 55 survived 与 more likely to survive 意思一致，所以保留。D 项表示老年人的工作时间更灵活，但文中只是强调比起薪水，重新开始工作的老年人更在意工作是否更有趣。所以答案为 C。

5 定位词：main purpose, this passage

文中对应点：全文大意

题目解析：这是一道概括题，需要总结全文以弄清作者的态度。分析文章结构可以发现，A 到 C 段主要说明公司解雇老年员工的原因并描述老年员工的缺点和不足，但 D 到 F 段为转折段，论述了老年员工具备的优势，并在 G 到 I 段针对老年员工的就业问题提出相应的解决措施和建议。根据上述文章结构的分析，作者的态度十分明显：老年员工在职场上的价值应被正确认识，所以答案为 B。

参考答案

1 B   **2** D   **3** D   **4** C   **5** B

Smell and Memory

Why does the scent of a fragrance or the mustiness of an old trunk trigger such powerful memories of childhood? New research has the answer, writes Alexandra Witze.

A You probably pay more attention to a newspaper with your eyes than with your nose, but lift the paper to your nostril and inhale. The smell of newsprint might carry you back to your childhood, when your parents perused the paper on Sunday mornings. Or maybe some other smell takes you back — the scent of your mother's perfume, the pungency of a driftwood campfire. Specific odours can spark a flood of reminiscences. Psychologists call it the 'Proustian phenomenon', after French novelist Marcel Proust. Near the beginning of the masterpiece *In Search of Lost Time*, Proust's narrator dunks a madeleine cookie into a cup of tea — and the scent and taste unleash a torrent of childhood memories for 3,000 pages.

B Now, this phenomenon is getting the scientific treatment. Neuroscientists Rachel Herz, a cognitive neuroscientist at Brown University in Providence, Rhode Island, have discovered, for instance, how sensory memories are shared across the brain, with different brain regions remembering the sights, smells, tastes and sounds of a particular experience. Meanwhile, psychologists have demonstrated that memories triggered by smells can be more emotional, as well as more detailed, than memories not related to smells. When you inhale, odour molecules set brain cells dancing within a region known as the amygdala, a part of the brain that helps control emotion. In contrast, the other senses, such as taste or touch, get routed through other parts of the brain before reaching the amygdala. The direct link between odours and the amygdala may help explain the emotional potency of smells. 'There is this unique connection between the sense of smell and the part of the brain that processes emotion,' says Rachel Herz.

C But the links don't stop there. Like an octopus reaching its tentacles outward, the memory of smells affects other brain regions as well. In recent experiments, neuroscientists at University College London (UCL) asked 15 volunteers to look at pictures while smelling unrelated odours. For instance, the subjects might see a photo of a duck paired with the scent of a rose, and then be asked to create a story linking the two. Brain scans taken at the time revealed that the volunteers' brains were particularly active in a region known as the olfactory cortex, which is known to be involved in processing smells. Five minutes later, the volunteers were shown the duck photo again, but without the rose smell. And in their brains, the olfactory cortex lit up again, the scientists reported recently. The fact that the olfactory cortex became active in the absence of the odour suggests that people's sensory memory of events is spread across different brain regions. Imagine going on a seaside holiday, says UCL team leader, Jay Gottfried. The sight of the waves becomes stored in one area, whereas the crash of the surf goes elsewhere, and the smell of seaweed in yet another place. There could be advantages to having memories spread around the brain. 'You can reawaken that memory from any one of the sensory triggers,' says Gottfried. 'Maybe the smell of the sun lotion, or a particular sound from that day, or the sight of a rock formation.' Or in the case of an early hunter and gatherer out on a plain — the sight of a lion might be enough to trigger the urge to flee, rather than having to wait for the sound of its roar and the stench of its hide to kick in as well.

D 'Remembered smells may also carry extra emotional baggage,' says Herz. Her research suggests that memories triggered by odours are more emotional than memories triggered by other cues. In one recent study, Herz recruited 5 volunteers who had vivid memories associated with a particular perfume, such as Opium for Women and Juniper Breeze from Bath and Body Works. She took images of the volunteers' brains as they sniffed that perfume and an unrelated perfume without knowing which was which. (They were also shown photos of each perfume bottle.) Smelling the specified perfume activated the volunteers' brains the most, particularly in the amygdala, and in a region called the hippocampus, which helps in memory formation. Herz published the work earlier this year in the journal *Neuropsychologia*.

E But she couldn't be sure that the other senses wouldn't also elicit a strong response. So in another study Herz compared smells with sounds and pictures. She had 70 people describe an emotional memory involving three items — popcorn, fresh-cut grass and a campfire. Then they compared the items through sights, sounds and smells. For instance, the person might see a picture of a lawnmower, then sniff the scent of grass and finally listen to the lawnmower's sound. Memories triggered by smell were more evocative than memories triggered by either sights or sounds.

F Odour-evoked memories may be not only more emotional, but more detailed as well. Working with colleague John Downes, psychologist Simon Chu of the University of Liverpool started researching odour and memory partly because of his grandmother's stories about Chinese culture. As generations gathered to share oral histories, they would pass a small pot of spice or incense around; later, when they wanted to remember the story in as much detail as possible, they would pass the same smell around again. 'Its kind of fits with a lot of anecdotal evidence on how smells can be really good reminders of past experiences,' Chu says. And scientific research seems to bear out the anecdotes. In one experiment, Chu and Downes asked 42 volunteers to tell a life story, then tested to see whether odours such as coffee and cinnamon could help them remember more details in the story. They could.

G Despite such studies, not everyone is convinced that Proust can be scientifically analysed. In the June issue of *Chemical Senses*, Chu and Downes exchanged critiques with renowned perfumer and chemist J. Stephan Jellinek. Jellinek chided the Liverpool researchers for, among other things, presenting the smells and asking the volunteers to think of memories, rather than seeing what memories were spontaneously evoked by the odours. But there's only so much science they can do to test a phenomenon that's inherently different for each person, Chu says. Meanwhile, Jellinek has also been collecting anecdotal accounts of Proustian experiences, hoping to find some common links between the experiences. 'I think there is a case to be made that surprise may be a major aspect of the Proust phenomenon,' he says. 'That's why people are so struck by these memories.' No one knows whether Proust ever experienced such a transcendental moment. But his notions of memory, written as fiction nearly a century ago, continue to inspire scientists of today.

Questions 1–4

Choose the correct letter, **A**, **B**, **C** or **D**.

Write the correct letter in boxes 1–4 on your answer sheet.

1   What does the experiment conducted by Herz show?

    A   Women are more easily addicted to opium medicine.
    B   Smell is superior to other senses in connection to the brain.
    C   Smell is more important than other senses.
    D   Amygdala is part of brain that stores and processes memory.

2   What does the second experiment conducted by Herz suggest?

    A   The result directly conflicts with the first one.
    B   The result of the first experiment is correct.
    C   Sights and sounds trigger memories at an equal level.
    D   The lawnmower is a perfect example in the experiment.

3   What is the outcome of the experiment conducted by Chu and Downes?

    A   Smell is the only one that functions under Chinese tradition.
    B   Half of volunteers told detailed story.
    C   Smells of certain odours assist story tellers.
    D   Odour of cinnamon is stronger than that of coffee.

4   What is the comment of Jellinek to Chu and Downes in the issue of Chemical Senses?

    A   Jellinek accused their experiment of being unscientific.
    B   Jellinek thought Liverpool is not a suitable place for experiment.
    C   Jellinek suggested that there was no further clue of what specific memories aroused.
    D   Jellinek stated that experiment could be remedied.

核心词汇

A 段

trigger ['trɪgə(r)] *vt.* 引发，引起；触发 *n.* 扳机

peruse [pə'ruːz] *vt.* 细读，精读

pungency ['pʌndʒənsi] *n.* 辛辣；刺激性 [拓] pungent *adj.* 辛辣的；刺激的；尖刻的

reminiscence [ˌremɪ'nɪsns] *n.* 回忆，回忆录 [拓] reminisce *vi.* 回忆，缅怀过去

unleash [ʌn'liːʃ] *vt.* 释放，发泄

B 段

cognitive ['kɒgnətɪv] *adj.* 认知的，认识的 [拓] cognition *n.* 认知；认识

sensory ['sensəri] *adj.* 感觉的，感官的，知觉的 [拓] sense *n.* 感觉；感官；理解力

inhale [ɪn'heɪl] *vi. & vt.* 吸入，吸气

process ['prəʊses] *vt.* 处理；加工 *vi.* 列队前进 *n.* 过程，进行；程序

C 段

olfactory [ɒ'fæktəri] *adj.* 嗅觉的；味道的

lotion ['ləʊʃn] *n.* 洗液；洗涤剂

D 段

recruit [rɪ'kruːt] *vi. & vt.* 招聘，招募；吸收 *vt.* 劝说，劝服

sniff [snɪf] *vi. & vt.* 嗅，闻 *n.* 闻；哼声

E 段

evocative [ɪ'vɒkətɪv] *adj.* 唤起感情的

F 段

anecdote ['ænɪkdəʊt] *n.* 轶事；奇闻 [拓] anecdotal *adj.* 轶事的，趣闻的

bear out 证实；支持

G 段

critique [krɪ'tiːk] *n.* 批评；评论文章 *vt.* 批判；评论

renowned [rɪ'naʊnd] *adj.* 著名的；有声望的

spontaneously [spɒn'teɪniəsli] *adv.* 自发地，自然地；率性地

inherently [ɪn'hɪərəntli] *adv.* 固有地，内在地

高频同义替换

trigger ▶ arouse, stimulate, invoke, cause, lead to, give rise to, bring about

detailed ▶ specific, explicit, particular, elaborate

assist ▶ aid, help

comment ▶ critique, criticise

题目解析

1. 定位词：experiment, Herz, brain, amygdala

   文中对应点：D 段倒数第二句

   题目解析：由题干中的定位词 experiment 和 Herz 定位至 D 段。A 项说女性更容易对鸦片药物上瘾，原文中并未提出对比，无从判断，所以排除。由 B 项中的 brain 定位到 D 段第四句 "She took images of the volunteers' brains as they sniffed that perfume and an unrelated perfume without knowing which was which."。其中，brains 为 brain 的复数形式。句意为，当志愿者在不知道香水是哪一种的情况下闻特定香水和一种不相关的香水时，她拍下了志愿者们的大脑图像。B 项说嗅觉比其他与大脑有关的感觉更高级。原文没有将嗅觉与其他与大脑有关的感觉进行比较，所以排除。C 项说嗅觉比其他感觉更重要。原文并没有将嗅觉与其他感官的重要性进行对比，所以排除。由 D 项中的 amygdala 定位到 D 段倒数第二句 "Smelling the specified perfume activated the volunteers' brains the most, particularly in the amygdala, and in a region called the hippocampus, which helps in memory formation."。句意为，闻到特定香水后的志愿者的大脑被激活最多，尤其是杏仁核区，以及一个帮助形成记忆力的叫做海马体的区域。原文与选项 D "杏仁核是大脑中储存和处理记忆的区域"意思一致。因此答案为 D。

2. 定位词：second experiment, Herz, result, lawnmower

   文中对应点：E 段倒数第一、二句

   题目解析：由题干中的定位词 second experiment, Herz 定位到 E 段 "So in another study Herz compared smells with sounds and pictures."。其中，第二句中的 another study 对应题干中的 second experiment，说明其后的内容是对该实验的分析。由 A 项中的 result 定位到 E 段倒数第一句 "Memories triggered by smell were more evocative than memories triggered by either sights or sounds."。句意为，由气味引起的记忆比由视觉或声音触发的记忆更能唤起回忆。第一项实验的结论在 D 段第二句，指出气味引发的记忆比其他感官引发的要更情感化，这与 E 段最后一句的内容相符，所以 A 项 "实验结果与第一项实验结果恰好相反"错误，所以排除。B 项说第一项试验的结果是正确的，这与原文内容意思一致，所以保留。C 项说视觉和声音能够引发相同程度的记忆。原文中没有提到视觉和听觉所引发的记忆是不是同等程度的比较，无从判断，所以排除。由 D 项中的 lawnmower 定位到 E 段倒数第二句 "For instance, the person might see a picture of a lawnmower, then sniff the scent of grass and finally listen to the lawnmower's sound."。句意为，例如这个人可能会看到一台割草机的照片，然后嗅出青草的气味，最后听到割草机的声音。D 项说割草机是试验中完美的例子。原文中仅提到割草机，但并未提及是否是完美的例子，无从判断，所以排除。因此答案为 B。

3 **定位词**：Chu and Downes, volunteers, assist, story, cinnamon, coffee
　文中对应点：F 段倒数第一、二句
　题目解析：由题干中的定位词 Chu and Downes 定位到 F 段。A 项说嗅觉是中国传统中唯一实用的。文中无对应点，所以排除。由 B 项中的 volunteers 定位到 F 段倒数第二句 "In one experiment, Chu and Downes asked 42 volunteers to tell a life story, then tested to see whether odours such as coffee and cinnamon could help them remember more details in the story."。句意为，在一项实验中，Chu 和 Downes 让 42 名志愿者讲述一个人生故事，然后测试看咖啡和肉桂等气味是否能帮助他们记住故事中的更多细节。B 项说半数的志愿者都讲述了细节性的故事。文中并未提到 half，所以排除。由 C 项中的 assist, story 定位到 F 段倒数第一、二句 "In one experiment, Chu and Downes asked 42 volunteers to tell a life story, then tested to see whether odours such as coffee and cinnamon could help them remember more details in the story. They could."。其中，help 与选项 C 中的 assist 为同义替换。句意为，两人的实验结果体现在最后两句，说明咖啡或肉桂皮这样的气味是否能够帮助志愿者记住故事中的更多细节，答案是肯定的——能。选项 C 项与定位句意思一致，所以保留。由 D 项中的 cinnamon, coffee 同样定位到 F 段倒数第二句，D 项说肉桂的气味比咖啡更加强烈。原文中 cinnamon 和 coffee 是并列关系，并无比较，所以排除。因此答案为 C。

4 **定位词**：comment of Jellinek, Liverpool
　文中对应点：G 段第三句
　题目解析：由题干中的定位词 comment of Jellinek 定位到 G 段。A 项说 Jellinek 指责他们的实验没有科学性。文中只是提到指责，但并未对其是否科学作出评价，无从判断，所以排除。由 B 项中的 Liverpool 定位到 G 段第三句 "Jellinek chided the Liverpool researchers for, among other things,..."。文中并未提到杰利内克是否认为利物浦不适合做实验，仅提到科学家来自利物浦，所以排除。由 C 项中的 Liverpool 定位到 G 段第三句 "...among other things, presenting the smells and asking the volunteers to think of memories, rather than seeing what memories were spontaneously evoked by the odours."。其中，rather than...by the odours 与选项 C 中的 no further clue of what specific memories aroused（杰利内克表示没有更进一步的证据表明所被引发的具体回忆）意思一致。句意为，Jellinek 斥责利物浦的研究人员，在某些方面，呈现气味的同时要求志愿者来记忆，而不是研究是什么样的回忆能自发地被气味所引发。保留 C 项。D 项说 Jellinek 声称这项实验能够被纠正。原文中只出现了对某些方面的责备，并没有提到是否要纠正这项实验，无从判断，所以排除。因此答案为 C。

参考答案

1 D　2 B　3 C　4 C

READING PASSAGE 4

The Origin of Ancient Writing

A The Sumerians, an ancient people of the Middle East, had a story explaining the invention of writing more than 5,000 years ago. It seems a messenger of the King of Uruk arrived at the court of a distant ruler so exhausted that he was unable to deliver the oracle message. So the king set down the words of his next messages on a clay tablet. A charming story, whose retelling at a recent symposium at the University of Pennsylvania amused scholars. They smiled at the absurdity of a letter which the recipient would not have been able to read.

B They also doubted that the earliest writing was a direct rendering of speech. Writing more likely began as a separate, symbolic system of communication and only later merged with spoken language.

C Yet in the story the Sumerians, who lived in Mesopotamia, in what is now southern Iraq, seemed to understand writing's transforming function. As Dr Holly Pittman, director of the University's Centre for Ancient Studies, observed, writing 'arose out of the need to store and transmit information...over time and space'.

D In exchanging interpretations and information, the scholars acknowledged that they still had no fully satisfying answers to the questions of how and why writing developed. Many favoured an explanation of writing's origins in the visual arts, pictures becoming increasingly abstract and eventually representing spoken words. Their views clashed with a widely held theory among archaeologists that writing developed from the pieces of clay that Sumerian accountants used as tokens to keep track of goods.

E Archaeologists generally concede that they have no definitive answer to the question of whether writing was invented only once, or arose independently in several places, such as Egypt, the Indus Valley, China, Mexico and Central America. The preponderance of archaeological data shows that the urbanising Sumerians were the first to develop writing, in 3 200 or 3 300 BC. These are the dates for many clay tablets in an early form of cuneiform, a script written by pressing the end of a sharpened stick into wet clay, found at the site of the ancient city of Uruk.

The baked clay tablets bore such images as pictorial symbols of the names of people, places and things connected with government and commerce. The Sumerian script gradually evolved from the pictorial to the abstract but did not at first represent recorded spoken language.

F Dr Peter Damerow, a specialist in Sumerian cuneiform at the Max Planck Institute for the History of Science in Berlin, said, it is likely that there were mutual influences of writing systems around the world. However, their great variety now shows that the development of writing, once initiated, attains a considerable degree of independence and flexibility to adapt to specific characteristics of the sounds of the language to be represented. Not that he accepts the conventional view that writing started as a representation of words by pictures. New studies of early Sumerian writing, he said, challenge this interpretation. The structures of this earliest writing did not, for example, match the structure of spoken language, dealing mainly in lists and categories rather than in sentences and narrative.

G For at least two decades, Dr Denise Schmandt-Besserat, a University of Texas archaeologist, has argued that the first writing grew directly out of a system practised by Sumerian accountants. They used clay tokens, each one shaped to represent a jar of oil, a container of grain or a particular kind of livestock. These tokens were sealed inside clay spheres, and then the number and type of tokens inside was recorded on the outside using impressions resembling the tokens. Eventually, the token impressions were replaced with inscribed signs, and writing had been invented.

H Though Dr Schmandt-Besserat has won much support, some linguists question her thesis, and others, like Dr Pittman, think it too narrow. They emphasise that pictorial representation and writing evolved together. 'There's no question that the token system is a forerunner of writing,' Dr Pittman said, 'but I have an argument with her evidence for a link between tokens and signs, and she doesn't open up the process to include picture making.'

I Dr Schmandt-Besserat vigorously defended her ideas. 'My colleagues say that pictures were the beginning of writing,' she said. 'But show me a single picture that becomes a sign in writing. They say that designs on pottery were the beginning of writing, but show me a single sign of writing you can trace back to a pot — it doesn't exist.' In its first 500 years, she asserted, cuneiform writing was used almost solely for recording economic information, and after that its uses multiplied and broadened.

J Yet other scholars have advanced different ideas. Dr. Piotr Michalowski, Professor of Near East Civilisations at the University of Michigan, said that the proto-writing of Sumerian Uruk was 'so radically different as to be a complete break with the past'. It no doubt served, he said, to store and communicate information, but also became a new instrument of power. Some scholars noted that the origins of writing may not always have been in economics. In Egypt, most early writing is high on monuments or deep in tombs. In this case, said Dr Pascal Vernus from a university in Paris, early writing was less administrative than sacred. It seems that only certainty in this field is that many questions remain to be answered.

Questions 1–4

*Choose the correct letter, **A**, **B**, **C**, or **D**.*

Write the correct letter in boxes 1–4 on your answer sheet.

1 The researchers at the symposium regarded the story of the King of Uruk as ridiculous because

   A   writing probably developed independently of speech.
   B   clay tablets had not been invented at that time.
   C   the distant ruler would have spoken another language.
   D   evidence of writing has been discovered from an earlier period.

2 According to the writer, the story of the King of Uruk

   A   is a probable explanation of the origins of writing.
   B   proves that early writing had a different function to writing today.
   C   provides an example of symbolic writing.
   D   shows some awareness amongst Sumerians of the purpose of writing.

3 There was disagreement among the researchers at the symposium about

   A   the area where writing began.
   B   the nature of early writing materials.
   C   the way writing began.
   D   the meaning of certain abstract images.

4 The opponents of the theory that writing developed from tokens believe that it

   A   grew out of accountancy.
   B   evolved from pictures.
   C   was initially intended as decoration.
   D   was unlikely to have been connected with commerce.

核心词汇

A 段

Sumerian [sjuːˈmɛərɪən] *n.* 苏美尔人
oracle [ˈɒrəkl] *n.* 神谕；宣示神谕的人
symposium [sɪmˈpəʊzɪəm] *n.* 讨论会
absurdity [əbˈsɜːdəti] *n.* 荒谬
recipient [rɪˈsɪpɪənt] *n.* 接受者

B 段

rendering [ˈrendərɪŋ] *n.* 表演，演奏

C 段

Mesopotamia [ˌmesəpəˈteimiə] *n.* 美索不达米亚

D 段

clash [klæʃ] *v.* 冲突，打斗
token [ˈtəʊkən] *n.* 表征；代币；记号

E 段

concede [kənˈsiːd] *v.* 承认；让步，认输
preponderance [prɪˈpɒndərəns] *n.* 数量上的优势
cuneiform [ˈkjuːnɪfɔːm] *n.* 楔形文字
pictorial [pɪkˈtɔːrɪəl] *adj.* 绘画的；形象化的

F 段

mutual [ˈmjuːtʃuəl] *adj.* 相互的，彼此的
attain [əˈteɪn] *v.* 得到，获得

G 段

inscribe [ɪnˈskraɪb] *v.* 印制；题写

H 段

forerunner [ˈfɔːrʌnə(r)] *n.* 先驱

I 段

vigorously [ˈvɪɡərəsli] *adv.* 强有力地

J 段

sacred [ˈseɪkrɪd] *adj.* 神的；神圣的；宗教的

高频同义替换

deliver	▸	take, pass
transmit	▸	release, send, communicate
eventually	▸	finally, ultimately, lastly
connect	▸	join, band, combine
mutual	▸	corporate, common, collective, joint
record	▸	register, keep track of, make notes of
impression	▸	infection, effect, influence, affection
argument	▸	discussion, debate, dispute
broaden	▸	enlarge, extend, exaggerate
communicate	▸	intercommunicate, affect, contract, convey, keep in touch with

题目解析

1 定位词：King of Uruk, ridiculous

文中对应点：A 段倒数第一句

题目解析：由题干中的定位词 King of Uruk 和 ridiculous 定位到 A 段倒数第一句 "They smiled at the absurdity of a letter which the recipient would not have been able to read."。其中，absurdity（荒谬）与题干中的 ridiculous 对应，recipient 与 C 项中的 distant ruler 对应，not have been able to read 与 C 项中的 have spoken another language 对应。句意为，他们对信使可能没办法读明白信件这个传说的荒谬之处报以微笑。其他选项原文均没有提及。因此答案为 C。

2 定位词：the story, the origins of writing, symbolic writing, Sumerians

文中对应点：B 段第二句和 C 段第一句

题目解析：由定位词 the story 和 symbolic writing 定位到 B 段。由 A 项中的 the origins of writing 定位到 B 段第二句 "Writing more likely began as a separate, symbolic system of communication and only later merged with spoken language."。其中，origins 与 began 对应，但原文中的 a separate, symbolic system of communication 与 the story of the King of Uruk 意思矛盾，所以排除 A 项。B 项说 King of Uruk 故事证明了早期文字与今天的文字有不同的作用，原文未提及。由 C 项中的 symbolic writing 同样定位到 B 段第二句，但说 King of Uruk 故事并不是证明 symbolic writing 实例。由 D 项中的 Sumerians 定位到 C 段第一句 "Yet in the story the Sumerians, who lived in Mesopotamia, in what is now southern Iraq, seemed to understand writing's transforming function."。其中，understand 与 some awareness 对应，writing's transforming function 与 the purpose of writing 对应。句意为，然而，在这个故事中，住在美索不达米亚，现在的伊拉克南部的苏美尔人，似乎理解书写的转换功能。D 项 "展示了苏美尔人对写作目的的一些认识" 与原文相符，所以保留。因此答案为 D。

3 定位词：symposium, writing began, abstract images

文中对应点：D 段第二句

题目解析：由题干中的定位词 symposium 定位到 A 段。A 段提及一个传说，因为一位远方的信使，路途遥远过度疲劳，没力气再口头传信息回去，因此，国王将要传回的内容写在粘土版上，这应该是最早的文字发明，但尾句提到"座谈会上的人都觉得这是荒唐可笑的"。由 A 和 C 项中的 writing began，D 项中的 abstract images 定位到 D 段第二句 "Many favoured an explanation of writing's origins in the visual arts, pictures becoming increasingly abstract and eventually representing spoken words."。其中，writing's origins 与 writing began 对应，pictures becoming increasingly abstract 与 abstract images 对应。句意为，许多人倾向于用视觉艺术解释文字起源，图片变得越来越抽象，并最终发展为口语。这与 C 项"文字开始的方式"意思一致。因此答案为 C。

4 定位词：opponents, tokens, accountancy, pictures

文中对应点：D 段倒数第一、二句和 H 段倒数第一句

题目解析：由题干中的定位词 opponents, tokens 定位到 D 段倒数第一句 "Their views clashed with a widely held theory among archaeologists that writing developed from the pieces of clay that Sumerian accountants used as tokens to keep track of goods."。其中，clashed with 对应 opponents。句意为，他们的观点与考古学家普遍持有的理论相冲突，他们认为古代文字发展于苏美尔人的会计作为标记来记录货物的粘土碎片。由 A 项中的 accountancy 同样定位到 D 段倒数第一句，其中，accountancy 与 accountants 为同根词，但 opponents 并不认为文字起源于 accountancy，所以排除。由 B 项中的 pictures 定位到 D 段倒数第二句 "...pictures becoming increasingly abstract and eventually representing spoken words." 以及 H 段倒数第一句 "'There's no question that the token system is a forerunner of writing,' Dr Pittman said, 'but I have an argument with her evidence for a link between tokens and signs, and she doesn't open up the process to include picture making.'"。其中，visual arts, pictures 与 B 项符合，意思与原文相符，所以保留。C 项说文字最初的目的是作为装饰，原文未提及。D 项说不太可能与商业联系在一起，这与 D 段倒数第一句提及的 ...Sumerian accountants used as tokens to keep track of goods 矛盾，所以排除。因此答案为 B。

参考答案

1 C 2 D 3 C 4 B

Compliance or Noncompliance for Children

A   Many Scientists believe that socialisation takes a long process, while compliance is the outset of it. Accordingly, compliance for education of children is the priority. Motivationally distinct forms of child compliance, mutually positive affect, and maternal control, observed in 3 control contexts in 103 dyads of mothers and their 26–41-month-old children, were examined as correlates of internalisation, assessed using observations of children while alone with prohibited temptations and maternal ratings. One form of compliance (committed compliance), when the child appeared committed wholeheartedly to the maternal agenda and eager to endorse and accept it, was emphasised. Mother-child mutually positive affect was both a predictor and a concomitant of committed compliance. Children who shared positive affect with their mothers showed a high level of committed compliance and were also more internalised. Differences and similarities between children's compliance to requests and prohibitions ('Do' vs. 'Don't' demand contexts) were also explored. Maternal 'Dos' appeared more challenging to toddlers than the 'Don't's. Some individual coherence of behaviour was also found across both demand contexts. The implications of committed compliance for emerging internalised regulators of conduct are discussed.

B   A number of parents were not easy to be aware of the compliance, some even overlooked their children's noncompliance. Despite good education, these children did not follow the words from their parents on several occasions, especially boys in certain ages. Fortunately, this rate was acceptable, some parents could be patient with the noncompliance. Someone held that noncompliance is probably not a wrong thing. In order to determine the effects of different parental disciplinary techniques on young children's compliance and noncompliance, mothers were trained to observe emotional incidents involving their own toddler-aged children. Reports of disciplinary encounters were analysed in terms of the types of discipline used (reasoning, verbal prohibition, physical coercion, love withdrawal, and combinations thereof) and children's responses to that discipline (compliance/noncompliance and avoidance). The relation between compliance/noncompliance and type of misdeed (harm to persons, harm to property, and lapses of self-control) was also analysed. Results indicated that love withdrawal combined with other techniques was most effective in securing children's compliance and that its effectiveness was not a function of the type of technique with which it was combined. Avoidant responses and affective reunification with the parent were more likely to follow love withdrawal than any other technique. Physical coercion was somewhat less effective than love withdrawal, while reasoning and verbal prohibition were not at all effective except when both were combined with physical coercion.

C   'Non-compliant children sometimes prefer to say no directly as they were younger, they are easy to deal with the relationship with contemporaries when they are growing up. During the period that children are getting elder, they may learn to use more advanced approaches for their noncompliance. They are more skilful to negotiate or give reasons for refusal rather than show their opposite idea to parents directly,' said Henry Porter, scholar working in Psychology Institute of UK. He indicated that noncompliance means growth in some way, which may have benefit for children. Many experts held different viewpoints in recent years and they tried drilling compliance into children. His collaborator Wallace Freisen believed in organising children's daily activities so that they occur in the same order each day as much as possible. This first strategy for defiant children is ultimately the most important. Developing a routine helps a child to know what to expect and increases the chances that he or she will comply with things such as chores, homework, and hygiene requests. When undesirable activities occur in the same order at optimal times during the day, they become habits that are not questioned, but done without thought. Chances are that you have developed some type of routine for yourself in terms of showering, cleaning your house, or doing other types of work. You have an idea in your mind when you will do these things on a regular basis and this helps you to know what to expect. In fact, you have probably already been using most of these compliance strategies for yourself without realising it. For children, without setting these expectations on a daily basis by making them part of a regular routine, they can become very upset. Just like adults, children think about what they plan to do that day and expect to be able to do what they want. So, when you come along and ask them to do something they weren't already planning to do that day, this can result in automatic refusals and other undesirable defiant behaviour. However, by using this compliance strategy with defiant children, these activities are done almost every day in the same general order and the child expects to already do them.

D Doctor Steven Walson addressed that organising fun activities to occur after frequently refused activities. This strategy also works as a positive reinforcer when the child complies with your requests. By arranging your day so that things often occur right before highly preferred activities, you are able to eliminate defiant behaviour and motivate your child's behaviour of doing the undesirable activity. This is not to be presented in a way that the preferred activity is only allowed if a defiant child does the non-preferred activity. However, you can word your request in a way so that your child assumes that you have to do the non-preferred activity before moving on to the next preferred activity. For example, you do not want to say something such as, 'If you clean your room we can play a game.' Instead word your request like this, 'As soon as you are done cleaning your room we will be able to play that really fun game you wanted to play.'

E Psychologist Paul Edith insisted praise is the best way to make children comply with parents. This is probably a common term you are used to hearing by now. If you praise your child's behaviour, he or she will be more likely to do that behaviour. So, it is essential to use praise when working with defiant children. It also provides your child with positive attention. However, it is important to know how to praise children in a way that encourages future automatic reinforcement for your child when doing a similar behaviour.

Questions 1–5

*Choose the correct letter, **A**, **B**, **C**, or **D**.*

Write the correct letter in boxes 1–5 on your answer sheet.

1 The children, especially boys, received good education may

    A always comply with their parents' words.
    B be good at maths.
    C have a high score at school.
    D disobey their parents' order sometimes.

2 Faced with their children's compliance and noncompliance, parents

    A must be aware of the compliance.
    B ask for help from their teachers.
    C may ignore their noncompliance.
    D pretend not to see.

3 According to Henry Porter, noncompliance for children

    A is entirely harmful.
    B may have positive effects.
    C needs medicine assistance.
    D should be treated by expert doctor.

4 When children are growing up, they

    A always try to directly say no.
    B are more skilful to negotiate.
    C learn to cheat instead of noncompliance.
    D tend to keep silent.

5 Which is the possible reaction the passage mentioned for elder children and younger ones if they don't want to comply with the order?

    A Elder children prefer to refuse directly.
    B Elder ones refuse to answer.
    C Younger children may reject directly.
    D Younger ones may save any words.

核心词汇

A 段

distinct [dɪˈstɪŋkt] *adj.* 明显的
correlate [ˈkɒrələt] *v.* 联系
concomitant [kənˈkɒmɪtənt] *adj.* 伴随的
toddler [ˈtɒdlə(r)] *n.* 蹒跚学步的婴儿

B 段

coercion [kəʊˈɜːʃn] *n.* 强制；强迫

C 段

drilling [drɪlɪŋ] *n.* 演练
collaborator [kəˈlæbəreɪtə(r)] *n.* 通敌者；协作者，合作者
ultimately [ˈʌltɪmətli] *adv.* 最后，最终；根本
optimal [ˈɒptɪməl] *adj.* 最佳的，最优的
refusal [rɪˈfjuːzl] *n.* 拒绝

D 段

reinforcer [riːɪnˈfɔːsə(r)] *n.* 强化刺激
defiant [dɪˈfaɪənt] *adj.* 挑衅的
assume [əˈsjuːm] *v.* 假定，认为

高频同义替换

temptation	▶	invitation, allurement, seduce
compliance	▶	commitment, obedience, obey
aware	▶	conscious, sensible, realise
determine	▶	condition, conclude, identify, drop, judge
negotiate	▶	confer, consult with, bargain
strategy	▶	method, plan, way, tactic
eliminate	▶	avoid, exclude, remove
comply	▶	conform, abide by, observe, adhere to, follow

题目解析

1. 定位词：boy, good education, their parents' words, disobey
   文中对应点：B 段第二句
   题目解析：由题干中的定位词 boy, good education, their parents' words 定位到 B 段第二句 "Despite good education, these children did not follow the words from their parents on several occasions, especially boys in certain ages."。其中，the words from their parents 与 A 项中的 their parents' words 为同义替换，但是 did not follow 与 A 项中的 always comply with 矛盾，所以排除 A 项。did not follow 与 D 项中的 disobey 同义替换，words 与 D 项中的 order 对应，D 项"有时不会遵从父母的命令"符合原文意思，保留 D 项。句意为，即使对于一些接受了良好教育的孩子，他们在很多情况下也不会听从父母的话，尤其是到了一定年纪的男孩子。B 项"擅长数学"和 C 项"在学校拥有更高的分数"，原文没有提及。因此答案为 D。

2. 定位词：compliance and noncompliance, parents
   文中对应点：B 段第一句
   题目解析：由题干中的定位词 compliance and noncompliance, parents 定位到 B 段第一句 "A number of parents were not easy to be aware of the compliance, some even overlooked their children's noncompliance."。其中，not easy to be aware of the compliance 与 A 项中的 must be aware of the compliance 矛盾，所以排除。B 项说向孩子的老师寻求帮助，原文没有提。原文的 overlooked 与 C 项中的 ignore 为同义替换，C 项说有些父母会忽略他们的不顺从，与原文相符，所以保留。D 项说父母假装没看见，与原文意思不一致。句意为，对于很多家长来说，让他们意识到听从这件事并不容易，一些家长甚至忽视孩子的不听从。因此答案为 C。

3. 定位词：Henry Porter, noncompliance
   文中对应点：C 段第四句
   题目解析：由题干中的定位词 Henry Porter, noncompliance 定位到 C 段第四句 "He indicated that noncompliance means growth in some way, which may have benefit for children."。句意为，他指出孩子不听话某种程度上来讲意味着他们在成长，这对他们也许有利。A 项说不遵从父母的行为是完全有害的，与原文 benefit for children 意思矛盾，所以排除。B 项中的 positive effects 与 benefit for 对应，意思与原文相符，所以保留。C 项"需要药物辅助治疗"和 D 项"需要专业的医生来处理"，原文没有提及。因此答案为 B。

4. 定位词：growing up, directly say no, more skillful to negotiate
   文中对应点：C 段第一和第三句
   题目解析：由题干中的定位词 growing up 定位到 C 段。由 A 项中的 directly say no 定位到 C 段第一句 "Non-compliant children sometimes prefer to say no directly as they were younger, they are easy to deal with the relationship with contemporaries when they are growing up."。其中，say no directly 与 directly say no 对应，但这是孩子 younger 时期的特点，而非题干中的 growing up，所以排除。由 B 项中的 more skillful to negotiate 定位到 C 段第三句 "They are more skilful to negotiate or give reasons for refusal rather than show their opposite idea to parents directly."。其中，more skilful to negotiate 为原文重现，而且也是 C 段第二句提及的孩子 getting elder 时期的特点，

意思与原文相符，所以保留。C 项"用欺骗来代替不听话"和 D 项"倾向于保持沉默"，原文没有提及。因此答案为 B。

5 定位词：elder children and younger ones, don't want to comply
  文中对应点：C 段第一到第三句
  题目解析：由题干中的定位词 elder children and younger ones, don't want to comply 直接定位到 C 段第一到三句 "Non-compliant children sometimes prefer to say no directly as they were younger, they are easy to deal with the relationship with contemporaries when they are growing up. During the period that children are getting elder, they may learn to use more advanced approaches for their noncompliance. They are more skilful to negotiate or give reasons for refusal rather than show their opposite idea to parents directly,' Said Henry Porter, scholar working in Psychology Institute of UK."。其中，elder children，younger ones 分别与 getting elder，younger 对应，don't want to comply 与 non-compliant 对应。A 项说较大的孩子喜欢直接拒绝，与原文 prefer to say no directly as they were younger 矛盾。B 项说较大的孩子拒绝回答，原文未提及。C 项说较小的孩子可能会直接拒绝，与原文意思一致，所以保留。D 项说较小的孩子可能不会说，与原文矛盾。因此答案为 C。

参考答案

1 D **2** C **3** B **4** B **5** C

Children's Acquiring the Principles of Mathematics and Science

A It has been pointed out that learning mathematics and science is not so much learning facts as learning ways of thinking. It has also been emphasised that in order to learn science, people often have to change the way they think in ordinary situations. For example, in order to understand even simple concepts such as heat and temperature, ways of thinking of temperature as a measure of heat must be abandoned and a distinction between 'temperature' and 'heat' must be learned. These changes in ways of thinking are often referred to as conceptual changes. But how do conceptual changes happen? How do young people change their ways of thinking as they develop and as they learn in school?

B Traditional instruction based on telling students how modern scientists think does not seem to be very successful. Students may learn the definitions, the formulae, the terminology, and yet still maintain their previous conceptions. This difficulty has been illustrated many times, for example, when instructed students are interviewed about heat and temperature. It is often identified by teachers as a difficulty in applying the concepts learned in the classroom; students may be able to repeat a formula but fail to use the concept represented by the formula when they explain observed events.

C The psychologist Piaget suggested an interesting hypothesis relating to the process of cognitive change in children. Cognitive change was expected to result from the pupils' own intellectual activity. When confronted with a result that challenges their thinking — that is, when faced with conflict — pupils realise that they need to think again about their own ways of solving problems, regardless of whether the problem is one in mathematics or in science. He hypothesised that conflict brings about disequilibrium, and then triggers equilibration processes that ultimately produce cognitive change. For this reason, according to Piaget and his colleagues, in order for pupils to progress in their thinking they need to be actively engaged in solving problems that will challenge their current mode of reasoning. However, Piaget also pointed out that young children do not always discard their ideas in the face of contradictory evidence. They may actually discard the evidence and keep their theory.

D Piaget's hypothesis about how cognitive change occurs was later translated into an educational approach which is now termed 'discovery learning'. Discovery learning initially took what is now considered the 'lone learner' route. The role of the teacher was to select situations that challenged the pupils' reasoning; and the pupils' peers had no real role in this process. However, it was subsequently proposed that interpersonal conflict, especially with peers, might play an important role in promoting cognitive change. This hypothesis, originally advanced by Perret-Clermont and Doise and Mugny, has been investigated in many recent studies of science teaching and learning.

E Christine Howe and her colleagues, for example, have compared children's progress in understanding several types of science concepts when they are given the opportunity to observe relevant events. In one study, Howe compared the progress of 8–12-year-old children in understanding what influences motion down a slope. In order to ascertain the role of conflict in group work, they created two kinds of groups according to a pre-test: one in which the children had dissimilar views, and a second in which the children had similar views. They found support for the idea that children in the groups with dissimilar views progressed more after their training sessions than those who had been placed in groups with similar views. However, they found no evidence to support the idea that the children worked out their new conceptions during their group discussions, because progress was not actually observed in a post-test immediately after the sessions of group work, but rather in a second test given around four weeks after the group work.

F In another study, Howe set out to investigate whether the progress obtained through pair work could be a function of the exchange of ideas. They investigated the progress made by 12–15-year-old pupils in understanding the path of falling objects, a topic that usually involves conceptual difficulties. In order to create pairs of pupils with varying levels of dissimilarity in their initial conceptions, the pupils' predictions and explanations of the path of falling objects were assessed before they were engaged in pair work. The work sessions involved solving computer-presented problems, again about predicting and explaining the paths of falling objects. A post-test, given to individuals, assessed the progress made by pupils in their conceptions of what influenced the path of falling objects.

Questions 1–3

*Choose the correct letter, **A**, **B**, **C** or **D**.*

Write the correct letter in boxes 1–3 on your answer sheet.

1   The 'lone learner' route is an educational approach which

   A   is the main approach for discovery learning in teaching now.
   B   requires help from the pupils' peers.
   C   relies heavily on how the teacher guides the students.
   D   missed an important part for discovery learning.

2   It can be inferred from the experiment in Paragraph E that

   A   children acquire more when learning in groups.
   B   children opposing each other would learn slower.
   C   researches should check feedback right after the first test.
   D   there can be a satisfying result thanks to the duration of it.

3   Howe set out the pair work experiment in order to

   A   study how 12–15-year-old pupils learn scientific concepts.
   B   assess whether teammates would have the features of exchange ideas.
   C   investigate pupils' ability of solving physics problems.
   D   predict and explain the path of falling objects.

核心词汇

A 段

distinction [dɪˈstɪŋkʃn] *n.* 分别，差别
conceptual [kənˈseptʃuəl] *adj.* 概念的，观念的

B 段

terminology [ˌtɜːmɪˈnɒlədʒi] *n.* 学术术语，专用术语

C 段

hypothesis [haɪˈpɒθəsɪs] *n.* 假说，假设
cognitive [ˈkɒɡnətɪv] *adj.* 认知的；认识过程的
hypothesise [haɪˈpɒθəsaɪz] *v.* 提出假说，提出假设
disequilibrium [ˌdɪsˌiːkwɪˈlɪbriəm] *n.* 不平衡，不稳定，失调
trigger [ˈtrɪɡə(r)] *v.* 引发
discard [dɪsˈkɑːd] *v.* 丢弃，抛弃

D 段

peer [pɪə(r)] *n.* 同龄人，同辈
motion [ˈməʊʃn] *n.* 运动，移动
slope [sləʊp] *n.* 坡度
ascertain [ˌæsəˈteɪn] *v.* （尤指经过努力后）查明，弄清，确定
dissimilar [dɪˈsɪmɪlə(r)] *adj.* 不一样的，不同的
conception [kənˈsepʃn] *n.* 概念，观念，想法

E 段

varying [ˈveəriŋ] *adj.* 多变的，不同的
assess [əˈses] *v.* 评估，评价

高频同义替换

instruction	▸	direction, order, command
illustrate	▸	clarify, elucidate, give an example
observe	▸	watch, perceive, detect, notice
investigate	▸	check into, inquire into, examine
dissimilar	▸	diverse, unlike, varying, unrelated, distinct
assess	▸	evaluate, estimate

题目解析

1. **定位词**：lone learner, discovery learning, pupils' peers
   文中对应点：D 段第二、三句
   题目解析：由题干中的定位词 lone learner 定位到 D 段。由 A 项中的 discovery learning 定位到 D 段第二句 "Discovery learning initially took what is now considered the 'lone learner' route."。句意为最初"发现学习"走了一条现在被称为"孤独学习"的道路。其中，A 项中的 discovery learning 为原文重现，意思与原文相符，所以保留。由 B 项中的 pupils' peers 定位到 D 段第三句 "The role of the teacher was to select situations that challenged the pupils' reasoning; and the pupils' peers had no real role in this process."。句意为，其他同学是没有任何实质的角色的，而非选项中的"需要来自于同伴的帮助"，所以排除。C 项说十分依赖于老师如何指导学生，在文中并未提及，所以排除。根据 D 项中的 discovery learning 同样定位到 D 段第二句，D 项"遗漏了发现式学习很重要的一步"与原文矛盾，所以排除。因此答案为 A。

2. **定位词**：Paragraph E, in groups, opposing each other, right after
   文中对应点：E 段第三到第五句
   题目解析：由题干中的定位词 Paragraph E 定位到 E 段。由 A 项中的 in groups 定位到 E 段第三句 "In order to ascertain the role of conflict in group work, they created two kinds of groups according to a pre-test..."。句意为，为了确定小组内矛盾的作用，他们根据预测把小孩分成了两组。A 项说组团学习的儿童获得更多知识，但原文提及的是两组都有组团，所以排除。由 B 项中的 opposing each other 定位到 E 段第四句 "They found support for the idea that children in the groups with dissimilar views progressed more after their training sessions than those who had been placed in groups with similar views."。其中，dissimilar views 与 opposing each other 对应，但 progressed more 与 learn slower 意思矛盾，所以排除。由 C 项中的 right after 定位到 E 段第五句 "...because progress was not actually observed in a post-test immediately after the sessions of group work, but rather in a second test given around four weeks after the group work."。其中，immediately after 与 C 项中的 right after 对应，意思与原文相符，所以保留。D 项说由于实验的持续性，应该有一个满意的结果产生，原文没提及，所以排除。因此答案为 C。

3. **定位词**：pair work
   文中对应点：F 段第一、二句
   题目解析：由题干中的定位词 pair work 定位到 F 段第一、二句 "In another study, Howe set out to investigate whether the progress obtained through pair work could be a function of the exchange of ideas. They investigated the progress made by 12–15-year-old pupils in understanding the path of falling objects, a topic that usually involves conceptual difficulties."。句意为，在另一项研究中，Howe 着手调查两个人一起学习是否能够借交换意见来推进学习进度。他们调查了 12–15 岁的学生理解物体坠落的路径的过程。其中，A 项 learn scientific concepts "学习科学概念"，C 项 "研究学生解决物理问题的能力" 以及 D 项 "预测和解释下降物体的路径"，均为研究内容而不是目的，所以排除。B 项中，assess 与 investigate 对应，the features of 与 a function of 对应，exchange ideas 与 the exchange of ideas 对应，与原文一致，因此答案为 B。

参考答案

1 A   2 C   3 B

Paul Nash

A Paul Nash, the elder son of William Nash and his first wife, Caroline Jackson, was born in London on 11th May, 1889. His father was a successful lawyer who became the Recorder of Abingdon. According to Ronald Blythe: 'In 1901 the family returned to its native Buckinghamshire, where the garden of Wood Lane House at Iver Heath, and the countryside of the Chiltern hills, with its sculptural beeches and chalky contours, were early influences on the development of the three children. Their lives were overshadowed by their mother's mental illness and Nash himself was greatly helped by his nurse who, with some elderly neighbours, introduced him to the universe of plants.'

B Nash was educated at St. Paul's School and the Slade School of Art, where he met Dora Carrington. Unlike some of his contemporaries at the Slade School, Nash remained untouched by the two post-impressionist exhibitions organised by Roger Fry in 1910 and 1912. Instead, he was influenced by the work of William Blake. He also became a close friend of Gordon Bottomley, who took a keen interest in his career.

C Nash had his first one-man show, of ink and wash drawings, at the Carfax Gallery in 1912. The following year he shared an exhibition at the Dorien Leigh Gallery with his brother, John Nash. Myfanwy Piper, has added: 'Nash had a noteworthy sense of order and of the niceties of presentation; his pictures were beautifully framed, drawings mounted, his studio precisely and decoratively tidy, and oddments which he collected were worked up into compositions.'

D Paul Nash was strongly attracted to Dora Carrington: He later recalled 'Carrington was the dominating personality, I got an introduction to her and eventually won her regard by lending her my braces for a fancy-dress party. We were on the top of a bus and she wanted them then and there.'

E On the outbreak Nash considered the possibility of joining the British Army. He told a friend: 'I am not keen to rush off and be a soldier. The whole damnable war is too horrible of course and I am all against killing anybody, speaking off hand, but beside all that I believe both Jack and I might be more useful as ambulance and red cross men and to that end we are training.' Nash enlisted in the Artists' Rifles. He told Gordon Bottomley: 'I have joined the Artists' London Regiment of Territorials the old Corps which started with Rossetti, Leighton and Millais as members in 1860. Every man must do his bit in this horrible business so I have given up painting. There are many nice creatures in my company and I enjoy the burst of exercise — marching, drilling all day in the open air about the pleasant parts of Regents Park and Hampstead Heath.'

F In March 1917 he was sent to the Western Front. Nash, who took part in the offensive at Ypres, had reached the rank of lieutenant in the Hampshire Regiment by 1916. Whenever possible,

Nash made sketches of life in the trenches. In May 1917 he was invalided home after a non-military accident. While recuperating in London, Nash worked from his sketches to produce a series of war paintings. This work was well-received when exhibited later that year. As a result of this exhibition, Charles Masterman, head of the government's War Propaganda Bureau (WPB), and the advice of Edward Marsh and William Rothenstein, it was decided to recruit Nash as a war artist. In November 1917 in the immediate aftermath of the battle of Passchendaele, Nash returned to France.

Nash was unhappy with his work as a member of War Propaganda Bureau. He wrote at the time: 'I am no longer an artist. I am a messenger who will bring back word from the men who are fighting to those who want the war to go on forever. Feeble, inarticulate will be my message, but it will have a bitter truth and may it burn their lousy souls.' However, as Myfanwy Piper has pointed out: 'The drawings he made then, of shorn trees in ruined and flooded landscapes, were the works that made Nash's reputation.' They were shown at the Leicester Galleries in 1918 together with his first efforts at oil painting, in which he was self-taught and quickly successful, though his drawings made in the field had more immediate public impact.

In 1919 Nash moved to Dymchurch in Kent, beginning his well-known series of pictures of the sea, the breakwaters, and the long wall that prevents the sea from flooding Romney Marsh. This included *Winter Sea* and *Dymchurch Steps*. Nash also painted the landscapes of the Chiltern Hills. In 1924 and 1928 he had successful exhibitions at the Leicester Galleries. Despite this popular acclaim in 1929 his work became more abstract. In 1933 Nash founded Unit One, the group of experimental painters, sculptors, and architects.

During the Second World War Nash was employed by the Ministry of Information and the Air Ministry and paintings produced by him during this period include the *Battle of Britain* and *Totes Meer*. His biographer, Myfanwy Piper, has argued: 'This war disturbed Nash but did not change his art as the last one had. His style and his habits were formed, and in the new war he treated his new subjects as he had treated those he had been thinking about for so long. His late paintings, both oils and watercolours, are alternately brilliant and sombre in colour with the light of setting suns and rising moons spreading over wooded and hilly landscapes.' Paul Nash died at 35 Boscombe Spa Road, Bournemouth, on 11th July, 1946.

Questions 1–4

*Choose FOUR letters, **A–G**.*

Write the correct letters in boxes 1–4 on your answer sheet.

What **FOUR** statements are correct concerning Nash's story?

- **A** He did not make an effort after becoming a high ranking official in the army.
- **B** He had a dream since his childhood.
- **C** He once temporarily ceased his painting career for some reason.
- **D** He was not affected by certain shows attractive to his other peers.
- **E** He had cooperation in art with his relative.
- **F** Some of his paintings were presented in a chaotic way.
- **G** His achievement after being enlisted in the army did not attract as much attention as his previous works.

核心词汇

A 段

sculptural [ˈskʌlptʃərəl] *adj.* 雕塑的

overshadow [ˌəʊvəˈʃædəʊ] *v.* 使失色

B 段

contemporary [kənˈtemprəri] *n.* 同时代的人，同辈

C 段

noteworthy [ˈnəʊtwɜːði] *adj.* 值得注意的

mount [maʊnt] *v.* 逐渐增加；安排

composition [ˌkɒmpəˈzɪʃn] *n.* 作品

E 段

outbreak [ˈaʊtbreɪk] *n.* 爆发

damnable [ˈdæmnəbl] *adj.* 恶劣的

march [mɑːtʃ] *v.* 行进，行军

F 段

lieutenant [lefˈtenənt] *n.* 中尉

trench [trentʃ] *n.* 战壕

invalided [ɪnˈvælɪdɪd] *adj.* 伤残的

aftermath [ˈɑːftəmæθ] *n.* 后果，余波

G 段

inarticulate [ˌɪnɑːˈtɪkjələt] *adj.* 不善辞令的

H 段

acclaim [əˈkleɪm] *v.* 称赞

I 段

hilly [ˈhɪli] *adj.* 多丘陵的

高频同义替换

mental	▸	spiritual, inner
exhibition	▸	expo, display, show, fair, manifestation
precisely	▸	accurately, exactly

possibility	⊙	probability, feasibility, potential, maybe, chance
horrible	⊙	terrible, awesome, fearful, dire, dreadful
recruit	⊙	supply, replenish

题目解析

1 定位词：did not make an effort, high ranking official

文中对应点：F 段第二、四句

题目解析：由 A 项中的定位词 high ranking official 定位到 F 段第二句 "Nash, who took part in the offensive at Ypres, had reached the rank of lieutenant in the Hampshire Regiment by 1916."。介绍保罗在军队中的级别（the rank of lieutenant），与 high ranking official 对应。接着 F 段第四句 "In May 1917 he was invalided home after a non-military accident." 句意为，他因非军事事故回家休养，这与 A 项中的 did not make an effort 对应。因此 A 项的陈述正确。

2 定位词：ceased, his painting career

文中对应点：E 段倒数第二句

题目解析：由 C 项中的定位词 ceased 定位到 E 段倒数第二句 "Every man must do his bit in this horrible business so I have given up painting."。其中，have given up 与 ceased 对应，painting 对应 painting career。句意为，每个人都必须在这个可怕的事情上尽自己的一份力量，所以我放弃了绘画。因此 C 项的陈述正确。

3 定位词：not affected by certain shows, other peers

文中对应点：B 段第二句

题目解析：由 D 项中的定位词 not affected by certain shows 和 attractive to 定位到 B 段第二句 "Unlike some of his contemporaries at the Slade School, Nash remained untouched by the two post-impressionist exhibitions organised by Roger Fry in 1910 and 1912."。其中，certain shows 与 the two post-impressionist exhibitions organised by Roger Fry in 1910 and 1912 对应，other peers 与 his contemporaries 对应，not affected by 与 remained untouched by 对应。句意为，Paul Nash 不像 Slade School 同时代的人，他不受 Roger Fry 在 1910 和 1912 年举办的两个后印象派展览影响。因此 D 项的陈述正确。

4 定位词：cooperation...with his relative

文中对应点：C 段第二句

题目解析：由 E 项中的定位词 cooperation...with his relative 定位到 C 段第二句 "The following year he shared an exhibition at the Dorien Leigh Gallery with his brother, John Nash."。其中，cooperation... with his relative 与 shared...with his brother 对应。句意为，Nash 与他的兄弟 John Nash 次年在 Dorien Leigh 画廊共同举办了一个画展。因此 E 项的陈述正确。

参考答案

1 A 2 C 3 D 4 E

READING PASSAGE 8

Coastal Archaeology of Britain

A The recognition of the wealth and diversity of England's coastal archaeology has been one of the most important developments of recent years. Some elements of this enormous resource have long been known. The so-called 'submerged forests' off the coasts of England, sometimes with clear evidence of human activity, had attracted the interest of antiquarians since at least the eighteenth century but serious and systematic attention has been given to the archaeological potential of the coast only since the early 1980s.

B It is possible to trace a variety of causes for this concentration of effort and interest. In the 1980s and 1990s scientific research into climate change and its environmental impact spilled over into a much broader public debate as awareness of these issues grew; the prospect of rising sea levels over the next century, and their impact on current coastal environments, has been a particular focus for concern. At the same time archaeologists were beginning to recognise that the destruction caused by natural processes of coastal erosion and by human activity was having an increasing impact on the archaeological resource of the coast.

C The dominant process affecting the physical form of England in the post-glacial period has been the rise in the altitude of sea level relative to the land, as the glaciers melted and the landmass readjusted. The encroachment of the sea, the loss of huge areas of land now under the North Sea and the English Channel, and especially the loss of the land bridge between England and France, which finally made Britain an island, must have been immensely significant factors in the lives of our prehistoric ancestors. Yet the way in which prehistoric communities adjusted to these environmental changes has seldom been a major theme in discussions of the period. One factor contributing to this has been that, although the rise in relative sea level is comparatively well documented, we know little about the constant reconfiguration of the coastline. This was affected by many processes, mostly quite, which have not yet been adequately researched. The detailed reconstruction of coastline histories and the changing environments available for human use will be an important theme for future research.

D So great has been the rise in sea level and the consequent regression of the coast that much of the archaeological evidence now exposed in the coastal zone, whether being eroded or exposed as a buried land surface, is derived from what was originally terrestrial occupation. Its current location in the coastal zone is the product of later unrelated processes, and it can tell us little about past adaptations to the sea. Estimates of its significance will need to be made in the context of other related evidence from dry land sites. Nevertheless, its physical environment means that preservation is often excellent, for example in the case of the Neolithic structure excavated at the Stumble in Essex.

E In some cases these buried land surfaces do contain evidence for human exploitation of what was a coastal environment, and elsewhere along the modern coast there is similar evidence. Where the evidence does relate to past human exploitation of the resources and the opportunities offered by the sea and the coast, it is both diverse and as yet little understood. We are not yet in a position to make even preliminary estimates of answers to such fundamental questions as the extent to which the sea and the coast affected human life in the past, what percentage of the population at any time lived within reach of the sea, or whether human settlements in coastal environments showed a distinct character from those inland.

F The most striking evidence for use of the sea is in the form of boats, yet we still have much to learn about their production and use. Most of the known wrecks around our coast are not unexpectedly of post-medieval date, and offer an unparalleled opportunity for research which has as yet been little used. The prehistoric sewn-plank boats such as those from the Humber estuary and Dover all seem to belong to the second millennium BC; after this there is a gap in the record of a millennium, which cannot yet be explained, before boats reappear, but built using a very different technology. Boatbuilding must have been an extremely important activity around much of our coast, yet we know almost nothing about it. Boats were some of the most complex artefacts produced by pre-modern societies, and further research on their production and use make an important contribution to our understanding of past attitudes to technology and technological change.

G Boats needed landing places, yet here again our knowledge is very patchy. In many cases the natural shores and beaches would have sufficed, leaving little or no archaeological trace, but especially in later periods, many ports and harbours, as well as smaller facilities such as quays, wharves, and jetties, were built. Despite a growth of interest in the waterfront archaeology of some of our more important Roman and medieval towns, very little attention has been paid to the multitude of smaller landing places. Redevelopment of harbour sites and other development and natural pressures along the coast are subjecting these important locations to unprecedented threats, yet few surveys of such sites have been undertaken.

H One of the most important revelations of recent research has been the extent of industrial activity along the coast. Fishing and salt production are among the better documented activities, but even here our knowledge is patchy. Many forms of fishing will leave little archaeological trace, and one of the surprises of recent survey has been the extent of past investment in facilities for procuring fish and shellfish. Elaborate wooden fish weirs, often of considerable extent and responsive to aerial photography in shallow water, have been identified in areas such as Essex and the Severn estuary. The production of salt, especially in the late Iron Age and early Roman periods, has been recognised for some time, especially in the Thames estuary and around the Solent and Poole Harbour, but the reasons for the decline of that industry and the nature of later coastal salt working are much less well understood. Other industries were also located along the coast, either because the raw materials outcropped there or for ease of working and transport: mineral resources such as sand, gravel, stone, coal, ironstone, and alum were all exploited. These industries are poorly documented, but their remains are sometimes extensive and striking.

I Some appreciation of the variety and importance or the archaeological remains preserved in the coastal zone, albeit only in preliminary form, can thus be gained from recent work, but the complexity of the problem of managing that resource is also being realised. The problem arises not only from the scale and variety of the archaeological remains, but also from two other sources: the very varied natural and human threats to the resource, and the complex web of organisations with authority over, or interests in, the coastal zone. Human threats include the redevelopment of historic towns and old dockland areas, and the increased importance of the coast for the leisure and tourism industries, resulting in pressure for the increased provision of facilities such as marinas. The larger size of ferries has also caused an increase in the damage caused by their wash to fragile deposits in the intertidal zone. The most significant natural threat is the predicted rise in sea level over the next century especially in the south and east of England. Its impact on archaeology is not easy to predict, and though it is likely to be highly localised, it will be at a scale much larger than that of most archaeological sites. Thus protecting one site may simply result in transposing the threat to a point further along the coast. The management of the archaeological remains will have to be considered in a much longer time scale and a much wider geographical scale than is common in the case of dry land sites, and this will pose a serious challenge for archaeologists.

Questions 1–3

Choose **THREE** letters, **A–G**.

Write the correct letters in boxes 1–3 on your answer sheet.

Which **THREE** of the following statements are mentioned in the passage?

- A Our prehistoric ancestors adjusted to the environmental change caused by the rising sea level by moving to higher lands.
- B It is difficult to understand how many people lived close to the sea.
- C Human settlements in coastal environment were different from those inland.
- D Our knowledge of boat evidence is limited.
- E The prehistoric boats were built mainly for collecting sand from the river.
- F Human development threatens the archaeological remains.
- G The reason for the decline of salt industry was the shortage of labourers.

核心词汇

A 段

archaeology [ˌɑːkiˈɒlədʒi] *n.* 考古学
submerged [səbˈmɜːdʒd] *adj.* 水面下的，在水中的
antiquarian [ˌæntɪˈkweəriən] *n.* 古文物研究者，古文物收藏家 *adj.* 古文物研究的；古文物的
systematic [ˌsɪstəˈmætɪk] *adj.* 系统化的，有条理的

B 段

public debate 公开辩论，公开讨论
archaeologist [ˌɑːkiˈɒlədʒɪst] *n.* 考古学家

C 段

dominant [ˈdɒmɪnənt] *adj.* 强大的，占优势的，处于统治地位的
readjust [ˌriːəˈdʒʌst] *vi.* 重新适应 *vt.* 重新调整
prehistoric [ˌpriːhɪˈstɒrɪk] *adj.* 史前的，陈旧的
reconfiguration [ˈriːkənfɪɡjʊˈreɪʃn] *n.* 重新配置，重新组合
adequately [ˈædɪkwətli] *adv.* 充分地，适当地，足够地

D 段

regression [rɪˈɡreʃn] *n.* 退步，退化
terrestrial [təˈrestriəl] *adj.* 地球的，陆地的，陆生的
excavate [ˈekskəveɪt] *vi.* & *vt.* 发掘，挖掘

E 段

exploitation [ˌeksplɔɪˈteɪʃn] *n.* 剥削；开发，开采；充分利用

F 段

unparalleled [ʌnˈpærəleld] *adj.* 无比的，无双的，空前未有的
artefact [ˈɑːtɪfækt] *n.* 人工制品，手工艺品

G 段

unprecedented [ʌnˈpresɪdentɪd] *adj.* 空前的，前所未有的

H 段

elaborate [ɪˈlæbərət] *adj.* 详尽的，复杂的；精心制作的 *vi. & vt.* 精心制作；详细阐述

exploit [ɪkˈsplɔɪt] *vt.* 剥削，压榨；充分利用，发挥

I 段

leisure [ˈleʒə(r)] *n.* 闲暇，空闲，业余时间

intertidal [ˌɪntəˈtaɪdəl] *adj.* 潮间带的，高潮线与低潮线之间的

geographical [ˌdʒiːəˈɡræfɪkl] *adj.* 地理的，地理学的

高频同义替换

recognition	▸	understand, understanding, recognise, realise, be aware of, awareness
diversity	▸	diverse, various of, a variety of, difference
important	▸	significant, remarkable, considerable
readjust	▸	redesign, reproduce, reproduction
evidence	▸	witness, evident, see, proof, testimony

题目解析

1 定位词：difficult to understand, how many people
文中对应点：E 段倒数第一句
题目解析：由 B 项中的定位词 difficult to understand, how many people 定位到 E 段倒数第一句 "We are not yet in a position to make even preliminary estimates of answers to such fundamental questions as the extent to which the sea and the coast affected human life in the past, what percentage of the population at any time lived within reach of the sea, or whether human settlements in coastal environments showed a distinct character from those inland."。其中，not yet in a position to make even preliminary estimates of answers 与 difficult to understand 对应，what percentage of the population 与 how many people 对应。句意为，我们没有能力对如此重要的问题（如海洋和海岸在过去对人类生活的影响程度、任何时候生活在海洋附近的人口百分比以及人类在海岸环境的定居是否与内陆定居有不同的特征）的答案进行哪怕是初步的估计。说明很难知道有多少人曾生活在海边，因此答案为 B，同时排除 C 项。

2 定位词：boat, limited
文中对应点：F 段第一句
题目解析：由 D 项中的定位词 boat, limited 定位到 F 段第一句 "The most striking evidence for use of the sea is in the form of boats, yet we still have much to learn about their production and use."。其中，boats 为 boat 的复数形式，still have much to learn about 与 limited 对应。句意为，

人们利用海洋的最显著的特征就是以船的形式。然而，关于它们的生产和使用，我们仍有很多地方需要去了解。说明我们对船的了解是有限的，因此答案为 D。

3 定位词：threatens, archaeological remains
文中对应点：I 段第三句
题目解析：由 F 项中的定位词 threatens, archaeological remains 定位到 I 段第三句 "Human threats include the redevelopment of historic towns and old dockland areas, and the increased importance of the coast for the leisure and tourism industries, resulting in pressure for the increased provision of facilities such as marinas."。其中，threats 为 threatens 的名词形式，historic towns and old dockland areas 与 archaeological remains 对应。句意为，人类的威胁包括对历史悠久的小镇和老旧港区的重建，以及由于休闲旅游业的发展而造成的对越来越重要的海岸地区的压力，该压力体现在人们需要建设更多的游船码头等设施。解释了 human threats 具体包括哪些因素，说明人类的发展威胁到考古遗迹，因此答案为 F。

参考答案

1 B **2** D **3** F

第五章　摘要填空题

READING PASSAGE 1

Global Warming: Prevent Poles from Melting

A Such is our dependence on fossil fuels, and such is the volume of carbon dioxide we have already released into the atmosphere, that most climate scientists agree that significant global warming is now inevitable — the best we can hope to do is keep it at a reasonable level, and even that is going to be an uphill task. At present, the only serious option on the table for doing this is cutting back on our carbon emissions, but while a few countries are making major strides in this regard, the majority are having great difficulty even stemming the rate of increase, let alone reversing it. Consequently, an increasing number of scientists are beginning to explore the alternatives. They all fall under the banner of geoengineering — generally defined as the intentional large-scale manipulation of the environment.

B Geoengineering has been shown to work, at least on a small, localised scale, for decades. May Day parades in Moscow have taken place under clear blue skies, aircraft having deposited dry ice, silver iodide and cement powder to disperse clouds. Many of the schemes now suggested look to do the opposite, and reduce the amount of sunlight reaching the planet. One scheme focuses on achieving a general cooling of the Earth and involves the concept of releasing aerosol sprays into the stratosphere above the Arctic to create clouds of sulphur dioxide, which would, in turn, lead to a global dimming. The idea is modeled on historical volcanic explosions, such as that of Mount Pinatubo in the Philippines in 1991; which led to a short-term cooling of global temperatures by 0.5℃. The aerosols could be delivered by artillery, high-flying aircraft or balloons.

C Instead of concentrating on global cooling, other schemes look specifically at reversing the melting at the poles. One idea is to bolster an ice cap by spraying it with water. Using pumps to carry water from below the sea ice, the spray would come out as snow or ice particles, producing thicker sea ice with a higher albedo (the ratio of sunlight reflected from a surface) to reflect summer radiation. Scientists have also scrutinised whether it is possible to block ice flow in Greenland with cables which have been reinforced, preventing icebergs from moving into the sea. Veli Albert Kallio, a Finnish scientist, says that such an idea is impractical, because the force of the ice would ultimately snap the cables and rapidly release a large quantity of frozen ice into the sea. However, Kallio believes that the sort of cables used in suspension bridges could potentially be used to divert, rather than halt, the southward movement of ice from Spitsbergen. 'It would stop the ice moving south, and local currents would see them float northwards,' he says.

D A number of geoengineering ideas are currently being examined in the Russian Arctic. These include planting millions of birch trees: the thinking, according to Kallio, is that their white bark would increase the amount of reflected sunlight. The loss of their leaves in winter would also enable the snow to reflect radiation. In contrast, the native evergreen pines tend to shade the snow and absorb radiation. Using ice-breaking vessels to deliberately break up and scatter coastal sea ice in both Arctic and Antarctic waters in their respective autumns, and diverting Russian rivers to increase cold-water flow to ice-forming areas, could also be used to slow down warming. Kallio says: 'You would need the wind to blow the right way, but in the right conditions, by letting ice float free and head north, you would enhance ice growth.'

E But will such ideas ever be implemented? The major counter-arguments to geoengineering schemes are, first, that they are a 'cop-cut' that allow us to continue living the way we do, rather reducing carbon emissions; and, second, even if they do work, would the side-effects outweigh the advantages? Then there's the daunting prospect of upkeep and repair of any scheme as well as the consequences of a technical failure. 'I think all of us agree that if we were to end geoengineering on a given day, then the planet would return to its pre-engineered condition very rapidly, and probably within 10 to 20 years,' says Dr Phil Rasch, chief scientist for climate change at the US-based Pacific Northwest National Laboratory. 'That's certainly something to worry about. I would consider geoengineering as a strategy to employ only while we manage the conversion to a non-fossil-fuel economy. The risk with geoengineering projects is that you can 'overshoot',' says Dr Dan Lunt, from the University of Bristol. 'You may bring global temperatures back to pre-industrial levels, but the risk is that the poles will still be warmer than they should be and the tropics will be cooler than before industrialisation.'

F The main reason why geoengineering is countenanced by the mainstream scientific community is that most researchers have little faith in the ability of politicians to agree — and then bring in — the necessary carbon cuts. 'Even leading conservation organisations believe the subject is worth exploring,' as Dr Martin Sommerkorn, a climate change advisor says. 'But human-induced climate change has brought humanity to a position where it is important not to exclude thinking thoroughly about this topic and its possibilities despite the potential drawbacks. If, over the coming years, the science tells us about an ever-increased climate sensitivity of the planet — and this isn't unrealistic — then we may be best served by not having to start our thinking from scratch.'

Questions 1–5

Complete the summary below.

Choose **NO MORE THAN TWO WORDS** from the passage for each answer.

Write your answers in boxes 1–5 on your answer sheet.

Geoengineering Projects

A range of geoengineering ideas has been put forward, which aims either to prevent the melting of the ice caps or to stop the general rise in global temperatures. One scheme to discourage the melting of ice and snow involves introducing **1** .... to the Arctic because of their colour.

The build-up of ice could be encouraged by dispersing ice along the coasts using special ships and changing the direction of some **2** .... , but this scheme is dependent on certain weather conditions. Another way of increasing the amount of ice involves using **3** .... to bring water to the surface. A scheme to stop ice moving would apply **4** .... but this method is more likely to be successful in preventing the ice from travelling in one direction rather than stopping it altogether. A suggestion for cooling global temperatures is based on what has happened in the past after **5** .... and it involves creating clouds of gas.

核心词汇

A 段

fossil fuel 化石燃料
carbon dioxide 二氧化碳
release [rɪ'liːs] *vt.* 排放；释放；发布；发行；松开
inevitable [ɪn'evɪtəbl] *adj.* 不可避免的，必然发生的
stem [stem] *vt.* 遏制，阻止；堵住，止住 *n.* 茎，梗，柄；词干 [拓] stem from 起源于……
intentional [ɪn'tenʃənl] *adj.* 蓄意的，故意的
manipulation [mə,nɪpju'leɪʃn] *n.* 控制；操纵；操作；推拿

B 段

cement powder 水泥粉
disperse [dɪ'spɜːs] *vi. & vt.* （使）消散；分散；驱散
spray [spreɪ] *vi.* 飞散，飞溅 *vt.* 喷，喷洒 *n.* 喷雾，喷剂；浪花，水沫

C 段

reinforce [,riːɪn'fɔːs] *vt.* 加固；增援；加强；强化
suspension [sə'spenʃn] *n.* 悬架，减震装置；暂停，中止 [拓] suspension bridge 吊桥，悬索桥
current ['kʌrənt] *n.* 水流；气流；电流；潮流 *adj.* 现时的，当前的，现行的

D 段

deliberately [dɪ'lɪbərətli] *adv.* 慎重地；故意地，蓄意地

E 段

conversion [kən'vɜːʃn] *n.* 转变，转换；换算；归附

F 段

mainstream ['meɪnstriːm] *adj.* 主流的，主要的 *n.* 主流 *vt.* 使纳入主流教育
conservation [,kɒnsə'veɪʃn] *n.* 保护；保存；节约
thorough ['θʌrə] *adj.* 彻底的，全面的，详尽的；缜密的 [拓] thoroughly *adv.* 仔细地；彻底地；全面地
drawback ['drɔːbæk] *n.* 缺点；不利因素

题目

disperse [dɪ'spɜːs] *vt.* 分数

高频同义替换

focus on	▸	concentrate on, devote oneself to, apply oneself to
reinforce	▸	strengthen, enhance, intensify
deliberate	▸	intentional, intended
outweigh	▸	take precedence over, outflank, override
consequence	▸	outcome, result, aftermath
employ	▸	use, utilise, exploit, adopt
thorough	▸	radical, complete, entire
drawback	▸	weakness, shortcoming, flaw, demerit

题目解析

1 定位词：involves, introducing, colour

文中对应点：D 段第二句

题目解析：通过题干中的定位词 involves, introducing, colour 定位到 D 段第二句 "These include planting millions of birch trees: the thinking, according to Kallio, is that their white bark would increase the amount of reflected sunlight."。其中，include 与 involves 为同义替换，planting 对应 introducing，white bark 对应 colour。句意为，这些想法包括种植数以百万计的桦树，根据卡里奥的考量，这是因为它们白色的树干将会增加日光的反射量。因此答案为 birch trees。

2 定位词：special ships, changing the direction, certain weather conditions

文中对应点：D 段最后两句

题目解析：通过题干中的定位词 special ships, changing the direction, certain weather conditions 定位到 D 段最后两句 "Using ice-breaking vessels to deliberately break up and scatter coastal sea ice in both Arctic and Antarctic waters in their respective autumns, and diverting Russian rivers to increase cold-water flow to ice-forming areas, could also be used to slow down warming. Kallio says: 'You would need the wind to blow the right way, but in the right conditions, by letting ice float free and head north, you would enhance ice growth.'"。其中，ice-breaking vessels 对应 special ships，right conditions 对应 certain weather conditions，diverting Russian rivers to increase cold-water flow to ice-forming areas 对应 changing the direction。句意为，在南极和北极各自的秋天里，使用破冰船有意地撞碎冰块并使冰块分散到水流中，以及改变俄罗斯河流的流向从而增加流进结冰区域的冰水，这两种方法都可以用来减缓全球变暖的速度。卡里奥说："你需要借助正确的风向，但是如果有适宜的条件，通过让冰块自由地向北漂流，也能增加冰块的大小。因此答案为 (Russian) rivers。

3 定位词：increasing the amount of ice, bring water to the surface

文中对应点：C 段第三句

题目解析：通过题干中的定位词 increasing the amount of ice, bring water to the surface 定位到 C

段第三句 "Using pumps to carry water from below the sea ice, the spray would come out as snow or ice particles, producing thicker sea ice with a higher albedo (the ratio of sunlight reflected from a surface) to reflect summer radiation."。其中，原文中的 producing thicker sea ice 对应题干中的 increasing the amount of ice，carry water from below the sea ice 对应 bring water to the surface。句意为，（具体方法为）先使用抽水机把冰块下面的水抽出来，这些水会以雪或冰粒的形式喷在冰块上，由此使得冰块变厚从而有更高的反射夏季辐射的反射率（反射光照的比例）。因此答案为 pumps。

4 定位词：stop ice moving
   文中对应点：C 段第四句
   题目解析：通过题干中的定位词 stop ice moving 定位到 C 段第四句 "Scientists have also scrutinised whether it is possible to block ice flow in Greenland with cables which have been reinforced, preventing icebergs from moving into the sea."。其中，block ice flow 对应 stop ice moving。句意为，同时，科学家们也仔细检查了用加固的缆绳是否能够封锁格陵兰岛的冰流，阻止冰山进入海洋。因此答案为 cables。

5 定位词：cooling global temperatures, in the past
   文中对应点：B 段倒数第二句
   题目解析：通过题干中的定位词 cooling global temperatures, in the past 定位到 B 段倒数第二句 "The idea is modeled on historical volcanic explosions, such as that of Mount Pinatubo in the Philippines in 1991; which led to a short-term cooling of global temperatures by 0.5℃."。其中，原文中的 cooling of global temperatures 对应题干中的 cooling global temperatures，historical 对应 in the past。句意为，这一想法模仿的是历史上的火山喷发，例如 1991 年菲律宾的皮那图博火山爆发，导致全球温度短期下降 0.5 摄氏度。因此答案为 volcanic explosions。

参考答案

1 birch trees   **2** (Russian) rivers   **3** pumps   **4** cables   **5** volcanic explosions

READING PASSAGE 2

Flight from Reality

Mobiles are barred, but passengers can tap away on their laptops to their hearts' content. Is one really safer than the other? In the US, a Congressional subcommittee grilled airline representatives and regulators about the issue last month. But the committee heard that using cellphones in planes may indeed pose a risk albeit a slight one. This would seem to vindicate the treatment of Manchester oil worker Neil Whitehouse, who was sentenced last summer to a year in jail by a British court for refusing to turn off his mobile phone on a flight home from Madrid. Although he was only typing a message to be sent on landing not actually making a call, the court decided that he was putting the flight at risk.

A The potential for problems is certainly there. Modern airliners are packed with electronic devices that control the plane and handle navigation and communications. Each has to meet stringent safeguards to make sure it doesn't emit radiation that would interfere with other devices in the plane — standards that passengers' personal electronic devices don't necessarily meet. Emissions from inside the plane could also interfere with sensitive antennae on the fixed exterior.

B But despite running a number of studies, Boeing, Airbus and various government agencies haven't been able to find clear evidence of problems caused by personal electronic devices, including mobile phones. 'We've done our own studies. We've found cellphones actually have no impact on the navigation system,' says Maryanne Greczyn, a spokeswoman for Airbus Industries of North America in Herndon, Virginia. 'Nor do they affect other critical systems,' she says. The only impact Airbus found? 'Sometimes when a passenger is starting or finishing a phone call, the pilot hears a wry slight beep in the headset,' she says.

C The best evidence yet of a problem comes from a report released this year by Britain's Civil Aviation Authority. Its researchers generated simulated cellphone transmissions inside two Boeing aircrafts. They concluded that the transmissions could create signals at a power and frequency that would not affect the latest equipment, but exceeded the safety threshold established in 1984 and might therefore affect some of the older equipment on board. This doesn't mean 'mission critical' equipment such as the navigation system and flight controls. But the devices that could be affected, such as smoke detectors and fuel level indicators, could still create serious problems for the flight crew if they malfunction.

D 'Many planes still use equipment certified to the older standards,' says Dan Hawkes, head of avionics at the CAA's Safely Regulation Group. The CAA study doesn't prove the equipment will actually fail when subjected to the signals, but does show there's a danger. 'We've taken some of the uncertainty out of these beliefs,' he says. 'Another study later this year will see if the cellphone signals actually cause devices to fail.'

E In 1996, RTCA, a consultant hired by the Federal Aviation Administration in the US to conduct tests, determined that potential problems from personal electronic devices were 'low'. Nevertheless, it recommended a ban on their use during 'critical' periods of flight, such as take-off and landing. RTCA didn't actually test cellphones, but nevertheless recommended their wholesale ban on flights. 'Better safe than sorry' is the current policy but it's applied inconsistently, according to Marshall Cross, the chairman of Mega Wave Corporation, based in Boylston, Massachusetts. Why are cellphones outlawed when no one considers a ban on laptops? 'It's like most things in life. The reason is a little bit technical, a little bit economic and a little bit political,' says Cross.

F The company wrote a report for the FAA in 1998 saying it is possible to build an on-board system that can detect dangerous signals from electronic devices. But Cross's personal conclusion is that mobile phones aren't the real threat. 'You'd have to stretch things pretty far to figure out how a cellphone could interfere with a plane's systems,' he says. Cellphones transmit in ranges of around 400, 800 or 1800 megahertz. Since no important piece of aircraft equipment operates at those frequencies, the possibility of interference is very low, Cross says. 'The use of computers and electronic game systems is much more worrying,' he says. They can generate very strong signals at frequencies that could interfere with plane electronics, especially if a mouse is attached (the wire operates as an antenna) or if their built-in shielding is somehow damaged. Some airlines are even planning to put sockets for laptops in seatbacks.

G There's fairly convincing anecdotal evidence that some personal electronic devices have interfered with systems. Air crew on one flight found that the autopilot was being disconnected, and narrowed the problem down to a passenger's portable computer. They could actually watch the autopilot disconnect when they switched the computer on. Boeing bought the computer, took it to the airline's labs and even tested it on an empty flight. But as with every other reported instance of interference, technicians were unable to replicate the problem.

H Some engineers, however, such as Bruce Donham of Boeing, say that common sense suggests phones are more risky than laptops. 'A device capable of producing a strong emission is not as safe as a device which does not have any intentional emission,' he says. Nevertheless, many experts think it's illogical that cellphones are prohibited when computers aren't. Besides, the problem is more complicated than simply looking at power and frequency. In the air, the plane operates in a soup of electronic emissions, created by its own electronics and by ground-based radiation. Electronic devices in the cabin — especially those emitting a strong signal — can behave unpredictably, reinforcing other signals, for instance, or creating unforeseen harmonics that disrupt systems.

I Despite the Congressional subcommittee hearings last month, no one seems to be working seriously on a technical solution that would allow passengers to use their phones. That's mostly because no one — besides cellphone users themselves — stands to gain a lot if the phones are allowed in the air. Even the cellphone companies don't want it. They are concerned that airborne signals could cause problems by flooding a number of the networks' base stations at once with the same signal. This effect, called big footing, happens because airborne cellphone signals tend to go to many base stations at once, unlike land calls which usually go to just one or two stations. In the US, even if FAA regulations didn't prohibit cellphones in the air, Federal Communications Commission regulations would.

J Possible solutions might be to enhance airliners' electronic insulation, or to fit detectors which warned flight staff when passenger devices were emitting dangerous signals. But Cross complains that neither the FAA, the airlines nor the manufacturers are showing much interest in developing these. So despite Congressional suspicions and the occasional irritated (or jailed) mobile user, the industry's 'better safe than sorry' policy on mobile phones seems likely to continue. In the absence of firm evidence that the international airline industry is engaged in a vast conspiracy to overcharge its customers, a delayed phone call seems a small price to pay for even the tiniest reduction in the chances of a plane crash. But you'll still be allowed to use your personal computer during a flight. And while that remains the case, airlines can hardly claim that logic has prevailed.

Questions 1–4

Complete the summary below.

Choose **NO MORE THAN THREE WORDS** from the passage for each answer.

Write your answers in boxes 1–4 on your answer sheet.

The would-be risk surely exists, since the avionic systems on modern aircraft are used to manage flight and deal with **1** .... Those devices are designed to meet the safety criteria which should be free from interrupting **2** .... or interior emission. The personal use of mobile phone may cause the sophisticated **3** .... outside of a plane to dysfunction. Though definite interference in piloting devices has not been scientifically testified, the devices such as those which detect **4** .... or indicate fuel load could be affected.

核心词汇

A 段

navigation [ˌnævɪˈgeɪʃn] *n.* 航行

stringent [ˈstrɪndʒənt] *adj.* 严格的；严厉的

radiation [ˌreɪdiˈeɪʃn] *n.* 辐射

emission [iˈmɪʃn] *n.* 散发；发射

antennae [ænˈtenɪː] *n.* 天线

B 段

wry [raɪ] *adj.* 歪斜的

C 段

simulated [ˈsɪmjuleɪtɪd] *adj.* 模拟的

transmission [trænsˈmɪʃn] *n.* 传递；传送

threshold [ˈθreʃhəʊld] *n.* 阈，起始点；门槛

malfunction [ˌmælˈfʌŋkʃn] *v.* 发生故障；不起作用

D 段

avionics [ˌeɪviˈɒnɪks] *n.* 航空电子设备

E 段

wholesale [ˈhəʊlseɪl] *adj.* 大规模的

outlaw [ˈaʊtlɔː] *v.* 宣布……为不合法

F 段

megahertz [ˈmegəhɜːts] *n.* 兆赫

shielding [ˈʃiːldɪŋ] *n.* 屏蔽；防护

socket [ˈsɒkɪt] *n.* 插座

G 段

anecdotal [ˌænɪkˈdəʊtl] *adj.* 轶事的

portable [ˈpɔːtəbl] *adj.* 手提的，便携式的

replicate [ˈreplɪkeɪt] *v.* 复制；折叠

H 段

illogical [ɪˈlɒdʒɪkl] *adj.* 不合逻辑的；不合常理的

unforeseen [ˌʌnfɔːˈsiːn] *adj.* 未预见到的；无法预料的

harmonic [hɑːˈmɒnɪk] *n.* 谐波

J 段

insulation [ˌɪnsjuˈleɪʃn] *n.* 绝缘；隔离
irritated [ˈɪrɪteɪtɪd] *adj.* 恼怒的，生气的

题目

dysfunction [dɪsˈfʌŋkʃn] *vi.&n.* 功能紊乱
testify [ˈtestɪfaɪ] *vt.* 证明

高频同义替换

necessarily	▶	inevitably, consequentially, positively
sensitive	▶	vulnerable, subtle
start	▶	institute, initiate, set out
release	▶	deliver, send, convey
affect	▶	influence, impact
interference	▶	conflict, disturbance, obstacle, collision
complicate	▶	aggravate, exacerbate, perplex
prohibit	▶	stem, block, dispute, discourage, stop, ban
hardly	▶	scarcely, barely

题目解析

1 定位词：would-be risk, deal with
文中对应点：A 段第一、二句
题目解析：通过题干中的定位词 would-be risk 和 deal with 定位到 A 段第一、二句 "The potential for problems is certainly there. Modern airliners are packed with electronic devices that control the plane and handle navigation and communications."。其中，potential for problems（潜在危险）与 would-be risk 对应，handle 与 deal with 对应。句意为，潜在的问题当然存在。现代客机上装有控制飞机和处理导航和通信的电子设备。因此答案为 navigation and communications。

2 定位词：safety criteria, interrupting
文中对应点：A 段第三句
题目解析：通过题干中的定位词 safety criteria 和 interrupting 定位到 A 段第三句 "Each has to meet stringent safeguards to make sure it doesn't emit radiation that would interfere with other devices in the plane — standards that passengers' personal electronic devices don't necessarily meet."。其中，safeguards 与 safety criteria 对应，interfere with 与 interrupting 对应。句意为，每个人都必须遵守严格的安全措施，以确保它不会发射出干扰飞机上其他设备的辐射，而乘客的个人电子设备不

一定会遇到这种情况。因此答案取其中的 radiation。

3　定位词：sophisticated, outside of a plane
　　文中对应点：A 段倒数第一句
　　题目解析：通过题干中的定位词 outside of a plane 定位到 A 段倒数第一句"Emissions from inside the plane could also interfere with sensitive antennae on the fixed exterior."。其中，sensitive 对应题干中的 sophisticated，fixed exterior（飞机外面）对应题干的 outside of a plane。句意为，飞机内部的排放也会干扰固定外部的敏感天线。因此答案就是这句话中的 antennae（天线）。

4　定位词：detect, indicate, fuel load
　　文中对应点：C 段倒数第一句
　　题目解析：通过题干中的定位词 detect, indicate, fuel load 定位到 C 段倒数第一句"But the devices that could be affected, such as smoke detectors and fuel level indicators, could still create serious problems for the flight crew if they malfunction."。其中，indicators 为 indicate 的同根词，fuel load 与 fuel level 对应，detectors 与 detect 为同根词。句意为，但那些可能受到影响的设备，如烟雾探测器和燃料指示器，如果它们出现故障，仍然会给机组人员带来严重的问题。因此答案为 smoke。

参考答案

1 navigation and communications　　**2** radiation　　**3** antennae　　**4** smoke

Plain English Campaign

A We launched Plain English Campaign in 1979 with a ritual shredding of appalling government and municipal council forms in Parliament Square, London. We had become so fed up of people visiting our advice centre in Salford, Greater Manchester, to complain about incomprehensible forms that we thought we ought to take action. At the time the shredding seemed like merely throwing sand in the eyes of the charging lion, but it briefly caught the public imagination and left an impression on government and business. Although we're pleased with the new Plain English awareness in government departments, many local councils and businesses maintain a stout resistance to change. One council began a letter to its tenants about a rent increase with two sentences averaging 95 words, full of bizarre housing finance jargon and waffle about Acts of Parliament. The London Borough of Ealing sent such an incomprehensible letter to ISO residents that 40 of them wrote or telephoned to complain and ask for clarification. Many were upset and frightened that the council was planning to imprison them if they didn't fill in the accompanying form. In fact, the letter meant nothing of the sort, and the council had to send another letter to explain.

B Plain legal English can be used as a marketing tactic. Provincial Insurance issued their Plain English Home Cover policy in 1983 and sold it heavily as such. In the first 18 months its sales rocketed, drawing in about an extra £1.5 million of business. Recently, the Eagle Star Group launched a Plain English policy to a chorus of congratulatory letters from policyholders. People, it seems, prefer to buy a policy they can understand.

C Two kinds of instructions give us a lot of concern — medical labels and do-it-yourself products. With medical labels there is a serious gap between what the professionals think is clear and what is really clear to patients. A survey by pharmacists Raynor and Sillito found that 31% of patients misunderstood the instruction on eyedrops 'To be instilled', while 33% misunderstood 'Use sparingly'. The instruction 'Take two tablets 4 hourly' is so prone to misunderstanding (for example, as 8 tablets an hour) that we think it should be banned. Unclear instructions on do-it-yourself products cause expense and frustration to customers. Writing the necessary instructions for these products is usually entrusted to someone who knows the product inside out, yet the best qualification for writing instructions is ignorance. The writer is then like a first-time user, discovering how to use the product in a step-by-step way. Instructions never seem to be tested with first-time users before being issued. So vital steps are missed out or components are mislabelled or not labelled at all. For example, the instructions for assembling a sliding door gear say: 'The pendant bolt centres are fixed and should be at an equal distance from the centre of the door.' This neglects to explain who should do the fixing and how the bolt centres will get into the correct position. By using an imperative and an active verb the instruction becomes much clearer: 'Make sure you fix the centres of the pendant bolts at an equal distance from the centre of the door.'

D Effectively, the Plain English movement in the US began with President Jimmy Carter's Executive Order 12044 of 23 March 1978, that required regulations to be written in plain language. There were earlier government efforts to inform consumers about their rights and obligations, such as The Truth in Lending Act (1969) and The Fair Credit Billing Act (1975), which emphasised a body of information that consumers need in simple language. But President Carter's executive order gave the prestige and force of a president to the movement. All over the country isolated revolts or efforts against legalistic gobbledygook at the federal, state and corporate levels seemed to grow into a small revolution. These efforts and advances between the years 1978 and 1985 are described in the panel 'The Plain English Scorecard'.

E The Bastille has not fallen yet. The forces of resistance are strong, as one can see from the case of Pennsylvania as cited in the Scorecard. In addition, President Ronald Reagan's executive order of 19 February 1981, revoking President Carter's earlier executive order, has definitely slowed the pace of Plain English legislation in the United States. There are three main objections to the idea of Plain English. They are given below, with the campaign's answers to them:

F The statute would cause unending litigation and clog the courts. Simply not true in all the ten states with Plain English laws for consumer contracts and the 34 states with laws or regulations for insurance policies. Since 1978 when Plain English law went into effect in New York there have been only four litigations and only two decisions. Massachusetts had zero cases. The cost of compliance would be enormous. Translation of legal contracts into nonlegal everyday language would be a waste of time and money. The experience of several corporations has proved that the cost of compliance is often outweighed by solid benefits and litigation savings. Citibank of New York made history in 1975 by introducing a simplified promissory note and afterwards simplified all their forms. Citibank counsel Carl Falsenfield says: 'We have lost no money and there has been no litigation as a result of simplification.' The cost effectiveness of clarity is demonstrable. A satisfied customer more readily signs on the bottom line and thus contributes to the corporation's bottom line. Some documents simply can't be simplified. Only legal language that has been tested for centuries in the courts is precise enough to deal with a mortgage, a deed, a lease, or an insurance policy. Here, too, the experience of several corporations and insurance companies has proved that contracts and policies can be made more understandable without sacrificing legal effectiveness.

G What does the future hold for the Plain English movement? Today, American consumers are buffeted by an assortment of pressures. Never before have consumers had as many choices in areas like financial services, travel, telephone services, and supermarket products. There are about 300 long-distance phone companies in the US. Not long ago, the average supermarket carried 9,000 items; today, it carries 22,000. More important, this expansion of options — according to a recent report — is faced by a staggering 30 million Americans lacking the reading skills to handle the minimal demands of daily living. The consumer's need, therefore, for information expressed in Plain English is more critical than ever.

H What is needed today is not a brake on the movement's momentum, but another push toward Plain English contracts from consumers. I still hear Plain English on the TV and in the streets, and read Plain English in popular magazines and best-sellers, but not yet in many functional documents. Despite some victories, the war against gobbledygook is not over yet. We do well to remember, the warning of Chrissie Maher, organiser of Plain English Campaign in the UK: 'People are not just injured when medical labels are written in gobbledygook — they die. Drivers are not just hurt when their medicines don't tell them they could fall asleep at the wheel — they are killed.'

Questions 1–8

Complete the summary below.

Choose **NO MORE THAN THREE WORDS** from the passage for each answer.

Write your answers in boxes 1–8 on your answer sheet.

Campaigners experienced a council renting document full of strange **1** .... of housing in terms of an Act. They were anxious in some other field, for instance, when they were reading a label of medicine, there was an obvious **2** .... between professionals and patients on labels. Another notable field was on **3** .... products; it not only additionally cost buyers, but caused **4** .... because the writer may not best qualified in writing thus regarded himself as a/an **5** .... However, oppositions against the Plain English Campaign are under certain circumstances, e.g., **6** .... language had been embellished as an accurate language used in the **7** .... The author suggested that nowadays new compelling force is needed from **8** ....

核心词汇

A 段

ritual [ˈrɪtʃuəl] n. 仪式，典礼；惯例 adj. 例行的，作为仪式一部分的

appalling [əˈpɔːlɪŋ] adj. 可怕的，令人震惊的；糟透了的

resistance [rɪˈzɪstəns] n. 抵抗，反抗，抗拒

complain [kəmˈpleɪn] vi. & vt. 抱怨，发牢骚

imprison [ɪmˈprɪzn] vt. 监禁，关押；束缚，限制

C 段

instruction [ɪnˈstrʌkʃn] n. 指令；说明（常用复数 instructions）

expense [ɪkˈspens] n. 损失，代价；消费；开支

frustration [frʌˈstreɪʃn] n. 懊恼，沮丧；挫折

entrust [ɪnˈtrʌst] vt. 委托，交付，托管

ignorance [ˈɪɡnərəns] n. 无知，愚昧

issue [ˈɪʃuː] vt. 发布，发行，发表 n. 议题，话题

vital [ˈvaɪtl] adj. 至关重要的，生死攸关的；生机勃勃的

component [kəmˈpəʊnənt] n. 部件，零件，组成部分 adj. 组成的，构成的

label [ˈleɪbl] vt. 贴上标签 n. 标签，标记

assemble [əˈsembl] vi. & vt. 集合，聚集 vt. 组装，装配

imperative [ɪmˈperətɪv] adj. 必要的，紧急的 n. 必要的事；观念，新信念；祈使语气

D 段

regulation [ˌreɡjuˈleɪʃn] n. 条例，规定，法令 adj. 符合规定的

obligation [ˌɒblɪˈɡeɪʃn] n. 义务，职责，责任

emphasise [ˈemfəsaɪz] vt. 强调，着重

E 段

executive [ɪɡˈzekjətɪv] adj. 行政的，管理的；豪华的 n. 经理，主管

F 段

litigation [ˌlɪtɪˈɡeɪʃn] n. 诉讼，起诉

compliance [kəmˈplaɪəns] n. 顺从，听从，遵守

enormous [ɪˈnɔːməs] adj. 庞大的，巨大的

sacrifice [ˈsækrɪfaɪs] vi. & vt. 献祭；奉献 vt. 牺牲，献出 n. 牺牲，祭品，供奉

contract [kənˈtrækt] n. 合同，合约 [kənˈtrækt] vi. & vt. 签合约 vi. 缩小，缩短 [kənˈtrækt] vt. 感染，患病

高频同义替换

additionally ▸ in addition, moreover, besides

cause ▸ reason, lead to, contribute to, as a result of

accurate ▸ precise, refined, strict, mathematical

题目解析

1 定位词：a council renting document, full of strange

文中对应点：A 段第五句

题目解析：通过题干中的定位词 a council renting document, full of strange 定位到 A 段第五句 "...full of bizarre housing finance jargon and waffle about Acts of Parliament."。其中，原文中的 full of 在题干中重现，原文中的 bizarre 对应题干中的 strange，原文中的 Acts of Parliament 对应题干中 an Act。句意为，……充斥着怪异的住宅信贷术语和国会法案的废话。因此答案为 jargon and waffle。

2 定位词：label of medicine, between professionals and patients

文中对应点：C 段第二句

题目解析：通过题干中的定位词 label of medicine, between professionals and patients 定位到 C 段第二句 "With medical labels there is a serious gap between what the professionals think is clear and what is really clear to patients."。其中，原文中的 label of medicine 在题干中重现，原文中的 serious 对应题干中的 obvious，而空格后面的 between professionals and patients，说明总结的是在阅读医药商标时专家和病人之间的对比。句意为，在医学标签上，专业人士认为清楚的东西和病人真正清楚的东西之间存在着巨大的差距。因此答案为 gap。

3 定位词：another noteble field

文中对应点：C 段第一句

题目解析：通过题干中的定位词 another notable field 定位到 C 段第一句 "Two kinds of instructions give us a lot of concern — medical labels and do-it-yourself products."。其中，原文中的 products 在题干中重现，题干前一空已经回答了 medical labels 的相关问题。句意为，两种说明书造成了许多担忧，分别是医疗标签和自制产品。因此答案为 do-it-yourself。

4 定位词：not only, cost buyers, cause

文中对应点：C 段第五句

题目解析：通过题干中的定位词 not only, cost buyers, cause 定位到 C 段第五句 "Unclear instructions on do-it-yourself products cause expense and frustration to customers."。其中，题干中已有 cause expense（cost buyers）这层意思，本题总结的是自制产品产生的相关问题。句意为，在自制产品上不明确的指示会给顾客造成损失，产生挫败感。因此答案为 frustration。

5 定位词：writer, regarded himself as

文中对应点：C 段第七句

题目解析：通过题干中的定位词 writer, regard himself as 定位到 C 段第七句 "The writer is then like a first-time user, discovering how to use the product in a step-by-step way."。其中，原文中的 like 对应题干中的 regarded himself as。句意为，编写标签说明的人就像一个初次使用者一样，一步步地发现如何使用产品。因此答案为 first-time user。

6 定位词：oppositions, Plain English Campaign, accurate language

文中对应点：F 段倒数第二句

题目解析：通过题干中的定位词 oppositions, Plain English Campaign, accurate language 定位到 F 段倒数第二句 "Only legal language that has been tested for centuries in the courts is precise enough to deal with a mortgage, a deed, a lease, or an insurance policy."。其中，原文中的 precise 对应题干中的 accurate，而且 E 段末尾提到 Plain English 主要有三种反对观点，可知后面的内容即是对此的具体介绍。句意为，只有在法庭上经过几个世纪考验的法律语言才能精确到足以处理抵押、契约、租赁或保险事物。因此答案为 legal。

7 定位词：used in

文中对应点：F 段倒数第二句

题目解析：通过题干中的定位词 used in 同样定位到 F 段倒数第二句 "Only legal language that has been tested for centuries in the courts is precise enough…"。其中，原文中的 has been tested for 与 used in 对应。题干暗示这种 accurate language 使用的场合，紧承前一问。因此答案为 courts。

8 定位词：nowadays, compelling force, needed from

文中对应点：H 段第一句

题目解析：通过题干中的定位词 nowadays, compelling force, needed from 定位到 H 段第一句 "What is needed today is not a brake on the movement's momentum, but another push toward Plain English contracts from consumers."。其中，原文中的 today 与题干中的 nowadays 对应，another 与 new 对应，push 对应 compelling force，from 对应 needed from。句意为，当今需要的并不是阻碍运动的声势，而是消费者对于使用简明英语的推力。因此答案为 consumers。

参考答案

1 jargon and waffle   **2** gap   **3** do-it-yourself   **4** frustration   **5** first-time user   **6** legal   **7** courts   **8** consumers

READING PASSAGE 4

London Swaying Footbridge

A In September 1996, a competition was organised by the *Financial Times* in association with the London Borough of Southwark to design a new footbridge across the Thames. The competition attracted over 200 entries and was won by a team comprising Amp (engineers), Foster and Partners (architects) and the sculptor Sir Anthony Caro.

B The bridge opened to the public on 10 June 2000. Up to 100,000 people crossed it that day with up to 2,000 people on the bridge at any one time. At first, the bridge was still. Then it began to sway, just slightly. Then, almost from one moment to the next, when large groups of people were crossing, the wobble intensified. This movement became sufficiently large for people to stop walking to retain their balance and sometimes to hold onto the hand rails for support. It was decided immediately to limit the number of people on the bridge, but even so the deck movement was sufficient to be uncomfortable and to raise concern for public safety so that on 12 June the bridge was closed until the problem could be solved.

C The embarrassed engineers found the videotape that day which showed the centre span swaying about 3 inches side to side every second. The engineers first thought that winds might be exerting excessive force on the many large flags and banners bedecking the bridge for its gala premiere.

D What's more, they also discovered that the pedestrians also played a key role. Human activities, such as walking, running, jumping, swaying, etc., could cause horizontal force which in turn could cause excessive dynamic vibration in the lateral direction of the bridge. As the structure began moving, pedestrians adjusted their gait to the same lateral rhythm as the bridge. The adjusted footsteps magnified the motion — just like when four people all stand up in a small boat at the same time. As more pedestrians locked into the same rhythm, the increasing oscillations led to the dramatic swaying captured on film.

E In order to design a method of reducing the movements, the force exerted by the pedestrians had to be quantified and related to the motion of the bridge. Although there are some descriptions of this phenomenon in existing literature, none of these actually quantifies the force. So there was no quantitative analytical way to design the bridge against this effect. An immediate research programme was launched by the bridge's engineering designers Ove Arup, supported by a number of universities and research organisations.

F The tests at the University of Southampton involved a person walking 'on the spot' on a small shake table. The tests at Imperial College involved persons walking along a specially built, 7.2-m-long platform which could be driven laterally at different frequencies amplitudes. Each type of test had its limitations. The Imperial College tests were only able to capture 7–8 footsteps, and the 'walking on the spot' tests, although monitoring many footsteps, could not investigate normal forward walking. Neither test could investigate any influence of other people in a crowd on the behaviour of the individual being tested.

G The results of the laboratory tests provided information which enabled the initial design of a retro-fit to be progressed. However, the limitations of these tests were clear and it was felt that the only way to replicate properly the precise conditions of the Millennium Bridge was to carry out crowd tests on the bridge deck itself. These tests done by the Arup engineers could incorporate factors not possible in the laboratory tests. The first of these was carried out with 100 people in July 2000. The results of these tests were used to refine the load model for the pedestrians. A second series of crowd tests was carried out on the bridge in December 2000. The purpose of these tests was to further validate the design assumptions and to load test a prototype damper installation. The test was carried out with 275 people.

H Unless the usage of the bridge was to be greatly restricted, only two generic options to improve its performance were considered feasible. The first was to increase the stiffness of the bridge to move all its lateral natural frequencies out of the range that could be excited by the lateral footfall forces, and the second was to increase the damping of the bridge to reduce the resonant response.

Questions 1–5

Complete the summary below.

Choose **NO MORE THAN THREE WORDS** from the passage for each answer.

Write your answers in boxes 1–5 on your answer sheet.

After the opening ceremony, the embarrassed engineers tried to find out the reason of the bridge's wobbling. Judged from the videotape, they thought that **1** .... and **2** .... might create excessive force on the bridge. The distribution of **3** .... resulted from human activities could cause **4** .... throughout the structure. This swaying prompted people to start adjusting the way they walk, which in turn reinforced the **5** ....

核心词汇

B 段

sway [sweɪ] *vi.* 摇摆，摇晃 *vt.* 影响；使……改变看法 *n.* 摇摆；影响力；支配，统治
wobble ['wɒbl] *n.* 轻微晃动，不稳定；游移不定 *vi.* 摇晃；犹豫不决 *vt.* 使……摇摆
intensify [ɪn'tensɪfaɪ] *vi. & vt.* （使）加剧，（使）增强
retain [rɪ'teɪn] *vt.* 保有，保留；保存；记住

C 段

span [spæn] *vt.* 持续，贯穿；跨越；包括 *n.* 期间，时距；持续时间；跨距；全长
exert [ɪɡ'zɜːt] *vt.* 施加；运用
gala ['ɡɑːlə] *n.* 庆典，演出盛会；运动会

D 段

pedestrian [pə'destrɪən] *n.* 行人，步行者 *adj.* 行人的；平淡无奇的，乏味的
horizontal [ˌhɒrɪ'zɒntl] *adj.* 水平的 *n.* 水平线；水平面
vibration [vaɪ'breɪʃn] *n.* 振动，颤动，震颤 [拓] vibrations *n.* （复数）感应，感受
lateral ['lætərəl] *adj.* 横向的；侧面的；平级的，同级的 [拓] laterally *adv.* 横向地；在侧面
gait [ɡeɪt] *n.* 步伐，步态
magnify ['mæɡnɪfaɪ] *vt.* 使……加重；放大；夸张，夸大
motion ['məʊʃn] *n.* 移动；手势；提议 *vi. & vt.* 做示意动作

E 段

quantify ['kwɒntɪfaɪ] *vt.* 测定……的数量；量化
quantitative ['kwɒntɪtətɪv] *adj.* 定量的；与数量有关的

F 段

frequency ['friːkwənsi] *n.* 频率，发生率
amplitude ['æmplɪtjuːd] *n.* 振幅

G 段

replicate ['replɪkeɪt] *vt.* 复制；自我复制；重做
incorporate [ɪn'kɔːpəreɪt] *vt.* 包含；把……并入 [拓] incorporation *n.* 合并；成立公司
refine [rɪ'faɪn] *vt.* 改进，完善；净化；提炼
validate ['vælɪdeɪt] *vt.* 证实；使生效；承认，认可
prototype ['prəʊtətaɪp] *n.* 原型，雏形；典型；样板

H 段

resonant [ˈrezənənt] *adj.* 共振的，共鸣的；回荡的

高频同义替换

create	▸	produce, generate, invent
excessive	▸	extravagant, undue
result from	▸	arise from, because of, on account of
cause	▸	create, induce, make, lead to
prompt	▸	motivate, cause, make, stimulate
reinforce	▸	strengthen, bolster, augment

题目解析

1-2 定位词：the embarrassed engineers, videotape, excessive force
文中对应点：C 段第二句
题目解析：题干中的定位词 the embarrassed engineers, excessive force 定位到 C 段第二句 "The engineers first thought that winds might be exerting excessive force on the many large flags and banners bedecking the bridge for its gala premiere."。其中，The engineers 对应 the embarrassed engineers，题干中空格所在句的主语指的正是 the embarrassed engineers，exerting excessive force 与 create excessive force 为同义替换。句意为，工程师们最初认为，首次亮相的桥上装饰了许多大型旗帜和横幅，风可能给它们施加了过大的压力。原文中第一个空对应的从句主语为 winds，因此答案为 winds。第二个空需要寻找与 winds 并列的词汇，顺读 C 段之后的内容没有找到相关内容。D 段第一句 "What's more, they also discovered that the pedestrians also played a key role." 而且，他们还发现行人也是一部分原因。what's more 和两个 also 表明并列的含义。因此第 2 个空填写 (the) pedestrians。

3 定位词：resulted from, human activities
文中对应点：D 段第二句
题目解析：通过题干中的定位词 resulted from, human activities 定位到 D 段第二句 "Human activities, such as walking, running, jumping, swaying, etc., could cause horizontal force which in turn could cause excessive dynamic vibration in the lateral direction of the bridge."。其中，原文中的 human activities 在题干中重现，原文中的 cause 对应题干中的 resulted from。句意为，人类活动，例如散步、跑步、跳跃、摇晃等可能会引起水平力，水平力转而引起桥梁侧面的过度的动力震动。因此答案为 horizontal force。

4 定位词：human activities, cause

文中对应点：D 段第二句

题目解析：通过题干中的定位词 human activities, cause 定位到 D 段第二句。其中，human activities, cause 在题干中重现，原文中的 in the lateral direction of the bridge 对应题干中空格后的 throughout the structure。空格处需要填写 cause 的宾语，受 throughtout the structure 限定，因此答案为原文中 in the lateral direction of the bridge 前的 (excessive dynamic) vibration。

5 定位词：adjusting, walk, reinforced

文中对应点：D 段第三、四句

题目解析：通过题干中的定位词 adjusting, walk, reinforced 定位到 D 段第三、四句 "As the structure began moving, pedestrians adjusted their gait to the same lateral rhythm as the bridge. The adjusted footsteps magnified the motion — just like when four people all stand up in a small boat at the same time."。其中，原文中的 adjusted 对应题干中的 adjusting，footsteps 对应 walk，magnified 对应 reinforced。句意为，当桥体结构开始移动的时候，行人调整他们的步态，与桥体晃动的节奏保持一致。调整后的脚步增强了桥体的晃动——就像是坐在小船里的四个人同时站起来一样。题干中需要填写 reinforced 的宾语，所以填写原文中 magnified 的宾语 motion。

参考答案

1 winds 2 (the) pedestrians 3 horizontal force 4 (excessive dynamic) vibration 5 motion

Making Copier

At first, nobody bought Chester Carlson's strange idea. But trillions of documents later, his invention is the biggest thing in printing since Gutenburg.

A Copying is the engine of civilisation: culture is behaviour duplicated. The oldest copier invented by people is language, by which an idea of yours becomes an idea of mine. The second great copying machine was writing. When the Sumerians transposed spoken words into stylus marks on clay tablets more than 5,000 years ago, they hugely extended the human network that language had created. Writing freed copying from the chain of living contact. It made ideas permanent, portable and endlessly reproducible.

B Until Johannes Gutenberg invented the printing press in the mid-1400s, producing a book in an edition of more than one generally meant writing it out again. Printing with moveable type was not copying, however. Gutenberg couldn't take a document that already existed, feed it into his printing press and run off facsimiles. The first true mechanical copier was manufactured in 1780, when James Watt, who is better known as the inventor of the modern steam engine, created the copying press. Few people today know what a copying press was, but you may have seen one in an antiques store, where it was perhaps called a book press. A user took a document freshly written in special ink, placed a moistened sheet of translucent paper against the inked surface and squeezed the two sheets together in the press, causing some of the ink from the original to penetrate the second sheet, which could then be read by turning it over and looking through its back. The high cost prohibits the widespread use of this copier.

C Among the first modern copying machines, introduced in 1950 by 3M, was the Thermo-Fax, and it made a copy by shining infrared light through an original document and a sheet of paper that had been coated with heat-sensitive chemicals. Competing manufacturers soon introduced other copying technologies and marketed machines called Dupliton, Dial-A-Matic Autostat, Verifax, Copease and Copymation. These machines and their successors were welcomed by secretaries, who had no other means of reproducing documents in hand, but each had serious drawbacks. All required expensive chemically treated papers. And all made copies that smelled bad, were hard to read, didn't last long and tended to curl up into tubes. The machines were displaced, beginning in the late 1800s, by a combination of two 19th century inventions: the typewriter and carbon paper. For those reasons, copying presses were standard equipment in offices for nearly a century and a half.

D None of those machines are still manufactured today. They were all made obsolete by a radically different machine, which had been developed by an obscure photographic-supply company. That company had been founded in 1906 as the Haloid Company and is known today as the Xerox Corporation. In 1959, it introduced an office copier called the Haloid Xerox 914, a machine that, unlike its numerous competitors, made sharp, permanent copies on ordinary paper — a huge breakthrough. The process, which Haloid called xerography (based on Greek words meaning 'dry' and 'writing'), was so unusual that physicists who visited the drafty warehouses where the first machines were built sometimes expressed doubt that it was even theoretically feasible.

E Remarkably, xerography was conceived by one person — Chester Carlson, a shy, soft-spoken patent attorney, who grew up in almost unspeakable poverty and worked his way through junior college and the California Institute of Technology. Chester Carlson was born in Seattle in 1906. His parents — Olof Adolph Carlson and Ellen Josephine Hawkins — had grown up on neighbouring farms in Grove City, Minnesota, a tiny Swedish farming community about 75 miles west of Minneapolis. Compared with competitors, Carlson was not a normal inventor in 20th-century. He made his discovery in solitude in 1937 and offered it to more than 20 major corporations, among them IBM, General Electric, Eastman Kodak and RCA. All of them turned him down, expressing what he later called 'an enthusiastic lack of interest' and thereby passing up the opportunity to manufacture what *Fortune* magazine would describe as 'the most successful product ever marketed in America'.

F Carlson's invention was indeed a commercial triumph. Essentially overnight, people began making copies at a rate that was orders of magnitude higher than anyone had believed possible. And the rate is still growing. In fact, most documents handled by a typical American office worker today are produced xerographically, either on copiers manufactured by Xerox and its competitors or on laser printers, which employ the same process (and were invented, in the 1970s, by a Xerox researcher). This year, the world will produce more than three trillion xerographic copies and laser-printed pages — about 500 for every human on earth.

G Xerography eventually made Carlson a very wealthy man. (His royalties amounted to something like a 16th of a cent for every Xerox copy made, worldwide, through 1965.) Nevertheless, he lived simply. He never owned a second home or a second car, and his wife had to urge him not to buy third-class train tickets when he travelled in Europe. People who knew him casually seldom suspected that he was rich or even well-to-do; when Carlson told an acquaintance he worked at Xerox, the man assumed he was a factory worker and asked if he belonged to a union. 'His possessions seemed to be composed of the number of things he could easily do without,' his second wife said. He spent the last years of his life quietly giving most of his fortune to charities. When he died in 1968, among the eulogists was the secretary general of the United Nations.

Questions 1–7

Complete the summary below.

Choose **NO MORE THAN THREE WORDS** from the passage for each answer.

Write your answers in boxes 1–7 on your answer sheet.

Carlson, unlike a 20th-century **1** ...., liked to work on his own. In 1937, he unsuccessfully invited 20 major **2** .... to make his discovery. However, this action was not welcome among shareholders at beginning, and all of them **3** .... Eventually Carlson's creation was undeniably a **4** .... Thanks for the discovery of Xerography, Carlson became a very **5** .... person. Even so, his life remained as simple as before. It looked as if he could live without his **6** .... At the same time, he gave lots of his money to **7** ....

核心词汇

A 段

duplicate [ˈdjuːplɪkeɪt] *v.* 复制；使加倍

transpose [trænˈspəʊz] *v.* 调换；颠倒顺序；移项

portable [ˈpɔːtəbl] *adj.* 手提的，便携式的；轻便的

reproducible [ˌriːprəˈdjuːsəbl] *adj.* 可再生的；可繁殖的；可复写的

B 段

facsimile [fækˈsɪməli] *n.* 传真机；复印本

translucent [trænsˈluːsnt] *adj.* 透明的；半透明的

penetrate [ˈpenətreɪt] *v.* 渗透；穿透；洞察

C 段

infrared [ˌɪnfrəˈred] *n.* 红外线 *adj.* 红外线的

D 段

obsolete [ˈɒbsəliːt] *adj.* 废弃的；老式的

feasible [ˈfiːzəbl] *adj.* 可行的；可实行的

E 段

conceive [kənˈsiːv] *v.* 构思；设想

attorney [əˈtɜːni] *n.* 律师；代理人；检察官

solitude [ˈsɒlɪtjuːd] *n.* 孤独；隐居；荒僻的地方

F 段

triumph [ˈtraɪʌmf] *n.* 胜利，凯旋

magnitude [ˈmæɡnɪtjuːd] *n.* 大小；量级；震级；重要性

G 段

eulogist [ˈjuːlədʒɪst] *n.* 赞颂者，称赞者

高频同义替换

extend	▸	stretch, enlarge, increase, prolong, spread
produce	▸	attract, cause, operate
document	▸	file, paper, matter
widespread	▸	extensive, universal, comprehensive, generalised

introduce	▸	present, recommend, prefer
serious	▸	acute, grave, solemn
unusual	▸	different, distinctive
discovery	▸	detection, occurrence, find
typical	▸	characteristic, representative, proper
casually	▸	randomly, temporarily, provisionally

题目解析

1 定位词：unlike, 20th-century

文中对应点：E 段第四句

题目解析：通过题干中的定位词 20th-century 定位到 E 段第四句 "Compared with competitors, Carlson was not a normal inventor in 20th-century."。其中，原文中的 compared with 与题干中的 unlike 对应。句意为，与竞争对手相比，卡尔松在 20 世纪并不是一个普通的发明家。因此答案为 inventor。

2 定位词：1937, more than 20

文中对应点：E 段第五句

题目解析：通过题干中的定位词 1937, more than 20 定位到 E 段第五句 "He made his discovery in solitude in 1937 and offered it to more than 20 major corporations, among them IBM, General Electric, Eastman Kodak and RCA."。句意为，1937 年，他独自创造了自己的发明，并将其提供给 20 多家大公司，其中包括 IBM、通用电气、伊斯曼柯达和 RCA。因此答案为 corporations。

3 定位词：all of them

文中对应点：E 段第六句

题目解析：通过题干中的定位词 all of them 定位到 E 段第六句 "All of them turned him down, expressing what he later called 'an enthusiastic lack of interest'…"。句意为，这些公司都拒绝了他，表达了他后来所说的"对兴趣缺乏热情"。因此答案就是 turned him down。

4 定位词：Carlson's creation, undeniably

文中对应点：F 段第一句

题目解析：通过题干中的定位词 Carlson's creation 定位到 F 段第一句 "Carlson's invention was indeed a commercial triumph."。其中，Carlson's invention 与 Carlson's creation 对应。句意为，卡尔松的发明确实是商业上的巨大成就。因此答案为 commercial triumph。

5 定位词：Xerography, person

文中对应点：G 段第一句

题目解析：通过题干中的定位词 Xerography 定位到 G 段第一句 "Xerography eventually made Carlson a very wealthy man."。其中，man 与 person 对应。句意为，静电复印最终使卡尔松成为一个非常富有的人。因此答案为 wealthy。

6 定位词：look as if, without

文中对应点：G 段倒数第三句

题目解析：根据 look as if 定位到 G 段倒数第三句 "'His possessions seemed to be composed of the number of things he could easily do without,' his second wife said."。其中，seemed to 与 look as if 对应。句子意思为，他的第二任妻子说，他的财产似乎是由他可以轻易不要的东西组成的。因此答案为 possessions。

7 定位词：gave lots of money to

文中对应点：G 段倒数第二句

题目解析：通过题干中的定位词 gave lots of money to 定位到 G 段倒数第二句 "He spent the last years of his life quietly giving most of his fortune to charities."。其中，giving 与 gave 为同根词，most of his fortune to 与 lots of money to 对应。句意为，他平静地度过了自己生命的最后几年里，并把大部分的财产都捐给了慈善机构。因此答案为 charities。

参考答案

1 inventor　**2** corporations　**3** turned him down　**4** commercial triumph　**5** wealthy　**6** possessions　**7** charities

What Are You Laughing At?

A We like to think that laughing is the height of human sophistication. Our big brains let us see the humour in a strategically positioned pun, an unexpected plot twist or a clever piece of word play. But while joking and wit are uniquely human inventions, laughter certainly is not. Other creatures, including chimpanzees, gorillas and even rats, chuckle. Obviously, they don't crack up at *Homer Simpson* or titter at the boss's dreadful jokes, but the fact that they laugh in the first place suggests that sniggers and chortles have been around for a lot longer than we have. It points the way to the origins of laughter, suggesting a much more practical purpose than you might think.

B There is no doubt that laughing typically involves groups of people. 'Laughter evolved as a signal to others — it almost disappears when we are alone,' says Robert Provine, a neuroscientist at the University of Maryland. Provine found that most laughter comes as a polite reaction to everyday remarks such as 'see you later', rather than anything particularly funny. And the way we laugh depends on the company we're keeping. Men tend to laugh longer and harder when they are with other men, perhaps as a way of bonding. Women tend to laugh more and at a higher pitch when men are present, possibly indicating flirtation or even submission.

C To find the origins of laughter, Provine believes we need to look at play. He points out that the masters of laughing are children, and nowhere is their talent more obvious than in the boisterous antics, and the original context is play. Well-known primate watchers, including Dian Fossey and Jane Goodall, have long argued that chimps laugh while at play. The sound they produce is known as a pant laugh. It seems obvious when you watch their behaviour — they even have the same ticklish spots as we do. But remove the context, and the parallel between human laughter and a chimp's characteristic pant laugh is not so clear. When Provine played a tape of the pant laughs to 119 of his students, for example, only two guessed correctly what it was.

D These findings underline how chimp and human laughter vary. When we laugh the sound is usually produced by chopping up a single exhalation into a series of shorter with one sound produced on each inward and outward breath. The question is: does this pant laughter have the same source as our own laughter? New research lends weight to the idea that it does. The findings come from Eke Zimmerman, head of the Institute for Zoology in Germany, who compared the sounds made by babies and chimpanzees in response to tickling during the first year of their life. Using sound spectrographs to reveal the pitch and intensity of vocalisations, she discovered that chimp and human baby laughter follow broadly the same pattern. Zimmerman believes the closeness of baby laughter to chimp laughter supports the idea that laughter was around long before humans arrived on the scene. What started simply as a modification of breathing associated with enjoyable and playful interactions has acquired a symbolic meaning as an indicator of pleasure.

E   Pinpointing when laughter developed is another matter. Humans and chimps share a common ancestor that lived perhaps 8 million years ago, but animals might have been laughing long before that. More distantly related primates, including gorillas, laugh, and anecdotal evidence suggests that other social mammals can do too. Scientists are currently testing such stories with a comparative analysis of just how common laughter is among animals. So far, though, the most compelling evidence for laughter beyond primates comes from research done by Jaak Panksepp from Bowling Green State University, Ohio, into the ultrasonic chirps produced by rats during play and in response to tickling.

F   All this still doesn't answer the question of why we laugh at all. One idea is that laughter and tickling originated as a way of sealing the relationship between mother and child. Another is that the reflex response to tickling is protective, alerting us to the presence of crawling creatures that might harm us or compelling us to defend the parts of our bodies that are most vulnerable in hand-to-hand combat. But the idea that has gained most popularity in recent years is that laughter in response to tickling is a way for two individuals to signal and test their trust in one another. This hypothesis starts from the observation that although a little tickle can be enjoyable, if it goes on too long it can be torture. By engaging in about of tickling, we put ourselves at the mercy of another individual, and laughing is what makes it a reliable signal of trust according to Tom Flamson, a laughter researcher at the University of California, Los Angeles. 'Even in rats, laughter, tickle, play and trust are linked. Rats chirp a lot when they play,' says Flamson. 'These chirps can be aroused by tickling. And they get bonded to us as a result, which certainly seems like a show of trust.'

G   We'll never know which animal laughed the first laugh, or why. But we can be sure it wasn't in response to a prehistoric joke. The funny thing is that while the origins of laughter are probably quite serious, we owe human laughter and our language-based humour to the same unique skill. While other animals pant, we alone can control our breath well enough to produce the sound of laughter. Without that control there would also be no speech and no jokes to endure.

Questions 1–4

Complete the summary using the list of words, **A–K**, below.

Write the correct letter, **A–K**, in boxes 1–4 on your answer sheet.

Some researchers believe that laughter first evolved out of **1** ……………… . Investigation has revealed that human and chimp laughter may have the same **2** ……………… . Besides, scientists have been aware that **3** ……………… laugh. However, it now seems that laughter might be more widespread than once we thought. Although the reasons why humans started to laugh are still unknown, it seems that laughter may result from the **4** ……………… we feel with another person.

A evolution	B chirps	C origins
D voice	E confidence	F rats
G primates	H response	I play
J children	K tickling	

核心词汇

A 段

sophistication [sə,fɪstɪ'keɪʃn] *n.* 复杂性；精密；老练

strategically [strə'tiːdʒɪkli] *adv.* 有用地，适合地；战略上，策略上 [拓] strategy *n.* 战略；计划，规划

uniquely [juː'niːkli] *adv.* 极好地；特别地；独特地

dreadful ['dredfl] *adj.* 糟糕透顶的，极其讨厌的；可怕的

snigger ['snɪɡə(r)] *n.* 暗笑，窃笑 *vi.* 暗笑，窃笑

B 段

flirtation [flɜː'teɪʃn] *n.* 调情

submission [səb'mɪʃn] *n.* 屈服，顺从；提交；意见

C 段

boisterous ['bɔɪstərəs] *adj.* 活跃的；喧闹的

ticklish ['tɪklɪʃ] *adj.* 易痒的，发痒的；棘手的 [拓] tickle *vi. & vt.* （使）发痒；（使）开心 *n.* 痒，发痒

parallel ['pærəlel] *n.* 相似之处，联系；纬线 *adj.* 平行的；相似的；同时发生的 *vt.* 与……同时发生；与……相似

D 段

exhalation [,ekshə'leɪʃn] *n.* 呼出，呼气 [拓] exhale *vi. & vt.* 呼气，呼出

reveal [rɪ'viːl] *vt.* 揭示，揭露，透露；展现，显露

intensity [ɪn'tensəti] *n.* 强度；强烈；剧烈程度 [拓] intense *adj.* 强烈的；紧张的；极为严肃的

modification [,mɒdɪfɪ'keɪʃn] *n.* 调整，修改，改变 [拓] modify *vt.* 修改；改进；修饰

indicator ['ɪndɪkeɪtə(r)] *n.* 指示物；指针；转向指示灯 [拓] indicate *vt.* 显示；指示，指出；代表

E 段

pinpoint ['pɪnpɔɪnt] *vt.* 查明；准确描述；为……准确定位 *n.* 极小的范围

compelling [kəm'pelɪŋ] *adj.* 令人信服的；极为有趣的；强烈的

F 段

originate [ə'rɪdʒɪneɪt] *vi.* 发源；开始；起源 *vt.* 创始，创造；发起 [拓] origin *n.*（常用复数 origins）起源，起因；血统 [拓] original *adj.* 最初的；新颖的；原作的 *n.* 原件

seal [siːl] *vt.* 密封；封闭；封锁；粘住 *n.* 海豹；密封条

reflex ['riːfleks] *n.*（常用复数 reflexes）反应能力；反射动作，反射作用 [拓] reflex response 反射性反应，本能反应

vulnerable ['vʌlnərəbl] *adj.* 易受攻击的；感情脆弱的，易受伤的

torture ['tɔːtʃə(r)] *n.* 折磨，煎熬；拷问 *vt.* 使……精神上受到折磨；拷问

G 段

endure [ɪnˈdjʊə(r)] *vi.* 持续存在，生活下去 *vt.* 忍耐；忍受

高频同义替换

reveal	❯	show, indicate, suggest, demonstrate, illustrate
same	❯	common, alike, uniform, as
be aware of	❯	be conscious of, understand, realise, begin to know
result from	❯	because, stem from, come from, in that, due to, owing to, thanks to
origin	❯	ancestor, first evolved out of, source, beginning
confidence	❯	trust, believe in, reliance

题目解析

1 定位词：laugher, first evolved out of

文中对应点：C 段第一句

题目解析：通过题干中的定位词 laugher, first evolved out of 定位到 C 段第一句 "To find the origins of laughter, Provine believes we need to look at play."。其中，原文中的 the origins of laughter 对应题干中的 first evolved out of，原文中的 Provine 对应题干中的 researchers，因此空格内需要填写 play 或其同义替换词，可在选项中看到原词 play。句意为，为了寻找笑的起源，普罗文认为我们需要关注玩耍。所以答案为 I。

2 定位词：human and chimp, same

文中对应点：E 段第二句

题目解析：通过题干中的定位词 human and chimp, same 定位于 E 段第二句 "Humans and chimps share a common ancestor that lived perhaps 8 million years ago, but animals might have been laughing long before that."。其中，原文中的 human and chimps 在题干中重现，原文中的 common 对应题干中的 same，因此空格内需要填写 ancestor 或其同义替换词，选项中的 origins 可替换 ancestor。句意为，人类和黑猩猩拥有共同的祖先——大约生活在 800 万年前，但早在那之前，动物可能就已经会笑了。所以答案为 C。

3 定位词：besides, aware, more widespread

文中对应点：E 段第三句

题目解析：通过题干中的定位词 besides, aware, more widespread 定位于 E 段第三句 "More distantly related primates, including gorillas, laugh, and anecdotal evidence suggests that other social mammals can do too."。其中，原文中的 other social mammals can do too 对应题干中的 laughter might be more widespread，因此空格内需要填写 primates 或其同义替换词，可在选项中

看到原词 primates。句意为，更远一点的亲戚——灵长类动物，包括大猩猩，也会笑，并且轶事证据暗示其他群居型的哺乳动物也会笑。所以答案为 G。

4 定位词：result from, another person
文中对应点：F 段第四句
题目解析：通过题干中的定位词 result from, feel, another person 根定位于 F 段第四句 "But the idea that has gained most popularity in recent years is that laughter in response to tickling is a way for two individuals to signal and test their trust in one another."。其中，signal and test 对应 result from, one another 对应 another person，因此空格内需要填写 trust 或其同义替换词，选项中的 confidence 可替换 trust。句意为，但是近几年最为流行的说法是，因为挠痒痒而笑是两个人去示意和检测彼此间信任的一种方式。所以答案为 E。

参考答案

1 I **2** C **3** G **4** E

第六章 完成句子题

READING PASSAGE 1

Ancient Chinese Chariots

A The Shang Dynasty or Yin Dynasty, according to traditional historiography, ruled in the Yellow River valley in the second millennium. Archaeological work at the Ruins of Yin (near modern-day Anyang), which has been identified as the last Shang capital, uncovered eleven major Yin royal tombs and the foundations of palaces and ritual sites, containing weapons of war and remains from both animal and human sacrifices.

B The Tomb of Fu Hao is an archaeological site at Yinxu, the ruins of the ancient Shang Dynasty capital Yin, within the modern city of Anyang in Henan Province, China. Discovered in 1976, it was identified as the final resting place of the queen and military general Fu Hao. The artefacts unearthed within the grave included jade objects, bone objects, bronze objects, etc. These grave goods are confirmed by the oracle texts, which constitute almost all of the first hand written record we possess of the Shang Dynasty. Below the corpse was a small pit holding the remains of six sacrificial dogs and along the edge lay the skeletons of human slaves, evidence of human sacrifice.

C The Terracotta Army was discovered on 29 March, 1974 to the east of Xi'an in Shaanxi. The terracotta soldiers were accidentally discovered when a group of local farmers was digging a well during a drought around 1.6 km (1 mile) east of the Qin Emperors tomb around at Mount Li (Lishan), a region riddled with underground springs and watercourses. Experts currently place the entire number of soldiers at 8,000 — with 130 chariots (130 cm long), 530 horses and 150 cavalry horses helping to ward off any dangers in the afterlife. In contrast, the burial of Tutankhamun yielded six complete but dismantled chariots of unparalleled richness and sophistication. Each was designed for two people (90 cm long) and had its axle sawn through to enable it to be brought along the narrow corridor into the tomb.

D Excavation of ancient Chinese chariots has confirmed the descriptions of them in the earliest texts. Wheels were constructed from a variety of woods: elm provided the hub, rose-wood the spokes and oak the felloes. The hub was drilled through to form an empty space into which the tampering axle was fitted, the whole being covered with leather to retain lubricating oil. Though the number of spokes varied, a wheel by the fourth century B.C. usually had eighteen to thirty-two of them. Records show how elaborate was the testing of each completed wheel: flotation and weighing were regarded as the best measures of balance, but even the empty spaces in the assembly were checked with millet grains. One outstanding constructional asset of the ancient Chinese wheel was dishing. Dishing refers to the dish-like shape of an advanced wooden wheel, which looks rather like a flat cone. On occasion they chose to strengthen a dished wheel with a pair of struts running from rim to rim on each of the hub. As these extra supports were inserted separately into the felloes, they would have added even greater strength to the wheel. Leather wrapped up the edge of the wheel aimed to retain bronze.

E Within a millennium, however, Chinese chariot-makers had developed a vehicle with shafts, the precursor of the true carriage or cart. This design did not make its appearance in Europe until the end of the Roman Empire. Because the shafts curved upwards, and the harness pressed against a horse's shoulders, not his neck, the shaft chariot was incredibly efficient. The halberd was also part of a chariot standard weaponry. This halberd usually measured well over 3 metres in length, which meant that a chariot warrior wielding it sideways could strike down the charioteer in a passing chariot. The speed of chariot which was tested on the sand was quite fast at speed these passes were very dangerous for the crews of both chariots.

F The advantages offered by the new chariots were not entirely missed. They could see how there were literally the warring states, whose conflicts lasted down the Qin unification of China. Qin Shi Huang was buried in the most opulent tomb complex ever constructed in China, a sprawling, city-size collection of underground caverns containing everything the emperor would need for the afterlife. Even a collection of terracotta armies called Terra-Cotta Warriors was buried in it. The ancient Chinese, along with many cultures including ancient Egyptians, believed that items and even people buried with a person could be taken with him to the afterlife.

Questions 1–6

Complete the sentences below.

*Choose **ONE WORD/NUMBER ONLY** from the passage for each answer.*

Write your answers in boxes 1–6 on your answer sheet.

1   The hub is made from the tree of ....

2   The room through the hub was to put tampering axle in which is wrapped up by leather aiming to retain ....

3   The number of spokes varied from .... to ....

4   The shape of wheel resembles a ....

5   Two .... were used to strengthen the wheel.

6   Leather wrapped up the edge of the wheel aimed to remain ....

核心词汇

A 段

millennium [mɪˈleniəm] *n.* 一千年，千年期

archaeological [ˌɑːkiəˈlɒdʒɪkl] *adj.* 考古的，考古学的 [拓] archaeology *n.* 考古学

ruin [ˈruːɪn] *n.* 废墟；破产，身败名裂 *vt.* 毁坏；使破产 [拓] the ruins of sth. ……的残余部分

uncover [ʌnˈkʌvə(r)] *vt.* 发现；揭露；揭开……的盖子

remains [rɪˈmeɪnz] *n.* 残骸；遗体；遗迹

sacrifice [ˈsækrɪfaɪs] *n.* 祭品，献祭；牺牲 *vt.* 献出；牺牲 *vi. & vt.* 献祭；以……作祭品

B 段

artefact [ˈɑːtɪfækt] *n.* 人工制品；手工艺品

unearth [ʌnˈɜːθ] *vt.* 发掘；发现；揭露

oracle [ˈɒrəkl] *n.* 神谕；传神谕者；提供意见（信息）的人

C 段

terracotta [ˌterəˈkɒtə] *n.* 赤陶土，赤陶；棕红色

drought [draʊt] *n.* 干旱，旱灾

ward off 防止，抵挡

dismantle [dɪsˈmæntl] *vt.* 拆开，拆卸；废除

sophistication [səˌfɪstɪˈkeɪʃn] *n.* 复杂；精密；老练

D 段

excavation [ˌekskəˈveɪʃn] *n.* 发掘；挖掘

drill [drɪl] *vi. & vt.* 钻孔；打眼 *vt.* 教……反复练习；操练 *n.* 钻机；训练；军事操练

elaborate [ɪˈlæbərət] *adj.* 精心制作的；详尽的 *vi. & vt.* 详尽说明；阐述

E 段

precursor [priːˈkɜːsə(r)] *n.* 前身；先驱

harness [ˈhɑːnɪs] *n.* 马具；系带 *vt.* 控制

wield [wiːld] *vt.* 拿起；使用，行使

F 段

opulent [ˈɒpjələnt] *adj.* 华丽的，奢侈的；阔绰的，极富有的

高频同义替换

| aim to | ▸ | propose, design, map |
| retain | ▸ | keep, sustain, hold, remain |

vary	▶	change, alter, differ
resemble	▶	like, be similar to, similarity
strengthen	▶	enhance, build up
remain	▶	keep, stay, retain

题目解析

1 定位词：hub, tree
文中对应点：D 段第二句
题目解析：通过题干中的定位词 hub, tree 定位到 D 段第二句 "Wheels were constructed from a variety of woods: elm provided the hub, rosewood the spokes and oak the felloes."。其中，elm, rosewood, oak 对应 tree。句意为，轮子是用不同种类的木材制成的：榆木制轮毂，花梨木制轮辐，橡木制轮辋。题干考查的是制作 hub 的木材，因此答案为 elm。

2 定位词：the room through the hub, tampering axle, leather, retain
文中对应点：D 段第三句
题目解析：通过题干中的定位词 the room through the hub, tampering axle, leather, retain 定位到 D 段第三句 "The hub was drilled through to form an empty space into which the tampering axle was fitted, the whole being covered with leather to retain lubricating oil."。其中，empty space 对应 the room through the hub。句意为，轮毂被钻透，以形成一个空间，方便轴的状态被改变以灵活适应操作需要，这些全部都被皮革包裹以保持润滑油不外漏。由于题目的字数限制，因此答案为 oil。

3 定位词：number of spokes
文中对应点：D 段第四句
题目解析：通过题干中的定位词 number of spokes 定位到 D 段第四句 "Though the number of spokes varied, a wheel by the fourth century B.C. usually had eighteen to thirty-two of them."。其中，number of spokes 为原文再现。句意为，尽管轮辐的数量各异，公元前四世纪的轮子通常有 18 到 32 个轮辐。因此答案为 18 和 32。

4 定位词：shape of wheel, resembles
文中对应点：D 段倒数第四句
题目解析：通过题干中的定位词 shape of wheel, resembles 定位到 D 段倒数第四句 "Dishing refers to the dish-like shape of an advanced wooden wheel, which looks rather like a flat cone."。其中，shape of an advanced wooden wheel 对应 shape of wheel，like 对应 resembles。句意为，盘形物指的是一种盘子形状的先进的木制车轮，看起来更像是一个平的圆锥体。因此答案为 dish。

5 定位词：two, strengthen
文中对应点：D 段倒数第三句
题目解析：通过题干中的定位词 two, strengthen 定位到 D 段倒数第三句 "On occasion they chose to strengthen a dished wheel with a pair of struts running from rim to rim on each of the hub."。

其中，a pair of 对应 two。句意为，有一种情况，他们是用每个轮毂上从一个边缘滑到另一个边缘的一组支杆来加固盘型车轮的。因此答案为 struts。

6 定位词：leather, edge
文中对应点：D 段最后一句
题目解析：通过题干中的定位词 leather, edge 定位到 D 段最后一句 "Leather wrapped up the edge of the wheel aimed to retain bronze."。其中，retain 对应 remain。句意为，皮革包裹着车轮的边缘，以裹住上面的青铜组件。因此答案为 bronze。

参考答案

1 elm   **2** oil   **3** 18, 32   **4** dish   **5** struts   **6** bronze

READING PASSAGE 2

Is Graffiti Art or Crime?

A The term *graffiti* derives from the Italian graffito meaning 'scratching' and can be defined as uninvited markings or writing scratched or applied to objects, built structures and natural features. It is not a new phenomenon: examples can be found on ancient structures around the world, in some cases predating the Greeks and Romans. In such circumstances, it has acquired invaluable historical and archaeological significance, providing a social history of life and events at that time. Graffiti is now a problem that has become pervasive, as a result of the availability of cheap and quick means of mark-making.

B It is usually considered a priority to remove graffiti as quickly as possible after it appears. This is for several reasons. The first is to prevent 'copy-cat' emulation which can occur rapidly once a clean surface is defaced. It may also be of a racist or otherwise offensive nature and many companies and councils have a policy of removing this type of graffiti within an hour or two of its being reported. Also, as paints, glues and inks dry out over time they can become increasingly difficult to remove and are usually best dealt with as soon as possible after the incident. Graffiti can also lead to more serious forms of vandalism and, ultimately, the deterioration of an area, contributing to social decline.

C Although graffiti may be regarded as an eyesore, any proposal to remove it from sensitive historic surfaces should be carefully considered: techniques designed for more robust or utilitarian surfaces may result in considerable damage. In the event of graffiti incidents, it is important that the owners of buildings or other structures and their consultants are aware of the approach they should take in dealing with the problem. Some owners may wish to attempt their own treatment. Others may prefer to appoint a suitable specialist contractor to deal with the incident. Whichever course is chosen, it is important that all those involved follow as far as possible a systematic approach which includes such considerations as putting in place preventive measures. The police should be informed as there may be other related attacks occurring locally. An incidence pattern can identify possible culprits, as can stylise signatures or nicknames, known as 'tags', which may already be familiar to local police.

D There are a variety of methods that are used to remove graffiti. Broadly these divide between chemical and mechanical systems. Chemical preparations are based on dissolving the media; these solvents can range from water to potentially hazardous chemical 'cocktails'. Mechanical systems such as wire-brushing and grit-blasting attempt to abrade or chip the media from the surface. Care should be taken to comply with health and safety legislation with regard to the protection of both passers-by and any person carrying out the cleaning. Operatives should follow product guidelines in terms of application and removal, and wear the appropriate protective equipment. Measures must be taken to ensure that run-off, aerial mists, drips and splashes do not threaten unprotected members of the public.

E   A variety of preventive strategies can be adopted to combat a recurring problem of graffiti at a given site. It is also clear that preventive measures will ultimately be cheaper, more effective and less damaging than multiple removal treatments. It is worth undertaking a site audit to look at where the vulnerable surfaces are located and where past graffiti attacks have occurred. Often these are readily accessible flat surfaces where the graffiti will have most impact, but this is not always the case and graffitists may scale walls or bridges for example to give their work greater impact.

F   As no two sites are the same, no one set of protection measures will be suitable for all situations. Each site must be looked at individually. Surveillance systems such as closed circuit television may also help. In cities and towns around the country, prominently placed cameras have been shown to reduce anti-social behaviour of all types including graffiti. Security patrols will also act as a deterrent to prevent recurring attacks. However, the cost of this may be too high for most situations. Physical barriers such as a wall, railings, doors or gates can be introduced to discourage unauthorised access to a vulnerable site. However, consideration has to be given to the impact measures have on the structure being protected. In the worst cases, they can be almost as damaging to the quality of the environment as the graffiti they prevent. In others, they might simply provide a new surface for graffiti.

Questions 1–6

Complete the sentences below.

Choose **NO MORE THAN TWO WORDS** from the passage for each answer.

Write your answers in boxes 1–6 on your answer sheet.

1   Ancient graffiti is significant, recording the .... of life details of that time.

2   .... has become a widespread problem because of the convenient ways of signs.

3   The police can recognise probable culprits according to the design of graffiti, and the signature that they are familiar with is called ....

4   In order to guard passers-by and other people, ... should be taken to obey the law.

5   Operatives ought to comply with relevant rules during the operation, and put on the suitable ....

6   We should take measures to make sure that the defenseless members of the .... would not be scared by the graffiti.

核心词汇

A 段

predate [ˌpriːˈdeɪt] *vt.* 早于……出现

pervasive [pəˈveɪsɪv] *adj.* 到处存在的，到处弥漫着的

B 段

priority [praɪˈɒrəti] *n.* 优先处理的事，当务之急；优先权 *adj.* 优先的

emulation [ˌemjuˈleɪʃn] *n.* 模仿，效仿

racist [ˈreɪsɪst] *n.* 种族主义者

incident [ˈɪnsɪdənt] *n.* 事件；冲突

vandalism [ˈvændəlɪzəm] *n.* 故意破坏财物的行为

ultimately [ˈʌltɪmətli] *adv.* 最后，最终

C 段

eyesore [ˈaɪsɔː(r)] *n.* 碍眼的事物；难看的东西

sensitive [ˈsensətɪv] *adj.* 需小心处理的；敏感的；善解人意的

consultant [kənˈsʌltənt] *n.* 顾问；会诊医生

culprit [ˈkʌlprɪt] *n.* 罪犯；问题的起因

D 段

mechanical system　机械系统

solvent [ˈsɒlvənt] *n.* 溶剂 *adj.* 有偿还能力的

hazardous [ˈhæzədəs] *adj.* 危险的，不安全的

comply with　遵守；服从

mist [mɪst] *n.* 薄雾，雾霭 *vt.* 使蒙上水汽

splash [splæʃ] *n.* 洒溅的斑点；飞溅声；少量液体 *vi.* 飞溅，溅落 *vt.* 泼；以大篇幅报道

F 段

surveillance [sɜːˈveɪləns] *n.* 监视；侦察；监察

prominently [ˈprɒmɪnəntli] *adv.* 显眼地；显著地

deterrent [dɪˈterənt] *n.* 制止物；威慑力量

高频同义替换

derive from	▶	extract, extraction, come from
acquire	▶	obtain, get, gain, earn

pervasive	▸	permeant, worldwide, spread, universal, widespread, catholic
comply with	▸	abide by, obey, observe, stand by
prominently	▸	conspicuously, remarkably, notably, noticeably, markedly

题目解析

1 定位词：ancient, significant, life details, that time
文中对应点：A 段倒数第二句
题目解析：通过题干中的定位词 ancient, significant, life details, that time 定位到 A 段倒数第二句 "In such circumstances, it has acquired invaluable historical and archaeological significance, providing a social history of life and events at that time."。其中，significance 为 significant 的名词形式，life and events 对应 life details，at that time 对应 that time。句意为，在这种情况下，它具有极其宝贵的历史和考古意义，为我们提供了当时社会生活和事件的历史写照。因此答案为 social history。

2 定位词：widespread, because of, convenient ways, signs
文中对应点：A 段最后一句
题目解析：通过题干中的定位词 widespread, because of, convenient ways, signs 定位到 A 段最后一句 "Graffiti is now a problem that has become pervasive, as a result of the availability of cheap and quick means of mark-making."。其中，pervasive 对应 widespread，as a result of 对应 because of，quick means 对应 convenient ways，mark-making 对应 signs。句意为，由于廉价的可用性和创作的便捷方式，涂鸦现在已经成为一个越来越普遍的问题。因此答案为 Graffiti。

3 定位词：probable culprits, signature, are familiar with
文中对应点：C 段最后一句
题目解析：通过题干中的定位词 probable culprits, signature, are familiar with 定位到 C 段最后一句 "An incidence pattern can identify possible culprits, as can stylise signatures or nicknames, known as 'tags', which may already be familiar to local police."。其中，possible culprits 对应 probable culprits，be familiar to 对应 are familiar with。句意为，一种发生规律能够识别可能的罪犯，因为程序化的鲜明签名或昵称——被称为"标记"，可能已经被当地警方所熟知。因此答案为 tags。

4 定位词：passers-by, law
文中对应点：D 段第五句
题目解析：通过题干中的定位词 probable culprits, signature, are familiar with 定位到 D 段第五句 "Care should be taken to comply with health and safety legislation with regard to the protection of both passers-by and any person carrying out the cleaning."。其中，legislation 对应题干中的 law, protection 对应题干中的 guard。句意为，应当谨慎遵守关于保护行人和清洁人员健康和安全的法规。因此答案为 care。

5 定位词：operatives, comply with, suitable
   文中对应点：D 段倒数第二句
   题目解析：通过题干中的定位词 operatives, comply with, suitable 定位到 D 段倒数第二句 "Operatives should follow product guidelines in terms of application and removal, and wear the appropriate protective equipment."。其中，follow 对应 comply with，wear 对应 put on，appropriate 对应 suitable。句意为，作业人员在应用产品和清理时应遵循产品使用指南，并佩戴适当的防护设备。因此答案为 protective equipment。

6 定位词：take measures, make sure, defenseless
   文中对应点：D 段倒数第一句
   题目解析：通过题干中的定位词 take measures, make sure, members 定位到 D 段倒数第一句 "Measures must be taken to ensure that run-off, aerial mists, drips and splashes do not threaten unprotected members of the public."。其中，measures must be taken 与 take measures 为同义替换，ensure 与 make sure 为同义替换，unprotected 对应 defenseless。句意为，必须采取措施确保径流、空中迷雾、水滴和滴溅不威胁到未受保护的公众的安全。因此答案为 public。

参考答案

1 social history   2 Graffiti   3 tags   4 care   5 protective equipment   6 public

第七章　简答题

READING PASSAGE 1

The Concept of Childhood in the Western Countries

The history of childhood has been a topic of interest in social history since the highly influential 1960 book Centuries of Childhood, written by French historian Philippe Aries. He argued that 'childhood' is a concept created by modern society.

A　One of the most hotly debated issues in the history of childhood has been whether childhood is itself a recent invention. The historian Philippe Aries argued that in Western Europe during the Middle Ages (up to about the end of the fifteenth century) children were regarded as miniature adults, with all the intellect and personality that this implies. He scrutinised medieval pictures and diaries, and found no distinction between children and adults as they shared similar leisure activities and often the same type of work. Aries, however, pointed out that this is not to suggest that children were neglected, forsaken or despised. The idea of childhood is not to be confused with affection for children; it corresponds to an awareness of the particular nature of childhood, that particular nature which distinguishes the child from the adult, even the young adult.

B　There is a long tradition of the children of the poor playing a functional role in contributing to the family income by working either inside or outside the home. In this sense children are seen as 'useful'. Back in the Middle Ages, children as young as 5 or 6 did important chores for their parents and, from the sixteenth century, were often encouraged (or forced) to leave the family by the age of 9 or 10 to work as servants for wealthier families or to be apprenticed to a trade.

C　With industrialisation in the eighteenth and nineteenth centuries, a new demand for child labour was created, and many children were forced to work for long hours, in mines, workshops and factories. Social reformers began to question whether labouring long hours from an early age would harm children's growing bodies. They began to recognise the potential of carrying out systematic studies to monitor how far these early deprivations might be affecting children's development.

D　Gradually, the concerns of the reformers began to impact on the working conditions of children. In Britain, *the Factory Act* of 1833 signified the beginning of legal protection of children from exploitation and was linked to the rise of schools for factory children. The worst forms of child exploitation were gradually eliminated, partly through factory reform but also through the influence of trade unions and economic changes during the nineteenth century which made some forms of child labour redundant. Childhood was increasingly seen as a time for play and education for all children, not just for a privileged minority. Initiating children into work as 'useful' children became less of a priority. As the age for starting full-time work was delayed, so childhood was increasingly understood as a more extended phase of dependency, development and learning. Even so, work continued to play a significant, if less central role in children's lives throughout the later nineteenth and twentieth century. And the 'useful child' has become a controversial image during the first decade of the twenty-first century especially in the context of global concern about large numbers of the world's children engaged in child labour.

E   The *Factory Act* of 1833 established half-time schools which allowed children to work and attend school. But in the 1840s, a large proportion of children never went to school, and if they did, they left by the age of 10 or 11. The situation was very different by the end of the nineteenth century in Britain. The school became central to images of 'a normal' childhood.

F   Attending school was no longer a privilege and all children were expected to spend a significant part of their day in a classroom. By going to school, children's lives were now separated from domestic life at home and from the adult world of work. School became an institution dedicated to shaping the minds, behaviour and morals of the young. Education dominated the management of children's waking hours, not just through the hours spent in classrooms but through 'home' work, the growth of 'after school' activities and the importance attached to 'parental' involvement.

G   Industrialisation, urbanisation and mass schooling also set new challenges for those responsible for protecting children's welfare, and promoting their learning. Increasingly, children were being treated as a group with distinctive needs and they were organised into groups according to their age. For example, teachers needed to know what to expect of children in their classrooms, what kinds of instruction were appropriate for different age groups and how best to assess children's progress. They also wanted tools that could enable them to sort and select children according to their abilities and potential.

Questions 1–6

Answer the questions below.

Choose **NO MORE THAN THREE WORDS** from the passage for each answer.

Write your answers in boxes 1–6 on your answer sheet.

1   What is the controversial topic that arises with the French historian Philippe Aries's concept?

    ....

2   What image for children did Aries believe to be like in Western Europe during the Middle Ages?

    ....

3   What historical event generated the need for great amount of children labour to work long time in 18th and 19th centuries?

    ....

4   What legal format initiated the protection of children from exploitation in 19th century?

    ....

5   What activities were more and more regarded as being preferable for almost all children time in 19th century?

    ....

6   Where has been the central area for children to spend largely of their day as people's expectation in modern society?

    ....

核心词汇

A 段

miniature [ˈmɪnətʃə(r)] *adj.* 微型的，很小的 *n.* 微型图

scrutinise [ˈskruːtənaɪz] *vt.* 认真查看；检查

forsake [fəˈseɪk] *vt.* 遗弃；戒掉；离开

despise [dɪˈspaɪz] *vt.* 轻视，鄙视

correspond [ˌkɒrəˈspɒnd] *vi.* 相一致；相当；通信 [拓] correspondence *n.* 信件；通信联系；关系

distinguish [dɪˈstɪŋgwɪʃ] *vt.* 区分；使有特色；认出 *vi.* 区分，辨别

B 段

apprentice [əˈprentɪs] *vt.* 当学徒 *n.* 学徒，徒弟

C 段

systematic [ˌsɪstəˈmætɪk] *adj.* 系统化的，有条理的；细致周到的 [拓] system *n.* 系统；体制

deprivation [ˌdeprɪˈveɪʃn] *n.* 缺少，匮乏 [拓] deprive sb. of sth. 剥夺某人的某物

D 段

exploitation [ˌeksplɔɪˈteɪʃn] *n.* 剥削；开发；充分利用 [拓] exploit *vt.* 剥削；充分利用；发挥

eliminate [ɪˈlɪmɪneɪt] *vt.* 消除，消灭；淘汰 [拓] elimination *n.* 消除；淘汰

redundant [rɪˈdʌndənt] *adj.* 多余的，过剩的

privileged [ˈprɪvəlɪdʒd] *adj.* 有特权的；幸运的；有权保密的

priority [praɪˈɒrəti] *n.* 优先处理的事；优先权 *adj.* 优先的 [拓] prior *adj.* 较早的；事先安排的 *n.* 犯罪前科

controversial [ˌkɒntrəˈvɜːʃl] *adj.* 矛盾的，可争议的

F 段

dedicate [ˈdedɪkeɪt] *vt.* 致力于；献给

moral [ˈmɒrəl] *n.* 道德准则（常用复数）；教育意义 *adj.* 道德的；道义上的；品行端正的

dominate [ˈdɒmɪneɪt] *vi.&vt.* 支配，控制，主宰 *vt.* 耸立于；俯视 [拓] dominant *adj.* 突出的；专横的；显性的

G 段

welfare [ˈwelfeə(r)] *n.* 健康；幸福；福利；救济金

distinctive [dɪˈstɪŋktɪv] *adj.* 独特的，与众不同的 [拓] distinct *adj.* 不同种类的；清晰的；确实存在的 [拓] distinction *n.* 区别；优秀；不同凡响

sort [sɔːt] *vt.* 将……分类；处理；安排妥当 *n.* 种类；类型

高频同义替换

believe to be ▸ regard as, treat as, see as, consider as

generate ▸ create, produce, bring about, give rise to, cause

need ▸ demand, request, requirement

initiate ▸ begin, start, commence, originate, pioneer

largely ▸ a significant part of, mainly, in abundance

题目解析

1 定位词：controversial topic

文中对应点：A 段第一句

题目解析：题干问，由法国历史学家菲利普·阿雷兹的概念引起的有争议的话题是什么？通过本题的疑问词部分 what，判断答案为名词。根据题干中的定位词 controversial topic，定位至 A 段第一句 "One of the most hotly debated issues in the history of childhood has been whether childhood is itself a recent invention."。其中，hotly debated issues 与 controversial topic 为同义替换。句意为，童年历史上争论最激烈的课题之一就是"童年"这个词本身是否是一个新兴的产物。由此句可以得出本题的答案，且要求不超过三个词，所以有争议的话题是童年历史。因此答案为 history of childhood。

2 定位词：believe to be, Western Europe during the Middle Ages

文中对应点：A 段第二句

题目解析：题干问，阿雷兹认为在中世纪的西欧孩子们是什么样的？通过本题的疑问词部分 what image，判断答案为名词。根据题干中的定位词 believe to be, Western Europe during the Middle Ages 定位至 A 段第二句 "The historian Philippe Aries argued that in Western Europe during the Middle Ages (up to about the end of the fifteenth century) children were regarded as miniature adults, with all the intellect and personality that this implies."。其中，were regarded as 对应 believe to be。句意为，历史学家菲利普·阿雷兹认为，在中世纪（直到约 15 世纪末）的欧洲西部，儿童被认为是缩小版的成年人，并且具备其所蕴含的一切智力与品性。因此答案为 miniature adults。

3 定位词：the need, child labour, in 18th and 19th century

文中对应点：C 段第一句

题目解析：题干问，什么历史事件导致了在 18 和 19 世纪大量的童工长时间工作？通过本题的疑问词部分 what historical event，判断答案为名词。根据题干中的定位词 the need, child labour, 18th and 19th centuries 定位至 C 段第一句 "With industrialisation in the eighteenth and nineteenth centuries, a new demand for child labour was created, and many children were forced to work for long hours, in mines, workshops and factories."。其中，new demand 对应 the need。句意为，随着 18 世纪和 19 世纪工业革命的发展，对于儿童劳动力的新需求出现了，很多儿童被迫在矿井、作坊和工厂进行长时间的工作。因此答案为 industrialisation。

4 定位词：legal format, protection of children from exploitation, in 19th century
   文中对应点：D 段第二句
   题目解析：题干问，在 19 世纪，什么法律开始保护儿童免受剥削？通过本题的疑问词部分 what legal format，判断答案为名词。根据题干中的定位词 legal format, protection of children from exploitation, in 19th century 定位至 D 段第二句"In Britain, the *Factory Act* of 1833 signified the beginning of legal protection of children from exploitation and was linked to the rise of schools for factory children."。其中，legal format 对应 *Factory Act*，1833 对应 19th century，句意为，英国 1833 年的《工厂法案》意味着对童工法律保护的开端和对工厂儿童开放学校的发展。因此答案为 *Factory Act*。

5 定位词：more and more, for all children time
   文中对应点：D 段第四句
   题目解析：题干问，在 19 世纪，什么样的活动被认为对几乎所有的孩子来说是更可取的？通过本题的疑问词部分 what activities，判断答案为名词。根据题干中的定位词 more and more, for all children time 定位至 D 段第四句"Childhood was increasingly seen as a time for play and education for all children, not just for a privileged minority."。其中，increasingly 对应 more and more，a time... for all children 对应 for all children time。句意为，童年时期越来越被认为是所有孩子玩耍和受教育的时期，而这并不仅限于享有特权的小部分群体。因此答案为 play and education。

6 定位词：largely, expectation
   文中对应点：F 段第一句
   题目解析：题干问，在现代社会，人们期望孩子们花费大部分时间的中心区域是哪里？通过本题的疑问词部分 where，判断答案为名词。根据题干中的定位词 largely, expectation 定位至 F 段第一句"Attending school was no longer a privilege and all children were expected to spend a significant part of their day in a classroom."。其中，expected 对应 expectation，a significant part 对应 largely。句意为，上学不再是一种特权，所有的孩子都应该在课堂上度过一天中有意义的一部分。因此答案为 classroom。

参考答案

1 history of childhood 2 miniature adults 3 industrialisation 4 Factory Act 5 play and education
6 classroom

READING PASSAGE 2

The Effect of Living in a Noisy World

Section A A Decibel Hell

It's not difficult for a person to encounter sound at certain levels that can cause adverse health effects. During a single day, people living in a typical urban environment can experience a wide range of sounds in many locations, even once-quiet locales have become polluted with noise. In fact, it's difficult today to escape sound completely. In its *1999 Guidelines for Community Noise*, the World Health Organisation (WHO) declared, 'Worldwide, noise-induced hearing impairment is the most prevalent irreversible occupational hazard, and it is estimated that 120 million people worldwide have disabling hearing difficulties.' Growing evidence also points to many other health effects of too much volume.

Mark Stephenson, a Cincinnati, Ohio-based senior research audiologist at the National Institute for Occupational Safety and Health (NIOSH), says his agency's definition of hazardous noise is sound that exceeds the time-weighted average of 85 dBA, meaning the average noise exposure measured over a typical eight-hour work day. Other measures and definitions are used for other purposes. For example, 'sound exposure level' accounts for variations in sound from moment to moment, while 'equivalent sound level' determines the value of a steady sound with the same dBA sound energy as that contained in a time-varying sound.

Section B Growing Volume

Meanwhile, there is no evidence to suggest things have gotten any quieter for residents since the EPA published its 1981 handbook. 'For many people in the United States, noise has drastically affected the quality of their lives,' says Arline L. Bronzaft, chair of the Noise Committee of the New York City Council of the Environment and a psychologist who has done pioneering research on the effects of noise on children's reading ability. 'My daughter lives near La Guardia airport in New York City, and she can't open a window or enjoy her backyard in the summer because of the airplane noise.'

Indeed, the term secondhand noise is increasingly used to describe noise that is experienced by people who did not produce it. Anti-noise activists say its effect on people is similar to that of secondhand smoke. 'Secondhand noise is really a civil rights issue,' says Les Blomberg, executive director of the Noise Pollution Clearinghouse, an anti-noise advocacy group based in Montpelier, Vermont. 'Like secondhand smoke, it's put into the environment without people's consent and then has effects on them that they don't have any control over.'

Noise is indeed everywhere, and experts expect no decrease in noise levels, given the powerful impact of technology on modern life. 'In the past three decades, we have built noisier and noisier devices that are not subject to any regulations,' Blomberg says. 'Think about it. The car alarm is a seventies invention, as is the leaf blower. The stereo sound systems we have in our cars are much louder than the sound system the Beatles used for their concerts in the sixties. All they had back then were three-hundred-amp speakers.'

Section C Scary Sound Effect

Numerous scientific studies over the years have confirmed that exposure to certain levels of sound can damage hearing. Prolonged exposure can actually change the structure of the hear cells in the inner ear, resulting in hearing loss. It can also cause tinnitus, a ringing, roaring, buzzing, or clicking in the ears.

William Luxford, medical director of the House Ear Clinic of St. Vincent Medical Centre in Los Angeles, points out one piece of good news: 'It's true that continuous noise exposure will lead to the continuation of hearing loss, but as soon as the exposure is stopped, the hearing loss stops. So a change in environment can improve a person's hearing health.'

Research is catching up with this anecdotal evidence. In the July 2001 issue of *Pediatrics*, researchers from the Centres for Disease Control and Prevention reported that, based on audiometric testing of 5,249 children as part of the Third National Health and Nutrition Examination Survey, an estimated 12.5% of American children have noise-induced hearing threshold shifts — or dulled hearing — in one or both ears. Most children with noise-induced hearing threshold shifts have only limited hearing damage, but continued exposure to excessive noise can lead to difficulties with high-frequency sound discrimination. The report listed stereos, music concerts, toys (such as toy telephones and certain rattles), lawn mowers, and fireworks as producing potentially harmful sounds.

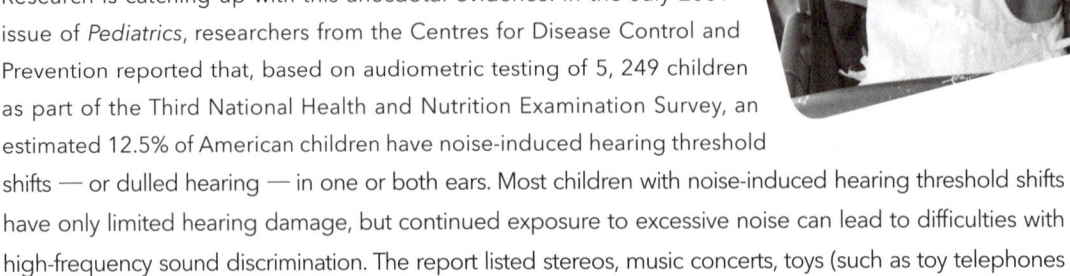

Section D Beyond the Ears

The effects of sound don't stop with the ears. Nonauditory effects of noise exposure are those effects that don't cause hearing loss but still can be measured, such as elevated blood pressure, loss of sleep, increased heart rate, cardiovascular constriction, laboured breathing, and changes in brain chemistry.

The nonauditory effects of noise were noted as early as 1930 in a study published by E.L. Smith and D.L. Laird in volume 2 of the *Journal of the Acoustical Society of America*. The results showed that exposure to noise caused stomach contractions in healthy human beings. Reports on noise's nonauditory effects published since that pioneering study have been both contradictory and controversial in some areas.

Bronzaft and the school principal persuaded the school board to have acoustical tile installed in the classrooms adjacent to the tracks. The Transit Authority also treated the tracks near the school to make them less noisy. A follow-up study published in the September 1981 issue of the *Journal of Environmental Psychology* found that children's reading scores improved after these interventions were put in place. 'After we did the study, more than twenty-five other studies were done examining the effect of noise on children's learning ability,' Bronzaft says. 'They have all found the same thing to be true: noise can affect children's learning.'

Section E Fighting for Quiet

Worldwide, airports have become a flash point for community frustration over noise pollution. In March 2003, representatives from eight neighbourhoods in Portland, Oregon, showed up for a city council hearing convened to discuss dozens of expansion projects for Portland International Airport. The airport was already a busy one: in 2002 it handled 12.2 million passengers and about 29,000 containers of air cargo. 'The impacts are tremendous on the neighbourhoods under the flight paths,' testified by one neighbourhood representative, Jean Ridings. 'People move in and move out. It's becoming a disaster.' In response, the airport has initiated a multiyear, multimillion-dollar effort to study the sound impact of the airport, which locals hope that will lead to a plan to reduce airport noise.

In the European Union, countries with cities of at least 250,000 people are creating noise maps of those cities to help leaders determine noise pollution policies. Paris has already prepared its first noise maps. The map data, which must be finished by 2007, will be fed into computer models that will help test the sound impact of street designs before construction begins.

Questions 1–3

Answer the questions below.

Choose **NO MORE THAN TWO WORDS** from the passage for each answer.

Write your answers in boxes 1–3 on your answer sheet.

1   What are the effects that can be measured without leading to hearing deficiency?

   ....

2   What are the classrooms equipped with besides the tracks?

   ....

3   What will the map data be fed into to help test the sound effect before the construction?

   ....

核心词汇

A 部分

decibel [ˈdesɪbel] *n.* 分贝

encounter [ɪnˈkaʊntə(r)] *vt.* 遇到；偶然碰到 *n.* 相遇；经历，遭遇

adverse [ˈædvɜːs] *adj.* 不利的；反面的

impairment [ɪmˈpeəmənt] *n.* 损伤

prevalent [ˈprevələnt] *adj.* 普遍的；流行的

irreversible [ˌɪrɪˈvɜːsəbl] *adj.* 不能治愈的；不可逆转的

hazard [ˈhæzəd] *n.* 危害，冒险，危险

audiologist [ˌɔːdiˈɒlədʒɪst] *n.* 听力学家；听觉病矫治专家

B 部分

advocacy [ˈædvəkəsi] *n.* 支持，拥护，提倡

consent [kənˈsent] *n.* 同意，赞成

C 部分

prolonged [prəˈlɒŋd] *adj.* 延长的

tinnitus [ˈtɪnɪtəs] *n.* 耳鸣

roar [rɔː(r)] *vi.* & *vt.* 咆哮，大声喊叫

buzz [bʌz] *vi.* 发出嗡嗡声；嗡嗡地飞；喧闹

continuation [kənˌtɪnjuˈeɪʃn] *n.* 持续，持续性

anecdotal [ˌænɪkˈdəʊtl] *adj.* 轶事的

threshold [ˈθreʃhəʊld] *n.* 门口，门槛；起始点

discrimination [dɪˌskrɪmɪˈneɪʃn] *n.* 鉴别力；歧视

D 部分

elevated [ˈelɪveɪtɪd] *adj.* 升高的

cardiovascular [ˌkɑːdiəʊˈvæskjələ(r)] *adj.* 心血管的

constriction [kənˈstrɪkʃn] *n.* 收缩；约束

acoustical [əˈkuːstɪkəl] *adj.* 听觉的；声音的

contraction [kənˈtrækʃn] *n.* 缩小

contradictory [ˌkɒntrəˈdɪktəri] *adj.* 矛盾的；抵触的

controversial [ˌkɒntrəˈvɜːʃl] *adj.* 有争议的，引起争论的

intervention [ˌɪntəˈvenʃn] *n.* 干预，干扰

E 部分

frustration [frʌ'streɪʃn] *n.* 不满，沮丧；受挫

convene [kən'viːn] *vi.*（为正式会议而）聚会，集会

高频同义替换

measure	▶	evaluate, size, estimate, survey
deficiency	▶	shortage, defect, need
equip	▶	prepare, provide
adjacent to	▶	beside, next to, near
effect	▶	impact, influence, cause
building	▶	construction, structure
impairment	▶	damage, hazard

题目解析

1 定位词：effects, without, hearing deficiency

文中对应点：Section D 第一段第二句

题目解析：题干问，暴露在噪音中不会造成听觉损伤但仍可被测量的影响是什么？通过本题的疑问词部分 what，判断答案为名词。根据题干中的定位词 effects, without, hearing deficiency 定位至 Section D 第一段第二句 "Nonauditory effects of noise exposure are those effects that don't cause hearing loss but still can be measured, such as elevated blood pressure, loss of sleep, increased heart rate, cardiovascular constriction, laboured breathing, and changes in brain chemistry."。其中，don't cause 对应 without，hearing loss 对应 hearing deficiency。句意为，暴露在噪音中的非听觉影响是指那些不会造成听觉损伤但仍可被测量的影响，比如血压升高、睡眠不足、心率增加、心血管收缩、呼吸困难以及大脑化学物质的变化。因此答案为 nonauditory effects。

2 定位词：classrooms, beside the tracks

文中对应点：Section D 第三段第一句

题目解析：题干问，轨道附近的教室都配备了什么？根据题干中的定位词 classrooms, beside the tracks 定位至 Section D 第三段第一句 "Bronzaft and the school principal persuaded the school board to have acoustical tile installed in the classrooms adjacent to the tracks."。其中，installed 对应 equipped with，adjacent to the tracks 对应 beside the tracks。句意为，布隆扎夫特和校长说服学校董事会在靠近轨道附近的教室安装隔音砖。因此答案为 acoustical tile。

3 定位词：map data, before the construction

文中对应点：Section E 第二段倒数第一句

题目解析：题干问，地图数据输入到哪里可以用来测试建造前的声音效果？根据题干中的定位词

map data, before the construction 定位至 Section E 第二段倒数第一句 "The map data, which must be finished by 2007, will be fed into computer models that will help test the sound impact of street designs before construction begins."。其中，sound impact 对应 sound effect。句意为，地图数据必须在 2007 年之前完成，也将被输入计算机模型当中。计算机模型将在建筑建造之前帮助测试街道设计的声音影响。因此答案为 computer models。

参考答案

1 nonauditory effects   **2** acoustical tile   **3** computer models

READING PASSAGE 3

The Culture of Chimpanzee

A The similarities between chimpanzees and humans have been studied for years, but in the past decade researchers have determined that these resemblances run much deeper than anyone first thought. For instance, the nut cracking observed in the Tai Forest is far from a simple chimpanzee behaviour; rather it is a singular adaptation found only in that particular part of Africa and a trait that biologists consider to be an expression of chimpanzee culture. Scientists frequently use the term 'culture' to describe elementary animal behaviours — such as the regional dialects of different populations of songbirds — but as it turns out, the rich and varied cultural traditions found among chimpanzees are second in complexity only to human traditions.

B During the past two years, an unprecedented scientific collaboration, involving every major research group studying chimpanzees, has documented a multitude of distinct cultural patterns extending across Africa, in actions ranging from the animals' use of tools to their forms of communication and social customs. This emerging picture of chimpanzees not only affects how we think of these amazing creatures but also alters human beings' conception of our own uniqueness and hints at ancient foundations for extraordinary capacity for culture.

C Homo sapiens and Pan troglodytes have coexisted for hundreds of millennia and share more than 98 percent of their genetic material, yet only 40 years ago we still knew next to nothing about chimpanzee behaviour in the wild. That began to change in the 1960s, when Toshisada Nishida of Kyoto University in Japan and Jane Goodall began their studies of wild chimpanzees at two field sites in Tanzania. (Goodall's research station at Gombe — the first of its kind — is more famous, but Nishida's site at Mahale is the second oldest chimpanzee research site in the world.)

D In these initial studies, as the chimpanzees became accustomed to close observation, the remarkable discoveries began. Researchers witnessed a range of unexpected behaviours, including fashioning and using tools, hunting, meat eating, food sharing and lethal fights between members of neighbouring communities.

E As early as 1973, Goodall recorded 13 forms of tool use as well as eight social activities that appeared to differ between the Gombe chimpanzees and chimpanzee populations elsewhere. She ventured that some variations had what she termed a cultural origin. But what exactly did Goodall mean by 'culture'? According to *the Oxford Encyclopedic English Dictionary*, culture is defined as 'the customs...and achievements of a particular time or people'. The diversity of human cultures extends from technological variations to marriage rituals, from culinary habits to myths and legends. Animals do not have myths and legends, of course. But they do have the capacity to pass on behavioural traits from generation to generation, not through their genes but by learning. For biologists, this is the fundamental criterion for a cultural trait: it must be something that can be learned by observing the established skills of others and thus passed on to future generations.

F What of the implications for chimpanzees themselves? We must highlight the tragic loss of chimpanzees, whose populations are being decimated just when we are at last coming to appreciate these astonishing animals more completely. Populations have plummeted in the past century and continue to fall as a result of illegal trapping, logging and, most recently, the bushmeat trade. The latter is particularly alarming: logging has driven roadways into the forests that are now used to ship wild-animal meat — including chimpanzee meat — to consumers as far afield as Europe. Such destruction threatens not only the animals themselves but also a host of fascinatingly different ape cultures.

G Perhaps the cultural richness of the ape may yet help in its salvation, however. Some conservation efforts have already altered the attitudes of some local people. A few organisations have begun to show videotapes illustrating the cognitive prowess of chimpanzees. One Zairian viewer was heard to exclaim, 'Ah, this ape is so like me, I can no longer eat him.'

H How an international team of chimpanzee experts conducted the most comprehensive survey of the animals ever attempted. Scientists have been investigating chimpanzee culture for several decades, but too often their studies contained a crucial flaw. Most attempts to document cultural diversity among chimpanzees have relied solely on officially published accounts of the behaviours recorded at each research site. But this approach probably overlooks a good deal of cultural variation for three reasons.

I First, scientists typically don't publish an extensive list of all the activities they do not see at a particular location. Yet this is exactly what we need to know — which behaviours were and were not observed at each site. Second, many reports describe chimpanzee behaviours without saying how common they are; without this information, we can't determine whether a particular action was a once-in-a-lifetime aberration or a routine event that should be considered part of the animals' culture. Finally, researchers' descriptions of potentially significant chimpanzee behaviours frequently lack sufficient detail, making it difficult for scientists working at other spots to record the presence or absence of the activities.

J To remedy these problems, the two of us decided to take a new approach. We asked field researchers at each site for a list of all the behaviours they suspected were local traditions. With this information in hand, we pulled together a comprehensive list of 65 candidates for cultural behaviours.

K Then we distributed our list to the team leaders at each site. In consultation with their colleagues, they classified each behaviour in terms of its occurrence or absence in the chimpanzee community studied. The key categories were customary behaviour (occurs in most or all of the able-bodied members of at least one age or sex class, such as all adult males), habitual (less common than customary but occurs repeatedly in several individuals), present (seen at the site but not habitual), absent (never seen), and unknown.

Questions 1–4

Answer the questions below.

Choose **NO MORE THAN THREE WORDS** from the passage for each answer.

Write your answers in boxes 1–4 on your answer sheet.

1   When did the unexpected discoveries of chimpanzee behaviour start?

   ....

2   Which country is the researching site of Toshisada Nishida and Jane Goodall in?

   ....

3   What did the chimpanzee have to get used to in the initial study?

   ....

4   What did Jane Goodall think is the reason chimpanzees have differences in using tools in 1973?

   ....

核心词汇

A 段

similarity [ˌsɪməˈlærəti] *n.* 相似之处

chimpanzee [ˌtʃɪmpænˈziː] *n.* 黑猩猩

resemblance [rɪˈzembləns] *n.* 相似，类似 [拓] resemble *vt.* 像，与……相似

crack [kræk] *vt.* 使裂开；重击；解决 *vi.* 破裂；崩溃；变嘶哑

adaptation [ˌædæpˈteɪʃn] *n.* 改变；适应；改编版

elementary [ˌelɪˈmentri] *adj.* 基本的；初级的；小学的

dialect [ˈdaɪəlekt] *n.* 方言，土语

complexity [kəmˈpleksəti] *n.* 复杂性；复杂之处

B 段

unprecedented [ʌnˈpresɪdentɪd] *adj.* 前所未有的

collaboration [kəˌlæbəˈreɪʃn] *n.* 合作，协作；勾结

a multitude of 大批的，众多的

alter [ˈɔːltə(r)] *vi. & vt.* （使）改变，（使）转变

C 段

Homo sapiens 智人，现代人

Pan troglodytes 黑猩猩

millennium [mɪˈleniəm] *n.* 千年期，一千年（复数形式为 millennia）

D 段

initial [ɪˈnɪʃl] *adj.* 最初的，开始的 *n.* 姓名的首字母

be accustomed to 习惯于……

E 段

venture [ˈventʃə(r)] *vt.* 小心地说；谨慎地做 *vi.* 冒险去…… *n.* 风险项目，风险投资

variation [ˌveəriˈeɪʃn] *n.* 差异；变化；变体；变奏

culinary [ˈkʌlɪnəri] *adj.* 厨房的；烹调用的

criterion [kraɪˈtɪəriən] *n.* 标准，准则

F 段

decimate [ˈdesɪmeɪt] *vt.* 大批杀害；十中抽一

plummet [ˈplʌmɪt] *vi.* （价格、水平等）骤然下跌

ape [eɪp] *n.* 猿 *vt.* 模仿，照搬

G 段

salvation [sæl'veɪʃn] *n.* 拯救；救助
illustrate ['ɪləstreɪt] *vt.* 举例说明，阐明；给……加插图
cognitive ['kɒgnətɪv] *adj.* 认知的，认识的
prowess ['praʊəs] *n.* 威力，超凡技术

H 段

comprehensive [ˌkɒmprɪ'hensɪv] *adj.* 彻底的；详尽的；全面的
flaw [flɔː] *n.* 瑕疵，缺点；错误

I 段

aberration [ˌæbə'reɪʃn] *n.* 失常；越轨

高频同义替换

resemblance	▶	resemble, like, look like
elementary	▶	primary, initial, primeval, at the beginning, original
collaboration	▶	cooperation, communication, synergism
a multitude of	▶	a number of, numbers of, a variety of, various of, all kinds of, many
alter	▶	transform, change, modify, shift
extraordinary	▶	excellent, outstanding, noted, notable, distinguished, remarkable, prominent, brilliant

题目解析

1 定位词：unexpected discoveries, start

文中对应点：C 段第二句和 D 段第二句

题目解析：题干问，黑猩猩的意外行为是什么时候发现的？通过本题的疑问词 when，判断答案为时间。根据题干中的定位词 start 定位到 C 段第二句："That began to change in the 1960s, when Toshisada Nishida of Kyoto University in Japan and Jane Goodall began their studies of wild chimpanzees at two field sites in Tanzania."。其中，原文中的 began 对应题干中的 start。句意为，这种情形从 20 世纪 60 年代开始改变，那时日本京都大学的西田利贞和珍妮·古道尔开始在坦桑尼亚的两处野外地点研究野生黑猩猩。但是该句没有提到有什么发现，所以需要向后找。根据题干中的定位词 unexpected discoveries 定位到 D 段第二句："Researchers witnessed a range of unexpected behaviours, including fashioning and using tools, hunting, meat eating, food sharing and lethal fights between members of neighbouring communities."。其中，原文中的 unexpected behaviours 对应题干中的 unexpected discoveries。句意为，研究者们见证了一系列的意外行为，包括制作和使用工具、打猎、食肉、分享食物以及邻近社群的成员间的殊死打斗。因此答案为 in the 1960s。

2. 定位词：researching site, Toshisada Nishida, Jane Goodall

   文中对应点：C 段第二句

   题目解析：题干问，Toshisada Nishida 和 Jane Goodall 的研究地点在哪个国家？通过本题的疑问词 which country，判断答案为国家名。根据题干中的定位词 Toshisada Nishida 和 Jane Goodall 定位到 C 段第二句："That began to change in the 1960s, when Toshisada Nishida of Kyoto University in Japan and Jane Goodall began their studies of wild chimpanzees at two field sites in Tanzania."。其中，原文中的 two field sites 对应题干中的 researching site，句意为，这种情形从 20 世纪 60 年代开始改变，那时日本京都大学的西田利贞和珍妮·古道尔开始在坦桑尼亚的两处野外地点研究野生黑猩猩。因此答案为 Tanzania。

3. 定位词：get used to, initial study

   文中对应点：D 段第一句

   题目解析：题干问，在最初的研究中，黑猩猩必须适应什么？通过本题的疑问词 what，判断答案为名词。根据题干中的定位词 initial study 定位到 D 段第一句："In these initial studies, as the chimpanzees became accustomed to close observation, the remarkable discoveries began."。其中，原文中的 these initial studies 对应题干中的 the initial study， accustomed to 对应 get used to。句意为，在这些最初的研究中，随着黑猩猩渐渐适应了近距离观察，他们开始有了不同寻常的发现。因此答案为 close observation。

4. 定位词：differences, 1973

   文中对应点：E 段第一、二句

   题目解析：题干问，珍妮·古道尔在 1973 年认为黑猩猩在使用工具方面不同是什么原因？通过本题的疑问词 what，判断答案为名词。根据题干中的定位词 1973 定位到 E 段第一、二句："As early as 1973, Goodall recorded 13 forms of tool use as well as eight social activities that appeared to differ between the Gombe chimpanzees and chimpanzee populations elsewhere. She ventured that some variations had what she termed a cultural origin."。其中，原文中的 variations 对应题干中的 differences，tool use 对应 using tools。句意为，早在 1973 年，古道尔不但记载了 13 种工具使用的形式，还记载了 8 种社会活动，这些特点似乎是贡贝地区的黑猩猩和其他地区黑猩猩群体的不同之处。她大胆地提出，有些变化有她所谓的文化根源。因此答案为 (a) cultural origin。

参考答案

1 in the 1960s **2** Tanzania **3** close observation **4** (a) cultural origin

READING PASSAGE 4

Thomas Young: The Last True Know-It-All

A   Thomas Young (1773–1829) contributed 63 articles to the *Encyclopaedia Britannica*, including 46 biographical entries (mostly on scientists and classicists) and substantial essays on 'Bridge', 'Chromatics', 'Egypt', 'Languages' and 'Tides'. Was someone who could write authoritatively about so many subjects, a polymath, a genius or a dilettante? In an ambitious new biography, Andrew Robinson argues that Young is a good contender for the epitaph 'the last man who knew everything'. Young has competition, however: the phrase, which Robinson takes for his title, also serves as the subtitle of two other recent biographies: Leonard Warren's 1998 life of paleontologist Joseph Leidy (1823–1891) and Paula Findlen's 2004 book on Athanasius Kircher (1602–1680), another polymath.

B   Young, of course, did more than write encyclopaedia entries. He presented his first paper to the Royal Society of London at the age of 20 and was elected a Fellow a week after his 21st birthday. In the paper, Young explained the process of accommodation in the human eye on how the eye focuses properly on objects at varying distances. Young hypothesised that this was achieved by changes in the shape of the lens. Young also theorised that light travelled in waves and he believed that, to account for the ability to see in colour, there must be three receptors in the eye corresponding to the three 'principal colours' to which the retina could respond: red, green, violet. All these hypothesis were subsequently proved to be correct.

C   Later in his life, when he was in his forties, Young was instrumental in cracking the code that unlocked the unknown script on the Rosetta Stone, a tablet that was 'found' in Egypt by the Napoleonic army in 1799. The stone contains text in three alphabets: Greek, something unrecognisable and Egyptian hieroglyphs. The unrecognisable script is now known as demotic and, as Young deduced, is related directly to hieroglyphic. His initial work on this appeared in his Britannica entry on Egypt. In another entry, he coined the term Indo-European to describe the family of languages spoken throughout most of Europe and northern India. These are the landmark achievements of a man who was a child prodigy and who, unlike many remarkable children, did not disappear into oblivion as an adult.

D   Born in 1773 in Somerset in England, Young lived from an early age with his maternal grandfather, eventually leaving to attend boarding school. He had devoured books from the age of two, and through his own initiative he excelled at Latin, Greek, mathematics and natural philosophy. After leaving school, he was greatly encouraged by his mother's uncle, Richard Brocklesby, a physician and Fellow of the Royal Society. Following Brocklesby's lead, Young decided to pursue a career in medicine. He studied in London, following the medical circuit, and then moved on to more formal education in Edinburgh, Gottingen and Cambridge. After completing his medical training at the University of Cambridge in 1808, Young set up practice as a physician in London. He soon became a Fellow of the Royal College of Physicians and a few years later was appointed physician at St. George's Hospital.

Young's skill as a physician, however, did not equal his skill as a scholar of natural philosophy or linguistics. Earlier, in 1801, he had been appointed to a professorship of natural philosophy at the Royal Institution, where he delivered as many as 60 lectures in a year. These were published in two volumes in 1807. In 1804 Young had become secretary to the Royal Society, a post he would hold until his death. His opinions were sought on civic and national matters, such as the introduction of gas lighting to London and methods of ship construction. From 1819 he was superintendent of the Nautical Almanac and secretary to the Board of Longitude. From 1824 to 1829 he was physician to and inspector of calculations for the Palladian Insurance Company. Between 1816 and 1825 he contributed his many and various entries to the *Encyclopaedia Britannica*, and throughout his career he authored numerous books, essays and papers.

Young is a perfect subject for a biography — perfect, but daunting. Few men contributed so much to so many technical fields. Robinson's aim is to introduce non-scientists to Young's work and life. He succeeds, providing clear expositions of the technical material (especially that on optics and Egyptian hieroglyphs). Some readers of this book will, like Robinson, find Young's accomplishments impressive; others will see him as some historians have — as a dilettante. Yet despite the rich material presented in this book, readers will not end up knowing Young personally. We catch glimpses of a playful Young, doodling Greek and Latin phrases in his notes on medical lectures and translating the verses that a young lady had written on the walls of a summerhouse into Greek elegiacs. Young was introduced into elite society, attended the theatre and learned to dance and play the flute. In addition, he was an accomplished horseman. However, his personal life looks pale next to his vibrant career and studies.

Young married Eliza Maxwell in 1804, and according to Robinson, 'their marriage was a happy one and she appreciated his work.' Almost all we know about her is that she sustained her husband through some rancorous disputes about optics and that she worried about money when his medical career was slow to take off. Very little evidence survives about the complexities of Young's relationships with his mother and father. Robinson does not credit them, or anyone else, with shaping Young's extraordinary mind. Despite the lack of details concerning Young's relationships, however, anyone interested in what it means to be a genius should read this book.

Questions 1–6

Answer the questions below.

Choose NO MORE THAN THREE WORDS AND/OR A NUMBER *from the passage for each answer.*

Write your answers in boxes 1–6 on your answer sheet.

1   How many life stories did Young write for *Encyclopaedia Britannica*?

   ....

2   What aspect of scientific research did Young do in his first academic paper?

   ....

3   What name did Young introduce to refer to a group of languages?

   ....

4   Who inspired Young to start the medical studies?

   ....

5   Where did Young get a teaching position?

   ....

6   What did Young introduce to London?

   ....

核心词汇

A 段

encyclopaedia [ɪnˌsaɪklə'piːdiə] *n.* 百科全书

polymath ['pɒlimæθ] *n.* 博学的人

dilettante [ˌdɪlə'tænti] *n.* 业余爱好者；半吊子 *adj.* 浅薄的，一知半解的

contender [kən'tendə(r)] *n.* 竞争者，争夺者

epitaph ['epɪtɑːf] *n.* 碑文，墓志铭

paleontologist [ˌpælɪɒn'tɒlədʒɪst] *n.* 古生物学者

B 段

varying ['veərɪŋ] *adj.* 各不相同的，变化的

hypothesis [haɪ'pɒθəsɪs] *n.* 假设，猜想（复数 hypotheses）

in the shape of 以……的形式；呈……的形状

retina ['retɪnə] *n.* 视网膜

C 段

instrumental [ˌɪnstrə'mentl] *adj.* 有帮助的

hieroglyph ['haɪərəglɪf] *n.* 象形文字

demotic [dɪ'mɒtɪk] *adj.* 通俗的，民众的

coin [kɔɪn] *vt.* 创造；铸造（货币）

prodigy ['prɒdədʒi] *n.* 天才，神童

oblivion [ə'blɪviən] *n.* 遗忘；漠视

D 段

devour [dɪ'vaʊə(r)] *vt.* 如饥似渴地阅读，狼吞虎咽地吃

E 段

superintendent [ˌsuːpərɪn'tendənt] *n.* 主管，负责人

F 段

daunting ['dɔːntɪŋ] *adj.* 吓人的；使人气馁的

doodle ['duːdl] *vi.* 涂鸦

accomplished [ə'kʌmplɪʃt] *adj.* 熟练的；造诣高的

G 段

rancorous ['ræŋkərəs] *adj.* 满怀恨意的

optic ['ɒptɪk] *adj.* 眼睛的，视觉的

extraordinary [ɪk'strɔːdnri] *adj.* 非凡的，特别的；令人惊奇的

高频同义替换

academic ▸ theoretical, collegial

inspire ▸ vitalise

medical ▸ iatrical

research ▸ investigation, study, survey, indagation

题目解析

1 定位词：how many, life stories, Encyclopaedia Britannica
文中对应点：A 段第一句
题目解析：题干问，杨为《大英百科全书》写了多少生活故事？通过本题的疑问词 How many，判断答案为数字。根据题干中的定位词 how many, life stories, Encyclopaedia Britannica 定位到 A 段第一句 "Thomas Young (1773-1829) contributed 63 articles to the *Encyclopaedia Britannica*, including 46 biographical entries (mostly on scientists and classicists) and substantial essays on 'Bridge', 'Chromatics', 'Egypt', 'Languages' and 'Tides'."。其中，biographical entries 指 "传记词条"，与题干中的 life stories 为同义替换。句意为，托马斯·杨 (1773-1829) 为《大英百科全书》贡献了 63 篇文章，包括 46 篇传记作品 (主要是关于科学家和古典学者的)，以及大量关于"桥""色彩学""埃及""语言"和"潮汐"的文章。因此本题答案为 46。

2 定位词：aspect of scientific research, first academic paper
文中对应点：B 段第二、三句
题目解析：题干问，在他的第一篇学术论文中，杨作了哪个方面的科学研究？通过本题的疑问词 what aspect of scientific research，判断答案为科研的方面。根据题干中的定位词 aspect of scientific research, first academic paper 定位到 B 段第二、三句 "He presented his first paper to the Royal Society of London at the age of 20 and was elected a Fellow a week after his 21st birthday. In the paper, Young explained the process of accommodation in the human eye on how the eye focuses properly on objects at varying distances."。其中，explained 对应 aspect of scientific research, first academic paper 与 first paper 对应。句意为，杨将自己的第一篇论文自荐给了伦敦皇家学会。在这篇论文中，杨解释了人眼在不同距离下如何正确聚焦于物体下的适应过程。杨主要讨论了人类眼球的调节机制。因此本题答案为 human eye 或 human eye accommodation。

3 定位词：a group of languages
文中对应点：C 段倒数第二句
题目解析：题干问，杨用了什么名字来指代一组语言？通过本题的疑问词 what name，判断答案为名称。根据题干中的定位词 a group of languages 定位到 C 段倒数第二句："In another entry, he coined the term Indo-European to describe the family of languages spoken throughout most of Europe and northern India."。其中，the family of languages spoken throughout most of Europe and northern India 与 a group of languages 对应。句意为，在另一篇文章中，他创造了"印欧语系"

这个词来描述欧洲大部分地区和印度北部使用的语言。因此本题答案为 Indo-European。

4　定位词：who, medical studies
　　文中对应点：D 段第四句
　　题目解析：题干问，是谁激励杨开始医学研究的？通过本题的疑问词 where，判断答案为位置。通过本题的疑问词 who，判断答案为某人。根据题干中的定位词 who, medical studies 定位到 D 段第四句 "Following Brocklesby's lead, Young decided to pursue a career in medicine."。其中，pursue a career in medicine 与 medical studies 对应。句意为，在布罗克兹比的引导下，杨决定发展医学事业，因此本题答案为 Brocklesby 或 Richard Brocklesby。

5　定位词：teaching position
　　文中对应点：E 段第二句
　　题目解析：题干问，杨在哪里得到一个教学职位？根据题干中的定位词 teaching position 定位到 E 段第二句："Earlier, in 1801, he had been appointed to a professorship of natural philosophy at the Royal Institution, where he delivered as many as 60 lectures in a year."。其中，professorship（教授职位）与 teaching position（教学职位）为同义替换。句意为，早在 1801 年，他就被任命为皇家学院自然哲学教授，在那里他一年发表了多达 60 次演讲。因此本题答案为 Royal Institution。

6　定位词：introduce, London
　　文中对应点：E 段第五句
　　题目解析：题干问，杨给伦敦带来什么？通过本题的疑问词 what contribution，判断答案为什么贡献。根据题干中的定位词 introduce, London 定位到 E 段第五句："His opinions were sought on civic and national matters, such as the introduction of gas lighting to London and methods of ship construction."。其中，such as 后面的例子都是杨所作出的贡献（contribution）。句意为，他在公民和国家事务上征求意见，例如在伦敦引进煤气照明和船舶建造方法。因此本题答案为 gas lighting。

参考答案

1　46　　2　human eye/human eye accommodation　　3　Indo-European
4　his mother's uncle/Brocklesby/Richard Brocklesby　　5　Royal Institution　　6　gas lighting

第八章　图表题

READING PASSAGE 1

Spider Silk

A strong, light bio-material made by genes from spiders could transform construction and industry

A Scientists have succeeded in copying the silk-producing genes of the Golden Orb Weaver spider and are using them to create a synthetic material which they believe is the model for a new generation of advanced bio-materials. The new material, biosilk, which has been spun for the first time by researchers at DuPont, has an enormous range of potential uses in construction and manufacturing.

B The attraction of the silk spun by the spider is a combination of great strength and enormous elasticity, which man-made fibres have been unable to replicate. On an equal-weight basis, spider silk is far stronger than steel and it is estimated that if a single strand could be made about 10 m in diameter, it would be strong enough to stop a jumbo jet in flight. A third important factor is that it is extremely light. Army scientists are already looking at the possibilities of using it for lightweight, bulletproof vests and parachutes.

C For some time, biochemists have been trying to synthesise the drag-line silk of the Golden Orb Weaver. The drag-line silk, which forms the radial arms of the web, is stronger than the other parts of the web and some biochemists believe a synthetic version could prove to be as important a material as nylon, which has been around for 50 years, since the discoveries of Wallace Carothers and his team ushered in the age of polymers.

D To recreate the material, scientists, including Randolph Lewis at the University of Wyoming, first examined the silk-producing gland of the spider. 'We took out the glands that produce the silk and looked at the coding for the protein material they make, which is spun into a web. We then went looking for clones with the right DNA,' he says.

E At DuPont, researchers have used both yeast and bacteria as hosts to grow the raw material, which they have spun into fibres. Robert Dorsch, DuPont's director of biochemical development, says the globules of protein, comparable with marbles in an egg, are harvested and processed. 'We break open the bacteria, separate out the globules of protein and use them as the raw starting material. With yeast, the gene system can be designed so that the material excretes the protein outside the yeast for better access,' he says.

F 'The bacteria and the yeast produce the same protein, equivalent to that which the spider uses in the drag lines of the web. The spider mixes the protein into a water-based solution and then spins it into a solid fibre in one go. Since we are not as clever as the spider and we are not using such sophisticated organisms, we substituted man-made approaches and dissolved the protein in chemical solvents, which are then spun to push the material through small holes to form the solid fibre.'

G Researchers at DuPont say they envisage many possible uses for a new biosilk material. They say that earthquake-resistant suspension bridges hung from cables of synthetic spider silk fibres may become a reality. Stronger ropes, safer seat belts, shoe soles that do not wear out so quickly and tough new clothing are among the other applications. Biochemists such as Lewis see the potential range of uses of biosilk as almost limitless. 'It is very strong and retains elasticity; there are no man-made materials that can mimic both these properties. It is also a biological material with all the advantages that has over petrochemicals,' he says.

H At DuPont's laboratories, Dorsch is excited by the prospect of new super-strong materials but he warns they are many years away. 'We are at an early stage but theoretical predictions are that we will wind up with a very strong, tough material, with an ability to absorb shock, which is stronger and tougher than the man-made materials that are conventionally available to us,' he says.

I The spider is not the only creature that has aroused the interest of material scientists. They have also become envious of the natural adhesive secreted by the sea mussel. It produces a protein adhesive to attach itself to rocks. It is tedious and expensive to extract the protein from the mussel, so researchers have already produced a synthetic gene for use in surrogate bacteria.

Questions 1–5

Complete the flow–chart below.

Choose **NO MORE THAN TWO WORDS** from the passage for each answer.

Write your answers in boxes 1–5 on your answer sheet.

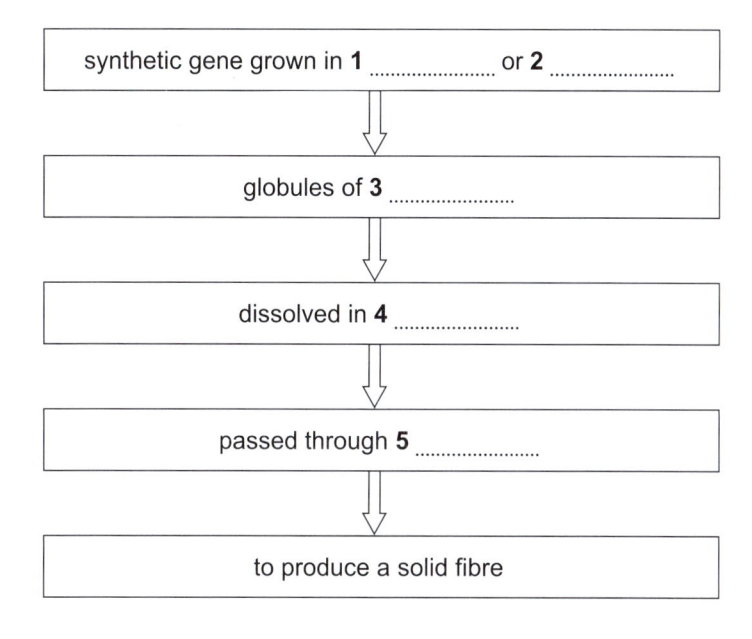

```
synthetic gene grown in 1 .............. or 2 ..............
                        ⇓
           globules of 3 ..............
                        ⇓
           dissolved in 4 ..............
                        ⇓
         passed through 5 ..............
                        ⇓
         to produce a solid fibre
```

核心词汇

A 段
synthetic [sɪn'θetɪk] *adj.* 合成的，人造的
enormous [ɪ'nɔːməs] *adj.* 庞大的，巨大的

B 段
elasticity [ˌelæ'stɪsəti] *n.* 弹性，弹力 [拓] elastic *n.* 弹力材料 *adj.* 有弹性的；灵活的
replicate ['replɪkeɪt] *vt.* 复制；重做 *vi. & vt.* 自我复制
strand [strænd] *n.* 股，缕；部分
bulletproof ['bʊlɪtpruːf] *adj.* 防弹的

C 段
usher ['ʌʃə(r)] *vt.* 引，领；招待 *n.* 引座员，迎宾员；门卫 [拓] usher in 开启，开创

E 段
yeast [jiːst] *n.* 酵母
excrete [ɪk'skriːt] *vi. & vt.* 分泌；排泄

F 段
spin [spɪn] *vt.* 纺织；吐丝结网；编造；使快速旋转 *vi.* 快速旋转；飞驰 *n.* 快速旋转；兜风
organism ['ɔːɡənɪzəm] *n.* 有机体，生物；有机组织
substitute ['sʌbstɪtjuːt] *vt.* 用……代替；替换 *vi.* 替代，顶替 *n.* 替代品；代替者
dissolve [dɪ'zɒlv] *vi. & vt.* （使）溶解；（使）消失 *vt.* 解散；解除
solvent ['sɒlvənt] *n.* 溶剂 *adj.* 有偿付能力的

G 段
envisage [ɪn'vɪzɪdʒ] *vt.* 设想；展望
mimic ['mɪmɪk] *vt.* 模仿；像 *n.* 善于模仿的人或动物
property ['prɒpəti] *n.* 特性；财产；房地产
petrochemical [ˌpetrəʊ'kemɪkl] *n.* 石油化学产品

H 段
wind up 以……告终；使……结束；关闭 [拓] wind sb. up 惹某人生气，逗弄某人
conventionally [kən'venʃənəli] *adv.* 照惯例地

I 段

envious [ˈenviəs] *adj.* 羡慕的；嫉妒的
adhesive [ədˈhiːsɪv] *n.* 粘合剂；胶黏剂
surrogate [ˈsʌrəgət] *adj.* 替代的；代理的 *n.* 替代品

高频同义替换

grow	▶	plant, cultivate, develop, raise, foster
or	▶	either, as well as, both...and..., not only...but also..., in addition to, apart from
pass	▶	push through, transit, hand
produce	▶	form, shape, manufacture

题目解析

1 定位词：grown in, or
　　文中对应点：E 段第一句
　　题目解析：根据题干定位词 grown in 及表示并列的词 or 定位至 E 段第一句 "At DuPont, researchers have used both yeast and bacteria as hosts to grow the raw material, which they have spun into fibres."。其中，use both yeast and bacteria as hosts to grow the raw material 与题干意义一致，use...to grow 与 grown in 为同义替换，both...and... 并列结构与 or 对应。句意为，在杜邦，研究人员用酵母和细菌作为寄主来生产原材料，并将其纺成纤维。因此答案为 yeast。

2 定位词：grown in, or
　　文中对应点：E 段第一句
　　题目解析：根据题干定位词 grown in 及并列的词 or 定位至 E 段第一句 "At DuPont, researchers have use both yeast and bacteria as hosts to grow the raw material..." 与题干意义一致，use...to grow 与 grown in 为同义替换，原文中的 both...and... 并列结构与题干中的 or 对应。因此答案为 bacteria。

3 定位词：globules of
　　文中对应点：E 段倒数第二句
　　题目解析：根据题干定位词 globules of 定位至 E 段倒数第二句 "We break open the bacteria, separate out the globules of protein and use them as the raw starting material."。其中，globules of 为原文重现。句意为，我们打开细菌，分离出蛋白质小球，用它们作为原料。因此答案为 protein。

4 定位词：dissolved in
　　文中对应点：F 段最后一句

题目解析：根据题干定位词 dissolved in 定位至 F 段最后一句 "Since we are not as clever as the spider and we are not using such sophisticated organisms, we substituted man-made approaches and dissolved the protein in chemical solvents, which are then spun to push the material through small holes to form the solid fibre.'"。其中，dissolved...in 与 dissolved in 意思相同。句意为，由于我们没有蜘蛛那么聪明，也没有使用这么复杂的生物，所以我们用人工方法，把蛋白质溶解在化学溶剂中，然后旋转，把物质推入小孔，形成固体纤维。因此答案为 chemical solvents。

5　定位词：passed through, produce, solid fibre
文中对应点：F 段最后一句
题目解析：根据题干定位词 passed through, produce, solid fibre 定位至 F 段最后一句 "Since we are not as clever as the spider and we are not using such sophisticated organisms, we substituted man-made approaches and dissolved the protein in chemical solvents, which are then spun to push the material through small holes to form the solid fibre.'"。其中，solid fibre 为原文重现，form 对应题干中的 produce，push...through 对应 passed through，因此答案为 small holes。

参考答案

1 yeast　　**2** bacteria　　**3** protein　　**4** chemical solvents　　**5** small holes

READING PASSAGE 2

Water Filter

A   An ingenious invention is set to bring clean water to the Third World, and while the science may be cutting edge, the materials are extremely down to earth. A handful of clay, yesterday's coffee grounds and some cow manure are the ingredients that could bring clean, safe drinking water to much of the Third World.

B   The simple new technology, developed by ANU materials scientist Mr. Tony Flynn, allows water filters to be made from commonly available materials and fired on the ground using cow manure as the source of heat, without the need for a kiln. The filters have been tested and shown to remove common pathogens (disease-producing organisms) including E. coli. Unlike other water filtering devices, the filters are simple and inexpensive to make. 'They are very simple to explain and demonstrate and can be made by anyone, anywhere,' says Mr. Flynn. 'They don't require any Western technology. All you need is terracotta clay, a compliant cow and a match.'

C   The production of the filters is extremely simple. Take a handful of dry, crushed clay, mix it with a handful of organic material, such as used tea leaves, coffee grounds or rice hulls, add enough water to make a stiff biscuit-like mixture and form a cylindrical pot that has one end closed, then dry it in the sun. According to Mr. Flynn, used coffee grounds have given the best results to date. Next, surround the pots with straw; put them in a mound of cow manure, light the straw and then top up the burning manure as required. In less than 60 minutes the filters are finished. The walls of the finished pot should be about as thick as an adult's index finger. The properties of cow manure are vital as the fuel can reach a temperature of 700 degrees in half an hour and will be up to 950 degrees after another 20 to 30 minutes. The manure makes a good fuel because it is very high in organic material that burns readily and quickly; the manure has to be dry and is best used exactly as found in the field. There is no need to break it up or process it any further.

D   'A potter's kiln is an expensive item and can take up to four or five hours to get up to 800 degrees. It needs expensive or scarce fuel, such as gas or wood to heat it and experience to run it. With no technology, no insulation and nothing other than a pile of cow manure and a match, none of these restrictions apply,' Mr. Flynn says.

E   It is also helpful that, like terracotta clay and organic material, cow dung is freely available across the developing world. 'A cow is a natural fuel factory. My understanding is that cow dung as a fuel would be pretty much the same wherever you would find it.' Just as using manure as a fuel for domestic uses is not a new idea, the porosity of clay is something that potters have known about for years, and something that as a former ceramics lecturer in the ANU School of Art, Mr. Flynn is well aware of. The difference is that rather than viewing the porous nature of the material as a problem — after all not many people want a pot that won't hold water — his filters capitalise on this property.

F Other commercial ceramic filters do exist, but, even if available, with prices starting at US$5 each, they are often outside the budgets of most people in the developing world. The filtration process is simple, but effective. The basic principle is that there are passages through the filter that are wide enough for water droplets to pass through, but too narrow for pathogens. Tests with the deadly E. coli bacterium have seen the filters remove 96.4 to 99.8 per cent of the pathogen — well within safe levels. Using only one filter it takes two hours to filter a litre of water. The use of organic material, which burns away leaving cavities after firing, helps produce the structure in which pathogens will become trapped. It overcomes the potential problems of finer clays that may not let water through and also means that cracks are soon halted. And like clay and cow dung, it is universally available.

G The invention was born out of a World Vision project involving the Manatuto community in East Timor. The charity wanted to help set up a small industry manufacturing water filters, but initial research found the local clay to be too fine — a problem solved by the addition of organic material. While the problems of producing a working ceramic filter in East Timor were overcome, the solution was kiln-based and particular to that community's materials and couldn't be applied elsewhere. Manure firing, with no requirement for a kiln, has make this zero technology approach available anywhere it is needed. With all the components being widely available, Mr. Flynn says there is no reason the technology couldn't be applied throughout the developing world, and with no plan to patent his idea, there will be no legal obstacles to it being adopted in any community that needs it. 'Everyone has a right to clean water, these filters have the potential to enable anyone in the world to drink water safely,' says Mr. Flynn.

Questions 1–6

Complete the flow-chart below.

Choose **NO MORE THAN TWO WORDS** from the passage for each answer.

Write your answers in boxes 1–6 on your answer sheet.

Guide to Making Water Filters

Step One: combination of **1** .... and organic material, with sufficient **2** .... to create a thick mixture
sun dried

Step Two: pack **3** .... around the cylinders and place them in
4 .... which is as burning fuel
for firing (maximum temperature: **5** ....)
filter being baked in under **6** ....

核心词汇

A 段

ingenious [ɪnˈdʒiːniəs] *adj.* 精巧的；机敏的
manure [məˈnjʊə(r)] *n.* 肥料；粪肥
ingredient [ɪnˈɡriːdiənt] *n.* 成分，食材；要素

B 段

pathogen [ˈpæθədʒən] *n.* 病原体
terracotta [ˌterəˈkɒtə] *n.* 赤陶土

C 段

organic [ɔːˈɡænɪk] *adj.* 有机的，绿色环保的
stiff [stɪf] *adj.* 硬的；僵直的；酸痛的 *n.* 死尸，尸体 *vt.* 不付钱给……

E 段

domestic [dəˈmestɪk] *adj.* 国内的；家庭的

F 段

commercial [kəˈmɜːʃl] *adj.* 商业的，商务的；营利的 *n.* 商业广告
filtration [fɪlˈtreɪʃn] *n.* 过滤
bacterium [bækˈtɪəriəm] *n.* 细菌（复数 bacteria）
halt [hɔːlt] *vt.* 阻止，停止 *n.* 停止，暂停
universally [ˌjuːnɪˈvɜːsəli] *adv.* 普遍地

G 段

charity [ˈtʃærəti] *n.* 慈善机构，慈善团体；施舍；宽厚
overcome [ˌəʊvəˈkʌm] *vt.* 控制；克服；征服
patent [ˈpætnt] *vt.* 取得……的专利权 *adj.* 专利的 *n.* 专利，专利证书
obstacle [ˈɒbstəkl] *n.* 障碍，干扰；妨害物
potential [pəˈtenʃl] *n.* 潜力，潜能；可能性；电势 *adj.* 潜在的，可能的

高频同义替换

combination	▸	alliance, unity, union, association
material	▸	stuff, ingredient
sufficient	▸	competent, plenty, wealthy, enough
place	▸	install, fix

题目解析

1 定位词：combination, organic material

文中对应点：C 段第二句

题目解析：根据题干定位词 combination, organic material 定位到 C 段第二句 "Take a handful of dry, crushed clay, mix it with a handful of organic material, such as used tea leaves, coffee grounds or rice hulls, add enough water to make a stiff biscuit-like mixture and form a cylindrical pot that has one end closed, then dry it in the sun."。其中，mix 与 combination 为同义替换，it 指代的是前面分句中的 clay。句意为，取一把干燥的粘土，与一些有机材料混合，比如用过的茶叶、咖啡渣或稻壳，加入足够的水，制成一种坚硬的饼干状混合物，形成一个一端封闭的圆柱形罐子，然后在阳光下晾干。因此答案为 clay。

2 定位词：sufficient, a thick mixture

文中对应点：C 段第二句

题目解析：根据题干定位词 sufficient, a thick mixture 确定本题与上一题定位为同一个句子，其中，题干中的 sufficient 与原文中 enough 为同义替换，a thick mixture 对应 a stiff biscuit-like mixture。因此答案为 water。

3 定位词：around the cylinders

文中对应点：C 段第四句

题目解析：根据题干定位词 around the cylinders 定位到 C 段第四句 "Next, surround the pots with straw; put them in a mound of cow manure, light the straw and then top up the burning manure as required."。其中，surround the pots 与 around the cylinders 为同义替换。句意为，接下来，用稻草把罐子围起来；把它们放在一堆牛粪里，点燃稻草，然后按要求装满燃烧的粪便。因此答案为 straw。

4 定位词：place them in

文中对应点：C 段第四句

题目解析：根据题干定位词 place them in 确定本题与上一题定位为同一个句子。其中，题干中的 place them in 与原文中的 put them in 为同义替换。因此答案为 cow manure。

5 定位词：maximum temperature

文中对应点：C 段倒数第三句

题目解析：根据题干定位词 maximum temperature 定位到 C 段倒数第三句 "The properties of cow manure are vital as the fuel can reach a temperature of 700 degrees in half an hour and will be up to 950 degrees after another 20 to 30 minutes."。其中，up to 对应 maximum temperature。句意为，牛粪的特性是至关重要的，因为这种燃料在半小时内可以达到 700 度的温度，再过 20 到 30 分钟就能达到 950 度。因此答案为 950 degrees。

6 定位词：being baked in, under
文中对应点：C 段第五句
题目解析：根据题干定位词 under 定位到 C 段第五句 "In less than 60 minutes the filters are finished."。其中，less than 与 under 为同义替换。句意为，不到 60 分钟，过滤器就制成了。因此答案为 60 minutes。

参考答案

1 clay 2 water 3 straw 4 cow manure 5 950 degrees 6 60 minutes

READING PASSAGE 3

Radio Automation – Forerunner of the Integrated Circuit

Today they are everywhere. Production lines controlled by computers and operated by robots. There's no chatter of assembly workers, just the whirr and click of machines. In the mid-1940s, the workerless factory was still the stuff of science fiction. There were no computers to speak of and electronics was primitive. Yet hidden away in the English countryside was a highly automated production line called ECME, which could turn out 1,500 radio receivers a day with almost no help from human hands.

A John Sargrove, the visionary engineer who developed the technology, was way ahead of his time. For more than a decade, Sargrove had been trying to figure out how to make cheaper radios. Automating the manufacturing process would help. But radios didn't lend themselves to such methods: there were too many parts to fit together and too many wires to solder. Even a simple receiver might have 30 separate components and 80 hand-soldered connections. At every stage, things had to be tested and inspected. Making radios required highly skilled labour — and lots of it.

B In 1944, Sargrove came up with the answer. His solution was to dispense with most of the fiddly bits by inventing a primitive chip — a slab of Bakelite with all the receiver's electrical components and connections embedded in it. This was something that could be made by machines, and he designed those too. At the end of the war, Sargrove built an automatic production line, which he called ECME (electronic circuit-making equipment), in a small factory in Effingham, Surrey.

C An operator sat at one end of each ECME line, feeding in the plates. She didn't need much skill, only quick hands. From now on, everything was controlled by electronic switches and relays. First stop was the sandblaster, which roughened the surface of the plastic so that molten metal would stick to it. The plates were then cleaned to remove any traces of grit. The machine automatically checked that the surface was rough enough before sending the plate to the spraying section. There, eight nozzles rotated into position and sprayed molten zinc over both sides of the plate. Again, the nozzles only began to spray when a plate was in place. The plate whizzed on. The next stop was the milling machine, which ground away the surface layer of metal to leave the circuit and other components in the grooves and recesses. Now the plate was a composite of metal and plastic. It sped on to be lacquered and have its circuits tested. By the time, it emerged from the end of the line, robot hands had fitted it with sockets to attach components such as valves and loudspeakers. When ECME was working flat out, the whole process took 20 seconds.

D ECME was astonishingly advanced. Electronic eyes, photocells that generated a small current when a panel arrived, triggered each step in the operation, so avoiding excessive wear and tear on the machinery. The plates were automatically tested at each stage as they moved along the conveyor. And if more than two plates in succession were duds, the machines were automatically adjusted — or if necessary halted. In a conventional factory, workers would test faulty circuits and repair them. But Sargrove's assembly line produced circuits so cheaply — they just threw away the faulty ones. Sargrove's circuit board was even more astonishing for the time. It predated the more familiar printed circuit, with wiring printed on aboard, yet was more sophisticated. Its built-in components made it more like a modern chip.

E   When Sargrove unveiled his invention at a meeting of the British Institution of Radio Engineers in February 1947, the assembled engineers were impressed. So was the man from *The Times*. 'ECME', he reported the following day, 'produces almost without human labour, a complete radio receiving set. This new method of production can be equally well applied to television and other forms of electronic apparatus.'

F   The receivers had many advantages over their predecessors. With less components they were more robust. Robots didn't make the sorts of mistakes human assembly workers sometimes did. 'Wiring mistakes just cannot happen,' wrote Sargrove. No wires also meant the radios were lighter and cheaper to ship abroad. And with no soldered wires to come unstuck, the radios were more reliable. Sargrove pointed out that the circuit boards didn't have to be flat. They could be curved, opening up the prospect of building the electronics into the cabinet of Bakelite radios.

G   Sargrove was all for introducing this type of automation to other products. It could be used to make more complex electronic equipment than radios, he argued. And even if only part of a manufacturing process were automated, the savings would be substantial. But while his invention was brilliant, his timing was bad. ECME was too advanced for its own good. It was only competitive on huge production runs because each new job meant retooling the machines. But disruption was frequent. Sophisticated as it was, ECME still depended on old-fashioned electromechanical relays and valves — which failed with monotonous regularity. The state of Britain's economy added to Sargrove's troubles. Production was dogged by power cuts and post-war shortages of materials. Sargrove's financial backers began to get cold feet.

H   There was another problem Sargrove hadn't foreseen. One of ECME's biggest advantages — the savings on the cost of labour — also accelerated its downfall. Sargrove's factory had two ECME production lines to produce the two circuits needed for each radio. Between them these did what a thousand assembly workers would otherwise have done. Human hands were needed only to feed the raw material in at one end and plug the valves into their sockets and fit the loudspeakers at the other. After that, the only job left was to fit the pair of Bakelite panels into a radio cabinet and check if it worked.

I   Sargrove saw automation as the way to solve post-war labour shortages. With somewhat Utopian idealism, he imagined his new technology would free people from boring, repetitive jobs on the production line and allow them to do more interesting work. 'Don't get the idea that we are out to rob people of their jobs,' he told the *Daily Mirror*, 'Our task is to liberate men and women from being slaves of machines.'

J   The workers saw things differently. They viewed automation in the same light as the everlasting light bulb or the suit that never wears out — as a threat to people's livelihoods. If automation spread, they wouldn't be released to do more exciting jobs. They'd be released to join the dole queue. Financial backing for ECME fizzled out. The money dried up. And Britain lost its lead in a technology that would transform industry just a few years later.

Questions 1–7

The following diagram explains the process of ECME.

Label the diagram below.

Choose **NO MORE THAN TWO WORDS** from the passage for each answer.

Write your answers in boxes 1–7 on your answer sheet.

Diagram for ECME line on Bakelite

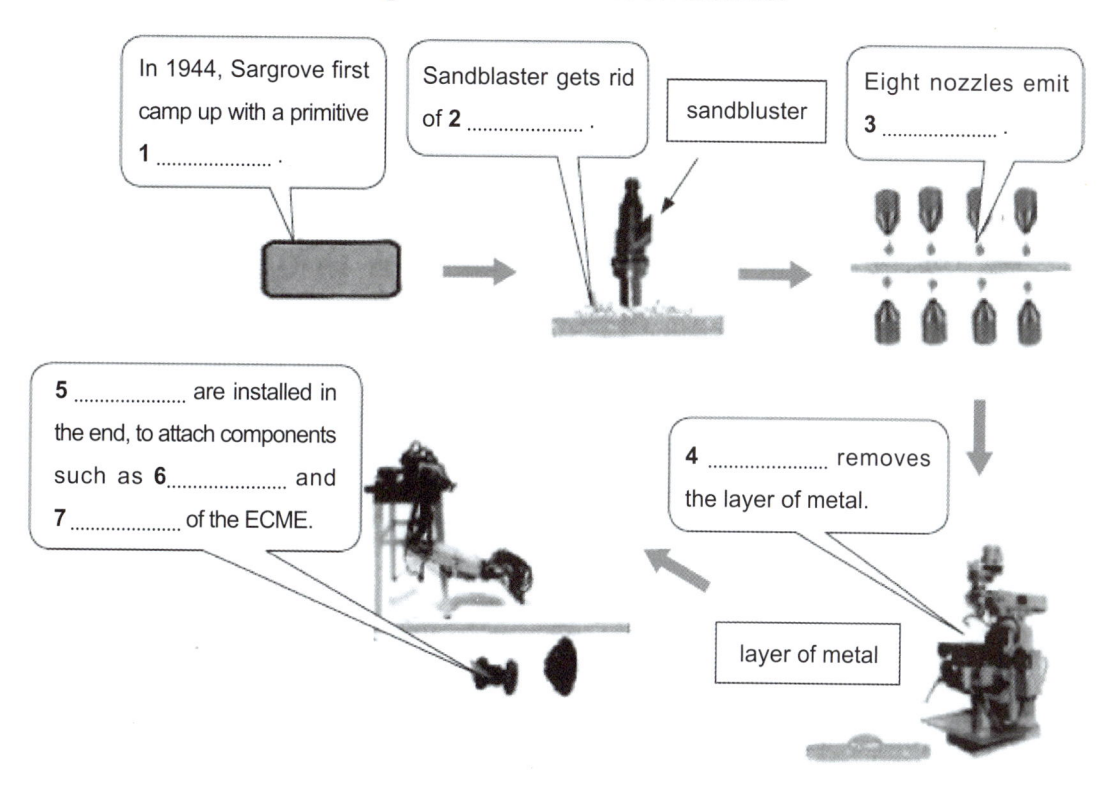

- In 1944, Sargrove first camp up with a primitive 1 ....
- Sandblaster gets rid of 2 ....
- sandbluster
- Eight nozzles emit 3 ....
- 4 .... removes the layer of metal.
- layer of metal
- 5 .... are installed in the end, to attach components such as 6 .... and 7 .... of the ECME.

核心词汇

A 段

visionary [ˈvɪʒənri] *adj.* 有眼界的；有先见之明的

wire [ˈwaɪə(r)] *n.* 电线

solder [ˈsəʊldə(r)] *v.* 焊接

B 段

dispense [dɪˈspens] *v.* 执行，施行

fiddly [ˈfɪdli] *adj.* 需要手巧的，要求高精度的

primitive [ˈprɪmətɪv] *adj.* 简单的；粗糙的；原始的

chip [tʃɪp] *n.* 芯片

slab [slæb] *n.* 厚板，平板

Bakelite [ˈbeɪkəlaɪt] *n.* 胶木；人造树胶

circuit [ˈsɜːkɪt] *n.* 电路；回路

C 段

plastic [ˈplæstɪk] *adj.* 塑料的

molten [ˈməʊltən] *adj.* 熔化的；铸造的

grit [ɡrɪt] *n.* 粗砂

spray [spreɪ] *v.* 喷，喷洒

nozzle [ˈnɒzl] *n.* 喷嘴

zinc [zɪŋk] *n.* 锌

milling [ˈmɪlɪŋ] *n.* 磨；制粉

groove [ɡruːv] *n.* 凹槽

recess [rɪˈses] *n.* 凹处

lacquer [ˈlækə(r)] *v.* 涂漆；使表面具有光泽

valve [vælv] *n.* 阀；真空管

D 段

succession [səkˈseʃn] *n.* 连续

dud [dʌd] *n.* 无用物

assembly [əˈsembli] *n.* 装配；集会

E 段

unveil [ˌʌnˈveɪl] *v.* 使公之于众，揭开

apparatus [ˌæpəˈreɪtəs] *n.* 装置，设备

F 段

predecessor [ˈpriːdɪsesə(r)] *n.* 前任；前辈；前身

robust [rəʊˈbʌst] *adj.* 强健的；粗野的

unstuck [ˌʌnˈstʌk] *adj.* 松开的

G 段

substantial [səbˈstænʃl] *adj.* 大量的

electromechanical [ɪˌlektrəʊmɪˈkænɪk(ə)l] *adj.* 电动机械的

monotonous [məˈnɒtənəs] *adj.* 单调的，无变化的

H 段

panel [ˈpænl] *n.* 嵌板；仪表板

I 段

Utopian [juːˈtəʊpiən] *adj.* 乌托邦的；空想的

slave [sleɪv] *n.* 奴隶

J 段

dole [dəʊl] *n.* 失业救济金

fizzle [ˈfɪzl] *v.* 失败

高频同义替换

process	●	manufacture, approach
require	●	exact, desire, order, command
rough	●	robust, tough, gross, coarse
faulty	●	vicious, imperfect, unfinished
complete	●	whole, thorough, absolute
substantial	●	massive, extensive, volume
interesting	●	funny, amusing, entertaining
view	●	observe, regard, comment

题目解析

1 定位词：1944, came up with

文中对应点：B 段第一、二句

题目解析：图表标题 Diagram for ECME line on Bakelite，表明这个图表的内容与 ECME 生产线有关。根据题干定位词 1944, came up with 定位至文章 B 段第一句，题目与原文比对后答案应该为 answer，但 answer 作为答案太抽象，这是一幅工序图，所以应填得具体一些，这个东西应该是下面各图或各工序中加工的对象，再往下文看：这一句为总述，下一句话会具体展开，看下一句 "His solution was to dispense with most of the fiddly bits by inventing a primitive chip — a slab of Bakelite with all the receiver's electrical components and connections embedded in it."。其中，solution 与 answer 是对应的，invent 与 came up with 也是对应的，所以应该填 invent 的宾语，即 chip，恰好其前面的修饰语为 primitive。句意为，他的解决方案是通过发明一个原始的芯片——一种集成了所有接收器电子元件和连接线嵌入其中的电木板，从而抛弃大多数的精细难做的小部件。因此答案为 chip。

2 定位词：sandblaster, get rid of

文中对应点：C 段的第四、五句

题目解析：从第二幅图及其内容描述得知，这是进入具体的操作步骤。根据题干定位词 sandblaster, get rid of 定位至文章 C 段第四、五句 "First stop is the sandblaster, which roughened the surface of the plastic so that molten metal would stick to it. The plates were then cleaned to remove any traces of grit."。其中，remove 与题干中的 get rid of 对应。句意为，第一步是喷砂器，它能使塑料表面变得粗糙以便熔融金属粘在上面。然后，这些平板被清理干净，以去除任何的砂砾。根据题目要求填写不得超过 2 个单词，只填 remove 核心的宾语。因此答案为 grit。

3 定位词：eight nozzles, emit

文中对应点：C 段第七句

题目解析：由第三幅图得知此处还是操作步骤描述，根据题干定位词 eight nozzles，emit 定位至文章 C 段第七句 "There, eight nozzles rotated into position and sprayed molten zinc over both sides of the plate."。其中，emit 与 spray 对应，所以填 spray 的宾语。句意为，在那里，8 个喷嘴旋转到位，并在平板两侧喷上熔融锌。因此答案为 molten zinc。

4 定位词：removers, layer of metal

文中对应点：C 段第十句

题目解析：由第四幅图得知此处还是操作步骤描述，根据题干定位词 removers, layer of metal 定位至文章 C 段第十句 "The next stop was the milling machine, which ground away the surface layer of metal to leave the circuit and other components in the grooves and recesses."。其中，ground away 对应 remove，layer of metal 为原文重现。句意为，下一步是铣床，它能够磨掉金属表面层从而在凹槽和角落印刷出电路和其他部件。题干让填 removes the layer of metal 的主语。因此答案为 milling machine。

5 定位词：installed, in the end

文中对应点：C 段倒数第二句

题目解析：根据题干定位词 in the end 定位至文章 C 段的倒数第二句 "By the time, it emerged from the end of the line, robot hands fitted it with sockets to attach components such as valves and loudspeakers."。其中，fit 与题干中的 install 对应，from the end of the line 与 in the end 对应。句意为，电路板出现在生产线的最后一步，机械手把插槽安装在电路板上，以安装诸如阀及扬声器之类的部件。按照题干 "___ are installed in the end, to attach components such as ___ and ___ of the ECME." 本题填 install 的宾语，且是 attach 这个动作的发出者，所以对应 fit 或 install 的宾语 sockets，同时 sockets 还是 attach 的动作发出者。因此答案为 sockets。

6 定位词：installed, in the end

文中对应点：C 段倒数第二句

题目解析：按照第 5 题的分析，本题填 attach 的宾语。因此答案为 loudspeakers (valves)。

7 定位词：installed, in the end

文中对应点：C 段最后第二句

题目解析：按照第 5 题的分析，本题填 attach 的宾语。因此答案为 valves (loudspeakers)。

参考答案

1 chip **2** grit **3** molten zinc **4** milling machine **5** sockets **6** loudspeakers / valves
7 valves / loudspeakers

READING PASSAGE 4

Travel Accounts

A There are many reasons why individuals have travelled beyond their own societies. Some travellers may have simply desired to satisfy curiosity about the larger world. Until recent times, however, trade, business dealings, diplomacy, political administration, military campaigns, exile, flight from persecution, migration, pilgrimage, missionary efforts, and the quest for economic or educational opportunities were more common inducements for foreign travel than was mere curiosity. While the travellers' accounts give much valuable information on these foreign lands and provide a window for the understanding of the local cultures and histories, they are also a mirror to the travellers themselves, for these accounts help them to have a better understanding of themselves.

B Records of foreign travel appeared soon after the invention of writing, and fragmentary travel accounts appeared in both Mesopotamia and Egypt in ancient times. After the formation of large, imperial states in the classical world, travel accounts emerged as a prominent literary genre in many lands, and they held especially strong appeal for rulers desiring useful knowledge about their realms. The Greek historian Herodotus reported on his travels in Egypt and Anatolia in researching the history of the Persian wars. The Chinese envoy Zhang Qian described much of central Asia as far west as Bactria (modern-day Afghanistan) on the basis of travels undertaken in the first century BC while searching for allies for the Han dynasty. Hellenistic and Roman geographers such as Ptolemy, Strabo, and Pliny the Elder relied on their own travels through much of the Mediterranean world as well as reports of other travellers to compile vast compendia of geographical knowledge.

C During the postclassical era (about 500 to 1500 CE), trade and pilgrimage emerged as major incentives for travel to foreign lands. Muslim merchants sought trading opportunities throughout much of the eastern hemisphere. They described lands, peoples, and commercial products of the Indian Ocean basin from east Africa to Indonesia, and they supplied the first written accounts of societies in sub-Saharan, West Africa. While merchants set out in search of trade and profit, devout Muslims travelled as pilgrims to Mecca to make their hajj and visit the holy sites of Islam. Since the prophet Muhammad's original pilgrimage to Mecca, untold millions of Muslims have followed his example, and thousands of hajj accounts have related their experiences. One of the best known Muslim travellers, Ibn Battuta, began his travels with the hajj but then went on to visit central Asia, India, China, sub-Saharan Africa, and parts of Mediterranean Europe before returning finally to his home in Morocco. East Asian travellers were not quite so prominent as Muslims during the postclassical era, but they too followed many of the highways and sea lanes of the eastern hemisphere. Chinese merchants frequently visited southeast Asia and India, occasionally venturing even to East Africa, and devout East Asian Buddhists undertook distant pilgrimages. Between the 5th and 9th century CE, hundreds and possibly even thousands of Chinese Buddhists travelled to India to study with Buddhist teachers, collect sacred texts, and visit holy sites. Written accounts recorded the experiences of many pilgrims, such as Faxian, Xuanzang, and Yijing. Though not so numerous as the Chinese pilgrims, Buddhists from Japan, Korea, and other lands also ventured abroad in the interests of spiritual enlightenment.

D Medieval Europeans did not hit the roads in such large numbers as their Muslim and east Asian counterparts during the early part of the postclassical era, although gradually increasing crowds of Christian pilgrims flowed to Jerusalem, Rome, Santiago de Compostela (in northern Spain), and other sites. After the 12th century, however, merchants, pilgrims, and missionaries from medieval Europe travelled widely and left numerous travel accounts, of which Marco Polo's description of his travels and sojourn in China is the best known. As they became familiar with the larger world of the eastern hemisphere — and the profitable commercial opportunities that it offered — European peoples worked to find new and more direct routes to Asian and African markets. Their efforts took them not only to all parts of the eastern hemisphere, but eventually to the Americas and Oceania as well.

E If Muslim and Chinese peoples dominated travel and travel-writing in postclassical times, European explorers, conquerors, merchants, and missionaries took centre stage during the early modern era (about 1500 to 1800 CE). By no means did Muslim and Chinese travel come to a halt in early modern times. But European peoples ventured to the distant corners of the globe, and European printing presses churned out thousands of travel accounts that described foreign lands and peoples for a reading public with an apparently insatiable appetite for news about the larger world. The volume of travel literature was so great that several editors, including Giambattista Ramusio, Richard Hakluyt, Theodore de Bry, and Samuel Purchas, assembled numerous travel accounts and made them available in enormous published collections.

F During the 19th century, European travellers made their way to the interior regions of Africa and the Americas, generating a fresh round of travel-writing as they did so. Meanwhile, European colonial administrators devoted numerous writings to the societies of their colonial subjects, particularly in Asian and African colonies they established. By mid-century, attention was flowing also in the other direction. Painfully aware of the military and technological prowess of European and Euro-American societies, Asian travellers in particular visited Europe and the United States in hopes of discovering principles useful for the reorganisation of their own societies. Among the most prominent of these travellers who made extensive use of their overseas observations and experiences in their own writings were the Japanese reformer Fukuzawa Yukichi and the Chinese revolutionary Sun Yat-sen.

G With the development of inexpensive and reliable means of mass transport, the 20th century witnessed explosions both in the frequency of long-distance travel and in the volume of travel-writing. While a great deal of travel took place for reasons of business, administration, diplomacy, pilgrimage, and missionary work, as in ages past increasingly effective modes of mass transport made it possible for new kinds of travel to flourish. The most distinctive of them was mass tourism, which emerged as a major form of consumption for individuals living in the world's wealthy societies. Tourism enabled consumers to get away from home to see the sights in Rome, take a cruise through the Caribbean, walk the Great Wall of China, visit some wineries in Bordeaux, or go on safari in Kenya. A peculiar variant of the travel account arose to meet the needs of these tourists: the guidebook, which offered advice on food, lodging, shopping, local customs, and all the sights that visitors should not miss seeing. Tourism has had a massive economic impact throughout the world, but other new forms of travel have also had considerable influence in contemporary times. Recent times have seen unprecedented waves of migration, for example, and numerous migrants have sought to record their experiences and articulate their feelings about life in foreign lands. Recent times have also seen an unprecedented development of ethnic consciousness, and many are the intellectuals and writers in diaspora who have visited the homes of their ancestors to see how much of their forebears' values and cultural traditions they themselves have inherited. Particularly notable among their accounts are the memoirs of Malcolm X and Maya Angelou describing their visits to Africa.

Questions 1–8

Complete the table below.

Choose **NO MORE THAN TWO WORDS** from the passage for each answer.

Write your answer in boxes 1–8 on your answer sheet.

TIME	DESTINATION	TRAVELLER	PURPOSE
Classical era	Egypt and Anatolia	Herodotus	To obtain information on **1** ....
1th century BC	Central Asia	Zhang Qian	To seek **2** ....
Roman Empire	Mediterranean	Ptolemy, Strabo, Pliny the Elder	To gather **3** ....
Postclassical era	Eastern hemisphere	Muslims	For business and **4** ....
5th to 9th century CE	India	Asian Buddhists	To study with **5** .... and for spiritual enlightenment
Early modern era	Distant places of the globe	The Europeans	To meet the public's expectation for the outside
19th century	Asia, Africa	Colonial administrator	To provide information on the **6** .... they conquer
By the mid-century of the 1800s	Europe and the United States	Sun Yat-sen, Fukuzawa Yukichi	To learn **7** .... for the reorganisation of their societies
20th century	Mass tourism	People from **8** .... countries	For entertainment

核心词汇

A 段
exile [ˈeksaɪl] *n.* 流亡；放逐
pilgrimage [ˈpɪlɡrɪmɪdʒ] *n.* 朝圣（之旅）

B 段
fragmentary [ˈfræɡməntri] *adj.* 不完整的；片段的
imperial [ɪmˈpɪəriəl] *adj.* 帝国的，皇帝的
compendia [kəmˈpendiə] *n.* 大全；手册（compendium 的复数）

C 段
incentive [ɪnˈsentɪv] *n.* 动力；激励
pilgrim [ˈpɪlɡrɪm] *n.* 朝圣者
prominent [ˈprɒmɪnənt] *adj.* 重要的；杰出的；著名的
venture [ˈventʃə(r)] *v.* 到（某处）去冒险

D 段
sojourn [ˈsɒdʒən] *n.* 逗留；暂住

E 段
come to a halt 停留
churn out （粗制滥造地）大量生产，制造
insatiable [ɪnˈseɪʃəbl] *adj.* 无法满足的，贪得无厌的

G 段
cruise [kruːz] *n.* 游览，航游
winery [ˈwaɪnəri] *n.* 葡萄酒厂，酿酒厂
variant [ˈveəriənt] *n.* 变体，变化形式
lodging [ˈlɒdʒɪŋ] *n.* 借宿，住宿
diaspora [daɪˈæspərə] *n.* （犹太人的）大流散；（任何民族的）大移居
forebear [ˈfɔːbeə(r)] *n.* 祖先，前辈

高频同义替换

common	▶	mutual, corporate, collective, usual, ordinary
valuable	▶	worthy, estimable
formation	▶	constitution, fabric, becoming, structure
appeal	▶	attract, implore
account	▶	interpret, count, guess
numerous	▶	many, multiple, hundred, plenty, plentiful

region	▸	area, extent, boundary, zone, territory
witness	▸	demonstrate, prove, argue
offer	▸	afford, undertake, tender
impact	▸	affect, influence, strike
notable	▸	obvious, remarkable, prominent, marked

题目解析

1 定位词：Herodotus, obtain
文中对应点：B 段第三句
题目解析：根据题干定位词 Herodotus，obtain 定位至文章 B 段第三句 "The Greek historian Herodotus reported on his travels in Egypt and Anatolia in researching the history of the Persian wars."。其中，in searching of 对应 obtain。句意为，希腊历史学家 Herodotus 在他的埃及和安纳托利亚之旅中，记录了有关波斯战争的考察。本题需要找出 Herodotus 旅行的目的，B 段第三句提及的目的是 in searching of the history of the Persian Wars。因此答案为 Persian Wars。

2 定位词：Zhang Qian, seek
文中对应点：B 段第四句
题目解析：根据题干定位词 Zhang Qian, seek 定位至文章 B 段第四句 "The Chinese envoy Zhang Qian described much of central Asia as far west as Bactria (modern-day Afghanistan) on the basis of travels undertaken in the first century BC while searching for allies for the Han dynasty."。其中，searching for 与 seek 对应。句意为，中国特使张骞为了给汉朝寻找盟友，以公元前一世纪的旅行为基础，描述了中亚大部分地区，最远西至巴克特里亚（现在的阿富汗）。本题需要找到张骞旅行的目的，因此答案为 allies。

3 定位词：Ptolemy, Strabo, Pliny the Elder
文中对应点：B 段倒数第一句
题目解析：根据题干定位词 Ptolemy, Strabo, Pliny the Elde 三个人物定位至文章 B 段倒数第一句 "Hellenistic and Roman geographers such as Ptolemy, Strabo, and Pliny the Elder relied on their own travels through much of the Mediterranean world as well as reports of other travelers to compile vast compendia of geographical knowledge."。其中，compile 对应 gather。句意为，希腊和罗马地理学家，如 Ptolemy，Strabo 和 Pliny 等，依靠自己在地中海区域的旅行以及其他旅行者的记录，编译了大量的地理知识概略。这三个地理学家的目的是 to compile vast compendia of geographical knowledge，因此答案为 geographical knowledge。

4 定位词：Postclassical era, business
文中对应点：C 段第一句
题目解析：根据题干定位词 postclassical area, Muslims, business 定位至文章 C 段第一句 "During the Postclassical era (about 500 to 1500 CE), trade and pilgrimage emerged as major incentives for travel to foreign lands."。其中，trade 与 business 为同义替换。句意为，在后古典主义时期（约公元 500 到 1500 年），贸易和朝圣成为人们去异国旅行的主要诱因。因此答案为 pilgrimage。

5 定位词：5th to 9th centuries, Asian Buddhists
文中对应点：C 段倒数第三句
题目解析：根据题干定位词 5th to 9th centuries, Asian Buddhists 定位至文章 C 段倒数第三句 "Between the 5th and 9th centuries CE, hundreds and possibly even thousands of Chinese Buddhists travelled to India to study with Buddhist teachers, collect sacred texts, and visit holy sites."。其中，5th to 9th centuries 与 between the 5th and 9th centuries CE 对应，Asian Buddhists 与 Chinese Buddhists 对应。句意为，公元 5-9 世纪之间，数以百计，甚至数以千计的中国佛教徒前往印度向佛教高僧求教，收集经文，并拜访佛教圣地。因此答案为 Buddhist teachers。

6 定位词：Colonial administrator, provide
文中对应点：F 段第二句
题目解析：根据题干定位词 Colonial administrator, provide 定位至文章 F 段第二句 "Meanwhile, European colonial administrators devoted numerous writings to the societies of their colonial subjects, particularly in Asian and African colonies they established."。其中，devoted 与 provide 对应。句意为，与此同时，欧洲殖民主义者向其殖民地，特别是他们在亚洲和非洲建立的殖民地，发放大量关于殖民地情况的游记。因此答案为 colonies。

7 定位词：Sun Yat-sen, Fukuzawa Yukichi, learn, for the reorganisation of their societies
文中对应点：F 段倒数第一、二句
题目解析：根据题干定位词 Sun Yat-sen, Fukuzawa Yukichi 定位至文章 F 段倒数第一、二句 "Painfully aware of the military and technological prowess of European and Euro-American societies, Asian travellers in particular visited Europe and the United States in hopes of discovering principles useful for the reorganisation of their own societies. Among the most prominent of these travellers who made extensive use of their overseas observations and experiences in their own writings were the Japanese reformer Fukuzawa Yukichi and the Chinese revolutionary Sun Yat-sen."。其中，discovering 与 learn 对应。句意为，当痛苦地意识到欧洲和欧美社会的军事和科技实力时，亚洲旅行者特别访问了欧洲和美国，希望发现适用于重建自己社会的准则。在游记中广泛应用自身的海外观察和经历的旅行者中，最著名的是日本改革家 Fukuzawa Yukichi 和中国革命先驱孙中山先生。因此答案为 principles。

8 定位词：mass tourism, people from, countries
文中对应点：G 段第三句
题目解析：根据题干定位词 mass tourism, people from, countries 定位至文章 G 段第三句 "The most distinctive of them was mass tourism, which emerged as a major form of consumption for individuals living in the world's wealthy societies."。其中，individuals living in 与 people from 为同义替换，societies 与 countries 对应。句意为，最独特的是大众旅游，这已成为世界上富裕人士的一个主要消费形式。这道题目答案需要填写进行 mass tourism 的人群，因此答案为 wealthy。

参考答案

1 Persian wars **2** allies **3** geographical knowledge **4** pilgrimage **5** Buddhist teachers
6 colonies **7** principles **8** wealthy

Vicky IELTS Practices

Part 3
雅思阅读机经套题及解析

第一章 机经套题

TEST 1

READING PASSAGE 1

You should spend about 20 minutes on Questions 1–13, which are based on Reading Passage 1 below.

Crisis! Fresh Water

A   As in New Delhi and Phoenix, policymakers worldwide wield great power over how water resources are managed. Wise use of such power will become increasingly important as the years go by because the world's demand for freshwater is currently overtaking its ready supply in many places, and this situation shows no sign of abating.

B   That the problem is well-known makes it no less disturbing: today one out of six people, more than a billion, suffer inadequate access to safe freshwater. By 2025, according to data released by the United Nations, the freshwater resources of more than half the countries across the globe will undergo either stress — for example, when people increasingly demand more water than is available or safe for use — or outright shortages. By mid-century as much as three quarters of the earth's population could face scarcities of freshwater.

C   Scientists expect water scarcity to become more common in large part because the world's population is rising and many people are getting richer (thus expanding demand) and because global climate change is exacerbating aridity and reducing supply in many regions. What is more, many water sources are threatened by faulty waste disposal, releases of industrial pollutants, fertiliser runoff and coastal influxes of saltwater into aquifers as groundwater is depleted.

D   Because lack of access to water can lead to starvation, disease, political instability and even armed conflict, failure to take action can have broad and grave consequences. Fortunately, to a great extent, the technologies and policy tools required to conserve existing freshwater and to secure more of it are known among which several seem particularly effective. What is needed now is action. Governments and authorities at every level have to formulate and execute concrete plans for implementing the political, economic and technological measures that can ensure water security now and in the coming decades.

E   The world's water problems requires, as a start, an understanding of how much freshwater each person requires, along with knowledge of the factors that impede supply and increase demand in different parts of the world. Malin Falkenmark of the Stockholm International Water Institute and other experts estimate that, on average, each person on the earth needs a minimum of 1,000 cubic metres (m³) of water. The minimum water each person requires for drinking, hygiene and growing food. The volume is equivalent to two fifths of an Olympic-size swimming pool.

F   Much of the Americas and northern Eurasia enjoy abundant water supplies. But several regions are beset by greater or lesser degrees of 'physical' scarcity — whereby demand exceeds local availability. Other areas, among them Central Africa, parts of the Indian subcontinent and Southeast Asia, contend with 'economic' water scarcity, where lack of technical training, bad governments or weak finances limit access even though sufficient supplies are available.

G   More than half of the precipitation that falls on land is never available for capture or storage because it evaporates from the ground or transpires from plants; this fraction is called green water. The remainder channels into so-called blue-water sources — rivers, lakes, wetlands and aquifers — that people can tap directly. Farm irrigation from these free-flowing bodies is the biggest single human use of freshwater. Cities and industries consume only tiny amounts of total freshwater resources, but the intense local demand they create often drains the surroundings of ready supplies.

H   Lots of Water, but not always where it is needed one hundred and ten thousand cubic kilometres of precipitation, nearly 10 times the volume of Lake Superior, falls from the sky onto the earth's land surface every year. This huge quantity would be enough to easily fulfil the requirements of everyone on the planet if the water arrived where and when people needed it. But much of it cannot be captured (top), and the rest is distributed unevenly (bottom). Green water (61.1% of total precipitation*): absorbed by soil and plants, then released back into the air; unavailable for withdrawal. Blue water (38.8% of total precipitation*): collected in rivers, lakes, wetlands and groundwater; available for withdrawal before it evaporates or reaches the ocean. These figures may not add up to 100% because of rounding. Only 1.5% is directly used by people.

I   Waters run away in tremendous wildfires in recent years. The economic actors had all taken their share reasonably enough; they just did not consider the needs of the natural environment, which suffered greatly when its inadequate supply was reduced to critical levels by drought. The members of the Murray-Darling Basin Commission are now frantically trying to extricate themselves from the disastrous results of their misallocation of the total water resource. Given the difficulties of sensibly apportioning the water supply within a single nation, imagine the complexities of doing so for international river basins such as that of the Jordan River, which borders on Lebanon, Syria, Israel, the Palestinian areas and Jordan, all of which have claims to the shared, but limited, supply in an extremely parched region. The struggle for freshwater has contributed to civil and military disputes in the area. Only continuing negotiations and compromise have kept this tense situation under control.

Questions 1–5

Do the following statements agree with the information given in Reading Passage 1?

In boxes 1–5 on your answer sheet, write

> **TRUE** if the statement agrees with the information
> **FALSE** if the statement contradicts the information
> **NOT GIVEN** if there is no information on this

1. The prospect for the need for the freshwater worldwide is obscure.
2. To some extent, the challenge for the freshwater is alleviated by the common recognition.
3. Researchers arrive at the specific conclusion about the water crisis based on persuasive consideration of several factors.
4. The fact that people do not actually cherish the usage of water also contributes to the water scarcity.
5. Controversy can't be avoided for adjacent nations over the water resource.

Questions 6–10

Reading Passage 1 has nine paragraphs, **A–I**.

Which paragraph contains the following information?

Write the correct letter, **A–I**, in boxes 6–10 on your answer sheet.

NB You may use any letter more than once.

6. the uneven distribution of water around the world
7. other factors regarding nature bothering people who make the policies
8. joint efforts needed to carry out the detailed solutions combined with various aspects
9. no always-in-time match available between the requirements and the actual rainfall
10. the lower limit of the amount of freshwater for a person to survive

Questions 11–13

Complete the summary below.

Choose **NO MORE THAN THREE WORDS** from the passage for each answer.

Write your answers in boxes 11–13 on your answer sheet.

The shortage of water sometimes for some areas seems **11** .... because of unavailability, but other regions suffer other kinds of scarcity for insufficient support. **12** .... of some rainfall cannot be achieved because of evaporation. Some other parts form the **13** which can be used immediately. Water to irrigate the farmland takes a considerable amount along with the use for cities and industries and the extended need from the people involved.

READING PASSAGE 2

You should spend about 20 minutes on Questions 14–26, which are based on Reading Passage 2 below.

The Dugong: Sea Cow

Dugongs are herbivorous mammals that spend their entire lives in the sea. Their close relatives the manatees also venture into or live in fresh water. Together dugongs and manatees make up the order sirenia or sea cows, so-named because dugongs and manatees are thought to have given rise to the myth of the mermaids or sirens of the sea.

A The dugong, which is a large marine mammal which, together with the manatees, looks rather like a cross between a rotund dolphin and a walrus. Its body, flippers and fluke resemble those of a dolphin but it has no dorsal fin. Its head looks somewhat like that of a walrus without the long tusks.

B Dugongs, along with other Sirenians, their diet consists mainly of sea-grass; and the distribution of dugongs very closely follows that of these marine flowering plants. As sea grasses grow rooted in the sediment, they are limited by the availability of light. Consequently they are found predominantly in shallow coastal waters, and so too are dugongs. But, this is not the whole story. Dugongs do not eat all species of seagrass, preferring seagrass of higher nitrogen and lower fibre content.

C Due to their poor eyesight, dugongs often use smell to locate edible plants. They also have a strong tactile sense, and feel their surroundings with their long sensitive bristles. They will dig up an entire plant and then shake it to remove the sand before eating it. The flexible and muscular upper lip is used to dig out the plants. When eating they ingest the whole plant, including the roots, although when this is impossible they will feed on just the leaves. A wide variety of seagrass has been found in dugong stomach contents, and evidence exists they will eat algae when seagrass is scarce. Although almost completely herbivorous, they will occasionally eat invertebrates such as jellyfish, sea squirts, and shellfish.

D A heavily grazed seagrass bed looks like a lawn mown by a drunk. Dugongs graze apparently at random within a seagrass bed, their trails meandering in all directions across the bottom. This is rather an inefficient means of removing seagrass that results in numerous small tufts remaining. And this is where the dugongs derive some advantage from their inefficiency. The species that recover most quickly from this disturbance, spreading out vegetative from the remaining tufts, are those that dugongs like to eat. In addition, the new growth found in these areas tends to be exactly what hungry dugongs like.

E Dugongs are semi-nomadic, often travelling long distances in search of food, but staying within a certain range their entire life. Large numbers often move together from one area to another. It is thought that these movements are caused by changes in seagrass availability. Their memory allows them to return to specific points after long travels. Dugong movements mostly occur within a localised area of seagrass beds, and animals in the same region show individualistic patterns of movement.

F Recorded numbers of dugongs are generally believed to be lower than actual numbers, due to a lack of accurate surveys. Despite this, the dugong population is thought to be shrinking, with a worldwide decline of 20 per cent in the last 90 years. They have disappeared from the waters of Hong Kong, Mauritius, and Taiwan, as well as parts of Cambodia, Japan, the Philippines and Vietnam. Further disappearances are likely. In the late 1960s, herds of up to 500 dugongs were observed off the coast of East Africa and nearby islands. However, current populations in this area are extremely small, numbering 50 and below, and it is thought likely they will become extinct. The eastern side of the Red Sea is the home of large populations numbering in the hundreds, and similar populations are thought to exist on the western side. In the 1980s, it was estimated there could be as many as 4,000 dugongs in the Red Sea. The Persian Gulf has the second-largest dugong population in the world, inhabiting most of the southern coast, and the current population is believed to be around 7,500. Australia is home to the largest population, stretching from Shark Bay in Western Australia to Moreton Bay in Queensland. The population of Shark Bay is thought to be stable with over 10,000 dugongs.

G Experience from various parts of northern Australia suggests that extreme weather such as cyclones and floods can destroy hundreds of square kilometres of seagrass meadows, as well as washing dugongs ashore. The recovery of seagrass meadows and the spread of seagrass into new areas, or areas where it has been destroyed, can take over a decade. For example, about 900 km^2 of seagrass was lost in Hervey Bay in 1992, probably because of murky water from flooding of local rivers, and run-off turbulence from a cyclone three weeks later. Such events can cause extensive damage to seagrass communities through severe wave action, shifting sand and reduction in saltiness and light levels. Prior to the 1992 floods, the extensive seagrasses in Hervey Bay supported an estimated 1,750 dugongs. Eight months after the floods the affected area was estimated to support only about 70 dugongs. Most animals presumably survived by moving to neighbouring areas. However, many died attempting to move to greener pastures, with emaciated carcasses washing up on beaches up to 900km away.

H If dugongs do not get enough to eat they may calve later and produce fewer young. Food shortages can be caused by many factors, such as a loss of habitat, death and decline in quality of seagrass, and a disturbance of feeding caused by human activity. Sewage, detergents, heavy metal, hypersaline water, herbicides, and other waste products all negatively affect seagrass meadows. Human activity such as mining, trawling, dredging, land-reclamation, and boat propeller scarring also cause an increase in sedimentation which smothers seagrass and prevents light from reaching it. This is the most significant negative factor affecting seagrass. One of the dugong's preferred species of seagrass, Halophila ovalis, declines rapidly due to lack of light, dying completely after 30 days.

I Despite being legally protected in many countries, the main causes of population decline remain anthropogenic and include hunting, habitat degradation, and fishing-related fatalities. Entanglement in fishing nets has caused many deaths, although there are no precise statistics. Most issues with industrial fishing occur in deeper waters where dugong populations are low, with local fishing being the main risk in shallower waters. As dugongs cannot stay underwater for a very long period, they are highly prone to deaths due to entanglement. The use of shark nets has historically caused large numbers of deaths, and they have been eliminated in most areas and replaced with baited hooks.

Questions 14–17

Complete the summary below.

Choose **NO MORE THAN THREE WORDS** from the passage for each answer.

Write your answers in boxes 14–17 on your answer sheet.

Dugongs are herbivorous mammals that spend their entire lives in the sea. Yet dugongs are picky on their feeding seagrass, and only chose seagrass with higher **14** .... and lower fibre. To compensate for their poor eyesight, they use their **15** .... to feel their surroundings. It is like that Dugongs are 'farming' seagrass. They often leave **16** .... randomly in all directions across the sea bed. Dugongs prefer eating the newly grown seagrass recovering from the tiny **17** .... left behind by the grazing dugongs.

Questions 18–22

Do the following statements agree with the information given in Reading Passage 2?

In boxes 18–22 on your answer sheet, write

TRUE if the statement agrees with the information
FALSE if the statement contradicts the information
NOT GIVEN if there is no information on this

18   The dugong will keep eating up the plant completely when they begin to feed.

19   It takes a very long time for the re-growth of seagrass where it has been only grazed by dugongs.

20   Even in facing food shortages, the strong individuals will not compete with weak small ones for food.

21   It is thought that the dugong rarely returned to the old habitats when they finished plant.

22   Industrial fishing poses the greatest danger to dugongs which are prone to be killed due to entanglement.

Questions 23–26

Answer the questions below.

*Choose **NO MORE THAN TWO WORDS AND/OR A NUMBER** from the passage for each answer.*

23 What is dugong in resemblance to yet as people can easily tell them apart from the manatees by the fins in its back?

24 What is the major reason as dugongs travelled long distances in herds from one place to another?

25 What number, has estimated to be, of dugong's population before the 1992 floods in Hervey Bay took place?

26 What is thought to be the lethal danger when dugongs were often trapped in?

You should spend about 20 minutes on Questions 27–40, which are based on Reading Passage 3 below.

Detection of a Meteorite Lake

A As the sun rose over picturesque Lake Bosumtwi, a team of Syracuse University prepared for another day of using state-of-the-art equipment to help unlock the mysteries hidden below the lake bottom. Nestled in the heart of Ghana, the lake holds an untapped reservoir of information that could help scientists predict future climate changes by looking at evidence from the past. This information will also improve the scientist's understanding of the changes that occur in a region stuck by a massive meteorite.

B The project, led by earth sciences professor Christopher Scholz of the College of Arts and Sciences and funded by the National Science Foundation (NSF), is the first large-scale effort to study Lake Bosumtwi, Earth's surface. The resulting crater is one of the largest and most well-preserved geologically young craters in the world, says Scholz, who is collaborating on the project with researchers from the University of South Carolina, the University of Rhode Island, and several Ghanaian institutions. 'Our data should provide information about what happens when an impact hits hard, Pre-Cambrian, crystalline rocks that are a billion years old,' he says.

C Equally important is the fact that the lake, which is about 8 kilometres in diameter, has no natural outlet. The rim of the crater rises about 240 metres above the water's surface. Streams flow into the lake, Scholz says, but the water leaves only by evaporation, or by seeping through the lake sediments. For the past million years, the lake has acted as a tropical rain gauge, filling and drying with changes in precipitation and the tropical climate. The record of those changes is hidden in sediment below the lake bottom. 'The lake is one of the best sites in the world for the study of tropical climate change,' Scholz says. 'The tropics are the heart engine for the Earth's climate. To understand global climate, we need to have records of climate changes from many sites around the world, including the tropics.'

D Before the researchers could explore the lake's surface, they need a boat with a large, working deck area that could carry eight tons of scientific equipment. The boat — dubbed R/V *Kilindi* — was built in Florida last year. It was constructed in modules that were dismantled, packed inside a shipping container, and reassembled over a 10-day period in late November and early December 1999 in the rural village of Abono, Ghana. The research team then spent the next two weeks testing the boat and equipment before returning to the United States for the holidays.

E   In mid-January, five members of the team — Keely Brooks, an earth sciences graduate student; Peter Cattaneo, a research analyst; and Kiram Lezzar, a postdoctoral scholar, all from SU; James McGill, a geophysical filed engineer; and Nick Peters, a Ph.D. student in geophysics from the University of Miami — returned to Abono to begin collecting data about the lake's subsurface using a technique called seismic reflection profiling. In this process, a high-pressure air gun is used to create small, pneumatic explosions in the water. The sound energy penetrates about 1,000 to 2,000 metres into the lake's subsurface before bouncing back to the surface of the water.

F   The reflected sound energy is detected by underwater microphones — called hydrophones — embedded in a 50-metre long cable that is towed behind the boat as it crosses the lake in a carefully designed grid pattern. On-board computers record the signals, and the resulting data are then processed and analysed in the laboratory. 'The results will give us a good idea of the shape of the basin, how thick the layer of sediment is, and when and where there were major changes in sediment accumulation,' Scholz says. 'We are now developing three-dimensional perspective of the lake's subsurface and the layers of sediment that have been laid down.'

G   Team members spent about four weeks in Ghana collecting the data. They worked seven days a week, arriving at the lake just after sunrise. On a good day, when everything went as planned, the team could collect data and be back at the dock by early afternoon. Except for a new relatively minor adjustments, the equipment and the boat worked well. Problems that arose were primarily non-scientific — tree stumps, fishing nets, cultural barriers, and occasional misunderstandings with local villagers.

H   Lake Bosumtwi, the largest natural freshwater lake in the country, is scared to the Ashanti people, who believe their souls come to the lake to bid farewell to their god. The lake is also the primary source of fish for the 26 surrounding villages. Conventional canoes and boats are forbidden. Fishermen travel on the lake by floating on traditional planks; they propel with small paddles. Before the research project could begin, Scholz and his Ghanaian counterparts had to secure special permission from tribal chiefs to put the R/V *Kilindi* on the lake.

I   When the team began gathering data, rumors flew around the lake as to why the researchers were there. 'Some thought we were dredging the lake for gold, others thought we were going to drain lake or that we had bought the lake,' Cattaneo says. 'But once the local people understood why we were there, they were very helpful.'

Questions 27–31

Do the following statements agree with the information given in Reading Passage 3?

In boxes 27–31 on your answer sheet, write

TRUE if the statement agrees with the information
FALSE if the statement contradicts the information
NOT GIVEN if there is no information on this

27 With the investigation of the lake, scientists may predict the climate changes in the future.

28 The crater resulted from a meteorite impact is the largest and most preserved one in the world.

29 The water stored in Lake Bosumtwi was gone only by seeping through the lake sediments.

30 Historical climate changes can be detected by the analysis of the sediment in the lake.

31 The greatest obstacle to research of scientists had been the interference by the locals due to their indigenous believes.

Questions 32–35

Complete the flow-chart below.

Choose **NO MORE THAN TWO WORDS** from the passage for each answer.

Write your answers in boxes 32–35 on your answer sheet.

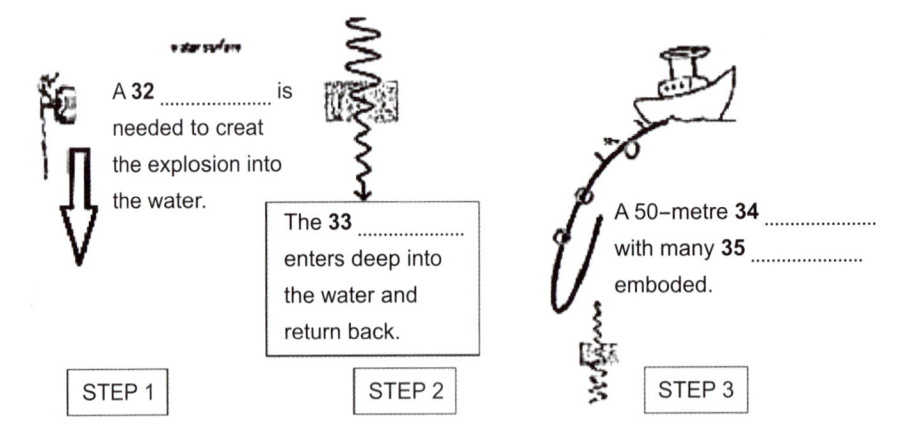

A 32 .... is needed to creat the explosion into the water.

STEP 1

The 33 .... enters deep into the water and return back.

STEP 2

A 50-metre 34 .... with many 35 .... emboded.

STEP 3

Questions 36–40

Complete the summary below.

Choose **NO MORE THAN THREE WORDS** from the passage for each answer.

Write your answers in boxes 36–40 on your answer sheet.

The boat dubbed R/V *Kilindi* was constructed in modules that were dismantled and stored in a **36** ………………. . The technology they used called **37** ………………. ; they created sound energy into 1,000–2,000 metres into the bottom of the lake, and separated equipment to collect the returned waves. Then the data had been analysed and processed in the **38** ………………. . Scholz also added that they were now building **39** ………………. view of the sediment or sub-image in the bottom of the lake. Whole set of equipment works well yet the ship should avoid physical barrier including tree stumps or **40** ………………. floating on the surface on the lake.

TEST 2

READING PASSAGE 1

You should spend about 20 minutes on Questions 1–13, which are based on Reading Passage 1 below.

Finches on Islands

A   Today, the quest continues. On Daphne Major — one of the most desolate of the Galipagos Islands, an uninhabited volcanic cone where cacti and shrubs seldom grow higher than a researcher's knee — Peter and Rosemary Grant, Biologists at Princeton University, have spent more than three decades watching Darwin's finch respond to the challenges of storms, drought and competition for food — the Grants know and recognise many of the individual birds on the island and can trace the birds' lineages hack back through time. They have witnessed Darwin's principle in action again and again, over many generations of finches.

B   The Grants' most dramatic insights have come from watching the evolving bill of the medium ground finch. The plumage of this sparrow-sized bird ranges from dull brown to jet black. At first glance, it may not seem particularly striking, but among scientists who study evolutionary biology, the medium ground finch is a superstar. Its bill is a middling example in the array of shapes and sizes found among Galapagos finches: heftier than that of the small ground finch, which specialises in eating small, soft seeds, but petite compared to that of the large ground finch, an expert at cracking and devouring big, hard seeds.

C   When the Grants began their study in the 1970s, only two species of finch lived on Daphne Major, the medium ground finch and the cactus finch. The island is so small that the researchers were able to count and catalogue every bird. When a severe drought hit in 1977, the birds soon devoured the last of the small, easily eaten seeds. Smaller members of the medium ground finch population, lacking the bill strength to crack large seeds, died out.

D   Bill and body size are inherited traits, and the next generation had a high proportion of big-billed individuals. The Grants had documented natural selection at work — the same process that, over many millennia, directed the evolution of the Galapagos' 14 unique finch species, all descended from a common ancestor that reached the islands a few million years ago.

E   Eight years later, heavy rains brought by an El Nino transformed the normally meager vegetation on Daphne Major. Vines and other plants that in most years struggle for survival suddenly flourished, choking out the plants that provide large seeds to the finches. Small seeds came to dominate the food supply, and big birds with big bills died out at a higher rate than smaller ones. 'Natural selection is observable,' Rosemary Grant says. 'It happens when the environment changes. When local conditions reverse themselves, so does the direction of adaptation.'

F Recently, the Grants witnessed another form of natural selection acting on the medium ground finch: competition from bigger, stronger cousins. In 1982, a third finch, the large ground finch, came to live on Daphne Major. The stout bills of these birds resemble the business end of a crescent wrench. Their arrival was the first such colonisation recorded on the Galapagos in nearly a century of scientific observation. 'We realised,' Peter Grant says, 'we had a very unusual and potentially important event to follow.' For 20 years, the large ground finch coexisted with the medium ground finch, which shared the supply of large seeds with its bigger-billed relative. Then, in 2002 and 2003, another drought struck. None of the birds nested that year, and many died out. Medium ground finches with large bills, crowded out of feeding areas by the more powerful large ground finches, were hit particularly hard.

G When wetter weather returned in 2004, and the finches nested again, the new generation of the medium ground finch was dominated by smaller birds with smaller bills, able to survive on smaller seeds. This situation, says Peter Grant, marked the first time that biologists have been able to follow the complete process of an evolutionary change due to competition between species and the strongest response to natural selection that he had seen in 33 years of tracking Galapagos finches.

H On the inhabited island of Santa Cruz, just south of Daphne Major, Andrew Hendry of McGill University and Jeffrey Podos of the University of Massachusetts at Amherst have discovered a new, man-made twist in finch evolution. Their study focused on birds living near the Academy Bay research station, on the fringe of the town of Puerto Ayora. The human population of the area has been growing fast — from 900 people in 1974 to 9,582 in 2001. 'Today Puerto Ayora is full of hotels and mai tai bars,' Hendry says. 'People have taken this extremely arid place and tried to turn it into a Caribbean resort.'

I Academy Bay records dating back to the early 1960s show that medium ground finches captured there had either small or large bills. Very few of the birds had mid-size bills. The finches appeared to be in the early stages of a new adaptive radiation: If the trend continued, the medium ground finch on Santa Cruz could split into two distinct subspecies, specialising in different types of seeds. But in the late 1960s and early 70s, medium ground finches with medium-sized bills began to thrive at Academy Bay along with small and large-billed birds. The booming human population had introduced new food sources, including exotic plants and bird feeding stations stocked with rice. Bill size, once critical to the finches' survival, no longer made any difference. 'Now an intermediate bill can do fine,' Hendry says.

J At a control site distant from Puerto Ayora, and relatively untouched by humans, the medium ground finch population remains split between large- and small-billed birds. On undisturbed parts of Santa Cruz, there is no ecological niche for a middling medium ground finch, and the birds continue to diversify. In town, though there are still many finches, once-distinct populations are merging.

K The finches of Santa Cruz demonstrate a subtle process in which human meddling can stop evolution in its tracks, ending the formation of new species. In a time when global biodiversity continues its downhill slide, Darwin's finches have yet another unexpected lesson to teach. 'If we hope to regain some of the diversity that's already been lost,' Hendry says, 'we need to protect not just existing creatures, but also the processes that drive the origin of new species.'

Questions 1–4

Complete the table below.

Choose **NO MORE THAN TWO WORDS** from the passage for each answer.

Write your answers in boxes 1–4 on your answer sheet.

Year	Climate	Finch's condition
1977	1	small-beak birds failing to survive, without the power to open 2 ....
1985	3 .... brought by El Nino	big-beak birds dying out, with 4 .... as the main food resource

Questions 5–8

Complete the summary below.

Choose **NO MORE THAN TWO WORDS** from the passage for each answer.

Write your answers in boxes 5–8 on your answer sheet.

On the remote island of Santa Cruz, Andrew Hendry and Jeffrey Podos conducted a study on reversal in 5 .... due to human activity. In the early 1960s medium ground finches were found to have a larger or smaller beak. But in the late 1960s and early 70s, finches with 6 .... flourished. The study speculates that it is due to the growing 7 .... who brought in alien plants with intermediate-size seeds into the area and the birds ate 8 .... sometimes.

Questions 9–13

Do the following statements agree with the information given in Reading Passage 1?

In boxes 9–13 on your answer sheet, write

>   **TRUE**   if the statement agrees with the information
>   **FALSE**   if the statement contradicts the information
>   **NOT GIVEN**   if there is no information on this

9   Grants' discovery has questioned Darwin's theory.

10 The cactus finches are less affected by food than the medium ground finch.

11 In 2002 and 2003, all the birds were affected by the drought.

12 The discovery of Andrew Hendry and Jeffrey Podos was the same as that of the previous studies.

13 It is shown that the revolution in finches on Santa Cruz is likely a response to human intervention.

READING PASSAGE 2

You should spend about 20 minutes on Questions 14–26, which are based on the passage below.

Questions 14–19

Reading Passage 2 has nine paragraphs, **A–I**.

Choose the correct heading for paragraphs **B–G** from the list of headings below.

Write the correct number, **i–x**, in boxes 14–19 on your answer sheet.

List of Headings

i	A description of the procedure and mechanism
ii	An international research project
iii	An experiment to investigate consumer responses
iv	Marketing with an alternative name
v	A misleading name for business
vi	A potentially profitable line of research
vii	Medical dangers of the technique
viii	Internal drawbacks to marketing tools
ix	Broadening applications
x	What is neuromarketing

Example	Answer
Paragraph A	x

14   Paragraph **B**

15   Paragraph **C**

16   Paragraph **D**

17   Paragraph **E**

18   Paragraph **F**

19   Paragraph **G**

What Does the Consumer Think?

A   Marketing people are no longer prepared to take your word for it that you favour one product over another. They want to scan your brain to see which one you really prefer. Using the tools of neuroscientists, such as electroencephalogram (EEG) mapping and functional magnetic-resonance imaging (fMRI), they are trying to learn more about the mental processes behind purchasing decisions. The resulting fusion of neuroscience and marketing is inevitably, being called 'neuromarketing'.

B   The first person to apply brain-imaging technology in this way was Gerry Zaltman of Harvard University, in the late 1990s. The idea remained in obscurity until 2001, when Bright House, a marketing consultancy based in Atlanta, Georgia, set up a dedicated neuromarketing arm, Bright House Neurostrategies Group. (Bright House lists Coca-Cola, Delta Airlines and Home Depot among its clients.) But the company's name may itself simply be an example of clever marketing. Bright House does not scan people while showing them specific products or campaign ideas, but bases its work on the results of more general fMRI-based research into consumer preferences and decision-making carried out at Emory University in Atlanta.

C   Can brain scanning really be applied to marketing? The basic principle is not that different from focus groups and other traditional forms of market research. A volunteer lies in an fMRI machine and is shown images or video clips. In place of an interview or questionnaire, the subject's response is evaluated by monitoring brain activity. fMRI provides real-time images of brain activity, in which different areas 'light up' depending on the level of blood flow. This provides clues to the subject's subconscious thought patterns. Neuroscientists know, for example, that the sense of self is associated with an area of the brain known as the medial prefrontal cortex. A flow of blood to that area while the subject is looking at a particular logo suggests that he or she identifies with that brand.

D   At first, it seemed that only companies in Europe were prepared to admit that they used neuromarketing. Two carmakers, Daimler Chrysler in Germany and Ford's European arm, ran pilot studies in 2003. But more recently, American companies have become more open about their use of neuromarketing. Lieberman Research Worldwide, a marketing firm based in Los Angeles, is collaborating with the California Institute of Technology (Caltech) to enable movie studios to make market-test film trailers. More controversially, the *New York Times* recently reported that a political consultancy, FKF Research, has been studying the effectiveness of campaign commercials using neuromarketing techniques.

E   Whether all this is any more than a modern-day version of phrenology, the Victorian obsession with linking lumps and bumps in the skull to personality traits, is unclear. There have been no large-scale studies, so scans of a handful of subjects may not be a reliable guide to consumer behaviour in general. Of course, focus groups and surveys are flawed too: strong personalities can steer the outcomes of focus groups, and some people may be untruthful in their responses to opinion pollsters. And even honest people cannot always explain their preferences.

F That is perhaps where neuromarketing has the most potential. When asked about cola drinks, most people claim to have a favourite brand, but cannot say why they prefer that brand's taste. An unpublished study of attitudes towards two well-known cola drinks, Brand A and Brand B, carried out last year in a college of medicine in the US found that most subjects preferred Brand B in a blind testing — fMRI scanning showed that drinking Brand B lit up a region called the ventral putamen, which is one of the brain's reward centres, far more brightly than Brand A. But when told which drink was which, most subjects said they preferred Brand A, which suggests that its stronger brand outweighs the more pleasant taste of the other drink.

G People form many unconscious attitudes that are obviously beyond traditional methods that utilise introspection, says Steven Quartz, a neuroscientist at Caltech who is collaborating with Lieberman Research. With over 100 billion dollars spent each year on marketing in America alone, any firm that can more accurately analyse how customers respond to brands could make a fortune.

H Consumer advocates are wary. Gary Ruskin of Commercial Alert, a lobby group, thinks existing marketing techniques are powerful enough. 'Already, marketing is deeply implicated in many serious pathologies', he says. 'That is especially true of children, who are suffering from an epidemic of marketing-related diseases, including obesity and type 2 diabetes. Neuromarketing is a tool to amplify these trends.' Dr. Quartz counters that neuromarketing techniques could equally be used for benign purposes. 'There are ways to utilise these technologies to create more responsible advertising,' he says. 'Brain-scanning could, for example, be used to determine when people are capable of making free choices, to ensure that advertising falls within those bounds.'

I Another worry is that brain-scanning is an invasion of privacy that information on the preferences of specific individuals will be misused. But neuromarketing studies rely on small numbers of volunteer subjects, so that seems implausible. Critics also object to the use of medical equipment for frivolous rather than medical purposes. But Tim Ambler, a neuromarketing researcher at the London Business School, says, 'A tool is a tool, and if the owner of the tool gets a decent rent for hiring it out, then that subsidises the cost of the equipment, and everybody wins.' Perhaps more brain-scanning will some day explain why some people like the idea of neuromarketing, but others do not.

Questions 20–22

Look at the following people (Questions 20–22) and the list of opinions below.

Match each person with the correct opinion, **A–F**.

Write the correct letter, **A–F**, in boxes 20–22 on your answer sheet.

20   Steven Quartz

21   Gary Ruskin

22   Tim Ambler

List of Opinions

A   Neuromarketing could be used to contribute towards the cost of medical technology.

B   Neuromarketing could use introspection as a tool in marketing research.

C   Neuromarketing could be a means of treating medical problems.

D   Neuromarketing could make an existing problem worse.

E   Neuromarketing could lead to the misuse of medical equipment.

F   Neuromarketing could be used to help the exploitation of consumers.

Questions 23–26

Complete the summary below.

Choose **ONE WORD ONLY** from the passage for each answer.

Write your answers in boxes 23–26 on your answer sheet.

Neuromarketing can provide valuable information on attitudes to particular **23** .... There are also drawbacks in surveys, where people can be **24** .... , or focus groups, where they may be influenced by others. It also allows researchers to identify the subject's **25** .... thought patterns. However, some people are concerned that it could lead to problems such as an increase in disease especially among **26** ....

READING PASSAGE 3

You should spend about 20 minutes on Questions 27–40, which are based on the passage below.

Questions 27–32

The passage has six paragraphs, **A–F**.

Choose the correct heading for each paragraph from the list of headings below.

Write the correct number, **i–x**, in boxes 27–32 on your answer sheet.

List of Headings

i	Paper continued as a sharing or managing must
ii	Piles can be more inspiring rather than disorganising
iii	Favourable situation that economists used paper pages
iv	Overview of an unexpected situation: paper survived
v	Comparison between efficiencies for using paper and using computer
vi	IMF's paperless office seemed to be a waste of papers
vii	Example of failure for avoidance of paper record
viii	Advantages of using a paper in offices
ix	Piles reflect certain characteristics in people's thought
x	Joy of having the paper square in front of computer

27 Paragraph **A**

28 Paragraph **B**

29 Paragraph **C**

30 Paragraph **D**

31 Paragraph **E**

32 Paragraph **F**

Paper or Computer?

A   Computer technology was supposed to replace paper. But that hasn't happened. Every country in the Western world uses more paper today, on a per-capita basis, than it did ten years ago. The consumption of uncoated free-sheet paper, for instance — the most common kind of office paper — rose almost fifteen per cent in the United States between 1995 and 2000. This is generally taken as evidence of how hard it is to eradicate old, wasteful habits and of how stubbornly resistant we are to the efficiencies offered by computerisation. A number of cognitive psychologists and ergonomics experts, however, don't agree. Paper has persisted, they argue, for very good reasons: when it comes to performing certain kinds of cognitive tasks, paper has many advantages over computers. The dismay people feel at the sight of a messy desk — or the spectacle of air-traffic controllers tracking flights through notes scribbled on paper strips — arises from a fundamental confusion about the role that paper plays in our lives.

B   The case for paper is made most eloquently in *The Myth of the Paperless Office*, by two social scientists, Abigail Sellen and Richard Harper. They begin their book with an account of a study they conducted at the International Monetary Fund, in Washington, D.C.. Economists at the I.M.F. spend most of their time writing reports on complicated economic questions, work that would seem to be perfectly suited to sitting in front of a computer. Nonetheless, the I.M.F. is awash in paper, and Sellen and Harper wanted to find out why. Their answer is that the business of reports — at least at the I.M.F. — is an intensely collaborative process, the professional judgments and contributions of many people. The economists bring drafts of reports to conference rooms, spread out the relevant pages, and negotiate changes with one other. They go back to their offices and jot down comments in the margin, taking advantage of the freedom offered by the informality of the handwritten note. Then they deliver the annotated draft to the author in person, taking him, page by page, through the suggested changes. At the end of the process, the author spreads out all the pages with comments on his desk and starts to enter them on the computer — moving the pages around as he works, organising and reorganising, saving and discarding.

C   Without paper, this kind of collaborative and iterative work process would be much more difficult. According to Sellen and Harper, paper has a unique set of 'affordances' — that is, qualities that permit specific kinds of uses. Paper is tangible: we can pick up a document, flip through it, read little bits here and there, and quickly get a sense of it. Paper is spatially flexible, meaning that we can spread it out and arrange it in the way that suits us best. And it's tailorable: we can easily annotate it, and scribble on it as we read, without altering the original text. Digital documents, of course, have their own affordances. They can be easily searched, shared, stored, and remotely, linked to other relevant material. But they lack the affordances that really matter to a group of people working together on a report.

D   Paper enables a certain kind of thinking. Picture, for instance, the top of your desk. Chances are that you have a keyboard and a computer screen off to one side, and a clear space roughly eighteen square inches in front of your chair. What covers the rest of the desktop is probably piles — piles of papers, journals, magazines, binders, postcards, videotapes, and all the other artifacts of the knowledge economy. The piles look like a mess, but they aren't. When a group at Apple Computer studied piling behaviour several years ago, they found that even the most disorderly piles usually make perfect sense to the piles, and that office workers could hold forth in great detail about the precise history and meaning of their piles. The pile closest to the cleared, eighteen-inch-square working area, for example, generally represents the most business, and within that pile the most important document of all is likely to be at the top. Piles are living, breathing archives. Over time, they get broken down and resorted, sometimes chronologically and sometimes thematically and sometimes chronologically and thematically; clues about certain documents may be physically embedded in the file by, say, stacking a certain piece of paper at an angle or inserting dividers into the stack.

E But why do we pile documents instead of filing them? Because piles represent the process of active, ongoing thinking. The psychologist Alison Kidd, whose research Sellen and Harper refer to extensively, argues that 'knowledge workers' use the physical space of the desktop to hold 'ideas which they cannot yet categorise or even decide how they might use'. The messy desk is not necessarily a sign of disorganisation. It may be a sign of complexity: those who deal with many unresolved ideas simultaneously cannot sort and file the papers on their desks, because they haven't yet sorted and filed the ideas in their head. Kidd writes that many of the people she talked to use the papers on their desks as contextual cues to 'recover a complex set of threads without difficulty and delay' when they come in on a Monday morning, or after their work has been interrupted by a phone call. What we see when we look at the piles on our desks is, in a sense, the contents of our brains.

F This idea that paper facilitates a highly specialised cognitive and social process is a far cry from the way we have historically thought about the stuff. Paper first began to proliferate in the workplace in the late nineteenth century as part of the move toward 'systematic management'. To cope with the complexity of the industrial economy, managers were instituting company-wide policies and demanding monthly, weekly, or even daily updates from their subordinates. Thus was born the monthly sales report, and the office manual and the internal company newsletter. The typewriter took off in the eighteen-eighties, making it possible to create documents in a fraction of the time it had previously taken, and that was followed closely by the advent of carbon paper, which meant that a typist could create ten copies of that document simultaneously. Paper was important not to facilitate creative collaboration and thought but as an instrument of control.

Questions 33–36

Complete the summary below.

Choose **NO MORE THAN THREE WORDS** from the passage for each answer.

Write your answers in boxes 33–36 on your answer sheet.

Compared with digital documents, paper has several advantages. It allows clerks to work more easily in a 33 .... process. Next, paper is not like virtual digital versions. It's 34 .... Finally, because it is 35 .... note or comments can be effortlessly added as related informational digital documents have affordances too. However, shortcoming comes at the absence of convenience on task which is for a 36 ....

Questions 37–40

Choose the correct letter, **A**, **B**, **C** or **D**.

Write the correct letter in boxes 37–40 on your answer sheet.

37 What do the economists from I.M.F. say that their way of writing documents?

 A They note down their comments for freedom on the drafts.
 B They finish all writing individually.
 C They share ideas on before electronic version was made.
 D They use electronic version fully.

38 What is the implication of the 'Piles' mentioned in the passage?

 A They have underlying orders.
 B They are necessarily a mess.
 C They are in time sequence order.
 D They are in alphabetic order.

39 What does the manager believe in sophisticated economy?

 A Recorded paper can be as management tool.
 B Carbon paper should be compulsory.
 C Teamwork is the most important.
 D Monthly report is the best way.

40 According to the end of this passage, what is the reason why paper is not replaced by electronic vision?

 A Paper is inexpensive to buy.
 B It contributed to management theories in Western countries.
 C People need time for changing their old habit.
 D It is collaborative and functional for tasks implement and management.

TEST 3

READING PASSAGE 1

You should spend about 20 minutes on Questions 1–13, which are based on the passage below.

Finding Our Way

A   'Drive 200 yards, and then turn right,' says the car's computer voice. You relax in the driver's seat, follow the directions and reach your destination without error. It's certainly nice to have the Global Positioning System (GPS) to direct you to within a few yards of your goal. Yet if the satellite service's digital maps become even slightly outdated, you can become lost. Then you have to rely on the ancient human skill of navigating in three-dimensional space. Luckily, your biological finder has an important advantage over GPS: it does not go awry if only one part of the guidance system goes wrong, because it works in various ways. You can ask questions of people on the sidewalk. Or follow a street that looks familiar. Or rely on a navigational rubric: 'If I keep the East River on my left, I will eventually cross 34th Street.' The human positioning system is flexible and capable of learning. Anyone who knows the way from point A to point B — and from A to C, can probably figure out how to get from B to C, too.

B   But how does this complex cognitive system really work? Researchers are looking at several strategies people use to orient themselves in space: guidance, path integration and route following. We may use all three or combinations thereof. And as experts learn more about these navigational skills, they are making the case that our abilities may underlie our powers of memory and logical thinking. Grand Central, please imagine that you have arrived in a place you have never visited — New York City. You get off the train at Grand Central Terminal in midtown Manhattan. You have a few hours to explore before you must return home. You head uptown to see popular spots you have been told about: Rockefeller Centre, Central Park, and the Metropolitan Museum of Art. You meander in and out of shops along the way. Suddenly, it is time to get back to the station. But how?

C   If you ask passersby for help, most likely you will receive information in many different forms. A person who orients herself by a prominent landmark would gesture southward: 'Look down there. See the tall, broad Met Life Building? Head for that, the station is right below it.' Neurologists call this navigational approach 'guidance', meaning that a landmark visible from a distance serves as the marker for one's destination.

D   Another city dweller might say, 'What places do you remember passing? Okay. Go toward the end of Central Park, then walk down to St. Patrick's Cathedral. A few more blocks, and Grand Central will be off to your left.' In this case, you are pointed toward the most recent place you recall, and you aim for it. Once you arrive in the next notable place, you can retrace your path. Your brain is adding together the individual legs of your trek into a cumulative progress report. Researchers call this strategy 'path integration'. Many animals rely primarily on path integration to get around, including insects, spiders, crabs and rodents. The desert ants of the genus Cataglyphis employ this method to return from foraging as far as 100 yards away. They note the general direction they came from and retrace their steps, using the polarisation of sunlight to orient themselves even under overcast skies. On their way back they are faithful to this inner homing vector. Even when a scientist picks up an ant and puts it in a totally different spot, the insect stubbornly proceeds in the originally determined direction until it has gone 'back' all of the distance it wandered from its nest. Only then does the ant realise it has not succeeded, and it begins to walk in successively larger loops to find its way home.

E Whether it is trying to get back to the anthill or the train station, any animal using path integration must keep track of its own movements, so it knows, while returning, which segments it has already completed. As you move, your brain gathers data from your environment sights, sounds, smells, lighting, muscle contractions, a sense of time passing — to determine which way your body has gone. The church spire, the sizzling sausages on that vendor's grill, the open courtyard, and the train station — all represent snapshots of memorable junctures during your journey.

F In addition to guidance and path integration, we use a third method for finding our way. An office worker you approach for help on a Manhattan street corner might say: 'Walk straight down Fifth, turn left on 47th, turn right on Park, go through the walkway under the Helmsley Building, then cross the street to the Met Life Building into Grand Central.' This strategy, called route following, uses landmarks such as buildings and street names, plus directions — straight, turn, go through — for reaching intermediate points. Route following is more precise than guidance or path integration, but if you forget the details and take a wrong turn, the only way to recover is to backtrack until you reach a familiar spot, because you do not know the general direction or have a reference landmark for your goal. The route-following navigation strategy truly challenges the brain. We have to keep all the landmarks and intermediate directions in our head. It is the most detailed and therefore most reliable method, but it can be undone by routine memory lapses. With path integration, our cognitive memory is less burdened; it has to deal with only a few general instructions and the homing vector. Path integration works because it relies most fundamentally on our knowledge of our body's general direction of movement, and we always have access to these inputs. Nevertheless, people often choose to give route-following directions, in part because saying 'Go straight that way!' just does not work in our complex, man-made surroundings.

G Road Map or Metaphor? On your next visit to Manhattan you will rely on your memory to get around. Most likely you will use guidance, path integration and route-following in various combinations. But how exactly do these constructs deliver concrete directions? Do we humans have, as an image of the real world, a kind of road map in our heads, with symbols for cities, train stations and churches; thick lines for highways, narrow lines for local streets? Neurobiologists and cognitive psychologists do call the portion of our memory that controls navigation a 'cognitive map'. The map metaphor is obviously seductive: maps are the easiest way to present geographic information for convenient visual inspection. In many cultures, maps were developed before writing, and today they are used in almost every society. It is even possible that maps derive from a universal way in which our spatial-memory networks are wired.

H Yet the notion of a literal map in our heads may be misleading; a growing body of research implies that the cognitive map is mostly a metaphor. It may be more like a hierarchical structure of relationships. To get back to Grand Central, you first envision the large scale — that is, you visualise the general direction of the station. Within that system you then imagine the route to the last place you remember. After that, you observe your nearby surroundings to pick out a recognisable storefront or street corner that will send you toward that place. In this hierarchical, or nested, scheme, positions and distances are relative, in contrast with a road map, where the same information is shown in a geometrically precise scale.

Questions 1–5

Look at the following statements (Questions *1–5*) and the list of navigation methods below.

Match each statement with the correct navigation method, **A–C**.

Write the correct letter, **A–C**, in boxes 1–5 on your answer sheet.

NB You may use any letter more than once.

1   Using basic direction from starting point and light intensity to move on.
2   Using combination of place and direction heading for destination.
3   Using an iconic building near your destination as orientation.
4   Using a retrace method from a known place if a mistake happens.
5   Using a passed spot as reference for a new integration.

List of Navigation Methods
A   Guidance
B   Path integration
C   Route-following

Questions 6–8

*Choose the correct letter, **A**, **B**, **C** or **D**.*

Write the correct letter in boxes 6–8 on your answer sheet.

6   What does the ant of Cataglyphis respond if it has been taken to another location according to the passage?

    A changes the orientation sensors improvingly
    B releases biological scent for help from others
    C continues to move by the original orientation
    D totally gets lost once disturbed

7   Which of the followings is true about 'cognitive map' in this passage?

    A There is not obvious difference contrast by real map.
    B It exists in our head and is always correct.
    C It only exists under some cultures.
    D It was managed by brain memory.

8   Which of following description of way findings correctly reflects the function of cognitive map?

    A It visualises a virtual route in a nested scheme.
    B It reproduces an exact details of every landmark.
    C Observation plays a more important role.
    D Store or supermarket is a must in the map.

Questions 9–13

Do the following statements agree with the information given in Reading Passage 1?

In boxes 9–13 on your answer sheet, write

    TRUE   *if the statement agrees with the information*
    FALSE   *if the statement contradicts the information*
    NOT GIVEN *if there is no information on this*

9   Biological navigation has a state of flexibility.

10   You will always receive good reaction when you ask direction.

11   When someone follows a route, he or she collects comprehensive perceptional information in mind on the way.

12   Path integration requires more thought from brain compared with route-following.

13   Intormation about positions and distances is shown in the same way between the cognitive map and a road map.

READING PASSAGE 2

You should spend about 20 minutes on Questions 14–26, which are based on the passage below.

The Success of Cellulose

A Not too long ago many investors made the bet that renewable fuels from bio-mass would be the next big thing in energy. Converting corn, sugarcane and soybeans into ethanol or diesel-type fuels lessens our nation's dependence on oil imports while cutting carbon dioxide emissions. But already the nascent industry faces challenges. Escalating demand is hiking food prices while farmers clear rain-forest habitats to grow fuel crops. And several recent studies say that certain biofuel-production processes either fail to yield net energy gains or release more carbon dioxide than they use.

B A successor tier of start-up ventures aims to avoid those problems. Rather than focusing on the starches, sugars and fats of food crops, many of the prototype bioethanol processes work with lignocellulose, the 'woody' tissue that strengthens the cell walls of plants, says University of Massachusetts Amherst chemical engineer George W. Huber. Although the cellulose breaks down less easily than sugars and starches and thus requires a complex series of enzyme-driven chemical reactions, its use opens the industry to nonfood plant feed-stocks such as agricultural wastes, wood chips and switchgrass. But no company has yet demonstrated a cost-competitive industrial process for making cellulosic biofuels.

C So scientists and engineers are working on dozens of possible biofuel-processing routes, reports Charles Wyman, a chemical engineer at the University of California, Riverside, who is a founder of Mascoma Corporation in Cambridge Mass, a leading developer of cellulosic ethanol processing. 'There's no miracle process out there,' he remarks. And fine-tuning a process involves considerable money and time. 'The oil companies say that it takes 10 years to fully commercialise an industrial processing route,' warns Huber, who has contributed some thermochemical techniques to another biomass start-up, Virent Energy Systems in Madison, Wis.

D One promising biofuel procedure that avoids the complex enzymatic chemistry to break down cellulose is now being explored by Coskata in Warrenville, a firm launched in 2006 by high-profile investors and entrepreneurs (General Motors recently took a minority stake in it as well). In the Coskata operation, a conventional gasification system will use heat to turn various feedstocks into a mixture of carbon monoxide and hydrogen called syngas, says Richard Tobey, vice president of Engineering and R&D. The ability to handle multiple plant feedstocks would boost the flexibility of the overall process because each region in the country has access to certain feedstocks but not others.

E   Instead of using thermochemical methods to convert the syngas to fuel — a process that can be significantly more costly because of the added expense of pressurising gases, according to Tobey — the Coskata Group chose a biochemical route. The group focused on five promising strains of ethanol-excreting bacteria that Ralph Tanner, a microbiologist at the University of Oklahoma, had discovered years before in the oxygen-free sediments of a swamp. These anaerobic bugs make ethanol by voraciously consuming syngas.

F   The 'heart and soul of the Coskata process,' as Tobey puts it, is the bioreactor in which the bacteria live. 'Rather than searching for food in the fermentation mash in a large tank, our bacteria wait for the gas to be delivered to them,' he explains. The firm's success relies on plastic tubes, the filter-fabric straws as thin as human hair. The syngas flows through the straws, and water is pumped across their exteriors. The gases diffuse across the selective membrane to the bacteria embedded in the outer surface of the tubes, which permits no water inside. 'We get efficient mass transfer with the tubes, which is not easy,' Tobey says. 'Our data suggest that in an optimal setting we could get 90 percent of the energy value of the gases into our fuel.' After the bugs eat the gases, they release ethanol into the surrounding water. Standard distillation or filtration techniques could extract the alcohol from the water.

G   Coskata researchers estimate that their commercialised process could deliver ethanol at under $1 per gallon — less than half of today's $2-per-gallon wholesale price, Tobey claims. Outside evaluators, a Argonne National Laboratory measured the input-output 'energy balance' of the Coskata process and found that, optimally, it can produce 7.7 times as much energy in the end product as it takes to make it.

H   The company plans to construct a 40,000-gallon-a-year pilot plant near the GM test track in Milford, Mich., by the end of this year and hopes to build a full-scale, 100 million-gallon-a-year plant by 2011. Coskata may have some company by then; Bioengineering Resources in Fayetteville, Ark, is already developing what seems to be a similar three-step pathway in which syngas is consumed by bacteria isolated by James Gaddy, a retired chemical engineer at the University of Arkansas. Considering the advances in these and other methods, plant cellulose could provide the greener ethanol everyone wants.

Questions 14–19

Look at the following statements (Questions **14–19**) and the list of people below.

Match each statement with the correct people, **A–D**.

Write the correct letter, **A–D**, in boxes 14–19 on your answer sheet.

NB You may use any letter more than once.

14 A key component to gain the success lies in the place where the bacteria / bugs survive.

15 Separating bacteria in fixed procedures to produce ethanol in a homologous biochemical way.

16 Assists to develop certain skills.

17 It needs arduous efforts to achieve an economical industrial process.

18 There is no shortcut to expedite the production process.

19 A combination of chemistry and biology can considerably lower the cost needed for the production company.

List of People
A George W. Huber
B James Gaddy
C Richard Tobey
D Charles Wyman

Questions 20–23

Do the following statements agree with the information given in Reading Passage 2?

In boxes 20–23 on your answer sheet, write

TRUE	if the statement agrees with the information
FALSE	if the statement contradicts the information
NOT GIVEN	if there is no information on this

20 A shift from conventionally targeted areas of the vegetation to get ethanol takes place.

21 It takes a considerably long way before a completely mature process is reached.

22 The Coskata group sees no bright future for the cost advantage available in the production of greener ethanol.

23 Some enterprises are trying to buy the shares of Coskata group.

Questions 24–26

Complete the summary below.

Choose **NO MORE THAN THREE WORDS** from the passage for each answer.

Write your answers in boxes 24–26 on your answer sheet.

Tobey has noticed that the Coskata process can achieve a huge success because it utilises **24** .... as the bioreactor on whose exterior surface the bactcria take the syngas going through **25** .... to produce the ethanol into the water outside which researchers will later **26** .... by certain techniques. The figures show a pretty high percentage of energy can be transferred into the fuel which is actually very difficult to be achieved.

READING PASSAGE 3

You should spend about 20 minutes on Questions 27–40, which are based on the passage below.

Questions 27–34

The reading passage has eight paragraphs, **A–H**.

Choose the correct heading for each paragraph from the list of headings below.

Write the correct number, *i–x*, in boxes 27–34 on your answer sheet.

List of Headings

i	Different personality types mentioned
ii	Recommendation of combined styles for group
iii	Historical explanation of understanding personality
iv	A lively and positive attitude person depicted
v	A personality likes challenge and direct communication
vi	different characters illustrated
vii	Functions of understanding communication styles
viii	Cautious and considerable person cited
ix	Calm and Factual personality illustrated
x	Self-assessment determines one's temperament

27 Section **A**

28 Section **B**

29 Section **C**

30 Section **D**

31 Section **E**

32 Section **F**

33 Section **G**

34 Section **H**

Communicating Conflict!

A As far back as Hippocrates' time (460-370 B.C.) people have tried to understand other people by characterising them according to personality type or temperament. Hippocrates believed there were four different body fluids that influenced four basic types of temperament. His work was further developed 500 years later by Galen. These days there are a number of self-assessment tools that relate to the basic descriptions developed by Galen, although we no longer believe the source to be the types of body fluid that dominate our systems.

B The values in self-assessments help determine personality style. Learning styles, communication styles, conflict-handling styles, or other aspects of individuals are that they help depersonalise conflict in interpersonal relationships. The depersonalisation occurs when you realise that others aren't trying to be difficult, but they need different or more information than you do. They're not intending to be rude: they are so focused on the task they forget about greeting people. They would like to work faster but not at the risk of damaging the relationships needed to get the job done. They understand there is a job to do. But it can only be done right with the appropriate information, which takes time to collect. When used appropriately, understanding communication styles can help resolve conflict on teams. Very rarely are conflicts true personality issues. Usually they are issues of style, information needs, or focus.

C Hippocrates and later Galen determined there were four basic temperaments: sanguine, phlegmatic, melancholic and choleric. These descriptions were developed centuries ago and are still somewhat apt, although you could update the wording. In today's world, they translate into the four fairly common communication styles described below:

D The sanguine person would be the expressive or spirited style of communication. These people speak in pictures. They invest a lot of emotion and energy in their communication and often speak quickly. Putting their whole body into it. They are easily sidetracked onto a story that may or may not illustrate the point they are trying to make. Because of their enthusiasm, they are great team motivators. They are concerned about people and relationships. Their high levels of energy can come on strong at times and their focus is usually on the bigger picture, which means they sometimes miss the details or the proper order of things. These people find conflict or differences of opinion invigorating and love to engage in a spirited discussion. They love change and are constantly looking for new and exciting adventures.

E Tile phlegmatic person — cool and persevering — translates into the technical or systematic communication style. This style of communication is focused on facts and technical details. Phlegmatic people have an orderly, methodical way of approaching tasks, and their focus is very much on the task, not on the people, emotions, or concerns that the task may evoke. The focus is also more on the details necessary to accomplish a task. Sometimes the details overwhelm the big picture and focus needs to be brought back to the context of the task. People with this style think the facts should speak for themselves, and they are not as comfortable with conflict. They need time to adapt to change and need to understand both the logic of it and the steps involved.

F   The melancholic person who is softhearted and oriented toward doing things for others translates into the considerate or sympathetic communication style. A person with this communication style is focused on people and relationships. They are good listeners and do things for other people — sometimes to the detriment of getting things done for themselves. They want to solicit everyone's opinion and make sure everyone is comfortable with whatever is required to get the job done. At times this focus on others can distract from the task at hand. Because they are so concerned with the needs of others and smoothing over issues, they do not like conflict. They believe that change threatens the status quo and tends to make people feel uneasy, so people with this communication style, like phlegmatic people, need time to consider the changes in order to adapt to them.

G   The choleric temperament translates into the bold or direct style of communication. People with this style are brief in their communication — the fewer words the better. They are big picture thinkers and love to be involved in many things at once. They are focused on tasks and outcomes and often forget that the people involved in carrying out the tasks have needs. They don't do detail work easily and as a result can often underestimate how much time it takes to achieve the task. Because they are so direct, they often seem forceful and can be very intimidating to others. They usually would welcome someone challenging them. But most other styles are afraid to do so. They also thrive on change, the more the better.

H   A well-functioning team should have all of these communication styles for true effectiveness. All teams need to focus on the task, and they need to take care of relationships in order to achieve those tasks. They need the big picture perspective or the context of their work, and they need the details to be identified and taken care of for success. We all have aspects of each style within us. Some of us can easily move from one style to another and adapt our style to the needs of the situation at hand — whether the focus is on tasks or relationships. For others, a dominant style is very evident, and it is more challenging to see the situation from the perspective of another style.

I   The work environment can influence communication styles either by the type of work that is required or by the predominance of one style reflected in that environment. Some people use one style at work and another at home. The good news about communication styles is that we have the ability to develop flexibility in our styles. The greater the flexibility we have, the more skilled we usually are at handling possible and actual conflicts. Usually it has to be relevant to us to do so, either because we think it is important or because there are incentives in our environment to encourage it. The key is that we have to want to become flexible with our communication style. As Henry Ford said, 'Whether you think you can or you can't, you're right!'

Questions 35–39

Do the following statements agree with the information given in the passage?

In boxes 35–39 on your answer sheet, write

> **TRUE** if the statement agrees with the information
> **FALSE** if the statement contradicts the information
> **NOT GIVEN** if there is no information on this

35 It is believed that sanguine people do not like variety.

36 Melancholic and phlegmatic people have similar characteristics.

37 It is the sanguine personality that needed most in the workplace.

38 It is possible for someone to change type of personality.

39 Work surrounding can affect communication style by the required type of work.

Question 40

Choose the correct letter, **A**, **B**, **C** or **D**.

Write your answers in box 40 on your answer sheet.

40 The author thinks self-assessment tools can be able to

   A assist to develop one's personality in a certain scenario.
   B help to understand colleagues and resolve problems.
   C improve relationship with boss of company.
   D change others behaviour and personality.

TEST 4

READING PASSAGE 1

You should spend about 20 minutes on Questions 1–13, which are based on the passage below.

Hunting Perfume in Madagascar!

A Ever since the unguentari plied their trade in ancient Rome, perfumers have to keep abreast of changing fashions. These days they have several thousand ingredients to choose from when creating new scents, but there is always demand for new combinations. The bigger the 'palette' of smells, the better the perfumer's chance of creating something fresh and appealing. Even with everyday products such as shampoo and soap, kitchen cleaners and washing powders, consumers are becoming increasingly fussy. And many of today's fragrances have to survive tougher treatment than ever before, resisting the destructive power of bleach or a high temperature wash cycle. Chemists can create new smells from synthetic molecules, and a growing number of the odours on the perfumer's palette are artificial. But nature has been in the business far longer.

B The island of Madagascar is an evolutionary hot spot; 85% of its plants are unique, making it an ideal source for novel fragrances. Last October, Quest International, a company that develops fragrances for everything from the most delicate perfumes to cleaning products, sent an expedition to Madagascar in pursuit of some of nature's most novel fragrances. With some simple technology, borrowed from the pollution monitoring industry, and a fair amount of ingenuity, the perfume hunters bagged 20 promising new aromas in the Madagascan rainforest. Each day the team set out from their 'hotel' — a wooden hut lit by kerosene lamps, and trailed up and down paths and animal tracks, exploring the thick vegetation up to 10 metres on either side of the trail. Some smells came from obvious places, often big showy flowers within easy reach. Others were harder to pin down. 'Often it was the very small flowers that were much more interesting,' says Clery. After the luxuriance of the rainforest, the little-known island of Nosy Hara was a stark, dry place — geologically and biologically very different from the mainland. 'Apart from two beaches, the rest of the island is impenetrable, except by hacking through the bush,' says Clery. One of the biggest prizes here was a sweet-smelling sap weeping from the gnarled branches of some ancient shrubby trees in the parched interior. So far no one has been able to identify the plant.

C With most flowers or fruits, the hunters used a technique originally designed to trap and identify air pollutants. The technique itself is relatively simple. A glass bell jar or flask is fitted over the flower. The fragrance molecules are trapped in this 'headspace' and can be extracted by pumping the air out over a series of filters which absorb different types of volatile molecules. Back home in the laboratory, the molecules are flushed out of the filters and injected into a gas chromatograph for analysis. If it is impossible to attach the headspace gear, hunters fix an absorbent probe close to the source of the smell. The probe looks something like a hypodermic syringe, except that the 'needle' is made of silicone rubber which soaks up molecules from the air. After a few hours, the hunters retract the rubber needle and seal the tube, keeping the odour molecules inside until they can be injected into the gas chromatograph in the laboratory.

D Some of the most promising fragrances were those given off by resins that oozed from the bark of trees. Resins are the source of many traditional perfumes, including frankincense and myrrh. The most exciting resin came from a Calophyllum tree, which produces a strongly scented medicinal oil. The sap of this Calophyllum smelt rich and aromatic, a little like church incense. But it also smelt of something like fragrance industry has learnt to live without, castoreum, a substance extracted from the musk glands of beavers and once a key ingredient in many perfumes. The company does not use animal products any longer, but it was wonderful to find a tree with an animal smell.

E The group also set out from the island to capture the smell of coral reefs. Odours that conjure up sun kissed seas are highly sought after by the perfume industry. 'From the ocean, the only thing we have is seaweed, and that has a dark and heavy aroma. We hope to find something unique among the corals,' says Dir. The challenge for the hunters was to extract a smell from water rather than air. This was an opportunity to try Clery's new 'aquaspace' apparatus — a set of filters that work underwater. On Nosy Hara, jars were fixed over knobs of coral about 2 metres down and water was pumped out over the absorbent filters. So what does coral smell like? 'It's a bit like lobster and crab,' says Clery. The team's task now is to recreate the best of their captured smells. First they must identify the molecules that make up each fragrance. Some ingredients may be quite common chemicals. But some may be completely novel, or they may be too complex or expensive to make in the lab. The challenge then is to conjure up the fragrances with more readily available materials. 'We can avoid the need to import plants from the rainforest by creating the smell with a different set of chemicals from those in the original material,' says Clery. 'If we get it right, you can sniff the sample and it will transport you straight back to the moment you smelt it in the rainforest.'

Questions 1–5

Reading passage 1 has five paragraphs, **A–E**.

Which paragraph contains the following information?

Write the correct letter, **A–E**, in boxes 1–5 on your answer sheet.

NB   You may use any letter more than once.

1   One currently preferred spot to pick up plants for novel finding.

2   A new device designed for capturing a smell under water.

3   The demanding conditions for fragrance to endure.

4   A substitute for substance no longer available to the perfume manufacture.

5   Description of an outdoor expedition on land chasing new fragrances.

Questions 6–10

Do the following statements agree with the information given in the passage?

In boxes 6–10 on your answer sheet, write

>   **TRUE**   if the statement agrees with the information
>   **FALSE**   if the statement contradicts the information
>   **NOT GIVEN**   if there is no information on this

6   Manufacturers can choose to use synthetic odours for the perfume nowadays.

7   Madagascar is chosen to be a place for hunting plants which are rare in other parts of the world.

8   Capturing the smell is one of the most important things for creating new aromas.

9   The technique the hunters used to trap fragrance molecules is totally out of their ingenuity.

10   Most customers prefer the perfume made of substance extracted from the musk glands of animals.

Questions 11–13

Label the diagram below.

Choose **ONE WORD ONLY** from the passage for each answer.

Write your answer in boxes 11–13 on your answer sheet.

A simple device used to trap molecules

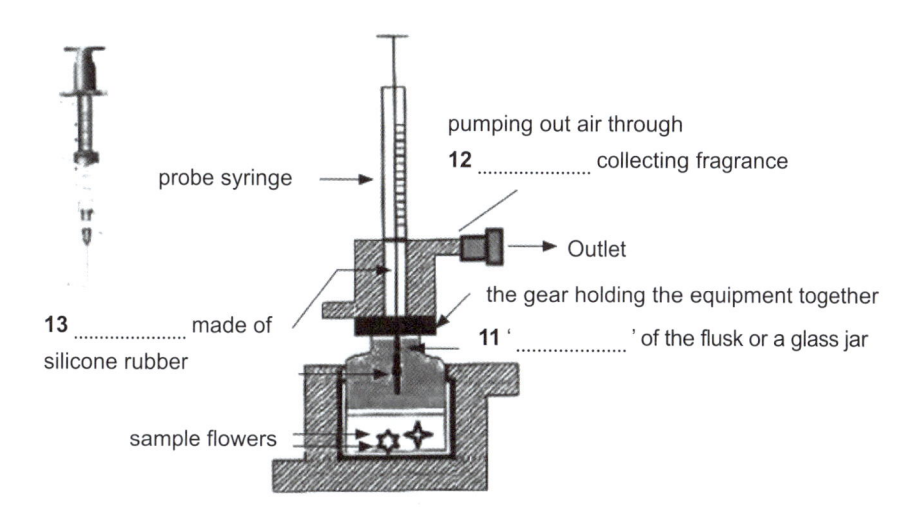

- probe syringe
- pumping out air through
- 12 .... collecting fragrance
- Outlet
- the gear holding the equipment together
- 11 '....................' of the flusk or a glass jar
- 13 .... made of silicone rubber
- sample flowers

389

READING PASSAGE 2

You should spend about 20 minutes on Questions 14–26, which are based on the passage below.

Questions 14–19

The reading passage has seven paragraphs, **A–G**.

*Choose the correct heading for paragraph **A–G** from the list below.*

*Write the correct number, **i–x**, in boxes 14–19 on your answer sheet.*

List of Headings

i   The search for the better-fit matching between the model and the gained figures to foresee the activities of the genes

ii   The definition of MEDUSA

iii   A flashback of a commencement for a far-reaching breakthrough

iv   A drawing of the gene map

v   An algorithm used to construct a specific model to discern the appearance of something new by the joint effort of Wiggins and another scientist

vi   An introduction of a background tracing back to the availability of mature techniques for detailed research on genes

vii   A way out to face the challenge confronting the scientist on the deciding of researchable data

viii   A failure to find out some specific genes controlling the production of certain proteins

ix   The use of a means from another domain for reference

x   A tough hurdle on the way to find the law governing the activities of the genes

---

Example	Answer
Paragraph **A**	iii

14   Paragraph **B**

15   Paragraph **C**

16   Paragraph **D**

17   Paragraph **E**

18   Paragraph **F**

19   Paragraph **G**

Life Code: Unlocked

A   On an airport shuttle bus to the Kavli Institute for Theoretical Physics in Santa Barbara, Calif, Chris Wiggins took a colleague's advice and opened a Microsoft Excel spreadsheet. It had nothing to do with the talk on biopolymer physics he was invited to give. Rather the columns and rows of numbers that stared back at him referred to the genetic activity of budding yeast. Specifically, the numbers represented the amount of messenger RNA (mRNA) expressed by all 6,200 genes of the yeast over the course of its reproductive cycle. 'It was the first time I ever saw anything like this,' Wiggins recalls of that spring day in 2002. 'How to make sense of all these data?'

B   Instead of shirking from this question, the 36-year-old applied mathematician and physicist at Columbia University embraced it — and now six years later he thinks he has an answer. By foraying into fields outside his own, Wiggins has drudged up tools from a branch of artificial intelligence called machine learning to model the collective proteinmaking activity of genes from real-world biological data. Engineers originally designed these tools in the late 1950s to predict output from input. Wiggins and his colleagues have now brought machine learning to the natural sciences and tweaked it so that it can also tell a story — one not only about input and output but also about what happens inside a model of gene regulation, the black box in between.

C   The impetus for this work began in the late 1990s, when high-throughput techniques generated more mRNA expression profiles and DNA sequences than ever before. 'Opening up a completely different way of thinking about biological phenomena,' Wiggins says. Key among these techniques were DNA microarrays, chips that provide a panoramic view of the activity of genes and their expression levels in any cell type, simultaneously and under myriad conditions. As noisy and incomplete as the data were, biologists could now query which genes turn on or off in different cells and determine the collection of proteins that give rise to a cell's characteristic features- healthy or diseased.

D   Yet predicting such gene activity requires uncovering the fundamental rules that govern it. 'Over time, these rules have been locked in by cells,' says theoretical physicist Harmen Bussemaker, now an associate professor of biology at Columbia. 'Evolution has kept the good stuff.' To find these rules, scientists needed statistics to infer the interaction between genes and the proteins that regulate them and to then mathematically describe this network's underlying structure — the dynamic pattern of gene and protein activity over time. But physicists who did not work with particles (or planets, for that matter) viewed statistics as nothing short of an anathema. 'If your experiment requires statistics,' British physicist Ernest Rutherford once said, 'you ought to have done a better experiment.'

E   But in working with microarrays, 'the experiment has been done without you,' Wiggins explains, 'And biology doesn't hand you a model to make sense of the data.' Even more challenging, the building blocks that make up DNA, RNA and proteins are assembled in myriad ways; moreover, subtly different rules of interaction govern their activity, making it difficult, if not impossible, to reduce their patterns of interaction to fundamental laws. Some genes and proteins are not even known. 'You are trying to find something compelling about the natural world in a context where you don't know very much,' says William Bialek, a biophysicist at Princeton University. 'You're forced to be agnostic.' 'Wiggins believes that many machine-learning algorithms perform precisely well under these conditions. When working with so many unknown variables, machine learning lets the data decide what's worth looking at,' he says.

F At the Kavli Institute, Wiggins began building a model of a gene regulatory network in yeast — the set of rules by which genes and regulators collectively orchestrate how DNA is vigorously transcribed into mRNA. As he worked with different algorithms, he started to attend discussions on gene regulation led by Christina Leslie, who ran the computational biology group at Columbia at the time. Leslie suggested using a specific machine-learning tool called a classifier. Say the algorithm must discriminate between pictures that have bicycles in them and pictures that do not. A classifier sifts through labeled examples and measures everything it can do about them, gradually learning the decision rules that govern the grouping. From these rules, the algorithm generates a model that can determine whether or not new pictures have bikes in them. In gene regulatory networks, the learning task becomes the problem of predicting whether genes increase or decrease their protein-making activity.

G The algorithm that Wiggins and Leslie began building in the fall of 2002 was trained on the DNA sequences and mRNA levels of regulators expressed during a range of conditions in yeast — when the yeast was cold, hot, starved, and so on. Specifically, this algorithm — MEDUSA (for motif element discrimination using sequence agglomeration) — scans every possible pairing between a set of DNA promoter sequences, called motifs, and regulators. Then, much like a child might match a list of words with their definitions by drawing a line between the two, MEDUSA finds the pairing that best improves the fit between the model and the data it tries to emulate. (Wiggins refers to these pairings as edges.) Each time MEDUSA finds a pairing, it updates the model by adding a new rule to guide its search for the next pairing. It then determines the strength of each pairing by how well the rule improves the existing model. The hierarchy of numbers enables Wiggins and his colleagues to determine which pairings are more important than others and how they can collectively influence the activity of each of the yeast's 6,200 genes. By adding one pairing at a time, MEDUSA can predict which genes ratchet up their RNA production or clamp that production down, as well as reveal the collective mechanisms that orchestrate an organism's transcriptional logic.

Questions 20–22

Do the following statements agree with the information given in the passage?

In boxes 20–22 on your answer sheet, write

> **TRUE** if the statement agrees with the information
> **FALSE** if the statement contradicts the information
> **NOT GIVEN** if there is no information on this

20 Wiggins is the first man to use DNA microarrays for the research on genes.

21 There is almost no possibility for the effort to decrease the patterns of interaction between DNA, RNA and proteins.

22 Wiggins holds a very positive attitude on the future of genetic research.

Questions 23–26

Complete the summary below.

Choose **NO MORE THAN THREE WORDS** from the passage for each answer.

Write your answers in boxes 23–26 on your answer sheet.

Wiggins states that the astoundingly rapid development of techniques concerning the components of genes aroused the researchers to look at **23** .... from a totally new way. **24** .... is the heart and soul of these techniques and no matter what the **25** .... were, at the same time they can offer a whole picture of the genes' activities as well as **26** .... in all types of cells. With these techniques scientists could locate the exact gene which was on or off to manipulate the production of the proteins.

Sunny Days for Silicon

A The old saw that 'the devil is in the details' characterises the kind of needling obstacles that prevent an innovative concept from becoming a working technology. It also often describes the type of problems that must be overcome to shave cost from the resulting product so that people will buy it. Emanuel Sachs of the Massachusetts Institute of Technology has struggled with many such little devils in his career-long endeavor to develop low-cost, high-efficiency solar cells. In his latest effort, Sachs has found incremental ways to boost the amount of electricity that common photovoltaics (PVs) generate from sunlight without increasing the costs. Specifically, he has raised the conversion efficiency of test cells made from multi-crystalline silicon from the typical 15.5 percent to nearly 20 percent — on par with pricier single-crystal silicon cells. Such improvements could bring the cost of PV power down from the current $1.90 to $2.10 per watt to $1.65 per watt. With additional tweaks, Sachs anticipates that creating within four years solar cells can be produced juice at a dollar per watt, a feat that would make electricity from the sun competitive with that from coal-burning power plants.

B Most PV cells, such as those on home rooftops, rely on silicon to convert sunlight into electric current. Metal interconnects then funnels the electricity out from the silicon to power devices or to feed an electrical grid. Since solar cells became practical and affordable three decades ago. Engineers have mostly favoured using single-crystal silicon as the active material, says Michael Rogol, managing director of Germany-based Photon Consulting. Wafers of the substance are typically sawed from an ingot consisting of one large crystal that has been pulled like taffy out of a vat of molten silicon. Especially at first, the high-purity ingots were left over from integrated-circuit manufacture, but later the process was used to make PV cells themselves, Rogol recounts. Although single-crystal cells offer high conversion efficiencies, they are expensive to make. The alternatives — multi-crystalline silicon cells, which factories fabricate from lower-purity, cast ingots composed of many smaller crystals — are cheaper to make, but unfortunately they are less efficient than single-crystal cells.

C Sachs, who has pioneered several novel ways to make silicon solar cells less costly and more effective, recently turned his focus to the details of multi-crystalline silicon cell manufacture. 'The first small improvement concerns the little silver fingers that gather electric current from the surface of the bulk silicon,' he explains. In conventional fabrication processes, cell manufacturers use screen-printing techniques ('like high-accuracy silk-screening of T-shirts,' Sachs notes) and inks containing silver particles to create these bus wires. The trouble is that standard silver wires come out wide and short, about 120 by 10 microns, and include many nonconductive voids. As a result, they block considerable sunlight and do not carry as much current as they should.

D   At his start-up company — Lexington, Mass-based 1,366 Technologies (the number refers to the flux of sunlight that strikes the earth's outer atmosphere: 1,366 watts per square metre) — Sachs is employing 'a proprietary wet' proces that can produce thinner and taller wires that are 20 by 20 microns. The slimmer bus wires use less costly silver and can be placed closer together so they can draw more current from the neighbouring active material, through which free electrons can travel only so far. At the same time, the wires block less incoming light than their standard counterparts.

E   The second innovation alters the wide, flat interconnect wires that collect current from the silver bus wires and electrically link adjacent cells. Interconnect wires at the top can shade as much as 5 per cent of the area of a cell. 'We place textured mirror surfaces on the faces of these rolled wires. These little mirrors reflect incoming light at a lower angle — around 30 degrees — so that when the reflected rays hit the glass layer at the top, they stay within the silicon wafer by way of total internal reflection,' Sachs explains. (Divers and snorkelers commonly see this optical effect when they view water surfaces from below.) The longer that light remains inside, the more chance it has to be absorbed and transformed into electricity.

F   Sachs expects that new antireflection coatings will further raise multi-crystalline cell efficiencies. One of his firm's future goals will be a switch from expensive silver bus wires to cheaper copper ones. And he has a few ideas regarding how to successfully make the substitution. 'Unlike silver, copper poisons the performance of silicon PVs,' Sachs says, 'so it will be crucial to include a low-cost diffusion barrier that stops direct contact between copper and the silicon.' In this business, it's always the little devilish details that count.

G   The cost of silicon solar cells is likely to fall as bulk silicon prices drop, according to the U.S. Energy Information Administration and the industry tracking firm Solarbuzz. A steep rise in solar panel sales in recent years had led to a global shortage of silicon because production capacity for the active material lagged behind, but now new silicon manufacturing plants are coming online. The reduced materials costs and resulting lower system prices will greatly boost demand for solar-electric technology, according to market watcher Michael Rogol of Photon Consulting.

Questions 27–31

Look at the following opinions or deeds (Questions 27–31) and the list of people below.

*Match each opinion or deed with the correct person, **A–C**.*

*Write the correct letter, **A–C**, in boxes 27–31 on your answer sheet.*

NB *You may use any letter more than once.*

27 Gives a brief account of the history of the common practice to manufacture silicon batteries for a long time.

28 Made a joint prediction with another national agency.

29 Established an enterprise with a meaningful name.

30 Led forward in the solar-electric field by reducing the cost while raising the efficiency.

31 Expects to lower the cost of solar cells to a level that they could contend with the traditional way to generate electricity.

List of People
A Emanuel Sach
B Michael Rogol
C Solarbuzz

Questions 32–35

Do the following statements agree with the information given in the passage?

In boxes 32–35 on your answer sheet, write

> **TRUE**   *if the statement agrees with the information*
> **FALSE**   *if the statement contradicts the information*
> **NOT GIVEN** *if there is no information on this*

32 Cells made from multi-crystalline silicon is cheaper than the single-crystalline silicon cells.

33 The multi-crystalline silicon cells are ideal substitutions for single-crystal cells.

34 Emanuel Sachs has some determining clues about the way to block the immediate contact between an alternative metal for silver and the silicon.

35 In the last few years, there is a sharp increase in the demand for solar panels.

Questions 36–40

Complete the summary below.

Choose **NO MORE THAN THREE WORDS** from the passage for each answer.

Write your answers in boxes 36–40 on your answer sheet.

Emanuel Sachs made two major changes to the particulars of the manufacture of **36** .... One is to take a **37** .... in the production of finer wires which means more current could be attracted from the **38** .... The other one is to set **39** .... above the interconnect silver bus wires to keep the incoming sunlight by **40** ....

TEST 5

READING PASSAGE 1

You should spend about 20 minutes on Questions 1–13, which are based on the passage below.

Coral Reefs

Coral reefs are underwater structures made from calcium carbonate secreted by corals. Coral reefs are colonies of tiny living animals found in marine waters that contain few nutrients. Most coral reefs are built from stony corals, which in turn consist of polyps that cluster in groups.

A Coral reefs are estimated to cover 284,300 km² just under 0.1% of the oceans' surface area, about half the area of France. The Indo-Pacific region accounts for 91.9% of this total area. Southeast Asia accounts for 32.3% of that figure, while the Pacific including Australia accounts for 40.8%. Atlantic and Caribbean coral reefs account for 7.6%. Yet often called 'rainforests of the sea', coral reefs form some of the most diverse ecosystems on Earth. They provide a home for 25% of all marine species, including fish, mollusks, worms, crustaceans, echinoderms, sponges, tunicates and other cnidarians. Paradoxically, coral reefs flourish even though they are surrounded by ocean waters that provide few nutrients. They are most commonly found at shallow depths in tropical waters, but deep water and cold water corals also exist on smaller scales in other areas. Although corals exist both in temperate and tropical waters, shallow-water reefs form only in a zone extending from 30°N to 30°S of the equator. Deep water coral can exist at greater depths and colder temperatures at much higher latitudes, as far north as Norway. Coral reefs are rare along the American and African west coasts. This is due primarily to upwelling and strong cold coastal currents that reduce water temperatures in these areas (respectively the Peru, Benguela and Canary streams). Corals are seldom found along the coastline of South Asia from the eastern tip of India (Madras) to the Bangladesh and Myanmar borders. They are also rare along the coast around northeastern South America and Bangladesh due to the freshwater release from the Amazon and Ganges Rivers, respectively.

B Coral reefs deliver ecosystem services to tourism, fisheries and coastline protection. The global economic value of coral reefs has been estimated at as much as US$375 billion per year. Coral reefs protect shorelines by absorbing wave energy, and many small islands would not exist without their reef to protect them.

C The value of reefs in biodiverse regions can be even higher. In parts of Indonesia and the Caribbean where tourism is the main use, reefs are estimated to be worth US$1 million per square kilometre, based on the cost of maintaining sandy beaches and the value of attracting snorkelers and scuba divers. Meanwhile, a recent study of the Great Barrier Reef in Australia found that the reef is worth more to the country as an intact ecosystem than an extractive reserve for fishing. Each year more than 1.8 million tourists visit the reef, spending an estimated AU$4.3 billion (Australian dollars) on reef-related industries from diving to boat rental to posh island resort stays. In the Caribbean, says UNEP, the net annual benefits from diver tourism was US$2 billion in 2000 with US$625 million spent directly on diving on reefs. Further, reef tourism is important source of employment, especially for some of the world's poorest people. UNEP says that of the estimated 30 million smallscale fishers in the developing world, most are dependent to a greater or lesser extent on coral reefs. In the Philippines, for example, more than one million small-scale fishers depend directly on coral reefs for their livelihoods. The report estimates that reef fisheries were worth between $15,000 and $150,000 per square kilometre a year, while fish caught for aquariums were worth $500 a kilogram against $6 for fish caught as food. The aquarium fish export industry supports around 50,000 people and generates some US$5.5 million a year in Sri Lanka along.

D Unfortunately, coral reefs are dying around the world. In particular, coral mining, agricultural and urban runoff, pollution (organic and inorganic), disease, and the digging of canals and access into islands and bays are localised threats to coral ecosystems. Broader threats are sea temperature rise, sea level rise and pH changes from ocean acidification, all associated with greenhouse gas emissions. Some current fishing practices are destructive and unsustainable. These include cyanide fishing, overfishing and blast fishing. Although cyanide fishing supplies live reef fish for the tropical aquarium market, most fish caught using this method are sold in restaurants, primarily in Asia, where live fish are prized for their freshness. To catch fish with cyanide, fishers dive down to the reef and squirt cyanide in coral crevices and on the fastmoving fish, to stun the fish making them easy to catch. Overfishing is another leading cause for coral reef degradation. Often, too many fish are taken from one reef to sustain a population in that area. Poor fishing practices, such as banging on the reef with sticks (muro-ami), destroy coral formations that normally function as fish habitat. In some instances, people fish with explosives (blast fishing), which blast apart the surrounding coral.

E Tourist resorts that empty their sewage directly into the water surrounding coral reefs contribute to coral reef degradation. Wastes kept in poorly maintained septic tanks can also leak into surrounding ground water, eventually seeping out to the reefs. Careless boating, diving, snorkeling and fishing can also damage coral reefs. Whenever people grab, kick, and walk on, or stir up sediment in the reefs, they contribute to coral reef destruction. Corals are also harmed or killed when people drop anchors on them or when people collect coral.

F To find answers for these problems, scientists and researchers study the various factors that impact reefs. The list includes the ocean's role as a carbon dioxide sink, atmospheric changes, ultraviolet light, ocean acidification, viruses, impacts of dust storms carrying agents to far flung reefs, pollutants, algal blooms and others. Reefs are threatened well beyond coastal areas. General estimates show approximately 10% of the world's coral reefs are dead. About 60% of the world's reefs are at risk due to destructive, humanrelated activities. The threat to the health of reefs is particularly strong in Southeast Asia, where 80% of reefs are endangered.

G In Australia, the Great Barrier Reef is protected by the Great Barrier Reef Marine Park Authority, and is the subject of much legislation, including a biodiversity action plan. Inhabitants of Ahus Island, Manus Province, Papua New Guinea, have followed a generations-old practice of restricting fishing in six areas of their reef lagoon. Their cultural traditions allow line fishing, but not net or spear fishing. The result is that both the biomass and individual fish sizes are significantly larger than in places where fishing is unrestricted.

Questions 1–6

The passage has seven paragraphs, **A–G**.

Which paragraph contains the following information?

Write the correct letter, **A–G**, in boxes 1–6 on your answer sheet.

NB You may use any letter more than once.

1 Geographical location of world's coral reef
2 How does coral reef benefit economy locally
3 The statistics of coral reefs economic significance
4 The listed reasons for declining number of coral reef
5 Physical approach to coral reef by people
6 Unsustainable fishing methods are applied in regions of the world

Questions 7–12

Do the following statement agree with the information given in the passage?

In boxes 7–12 on your answer sheet, write

> **TRUE** if the statement agrees with the information
> **FALSE** if the statement contradicts the information
> **NOT GIVEN** if there is no information on this

7 Coral reefs provide habitat to variety of marine life.
8 Coral reefs distribute around the ocean disproportionally.
9 Coral reef is increasingly important for scientific purpose.
10 Coral reefs are greatly exchanged among and exported to other countries.
11 Reef tourism is of economic essence generally for some poor people.
12 As with other fishing business, coral fishery is not suitable to women and children.

Question 13

*Choose the correct letter, **A**, **B**, **C** or **D**.*

Write your answers in box 13 on your answer sheet.

13 What is the main purpose of this passage?

- **A** To demonstrate how coral reefs grow in the ocean
- **B** To tell that coral reef is widely used as a scientific project
- **C** To present the general benefits and an alarming situation of coral reef
- **D** To show the vital efforts made to protect coral reef in Australia

Can Scientists Tell Us: What Happiness Is?

A   Economists accept that if people describe themselves as happy, then they are happy. However, psychologists differentiate between levels of happiness. The most immediate type involves a feeling; pleasure or joy. But sometimes happiness is a judgment that life is satisfying, and does not imply an emotional state. Esteemed psychologist Martin Seligman has spearheaded an effort to study the science of happiness. The bad news is that we're not wired to be happy. The good news is that we can do something about it. Since its origins in a Leipzig laboratory 130 years ago, psychology has had little to say about goodness and contentment. Mostly psychologists have concerned themselves with weakness and misery. There are libraries full of theories about why we get sad, worried, and angry. It hasn't been respectable science to study what happens when lives go well. Positive experiences, such as joy, kindness, altruism and heroism, have mainly been ignored. For every 100 psychology papers dealing with anxiety or depression, only one concerns a positive trait.

B   A few pioneers in experimental psychology bucked the trend. Professor Alice Isen of Cornell University and colleagues have demonstrated how positive emotions make people think faster and more creatively. Showing how easy it is to give people an intellectual boost, Isen divided doctors making a tricky diagnosis into three groups: one received candy, one read humanistic statements about medicine, one was a control group. The doctors who had candy displayed the most creative thinking and worked more efficiently. Inspired by Isen and others, Seligman got stuck in. He raised millions of dollars of research money and funded 50 research groups involving 150 scientists across the world. Four positive psychology centres opened, decorated in cheerful colours and furnished with sofas and baby-sitters. There were get-togethers on Mexican beaches where psychologists would snorkel and eat fajitas, then form 'pods' to discuss subjects such as wonder and awe. A thousand therapists were coached in the new science.

C   But critics are demanding answers to big questions. What is the point of defining levels of happiness and classifying the virtues? Aren't these concepts vague and impossible to pin down? Can you justify spending funds to research positive states when there are problems such as famine, flood and epidemic depression to be solved? Seligman knows his work can be belittled alongside trite notions such as 'the power of positive thinking'. His plan to stop the new science floating 'on the waves of self-improvement fashions' is to make sure it is anchored to positive philosophy above, and to positive biology below.

D   And this takes us back to our evolutionary past. Homo sapiens evolved during the Pleistocene era (1.8 m to 10,000 years ago), a time of hardship and turmoil. It was the

Ice Age, and our ancestors endured long freezes as glaciers formed, then ferocious floods as the ice masses melted. We shared the planet with terrifying creatures such as mammoths, elephant-sized ground sloths and sabre-toothed cats. But by the end of the Pleistocene, all these animals were extinct. Humans, on the other hand, had evolved large brains and used their intelligence to make fire and sophisticated tools, to develop talk and social rituals. Survival in a time of adversity forged our brains into a persistent mould. Professor Seligman says: 'Because our brain evolved during a time of ice, flood and famine, we have a catastrophic brain. The way the brain works is looking for what's wrong. The problem is that, worked in the Pleistocene era, it favoured you, but it doesn't work in the modern world.'

E   Although most people rate themselves as happy, there is a wealth of evidence to show that negative thinking is deeply ingrained in the human psyche. Experiments show that we remember failures more vividly than successes. We dwell on what went badly, not what went well. Of the six universal emotions, four anger, fear, disgust and sadness are negative and only one, joy, is positive. The sixth is, surprise. THE is psychologist Daniel Nettle, author of Happiness, and one of the Royal Institution lecturers, believes that the negative emotions each tell us 'something bad has happened' and suggest a different course of action.

F   What is it about the structure of the brain that underlies our bias towards negative thinking? And is there a biology of joy? At Iowa University, neuroscientists studied what happens when people are shown pleasant and unpleasant pictures. When subjects see landscapes or dolphins playing, part of the frontal lobe of the brain becomes active. But when they are shown unpleasant images like a bird covered in oil, or a dead soldier with part of his face missing, the response comes from more primitive parts of the brain. The ability to feel negative emotions derives from an ancient danger-recognition system formed early in the brain's evolution. The pre-frontal cortex, which registers happiness, is the part used for higher thinking, an area that evolved later in human history.

G   Our difficulty, according to Daniel Nettle, is that the brain systems for liking and wanting are separate. Wanting involves two ancient regions, the amygdala and the nucleus accumbens that communicate using the chemical dopamine to form the brain's reward system. They are involved in anticipating the pleasure of eating and in addiction to drugs. A rat will press a bar repeatedly, ignoring sexually available partners, to receive electrical stimulation of the 'wanting' parts of the brain. But having received brain stimulation, the rat eats more but shows no sign of enjoying the food it craved. In humans, a drug like nicotine produces much craving but little pleasure.

H   In essence, what the biology lesson tells us is that negative emotions are fundamental to the human condition, and it's no wonder they are difficult to eradicate. At the same time, by a trick of nature, our brains are designed to crave but never really achieve lasting happiness.

Questions 14–20

The reading passage has seven paragraphs, **A–H**.

Which paragraph contains the following information?

*Write the correct letter, **A–H**, in boxes 14–20 on your answer sheet.*

14   an experiment involving dividing several groups one of which received positive icon

15   review of a poorly researched psychology area

16   contrast being made about the brain's action as response to positive or negative stimulus

17   the skeptical attitude toward the research seemed to be a waste of fund

18   a substance that produces much wanting instead of much liking

19   a conclusion that lasting happiness is hardly obtained because of the nature of brains

20   one description that listed the human emotional categories

Questions 21–25

Complete the summary below.

Choose **NO MORE THAN FOUR WORDS** *from the passage for each answer.*

Write your answers in boxes 21–35 on your answer sheet.

A few pioneers in experimental psychology study what happens when lives go well. Professor Alice divided doctors, making a tricky experiment, into three groups: besides the one control group, the other two either are asked to read humanistic statements about drugs, or received **21** .... The latter displayed the most creative thinking and worked more efficiently. Since critics are questioning the significance of the **22** .... for both levels of happiness and classification for the virtues. Professor Seligman countered in an evolutionary theory: survival in a time of adversity forged our brains into the way of thinking for what's wrong because we have a **23** ....

There is bountiful of evidence to show that negative thinking is deeply built in the human psyche. Later, at Iowa University, neuroscientists studied the active parts in brains to contrast when people are shown pleasant and unpleasant pictures. When positive images like **24** .... are shown, part of the frontal lobe of the brain becomes active. But when they are shown unpleasant image, the response comes from **25** .... of the brain.

Question 26

*Choose the correct letter, **A**, **B**, **C** or **D**.*

Write the correct letter in box 26 on your answer sheet.

26 According to Daniel Nettle in the last two paragraphs, what is true as the scientists can tell us about happiness?

    A Brain systems always mix liking and wanting together.
    B Negative emotions can be easily rid of if we think positively.
    C Happiness is like nicotine we are craving for but get little pleasure.
    D The inner mechanism of human brains does not assist us to achieve durable happiness.

READING PASSAGE 3

You should spend about 20 minutes on Questions 27–40, which are based on the passage below.

Changes in Air

A   A federal ban on ozone-depleting chlorofluorocarbons (CFCs), to conform with the Clean Air Act, is, ironically, affecting 22.9 million people in the U.S. who suffer from asthma. Generic inhaled albuterol, which is the most commonly prescribed short-acting asthma medication and requires CFCs to propel it into the lungs, will no longer be legally sold after December 31, 2008. Physicians and patients are questioning the wisdom of the ban, which will have an insignificant effect on ozone but a measurable impact on wallets: the reformulated brand-name alternatives can be three times as expensive, raising the cost to about $40 per inhaler. The issue is even more disconcerting considering that asthma disproportionately affects the poor and that, according to recent surveys, an estimated 20 percent of asthma patients are uninsured.

B   'The decision to make the change was political, not medical or scientific,' says pharmacist Leslie Hendeles of the University of Florida, who co-authored a 2007 paper in the *New England Journal of Medicine* explaining the withdrawal and transition. In 1987 Congress signed on to the Montreal Protocol on Substances That Deplete the Ozone Layer, an international treaty requiring the phasing out of all nonessential uses of CFCs. At that time, medical inhalers were considered an essential use because no viable alternative propellant existed. In 1989 pharmaceutical companies banded together and eventually, in 1996, reformulated albuterol with hydrofluoroalkane.

C   The transition began quietly, but as more patients see their prescriptions change and costs go up, many question why this ban must begin before generics become available. At least one member of the FDA advisory committee, Nicholas J. Gross of the Stritch-Loyola School of Medicine, has publicly regretted the decision, recanting his support and requesting that the ban be pushed back until 2010, when the first patent expires.

D   Gross notes that the decision had nothing to do with the environment. Albuterol inhalers contributed less than 0.1 percent of the CFCs released when the treaty was signed. 'It's a symbolic issue,' Gross remarks. Some skeptics instead point to the billions of dollars to be gained by the three companies holding the patents on the available HFA albuterol inhalers, namely Glaxo-SmithKline, Schering-Plough and Teva. Although the FDA advisory committee recognised that the expenses would go up, Hendeles says, it also believed that the companies would help defray the added costs for individuals. Firms, for instance, had committed to donating a million HFA inhalers to clinics around the country. According to Hendeles, GlaxoSmithKline did not follow through, although Schering-Plough and Teva did. GlaxoSmithKline did not respond to requests for comment.

E   The issue now, Hendeles says, is that pharmaceutical-grade CFCs are in short supply, and the public faces the risk of a shortage of albuterol inhalers if the FDA does not continue promoting the production of HFA inhalers. He posits that even costs of generics would go up as CFCs become scarcer. Gross disagrees, saying that the inhaler shortage and the closure of CFC manufacturing plants are a result of the ban.

F   The HFA inhalers also have encountered resistance because some asthmatics insist that they do not work as well as the CFC variety. But, Hendeles says, the differences are in the mechanics and maintenance — unlike CFC inhalers, the HFA versions must be primed more diligently and rinsed to accommodate the stickier HFA formulation. They also run out suddenly without the warning with a CFC inhaler, that the device is running low. 'Pharmacists may not tell people of these things, and the doctors don't know,' Hendeles says.

G   The main public health issue in this decision may be the side effects of the economics, not the drug chemistry. Multiple studies have shown that raising costs leads to poorer adherence to treatment. One study discovered that patients took 30 percent less antiasthma medication when their co-pay doubled. In the case of a chronic disease such as asthma, it is particularly difficult to get people to follow regular treatment plans. 'Generally speaking, for any reason you don't take medication, cost makes it more likely that you do not,' comments Michael Chemew, a health policy expert at Harvard Medical School.

H   Such choices to forgo medication could affect more than just the patients themselves. 'For example,' Hendeles points out, 'in a pregnant mother with untreated asthma, less oxygen is delivered to the fetus, which can lead to congenital problems and premature birth.' And considering that the disease disproportionately strikes the poor, what seemed to be a good, responsible environmental decision might in the end exact an unexpected human toll.

Questions 27–31

Look at the following opinions or deeds (Questions 27–31) and the list of people below.

Match each opinion or deed with the correct person, **A–C**.

Write the correct letter, **A–C**, in boxes 27–31 on your answer sheet.

NB   You may use any letter more than once.

27   Put forward that the increase in the price of drugs would contribute to the patients' negative decision on the treatment.

28   Spoke out a secret that the druggists try to hold back.

29   Pointed out that the protocol itself is not concerning the environment.

30   Demonstrated that the stop of providing alternatives for CFCs would worsen rather than help with the situation.

31   In public repented of his previous backing up of the prohibition proposal.

List of People

A	Nicholas J. Gross
B	Michael Cherncw
C	Leslie Hendeles

Questions 32–35

Do the following statements agree with the information given in the passage?

In boxes 32–35 on your answer sheet, write

> **TRUE**   if the statement agrees with the information
> **FALSE**   if the statement contradicts the information
> **NOT GIVEN**   if there is no information on this

32   It took almost a decade before the replacement drug for the asthma therapy was ultimately developed by the joint effort of several drug companies.

33   One of the FDA committee members had a decisive impact on the implement of the ban on chlorofluorocarbons.

34   As a matter of fact, the emitted chlorofluorocarbons in asthma treatment took up quite an insignificant amount at the time when the pact was reached.

35   The HFA and CFC inhalers have something different regarding the therapeutic effect.

Questions 36–40

Complete the summary below.

Choose **NO MORE THAN THREE WORDS** from the passage for each answer.

Write your answers in boxes 36–40 on your answer sheet.

American people with asthma would be impacted by **36** .... about chlorofluorocarbons which would consume the ozone layer. The usually used **37** .... would be considered illegal because it needs the propelment of **38** .... The **39** .... would cost the patients considerably more money. Impoverished people are far more likely to suffer from asthma and what makes it even worse is that some of them are in **40** .... condition.

第二章　机经套题解析

TEST 1

READING PASSAGE 1

参考答案

1	FALSE	2	FALSE	3	TRUE
4	NOT GIVEN	5	TRUE	6	H
7	I	8	D	9	H
10	E	11	physical	12	Capture or shortage
13	blue-water sources				

Crisis! Fresh Water

A As in New Delhi and Phoenix, policymakers worldwide wield great power over how water resources are managed. Wise use of such power will become increasingly important as the years go by because the world's demand for freshwater is currently overtaking its ready supply in many places, and this situation shows no sign of abating. (1)

B That the problem is well-known makes it no less disturbing: today one out of six people, more than a billion, suffer inadequate access to safe freshwater. (2) By 2025, according to data released by the United Nations, the freshwater resources of more than half the countries across the globe will undergo either stress — for example, when people increasingly demand more water than is available or safe for use — or outright shortages. By mid-century as much as three quarters of the earth's population could face scarcities of freshwater.

C Scientists expect water scarcity to become more common in large part because the world's population is rising and many people are getting richer (thus expanding demand) and because global climate change is exacerbating aridity and reducing supply in many regions. (3/4) What is more, many water sources are threatened by faulty waste disposal, releases of industrial pollutants, fertiliser runoff and coastal influxes of saltwater into aquifers as groundwater is depleted.

D Because lack of access to water can lead to starvation, disease, political instability and even armed conflict, failure to take action can have broad and grave consequences. Fortunately, to a great extent, the technologies and policy tools required to conserve existing freshwater and to secure more of it are known among which several seem particularly effective. What is needed now is action. Governments and authorities at every level have to formulate and execute concrete plans for implementing the political, economic and technological measures that can ensure water security now and in the coming decades. (8)

E The world's water problems requires, as a start, an understanding of how much freshwater each person requires, along with knowledge of the factors that impede supply and increase demand in different parts of the world. Malin Falkenmark of the Stockholm International Water Institute and other experts estimate that, on average, each person on the earth needs a minimum of 1,000 cubic metres (m³) of water. (10) The minimum water each person requires for drinking, hygiene and growing food. The volume is equivalent to two fifths of an Olympic-size swimming pool.

F Much of the Americas and northern Eurasia enjoy abundant water supplies. But several regions are beset by greater or lesser degrees of 'physical' scarcity — whereby demand exceeds local availability. (11) Other areas, among them Central Africa, parts of the Indian subcontinent and Southeast Asia, contend with 'economic' water scarcity, where lack of technical training, bad governments or weak finances limit access even though sufficient supplies are available.

G More than half of the precipitation that falls on land is never available for capture or storage because it evaporates from the ground or transpires from plants; (12) this fraction is called green water. The remainder channels into so-called blue-water sources — rivers, lakes, wetlands and aquifers — that people can tap directly. (13) Farm irrigation from these free-flowing bodies is the biggest single human use of freshwater. Cities and industries consume only tiny amounts of total freshwater resources, but the intense local demand they create often drains the surroundings of ready supplies.

Lots of Water, but not always where it is needed one hundred and ten thousand cubic kilometres of precipitation, nearly 10 times the volume of Lake Superior, falls from the sky onto the earth's land surface every year. This huge quantity would be enough to easily fulfil the requirements of everyone on the planet if the water arrived where and when people needed it. (9) But much of it cannot be captured (top), and the rest is distributed unevenly (bottom). (6) Green water (61.1% of total precipitation*): absorbed by soil and plants, then released back into the air; unavailable for withdrawal. Blue water (38.8% of total precipitation*): collected in rivers, lakes, wetlands and groundwater; available for withdrawal before it evaporates or reaches the ocean. These figures may not add up to 100% because of rounding. Only 1.5% is directly used by people.

Waters run away in tremendous wildfires in recent years. The economic actors had all taken their share reasonably enough; they just did not consider the needs of the natural environment, which suffered greatly when its inadequate supply was reduced to critical levels by drought. (7) The members of the Murray-Darling Basin Commission are now frantically trying to extricate themselves from the disastrous results of their misallocation of the total water resource. Given the difficulties of sensibly apportioning the water supply within a single nation, imagine the complexities of doing so for international river basins such as that of the Jordan River, which borders on Lebanon, Syria, Israel, the Palestinian areas and Jordan, all of which have claims to the shared, but limited, supply in an extremely parched region. The struggle for freshwater has contributed to civil and military disputes in the area. Only continuing negotiations and compromise have kept this tense situation under control. (5)

核心词汇

A 段

overtake [ˌəʊvəˈteɪk] *v.* 赶上；超车

abate [əˈbeɪt] *v.* 使减少；使缓和；废除（法律）

B 段

undergo [ˌʌndəˈgəʊ] *v.* 经历，经受；忍受

outright [ˈaʊtraɪt] *adj.* 完全的，彻底的

scarcity [ˈskeəsəti] *n.* 不足；缺乏

C 段

aridity [əˈrɪdəti] *n.* 干旱；乏味

disposal [dɪˈspəʊzl] *n.* 处理；支配；清理；安排

runoff [ˈrʌnɒf] *n.* 径流；决赛

D 段

starvation [stɑːˈveɪʃn] *n.* 饿死；挨饿

conflict [ˈkɒnflɪkt] *n.* 冲突，矛盾；斗争；争执

execute [ˈeksɪkjuːt] *v.* 实行；执行；处死

E 段

hygiene [ˈhaɪdʒiːn] *n.* 卫生；卫生学

equivalent [ɪˈkwɪvələnt] *adj.* 等价的，相等的；同意义的

F 段

abundant [əˈbʌndənt] *adj.* 丰富的；充裕的；盛产的

availability [əˌveɪləˈbɪləti] *n.* 可用性；有效性；实用性

subcontinent [ˌsʌbˈkɒntɪnənt] *n.* 次大陆

G 段

precipitation [prɪˌsɪpɪˈteɪʃn] *n.* 降水；降水量；沉淀，沉淀物

irrigation [ˌɪrɪˈgeɪʃn] *n.* 灌溉；冲洗；冲洗法

H 段

distribute [dɪˈstrɪbjuːt] *v.* 分配；散布

I 段

tremendous [trəˈmendəs] *adj.* 极大的，巨大的；惊人的
disastrous [dɪˈzɑːstrəs] *adj.* 灾难性的；损失惨重的；悲伤的
complexity [kəmˈpleksəti] *n.* 复杂，复杂性；复杂错综的事物
negotiation [nɪˌɡəʊʃiˈeɪʃn] *n.* 谈判；协商

淡水资源危机

A 就像在新德里和凤凰城一样,世界各地的政策制定者对水资源的管理行使巨大的权力。随着时间的推移,明智地行使这种权力将变得越来越重要,因为目前在许多地方世界对淡水的需求正在超过其现有供给,而且这种情况并没有减弱的迹象。

B 这个问题是众所周知的,但依然让人感到不安:今天,六分之一的人口(超过10亿人)无法获得充足的、安全的淡水。根据联合国发布的数据,到2025年,全球一半以上的国家的淡水资源或将承受压力——例如,当人们对用水的需求越来越多,超过现有的或者安全的河用水时,或甚至将完全短缺。到本世纪中叶,多达四分之三的地球人口将面临淡水资源短缺的问题。

C 科学家们预计,水资源短缺将在很大程度上变得更加普遍,因为世界人口正在增长,许多人变得更加富有(从而扩大了需求),而且全球气候变化正在加剧许多地区的干旱,减少了水资源的供应。更严重的是,随着地下水枯竭,许多水源受到不良废物处理方法、工业污染物排放、肥料流失和海水流入含水层的威胁。

D 由于缺乏水资源可能导致饥饿、疾病、政治不稳定甚至武装冲突,不采取行动可能会产生广泛而严重的后果。幸运的是,在很大程度上,保护现存淡水和确保获取更多的淡水所需的技术和政策工具已被了解,并且其中一些似乎特别有效。现在需要的就是行动。各级政府和有关部门必须制订和执行具体的计划,以实施政治、经济和技术措施,来确保现在和未来几十年的水资源安全。

E 首先,关于世界上的水源问题,需要了解每个人需要多少淡水,同时还要了解阻碍世界各地淡水供应和增加淡水需求的因素。斯德哥尔摩国际水资源研究所的马林·法尔肯马克和其他专家估计,地球上的每个人平均需要至少1,000立方米的水。每个人所需的最低水量包括饮用水、卫生用水和种植粮食用水。这个体积相当于一个奥运会游泳池容量的五分之二的水。

F 美洲和欧亚大陆北部的大部分地区都有丰富的水源供应。但是,一些地区会受到或多或少的"物理性"稀缺程度的困扰,即需求超过了当地的可用水量。其他地区,包括中非、印度次大陆和东南亚的部分地区,都在与"经济性"水资源短缺作斗争。即便有足够的供应,但那里技术培训的缺乏、糟糕的政府或贫穷的财政状况,也限制了水资源的获取。

G 因为地表蒸发或植物蒸腾作用,落在陆地上的超过一半的降水,是永远无法捕获或储存的,这部分水被称为绿色水。剩下的进入所谓的蓝色水源——河流、湖泊、湿地和地下蓄水层——人们可以直接利用这部分水资源。利用这些自由流动的水体进行农业灌溉是人类消耗淡水最大的部分。城市和工业消耗的淡水资源只是很少一部分,但它们所创造的强大的当地需求往往会消耗掉周围的现有供应。

H 大量的水(但并不总是需要11.5万千立方千米的降水,几乎是苏比略湖的10倍),每年从天上落到地球的陆地表面。这个巨大的降水量足以轻松满足地球上每个人的需求——如果水降到了人们需要的地方而且正是人们需要的时候。但是其中的大部分不能被捕获(顶部),而剩下的分布是不均匀的(底部)。绿色水(占总降水量的61.1%)被土壤和植物吸收,然后释放回空气中,无法提取利用。蓝色水(占总降水量的38.8%)汇集于河流、湖泊、湿地和地下水,可以在它蒸发或流入海洋之前进行提取利用。由于四舍五入,这些数字可能加起来无法达到百分之百。只有1.5%被人类直接使用。

近年来，洪水在大火中肆虐。经济参与者们都已经足够合理地利用了他们的份额；他们只是没有考虑到自然环境的需要——由于干旱，水资源供应不足，锐减到临界水平，自然环境遭到重创。墨累–达令流域委员会的成员们现在正疯狂地试图从他们的水资源分配不当的灾难性后果中解脱出来。考虑到在一个国家内明智地分配水资源供应的困难，想象一下国际河流流域这样做的复杂性，比如约旦河，与黎巴嫩、叙利亚、以色列、巴勒斯坦地区，约旦的接壤，所有这几个国家都要求在极其干旱的地区共享有限的水资源。对淡水的争夺导致了该地区的民事和军事纠纷。只有持续的谈判和妥协才能使这种紧张局势得到控制。

READING PASSAGE 2

参考答案

14	nitrogen	15	(long) sensitive bristles	16	trails
17	tufts	18	TRUE	19	FALSE
20	NOT GIVEN	21	FALSE	22	NOT GIVEN
23	Dolphin	24	Seagrass availability	25	1,750
26	Fishing net				

The Dugong: Sea Cow

Dugongs are herbivorous mammals that spend their entire lives in the sea. Their close relatives the manatees also venture into or live in fresh water. Together dugongs and manatees make up the order sirenia or sea cows, so-named because dugongs and manatees are thought to have given rise to the myth of the mermaids or sirens of the sea.

A The dugong, which is a large marine mammal which, together with the manatees, looks rather like a cross between a rotund dolphin and a walrus. Its body, flippers and fluke resemble those of a dolphin but it has no dorsal fin. (23) Its head looks somewhat like that of a walrus without the long tusks.

B Dugongs, along with other Sirenians, their diet consists mainly of sea-grass; and the distribution of dugongs very closely follows that of these marine flowering plants. As sea grasses grow rooted in the sediment, they are limited by the availability of light. Consequently they are found predominantly in shallow coastal waters, and so too are dugongs. But, this is not the whole story. Dugongs do not eat all species of seagrass, preferring seagrass of higher nitrogen and lower fibre content. (14)

C Due to their poor eyesight, dugongs often use smell to locate edible plants. They also have a strong tactile sense, and feel their surroundings with their long sensitive bristles. (15) They will dig up an entire plant and then shake it to remove the sand before eating it. The flexible and muscular upper lip is used to dig out the plants. When eating they ingest the whole plant, including the roots, although when this is impossible they will feed on just the leaves. (18) A wide variety of seagrass has been found in dugong stomach contents, and evidence exists they will eat algae when seagrass is scarce. Although almost completely herbivorous, they will occasionally eat invertebrates such as jellyfish, sea squirts, and shellfish.

D A heavily grazed seagrass bed looks like a lawn mown by a drunk. Dugongs graze apparently at random within a seagrass bed, their trails meandering in all directions across the bottom. (16) This is rather an inefficient means of removing seagrass that results in numerous small tufts remaining. And this is where the dugongs derive some advantage from their inefficiency. The species that recover most quickly from this disturbance, spreading out vegetative from the remaining tufts, are those that dugongs like to eat. (17&19) In addition, the new growth found in these areas tends to be exactly what hungry dugongs like.

E Dugongs are semi-nomadic, often travelling long distances in search of food, but staying within a certain range their entire life. Large numbers often move together from one area to another. It is thought that these movements are caused by changes in seagrass availability. (24) Their memory allows them to return to specific points after long travels. (21) Dugong movements mostly occur within a localised area of seagrass beds, and animals in the same region show individualistic patterns of movement.

F Recorded numbers of dugongs are generally believed to be lower than actual numbers, due to a lack of accurate surveys. Despite this, the dugong population is thought to be shrinking, with a worldwide decline of 20 per cent in the last 90 years. They have disappeared from the waters of Hong Kong, Mauritius, and Taiwan, as well as parts of Cambodia, Japan, the Philippines and Vietnam. Further disappearances are likely. In the late 1960s, herds of up to 500 dugongs were observed off the coast of East Africa and nearby islands. However, current populations in this area are extremely small, numbering 50 and below, and it is thought likely they will become extinct. The eastern side of the Red Sea is the home of large populations numbering in the hundreds, and similar populations are thought to exist on the western side. In the 1980s, it was estimated there could be as many as 4,000 dugongs in the Red Sea. The Persian Gulf has the second-largest dugong population in the world, inhabiting most of the southern coast, and the current population is believed to be around 7,500. Australia is home to the largest population, stretching from Shark Bay in Western Australia to Moreton Bay in Queensland. The population of Shark Bay is thought to be stable with over 10,000 dugongs.

G Experience from various parts of northern Australia suggests that extreme weather such as cyclones and floods can destroy hundreds of square kilometres of seagrass meadows, as well as washing dugongs ashore. The recovery of seagrass meadows and the spread of seagrass into new areas, or areas where it has been destroyed, can take over a decade. For example, about 900 km^2 of seagrass was lost in Hervey Bay in 1992, probably because of murky water from flooding of local rivers, and run-off turbulence from a cyclone three weeks later. Such events can cause extensive damage to seagrass communities through severe wave action, shifting sand and reduction in saltiness and light levels. Prior to the 1992 floods, the extensive seagrasses in Hervey Bay supported an estimated 1,750 dugongs. (25) Eight months after the floods the affected area was estimated to support only about 70 dugongs. Most animals presumably survived by moving to neighbouring areas. However, many died attempting to move to greener pastures, with emaciated carcasses washing up on beaches up to 900km away.

H If dugongs do not get enough to eat they may calve later and produce fewer young. Food shortages can be caused by many factors, such as a loss of habitat, death and decline in quality of seagrass, and a disturbance of feeding caused by human activity. Sewage, detergents, heavy metal, hypersaline water, herbicides, and other waste products all negatively affect seagrass meadows. Human activity such as mining, trawling, dredging, land-reclamation, and boat propeller scarring also cause an increase in sedimentation which smothers seagrass and prevents light from reaching it. This is the most significant negative factor affecting seagrass. One of the dugong's preferred species of seagrass, Halophila ovalis, declines rapidly due to lack of light, dying completely after 30 days.

I Despite being legally protected in many countries, the main causes of population decline remain anthropogenic and include hunting, habitat degradation, and fishing-related fatalities. (22) Entanglement in fishing nets has caused many deaths, although there are no precise statistics. (26) Most issues with industrial fishing occur in deeper waters where dugong populations are low, with local fishing being the main risk in shallower waters. As dugongs cannot stay underwater for a very long period, they are highly prone to deaths due to entanglement. The use of shark nets has historically caused large numbers of deaths, and they have been eliminated in most areas and replaced with baited hooks.

核心词汇

A 段

marine [məˈriːn] *adj.* 海的，海洋的
mammal [ˈmæml] *n.* 哺乳动物
resemble [rɪˈzembl] *v.* 像，相似

B 段

distribution [ˌdɪstrɪˈbjuːʃn] *n.* 分布；分配
sediment [ˈsedɪmənt] *n.* 沉积；沉积物
predominantly [prɪˈdɒmɪnəntli] *adv.* 占主导地

C 段

edible [ˈedəbl] *adj.* 可食的
tactile [ˈtæktaɪl] *adj.* 有触觉的
ingest [ɪnˈdʒest] *v.* 咽下；吸收

D 段

graze [ɡreɪz] *v.* 放牧；（让动物）吃草
inefficient [ˌɪnɪˈfɪʃnt] *adj.* 无效率的；徒劳的
disturbance [dɪˈstɜːbəns] *n.* 干扰，打扰

E 段

availability [əˌveɪləˈbɪləti] *n.* 可利用性；可得到的东西；有效
pattern [ˈpætn] *n.* 模式

F 段

shrink [ʃrɪŋk] *v.* 减少
disappearance [ˌdɪsəˈpɪərəns] *n.* 消失
extinct [ɪkˈstɪŋkt] *adj.* 灭绝的

G 段

murky [ˈmɜːki] *adj.* 混浊的；脏的；阴暗的
turbulence [ˈtɜːbjələns] *n.* 湍流，骚乱
presumably [prɪˈzjuːməbli] *adv.* 大概

H 段

sewage [ˈsuːɪdʒ] *n.* 污水；下水道
trawl [trɔːl] *v.* 拖网捕鱼
reclamation [ˌrekləˈmeɪʃn] *n.* 开垦；开拓

I 段

anthropogenic [ˌænθrəpəˈdʒenɪk] *adj.* 人为的
degradation [ˌdegrəˈdeɪʃn] *n.* 退化；恶化；堕落
entanglement [ɪnˈtæŋɡlmənt] *n.* 缠住；牵连

儒艮：海牛

儒艮是终身生活在海里的草食性哺乳动物。它们的近亲海牛会冒险进入淡水流域生活。儒艮和海牛组成了海牛目，之所以如此命名是因为人们认为是儒艮和海牛引发了有关美人鱼或海中女妖的传说。

A 儒艮是一种大型的海洋哺乳动物，和海牛一样，它们看起来像是圆圆胖胖的海豚和海象的杂交后代。它的体形、鳍肢和鳍脚像海豚，但没有背鳍。它的头看起来有点像失去长牙的海象。

B 儒艮，和其他海牛目物种一样，主要以海草为食，它们的分布与海洋中开花植物的分布有着密切关系。由于海草扎根于海洋的沉积物里，所以其生长受制于所能获取的光照。因此，海草主要出现在浅海水域，儒艮也主要在浅海水域活动。但事实并非完全如此。儒艮不是什么海草都吃，它们更喜欢吃氮含量较高、纤维含量较低的海草。

C 由于视力差，儒艮常用嗅觉来定位可食植物。它们的触觉也很灵敏，用其长而敏感的体毛去感应周围的环境。它们会将整株植物拔起，然后在吃之前抖掉上面的沙子。灵活并且强健的上唇被用来拔植物。吃的时候它们会咽下整株植物，包括根部，但有时没法弄到整株植物，它们就会只吃叶子。在儒艮胃里的残留物中发现了各种各样的海草，也有证据说当海草不足时它们也会吃藻类植物。尽管儒艮几乎完全是食草性的动物，但偶尔也会吃无脊椎动物，如水母、海鞘类和贝类。

D 被重度啃食过的海草床看起来就像一片被醉汉修剪过的草坪，儒艮显然在海草床上肆意乱吃，掠食痕迹遍布。这是一种相当低效的拔草方式，会落下很多小簇的海草，而这也正是儒艮从该低效行为中所获得的好处。那一簇簇掠食后而残留下来的海草会迅速重生、并繁殖散播，这种海草正是儒艮喜欢吃的。此外，这些地方长出来的新海草也往往正是饥饿的儒艮喜欢吃的。

E 儒艮是半游牧的，经常会为了寻觅食物而长途跋涉，但一生中只会在特定范围内活动。它们经常成群结队地从一个地方游到另一个地方。据说这些活动是因为海草的可获得程度发生了变化。儒艮的记忆力能让它们在经过长途旅行后回到特定的地方。儒艮的活动大多发生在海草床的附近区域，同一区域内的儒艮有着不同的活动方式。

F 由于缺少精准的调查，人们普遍认为儒艮记录在案的数量低于实际数量。尽管如此，儒艮的数量正在减少，过去90年间全球范围内其数量减少了20%。它们已经从香港、毛里求斯、台湾以及柬埔寨、日本、菲律宾和越南的部分海域消失。可能还会进一步消失。（20世纪60年代末，在东非及其周边岛屿的海域发现了约500头的儒艮群。然而现在该地区的儒艮数量很少，不足50头，据说它们可能会濒临灭绝。红海东海岸是多达数百头儒艮的聚居地，西海岸也拥有相当数量的儒艮。20世纪80年代，据估计，红海海域有多达4,000头儒艮。波斯湾是世界第二大儒艮聚集区，它们主要生活在南部海岸，据说目前数量约为7,500头。澳大利亚是最大的聚居区，范围从澳大利亚西部的鲨鱼湾一直到昆士兰州的摩顿湾。据说鲨鱼湾儒艮的数量稳定在10,000头以上。）

G 澳大利亚北部各地的经历表明，像旋风和洪灾这种极端天气可以毁掉数百万平方公里的海草区，也能把儒艮冲上岸。海草区的恢复、海草在新地方或原区域的散播需要十年以上。例如，1992年赫维湾约900平方公里的海草被毁，这可能是因为当地河流泛滥造成的浑水以及三周后旋风引起的湍流。

通过剧烈的波浪作用、流沙、盐度降低和光照水平减弱，这种事件会大面积破坏海草群。在 1992 年洪灾之前，赫维湾的大量海草供养着约 1,750 头儒艮。洪灾过后 8 个月，据估计受灾区只能养活约 70 头儒艮。大部分许多动物可能是通过游到附近区域才得以生存。然而，很多动物在尝试游向更为茂盛的牧场时死去，瘦弱的尸体被冲到 900 千米之外的海滩上。

H 如果儒艮吃不饱，它们可能会推迟并减少产仔。食物短缺可能由多种因素造成，如栖息地消失、海草死亡或质量下降以及由人为活动造成的进食干扰。污水、洗涤剂、重金属、超咸水、除草剂和其他废弃物都会给海草区带来不利影响。人为活动如采矿、拖网捕鱼、清淤、土地开垦和船桨干扰作用都会增加沉积物，致使海草被完全覆盖，无法接受光照。这是最主要的影响海草的生长的不利因素。喜盐草是儒艮偏爱的海草之一，因为光照不足，其数量正在急剧下降，30 天后它们就会彻底死去。

I 尽管在很多国家儒艮都受到法律保护，但其数量减少的主要原因依然是人为的，包括狩猎、栖息地恶化、捕鱼相关行为致死。尽管并没有确切的数据，渔网缠绕也导致很多儒艮死亡。很多有关工业捕鱼的案例都发生在比较深的海域，这里儒艮的数量较少，而位于浅海海域的当地渔业成为主要危险。由于儒艮不能长时间待在水下，它们极易因渔网缠绕而致死。历史上捕鲨网的使用也曾导致儒艮大量死亡，多数地区已不再使用，而是用被装了鱼饵的鱼钩替代。

READING PASSAGE 3

参考答案

27	TRUE	28	NOT GIVEN	29	FALSE
30	TRUE	31	FALSE	32	air gun
33	sound energy	34	cable	35	hydrophones/underwater microphones
36	shipping container	37	seismic reflection profiling	38	laboratory
39	three-dimensional	40	fishing nets		

Detection of a Meteorite Lake

A   As the sun rose over picturesque Lake Bosumtwi, a team of Syracuse University prepared for another day of using state-of-the-art equipment to help unlock the mysteries hidden below the lake bottom. Nestled in the heart of Ghana, the lake holds an untapped reservoir of information that could help scientists predict future climate changes by looking at evidence from the past. (27) This information will also improve the scientist's understanding of the changes that occur in a region stuck by a massive meteorite.

B   The project, led by earth sciences professor Christopher Scholz of the College of Arts and Sciences and funded by the National Science Foundation (NSF), is the first large-scale effort to study Lake Bosumtwi, Earth's surface. The resulting crater is one of the largest and most well-preserved geologically young craters in the world, (28) says Scholz, who is collaborating on the project with researchers from the University of South Carolina, the University of Rhode Island, and several Ghanaian institutions. 'Our data should provide information about what happens when an impact hits hard, Pre-Cambrian, crystalline rocks that are a billion years old,' he says.

C   Equally important is the fact that the lake, which is about 8 kilometres in diameter, has no natural outlet. The rim of the crater rises about 240 metres above the water's surface. Streams flow into the lake, Scholz says, but the water leaves only by evaporation, or by seeping through the lake sediments. (29) For the past million years, the lake has acted as a tropical rain gauge, filling and drying with changes in precipitation and the tropical climate. The record of those changes is hidden in sediment below the lake bottom. (30) 'The lake is one of the best sites in the world for the study of tropical climate change,' Scholz says. 'The tropics are the heart engine for the Earth's climate. To understand global climate, we need to have records of climate changes from many sites around the world, including the tropics.'

D   Before the researchers could explore the lake's surface, they need a boat with a large, working deck area that could carry eight tons of scientific equipment. The boat — dubbed R/V *Kilindi* — was built in Florida last year. It was constructed in modules that were dismantled, packed inside a shipping container, (36) and reassembled over a 10-day period in late November and early December 1999 in the rural village of Abono, Ghana. The research team then spent the next two weeks testing the boat and equipment before returning to the United States for the holidays.

E   In mid-January, five members of the team — Keely Brooks, an earth sciences graduate student; Peter Cattaneo, a research analyst; and Kiram Lezzar, a postdoctoral scholar, all from SU; James McGill, a geophysical filed engineer; and Nick Peters, a Ph.D. Student in geophysics from the University of Miami-returned to Abono to begin collecting data about the lake's subsurface using a technique called seismic reflection profiling. (37) In this process, a high-pressure air gun is used to create small, pneumatic explosions in the water. (32) The sound energy penetrates about 1,000 to 2,000 metres into the lake's subsurface before bouncing back to the surface of the water. (33)

F The reflected sound energy is detected by underwater microphones — called hydrophones — embedded in a 50-metre long cable that is towed behind the boat as it crosses the lake in a carefully designed grid pattern. (35/34) On-board computers record the signals, and the resulting data are then processed and analysed in the laboratory. (38) 'The results will give us a good idea of the shape of the basin, how thick the layer of sediment is, and when and where there were major changes in sediment accumulation,' Scholz says. 'We are now developing three-dimensional perspective of the lake's subsurface and the layers of sediment that have been laid down.' (39)

G Team members spent about four weeks in Ghana collecting the data. They worked seven days a week, arriving at the lake just after sunrise. On a good day, when everything went as planned, the team could collect data and be back at the dock by early afternoon. Except for a new relatively minor adjustments, the equipment and the boat worked well. Problems that arose were primarily non-scientific — tree stumps, fishing nets, cultural barriers, and occasional misunderstandings with local villagers. (40)

H Lake Bosumtwi, the largest natural freshwater lake in the country, is scared to the Ashanti people, who believe their souls come to the lake to bid farewell to their god. The lake is also the primary source of fish for the 26 surrounding villages. Conventional canoes and boats are forbidden. Fishermen travel on the lake by floating on traditional planks; they propel with small paddles. Before the research project could begin, Scholz and his Ghanaian counterparts had to secure special permission from tribal chiefs to put the R/V *Kilindi* on the lake.

I When the team began gathering data, rumors flew around the lake as to why the researchers were there. 'Some thought we were dredging the lake for gold, others thought we were going to drain lake or that we had bought the lake,' Cattaneo says. 'But once the local people understood why we were there, they were very helpful.' (31)

核心词汇

A 段

picturesque [ˌpɪktʃəˈresk] *adj.* 生动的；风景如画般的

unlock [ˌʌnˈlɒk] *v.* 开启；解开

untapped [ˌʌnˈtæpt] *adj.* 未开发的；未使用的

reservoir [ˈrezəvwɑː(r)] *n.* 储藏；水库，蓄水池

meteorite [ˈmiːtiəraɪt] *n.* 陨星；流星

B 段

crater [ˈkreɪtə(r)] *n.* 火山口；弹坑

Pre-Cambrian [priːˈkæmbriən] *n.* 前寒武纪

crystalline [ˈkrɪstəlaɪn] *adj.* 结晶质的；透明的；水晶般的

C 段

diametre [daɪˈæmɪtə(r)] *n.* 直径

evaporation [ɪˌvæpəˈreɪʃn] *n.* 蒸发；消失

seep [siːp] *v.* 漏；渗出

sediment [ˈsedɪmənt] *n.* 沉积；沉淀物

gauge [ɡeɪdʒ] *n.* 测量标准；测量仪器

precipitation [prɪˌsɪpɪˈteɪʃn] *n.* 降水，降水量

D 段

dub [dʌb] *v.* 授予称号

module [ˈmɒdjuːl] *n.* 模块；组件

dismantle [dɪsˈmæntl] *v.* 拆除

E 段

postdoctoral [ˌpəʊstˈdɒktərəl] *adj.* 博士后的

geophysical [ˌdʒiːəʊˈfɪzɪkl] *adj.* 地球物理学的

seismic [ˈsaɪzmɪk] *adj.* 地震的

profile [ˈprəʊfaɪl] *v.* 给……画侧面图，给……作纵断面图

pneumatic [njuːˈmætɪk] *adj.* 气动的

penetrate [ˈpenətreɪt] *v.* 穿透，渗透

F 段

hydrophone [ˈhaɪdrəfəʊn] *n.* 水中听音器；水诊器

embed [ɪmˈbed] *v.* 使嵌入，使插入

three-dimensional [ˌθriːdaɪˈmenʃənl] *adj.* 三维的；立体的

perspective [pəˈspektɪv] *n.* 透视图

G 段

dock [dɒk] *n.* 码头

stump [stʌmp] *n.* 树桩

H 段

farewell [ˌfeəˈwel] *n.* 告别，辞别

plank [plæŋk] *n.* 厚木板

paddle [ˈpædl] *n.* 桨

I 段

dredge [dredʒ] *v.* 疏浚，挖掘，捞取

探测陨石湖

A 当太阳从风景如画的博苏姆推湖上空升起时，雪城大学的一个团队使用最先进的设备做准备，来帮助解开隐藏在湖底的秘密。该湖坐落在加纳的心脏地带，它拥有一个尚未开发的信息库，可以通过观察过去的证据来帮助科学家预测未来的气候变化。这一信息也将提高科学家对一个被巨大陨石所击中的区域所发生的变化的认识。

B 该项目是由艺术与科学学院的地球科学教授克里斯托弗·肖尔茨领导，并由美国国家科学基金会资助，是对地球表面的博苏姆推湖进行的首次大规模的研究。肖尔茨说，该陨石坑是世界上最大、保存最完好的地质上最年轻的陨石坑之一。他与来自南卡罗来纳大学和罗德岛大学以及加纳的几家机构的研究人员合作开展了这个项目。他说："我们的数据应该提供有关当时撞击发生时的信息。这些撞击是在前寒武纪水晶岩石中发生的，这些岩石已有10亿年的历史了。"

C 同样重要的是，这个直径约8公里的湖泊没有天然的出水口。火山口的边缘比水平面高出大约240米。肖尔茨说，溪流流入湖中，但水的消逝只能通过蒸发，或者通过湖底沉积物渗透。在过去的一百万年里，这座湖充当了一个热带雨量计，湖水的盈亏随着降雨量和热带气候的变化而变化。这些变化的记录隐藏在湖底的沉积物中。肖尔茨说："这座湖是世界上研究热带气候变化的最佳地点之一。热带地区是地球气候的核心引擎。要了解全球气候，我们需要记录世界各地的气候变化，包括热带地区。"

D 在研究人员探索湖泊的表面之前，他们需要一艘有大型工作甲板区域的船，可以携带8吨重的科学设备。这艘被称为基林迪的考察船是去年在佛罗里达州建造的。它是在被拆卸的堆放在集装箱内的模块中建造的并在1999年11月下旬到12月初在加纳的阿邦诺村庄里于十天内重新组装完成。研究小组随后在接下来的两周时间里测试船只和设备，之后返回美国度假。

E 1月中旬，团队的五名成员——基里·布鲁克斯，一名地球科学专业的研究生；彼得·卡塔内奥，一位研究分析师；还有基拉姆·莱扎，一名博士后学者，他们都来自于雪城大学。詹姆士·麦克基尔，一位地球物理工程师；尼克·彼得斯是迈阿密大学地球物理学的一名博士生，他回到了阿邦诺，使用一种名为"地震反射剖面法"的技术开始收集有关湖泊湖面以下的数据。在这个过程中，高压气枪用于在水中制造小型的气动爆炸。声音能量穿透到大约1,000到2,000米的水下，然后反弹回水面。

F 这种反射的声音能量是由水下的扩音器探测到的，它被称为"水诊器"，水诊器被嵌入在一根拖在船后的长为50米的电缆中，穿过湖中经过精心设计的网格结构，船载计算机记录信号，然后在实验室中处理和分析产生的数据。"研究结果将使我们对盆地的地形有一个很好的认识，比如沉积物有多厚，以及在沉积物中何时何地有重大变化，"肖尔茨说，"我们现在正在开发湖面以下以及湖底沉积物层的三维透视网。"

G 团队成员在加纳花了大约四个星期的时间收集数据。他们日出后到达湖边，一周工作七天。在天气好的日子里，一切按计划进行，团队可以收集数据，并在下午早些时候回到码头。除了一个新的相对较小的调整外，设备和船运行良好。出现的问题主要是非科学性质的——树桩、渔网、文化障碍，以及与当地村民偶尔的误会。

H 博苏姆推湖是这个国家最大的天然淡水湖。阿善堤人很敬畏这个湖,他们相信自己的灵魂会来到这个湖,向他们的上帝告别。这湖也是周边 26 个村庄的主要鱼类来源。普通的独木舟和船只是被禁止进入湖中的。渔民们利用传统的木板漂浮在湖上,用小桨推动。在这个研究项目开始之前,肖尔茨和他的加纳同行们必须得到部落首领的特别许可,才能把考察船基林迪驶入湖中。

I 当研究小组开始收集数据时,关于为什么研究人员在那里的谣言满天飞。"有些人认为我们是在挖湖寻找金子,另一些人则认为我们要去排水,或者我们买下了这座湖,"卡塔内奥说,"但一旦当地人明白了我们为什么会在那里,他们就会乐于帮忙。"

TEST 2

READING PASSAGE 1

参考答案

1	drought	2	large seeds	3	heavy rains
4	small seeds	5	finch evolution	6	medium-sized bills
7	human population	8	rice	9	FALSE
10	NOT GIVEN	11	TRUE	12	FALSE
13	TRUE				

Finches on Islands

A   Today, the quest continues. On Daphne Major — one of the most desolate of the Galipagos Islands, an uninhabited volcanic cone where cacti and shrubs seldom grow higher than a researcher's knee — Peter and Rosemary Grant, Biologists at Princeton University, have spent more than three decades watching Darwin's finch respond to the challenges of storms, drought and competition for food — the Grants know and recognise many of the individual birds on the island and can trace the birds' lineages back through time. They have witnessed Darwin's principle in action again and again, over many generations of finches. (9)

B   The Grants' most dramatic insights have come from watching the evolving bill of the medium ground finch. The plumage of this sparrow-sized bird ranges from dull brown to jet black. At first glance, it may not seem particularly striking, but among scientists who study evolutionary biology, the medium ground finch is a superstar. Its bill is a middling example in the array of shapes and sizes found among Galapagos finches: heftier than that of the small ground finch, which specialises in eating small, soft seeds, but petite compared to that of the large ground finch, an expert at cracking and devouring big, hard seeds.

C   When the Grants began their study in the 1970s, only two species of finch lived on Daphne Major, the medium ground finch and the cactus finch. (10) The island is so small that the researchers were able to count and catalogue every bird. When a severe drought hit in 1977, the birds soon devoured the last of the small, easily eaten seeds. (1) Smaller members of the medium ground finch population, lacking the bill strength to crack large seeds, died out. (2)

D   Bill and body size are inherited traits, and the next generation had a high proportion of big-billed individuals. The Grants had documented natural selection at work — the same process that, over many millennia, directed the evolution of the Galapagos' 14 unique finch species, all descended from a common ancestor that reached the islands a few million years ago.

E   Eight years later, heavy rains brought by an El Nino transformed the normally meager vegetation on Daphne Major. (3) Vines and other plants that in most years struggle for survival suddenly flourished, choking out the plants that provide large seeds to the finches. Small seeds came to dominate the food supply, and big birds with big bills died out at a higher rate than smaller ones. (4) 'Natural selection is observable,' Rosemary Grant says. 'It happens when the environment changes. When local conditions reverse themselves, so does the direction of adaptation.'

F   Recently, the Grants witnessed another form of natural selection acting on the medium ground finch: competition from bigger, stronger cousins. In 1982, a third finch, the large ground finch, came to live on Daphne Major. The stout bills of these birds resemble the business end of a crescent wrench. Their arrival was the first such colonisation recorded on the Galapagos in nearly a century of scientific observation. 'We realised,' Peter Grant says, 'we had a very unusual and potentially important event to follow.' For 20 years, the large ground finch coexisted with the medium ground finch, which shared the supply of large seeds with its bigger-billed relative. Then, in 2002 and 2003, another drought struck. None of the birds nested that year, and many died out. Medium ground finches with large bills, crowded out of feeding areas by the more powerful large ground finches, were hit particularly hard. (11)

G When wetter weather returned in 2004, and the finches nested again, the new generation of the medium ground finch was dominated by smaller birds with smaller bills, able to survive on smaller seeds. This situation, says Peter Grant, marked the first time that biologists have been able to follow the complete process of an evolutionary change due to competition between species and the strongest response to natural selection that he had seen in 33 years of tracking Galapagos finches.

H On the inhabited island of Santa Cruz, just south of Daphne Major, Andrew Hendry of McGill University and Jeffrey Podos of the University of Massachusetts at Amherst have discovered a new, man-made twist in finch evolution. (5/12) Their study focused on birds living near the Academy Bay research station, on the fringe of the town of Puerto Ayora. The human population of the area has been growing fast — from 900 people in 1974 to 9,582 in 2001. 'Today Puerto Ayora is full of hotels and mai tai bars,' Hendry says. 'People have taken this extremely arid place and tried to turn it into a Caribbean resort.'

I Academy Bay records dating back to the early 1960s show that medium ground finches captured there had either small or large bills. Very few of the birds had mid-size bills. The finches appeared to be in the early stages of a new adaptive radiation: If the trend continued, the medium ground finch on Santa Cruz could split into two distinct subspecies, specialising in different types of seeds. But in the late 1960s and early 70s, medium ground finches with medium-sized bills began to thrive at Academy Bay along with small and largebilled birds. (6) The booming human population had introduced new food sources, including exotic plants and bird feeding stations stocked with rice. Bill size, once critical to the finches' survival, no longer made any difference. 'Now an intermediate bill can do fine,' Hendry says. (13)

J At a control site distant from Puerto Ayora, and relatively untouched by humans, the medium ground finch population remains split between large- and small-billed birds. On undisturbed parts of Santa Cruz, there is no ecological niche for a middling medium ground finch, and the birds continue to diversify. In town, though there are still many finches, once-distinct populations are merging.

K The finches of Santa Cruz demonstrate a subtle process in which human meddling can stop evolution in its tracks, ending the formation of new species. In a time when global biodiversity continues its downhill slide, Darwin's finches have yet another unexpected lesson to teach. (12) 'If we hope to regain some of the diversity that's already been lost,' Hendry says, 'we need to protect not just existing creatures, but also the processes that drive the origin of new species.'

核心词汇

A 段

desolate [ˈdesələt] *adj.* 荒凉的

uninhabited [ˌʌnɪnˈhæbɪtɪd] *adj.* 无人居住的，杳无人迹的

cacti [ˈkæktaɪ] *n.* 仙人掌（cactus 的复数形式）

shrub [ʃrʌb] *n.* 灌木丛

finch [fɪntʃ] *n.* 雀类

lineage [ˈlɪniɪdʒ] *n.* 血统；家系

B 段

insight [ˈɪnsaɪt] *n.* 洞察力

sparrow [ˈspærəʊ] *n.* 麻雀

striking [ˈstraɪkɪŋ] *adj.* 显著的；惊人的

petite [pəˈtiːt] *adj.* 娇小的；柔弱的

crack [kræk] *v.* 使破裂

devour [dɪˈvaʊə(r)] *v.* 吞食

C 段

catalogue [ˈkætəlɒg] *v.* 登记分类，把……编入目录

D 段

inherited [ɪnˈherɪtd] *adj.* 遗传的

millennia [mɪˈleniə] *n.* 千年期；一千年（millennium 的复数形式）

descend [dɪˈsend] *v.* 遗传

E 段

meager [ˈmiːgə(r)] *adj.* 贫乏的

choke [tʃəʊk] *v.* 阻止，使窒息；阻塞

reverse [rɪˈvɜːs] *v.* 倒退，颠倒；倒转

F 段

stout [staʊt] *adj.* 结实的

resemble [rɪˈzembl] *v.* 类似，像

crescent [ˈkresnt] *adj.* 新月状的

wrench [rentʃ] *n.* 扳手，扳钳

H 段

twist [twɪst] *n.* 旋转

fringe [frɪndʒ] *n.* 边缘

resort [rɪˈzɔːt] *n.* 度假胜地；常去之地

I 段

subspecies [ˈsʌbspiːʃiːz] *n.* 亚种

thrive [θraɪv] *v.* 繁荣，兴旺

exotic [ɪɡˈzɒtɪk] *adj.* 异国的；外来的

intermediate [ˌɪntəˈmiːdiət] *adj.* 中间的，中级的

J 段

undisturbed [ˌʌndɪˈstɜːbd] *adj.* 未被扰乱的

niche [niːʃ] *n.* 合适的位置，壁龛

K 段

meddling [ˈmedlɪŋ] *n.* 干预

biodiversity [ˌbaɪəʊdaɪˈvɜːsəti] *n.* 生物多样性

岛上的雀鸟

A 如今探索仍在继续。在大达夫尼岛的（加拉帕戈斯群岛中最荒凉的岛屿之一）一个无人居住的火山锥上，这里的仙人掌和灌木丛很少能长得超过研究人员的膝盖，普林斯顿大学的生物学家彼得·格兰特和罗斯玛丽·格兰特已经花了 30 多年的时间来观察达尔文地雀如何对抗风暴、干旱和食物竞争所带来的挑战。格兰特夫妇了解并识别了岛上的很多鸟类，还追溯到这些鸟类的血统，他们通过很多代的雀鸟反复见证了达尔文理论的实际应用。

B 格兰特夫妇最激动人心的发现就是观察到了中嘴地雀鸟喙的进化。这种鸟体形近似麻雀，羽毛从暗淡的棕色到深黑色。乍看之下，它可能并不是特别引人注目，但对于那些研究进化生物学的科学家们而言，中嘴地雀就是一个超级明星。加拉帕戈斯群岛上那些雀鸟的鸟喙形状各异、大小不一，中嘴地雀的喙属于中等类鸟喙：它的喙比小嘴地雀的喙更粗大，这特别适合吃又小又软的种子；但跟大嘴地雀的喙相比又显得窄小，大嘴地雀很擅长啄碎并吞食又大又硬的种子。

C 格兰特夫妇在 20 世纪 70 年代刚开始他们的研究时，只有两种雀鸟生活在大达夫尼岛上——中嘴地雀和仙人掌地雀。这个岛太小了，以至于研究者能数清并登记分类每一种鸟。1977 年一场严重的干旱来袭，这些鸟很快就吃完了剩下的那些小的、易食的种子。中嘴地雀的数量越来越少，并因其鸟喙不够强壮无法啄碎大种子而逐渐消失。

D 喙型和体形的大小都是可以遗传的特性，因此下一代中有很大一部分是大喙雀鸟。格兰特夫妇记录了自然选择的作用——几千年来也正是这种过程引导着加拉帕戈斯群岛上 14 种独有雀鸟种类的进化，它们都源自几百万年前来到该岛的同一个祖先。

E 八年后，厄尔尼诺现象导致的强降雨一改大达夫尼岛平日里植被贫瘠的面貌。过去多年来极力求生的那些藤本植物和其他植物突然茂盛起来，使那些为雀鸟提供大种子的植物无法成活。小种子在食物供应中占据主导，大喙地雀的灭绝率要高于小喙地雀。罗斯玛丽·格兰特说："自然选择是能观察到的，环境发生变化时就会发生自然选择的现象。当本地的自然环境不适合雀鸟们生存时，它们也会反过来去适应自然选择。"

F 最近格兰特夫妇见证了发生在中嘴地雀身上的另一种自然选择形式：来自更大型、更强壮的地雀的同类竞争。1982 年，第三种地雀，大嘴地雀来到大达夫尼岛生活。这些雀鸟厚实的鸟喙就像月牙形扳手的头部。它们到来的此种建群现象被首次记录在加拉帕戈斯群岛近一个世纪以来的科学观察资料中，彼得·格兰特说："我们意识到有一件非同寻常的、可能很重要的事情需要我们去跟进。"20 年来，大嘴地雀与中嘴地雀和平共处，和这些鸟喙更大的同类分享大种子。然后在 2002 年到 2003 年间，另一场干旱来袭。这一年没有地雀繁殖，很多都灭绝了。大喙中嘴地雀受到了很强烈的攻击，被那些更强大的大嘴地雀从取食的地方挤了出来。

G 2004 年气候渐渐湿润，雀鸟又开始繁殖，新一代的中嘴地雀主要是那些鸟喙更小、体形也更小的雀鸟，它们靠较小的种子就能存活。彼得·格兰特说这种情况意味着生物学家首次跟踪到因种群竞争而发生进化变异的完整过程，这也是他 33 年来追踪加拉帕戈斯群岛雀鸟过程中发现的雀鸟面对自然选择的最强反应。

H 在有人居住的圣克鲁斯岛上，它位于大达夫尼岛的南边，麦吉尔大学的安德鲁·亨德利和艾摩斯特市马萨诸塞州立大学的杰弗里·波多斯发现了有关雀鸟进化一事的一个人为的新转折。他们主要研究生活在科学院湾研究站（在阿约拉港镇边上）附近的鸟类。该地区人口数量增长很快，从 1974 年的 900 人增至 2001 年的 9,582 人。亨德利说："如今阿约拉港到处都是宾馆和麦泰酒吧，人们已经接受了这个极其干旱的地方，并试着将它变成一个加勒比海度假胜地。"

I 追溯至 20 世纪 60 年代初，科学院湾的相关记录显示，在这里捕获的中嘴地雀的鸟喙非大即小，很少有中等大小的。这些雀鸟似乎还处在新的适应辐射过程的初级阶段：如果这种趋势继续下去，圣克鲁斯岛上的中等地雀可能会分化成两个明显不同的亚种，以适应食用不同的种子。但在 20 世纪 60 年代末到 70 年代初，中嘴中等地雀和小嘴雀鸟、大嘴雀鸟都开始在此茁壮成长。迅速增长的人口数量引入了新的食物来源，包括外来植物和围满稻米的鸟类饲养站。曾对雀鸟存活至关重要的鸟喙的大小，再也不会造成什么不同的影响。亨德利说："如今即使只有中等大小的鸟喙，也可以让雀鸟很好地生存下去。"

J 在阿约拉港远处一个几乎无人到访的控制站里，中嘴地雀仍然被分成大嘴中嘴地雀和小嘴中嘴地雀两种。在圣克鲁斯岛上安静的边远地区，是没有中嘴中嘴地雀的生态位的，而且这些雀鸟继续多样化发展。在城里，虽然还有很多雀鸟，但曾经分类清晰的群体正在互相融合。

K 圣克鲁斯岛上的雀鸟揭示了一种微妙的过程，在这个过程中人为干预能够阻止它们的进化，终止新物种的形成。在全球生物多样性走下坡路的这段时期，我们可以从达尔文地雀身上汲取到另一个意想不到的教训。亨德利说："如果我们希望重获一些已经失去的生物多样性，不仅需要保护现存的生物，也要保护促使新物种血统形成的进化过程。"

READING PASSAGE 2

参考答案

14	v	15	i	16	ix
17	viii	18	iii	19	vi
20	F	21	D	22	A
23	logo	24	untruthful	25	unconscious
26	children				

What Does the Consumer Think?

A Marketing people are no longer prepared to take your word for it that you favour one product over another. They want to scan your brain to see which one you really prefer. Using the tools of neuroscientists, such as electroencephalogram (EEG) mapping and functional magnetic-resonance imaging (fMRI), they are trying to learn more about the mental processes behind purchasing decisions. The resulting fusion of neuroscience and marketing is inevitably, being called 'neuromarketing'.

B The first person to apply brain-imaging technology in this way was Gerry Zaltman of Harvard University, in the late 1990s. The idea remained in obscurity until 2001, when Bright House, a marketing consultancy based in Atlanta, Georgia, set up a dedicated neuromarketing arm, Bright House Neurostrategies Group. (Bright House lists Coca-Cola, Delta Airlines and Home Depot among its clients.) But the company's name may itself simply be an example of clever marketing. (14) Bright House does not scan people while showing them specific products or campaign ideas, but bases its work on the results of more general fMRI-based research into consumer preferences and decision-making carried out at Emory University in Atlanta.

C Can brain scanning really be applied to marketing? The basic principle is not that different from focus groups and other traditional forms of market research. A volunteer lies in an fMRI machine and is shown images or video clips. In place of an interview or questionnaire, the subject's response is evaluated by monitoring brain activity. fMRI provides real-time images of brain activity, in which different areas 'light up' depending on the level of blood flow. This provides clues to the subject's subconscious thought patterns. (25) Neuroscientists know, for example, that the sense of self is associated with an area of the brain known as the medial prefrontal cortex. (15) A flow of blood to that area while the subject is looking at a particular logo suggests that he or she identifies with that brand. (23)

D At first, it seemed that only companies in Europe were prepared to admit that they used neuromarketing. Two carmakers, Daimler Chrysler in Germany and Ford's European arm, ran pilot studies in 2003. But more recently, American companies have become more open about their use of neuromarketing. (16) Lieberman Research Worldwide, a marketing firm based in Los Angeles, is collaborating with the California Institute of Technology (Caltech) to enable movie studios to make market-test film trailers. More controversially, the *New York Times* recently reported that a political consultancy, FKF Research, has been studying the effectiveness of campaign commercials using neuromarketing techniques.

E Whether all this is any more than a modern-day version of phrenology, the Victorian obsession with linking lumps and bumps in the skull to personality traits, is unclear. There have been no large-scale studies, so scans of a handful of subjects may not be a reliable guide to consumer behaviour in general. Of course, focus groups and surveys are flawed too: strong personalities can steer the outcomes of focus groups, and some people may be untruthful in their responses to opinion pollsters. And even honest people cannot always explain their preferences. (17/24)

439

F That is perhaps where neuromarketing has the most potential. When asked about cola drinks, most people claim to have a favourite brand, but cannot say why they prefer that brand's taste. An unpublished study of attitudes towards two well-known cola drinks, Brand A and Brand B, carried out last year in a college of medicine in the US found that most subjects preferred Brand B in a blind testing — fMRI scanning showed that drinking Brand B lit up a region called the ventral putamen, which is one of the brain's reward centres, far more brightly than Brand A. But when told which drink was which, most subjects said they preferred Brand A, which suggests that its stronger brand outweighs the more pleasant taste of the other drink. (18)

G People form many unconscious attitudes that are obviously beyond traditional methods that utilise introspection, says Steven Quartz, a neuroscientist at Caltech who is collaborating with Lieberman Research. (20) With over 100 billion dollars spent each year on marketing in America alone, any firm that can more accurately analyse how customers respond to brands could make a fortune. (19)

H Consumer advocates are wary. Gary Ruskin of Commercial Alert, a lobby group, thinks existing marketing techniques are powerful enough. 'Already, marketing is deeply implicated in many serious pathologies', he says. 'That is especially true of children, who are suffering from an epidemic of marketing-related diseases, including obesity and type 2 diabetes. Neuromarketing is a tool to amplify these trends.' (21/26) Dr. Quartz counters that neuromarketing techniques could equally be used for benign purposes. 'There are ways to utilise these technologies to create more responsible advertising,' he says. 'Brain-scanning could, for example, be used to determine when people are capable of making free choices, to ensure that advertising falls within those bounds.'

I Another worry is that brain-scanning is an invasion of privacy and that information on the preferences of specific individuals will be misused. But neuromarketing studies rely on small numbers of volunteer subjects, so that seems implausible. Critics also object to the use of medical equipment for frivolous rather than medical purposes. But Tim Ambler, a neuromarketing researcher at the London Business School, says, 'A tool is a tool, and if the owner of the tool gets a decent rent for hiring it out, then that subsidises the cost of the equipment, and everybody wins.' (22) Perhaps more brain-scanning will some day explain why some people like the idea of neuromarketing, but others do not.

核心词汇

A 段
neuroscientist [ˈnjʊərəʊsaɪəntɪst] *n.* 神经科学家，神经系统学家
magnetic-resonance imaging 核磁共振成像
fusion [ˈfjuːʒn] *n.* 融合
inevitably [ɪnˈevɪtəbli] *adv.* 无法避免地

B 段
obscurity [əbˈskjʊərəti] *n.* 默默无闻；模糊

C 段
subconscious [ˌsʌbˈkɒnʃəs] *adj.* 潜意识的

D 段
pilot [ˈpaɪlət] *adj.* 实验性的

E 段
phrenology [frəˈnɒlədʒi] *n.* 颅相学
obsession [əbˈseʃn] *n.* 痴迷
lump [lʌmp] *n.* 块，肿块
bump [bʌmp] *n.* 隆起物，肿块
skull [skʌl] *n.* 头盖骨
trait [treɪt] *n.* 特点

F 段
outweigh [ˌaʊtˈweɪ] *v.* 超过，大于

H 段
wary [ˈweəri] *adj.* 谨慎的，警惕的

I 段
implausible [ɪmˈplɔːzəbl] *adj.* 难以置信的，似乎不合情理的
object to 反对
frivolous [ˈfrɪvələs] *adj.* 毫无意义的；轻率的
decent [ˈdiːsnt] *adj.* 相当好的，恰当的，得体的
subsidise [ˈsʌbsɪdaɪz] *v.* 给补助，给津贴

消费者在想什么？

A 营销人员不会再相信你口头所说的喜欢某种产品胜过另一种这样的话了。他们想扫描你的大脑，看看哪个才是你真正喜欢的产品。通过使用神经学家的手段，如脑电图和功能磁共振成像，他们试图更多地了解消费者购买决定背后的心理过程。神经科学与市场营销的融合是一种必然，其结果产生了"神经营销学"。

B 20世纪90年代末，哈佛大学的格里·萨尔特曼第一次将大脑成像技术应用于营销领域。这个想法一直默默无闻，直到2001年，一家位于佐治亚州亚特兰大的叫做"聪明屋"的营销咨询公司成立专门的神经营销部门——聪明屋神经战略集团。（聪明屋的客户有可口可乐、达美航空和家得宝公司。）从公司名称可以看出，它只是希望自己能成为巧妙营销的典范。在给消费者展示具体产品或活动理念时，聪明屋并不扫描他们的大脑，但是他们的工作是以亚特兰大埃默里大学（Emory University）的研究结果为基础的。该大学针对消费者的偏好和决策过程进行更广泛的功能磁共振成像研究。

C 大脑扫描真能应用到市场营销吗？其基本原则与焦点小组和其他传统的市场调查并无差异。志愿者躺在功能磁共振机里，实验者向其展示图像或视频片段。取代了面谈或调查问卷，通过监测大脑活动即可评估实验对象的心理反应。功能磁共振成像提供了实时的大脑活动图像，根据血流量不同，不同的区域就会发亮。这就为受试者的潜意识思维模式提供了线索。例如，神经科学家知道自我意识与大脑的一个叫做内侧前额叶皮质的区域相联系。当受试者观看某一商标时，如果有血流通往那个区域就表明他或她支持那个品牌。

D 起初，似乎只有欧洲的公司准备承认他们使用了神经营销手段。在2003年，德国的戴姆勒-克莱斯勒和福特欧洲分部这两家汽车制造商对此进行了实验性的研究。然而近年来，美国的公司则越来越公开地使用神经营销手段。总部位于洛杉矶的营销公司，利柏曼全球研究所正在与加州理工学院合作，使电影公司制作用于市场测试的电影预告片。更有争议的是，《纽约时报》最近报道，一家名为"FKF研究"的政治咨询公司通过使用神经营销技巧来研究政治活动广告的有效性。

E 通过颅骨上的凹凸不平来判断一个人的个性特点是一种维多利亚式的迷恋。是否这一切只是现代版的颅相学目前还不清楚。科学家并没有对神经营销进行大规模的研究，因此，对少数受试者的大脑扫描可能并不能可靠地指导普遍的消费行为。当然，焦点小组和调查也存在不足：实验对象强烈的个性会影响焦点小组的调查结果，在问卷调查中，一些人的回答也许并不真实。即便是诚实的人也未必总能说清自己的偏好。

F 这也许就是神经营销学最有潜力的地方所在。当被问到可乐饮料时，大多数人都声称有自己最喜欢的品牌，但又说不清自己为什么喜欢那个品牌的口味。美国一所医学院去年就人们对两大知名可乐（A品牌和B品牌）口味的喜好进行了研究，该项未发表的研究表明，在盲饮的情况下，大多数受试者更喜欢B品牌。功能磁共振成像扫描显示，在喝B品牌可乐时，受试者的大脑腹侧外壳——大脑的受赏中心之一会出现反应，比喝A品牌可乐时的反应明显很多。但当被告知品尝的是哪种品牌时，大多数受试者表示更喜欢A品牌。这表明A产品强大的品牌效应胜过B品牌更可口的味道。

G 正与利伯曼全球研究合作的加州理工学院神经科学家史蒂芬·科兹说,在判断事物时,人们形成的许多潜意识看法明显超越了传统的内省方法。仅在美国,每年花费在市场营销上的资金就超过1,000亿美元。任何公司只要能更加准确地分析出客户对品牌的反应就能够大赚一笔。

H 消费者保护团体则持谨慎态度。一个游说团体,广告警示协会的盖里·拉斯金认为现有的营销技巧已经足够强大。他说,"市场营销已经成为导致许多严重疾病的原因。对于孩子们更是如此,市场营销类疾病的蔓延,使他们深受折磨如肥胖症、2型糖尿病。神经营销学是加剧这些趋势的一种手段。"科兹博士反驳说,神经营销技巧同样也能应用于良性目的。他说:"人们有办法利用这些技术来创造更负责任的广告,例如大脑扫描能被用于决定人们何时能够作出自由选择,从而确保广告刚好能在这个自由选择的范围之内"。

I 另一个担忧是大脑扫描是侵犯隐私的行为,这些关于个人偏好的信息会被滥用。但神经营销研究靠的是少数志愿受试者,因此这似乎并不可信。批评者也反对将医疗设备用于医疗目的之外的那些无关痛痒的研究上。但伦敦商学院的神经营销研究员蒂姆·安姆布勒说:"工具仅仅是工具,如果工具的主人能够通过出租工具获得可观的租金,那么这笔租金就能够资助设备的成本,这样一来人人都是赢家。"也许有一天,更多的大脑扫描将会解释为什么有些人喜欢神经营销这个想法,但其他人却不喜欢。

READING PASSAGE 3

参考答案

27	iv	28	iii	29	viii
30	ii	31	ix	32	i
33	collaborative and iterative	34	tangible	35	tailorable
36	group of people	37	C	38	A
39	A	40	D		

Paper or Computer?

A   Computer technology was supposed to replace paper. But that hasn't happened. (27) Every country in the Western world uses more paper today, on a per-capita basis, than it did ten years ago. The consumption of uncoated free-sheet paper, for instance — the most common kind of office paper — rose almost fifteen per cent in the United States between 1995 and 2000. This is generally taken as evidence of how hard it is to eradicate old, wasteful habits and of how stubbornly resistant we are to the efficiencies offered by computerisation. A number of cognitive psychologists and ergonomics experts, however, don't agree. Paper has persisted, they argue, for very good reasons: when it comes to performing certain kinds of cognitive tasks, paper has many advantages over computers. The dismay people feel at the sight of a messy desk — or the spectacle of air-traffic controllers tracking flights through notes scribbled on paper strips — arises from a fundamental confusion about the role that paper plays in our lives.

B   The case for paper is mode most eloquently in *The Myth of the Paperless Office*, by two social scientists, Abigail Sellen and Richard Harper. They begin their book with an account of a study they conducted at the International Monetary Fund, in Washington, D.C.. Economists at the I.M.F. spend most of their time writing reports on complicated economic questions, work that would seem to be perfectly suited to sitting in front of a computer. Nonetheless, the I.M.F. is awash in paper, and Sellen and Harper wanted to find out why. Their answer is that the business of reports — at least at the I.M.F. — is an intensely collaborative process, the professional judgments and contributions of many people. The economists bring drafts of reports to conference rooms, spread out the relevant pages, and negotiate changes with one other. They go back to their offices and jot down comments in the margin, taking advantage of the freedom offered by the informality of the handwritten note. Then they deliver the annotated draft to the author in person, taking him, page by page, through the suggested changes. At the end of the process, the author spreads out all the pages with comments on his desk and starts to enter them on the computer — moving the pages around as he works, organising and reorganising, saving and discarding. (28/37)

C   Without paper, this kind of collaborative and iterative work process would be much more difficult. (33) According to Sellen and Harper, paper has a unique set of 'affordances' — that is, qualities that permit specific kinds of uses. (29) Paper is tangible: we can pick up a document, flip through it, read little bits here and there, and quickly get a sense of it. (34) Paper is spatially flexible, meaning that we can spread it out and arrange it in the way that suits us best. And it's tailorable: we can easily annotate it, and scribble on it as we read, without altering the original text. (35) Digital documents, of course, have their own affordances. They can be easily searched, shared, stored, and remotely, linked to other relevant material. But they lack the affordances that really matter to a group of people working together on a report. (36)

D   Paper enables a certain kind of thinking. Picture, for instance, the top of your desk. Chances are that you have a keyboard and a computer screen off to one side, and a clear space roughly eighteen square inches in front of your chair. What covers the rest of the desktop is probably piles —

piles of papers, journals, magazines, binders, postcards, videotapes, and all the other artifacts of the knowledge economy. The piles look like a mess, but they aren't. (30/38) When a group at Apple Computer studied piling behaviour several years ago, they found that even the most disorderly piles usually make perfect sense to the piles, and that office workers could hold forth in great detail about the precise history and meaning of their piles. The pile closest to the cleared, eighteen-inch-square working area, for example, generally represents the most business, and within that pile the most important document of all is likely to be at the top. Piles are living, breathing archives. (30/38) Over time, they get broken down and resorted, sometimes chronologically and sometimes thematically and sometimes chronologically and thematically; clues about certain documents may be physically embedded in the file by, say, stacking a certain piece of paper at an angle or inserting dividers into the stack.

E But why do we pile documents instead of filing them? Because piles represent the process of active, ongoing thinking. (31) The psychologist Alison Kidd, whose research Sellen and Harper refer to extensively, argues that 'knowledge workers' use the physical space of the desktop to hold 'ideas which they cannot yet categorise or even decide how they might use'. The messy desk is not necessarily a sign of disorganisation. It may be a sign of complexity: those who deal with many unresolved ideas simultaneously cannot sort and file the papers on their desks, because they haven't yet sorted and filed the ideas in their head. Kidd writes that many of the people she talked to use the papers on their desks as contextual cues to 'recover a complex set of threads without difficulty and delay' when they come in on a Monday morning, or after their work has been interrupted by a phone call. What we see when we look at the piles on our desks is, in a sense, the contents of our brains. (31)

F This idea that paper facilitates a highly specialised cognitive and social process is a far cry from the way we have historically thought about the stuff. Paper first began to proliferate in the workplace in the late nineteenth century as part of the move toward 'systematic management'. To cope with the complexity of the industrial economy, managers were instituting company-wide policies and demanding monthly, weekly, or even daily updates from their subordinates. Thus was born the monthly sales report, and the office manual and the internal company newsletter. The typewriter took off in the eighteen-eighties, making it possible to create documents in a fraction of the time it had previously taken, and that was followed closely by the advent of carbon paper, which meant that a typist could create ten copies of that document simultaneously. Paper was important not to facilitate creative collaboration and thought but as an instrument of control. (32/39/40)

核心词汇

A 段

per-capita basis 每人平均基础
eradicate [ɪˈrædɪkeɪt] v. 根除，消灭
scribble [ˈskrɪbl] v. 潦草地写，乱写

B 段

eloquently [ˈeləkwəntli] adv. 有说服力地，善变地；富于表现力地
jot down 草草记下
annotated [ˈænəteɪtɪd] adj. 有注释的
discard [dɪsˈkɑːd] v. 丢弃

C 段

iterative [ˈɪtərətɪv] adj. 重复的；迭代的
tangible [ˈtændʒəbl] adj. 有形的
tailorable [ˈteɪlərəbl] adj. 可裁剪的

D 段

hold forth 滔滔不绝地说，长篇大论地讲
chronologically [ˌkrɒnəˈlɒdʒɪkli] adv. 按时间的前后顺序排列地
embed [ɪmˈbed] v. 使嵌入

E 段

disorganisation [dɪsˌɔːgənaɪˈzeɪʃn] n. 混乱

F 段

proliferate [prəˈlɪfəreɪt] v. 激增
subordinate [səˈbɔːdɪnət] n. 下属
simultaneously [ˌsɪmlˈteɪniəsli] adv. 同时地

纸张还是电脑？

A 计算机技术被期望取代纸张。但是这并没有发生。今天，所有的西方国家，以人均计算，反而比十年前用纸更多。例如，在 1995 年至 2000 年期间，美国最常见的一种不加涂层的办公用纸的消耗增长了近 15%。这通常被认为是难以消除旧的、浪费的习惯以及我们对计算机化所提供效率的顽固抵抗的证据。然而，许多认知心理学家和人类工程学专家并不认同这一观点。他们认为，纸张之所以被持续使用，是有充分理由的：当涉及执行某些类型的认知任务时，纸张比计算机更有优势。人们看到凌乱的办公桌时，或者看到空中交通管制员在纸条上草草记下航班的景象时感到沮丧，都源于人们对纸张在我们生活中所扮演的角色产生了根本性的困惑。

B 在《无纸化办公室的神话》一书中，两名社会学家阿比盖尔·塞伦和理查德·哈珀对纸张的观点进行了最有力的阐述。他们以讲述一项他们在华盛顿国际货币基金组织所做的研究作为该书的开端。国际货币基金组织的经济学家们大部分时间都在撰写关于复杂经济问题的报告，这些工作似乎非常适合坐在电脑前完成。然而，国际货币基金组织还是充斥着大量的纸张，塞伦和哈珀想要找出原因。他们的回答是：至少在国际货币基金组织中报告的业务是一个高度合作的过程，是许多人的专业判断和贡献。经济学家将报告草稿带到会议室，展开相关的页面，并与另一个人协商变更。他们回到自己的办公室，利用非正式手写便条提供的自由，在空白处草草记下评论。然后，他们亲自将带注释的草稿交给作者，并逐页地指明建议改动的地方。在这个过程的最后，作者把所有带评论的页面都放在他的桌子上，然后开始在电脑上输入——在他工作的时候移动页面，组织和重组，保存和丢弃。

C 如果没有纸张，这种协作和反复的工作过程将会困难得多。根据塞伦和哈珀的说法，纸张有一组独特的"可供性"——也就是允许特定类型使用的特性。纸张是有形的：我们可以拿起一份文件，翻阅它，随处都能读一点儿，然后很快就能把握它（的大致意思）。纸张在空间上是灵活的，这意味着我们可以把它展开，并以最适合我们的方式排列。而且它是可改变的：我们可以轻松注释它，并且在我们阅读的时候在上面乱涂乱画，而不改变原来的文本。当然，电子文档也有自己的可供性。它们可以很容易地搜索、共享、存储和远程链接到其他相关的材料。但它们缺乏对一群人在一份报告上合作的可供性。

D 纸张能使人产生某种思维。例如，想象一下你的桌面。很有可能在桌子的一边你有一个键盘和一个电脑屏幕，在你的椅子前面有一个大约 18 平方英寸的空间。覆盖桌面的剩余部分可能是成堆的文件、期刊、杂志、活页夹、明信片、录像带，以及所有其他知识经济的产物。这成堆的东西看起来很乱，但事实并非如此。几年前，当苹果电脑的一群人研究了"堆起"的行为时，他们发现，即使是最杂乱的一堆，通常也能对成堆的东西产生完美的感觉，而办公室的工作人员可以详细地讲述他们"成堆"的确切历史和意义。例如，最靠近被清理的 18 平方英寸的工作区域的"堆起"，通常代表着最多的业务，而在这一堆中，最重要的文件可能是在最上面的。"成堆"的是活的，会呼吸的档案。随着时间的推移，它们会被分解和采用，有时是按时间顺序的，有时是按主题顺序的，有时两者兼而有之。某些文档的线索可能会被物理性地嵌入到文件中，比如，将一张纸以一个角度插入，或者将分隔物插入到文件堆中。

E 但是为什么我们要把文件堆起来而不是归档呢？因为成堆代表了活跃的、正在进行的思考过程。塞伦和哈珀广泛地提到心理学家艾利森·基德的研究，她认为"知识工作者"使用桌面的物理空间来持有"他们还不能分类或者甚至还未决定如何使用的想法"。凌乱的办公桌并不一定是组织混乱的标志。这可能是一种复杂性的表现：那些同时处理许多未解决的想法的人不能分类和归档他们的办公桌上的文件，因为他们还没有对头脑里的想法进行分类和归档。基德写道，她交谈过的许多人都把桌子上的文件作为背景线索，在周一早上的时候，或者在他们的工作被电话打断后，"在没有困难和延迟的情况下恢复一组复杂的思路"。从某种意义上说，当我们看到桌子上成堆的东西时，我们看到的是我们大脑的内容。

F 这种纸张促进了高度专业化的认知和社会过程的观点，与我们以往对事物的看法大相径庭。在19世纪后期，作为"系统管理"运行的一部分，纸张开始在工作场所激增。为了应对工业经济的复杂性，经理们制定了全公司范围的政策，要求下属每月、每周甚至每天更新信息。由此诞生了月度销售报告，以及办公室手册和内部公司通信。打字机在19世纪80年代投入使用，使其能够在比以前更短的时间内创造出文件，而紧随其后的是碳素纸的出现，这意味着打字员可以同时创造出十份文件。纸张不仅对于促进创造性的协作和思考是很重要的，它同时也是一种控制工具。

TEST 3

READING PASSAGE 1

参考答案

1	B	2	C	3	A
4	C	5	B	6	C
7	D	8	A	9	TRUE
10	NOT GIVEN	11	TRUE	12	FALSE
13	FALSE				

Finding Our Way

A 'Drive 200 yards, and then turn right,' says the car's computer voice. You relax in the driver's seat, follow the directions and reach your destination without error. It's certainly nice to have the Global Positioning System (GPS) to direct you to within a few yards of your goal. Yet if the satellite service's digital maps become even slightly outdated, you can become lost. Then you have to rely on the ancient human skill of navigating in three-dimensional space. Luckily, your biological finder has an important advantage over GPS: it does not go awry if only one part of the guidance system goes wrong, because it works in various ways. You can ask questions of people on the sidewalk. Or follow a street that looks familiar. Or rely on a navigational rubric: 'If I keep the East River on my left, I will eventually cross 34th Street.' The human positioning system is flexible and capable of learning. (9) Anyone who knows the way from point A to point B — and from A to C, can probably figure out how to get from B to C, too.

B But how does this complex cognitive system really work? Researchers are looking at several strategies people use to orient themselves in space: guidance, path integration and route following. We may use all three or combinations thereof. And as experts learn more about these navigational skills, they are making the case that our abilities may underlie our powers of memory and logical thinking. Grand Central, please imagine that you have arrived in a place you have never visited — New York City. You get off the train at Grand Central Terminal in midtown Manhattan. You have a few hours to explore before you must return home. You head uptown to see popular spots you have been told about: Rockefeller Centre, Central Park, and the Metropolitan Museum of Art. You meander in and out of shops along the way. Suddenly, it is time to get back to the station. But how?

C If you ask passersby for help, most likely you will receive information in many different forms. (10) A person who orients herself by a prominent landmark would gesture southward: 'Look down there. See the tall, broad Met Life Building? Head for that, the station is right below it.' Neurologists call this navigational approach 'guidance', meaning that a landmark visible from a distance serves as the marker for one's destination. (3)

D Another city dweller might say, 'What places do you remember passing? Okay. Go toward the end of Central Park, then walk down to St. Patrick's Cathedral. A few more blocks, and Grand Central will be off to your left.' In this case, you are pointed toward the most recent place you recall, and you aim for it. Once you arrive in the next notable place, you can retrace your path. Your brain is adding together the individual legs of your trek into a cumulative progress report. Researchers call this strategy 'path integration'. (5) Many animals rely primarily on path integration to get around, including insects, spiders, crabs and rodents. The desert ants of the genus Cataglyphis employ this method to return from foraging as far as 100 yards away. They note the general direction they came from and retrace their steps, using the polarisation of sunlight to orient themselves even under overcast skies. (1) On their way back they are faithful to this inner homing vector. Even when a scientist picks up an ant and puts it in a totally different spot, the insect stubbornly proceeds in the originally determined direction until it has gone 'back' all of the distance it wandered from its nest. (6) Only then does the ant realise it has not succeeded, and it begins to walk in successively larger loops to find its way home.

E   Whether it is trying to get back to the anthill or the train station, any animal using path integration must keep track of its own movements, so it knows, while returning, which segments it has already completed. As you move, your brain gathers data from your environment sights, sounds, smells, lighting, muscle contractions, a sense of time passing — to determine which way your body has gone. (11) The church spire, the sizzling sausages on that vendor's grill, the open courtyard, and the train station-all represent snapshots of memorable junctures during your journey.

F   In addition to guidance and path integration, we use a third method for finding our way. An office worker you approach for help on a Manhattan street corner might say: 'Walk straight down Fifth, turn left on 47th, turn right on Park, go through the walkway under the Helmsley Building, then cross the street to the Met Life Building into Grand Central.' This strategy, called route following, uses landmarks such as buildings and street names, plus directions — straight, turn, go through — for reaching intermediate points. (2) Route following is more precise than guidance or path integration, but if you forget the details and take a wrong turn, the only way to recover is to backtrack until you reach a familiar spot, because you do not know the general direction or have a reference landmark for your goal. (4) The route-following navigation strategy truly challenges the brain. We have to keep all the landmarks and intermediate directions in our head. It is the most detailed and therefore most reliable method, but it can be undone by routine memory lapses. With path integration, our cognitive memory is less burdened; (12) it has to deal with only a few general instructions and the homing vector. Path integration works because it relies most fundamentally on our knowledge of our body's general direction of movement, and we always have access to these inputs. Nevertheless, people often choose to give route-following directions, in part because saying 'Go straight that way!' just does not work in our complex, man-made surroundings.

G   Road Map or Metaphor? On your next visit to Manhattan you will rely on your memory to get around. Most likely you will use guidance, path integration and route-following in various combinations. But how exactly do these constructs deliver concrete directions? Do we humans have, as an image of the real world, a kind of road map in our heads, with symbols for cities, train stations and churches; thick lines for highways, narrow lines for local streets? Neurobiologists and cognitive psychologists do call the portion of our memory that controls navigation a 'cognitive map'. (7) The map metaphor is obviously seductive: maps are the easiest way to present geographic information for convenient visual inspection. In many cultures, maps were developed before writing, and today they are used in almost every society. It is even possible that maps derive from a universal way in which our spatial-memory networks are wired.

H   Yet the notion of a literal map in our heads may be misleading; a growing body of research implies that the cognitive map is mostly a metaphor. It may be more like a hierarchical structure of relationships. To get back to Grand Central, you first envision the large scale — that is, you visualise the general direction of the station. Within that system you then imagine the route to the last place you remember. After that, you observe your nearby surroundings to pick out a recognisable storefront or street corner that will send you toward that place. In this hierarchical, or nested, scheme, positions and distances are relative, in contrast with a road map, where the same information is shown in a geometrically precise scale. (8/13)

核心词汇

A 段

navigate [ˈnævɪgeɪt] *v.* 导航

three-dimensional [ˌθriːdaɪˈmenʃənl] *adj.* 三维的

awry [əˈraɪ] *adj.* 出岔子的，出错的

rubric [ˈruːbrɪk] *n.* 说明，规定

B 段

thereof [ˌðeərˈɒv] *adv.* 在其中

underlie [ˌʌndəˈlaɪ] *v.* 为……的起因；构成……的基础

meander [miˈændə(r)] *v.* 漫步，闲逛，蜿蜒而行

C 段

passersby [ˌpɑːsəˈbaɪ] *n.* 路人

prominent [ˈprɒmɪnənt] *adj.* 重要的，杰出的，著名的

D 段

dweller [ˈdwelə(r)] *n.* 居民

retrace [rɪˈtreɪs] *v.* 沿（原路）返回

trek [trek] *n.* 行进，远足

cumulative [ˈkjuːmjələtɪv] *adj.* 渐增的，聚集的，累积的

rodent [ˈrəʊdnt] *n.* 啮齿动物

forage [ˈfɒrɪdʒ] *v.* 外出觅食

polarisation [ˌpəʊləraɪˈzeɪʃn] *n.* 极化，分化

vector [ˈvektə(r)] *n.* 矢量，向量

loop [luːp] *n.* 圈

E 段

anthill [ˈænthɪl] *n.* 蚁丘

segment [ˈsegmənt] *n.* 部分

contraction [kənˈtrækʃn] *n.* 收缩

spire [ˈspaɪə(r)] *n.* （教堂等建筑物的）尖顶

sizzle [ˈsɪzl] *v.* 发出咝咝声

juncture [ˈdʒʌŋktʃə(r)] *n.* 时刻，关键时刻

F 段

backtrack ['bæktræk] *v.* 原路返回
lapse [læps] *n.* 小错,疏忽

G 段

metaphor ['metəfə(r)] *n.* 隐喻,象征
seductive [sɪ'dʌktɪv] *adj.* 非常吸引人的
derive [dɪ'raɪv] *v.* 起源,来自于

H 段

hierarchical [ˌhaɪə'rɑːkɪkl] *adj.* 等级制度的

寻路

A   "开200码,然后向右转,"汽车的电脑声音说。你放松地坐在驾驶员的座位上,按照指示到达目的地,没有任何错误。让全球定位系统(GPS)将你带到你目的地的几码之内当然是件美好的事。然而,如果卫星服务的数字地图有一丁点儿陈旧,你可能就会迷失方向。然后你必须依靠人类在三维空间中导航的老式技能。幸运的是,你的生物导航有一个超越GPS的重要优势:如果导航系统中会有一部分出错,生物导航是不会出错的,因为它以多种方式工作。你可以在人行道上向别人问路,或者沿着一条看起来很熟悉的街道走,或者依赖于一个导航的标题:"如果东河始终在我的左边,我最终会穿过第34大街。""人类定位系统是灵活的,并且具备学习的能力。"任何知道如何从A点走到B点和从A走到C的人,都可能知道如何从B走到C。

B   那么这个复杂的认知系统是如何运作的呢?研究人员正在研究人们用于在空间中定位自己的几种策略:指导、路径整合和路线跟踪。我们可以使用这三种或其组合。随着专家们对这些导航技能的了解越来越多,他们认为我们的能力可能是我们记忆力和逻辑思维能力的基础。请想象你已经到达了一个你从未去过的地方——纽约市的中央车站。你在曼哈顿市中心的中央车站下车。在你必须回家之前,你有几个小时的时间去探索。你到上城区去看你知道的热门景点:洛克菲勒中心、中央公园和大都会艺术博物馆。你在沿途的商店里进进出出。突然,是时候回到车站了。但怎么才能回到车站?

C   如果你向路人寻求帮助,很可能你会得到许多不同形式的信息。以突出的地标来定位的人会打着向南的手势,说道:"往南看。看到高大的大都会建筑了吗?往那里走,车站就在它的正下方。"神经学家把这种导航方法称为"指导"。这意味着远处可见的地标可以作为目的地的标志。

D   另一个城市居民可能会说:"你记得经过什么地方了吗?好吧。走到中央公园的尽头,然后走到圣帕特里克大教堂。再走几个街区,中央车站就在你的左边。"在这种情况下,你会被指向你所记起的最近的地方,而你就向它走去。一旦你到达下一个比较著名的地方,你就可以重新追踪你的方位。你的大脑将你的每一处旅程都加在一起,形成一个累积的进度报告。研究人员称这种策略为"路径整合"。许多动物都基本依赖于路径整合去走动,包括昆虫、蜘蛛、螃蟹和啮齿动物。一种叫箭蚁的沙漠蚂蚁就是利用这种方法从一百码远的地方觅食再返回。它们注意到它们来时的大致方向,并重新追踪它们的脚步,利用阳光的偏折,即便是在阴暗的天空下也可以定位自己的方向。在它们回来的路上,它们忠实于这个内在的归巢的向量。甚至当一个科学家捉起一只蚂蚁,把它放在一个完全不同的地方时,这种昆虫也会顽固地沿着最初确定的方向前进,直到它"回到"它从巢穴中走出来的所有距离。只有在蚂蚁意识到它没有成功之后,它才开始在更大的循环圈中不断行走,以找到回家的路。

E   无论是试图回到蚁丘还是火车站,使用路径整合的任何动物都必须记录自己的动作,因此,在返回的时候,它会知道已经完成了哪些部分。当你移动的时候,你的大脑会从周围的环境景观、声音、气味、灯光、肌肉收缩、时间的流逝感中收集数据,从而确定你走过哪条路。教堂的尖顶,小贩烤架上的铁板香肠、开放的院子和火车站——都代表着在你旅途中可记忆时刻的快照。

F   除了指导和路径整合之外,我们还使用第三种方法来寻找我们的路。你在曼哈顿街角向某个办公室职员求助,他可能会说:"径直走到第五大道,在第47街左转,在公园右转,穿过汉姆斯利大厦下的人行道,然后穿过街道,进入大都会大厦,进入中央车站。"这一策略被称为"路线跟踪",它使用建筑物和街道名称等地标，再加上方向——直走、转弯、通过，来到达中间点。路线跟踪比指导或路径整合更精确，但是如果你忘记细节或转错了弯，恢复的唯一方式就是原路返回，直到到达一个你熟悉的地方，因为你不知道大致方向，也没有选取一个参考地标来作为你的目标。路线跟踪的导航策略确实挑战了大脑。我们必须把所有的地标和中间方向记在我们的大脑里。它是最详细也是最可靠的方法，但它可以被常规的记忆力衰退所破坏。对于路径整合，我们的认知记忆负担减轻了；它只需要处理一些一般的指令和归巢的向量。路径整合是有效的，因为它从最根本上依赖于我们对身体运动的一般方向的认识，并且我们总是能够获得这些认识。尽管如此，人们通常会选择按路线走：单单说"直走！"在我们复杂的、人造的环境中是行不通的。

G 路线图或是比喻？在下次去曼哈顿的时候，你会依靠你的记忆四处走动。很可能你会各种组合使用指导、路径整合和路线跟踪。但是这些结构到底是如何传递具体的方向的呢？作为真实世界的一种图像，我们人类的头脑中有一种地图吗？上面标有城市、火车站和教堂的符号；公路的粗线或街道的细线？神经生物学家和认知心理学家确实把我们控制导航的记忆部分称为"认知地图"。地图的比喻显然是有吸引力的：地图是提供地理信息最简单的方式，方便视觉检查。在许多文化中，地图是在写作之前发展起来的，而今天，几乎每个社会中都使用地图。甚至有可能，地图来源于我们的空间记忆网络连接的通用方式。

H 然而，我们头脑中文字地图的概念可能具有误导性。越来越多的研究表明，认知地图主要是一种隐喻。它可能更像是一种关系的等级结构。要回到中央车站，你首先想到的是大范围，即你可以想象车站的大致方向。在这个系统中，你接着想象你记得的最后一个地方的路线。在那之后，你会观察附近的环境，挑选一个可辨认的店面或街道、角落，把你引向那个地方。对比以几何精确比例显示同样信息的路线图而言，在这个等级化或嵌套的方案中，位置和距离是相对的。

READING PASSAGE 2

参考答案

14	C	15	B	16	C
17	A	18	D	19	C
20	TRUE	21	TRUE	22	FALSE
23	NOT GIVEN	24	plastic tubes/the filter fabric straws	25	the selective membrane
26	extract				

The Success of Cellulose

A Not too long ago many investors made the bet that renewable fuels from bio-mass would be the next big thing in energy. Converting corn, sugarcane and soybeans into ethanol or diesel-type fuels lessens our nation's dependence on oil imports while cutting carbon dioxide emissions. But already the nascent industry faces challenges. Escalating demand is hiking food prices while farmers clear rain-forest habitats to grow fuel crops. And several recent studies say that certain biofuel-production processes either fail to yield net energy gains or release more carbon dioxide than they use.

B A successor tier of start-up ventures aims to avoid those problems. Rather than focusing on the starches, sugars and fats of food crops, many of the prototype bioethanol processes work with lignocellulose, the 'woody' tissue that strengthens the cell walls of plants, says University of Massachusetts Amherst chemical engineer George W. Huber. Although the cellulose breaks down less easily than sugars and starches and thus requires a complex series of enzyme-driven chemical reactions, its use opens the industry to nonfood plant feed-stocks such as agricultural wastes, wood chips and switchgrass. (20) But no company has yet demonstrated a cost-competitive industrial process for making cellulosic biofuels. (17)

C So scientists and engineers are working on dozens of possible biofuel-processing routes, reports Charles Wyman, a chemical engineer at the University of California, Riverside, who is a founder of Mascoma Corporation in Cambridge Mass, a leading developer of cellulosic ethanol processing. 'There's no miracle process out there,' he remarks. And fine-tuning a process involves considerable money and time. (18) 'The oil companies say that it takes 10 years to fully commercialise an industrial processing route,' warns Huber, who has contributed some thermochemical techniques to another biomass start-up, Virent Energy Systems in Madison, Wis. (21)

D One promising biofuel procedure that avoids the complex enzymatic chemistry to break down cellulose is now being explored by Coskata in Warrenville, a firm launched in 2006 by high-profile investors and entrepreneurs (General Motors recently took a minority stake in it as well). (22) In the Coskata operation, a conventional gasification system will use heat to turn various feedstocks into a mixture of carbon monoxide and hydrogen called syngas, says Richard Tobey, vice president of Engineering and R&D. The ability to handle multiple plant feedstocks would boost the flexibility of the overall process because each region in the country has access to certain feedstocks but not others. (20)

E Instead of using thermochemical methods to convert the syngas to fuel — a process that can be significantly more costly because of the added expense of pressurising gases, according to Tobey — the Coskata Group chose a biochemical route. (19) The group focused on five promising strains of ethanol-excreting bacteria that Ralph Tanner, a microbiologist at the University of Oklahoma, had discovered years before in the oxygen-free sediments of a swamp. These anaerobic bugs make ethanol by voraciously consuming syngas.

F The 'heart and soul of the Coskata process,' as Tobey puts it, is the bioreactor in which the bacteria live. (14) 'Rather than searching for food in the fermentation mash in a large tank, our bacteria wait for the gas to be delivered to them,' he explains. The firm's success relies on plastic tubes, the filter-fabric straws as thin as human hair. (24) The syngas flows through the straws, and water is pumped across their exteriors. The gases diffuse across the selective membrane to the bacteria embedded in the outer surface of the tubes, which permits no water inside. (25) 'We get efficient mass transfer with the tubes, which is not easy,' Tobey says. 'Our data suggest that in an optimal setting we could get 90 percent of the energy value of the gases into our fuel.' (16) After the bugs eat the gases, they release ethanol into the surrounding water. Standard distillation or filtration techniques could extract the alcohol from the water. (26)

G Coskata researchers estimate that their commercialised process could deliver ethanol at under $1 per gallon — less than half of today's $2-per-gallon wholesale price, Tobey claims. (22) Outside evaluators, a Argonne National Laboratory measured the input-output 'energy balance' of the Coskata process and found that, optimally, it can produce 7.7 times as much energy in the end product as it takes to make it.

H The company plans to construct a 40,000-gallon-a-year pilot plant near the GM test track in Milford, Mich., by the end of this year and hopes to build a full-scale, 100 million-gallon-a-year plant by 2011. Coskata may have some company by then; Bioengineering Resources in Fayetteville, Ark, is already developing what seems to be a similar three-step pathway in which syngas is consumed by bacteria isolated by James Gaddy, a retired chemical engineer at the University of Arkansas. Considering the advances in these and other methods, plant cellulose could provide the greener ethanol everyone wants. (15)

核心词汇

A 段

convert [kən'vɜːt] *v.* 转化

sugarcane ['ʃʊgə,ken] *n.* 甘蔗

ethanol ['eθənɒl] *n.* 乙醇

nascent ['næsnt] *adj.* 初期的

escalating ['eskəleɪtɪŋ] *adj.* 逐步扩大的

B 段

venture ['ventʃə(r)] *n.* 冒险事业，商业冒险

cellulose ['seljuləʊs] *n.* 纤维素

starch [stɑːtʃ] *n.* 淀粉

cellulosic [,seljʊ'ləʊsɪk] *adj.* 有纤维质的

C 段

commercialise [kə'mɜːʃəlaɪz] *v.* 商业化，使成为营利手段

D 段

entrepreneur [,ɒntrəprə'nɜː(r)] *n.* 企业家，主办人，承包人

gasification [,gæsəfə'keʃən] *n.* 气化，渗碳

syngas ['singæs] *n.* 合成气

E 段

pressurise ['preʃəraɪz] *v.* 加压，增压

anaerobic [,æneə'rəʊbɪk] *adj.* 厌氧菌的，无氧的

voraciously [və'reɪʃəsli] *adv.* 贪婪地

F 段

fermentation [,fɜːmen'teɪʃn] *n.* 发酵；激动，纷扰

diffuse [dɪ'fjuːs] *v.* 传播；四散

membrane ['membreɪn] *n.* 隔膜

optimal ['ɒptɪməl] *adj.* 最佳的

distillation [,dɪstɪ'leɪʃn] *n.* 蒸馏；升华

filtration [fɪl'treɪʃn] *n.* 过滤

纤维素的成功

A 就在不久前,许多投资者还押注于生物量的可再生燃料将成为能源领域的下一个大事件。将玉米、甘蔗和大豆转化为乙醇或柴油型燃料,减少了我们国家对石油进口的依赖,同时减少了二氧化碳的排放。但这个新生行业已经面临挑战。不断增长的需求提高了食品价格,而农民则清除雨林栖息地来种植燃料作物。最近的几项研究表明,某些生物燃料的生产过程或不能产生净能量收益,或释放出更多的二氧化碳。

B 初创的冒险事业的后继层旨在避免这些问题。马萨诸塞大学爱摩斯特分校的化学工程师乔治·W·胡贝尔说,许多生物乙醇的原型加工不是把重点放在食物作物的淀粉、糖和脂肪上,而是使用它的木质素纤维素,一种加强植物细胞壁的"木本"组织。尽管纤维素不像糖和淀粉那么容易分解,因此需要一系列复杂的酶驱动的化学反应,但它的使用使该行业向非食品植物原料开放,如农业废料、木片和柳枝稷等。但是,还没有一家公司在生产纤维素生物燃料原料中展示过一个具有成本竞争力的工业过程。

C 因此,加州大学河滨分校的化学工程师查尔斯·威曼报告说,科学家和工程师们正在研究几十种可能的生物燃料加工途径。他是马萨诸塞州剑桥市麦斯科马公司的创始人,该公司是纤维素乙醇加工的主要开发商。他说:"没有什么奇迹工程。"对一个过程进行微调需要花费大量的金钱和时间。胡贝尔提醒道:"石油公司说,要把一个工业加工途径完全商业化需要十年时间。"他曾为另一家生物质能初创企业——威斯康星州威斯特能源系统公司——提供了一些热化学技术。

D 2006年由著名的投资者和企业家在沃伦维尔成立的科斯卡塔公司(通用汽车最近也收购了它的少数股权)正在探索一个很有前景的生物燃料途径,它避免了复杂的酶化学分解纤维素。工程和研发部门的副总裁理查德·托比说,在科斯卡塔的操作中,传统的气化系统将使用热量将各种原料转化为一氧化碳和氢气的混合物,称为合成气。处理多种植物原料的能力将提高整个过程的灵活性,因为这个国家的每个地区都可以获得其中某些原料,而不是其他的原料。

E 根据托比的说法,科斯卡塔小组选择了一种生化途径,而不是使用热化学方法将合成气转化为燃料——这一过程可能会因为增压气体的费用而产生更大的成本。该小组关注的是五种有前景的释放乙醇的细菌,该细菌是俄克拉荷马大学的微生物学家拉尔夫·坦纳多年前在沼泽地的无氧沉积物中发现的。这些厌氧菌通过贪婪地消耗合成气来制造乙醇。

F 正如托比所说,科斯卡塔加工过程中的"心脏和灵魂"是细菌生存的生物反应器。他解释说:"我们的细菌不是在一个大水箱里寻找正在发酵的食物,而是等待气体被输送到它们体内。"公司的成功依赖于这些塑料管,这些细如发丝的滤布吸管。合成气流经吸管,水被泵到它们的外表面。这些气体散布在选择性隔膜上,扩散到附着在管道外表面的细菌中,这种细菌不允许内部有水。托比说:"我们用这些管子进行有效的大规模转移,这并不容易。我们的数据表明,在最理想的情况下,我们可以将气体90%的能量转化为燃料。"在厌氧菌吃掉这些气体之后,它们会把乙醇释放到周围的水里。标准蒸馏或过滤技术可以从水中提取酒精。

G 科斯卡塔的研究人员估计,他们的商业化途径释放的乙醇,价格低于每加仑1美元。托比说,这不到今天每加仑2美元的批发价格的一半。除了评估者,阿贡国家实验室测量了科斯卡塔过程中的输入—输出"能量平衡",并发现,最理想的情况是,在最终产品中,它能产生制作过程中消耗的 7.7 倍的能量。

H到今年年底,在密歇根州米尔福德的通用测试轨道附近,该公司计划建造一座每年 4 万加仑的试验工厂,并希望在 2011 年之前建立一座完整规模的 1 亿加仑的工厂。科斯卡塔到那时可能会有合作者;阿肯色州费耶特维尔的生物工程已经在开发一种类似的三步走的资源途径,在这个计划中,一位来自阿肯色大学的退休化学工程师詹姆斯·加迪隔离细菌以消耗合成气。考虑到这些和其他方法的进步,植物纤维素可以提供每个人都想要的更环保的乙醇。

READING PASSAGE 3

参考答案

27	iii	28	vii	29	i
30	iv	31	ix	32	viii
33	v	34	ii	35	FALSE
36	TRUE	37	NOT GIVEN	38	TRUE
39	TRUE	40	B		

Communicating Conflict!

A As far back as Hippocrates' time (460-370 B.C.) people have tried to understand other people by characterising them according to personality type or temperament. Hippocrates believed there were four different body fluids that influenced four basic types of temperament. His work was further developed 500 years later by Galen. (27) These days there are a number of self-assessment tools that relate to the basic descriptions developed by Galen, although we no longer believe the source to be the types of body fluid that dominate our systems.

B The values in self-assessments help determine personality style. (28) Learning styles, communication styles, conflict-handling styles, or other aspects of individuals are that they help depersonalise conflict in interpersonal relationships. The depersonalisation occurs when you realise that others aren't trying to be difficult, but they need different or more information than you do. They're not intending to be rude: they are so focused on the task they forget about greeting people. They would like to work faster but not at the risk of damaging the relationships needed to get the job done. They understand there is a job to do. But it can only be done right with the appropriate information, which takes time to collect. When used appropriately, understanding communication styles can help resolve conflict on teams. (40) Very rarely are conflicts true personality issues. Usually they are issues of style, information needs, or focus.

C Hippocrates and later Galen determined there were four basic temperaments: sanguine, phlegmatic, melancholic and choleric. (29) These descriptions were developed centuries ago and are still somewhat apt, although you could update the wording. In today's world, they translate into the four fairly common communication styles described below:

D The sanguine person would be the expressive or spirited style of communication. (30) These people speak in pictures. They invest a lot of emotion and energy in their communication and often speak quickly. Putting their whole body into it. They are easily sidetracked onto a story that may or may not illustrate the point they are trying to make. Because of their enthusiasm, they are great team motivators. They are concerned about people and relationships. Their high levels of energy can come on strong at times and their focus is usually on the bigger picture, which means they sometimes miss the details or the proper order of things. These people find conflict or differences of opinion invigorating and love to engage in a spirited discussion. They love change and are constantly looking for new and exciting adventures. (35)

E Tile phlegmatic person—cool and persevering—translates into the technical or systematic communication style. This style of communication is focused on facts and technical details. (31) Phlegmatic people have an orderly, methodical way of approaching tasks, and their focus is very much on the task, not on the people, emotions, or concerns that the task may evoke. The focus is also more on the details necessary to accomplish a task. Sometimes the details overwhelm the big picture and focus needs to be brought back to the context of the task. People with this style think the facts should speak for themselves, and they are not as comfortable with conflict. They need time to adapt to change and need to understand both the logic of it and the steps involved.

F The melancholic person who is softhearted and oriented toward doing things for others translates into the considerate or sympathetic communication style. (32) A person with this communication style is focused on people and relationships. They are good listeners and do things for other people — sometimes to the detriment of getting things done for themselves. They want to solicit everyone's opinion and make sure everyone is comfortable with whatever is required to get the job done. At times this focus on others can distract from the task at hand. Because they are so concerned with the needs of others and smoothing over issues, they do not like conflict. They believe that change threatens the status quo and tends to make people feel uneasy, so people with this communication style, like phlegmatic people, need time to consider the changes in order to adapt to them. (36)

G The choleric temperament translates into the bold or direct style of communication. (33) People with this style are brief in their communication — the fewer words the better. They are big picture thinkers and love to be involved in many things at once. They are focused on tasks and outcomes and often forget that the people involved in carrying out the tasks have needs. They don't do detail work easily and as a result can often underestimate how much time it takes to achieve the task. Because they are so direct, they often seem forceful and can be very intimidating to others. They usually would welcome someone challenging them. But most other styles are afraid to do so. They also thrive on change, the more the better.

H A well-functioning team should have all of these communication styles for true effectiveness. (34) All teams need to focus on the task, and they need to take care of relationships in order to achieve those tasks. They need the big picture perspective or the context of their work, and they need the details to be identified and taken care of for success. We all have aspects of each style within us. Some of us can easily move from one style to another and adapt our style to the needs of the situation at hand — whether the focus is on tasks or relationships. (38) For others, a dominant style is very evident, and it is more challenging to see the situation from the perspective of another style.

I The work environment can influence communication styles either by the type of work that is required or by the predominance of one style reflected in that environment. (39) Some people use one style at work and another at home. The good news about communication styles is that we have the ability to develop flexibility in our styles. The greater the flexibility we have, the more skilled we usually are at handling possible and actual conflicts. Usually it has to be relevant to us to do so, either because we think it is important or because there are incentives in our environment to encourage it. The key is that we have to want to become flexible with our communication style. As Henry Ford said, 'Whether you think you can or you can't, you're right!'

核心词汇

A 段

fluid ['fluːɪd] *n.* 液体

B 段

depersonalise [diːˈpɜːsənəlaɪz] *v.* 使非个性化

C 段

sanguine [ˈsæŋgwɪn] *adj.* 乐天的，乐观的
phlegmatic [flegˈmætɪk] *adj.* 临危不惧的，冷静的，沉着的
melancholic [ˌmelənˈkɒlɪk] *adj.* 忧郁的，忧伤的
choleric [ˈkɒlərɪk] *adj.* 脾气火爆的，暴躁易怒的

D 段

spirited [ˈspɪrɪtɪd] *adj.* 精力充沛的；激烈的
sidetrack [ˈsaɪdtræk] *v.* 使转变话题，使转移目标
invigorating [ɪnˈvɪgəreɪtɪŋ] *adj.* 令人精神振奋的，令人充满生气的

E 段

evoke [ɪˈvəʊk] *v.* 引起，召唤

F 段

solicit [səˈlɪsɪt] *v.* 征求……的意见
status quo 现状，状况

G 段

bold [bəʊld] *adj.* 大胆的，无谓的
intimidating [ɪnˈtɪmɪdeɪtɪŋ] *adj.* 令人胆怯的，令人畏惧的

I 段

predominance [prɪˈdɒmɪnəns] *n.* 优势，主导地位，支配地位
incentive [ɪnˈsentɪv] *n.* 动机，刺激

沟通冲突

A 早在希波克拉底的时代（公元前 460—公元前 370 年），人们就试图根据性格类型或气质来理解他人。希波克拉底认为，有四种不同的体液影响了四种基本类型的气质。500 年后盖伦进一步发展了他的成果。如今，尽管我们不再相信体液类型是支配我们身体系统的源头，但仍有许多由盖伦开发的有关基本描述的自我评估工具。

B 自我评估中的价值观有助于决定个性风格。学习方式、沟通方式、冲突处理方式或个人的其他方面，都有助于人际关系中的冲突非个性化。当你意识到别人并不是在试图变得不随和，而是他们需要不同的或者比你更多的信息时，非个性化就发生了。他们不是故意粗鲁无礼：他们只是太专注于任务，以至于忘记了照顾别人的情感。他们想要更快地工作，但不会冒着所需要的破坏关系的风险来完成工作。他们知道有工作要做。但工作只能通过合适的信息才能以正确的方式完成，这需要时间来收集。如果使用得当，理解沟通方式可以帮助解决团队之间的冲突。冲突很少是真正的性格问题。通常冲突是方式、信息需求或焦点的问题。

C 希波克拉底和后来的盖伦认为有四种基本的性情：多血质、粘液质、神经质和胆汁质。这些描述是在几个世纪前发展起来的，尽管你可以更新措辞，但今天仍然比较恰当。在当今世界，它们解释为以下四种相当普遍的交流方式：

D 多血质者将会是采用富有表现力的或充满活力的交流方式。这些人说话很有画面感。他们在交流中投入了大量的情感和精力，并且通常语速很快。他们把整个身体都投入进去。他们很容易转换话题，以至于可能或无法阐释清他们想要阐述的观点。由于他们的热情，他们是团队杰出的激励者。他们关心人以及人之间的关系。他们的高级别的能量有时会变得很强大，他们的注意力通常集中在更大的范围上，这意味着他们有时会忽略细节或事物的正确顺序。这些人发现冲突或意见的分歧时会精神振奋，喜欢进行热烈的讨论。他们喜欢变化，并且不断地寻找新的令人兴奋的冒险。

E 黏液质者——冷静而坚忍——解释为技术或系统的沟通方式。这种交流方式主要集中在事实和技术细节上。黏液质者有一种有序的、有条不紊的方法来完成任务，他们的注意力主要集中在任务上，而不是任务可能引起的相关的人、情感或担忧上，关注点还在于完成一项任务所必需的细节。有时，细节压倒全局，焦点需要回到任务的框架中。有这种风格的人认为应该用事实说话，他们对冲突会觉得不那么舒服。他们需要时间来适应变化，需要理解相关的逻辑和步骤。

F 神经质者，心软，倾向于为他人做事，被理解为体贴或同情的沟通方式。具有这种沟通风格的人专注于人与关系。他们是很好的倾听者，为他人做事——有时甚至会损害自己的工作。他们想要征求每个人的意见，并希望确保每个人都能接受完成工作所需要的一切。有时，这种对他人的关注会分散他们对手头工作的注意力。因为他们非常关心别人的需要，并希望平息问题，他们不喜欢冲突。他们相信变化会威胁到现状，往往会让人感到不安，所以有这种沟通方式的人，像黏液质者一样，需要时间来考虑这些变化，以适应它们。

G 胆汁质的性情被解释为大胆或直接的沟通方式。这种风格的人在交流中很简洁——话越少越好。他们是大局面的思考家，喜欢同时参与许多事情。他们专注于任务和结果，往往忘记了参与执行任务的人也有需求。他们不擅长做细节工作，因此往往会低估完成任务所需的时间。因这类人是如此的直接，他们常常让人感觉坚定有力而令人生畏。他们通常欢迎有人挑战他们。但大多数其他风格的人都不敢这么做。他们也喜欢变化，并且越多越好。

H一个运转良好的团队应该具备所有这些沟通方式，以达到真正的效果。所有的团队都需要专注于任务，他们需要处理好关系来完成这些任务。他们需要全局的视角或者着眼整体工作的环境，他们需要确定细节，并为成功做好准备。我们每个人都有自己的风格。我们中的一些人可以很容易地从一种风格转变到另一种风格，并根据手头情况的需要调整我们的风格——无论是专注于任务还是人际关系。对另一些人来说，某种主导风格显而易见，从另一种风格的角度来看待这种情况则更具挑战性。

I通过所需要的工作类型或在该环境中能反映一种风格优势的工作环境可以影响沟通方式。有些人在工作时使用一种风格，在家里则用另一种风格。关于沟通方式的好消息是，我们有能力在我们的风格中发展灵活性。我们拥有的灵活性越大，在处理可能的和实际的冲突时我们就更熟练。通常情况下，它必须与我们相关才能这么做，要么是因为我们认为它很重要，要么是因为我们的环境中有激励它的动机。关键是我们必须要灵活运用我们的沟通方式。正如亨利·福特所说，"不管你认为你能还是不能，你都是对的！"

TEST 4

READING PASSAGE 1

参考答案

1	B	2	E	3	A
4	D	5	B	6	TRUE
7	TRUE	8	NOT GIVEN	9	FALSE
10	NOT GIVEN	11	headspace	12	filters
13	needle				

Hunting Perfume in Madagascar!

A Ever since the unguentari plied their trade in ancient Rome, perfumers have to keep abreast of changing fashions. These days they have several thousand ingredients to choose from when creating new scents, but there is always demand for new combinations. The bigger the 'palette' of smells, the better the perfumer's chance of creating something fresh and appealing. Even with everyday products such as shampoo and soap, kitchen cleaners and washing powders, consumers are becoming increasingly fussy. And many of today's fragrances have to survive tougher treatment than ever before, resisting the destructive power of bleach or a high temperature wash cycle. (3) Chemists can create new smells from synthetic molecules, and a growing number of the odours on the perfumer's palette are artificial. (6) But nature has been in the business far longer.

B The island of Madagascar is an evolutionary hot spot; 85% of its plants are unique, making it an ideal source for novel fragrances. (1/7) Last October, Quest International, a company that develops fragrances for everything from the most delicate perfumes to cleaning products, sent an expedition to Madagascar in pursuit of some of nature's most novel fragrances. With some simple technology, borrowed from the pollution monitoring industry, and a fair amount of ingenuity, the perfume hunters bagged 20 promising new aromas in the Madagascan rainforest. (9) Each day the team set out from their 'hotel' — a wooden hut lit by kerosene lamps, and trailed up and down paths and animal tracks, exploring the thick vegetation up to 10 metres on either side of the trail. (5) Some smells came from obvious places, often big showy flowers within easy reach. Others were harder to pin down. 'Often it was the very small flowers that were much more interesting,' says Clery. After the luxuriance of the rainforest, the little-known island of Nosy Hara was a stark, dry place — geologically and biologically very different from the mainland. 'Apart from two beaches, the rest of the island is impenetrable, except by hacking through the bush,' says Clery. One of the biggest prizes here was a sweet-smelling sap weeping from the gnarled branches of some ancient shrubby trees in the parched interior. So far no one has been able to identify the plant.

C With most flowers or fruits, the hunters used a technique originally designed to trap and identify air pollutants. The technique itself is relatively simple. A glass bell jar or flask is fitted over the flower. The fragrance molecules are trapped in this 'headspace' and can be extracted by pumping the air out over a series of filters which absorb different types of volatile molecules. (11/12) Back home in the laboratory, the molecules are flushed out of the filters and injected into a gas chromatograph for analysis. If it is impossible to attach the headspace gear, hunters fix an absorbent probe close to the source of the smell. The probe looks something like a hypodermic syringe, except that the 'needle' is made of silicone rubber which soaks up molecules from the air. (13) After a few hours, the hunters retract the rubber needle and seal the tube, keeping the odour molecules inside until they can be injected into the gas chromatograph in the laboratory.

D Some of the most promising fragrances were those given off by resins that oozed from the bark of trees. Resins are the source of many traditional perfumes, including frankincense and myrrh. The most exciting resin came from a Calophyllum tree, which produces a strongly scented medicinal oil. The sap of this Calophyllum smelt rich and aromatic, a little like church incense. But it also smelt of something like fragrance industry has learnt to live without, castoreum, a substance extracted from the musk glands of beavers and once a key ingredient in many perfumes. The company does not use animal products any longer, but it was wonderful to find a tree with an animal smell. (4/10)

E The group also set out from the island to capture the smell of coral reefs. Odours that conjure up sun kissed seas are highly sought after by the perfume industry. 'From the ocean, the only thing we have is seaweed, and that has a dark and heavy aroma. We hope to find something unique among the corals,' says Dir. The challenge for the hunters was to extract a smell from water rather than air. This was an opportunity to try Clery's new 'aquaspace' apparatus — a set of filters that work underwater. (2) On Nosy Hara, jars were fixed over knobs of coral about 2 metres down and water was pumped out over the absorbent filters. So what does coral smell like? 'It's a bit like lobster and crab,' says Clery. The team's task now is to recreate the best of their captured smells. First they must identify the molecules that make up each fragrance. Some ingredients may be quite common chemicals. But some may be completely novel, or they may be too complex or expensive to make in the lab. The challenge then is to conjure up the fragrances with more readily available materials. 'We can avoid the need to import plants from the rainforest by creating the smell with a different set of chemicals from those in the original material,' says Clery. 'If we get it right, you can sniff the sample and it will transport you straight back to the moment you smelt it in the rainforest.'

核心词汇

A 段

ply [plaɪ] v. 经营生意

keep abreast of 与……并驾齐驱

scent [sent] n. 气味

palette ['pælət] n. 调色盘

bleach [bliːtʃ] n. 漂白剂

synthetic [sɪn'θetɪk] adj. 合成的；人造的

molecule ['mɒlɪkjuːl] n. 分子

odour ['əʊdə(r)] n. 味道

artificial [ˌɑːtɪ'fɪʃl] adj. 人工的

B 段

aroma [ə'rəʊmə] n. 芳香

kerosene lamp 煤油灯

showy ['ʃəʊi] adj. 艳丽的

luxuriance [lʌg'ʒʊəriəns] n. 茂盛

stark [stɑːk] adj. 荒凉的

impenetrable [ɪm'penɪtrəbl] adj. 不可通过的

hack through 在……中开路

sap [sæp] n. 树液

gnarled [nɑːld] adj. 长满树瘤的；粗糙多节的

shrubby ['ʃrʌbi] adj. 灌木的

parched [pɑːtʃt] adj. 炎热的；干燥的

C 段

pollutant [pə'luːtənt] n. 污染物

bell jar 钟形容器，钟罩

flask [flɑːsk] n. 烧瓶

extract ['ekstrækt] v. 萃取

volatile ['vɒlətaɪl] adj. 挥发性的

gas chromatograph 气相色谱仪

absorbent [əb'zɔːbənt] adj. 能吸收的

probe [prəʊb] n. 探针

hypodermic [ˌhaɪpə'dɜːmɪk] adj. 皮下的

syringe [sɪ'rɪndʒ] n. 注射器

silicone rubber 硅胶

soak up 吸收

retract [rɪ'trækt] v. 缩进；撤回

D 段

resin ['rezɪn] n. 树脂

ooze [uːz] v. 渗出

frankincense ['fræŋkɪnsens] n. 乳香

myrrh [mɜː(r)] n. 没药

aromatic [ˌærə'mætɪk] adj. 芳香的

incense ['ɪnsens] n. 香

castoreum [kæ'stɔːrɪəm] n. 海狸香

substance ['sʌbstəns] n. 物质

musk [mʌsk] n. 麝香

gland [glænd] n. 腺

E 段

coral reef 珊瑚礁

conjure up 想起

seaweed ['siːwiːd] n. 海藻

apparatus [ˌæpə'reɪtəs] n. 装置

在马达加斯加猎香

A 自从玻璃器皿在古罗马进行交易以来，香水师们就必须跟上潮流的变化。如今，在创造新气味时，他们有几千种成分可供选择，但总有新的组合需求。气味的"调色板"越大，香水师创造出新鲜和吸引人的香水的机会就越大。即使有洗发水、香皂、厨房清洁剂和洗衣粉这样的日常用品，消费者也变得越来越挑剔。今天的许多芳香剂必须经受比以往任何时候更严格的处理，抵抗漂白或高温洗涤循环的破坏性力量。化学家可以从合成分子中制造出新的气味，而在香水师的调色板上，越来越多的气味是人造的。但大自然在这方面的历史更悠久。

B 马达加斯加岛是一个正在发展中的热点；岛上85%的植物都是独一无二的，这使它成为新香味的理想来源。奎斯特国际公司，致力于开发用于各种产品的芳香剂，从最精致的香水到清洁用品等。为了寻求大自然最新颖的香味，去年十月该公司派出了一支考察队到马达加斯加。利用一些从污染监测行业借鉴而来的简单的技术，以及相当多的独创性，香水猎人在马达加斯加雨林中收获了20种有前景的新香味。每天，这支队伍从他们的"旅馆"出发——一间煤油灯照明的木屋，沿着小路和动物的足迹，探索小径两侧高达10米的茂密的植物。有些气味来自于明显的地方，通常是容易够到的又大又艳丽的花朵。其他的则较难采到。克利里说："通常是那些非常小的花更有趣。"位于繁茂的热带雨林之后，鲜为人知的诺西哈拉岛是一个荒凉、干燥的地方——从地理和生物方面来说，与大陆截然不同。克利里说："除了两个海滩外，岛上的其他地方都是无法穿越的，只能在灌木丛中开辟道路。"这里最大的奖赏之一是：在干燥的岛内，一种古老的灌木树的长满树瘤的树枝上流出一种散发着甜味的树液。到目前为止，还没有人能够识别这种植物。

C 对于大多数的花或水果，猎人们使用一种最初设计用来捕捉和识别空气污染物的技术。这项技术本身相对简单。在花上安装一个玻璃钟罩或烧瓶。香味分子被困在"顶部空间"里，通过将空气抽出并经过一系列过滤器吸收不同类型的挥发性分子，可以将其提取出来。回到实验室里，将这些分子从过滤器中抽出并注入气相色谱仪进行分析。如果不可能连接到顶部空间装置，猎香者们就会在靠近气味源的地方固定一个吸收探针。这个探针看起来像一个皮下注射器，只不过"针"是由硅胶制成的，它可以从空气中吸收分子。几小时后，猎香者们收回橡胶针并封住管子，将气味分子留在里边，直到它们能被注射到实验室的气相色谱仪中。

D 一些最有市场前景的香味是那些从树皮上渗出来的树脂散发出来的。树脂是许多传统香水的来源，包括乳香和没药。最令人兴奋的树脂来自于一棵美珊瑚树，这棵树能产生一种强烈香味的药用油。这种树的汁液闻起来浓郁而芳香，有点像教堂的熏香。但它闻起来也像香水行业里已经不使用的海狸香，一种从海狸的麝腺中提取出来的物质，曾经是许多香水的关键成分。该公司不再使用动物产品，但找到一棵带有动物气味的树真是太好了。

E 该组织还从岛上出发，捕捉珊瑚礁的气味。一种能让人联想到太阳亲吻海洋的香味，备受香水行业青睐。"从海洋中，我们唯一拥有的就是海藻，它有一种深沉而浓郁的香气。我们希望能在珊瑚中找到一些独特的东西，"迪尔说。猎香者们面临的挑战是：要从水中而不是空气中提取出一种气味。这是试用克利里的"水下空间"仪器的一个机会——一套在水下工作的过滤器。在诺西哈拉岛上，罐子被固定在水下大约两米深的珊瑚旋钮上，水从吸收剂过滤器中抽出来。那么，珊瑚的气味是什么样的呢？"有点像龙虾和螃蟹，"克利里说。这个团队现在的任务是重新创造出他们所捕获的气味中最好的香味。首先，他们必须识别出形成每一种香味的分子。有些成分可能是很常见的化学物质。但是有些可能是完全新颖的，或者它们可能太复杂或太昂贵而不能在实验室里制造出来。挑战则是采用更容易获得的材料创造这些香味。"我们可以避免从雨林中进口植物的需要，通过使用不同于原材料的化学物质创造出这种香味，"克瑞里说，"如果我们成功了，你可以嗅样本，它会把你直接带回到在雨林中闻到的那一刻。"

READING PASSAGE 2

参考答案

14	ix	15	vi	16	x
17	vii	18	v	19	i
20	NOT GIVEN	21	TRUE	22	NOT GIVEN
23	biological phenomena	24	DNA microarrays	25	(myriad) conditions
26	their expression levels				

Life Code: Unlocked

A On an airport shuttle bus to the Kavli Institute for Theoretical Physics in Santa Barbara, Calif, Chris Wiggins took a colleague's advice and opened a Microsoft Excel spreadsheet. It had nothing to do with the talk on biopolymer physics he was invited to give. Rather the columns and rows of numbers that stared back at him referred to the genetic activity of budding yeast. Specifically, the numbers represented the amount of messenger RNA (mRNA) expressed by all 6,200 genes of the yeast over the course of its reproductive cycle. 'It was the first time I ever saw anything like this,' Wiggins recalls of that spring day in 2002. 'How to make sense of all these data?'

B Instead of shirking from this question, the 36-year-old applied mathematician and physicist at Columbia University embraced it — and now six years later he thinks he has an answer. By foraying into fields outside his own, Wiggins has drudged up tools from a branch of artificial intelligence called machine learning to model the collective proteinmaking activity of genes from real-world biological data. (14) Engineers originally designed these tools in the late 1950s to predict output from input. Wiggins and his colleagues have now brought machine learning to the natural sciences and tweaked it so that it can also tell a story — one not only about input and output but also about what happens inside a model of gene regulation, the black box in between.

C The impetus for this work began in the late 1990s, when high-throughput techniques generated more mRNA expression profiles and DNA sequences than ever before. 'Opening up a completely different way of thinking about biological phenomena,' Wiggins says. (23) Key among these techniques were DNA microarrays, (24) chips that provide a panoramic view of the activity of genes and their expression levels in any cell type, (26) simultaneously and under myriad conditions. (15/20/25) As noisy and incomplete as the data were, biologists could now query which genes turn on or off in different cells and determine the collection of proteins that give rise to a cell's characteristic features — healthy or diseased.

D Yet predicting such gene activity requires uncovering the fundamental rules that govern it. (16) 'Over time, these rules have been locked in by cells,' says theoretical physicist Harmen Bussemaker, now an associate professor of biology at Columbia. 'Evolution has kept the good stuff.' To find these rules, scientists needed statistics to infer the interaction between genes and the proteins that regulate them and to then mathematically describe this network's underlying structure — the dynamic pattern of gene and protein activity over time. But physicists who did not work with particles (or planets, for that matter) viewed statistics as nothing short of an anathema. (16) 'If your experiment requires statistics,' British physicist Ernest Rutherford once said, 'you ought to have done a better experiment.'

E But in working with microarrays, 'the experiment has been done without you,' Wiggins explains, 'And biology doesn't hand you a model to make sense of the data.' Even more challenging, the building blocks that make up DNA, RNA and proteins are assembled in myriad ways; moreover, subtly different rules of interaction govern their activity, making it difficult, if not impossible, to reduce their patterns of interaction to fundamental laws. (17/21) Some genes and proteins are not even known. 'You are trying to find something compelling about the natural world in a context where you don't know very much,' says William Bialek, a biophysicist at Princeton University. 'You're forced to be agnostic.' Wiggins believes that many machine-learning algorithms perform precisely well under these conditions. 'When working with so many unknown variables, machine learning lets the data decide what's worth looking at,' he says.

F At the Kavli Institute, Wiggins began building a model of a gene regulatory network in yeast — the set of rules by which genes and regulators collectively orchestrate how DNA is vigorously transcribed into mRNA. As he worked with different algorithms, he started to attend discussions on gene regulation led by Christina Leslie, who ran the computational biology group at Columbia at the time. Leslie suggested using a specific machine-learning tool called a classifier. (18) Say the algorithm must discriminate between pictures that have bicycles in them and pictures that do not. A classifier sifts through labeled examples and measures everything it can do about them, gradually learning the decision rules that govern the grouping. From these rules, the algorithm generates a model that can determine whether or not new pictures have bikes in them. In gene regulatory networks, the learning task becomes the problem of predicting whether genes increase or decrease their protein-making activity.

G The algorithm that Wiggins and Leslie began building in the fall of 2002 was trained on the DNA sequences and mRNA levels of regulators expressed during a range of conditions in yeast — when the yeast was cold, hot, starved, and so on. Specifically, this algorithm — MEDUSA (for motif element discrimination using sequence agglomeration) — scans every possible pairing between a set of DNA promoter sequences, called motifs, and regulators. Then, much like a child might match a list of words with their definitions by drawing a line between the two, MEDUSA finds the pairing that best improves the fit between the model and the data it tries to emulate. (Wiggins refers to these pairings as edges.) Each time MEDUSA finds a pairing, it updates the model by adding a new rule to guide its search for the next pairing. It then determines the strength of each pairing by how well the rule improves the existing model. The hierarchy of numbers enables Wiggins and his colleagues to determine which pairings are more important than others and how they can collectively influence the activity of each of the yeast's 6,200 genes. By adding one pairing at a time, MEDUSA can predict which genes ratchet up their RNA production or clamp that production down, as well as reveal the collective mechanisms that orchestrate an organism's transcriptional logic. (19)

核心词汇

A 段

spreadsheet ['spredʃi:t] *n.* 电子表格程序

biopolymer [baɪəʊ'pɒlɪmə(r)] *n.* 生物高聚物

B 段

embrace [ɪm'breɪs] *v.* 接受

foray ['fɒreɪ] *n.&v.* 侵略；涉足

drudge [drʌdʒ] *v.* 做苦工；操劳

tweak [twi:k] *v.* 稍稍调整

C 段

impetus ['ɪmpɪtəs] *n.* 动力

microarray [ˌmaɪkrəʊə'reɪ] *n.* 微阵列

panoramic [ˌpænə'ræmɪk] *adj.* 全景的；全貌的

simultaneously [ˌsɪml'teɪnɪəsli] *adv.* 同时地

myriad ['mɪriəd] *adj.* 无数的

D 段

fundamental [ˌfʌndə'mentl] *adj.* 基础的

particle ['pɑ:tɪkl] *n.* 微粒

anathema [ə'næθəmə] *n.* 可憎的事物

E 段

compelling [kəm'pelɪŋ] *adj.* 引人入胜的

algorithm ['ælgərɪðəm] *n.* 演算法，运算法则，计算程序

F 段

classifier ['klæsɪfaɪə(r)] *n.* 分类者

discriminate [dɪ'skrɪmɪneɪt] *v.* 区别，辨出

G 段

sequence ['si:kwəns] *n.* 序列，顺序

motif [məʊ'ti:f] *n.* 主题

emulate ['emjuleɪt] *v.* 仿真

hierarchy ['haɪərɑ:ki] *n.* 分层，层次；等级制度

ratchet up （使）小幅增加

transcriptional [træn'skrɪpʃənəl] *adj.* 转录的

生命代码：解锁

A 在一辆去往加州圣巴巴拉市的科维里理论物理研究所的机场巴士上，克里斯·威金斯接受了一位同事的建议，打开了一个微软 Excel 电子表格。这与他被邀请去做的生物聚合物物理的演讲没有任何关系。相反，那些他面对的一列列和一排排的数字显示的是出芽酵母的基因活性。具体地说，这些数字代表了 6,200 个酵母基因在其生殖周期过程中所体现的信使 RNA 的数量。"这是我第一次看到这样的事情，"威金斯回忆起 2002 年的春天，"如何理解所有这些数据？"

B 这位 36 岁的哥伦比亚大学的应用数学家和物理学家接受了这个问题，而不是逃避这个问题，六年后的现在，他认为自己有了答案。通过涉足自己领域外的研究，威金斯已经从一个叫做机器学习的人工智能分支中获取了一些工具，从而模拟了来自真实世界生物数据的基因的集体蛋白生成活动。工程师们最初在 20 世纪 50 年代末设计了这些工具来从输入预测输出。威金斯和他的同事们现在把机器学习运用到自然科学领域，并对其进行了微调，使其能够讲述一个故事——不仅关于输入和输出，还包括基因调控模型中发生的事情，即介于两者之间的黑盒子。

C 这项工作的动力始于 20 世纪 90 年代末，当时高通量技术产生了比以往更多的信使 RNA 表达谱和 DNA 序列。"开启了一种关于生物现象的完全不同的思考方式。"威金斯说。这些技术中的关键是 DNA 微阵列，在任何细胞类型中，同时在各种条件下，这些芯片可以提供基因活动的全景视图和它们的表达水平。尽管数据是杂乱而不完整的，生物学家现在可以查询在不同的细胞中哪些基因开启或关闭，并确定产生细胞属性特征的蛋白质集合——健康的或患病的。

D 然而，预测这种基因活动需要揭示支配它的基本规则。"随着时间的推移，这些规则已经被锁定在细胞里了。"理论物理学家哈门·布斯马克尔说，他现在是哥伦比亚大学的生物学副教授。"进化保留了好东西。"为了找到这些规则，科学家们需要统计数据来推断基因和调节它们的蛋白质之间的相互作用，然后用数学方法描述这个网络的底层结构——基因和蛋白质随着时间推移活动的动态模式。但是，那些没有研究粒子（或行星）的物理学家们把统计数据看作讨厌的事物。"如果你的实验需要统计数据，"英国物理学家欧内斯特·卢瑟福曾经说过，"你应该做一个更好的实验。"

E 但是在使用微阵列时，威金斯解释说，"在没有你的情况下实验已经完成了，而生物学并没有给你一个模型来理解数据。"更有挑战性的是，构成 DNA、RNA 和蛋白质的组成部分以多种方式组合在一起；此外，微妙的不同的互动规则支配着他们的活动，即使可能使他们很难减少他们与基本法则的互动模式。一些基因和蛋白质甚至不为人所知。普林斯顿大学的生物物理学家威廉比亚莱克说，"在一个不太了解的环境中发现一些关于自然世界引人注目的东西。你被迫成为不可知论者。"威金斯认为，许多机器学习算法恰好在这些条件下表现良好。他说："在处理如此多的未知变量时，机器工作可以让数据决定什么是值得看的。"

F 在科维里研究所，威金斯开始在酵母里建立一个基因调控网络的模型——通过这套规则，基因和调控器共同安排了 DNA 被积极转录成信使 RNA 的过程。当他使用不同的算法时，他开始参加由克里斯蒂娜·莱斯利领导的关于基因调控的讨论，她当时在哥伦比亚大学负责计算生物学小组。莱斯利建议使用一种叫做分类器的特殊机器学习工具。假设这个算法必须区分有自行车的图片和没有自行车的图片。一个分类器通过标记的示例进行筛选，并度量它所能做的一切，逐步学习控制分组的决策规则。

从这些规则中，该算法生成一个模型，可以确定新图片中是否有自行车。在基因调控网络中，学习任务是预测基因是否增加或减少其蛋白质制造活动的问题。

G 威金斯和莱斯利在 2002 年秋天开始建立的算法，是当酵母在寒冷、炎热、饥饿等一系列条件下，对 DNA 序列和调节器的信使 RNA 水平进行训练的。具体来说，美杜莎（使用序列聚集用于主题元素的识别）——这个算法扫描主题（一组 DNA 启动序列）和调控器之间的所有可能的配对。然后，就像一个孩子可能通过在一列单词和它们的定义之间画一条线来匹配，美杜莎发现这种配对最能提高模型与它试图模仿的数据之间的匹配度。（威金斯把这些配对称为边。）每次美杜莎找到配对时，它都会通过添加一条新规则来更新模型，以指导它对下一个配对的搜索。然后，它通过规则改进现有模型的程度来确定每个配对的强度。数字的层次结构使威金斯和他的同事们能够确定哪些配对比其他的更重要，以及它们如何共同影响酵母的 6,200 个基因的每个活动。通过每次增加一个配对，美杜莎可以预测哪些基因会增加或者抑制它们的 RNA 的产生，同时也能揭示编排生物体转录逻辑的集体机制。

READING PASSAGE 3

参考答案

27	B	28	B	29	A
30	A	31	A	32	TRUE
33	FALSE	34	NOT GIVEN	35	TRUE
36	multi-crystalline silicon cell	37	proprietary wet process	38	neighbouring active material
39	textured mirror surfaces	40	total internal reflection		

Sunny Days for Silicon

A   The old saw that 'the devil is in the details' characterises the kind of needling obstacles that prevent an innovative concept from becoming a working technology. It also often describes the type of problems that must be overcome to shave cost from the resulting product so that people will buy it. Emanuel Sachs of the Massachusetts Institute of Technology has struggled with many such little devils in his career-long endeavor to develop low-cost, high-efficiency solar cells. (30) In his latest effort, Sachs has found incremental ways to boost the amount of electricity that common photovoltaics (PVs) generate from sunlight without increasing the costs. Specifically, he has raised the conversion efficiency of test cells made from multi-crystalline silicon from the typical 15.5 percent to nearly 20 percent — on par with pricier single-crystal silicon cells. (32) Such improvements could bring the cost of PV power down from the current $1.90 to $2.10 per watt to $1.65 per watt. With additional tweaks, Sachs anticipates that within four years solar cells can be produced at a dollar per watt, a feat that would make electricity from the sun competitive with that from coal-burning power plants.

B   Most PV cells, such as those on home rooftops, rely on silicon to convert sunlight into electric current. Metal interconnects then funnels the electricity out from the silicon to power devices or to feed an electrical grid. Since solar cells became practical and affordable three decades ago. Engineers have mostly favoured using single-crystal silicon as the active material, says Michael Rogol, managing director of Germany-based Photon Consulting. (27) Wafers of the substance are typically sawed from an ingot consisting of one large crystal that has been pulled like taffy out of a vat of molten silicon. Especially at first, the high-purity ingots were left over from integrated-circuit manufacture, but later the process was used to make PV cells themselves, Rogol recounts. Although single-crystal cells offer high conversion efficiencies, they are expensive to make. The alternatives — multi-crystalline silicon cells, which factories fabricate from lower-purity, cast ingots composed of many smaller crystals — are cheaper to make, but unfortunately they are less efficient than single-crystal cells. (33)

C   Sachs, who has pioneered several novel ways to make silicon solar cells less costly and more effective, recently turned his focus to the details of multi-crystalline silicon cell manufacture. (36) 'The first small improvement concerns the little silver fingers that gather electric current from the surface of the bulk silicon,' he explains. (36) In conventional fabrication processes, cell manufacturers use screen-printing techniques ('like high-accuracy silk-screening of T-shirts,' Sachs notes) and inks containing silver particles to create these bus wires. The trouble is that standard silver wires come out wide and short, about 120 by 10 microns, and include many nonconductive voids. As a result, they block considerable sunlight and do not carry as much current as they should. (33)

D   At his start-up company — Lexington, Mass based 1,366 Technologies (the number refers to the flux of sunlight that strikes the earth's outer atmosphere: 1,366 watts per square metre) (29) — Sachs is employing 'a proprietary wet' process that can produce thinner and taller wires that are 20 by 20 microns. (37) The slimmer bus wires use less costly silver and can be placed closer together so they can draw more current from the neighbouring active material, through which free electrons can travel only so far. (38) At the same time, the wires block less incoming light than their standard counterparts. (31)

E The second innovation alters the wide, flat interconnect wires that collect current from the silver bus wires and electrically link adjacent cells. Interconnect wires at the top can shade as much as 5 per cent of the area of a cell. 'We place textured mirror surfaces on the faces of these rolled wires. (39) These little mirrors reflect incoming light at a lower angle — around 30 degrees — so that when the reflected rays hit the glass layer at the top, they stay within the silicon wafer by way of total internal reflection,' (40) Sachs explains. (Divers and snorkelers commonly see this optical effect when they view water surfaces from below.) The longer that light remains inside, the more chance it has to be absorbed and transformed into electricity.

F Sachs expects that new antireflection coatings will further raise multi-crystalline cell efficiencies. One of his firm's future goals will be a switch from expensive silver bus wires to cheaper copper ones. And he has a few ideas regarding how to successfully make the substitution. 'Unlike silver, copper poisons the performance of silicon PVs,' Sachs says, 'so it will be crucial to include a low-cost diffusion barrier that stops direct contact between copper and the silicon.' (34) In this business, it's always the little devilish details that count.

G The cost of silicon solar cells is likely to fall as bulk silicon prices drop, according to the U.S. Energy Information Administration and the industry tracking firm Solarbuzz. A steep rise in solar panel sales in recent years had led to a global shortage of silicon because production capacity for the active material lagged behind, but now new silicon manufacturing plants are coming online. (35) The reduced materials costs and resulting lower system prices will greatly boost demand for solar-electric technology, according to market watcher Michael Rogol of Photon Consulting. (28)

核心词汇

A 段

obstacle [ˈɒbstəkl] *n.* 障碍物

endeavor [ɪnˈdevə(r)] *n.* 努力

silicon [ˈsɪlɪkən] *n.* 硅

B 段

grid [ɡrɪd] *n.* （输电线路等）系统网络；网格

ingot [ˈɪŋɡət] *n.* 铸块

integrated [ˈɪntɪɡreɪtɪd] *adj.* 结合的；完整的

C 段

manufacture [ˌmænjuˈfæktʃə(r)] *v.&n.* 生产，制造

bulk [bʌlk] *n.* 大块

particle [ˈpɑːtɪkl] *n.* 微粒

D 段

flux [flʌks] *n.* 流量

proprietary [prəˈpraɪətri] *adj.* 专有的；专利的

counterpart [ˈkaʊntəpɑːt] *n.* 与对方地位相当的人或物

E 段

adjacent [əˈdʒeɪsnt] *adj.* 邻近的

internal [ɪnˈtɜːnl] *adj.* 内部的

transform [trænsˈfɔːm] *v.* 改变

F 段

copper [ˈkɒpə(r)] *n.* 铜

substitution [ˌsʌbstɪˈtjuːʃn] *n.* 替代

devilish [ˈdevəlɪʃ] *adj.* 残忍的；魔鬼似的

G 段

track [ˈtræk] *v.* 跟踪

panel [ˈpænl] *n.* 板

lag behind 落后于

硅的美好明天

A 认为"魔鬼在细节中"的旧观点是一种小障碍,它阻止了一个创新概念成为一种工作技术。它还经常描述必须克服的问题类型,以便从最终的产品中节省成本,这样人们就可以购买它。麻省理工学院的伊曼纽尔·萨克斯在他的职业生涯中长期努力与许多这样的小恶魔作斗争,以开发低成本、高效率的太阳能电池。在他的最新研究中,萨克斯已经找到了一些增量方法来提高普通光伏从太阳光中产生的电能,而不会增加成本。具体来说,他已经提高了由多晶体硅制成的测试单元的转换效率,从典型的 15.5% 提高到接近 20%——与昂贵的单晶硅电池一样。这样的改进将使光伏发电的成本从目前的每瓦 1.90 美元到 2.10 美元,降至每瓦 1.65 美元。通过额外的调整,萨克斯预计将在 4 年内创造出每瓦 1 美元价格的太阳能电池,这一壮举将使太阳能发电与燃煤电厂发电产生竞争。

B 大多数的光伏电池,如家庭屋顶上的太阳能电池,都依靠硅来将阳光转化为电流。金属相互连接,然后将电能从硅输出为设备或电网供电。太阳能电池在 30 年前已经变得实用且价格实惠。总部位于德国的光子咨询公司的总经理迈克尔·罗戈尔说,工程师们大多赞成使用单晶体硅作为活性材料。这种物质的晶片通常是从一大块晶体组成的钢锭锯下的,而这种晶体就像太妃糖一样从一大桶熔融硅中提取出来。特别是一开始,高纯度的钢锭被集成电路制造遗留下来,但后来这个过程被用来制造光伏电池,罗戈尔说。尽管单晶体电池提供高转换效率,但它们的制造成本很高。而多晶硅电池这种替代品,它是从低纯度的,由很多较小晶体组成的铸锭制造而来,成本更低,但不幸的是,它们的效率比单晶硅电池低。

C 萨克斯已经开创了几种能使硅太阳能电池变得更便宜、更有效的新方法,他最近把注意力转向了多晶硅电池制造的细节。他解释说:"第一个小的改进是从块状硅的表面收集电流的小银手指。"在常规制造过程中,电池制造商使用丝网印刷技术("像 T 恤的高精度丝网,"萨克斯指出)和含有银颗粒的墨水来制造这些汇流线。问题是,标准的银线宽而短,大约 120×10 微米,包括许多不导电的空隙。因此,它们阻挡了相当多的阳光,并且不能携带符合本身能力的电流。

D 在他的初创公司——名为"1366 技术"位于马萨诸塞州的列克星敦市,"1366 技术"(这个数字指的是撞击地球外部大气层的阳光的流量:每平方米 1,366 瓦特)——萨克斯采用了一种"专有的湿法",可以生产 20×20 微米的更细、更长的电线。更细的汇流线使用更便宜的银,而且可以放置得更近,这样它们就能从邻近的活性物质中汲取更多的电流,通过这些活性材料,自由电子只能移动这么远。与此同时,比起标准电线,这些电线阻挡进来的光线要更少。

E 第二个创新改变了从银质汇流线收集电流和连接相邻电池的又宽又平的互连线。顶部的互连线可以遮盖电池面积多达 5%。"我们在这些卷线的表面上放置有纹理的镜面。这些小镜子以较低的角度反射入射光线——大约 30 度——这样当反射光线照射到顶部的玻璃层时,通过全内反射的方式它们就会留在硅晶片内。"萨克斯解释道。(当潜水者和浮潜者在水下观察水面时,通常会看到这种光学效应。)光留在里面的时间越长,它就越有可能被吸收并转化为电能。

F 萨克斯预计新的抗反射涂层将进一步提高多晶电池的效率。他的公司未来的目标之一将是从昂贵的银质汇流线转向更便宜的铜线。关于如何成功地进行替换,他有一些想法。萨克斯说:"与银不同,铜会损坏硅光伏的性能。因此,至关重要的是,要包括一个低成本的扩散膜,以阻止铜和硅之间的直接接触。"在这个行业里,总是有一些魔鬼似的细节很重要。

G 根据美国能源情报署和行业追踪公司 Solarbuzz 的数据，硅太阳能电池的成本很可能会随着大量硅价格的降低而下降。近年来，因为活性材料的生产能力落后，太阳能电池板销售的急剧增长导致了全球硅的短缺，但现在新的硅制造工厂正在上线。据光子咨询公司的市场观察人士迈克尔·罗戈尔称，材料成本的降低和由此导致的系统价格下降将极大地促进对太阳能技术的需求。

TEST 5

READING PASSAGE 1

参考答案

1	A	2	C	3	C
4	D	5	E	6	D
7	TRUE	8	TRUE	9	NOT GIVEN
10	NOT GIVEN	11	TRUE	12	NOT GIVEN
13	C				

Coral Reefs

Coral reefs are underwater structures made from calcium carbonate secreted by corals. Coral reefs are colonies of tiny living animals found in marine waters that contain few nutrients. Most coral reefs are built from stony corals, which in turn consist of polyps that cluster in groups.

A Coral reefs are estimated to cover 284,300 km² just under 0.1% of the oceans' surface area, about half the area of France. The Indo-Pacific region accounts for 91.9% of this total area. Southeast Asia accounts for 32.3% of that figure, while the Pacific including Australia accounts for 40.8%. Atlantic and Caribbean coral reefs account for 7.6%. (1/8) Yet often called 'rainforests of the sea', coral reefs form some of the most diverse ecosystems on Earth. They provide a home for 25% of all marine species, including fish, mollusks, worms, crustaceans, echinoderms, sponges, tunicates and other cnidarians. (7) Paradoxically, coral reefs flourish even though they are surrounded by ocean waters that provide few nutrients. They are most commonly found at shallow depths in tropical waters, but deep water and cold water corals also exist on smaller scales in other areas. Although corals exist both in temperate and tropical waters, shallow-water reefs form only in a zone extending from 30°N to 30°S of the equator. Deep water coral can exist at greater depths and colder temperatures at much higher latitudes, as far north as Norway. Coral reefs are rare along the American and African west coasts. This is due primarily to upwelling and strong cold coastal currents that reduce water temperatures in these areas (respectively the Peru, Benguela and Canary streams). Corals are seldom found along the coastline of South Asia from the eastern tip of India (Madras) to the Bangladesh and Myanmar borders. They are also rare along the coast around northeastern South America and Bangladesh due to the freshwater release from the Amazon and Ganges Rivers, respectively.

B Coral reefs deliver ecosystem services to tourism, fisheries and coastline protection. The global economic value of coral reefs has been estimated at as much as US$375 billion per year. Coral reefs protect shorelines by absorbing wave energy, and many small islands would not exist without their reef to protect them.

C The value of reefs in biodiverse regions can be even higher. In parts of Indonesia and the Caribbean where tourism is the main use, reefs are estimated to be worth US$1 million per square kilometre, based on the cost of maintaining sandy beaches and the value of attracting snorkelers and scuba divers. (2) Meanwhile, a recent study of the Great Barrier Reef in Australia found that the reef is worth more to the country as an intact ecosystem than an extractive reserve for fishing. Each year more than 1.8 million tourists visit the reef, spending an estimated AU$4.3 billion (Australian dollars) on reef-related industries from diving to boat rental to posh island resort stays. In the Caribbean, says UNEP, the net annual benefits from diver tourism was US$2 billion in 2000 with US$625 million spent directly on diving on reefs. (3) Further, reef tourism is important source of employment, especially for some of the world's poorest people. (11) UNEP says that of the estimated 30 million smallscale fishers in the developing world, most are dependent to a greater or lesser extent on coral reefs. In the Philippines, for example, more than one million small-scale fishers depend directly on coral reefs for their livelihoods. The report estimates that reef fisheries were worth between $15,000 and $150,000 per square kilometre a year, while fish caught for aquariums were worth $500 a kilogram against $6 for fish caught as food. The aquarium fish export industry supports around 50,000 people and generates some US$5.5 million a year in Sri Lanka along. (3)

D   Unfortunately, coral reefs are dying around the world. In particular, coral mining, agricultural and urban runoff, pollution (organic and inorganic), disease, and the digging of canals and access into islands and bays are localised threats to coral ecosystems. Broader threats are sea temperature rise, sea level rise and pH changes from ocean acidification, all associated with greenhouse gas emissions. (4) Some current fishing practices are destructive and unsustainable. These include cyanide fishing, overfishing and blast fishing. (6) Although cyanide fishing supplies live reef fish for the tropical aquarium market, most fish caught using this method are sold in restaurants, primarily in Asia, where live fish are prized for their freshness. To catch fish with cyanide, fishers dive down to the reef and squirt cyanide in coral crevices and on the fastmoving fish, to stun the fish making them easy to catch. Overfishing is another leading cause for coral reef degradation. Often, too many fish are taken from one reef to sustain a population in that area. Poor fishing practices, such as banging on the reef with sticks (muro-ami), destroy coral formations that normally function as fish habitat. In some instances, people fish with explosives (blast fishing), which blast apart the surrounding coral.

E   Tourist resorts that empty their sewage directly into the water surrounding coral reefs contribute to coral reef degradation. Wastes kept in poorly maintained septic tanks can also leak into surrounding ground water, eventually seeping out to the reefs. Careless boating, diving, snorkeling and fishing can also damage coral reefs. Whenever people grab, kick, and walk on, or stir up sediment in the reefs, they contribute to coral reef destruction. Corals are also harmed or killed when people drop anchors on them or when people collect coral. (5)

F   To find answers for these problems, scientists and researchers study the various factors that impact reefs. The list includes the ocean's role as a carbon dioxide sink, atmospheric changes, ultraviolet light, ocean acidification, viruses, impacts of dust storms carrying agents to far flung reefs, pollutants, algal blooms and others. Reefs are threatened well beyond coastal areas. General estimates show approximately 10% of the world's coral reefs are dead. About 60% of the world's reefs are at risk due to destructive, humanrelated activities. The threat to the health of reefs is particularly strong in Southeast Asia, where 80% of reefs are endangered.

G   In Australia, the Great Barrier Reef is protected by the Great Barrier Reef Marine Park Authority, and is the subject of much legislation, including a biodiversity action plan. Inhabitants of Ahus Island, Manus Province, Papua New Guinea, have followed a generations-old practice of restricting fishing in six areas of their reef lagoon. Their cultural traditions allow line fishing, but not net or spear fishing. The result is that both the biomass and individual fish sizes are significantly larger than in places where fishing is unrestricted.

核心词汇

A 段

diverse [daɪˈvɜːs] *adj.* 不同的；多种多样的；变化多的
ecosystem [ˈiːkəʊsɪstəm] *n.* 生态系统
marine [məˈriːn] *adj.* 海的
paradoxically [ˌpærəˈdɒksɪkli] *adv.* 自相矛盾地；似非而是地；反常地
flourish [ˈflʌrɪʃ] *v.* 繁荣，兴旺；茂盛；活跃；处于旺盛时期
nutrient [ˈnjuːtriənt] *n.* 营养物；滋养物
tropical [ˈtrɒpɪkl] *adj.* 热带的
latitude [ˈlætɪtjuːd] *n.* 纬度

C 段

intact [ɪnˈtækt] *adj.* 完整的；原封不动的；未受损伤的
extractive [ɪkˈstræktɪv] *adj.* 提取的；可萃取的
resort [rɪˈzɔːt] *n.* 度假胜地；常去之地

D 段

localised [ˈləʊkəlaɪzd] *adj.* 局部的；地区的；小范围的
emission [iˈmɪʃn] *n.* 排放；（光、热等的）发射，散发；喷射；发行
destructive [dɪˈstrʌktɪv] *adj.* 破坏的；毁灭性的；有害的，消极的
unsustainable [ˌʌnsəˈsteɪnəbl] *adj.* 不能持续的
squirt [skwɜːt] *v.* 喷射
crevice [ˈkrevɪs] *n.* 裂缝；裂隙
degradation [ˌdegrəˈdeɪʃn] *n.* 退化；降格，降级；堕落

F 段

endangered [ɪnˈdeɪndʒəd] *adj.* 濒临灭绝的；有生命危险的

G 段

legislation [ˌledʒɪsˈleɪʃn] *n.* 立法；法律
biomass [ˈbaɪəʊmæs] *n.* （单位面积或体积内的）[生态] 生物量

珊瑚礁

珊瑚礁是珊瑚虫分泌的碳酸钙在水下形成的一种结构。它们是海水中几乎不含营养物质的小型活体动物群。大多数珊瑚礁是由石珊瑚构成的，反过来这些石珊瑚又是由聚居在一起的珊瑚虫构成的。

A 据估计，珊瑚礁的覆盖面积为 28.43 万平方千米，还不足海洋面积的 0.1%，大约是法国国土面积的一半。其中印太地区占总面积的 91.9%，东南亚占 32.3%，而太平洋（包括澳大利亚）占 40.8%，大西洋和加勒比海占 7.6%。虽然常被称为"海洋中的热带雨林"，珊瑚礁形成了地球上最多样化的生态系统。它们为 25% 的海洋物种提供了生活环境，包括鱼类、软体动物、蠕虫、甲壳类动物、棘皮动物、海绵、被囊动物和其他刺胞动物。矛盾的是，即使周围水里的营养物质很少，珊瑚礁仍能大量增长。珊瑚礁通常出现在热带水域的浅水区，但在其他地方也有小范围的深水珊瑚群和冷水珊瑚群存在。尽管珊瑚礁在温带水域和热带水域中都能生存，但浅水珊瑚礁只能在南北纬 30° 之间的海域中形成。深水的珊瑚礁可以在位于更高维度的、更低温和更深的水域形成，往北一直可以到挪威。珊瑚礁在美国和非洲西海岸很少见，这主要是因为海洋上升流和强冷的沿岸流降低了这些地区的水温（分别是秘鲁寒流、本格拉寒流和加纳利寒流）。印度最东部（马德拉斯）到孟加拉国再到缅甸边界的南亚海岸也很少有珊瑚礁，这是因为有淡水分别从亚马逊河和恒河排出。

B 珊瑚礁为旅游业、渔业和海岸线保护提供生态系统服务。据估计，珊瑚礁每年在全球范围内产生的经济价值约为 3,750 亿美元。珊瑚礁通过吸收潮汐能保护海岸线，如果没有珊瑚礁的保护很多小岛将不复存在。

C 在生物种类丰富的地区，珊瑚礁的价值可能会更高。在作为旅游胜地的印度尼西亚和加勒比海部分地区，因为维护沙质海滩的花费和吸引浮潜者和水肺潜水者的价值，每平方千米的珊瑚礁估价约一百万美元。与此同时，有关澳大利亚大堡礁的一项近期研究发现，对这个国家而言，珊瑚礁作为一个完整生态系统的价值要高于其作为渔业捕捞资源的价值。每年有 180 多万游客前来观赏珊瑚礁，据估从潜水到租船再到奢华的海岛度假，他们在珊瑚礁相关游玩项目上的花费约为 43 亿澳元。联合国环境规划署称，2000 年加勒比海潜水旅游的年净收益达 20 亿美元，其中 62,500 万美元直接来自珊瑚礁浅水上。而且，珊瑚礁旅游是重要的就业来源，尤其对一些世界上最穷的人而言。联合国环境规划署称，发展中国家约有 3,000 万小规模作业的渔民，他们当中很多人都在不同程度上依靠珊瑚礁维持。例如在菲律宾，一百多万小规模作业的渔民就直接靠珊瑚礁谋生。该报告预估珊瑚礁渔场每年每平方千米的产值在 1.5 万美元到 15 万美元之间，相对于每千克 6 美元捕获作为食物的鱼来说，为水族馆捕取的鱼每千克价值 500 美元。斯里兰卡的观赏鱼出口行业供养了 5 万人，每年总产值约 550 万美元。

D 不幸的是，珊瑚礁正在全球范围内消亡。尤其是珊瑚矿业、农田径流和城市径流、污染（有机和无机）、疾病、开挖运河和海岛造路，都是对珊瑚礁生态系统的局部的威胁。更广泛的威胁还包括水温上升、海平面上升和由于海洋酸化引起的 PH 值变化，这些都与温室气体排放有关。目前的一些捕鱼手段是毁灭性的、无法持续的。这些手段包括使用氰化物捕鱼、过度捕捞和使用炸药捕鱼。尽管使用氰化物捕鱼的方法能为热带鱼水族馆市场提供活生生的岩礁鱼类，但用这种手段捕捞到的大部分鱼成了餐馆里菜品，主要是在亚洲国家的餐馆里，因为这里很看重鱼的新鲜度。用氰化物捕鱼，渔民要潜水靠近珊瑚礁，向缝隙和快速移动的鱼喷洒氰化物，使其昏迷后可以更轻易地捕捞。过度捕捞是导致珊瑚礁退化的另一个主要原因。为了供养那个地区的人类，通常过多的鱼都取自同一片珊瑚礁。不良的捕鱼手段，如用棍子直接重击礁石（muro-ami 捕鱼手段），破坏了这些常被作为鱼类栖息地的珊瑚礁的结构。在某些情况下，人们还使用炸药捕鱼，这把其周围的珊瑚礁也炸开了。

E 旅游胜地的污水被直接倒进珊瑚礁周围的水域中，这也会导致珊瑚礁退化。维护不善的化粪池里的垃圾也会渗漏到周围的地下水中，最终渗到礁石上。肆意的划船、潜水、浮潜和捕鱼也都会破坏珊瑚礁。每当人们抓取、踢、行走或搅拌这些礁石上的沉淀物时，就会造成珊瑚礁破坏。当人们在礁石上抛锚固定或采集珊瑚时，也会使珊瑚礁损伤或死亡。

F 为了找到这些问题的答案，科学家和研究员研究了影响珊瑚礁系统的各种因素。这些因素的列表中包括海洋对二氧化碳的吸收作用、大气层的变化、紫外线的影响、海洋酸化、病毒、沙暴将病菌带到远海珊瑚礁的影响，污染物、藻类的过度繁殖和其他因素。受到威胁的不仅仅只是这些近海的珊瑚礁。粗略估计全球约 10% 的珊瑚礁近乎死亡，约 60% 的珊瑚礁因为人类破坏性的活动而面临危险。东南亚地区珊瑚礁面临的健康风险最大，这里 80% 的珊瑚礁正濒临灭绝。

G 在澳大利亚，大堡礁受到了大堡礁海洋公园管理局的保护，它也是很多法律的保护对象，包括一项生物多样性行动计划。巴布亚新几内亚马努斯省阿赫斯岛上的居民遵循着一种世代相传的做法，将捕鱼限制在环礁湖的六个区域内。他们的文化传统允许用绳子钓鱼，但不允许拖网或使用长矛捕鱼。这样做的结果就是，相比对捕鱼没有限制的地方，这里单位面积内的鱼群数量要多很多以及鱼的个头要大很多。

READING PASSAGE 2

参考答案

14	B	15	A	16	F
17	C	18	G	19	H
20	E	21	Candy	22	definition
23	a catastrophic brain	24	landscapes or dolphins playing	25	(more) primitive parts
26	D				

Can Scientists Tell Us: What Happiness Is?

A Economists accept that if people describe themselves as happy, then they are happy. However, psychologists differentiate between levels of happiness. The most immediate type involves a feeling; pleasure or joy. But sometimes happiness is a judgment that life is satisfying, and does not imply an emotional state. Esteemed psychologist Martin Seligman has spearheaded an effort to study the science of happiness. The bad news is that we're not wired to be happy. The good news is that we can do something about it. Since its origins in a Leipzig laboratory 130 years ago, psychology has had little to say about goodness and contentment. Mostly psychologists have concerned themselves with weakness and misery. There are libraries full of theories about why we get sad, worried, and angry. It hasn't been respectable science to study what happens when lives go well. Positive experiences, such as joy, kindness, altruism and heroism, have mainly been ignored. For every 100 psychology papers dealing with anxiety or depression, only one concerns a positive trait. (15)

B A few pioneers in experimental psychology bucked the trend. Professor Alice Isen of Cornell University and colleagues have demonstrated how positive emotions make people think faster and more creatively. Showing how easy it is to give people an intellectual boost, Isen divided doctors making a tricky diagnosis into three groups: one received candy, one read humanistic statements about medicine, one was a control group. (14/21) The doctors who had candy displayed the most creative thinking and worked more efficiently. Inspired by Isen and others, Seligman got stuck in. He raised millions of dollars of research money and funded 50 research groups involving 150 scientists across the world. Four positive psychology centres opened, decorated in cheerful colours and furnished with sofas and baby-sitters. There were get-togethers on Mexican beaches where psychologists would snorkel and eat fajitas, then form 'pods' to discuss subjects such as wonder and awe. A thousand therapists were coached in the new science.

C But critics are demanding answers to big questions. What is the point of defining levels of happiness and classifying the virtues? (22) Aren't these concepts vague and impossible to pin down? Can you justify spending funds to research positive states when there are problems such as famine, flood and epidemic depression to be solved? (17) Seligman knows his work can be belittled alongside trite notions such as 'the power of positive thinking'. His plan to stop the new science floating 'on the waves of self-improvement fashions' is to make sure it is anchored to positive philosophy above, and to positive biology below.

D And this takes us back to our evolutionary past. Homo sapiens evolved during the Pleistocene era (1.8 m to 10,000 years ago), a time of hardship and turmoil. It was the Ice Age, and our ancestors endured long freezes as glaciers formed, then ferocious floods as the ice masses melted. We shared the planet with terrifying creatures such as mammoths, elephant-sized ground sloths and sabre-toothed cats. But by the end of the Pleistocene, all these animals were extinct. Humans, on the other hand, had evolved large brains and used their intelligence to make fire and sophisticated tools, to develop talk and social rituals. Survival in a time of adversity forged our brains into a persistent mould. Professor Seligman says: 'Because our brain evolved during a time of ice, flood and famine, we have a catastrophic brain. (23) The way the brain works is looking for what's wrong. The problem is that, worked in the Pleistocene era, it favoured you, but it doesn't work in the modem world.'

E   Although most people rate themselves as happy, there is a wealth of evidence to show that negative thinking is deeply ingrained in the human psyche. Experiments show that we remember failures more vividly than successes. We dwell on what went badly, not what went well. Of the six universal emotions, four anger, fear, disgust and sadness are negative and only one, joy, is positive. The sixth is surprise. (20) The psychologist Daniel Nettle, author of Happiness, and one of the Royal Institution lecturers, believes that the negative emotions each tell us 'something bad has happened' and suggest a different course of action.

F   What is it about the structure of the brain that underlies our bias towards negative thinking? And is there a biology of joy? At Iowa University, neuroscientists studied what happens when people are shown pleasant and unpleasant pictures. When subjects see landscapes or dolphins playing, part of the frontal lobe of the brain becomes active. (24) But when they are shown unpleasant images, like a bird covered in oil, or a dead soldier with part of his face missing, the response comes from more primitive parts of the brain. (16/25) The ability to feel negative emotions derives from an ancient danger-recognition system formed early in the brain's evolution. The pre-frontal cortex, which registers happiness, is the part used for higher thinking, an area that evolved later in human history.

G   Our difficulty, according to Daniel Nettle, is that the brain systems for liking and wanting are separate. (26A) Wanting involves two ancient regions the amygdala and the nucleus accumbens that communicate using the chemical dopamine to form the brain's reward system. (18) They are involved in anticipating the pleasure of eating and in addiction to drugs. A rat will press a bar repeatedly, ignoring sexually available partners, to receive electrical stimulation of the 'wanting' parts of the brain. But having received brain stimulation, the rat eats more but shows no sign of enjoying the food it craved. In humans, a drug like nicotine produces much craving but little pleasure. (26C)

H   In essence, what the biology lesson tells us is that negative emotions are fundamental to the human condition, and it's no wonder they are difficult to eradicate. (26B) At the same time, by a trick of nature, our brains are designed to crave but never really achieve lasting happiness. (19/26D)

核心词汇

A 段

differentiate [ˌdɪfəˈrenʃieɪt] v. 区别，区分对待

spearhead [ˈspɪəhed] v. 带头

contentment [kənˈtentmənt] n. 满足

altruism [ˈæltruɪzəm] n. 利他主义，无私

B 段

snorkel [ˈsnɔːkl] v. 用通气管潜泳，浮潜

fajita [fəˈhiːtə] n. 墨西哥烤肉，法士达

therapist [ˈθerəpɪst] n. 治疗专家

C 段

virtue [ˈvɜːtʃuː] n. 美德，价值

vague [veɪɡ] adj. 模糊不清楚的

epidemic [ˌepɪˈdemɪk] adj. 流行性的，盛行的

trite [traɪt] adj. 老生常谈的

anchor [ˈæŋkə(r)] v. 抛锚，把……系住

D 段

turmoil [ˈtɜːmɔɪl] n. 混乱，焦虑

ferocious [fəˈrəʊʃəs] adj. 残忍的，凶猛的

mammoth [ˈmæməθ] n. 猛犸象

forge [fɔːdʒ] v. 锻造

mould [məʊld] n. 铸模，模型

E 段

ingrain [ɪnˈɡreɪn] v. 使根深蒂固

dwell [dwel] v. 细想某事；居住，存在于

disgust [dɪsˈɡʌst] n.&v. 使厌恶，使反感

F 段

primitive [ˈprɪmətɪv] adj. 原始的

derive [dɪˈraɪv] v. 得到，来自于

cortex [ˈkɔːteks] n. 大脑皮层，皮质，树皮

G 段

amygdala [ə'mɪgdələ] *n.* 扁桃形结构
nucleus accumbens 依伏神经核
dopamine ['dəʊpəmiːn] *n.* 多巴胺
crave [kreɪv] *v.* 渴望

H 段

eradicate [ɪ'rædɪkeɪt] *v.* 根除,摧毁

科学家能告诉我们什么是幸福吗？

A 经济学家相信如果人们描述自己是幸福的，那他们就是幸福的。然而，心理学家却把幸福的层次加以区别。最直接的幸福是一种高兴或快乐的感觉。但有时候幸福是对生活满意度的一种评判，并不暗示某种情感状态。受人尊敬的心理学家马丁·塞利格曼带头致力于研究幸福的科学。坏消息是我们不会天生就很幸福，好消息是我们可以通过做一些事情来获得幸福。对幸福的研究可以追溯到130年前的莱比锡实验室，在这之前有关善良和满足感的心理学鲜有论及。通常心理学家都只关心人性的弱点和痛苦。图书馆里都是有关我们为什么会伤心、焦虑和生气的各种理论。研究人们身处顺境时的心理状况还没有成为一种受人尊敬的科学。像快乐、善良、利他主义和英雄主义这些积极情绪体验大都被忽略了。每100篇有关焦虑或抑郁的心理学论文中，只有一篇会涉及某种积极的人格特质。

B 一些实验心理学领域的先驱者抗议过这种趋势。康奈尔大学的爱丽丝·艾森教授和她的同事们已经证明了积极情绪是如何让人们的思考变得更敏感、更有创造性的。为了展示提升人们的智力是一件很容易的事情，艾森把那些需要对复杂病情做出诊断的医生分成了三组：一组收到了糖果，一组要宣读医学人道主义誓言，还有一组是对照组。收到糖果的那组医生的思维最具创造性且工作也更高效。受到艾森和其他人的启发后，塞利格曼开始加紧这方面的研究。他筹集到了数百万美元的研究经费，成立了50个研究小组，涉及世界各国150名科学家。四家积极心理学中心开始运营，用令人愉悦的颜色加以装饰并配备了沙发和保姆。墨西哥的沙滩上有各种聚会，心理学家们在这里潜水、吃法士达，还分组去讨论一些令人惊奇或敬畏的话题。一千名治疗专家接受了这门新兴科学的相关培训。

C 但是评论家需要一些重大问题的答案。界定幸福层次和划分美德的意义是什么？这些概念会不会含糊不清或根本无法清楚地表述？在饥饿、洪灾和普遍萧条的问题还没有解决之时，花经费去研究积极的心态是否说得过去？塞利格曼知道自己的研究会因与传统观念一致而被轻视，比如说都是赞同"积极思考的力量"。所以他的计划就是要防止这门新兴的科学浮留在"自我提升趋势的浪潮"上，要确保该科学扎根于这样一类体系，上有积极哲学做指导，下有积极生物学做支撑。

D 这就需要我们回顾下人类过去的进化史。现代人类的进化发生在更新世时期（从180万年前到1万年前），这是一个充满艰难和混乱的时代。这是冰河时期，我们的祖先在冰川形成时忍耐漫长的严寒期，又在冰川融化时度过了凶猛的洪灾期。我们和耸人听闻的生物共享着一个星球，比如猛犸象、跟大象体型差不多的大地獭和长着长牙的猫科动物。但到了更新世末期，所有这些动物都灭绝了。而另一方面人类进化拥有更大的脑容量，并用自己的智慧生火、制作复杂的工具、学着说话并发展社会礼仪。逆境生存使我们的大脑进入一种持续模式。塞利格曼教授说："由于我们的大脑是在冰川、洪灾和饥饿时期发生的进化，我们的大脑里存储的都是各类灾难，所以大脑运转的方式就是探寻是哪里出了差错。问题是在更新世时期这样的大脑能起作用，对你有利，但在目前这个时期行不通。"

E 尽管很多人都评价说自己很幸福，但也有大量证据表明负面思维在人类的心智中也是根深蒂固的。试验表明，相比成功我们对失败记得更清楚。我们会深思糟糕的事情，而不是进展顺利的事情。在六种基本情绪中，愤怒、恐惧、厌恶和悲伤四种都是负面情绪，只有快乐一种是积极情绪。第六种情绪是惊讶。心理学家丹尼尔·内特尔是《幸福》一书的作者，也是皇家学会的一名讲师，他相信这些消极情绪都是在告诉我们"有坏事发生"，暗示我们换一种做法。

F 究竟是大脑的什么结构让我们更倾向于负面思维方式呢？是否有生物学原理可以解释快乐情绪的产生？在爱荷华大学，神经系统科学家们研究了人们看到令人开心的图片或令人不开心的图片时的表现。当研究对象看到风景图或者海豚玩耍的图片时，大脑额叶的部分区域就会活跃起来。但当给他们展示令人不开心的图片时，比如满身是油的小鸟或者一个脸部不完整的死去的战士，大脑的更原始的区域就会有反应。感知消极情绪的能力来自于一种古老的危险识别系统，这种系统形成于大脑进化的早期。可以记录幸福感的前额叶皮层是用来进行高级思考的，这是在人类历史后期发生的进化。

G 根据丹尼尔·内特尔的说法，我们的难题在于，表达喜欢和欲望的大脑系统是分开的。欲望涉及两个最初形成的大脑区域,杏仁核和伏核，它们通过化学物质多巴胺传达信息并形成大脑奖励机制。这些区域让人类期待吃东西的快感并对药物上瘾。一只老鼠无视异性伙伴，为了获得大脑"欲望"区的电击，不停地按笼闩。受到电击后老鼠会吃得更多，但并没有信号显示它们很享受渴望得来的食物。对人类而言，使用像尼古丁这类药物能让人产生很多欲望，却得不到多少快感。

H 实质上，生物课告诉我们的是：消极情绪是人类生存所必需的，所以很难消除这些消极情绪就一点也不奇怪了。与此同时，这是一个大自然玩儿的诡计，它对大脑的设计让人产生欲望，却又永远无法获得长久的幸福感。

READING PASSAGE 3

参考答案

27	B	28	C	29	A
30	C	31	A	32	TRUE
33	NOT GIVEN	34	TRUE	35	FALSE
36	a federal ban	37	Generic inhaled albuterol	38	CFCs/ chlorofluorocarbons
39	Reformulated brandname alternatives	40	uninsured		

Changes in Air

A. A federal ban on ozone-depleting chlorofluorocarbons (CFCs), to conform with the Clean Air Act, is, ironically, affecting 22.9 million people in the U.S. who suffer from asthma. (36) Generic inhaled albuterol, which is the most commonly prescribed short-acting asthma medication and requires CFCs to propel it into the lungs, will no longer be legally sold after December 31, 2008. (37/38) Physicians and patients are questioning the wisdom of the ban, which will have an insignificant effect on ozone but a measurable impact on wallets: the reformulated brand-name alternatives can be three times as expensive, raising the cost to about $40 per inhaler. (39) The issue is even more disconcerting considering that asthma disproportionately affects the poor and that, according to recent surveys, an estimated 20 percent of asthma patients are uninsured. (40)

B. 'The decision to make the change was political, not medical or scientific,' says pharmacist Leslie Hendeles of the University of Florida, who co-authored a 2007 paper in the New England Journal of Medicine, explaining the withdrawal and transition. In 1987 Congress signed on to the Montreal Protocol on Substances That Deplete the Ozone Layer, an international treaty requiring the phasing out of all nonessential uses of CFCs. At that time, medical inhalers were considered an essential use because no viable alternative propellant existed. In 1989 pharmaceutical companies banded together and eventually, in 1996, reformulated albuterol with hydrofluoroalkane. (32)

C. The transition began quietly, but as more patients see their prescriptions change and costs go up, many question why this ban must begin before generics become available. At least one member of the FDA advisory committee, Nicholas J. Gross of the Stritch-Loyola School of Medicine, has publicly regretted the decision, recanting his support and requesting that the ban be pushed back until 2010, when the first patent expires. (31/33)

D. Gross notes that the decision had nothing to do with the environment. Albuterol inhalers contributed less than 0.1 percent of the CFCs released when the treaty was signed. (3) 'It's a symbolic issue,' Gross remarks. (29/34) Some skeptics instead point to the billions of dollars to be gained by the three companies holding the patents on the available HFA albuterol inhalers, namely Glaxo-SmithKline, Schering-Plough and Teva. Although the FDA advisory committee recognised that the expenses would go up, Hendeles says, it also believed that the companies would help defray the added costs for individuals. Firms, for instance, had committed to donating a million HFA inhalers to clinics around the country. According to Hendeles, GlaxoSmithKline did not follow through, although Schering-Plough and Teva did. GlaxoSmithKline did not respond to requests for comment.

E. The issue now, Hendeles says, is that pharmaceutical-grade CFCs are in short supply, and the public faces the risk of a shortage of albuterol inhalers if the FDA does not continue promoting the production of HFA inhalers. He posits that even costs of generics would go up as CFCs become scarcer. Gross disagrees, saying that the inhaler shortage and the closure of CFC manufacturing plants are a result of the ban.

F   The HFA inhalers also have encountered resistance because some asthmatics insist that they do not work as well as the CFC variety. But, Hendeles says, the differences are in the mechanics and maintenance — unlike CFC inhalers, the HFA versions must be primed more diligently and rinsed to accommodate the stickier HFA formulation. (35) They also run out suddenly without the warning with a CFC inhaler that the device is running low. 'Pharmacists may not tell people of these things, and the doctors don't know,' Hendeles says. (28)

G   The main public health issue in this decision may be the side effects of the economics, not the drug chemistry. Multiple studies have shown that raising costs leads to poorer adherence to treatment. One study discovered that patients took 30 percent less antiasthma medication when their co-pay doubled. In the case of a chronic disease such as asthma, it is particularly difficult to get people to follow regular treatment plans. 'Generally speaking, for any reason you don't take medication, cost makes it more likely that you do not,' comments Michael Chemew, a health policy expert at Harvard Medical School. (27)

H   Such choices to forgo medication could affect more than just the patients themselves. 'For example,' Hendeles points out, 'in a pregnant mother with untreated asthma, less oxygen is delivered to the fetus, which can lead to congenital problems and premature birth.' (30) And considering that the disease disproportionately strikes the poor, what seemed to be a good, responsible environmental decision might in the end exact an unexpected human toll.

核心词汇

A 段

federal [ˈfedərəl] *adj.* 联邦的
conform [kənˈfɔːm] *v.* 遵从，遵守
inhaler [ɪnˈheɪlə(r)] *n.* 吸入器
disconcerting [ˌdɪskənˈsɜːtɪŋ] *adj.* 令人不安的，令人困惑的
disproportionately [ˌdɪsprəˈpɔːʃənətli] *adv.* 不成比例地

B 段

withdrawal [wɪðˈdrɔːəl] *n.* 撤回
transition [trænˈzɪʃn] *n.* 过度；转变
phrase out 逐步淘汰
alternative [ɔːlˈtɜːnətɪv] *adj.* 替代的

C 段

prescription [prɪˈskrɪpʃn] *n.* 处方
generics [dʒəˈnerɪks] *n.* 无商标的药物，非专利药品
recant [rɪˈkænt] *v.* 撤回

D 段

symbolic [sɪmˈbɒlɪk] *adj.* 标志性的
donate [dəʊˈneɪt] *v.* 捐赠

E 段

closure [ˈkləʊʒə(r)] *n.* 关闭

F 段

encounter [ɪnˈkaʊntə(r)] *v.* 遇到；遭遇
maintenance [ˈmeɪntənəns] *n.* 维护；维持
accommodate [əˈkɒmədeɪt] *v.* 适应

G 段

side effects 副作用
adherence [ədˈhɪərəns] *n.* 遵守，遵循

H 段

pregnant [ˈpregnənt] *adj.* 怀孕的

fetus [ˈfiːtəs] *n.* 胚胎

congenital [kənˈdʒenɪtl] *adj.* 先天的

premature [ˈpremətʃə(r)] *adj.* 不成熟的；早产的

大气变化

A 为了配合《空气洁净法》，联邦政府颁布了一项针对臭氧的禁令，禁止消耗使用氯氟烃。讽刺的是，这项禁令影响了美国2,290万的哮喘患者。通用吸入性沙丁胺醇是最常用的速效哮喘处方药物，它需要氯氟烃将其推进肺部，2008年12月31日之后这种药物将禁止合法销售。医生和病人都在质疑这一禁令是否明智，它对臭氧的影响微不足道，却对人们钱包的影响重大：重新制造替代的品牌药物将每只吸入器的成本提高到40美元左右，是原来价格的三倍。考虑到哮喘对穷人的影响更为严重，而最近的调查显示估计有20%的哮喘患者没有医疗保险，这项禁令无疑更令人不安。

B "做出这一改变的决定是出于政治考虑，而不是出于医学或科学的原因"，佛罗里达大学的药剂师莱斯利·亨德尔斯说。2007年他在《新英格兰医学杂志》上与其他作者合著了一篇论文，解释了撤销和改变使用氯氟烃。1987年，国会签署了国际条约《关于消耗臭氧层物质的蒙特利尔议定书》，要求逐步淘汰氯氟烃的所有非必要用途。当时，医用吸入器被认为是必不可少的用途，因为没有可行的替代推进剂。1989年，制药公司联合起来并最终在1996年用氢氟烷烃重新合成了沙丁胺醇。

C 这一转变是悄然开始的，但随着越来越多的病人看到他们处方的改变以及费用的上涨，许多人开始质疑为什么这项禁令必须在非专利药品出现之前就开始实施。食品和药品监督管理局顾问委员会中至少有一名成员公开对这一决定表示了遗憾。顾问委员会中的斯特里奇忠臣医学院的尼古拉斯·J·格罗斯撤回了自己的支持，并要求将禁令推迟到2010年，也就是第一项专利到期时。

D 格罗斯意识到禁令与环境保护无关。签署条约时沙丁胺醇吸入剂的氯氟烃释放比例不到0.1%。"这只是一个象征性的决议"，罗格斯说。一些对禁令持怀疑态度的人则指出，拥有可用氢氟烷烃沙丁胺醇吸入器专利的三家公司，即葛兰素史克、先灵葆雅和梯瓦，将获得数十亿美元的收益。亨德尔斯认为，虽然食品和药品监督管理局顾问委员会认识到药品费用将会上升，但是他们也相信这些公司将会帮助支付个人增加的费用。例如，一些公司已经承诺向全国各地的诊所捐赠一百万氢氟烷烃吸入器。亨德尔斯说尽管先灵葆雅和梯瓦进行了承诺，葛兰素史克却没有。对此，葛兰素史克没有回复要求置评的请求。

E 亨德尔斯认为现在的问题是，医用级氯氟烃供应短缺，如果食品和药品监督管理局不继续敦促氢氟烷烃吸入器的生产，那么公众就面临着缺乏沙丁胺醇吸入剂的风险。他认为随着氯氟烃的稀缺，非专利药品的成本也会上涨。格罗斯则不同意这种说法，他认为吸入器短缺和氯氟烃制造厂的关闭都是禁令的结果。

F 氢氟烷烃吸入器也遇到了阻力，因为一些哮喘病患者坚持认为它们不像氯氟烃吸入器那样有效。然而亨德尔斯指出，两者的差异在于操作方法和保存上。不同于氯氟烃吸入器，氢氟烷烃版本必须更加细心地填充和清洗以适应更黏稠的氢氟烷烃配方。而且它们会突然就用光了，不像氯氟烃吸入器那样在药剂含量低时有警告提示。"药剂师可能不会告诉人们这些东西，而医生也不知道"，亨德尔斯说。

G 这一禁令产生的主要公共健康问题是经济的不良影响，而不是药物化学。多项研究表明，成本的上升会导致治疗的依从性降低。一项研究发现，当患者的分摊付款额增加一倍时，他们服用的抗哮喘药物减少了30%。对于像哮喘这样的慢性病来说，要让人们遵守常规的治疗计划尤其困难。哈佛大学医学院的健康政策专家迈克尔·切莫评论说："总的来说，放弃药物治疗的理由中，费用是最有可能的因素。"

H　放弃药物治疗的选择影响的不仅是病人本身。亨德尔斯指出："举例来说，如果患哮喘的孕妇得不到治疗，胎儿便没有足够的氧气输入，这会导致先天性疾病以及早产。"考虑到这种疾病对穷人的影响更为严重，这个看似合理的、负责任的环境决议最终可能会导致意想不到的人员伤亡。